# USA by Rail

This fifth edition published in 2003 by Bradt Travel Guides Ltd,
19 High Street, Chalfont St Peter, Bucks SL9 9QE, England
web: www.bradt-travelguides.com
Published in the USA by The Globe Pequot Press Inc, 246 Goose Lane,
PO Box 480, Guilford, Connecticut 06475-0480

First published in 1992 by Bradt Publications

**British Library Cataloguing in Publication Data**
A catalogue record for this book is available from the British Library

ISBN 1 84162 069 6

**Photographs**
*Front cover* Capitol Limited, Pennsylvania (Amtrak)
*Text* Amtrak, Conway Scenic Railroad (CSR), Stephen Coyne/Sylvia Cordaiy
Photo Library Ltd (SC), Peter Cross (PC), Glyn Edmunds/Sylvia Cordaiy Photo
Library Ltd (GE), David William Gibbons/Sylvia Cordaiy Photo Library Ltd (DG),
Kenai Fiords Tours (KFT), Scott Rowed (SR), Geoffrey Roy/Kaa Photographics
(GR), Ron Ruhoff (RR), Neil Setchfield (NS),

**Illustrations** Emma Hill
**Maps** Steve Munns
**Route plans** Donald Sommerville

Typeset from the author's disc by Wakewing
Printed and bound in Italy by Legoprint SpA, Trento

# USA
# by Rail

### Fifth Edition

## John Pitt

Bradt Travel Guides Ltd, UK
The Globe Pequot Press Inc, USA

# Contents

**Maps**                               **VI**

USA Railways VI, The Pacific Northwest VIII, California IX,
The Midwest X, The Northeast XI, Florida XII

**Introduction**                         **XIII**

**Acknowledgements/List of maps**       **XIV**

**PART ONE**     **HISTORY AND TRAVEL FACTS**     **I**

**Chapter I**     **From Horsepower to Amtrak**     **3**
The Iron Horse 3, The Golden Age 4, The Twentieth
Century 9

**Chapter 2**     **American Trains Today**     **13**
Amtrak trains today 13, Non-Amtrak services 15,
Amtrak facilities and services 16

**Chapter 3**     **For The Visitor From Overseas**     **33**
Documents 33, When to visit 35, Getting there 35,
Money 36, Food 37, Drink 38, Accommodation 38,
Sightseeing 40, Telephones 40, On-line
communications 41, Postal service 41, Newspapers 42,
Tipping 42, Car travel 42, Medical insurance 43,
Crime 44, Drugs 44, Sex 45, Time zones 45, Public
holidays 45, Working 46

**PART TWO**     **TRAINS AND ROUTES IN THE UNITED STATES**     **47**
How to use Part Two 48

**Chapter 4**     **The *Coast Starlight***     **Seattle–Los Angeles**     **49**

**Chapter 5**     **The *California Zephyr***     **Chicago–Emeryville (for San Francisco)**     **75**

**Chapter 6**     **The *San Joaquins***     **San Francisco–Bakersfield (via Oakland)**     **98**

**Chapter 7**     **The *Pacific Surfliner***     **Los Angeles–San Diego**     **102**

**Chapter 8**     **The *Empire Builder***     **Chicago–Seattle**     **108**

**Chapter 9**     **The *Empire Builder***     **Spokane–Portland**     **124**

**Chapter 10**     **The *Southwest Chief***     **Chicago–Los Angeles**     **127**

| | | | |
|---|---|---|---|
| Chapter 11 | The *Sunset Limited* | Orlando–Los Angeles | 144 |
| Chapter 12 | The *Texas Eagle* | Chicago–San Antonio (for Los Angeles) | 168 |
| Chapter 13 | The *City of New Orleans* | Chicago–New Orleans | 182 |
| Chapter 14 | The Northeast Corridor | Boston–Washington | 189 |
| Chapter 15 | The Northeast Corridor | New Haven–Springfield (for Boston) | 209 |
| Chapter 16 | The *Crescent* | New York–New Orleans | 211 |
| Chapter 17 | The *Silver Star* | New York–Miami | 222 |
| Chapter 18 | The *Silver Meteor* | New York–Miami | 237 |
| Chapter 19 | The *Palmetto* | New York–Miami (via Tampa) | 242 |
| Chapter 20 | The *Twilight Shoreliner* | Boston–Newport News | 246 |
| Chapter 21 | The *Cardinal* | Washington–Chicago | 250 |
| Chapter 22 | The *Adirondack* | New York–Montreal | 260 |
| Chapter 23 | The *Vermonter* | Washington–St Albans (for Montreal) | 270 |
| Chapter 24 | The *Lake Shore Limited* | Boston/New York–Chicago | 275 |
| Chapter 25 | The *Capitol Limited* | Washington–Chicago | 286 |
| Chapter 26 | The *Three Rivers* | New York–Chicago | 294 |
| Chapter 27 | The *Maple Leaf* | New York–Toronto | 300 |
| Chapter 28 | The *Lake Cities* | Chicago–Pontiac | 306 |
| Chapter 29 | **Other Amtrak Trains** General information 312, The trains 312 | | 312 |
| Chapter 30 | **US Steam Today** Trains and routes 318 | | 317 |
| **PART THREE** | **ON CANADIAN RAILS** | | 337 |
| Chapter 31 | **Canada's Trains Today** VIA Rail 340, The Routes 348, Steam Trains in Canada 366 | | 339 |
| Appendix 1 | **The Internet** | | 369 |
| Appendix 2 | **Useful Addresses** | | 372 |
| Appendix 3 | **Ticketing Agents** | | 377 |
| Appendix 4 | **Further Reading** | | 381 |
| **Index** | | | 383 |

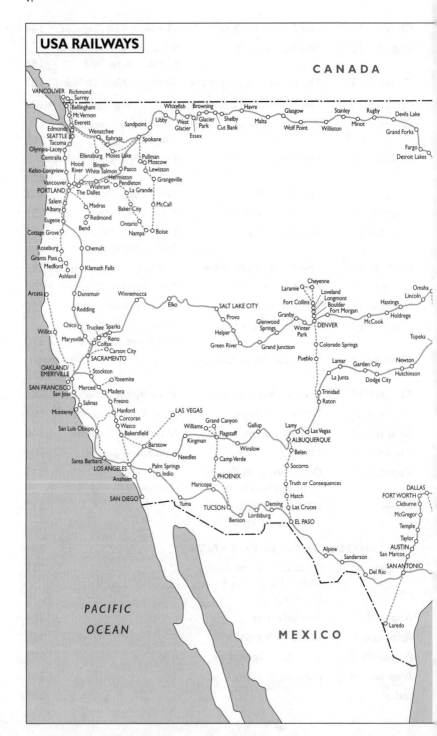

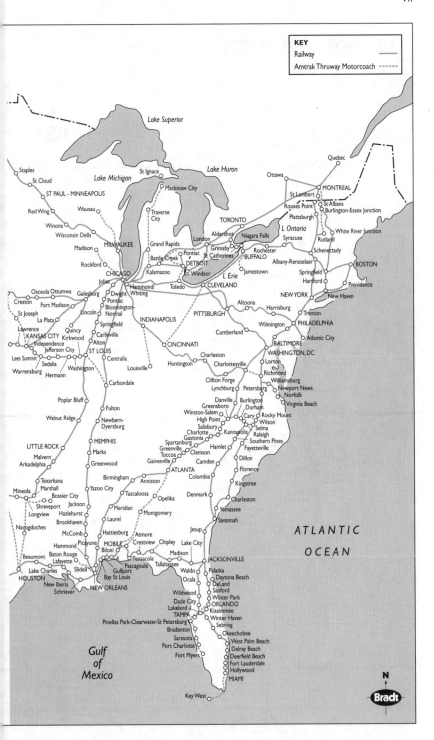

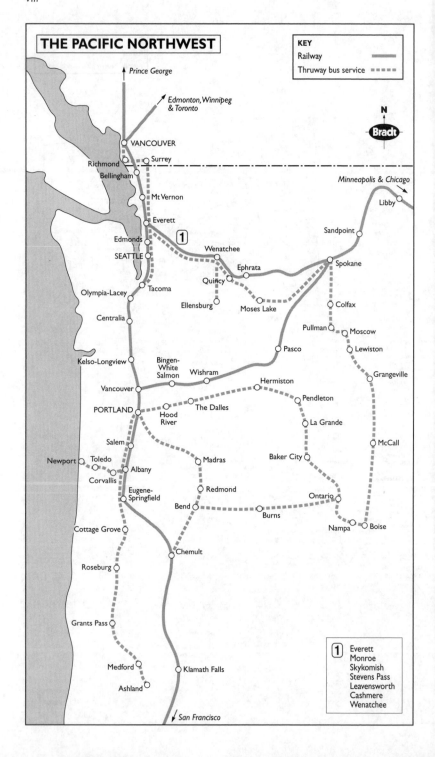

THE PACIFIC NORTHWEST

KEY
Railway
Thruway bus service

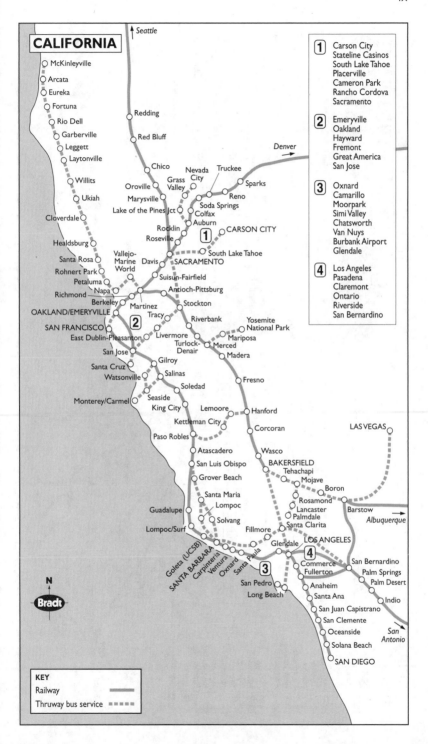

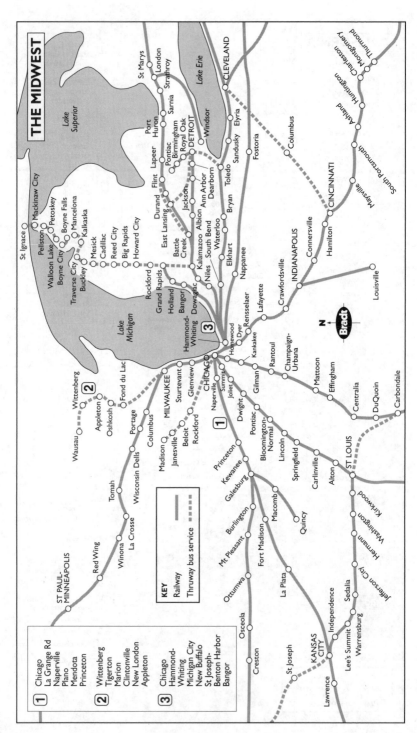

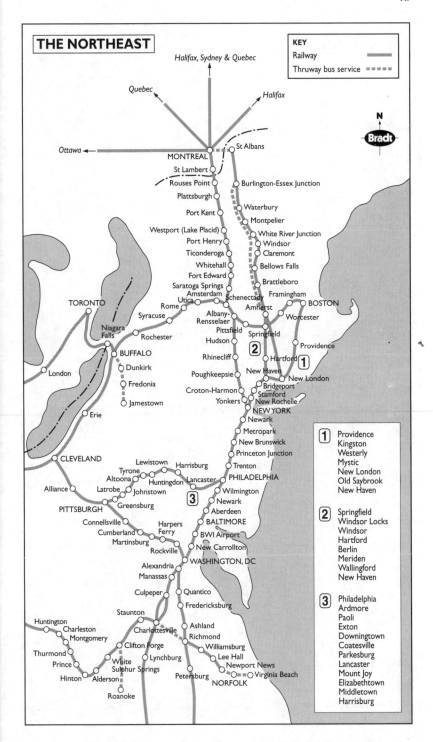

THE NORTHEAST

KEY
Railway
Thruway bus service

N
Bradt

Halifax, Sydney & Quebec
Quebec
Halifax
Ottawa
MONTREAL
St Albans
St Lambert
Rouses Point
Burlington-Essex Junction
Plattsburgh
Waterbury
Port Kent
Montpelier
Westport (Lake Placid)
White River Junction
Port Henry
Windsor
Ticonderoga
Claremont
Whitehall
Bellows Falls
Fort Edward
Brattleboro
Saratoga Springs
Amsterdam
Framingham
TORONTO
Rome
Utica
Schenectady
BOSTON
Syracuse
Albany-Rensselaer
Amherst
Worcester
Niagara Falls
Pittsfield
Springfield
Rochester
Hudson
Providence
BUFFALO
Rhinecliff
Hartford
Dunkirk
Poughkeepsie
New Haven
London
Fredonia
Croton-Harmon
New London
Jamestown
Yonkers
Bridgeport
Stamford
New Rochelle
Erie
NEW YORK
Newark
Metropark
CLEVELAND
New Brunswick
Lewistown
Harrisburg
Princeton Junction
Tyrone
Trenton
Altoona
Huntingdon
Lancaster
PHILADELPHIA
Alliance
Latrobe
Johnstown
Wilmington
PITTSBURGH
Greensburg
Newark
Aberdeen
Connellsville
Harpers Ferry
BALTIMORE
Cumberland
BWI Airport
Martinsburg
New Carrollton
Rockville
WASHINGTON, DC
Alexandria
Manassas
Culpeper
Quantico
Huntington
Fredericksburg
Charleston
Staunton
Montgomery
Charlottesville
Ashland
Thurmond
Clifton Forge
Richmond
Prince
White Sulphur Springs
Lynchburg
Williamsburg
Hinton
Alderson
Lee Hall
Petersburg
Newport News
Roanoke
NORFOLK
Virginia Beach

1  Providence
   Kingston
   Westerly
   Mystic
   New London
   Old Saybrook
   New Haven

2  Springfield
   Windsor Locks
   Windsor
   Hartford
   Berlin
   Meriden
   Wallingford
   New Haven

3  Philadelphia
   Ardmore
   Paoli
   Exton
   Downingtown
   Coatesville
   Parkesburg
   Lancaster
   Mount Joy
   Elizabethtown
   Middletown
   Harrisburg

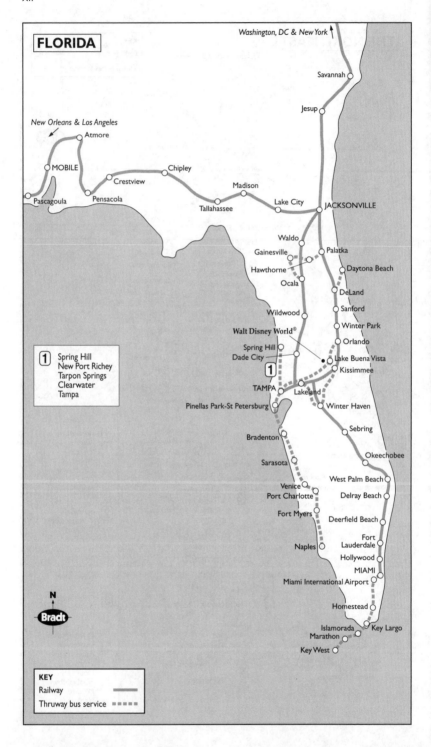

**FLORIDA**

Washington, DC & New York ↑

Savannah

Jesup

New Orleans & Los Angeles
Atmore

MOBILE

Chipley

Crestview

Madison

Pascagoula

Pensacola

Tallahassee

Lake City

JACKSONVILLE

Waldo

Gainesville

Palatka

Hawthorne

Daytona Beach

Ocala

DeLand

Sanford

Wildwood

Winter Park

Walt Disney World®

Orlando

Spring Hill

Lake Buena Vista

Dade City

Kissimmee

**1**  Spring Hill
New Port Richey
Tarpon Springs
Clearwater
Tampa

**1**

TAMPA

Lakeland

Pinellas Park-St Petersburg

Winter Haven

Sebring

Bradenton

Okeechobee

Sarasota

West Palm Beach

Venice

Delray Beach

Port Charlotte

Fort Myers

Deerfield Beach

Fort
Lauderdale

Naples

Hollywood

MIAMI

Miami International Airport

Homestead

N

Bradt

Islamorada

Key Largo

Marathon

Key West

**KEY**
Railway
Thruway bus service ▪▪▪▪▪

# Introduction

## ALL ABOARD!

Ever since they came on the scene, American trains have had a strong hold on the popular imagination, inspiring countless stories, songs, scandals, films and legends. Their rugged charm sets them apart from more mundane means of transport and their ecological soundness is again in fashion. Trains pollute less, rarely suffer from weather delays and won't give you jet lag. You can choose your companions, read a book, let your thoughts unfurl, take a snooze, sleep horizontally and generally enjoy most of the comforts of home. One reason for travelling by train is especially compelling: it's much more fun.

American passenger trains go to most big cities as well as to Disney World, Niagara Falls and the Grand Canyon. Pampered by helpful attendants, you can travel from coast to coast, explore the Rocky Mountains and ride directly alongside two oceans. You cross many rivers, lakes and deserts, often seeing places which can not be visited any other way. Less expensive than flying, more comfortable than the bus, trains keep you relaxed and in touch with an ever-changing landscape as the world becomes a moving picture, framed.

Amtrak coaches have generous reclining seats, air-conditioning, bright observation domes and snug bunks. This may not be the fastest way to travel but the civilised pace is perfect for sightseeing. If the scenery palls you can always go for a stroll, enjoy a meal, make friends in the bar or watch a movie. At night a gentle rocking and the steady, muffled rhythm of the wheels are sure to lull you to sleep.

Not many people would mourn buses if they became obsolete, and few entertain fond thoughts about airports, but children still count freight cars and wave as the train goes by. Instead of leaving you exhausted and surly, trains create a sense of adventure and romance. No wonder many still find the sound of a locomotive whistle at midnight a sure sign that it's time to move on. As the bell clangs and the conductor calls out 'All aboo-aard!', you soon discover why North American rail travel remains such a beguiling experience.

# Author/Acknowledgements

## AUTHOR

John Pitt studied economics and philosophy at East Anglia University before working at the Ministry of Defence and in local government. Since 1990 he has travelled extensively in North America, including over 65,000 miles by train, and has written on travel for Thomas Cook as well as for magazines and newspapers such as the *Sunday Times*, the *Telegraph* and the *Daily Mail*.

## ACKNOWLEDGEMENTS

The author would like to thank the following for their generous help in the preparation of this book. Malcolm Smith, Barbara Rizzi, Theresa Gren and George Genge at Amtrak; Guy Faulkner at VIA Rail; Kerry Mullin and Murray Atherton at Rocky Mountaineer Railtours; Nora Weber at Terracom Communications; Peter Boese and Christie Zielinski at American Orient Express; Heather Jeal at Leisurail; Jim Williams at the USA Hostel Handbook; Jerry Thull at the Grand Canyon Railway; Pam Butler at the Durango & Silverton Railroad; Craig S O'Connell and other Friends of Amtrak; Stephen Grande; Pat Fitzburgh; David Othen; Wanie Biggs in San Francisco; Raymond Parker in New Orleans; Ann Terry in Washington, DC; Nelson Sanchez and Tom Bynum in New York; Heidi Gardner at Trailfinders; Rita Plahetka; Eileen Rose; Marjorie and Wayne Preston in Florida; Anna Lander; Vangie S Palacios; Lynne Williams.

## LIST OF MAPS

| | | | | | |
|---|---|---|---|---|---|
| California | IX | Chicago to Portland | 125 | New York City to | |
| Canada railways | 338 | Chicago to San Antonio | 169 | Savannah | 238 |
| Florida | XII | Chicago to San Francisco | 76 | New York City to | |
| The midwest | X | Chicago to Seattle | 109 | Toronto | 301 |
| The northeast | XI | Jasper and Calgary to | | New York City to Winter | |
| The Pacific northwest | VIII | Vancouver | 354 | Haven | 243 |
| USA railways | VI–VII | Jasper to Prince Rupert | 349 | Orlando to Los Angeles | 145 |
| | | Los Angeles to San | | Pontiac to Chicago | 307 |
| **Route maps** | | Diego | 103 | Quebec to Montreal | 351 |
| Boston to Chicago | 276 | Montreal to Amherst | 271 | San Francisco to | |
| Boston to New Haven | 210 | Montreal to Washington | 261 | Bakersfield | 99 |
| Boston to Newport | | New York City to | | Seattle to Los Angeles | 50 |
| News | 247 | Chicago | 295 | Toronto to Vancouver | 348 |
| Boston to Washington | 190 | New York City to Miami | 223 | Washington to Chicago | 251 |
| Chicago to Los Angeles | 128 | New York City to New | | Washington to Cleveland | 287 |
| Chicago to New Orleans | 183 | Orleans | 212 | | |

# Part One

# History and Travel Facts

# From Horsepower to Amtrak

## THE IRON HORSE

The development of the United States in the 19th and early 20th centuries largely coincided with the epic story of its railroads. Trains contributed hugely to prosperity and provided a sense of national identity, coming to symbolise the country's strength, optimism and pioneering spirit. For over 170 years Americans have been proud to call themselves 'locomotive people'.

It may be symbolic that one of the country's first railroads had as its purpose the hauling of granite for the Bunker Hill Monument, which was being built to commemorate a defining episode in America's War Of Independence. Gridley Bryant's Granite Railway used horsepower to operate over three miles of track at Quincy, Massachusetts, in 1826. America's first steam-powered locomotive was the English-built *Stourbridge Lion*, inaugurated in August 1829 on the Delaware & Hudson Canal Company's line at Honesdale, Pennsylvania. But the story really began on February 19 1827, when a group of Baltimore residents decided to build the country's first public railroad between their city and the Ohio River. Charles Carroll, by then the only surviving signatory of the Declaration of Independence, laid the cornerstone on July 4 1828 and two years later the experimental engine *Tom Thumb*, weighing less than a ton, reached 18mph on 13 miles of Baltimore & Ohio track.

America's first (and the world's second) regular steam train service went into operation on Christmas Day 1830 on the South Carolina Canal & Railroad, when the *Best Friend of Charleston* took a passenger train out of Charleston on a line built to transport cotton from central Georgia. Completed three years later, the Charleston & Hamburg was for a time the world's longest railway (135 miles/217km).

Other lines soon followed, most notably the New York Central from Albany to Buffalo and the Philadelphia & Columbia (the first to be government-sponsored). Like most early lines, they served local needs and few people imagined the railway's full potential. Canal owners and road transport companies opposed them, partly on safety grounds, and doctors warned of the dangers inherent in such reckless speeds. Indeed, accidents did often happen. Few rights-of-way were fenced off and early railroad cars were little more than stage-coaches with flanged wheels, whose grip on the track was sometimes uncertain.

Despite these problems, total trackage increased to 3,000 miles by the early 1840s and to 9,000 miles (4,800km–14,500km) by 1850 (when it was three times the length of the canal system). By the late 1850s America had built half the world's railroad mileage in existence.

Early locomotives such as *Tom Thumb* and the *Best Friend of Charleston* had upright boilers but these were soon replaced by engines using horizontal, English-style boilers which allowed greater capacity. Mid-century engines were most usually handsome American-type (4-4-0) wood-burners, brightly painted and extravagantly decorated with polished brass. Other elegant innovations included a bell, whistle, headlight and pilot (or cowcatcher) to remove any obstacles ahead. A cab gave weather protection to the crew and a sandbox was added to improve traction. Typical examples from this period can be seen in the 1903 silent film *The Great Train Robbery* and in DW Griffith's 1916 epic *Intolerance*.

The first ticket offices were at stage-coach stops or in hotels, but characteristic railroad depots soon developed, usually as one-storey buildings located parallel to the tracks. Large cantilevered canopies protected passengers and freight from inclement weather. Clocktowers were often added at a later date as stations became more elaborate and companies adopted distinctive styles of architecture to make their railroads easily identifiable.

The New York Central brought together 10 small railroads in the northeast whose lines ran roughly parallel with the Erie Canal, later extending them to St Louis. The Erie Railroad went from the Hudson River north of New York to Lake Erie and Chicago, enabling New York City to enjoy fresh milk every day and consume more strawberries than anywhere else on earth. Chicago by this time had 11 railways and saw 70 trains a day, making it the busiest rail centre in the world.

From 1856 the Illinois Central linked Chicago to Cairo, at the junction of the Mississippi and Ohio Rivers, with Federal land grants assisting the line's construction through 700 miles (1,130km) of thinly populated country. The far west's first railway, the Sacramento Valley, opened in the same year between Sacramento and the gold mines at Folsom.

Southern railways made slower progress, but by the 1860s a thousand miles (1,600km) of track existed in each of Georgia, Tennessee and Virginia, and a network of lines served all states west of the Mississippi. This proved vital to both sides during the Civil War, when railroads and trains became major targets. In 1862 General Bragg's army of 30,000 men travelled nearly 800 miles (1,300km) to the key rail centre of Chattanooga from Mississippi by Confederate railway. The following year, 23,000 Union troops and their equipment journeyed 1,200 miles (1,900km) from Virginia to relieve Chattanooga. Their expedition took 12 days and required 30 trains with a total of 600 coaches. More than 35,000 lives were lost in bitter fighting before the battle ended. Later in the war, General Sherman's army of 100,000 men in Georgia needed 16 trains a day to keep it supplied. Without railways the North might never have broken Confederate resistance.

## THE GOLDEN AGE

Even before the Civil War, railroads had come to represent unity for a country divided by geography and culture. In 1862, at a crucial time for the Union,

President Lincoln signed the Pacific Railway Act making possible America's first transcontinental route. The Central Pacific Railroad set out to build a line eastwards from Sacramento, California, while the Union Pacific Railroad would go west from the Missouri River. Each company received generous Federal loans and was given ownership of huge tracts of land – 10 sections (each one mile square) for every completed mile.

Track was laid at a phenomenal rate, using mostly Irish or ex-army labour on the Union Pacific and Chinese immigrants on the Central Pacific. The thousands of workers from Kwantung Province imported by the CP became known as 'Celestials' after their 'Celestial Kingdom' homeland. They were often lowered down sheer cliff faces in baskets attached to ropes to drill into rock, pack in explosives and light a fuse before making a rapid return up the rope. Many 'basket men' failed to make it to safety before the explosion took place. A total of 19 tunnels (15 of them on the Central Pacific) were blasted out of solid rock with black powder at the rate of 14 inches a day. Nitroglycerine was tried in 1867 but had to be abandoned when it was found to be dangerously unstable.

At 10 spikes to the rail and 400 rails to the mile, it required approximately 21 million strokes of the hammer to complete the line. In 1867 alone, 235 miles of track were finished and Charles Crocker's Central Pacific team won a $10,000 bet from Thomas Durant of the Union Pacific after workers each lifted more than a hundred tons of steel to lay 10 miles in a single day (still a record). At one time the Union Pacific employed 10,000 labourers and an equal number of working animals. Hunters slaughtered vast quantities of buffalo to keep the workers supplied with meat and ramshackle tent towns sprang up along the way. These 'Hell on Wheels' settlements became notorious for land speculators, gambling, drinking and prostitution. Most collapsed as soon as the railroad moved on but some remained to become permanent towns.

Over 1,774 miles (2,860km) of track had been constructed by the time the two lines met ahead of schedule at Promontory Point, north of Utah's Great Salt Lake. Half a million people, including newspapermen, dignitaries and railway employees, gathered on May 10 1869 to watch the Golden Spike ceremony complete one of the greatest engineering feats of the century. The ceremony was rather disorganized, partly due to the size of the crowd. Leland Stanford of the Central Pacific had brought four ceremonial spikes, the famed 'Golden Spike' being presented by David Hewes, a San Francisco construction magnate. It was inscribed with the names of Central Pacific directors as well as the words 'The Last Spike' and 'May God continue the Unity of our Country as this Railroad unites the two great oceans of the world'.

A second gold spike was presented by the San Francisco *News Letter*, a silver spike by Nevada and a spike made from iron, silver and gold by Arizona. All four were dropped into a pre-bored laurel wood tie during the ceremony and at 12.47pm the actual last spike – an ordinary iron one – was driven into a regular tie. The spike had been wired to send the sound of the strikes over the telegraph to the nation but Leland Stanford and the Union Pacific's Thomas Durant frequently missed their aim as they took turns to drive it home. A single word, 'done', was telegraphed to the nation anyway, resulting in widespread celebrations. Meanwhile, construction supervisors actually drove in the final spike.

The Central Pacific's *Jupiter* and the Union Pacific's *No. 119* were present at the ceremony and replicas of both appear in the final scenes of John Ford's excellent 1924 pictorial history *The Iron Horse*. Cecil B De Mille told the story less convincingly in *Union Pacific*. The original 'Golden Spike' is now on display behind glass at Stanford University in Palo Alto, California. The temporary town of Promontory remained as a 'Hell on Wheels' settlement for a few weeks but never became a permanent city.

The first engines to cross the continent were the Central Pacific's *Success* and *Excelsior*, built by Rogers and delivered by rail. The first trains to carry passengers and cargo along the route ran on May 11 1869, with emigrants travelling west and a consignment of Japanese teas going east. The *Jupiter* was scrapped for iron in 1901 and the Union Pacific's *No. 119* went the same way two years later. The Lucin Cutoff took most traffic away from Promontory in 1904 and the last tie of laurel was destroyed in the 1906 San Francisco earthquake. The old rails over the 123-mile (197km) Promontory Summit line were salvaged in 1942 for the war effort in ceremonies marking the 'Undriving of the Golden Spike', when collectors picked over the area for ties and materials.

A re-enactment of the last spike ceremony took place in 1948, using miniature locomotives provided by the Southern Pacific, and in 1951 a monument to the event was erected at Ogden's Union Station. Congress established a seven-acre (2.8ha) piece of land as the Golden Spike National Historic Site and the National Golden Spike Society was formed to promote it. The site was enlarged to 2,176 acres (880ha) in 1965 and is now administered by the National Park Service. To mark the centennial of the transcontinental railroad, the Golden Spike Monument was moved 150ft (46m) northwest and the National Park Service began the reconstruction of two railroad and telegraph lines, together with switches and siding connections.

The engines used in the 1969 ceremonies were modified to resemble the originals and from then until 1980 the annual re-enactment used vintage locomotives on loan from Nevada. In 1980, with water from Liberty Island in New York harbour and Fort Point in San Francisco Bay, two replica locomotives, built by Chadwell O'Connor Engineering of Costa Mesa, California, were introduced. Costing $1.5 million, these were the first steam engines to be manufactured in the United States for a quarter of a century, and today they operate from May until August and from Christmas to New Year's Day. Visitors can also walk and drive along the old grades and see exhibitions relating to the railroad's construction.

Elsewhere, the Southern Pacific linked southern California to New Orleans in 1883 and two years later the Atchison, Topeka & Santa Fe line ran from Kansas City to Los Angeles along the Southern Pacific route. Cross-country travel now took five days instead of a month. When the Santa Fe first reached Los Angeles only 10,000 people lived in southern California, but more soon arrived as competition brought fares from New York down to as little as one dollar. Many farmers in the south returned from the Civil War to find themselves homeless and impoverished and so took the only jobs they could find – building railroads. Being farmers, they were often referred to as 'hoe boys' or 'hobos'. Unable to settle, many later went on to wander the country, riding on the same rails they had built.

The Iron Horse began to open up the west and create rapid development in cities along the way. Colonisation agents were employed to recruit people in the east or from abroad, urging them to settle where the air was clean and the land dirt cheap. Some immigrants travelled west free, sharing a wagon with their personal belongings, livestock and machinery. Educational trains up to 10 coaches long were sent out to teach farmers how to grow more and better crops – the Poultry Train featured a famous talking rooster. In a remarkably short time the railways transformed America's heartland into one of the most productive food-growing areas on earth.

Tourists also began to arrive. The Santa Fe railway cleverly publicised its route along the Santa Fe Trail by naming its trains the *Chief* and *Superchief*, and using the slogan 'see Indian country by train' on calendars and posters. Native Americans were recruited to present a romanticised picture of the west and artists were commissioned to paint both landscape and people. Detours were made, allowing urban Americans to see the outback for the first time and feel a sense of adventure as they overcame their fear of the west.

Other railways tried different means to attract passengers, selling or giving away such items as ashtrays, letter openers, match safes, spoons and scissors. Almost anything which could be stamped with a name or slogan was tried, including paperweights in the shape of locomotives or, in one instance, an Idaho baking potato. Such promotional items are now greatly sought after by rail fans, as are early books, posters, timetables, railroad songs and train recordings. Some people collect hardware such as destination signs, lanterns, silverware, locks, keys, telegraph instruments and hand brakes, or even bricks from demolished stations.

The Northern Pacific Railroad opened up the northwest in the 1880s and James J Hill built a similar transcontinental route, the Great Northern, between St Paul, Minnesota, and Seattle. Born in Rockwood, Ontario, Hill arrived in St Paul by steamboat in 1856 and started working for the Mississippi River Steamboat Company, fixing freight and passenger rates. After the Civil War he joined the St Paul & Pacific Railroad, which he later bought. He also advised on the construction of the Canadian Pacific but resigned when he saw that it would become a competitor to his own transcontinental line, which he built without government funds or loans.

Construction of the Great Northern reached Great Falls in 1887, the fast rate of laying track being ensured by excellent planning and the use of 8,000 men and 3,300 teams of horses. Immigrants were carried west for $10 provided they agreed to settle along the route and farmers were offered free imported cattle. More than six million acres of Montana were settled in two years and the line reached Puget Sound in 1893. The success of his railroad meant that Hill was able to take over the Northern Pacific in 1896.

Unlike the Northern Pacific, most railroad construction west of the Mississippi received Federal land grants, eventually totalling 131 million acres. Rail companies charged reduced rates for government traffic in return. As well as the four great transcontinental routes, many smaller lines were built throughout the west and by 1890 a network of 164,000 miles (264,000km) covered virtually the whole country. Few Americans then lived more than 25 miles (40km) from the track. Large, often grandiose, new stations opened at South Street, Boston (1890), St Louis (1894), Washington, DC (1907) and New York (Pennsylvania 1910, Grand Central 1913).

Standard gauge track and Standard Time (adopted in 1883) helped integration. Railroad timekeeping became so good that farmers set their clocks according to passing trains. Safety innovations included air brakes and automatic coupling. Trains became longer, faster and more efficient as coal-burning engines replaced less powerful wood-burners. 'American' types gave way to heavier Atlantics (4-4-2) and Pacifics (4-6-2). Refrigerated wagons were introduced to ship beef from Chicago and oranges from Florida as the railways brought increasing control over nature.

Compressed gas and electricity superseded candlelight in passenger carriages and hot-water heating replaced wood-burning stoves after the Civil War, with corridors and steam heat arriving by the turn of the century. The paint on these new 85ft-(25m)long coaches was varnished to make it shiny, and the word 'varnish' is still slang for a first-class passenger car. Express services for passengers and special freight were introduced as the economy grew at an ever greater pace.

Sleeping and dining cars, rarely seen before the Civil War, afterwards became much more common. George Pullman's $20,000 *Pioneer* sleeper boasted thick carpets, chandeliers, polished walnut, crimson plush upholstery and marble wash-stands. Pullman, originally a cabinet maker by trade, instructed his craftsmen to build 'palaces on wheels' in which the wealthy would wish to travel. The owner of the Penn Railroad was one of the first to buy a lavishly-equipped private coach complete with drawing room, dining room and private galley. Delmonico dining cars, introduced in 1868, meant passengers no longer had to snatch hurried meals at scheduled stops along the way. Parlour cars, forerunners of present day lounge and club cars, also went into service at about this time. The rich could buy their own lavish private vehicle or hire an entire 'hotel train', complete with barbershop and dance floor.

Railroads became America's first big business, dominating economic life for three-quarters of a century, but the golden age had its less appealing aspects. Unionisation brought better pay, at least for train crews, but a dispute on the Baltimore & Ohio in 1877 spread to other companies and resulted in riots. Following wage cuts, a strike at the Pullman factory in 1894 led to sympathy action throughout the Midwest. Rail traffic in America came to a halt as the dispute turned violent. People were threatened, property burnt and at least 34 people died when the government sent in 12,000 troops to break up the strike. Union leader Eugene Debs was jailed.

Fraud, corruption and coercion became commonplace. The huge profits attracted a profusion of crooks and bribery sometimes appeared the only way to get business done. Owners often bought up newspapers, politicians and even the law. Jay Gould, 'Commodore' Cornelius Vanderbilt ('the public interest be damned') and the Central Pacific's 'scrupulously dishonest' Collis Huntington were famous for their ruthlessness. 'Jubilee Jim' Fisk defrauded Erie Railroad stockholders of $64 million. Competition increased in some places but the railways too often exploited their monopoly and public opinion turned against them. The Interstate Commerce Commission was set up in 1887 to control their excesses and the financier Pierpoint Morgan, whose business fortune was said to total more than the combined value of all other property in the 22 states west of the Mississippi, was surprised and hurt when forced to break up his railroad empire.

Nevertheless, the country had reason to be grateful for the railroads. They brought prosperity, opened up the west, carried the mails and helped turn the United States into a major world power. Railroads made many people rich and gave even penniless hobos a means of transport they could afford. Trains became an indelible part of national culture, inspiring countless stories and featuring in folk songs, blues and gospel music. *Midnight Special* was one of many songs in which a train symbolised the American desire for escape. *Bound For Glory*, *Heavenbound Train* and *Downbound Train* made the railway journey a metaphor for life. On *The Black Diamond Express To Hell*, Sin was the engineer, Pleasure the headlight and the conductor was the Devil, and it was down by the railroad track that *Johnny B Goode* learnt to play guitar so well.

## THE TWENTIETH CENTURY

The New York Central's *Twentieth Century Limited* was inaugurated on the Water Level route in 1902, becoming the fastest and most luxurious way to travel between New York and Chicago. The *Twentieth Century* was the pride of the fleet and a national institution, its name synonymous with prestige and comfort. Another luxury train, the *Overland Limited*, provided passengers with fresh flowers and Persian carpets and served champagne for breakfast. By the late 1920s most city-to-city travel was by rail, with more than 15,000 passenger trains running every day over 254,000 miles (405,000km) of track. The 1932 film *Union Depot* gives a vivid picture of the atmosphere inside a busy station of the time.

In the beginning, the Pullman Company would hire only African-American men for the job of porter, which was eventually to have significant cultural and political consequences when A Philip Rudolph used the power of the labour union and the unity it represented to demand substantial social changes for African-Americans. The Brotherhood of Sleeping Car Porters, which he founded, became the first African-American union to gain a contract with a major US corporation. Rudolph later went on to become an important figure in the 1960s civil rights movement.

The 20th century brought other dramatic changes. The First World War made heavy demands for the movement of freight and people which led

President Wilson to set up the Railroad Administration to put the whole network under government control. With this extra workload the unions became more powerful, demanding an eight-hour day and the end of piecework. Over 100,000 women were recruited, mostly in clerical positions, but nearly all lost their jobs when the railways became private again after the war.

Many women recruited during the Second World War were given more responsible jobs and some remained for another 40 years. A few women had worked on the railways ever since the mid-19th century, sometimes making a living as professional gamblers. Former slave women sold food to passengers on the Chesapeake & Ohio line and attractive females were always in demand to christen a new engine or stretch of track.

Engines continued to become more efficient as 'compounding' (using steam more than once) and 'articulation', together with huge Mallet-type locomotives, allowed prodigious numbers of freight cars to be moved in a single train. Larger fireboxes and 'superheating' also improved productivity. Steam railroads served almost every large community by 1920 and were augmented by many local electric and street railways providing passenger services and encouraging cities to expand.

As the 20th century progressed, diesel replaced steam as the chief source of power. Steam engine numbers reached a peak of 72,000 in the 1920s but no more were put into service after 1953. The last regular service operating under steam was on the Norfolk & Western in April 1960. The first successful diesel service had been the streamlined *Pioneer Zephyr*, which in 1935 averaged 77.5mph (125km/h) on its inaugural run from Denver to Chicago. Streamliner designers boasted that they took their engines from trucks and their styling from automobiles. These trains were undeniably luxurious but rarely attracted enough passengers to pay their way.

Railroads were badly hit by the Great Depression, when increasing numbers of hobos rode box cars and flats to search for work. A million Americans are thought to have 'caught out' (jumped) trains during the 1930s, although it was a dangerous pursuit and thousands died from being crushed between carriages or falling from moving trains.

Even today 'riding the rods' offers the chance to travel free and hobo encampments can sometimes be seen alongside the track. 'First class' hobo travel means a boxcar offering protection from the elements and great panoramic views through the open doors. A wise hobo stays near the front of the car so that he is not thrown out of the door if the train suddenly stops. He tries never to walk between the rails, cross under couplers or carriages, 'catch out on the fly' (jump on a moving train) or join anyone else in a boxcar. Even with this guidance, being a hobo remains hazardous. Many were horrifically murdered during the 1990s in a series of killings for which there have been few arrests.

Hobos such as Danville Dan, Steamtrain Maury and Guitar Whitey continued to ride the rails in the 1960s and 70s, sharing food, cigarettes and alcohol as they roamed 200,000 miles of track across the land. Evading the 'bulls' (railroad security guards) they became part of an underworld culture that would later attract students, accountants and other 'weekend riders' looking for thrills. The writer James Michener described this as 'the last red-blooded American adventure'.

As the century progressed, mass car ownership, improved highways and air travel took away rail traffic, reducing revenues. America was the world's first nation to transfer its affection from trains to the automobile. Almost 98% of inter-city passengers travelled by rail in 1916 but by 1975 the figure was down to 6% and falling. Freight traffic also declined, although less rapidly.

Despite improved efficiency and lower wages, railways increasingly ran into massive deficit. By the end of the Depression half were bankrupt and many of those which remained were only rescued temporarily, by the Second World War. Military and civilian traffic in 1944 totalled an amazing 97 billion miles (155 billion km). After the war more streamlined trains were introduced, along with domed observation cars, high-level seating and economy sleepers. The Santa Fe slogan was 'If you want to feel like a star, travel like a star' and for a while the railways continued to carry more traffic than all other means of transport put together. The Interstate Commerce Commission insisted that they operate passenger services but by 1970 only 500 inter-city trains existed.

Tracks started turning to rust as railways merged or were forced into bankruptcy. The greatest collapse was that of the Penn Central (formed only two years earlier) in 1970. Ironically, the last time many lines made a profit was when hauling concrete to build the new interstate highways. To stay in business, the Union Pacific halved its work force and increased productivity by 55% in less than 10 years.

Federal government, under pressure to save America's trains, passed the 1970 Rail Passenger Service Act, and a year later the Railroad Passenger Corporation set up Amtrak (short for American Trackage) to take over most long-distance passenger routes. The Southern Railway, the Denver & Rio Grande Western and the Chicago, Rock Island & Pacific were the only lines to stay independent, but all three gave up their passenger services soon afterwards. The Chicago, Rock Island & Pacific line, which last saw trains more than twenty years ago, has recently been leased by the Union Pacific Railroad to the Missouri Central Railroad, which hopes soon to restore freight and possibly passenger trains.

The dire state of the freight industry in the early 1970s also forced the government to set up Conrail (the Consolidated Rail Corporation) to take over six bankrupt railroads in the northeast. An estimated $13 billion in subsidy was spent before the company was privatised in 1987. Like other private rail companies, Conrail shed labour, cut costs and sought new business. Services and revenues gradually improved, helped by a change in the government regulations which had put railroads at a disadvantage to truckers. Freight could now be transferred more easily between trains, trucks and ships. Containers gave faster delivery times and rates were cut by two thirds. More powerful and efficient locomotives were introduced, train crew size reduced and unprofitable routes abandoned or sold, leaving the remaining lines more profitable. For the first time in decades, business found it could save on transport costs by using rail instead of road. Consequently, since the mid-1980s, haulage has increased by a third and revenues have reached more than $31 billion.

This remarkable recovery has led to a series of mergers, resulting in further cost savings as fewer freight cars need to be shunted into sidings or change trains before reaching their destination. From 31 rail companies in 1980 there are now eight, four of which control 90% of the traffic. The Burlington Northern and Santa Fe Pacific joined forces in 1995, and in 1996 the Union Pacific and Pacific Rail merged to create a giant of the west. Conrail was valued at $10 billion in 1997 when its operations were competed for by the CSX and Norfolk Southern, both based in Virginia. Further mergers seem likely, antitrust rules permitting, bringing shorter routes and more cost savings.

Today's railroads employ 192,000 people to maintain and operate almost 200,000 miles of track, with 26,000 locomotives pulling 1.6 million freight and passenger cars. More rational line usage by freight companies should result in fewer delays for Amtrak passengers and the corporation's future seems much more assured. New equipment and other improvements continue to be introduced and Amtrak has received more than $15 billion from the government since 1971, although funding has lately been reduced. Amtrak's management personnel numbers have been cut by over a third in recent years and the work force as a whole by several thousand, making it one of the world's most efficient rail operators.

Even in the age of cyberspace, trains still have their uses. President Bill Clinton took a four-day train journey through West Virginia, Kentucky, Ohio, Indiana and Michigan on his way to the 1996 Democratic convention in Chicago, travelling aboard the *21st Century Express* on the kind of whistle-stop campaign not seen since the days of Harry Truman. Clinton went from the blue-collar mining and steel towns of Appalachia to Lake Michigan. At stops en route he could wave to cheering crowds from the train's podium as he drummed up interest in his campaign and made a series of proposals designed to appeal to America's heartland. The bullet-proof royal blue car with gold drapes and dark wood panelling had formerly been used by Franklin Roosevelt. Other sections of the 16-car train contained Secret Service personnel, satellite communications equipment and enough gadgetry to start a small war.

When terrorists attacked and destroyed New York City's World Trade Center on September 11 2001, Amtrak trains continued to operate throughout the crisis, bringing crucial emergency supplies and personnel to the scene. As well as providing such essential services, environment-friendly trains relieve traffic congestion and conserve energy. They use fuel efficiently, are not greedy for land and encourage economic growth. They are also the most enjoyable way to see America, which has some of the world's finest long-distance routes, and by using them as often as possible you can help ensure their survival and prosperity.

# American Trains Today

## AMTRAK TRAINS TODAY

The system Amtrak inherited in 1971 was dilapidated after being starved of investment for many years. Rolling stock was falling apart, roadbeds crumbling, stations dangerous and staff, not surprisingly, felt demoralised. The corporation initially served just 340 cities, with 21 routes operating over 20,000 miles (32,000km) of track. Most employees still worked for the rail companies Amtrak had taken over and continuing losses seemed inevitable. Things improved surprisingly quickly, though, as extra trains were scheduled and modern equipment purchased. Train reservations and tickets were still laboriously written by hand until Amtrak introduced an automatic system with computerised ticketing, well before airlines caught on to the same development.

Amtrak's slogan – 'the tracks are back' – was emblazoned on everything from lapel badges to bumper stickers. Stations were spruced up and made secure, running times significantly improved and staff again had reason to be cheerful. In Amtrak's first year passengers travelled over three billion miles, rediscovering historic trains like the *California Zephyr* and *Sunset Limited*. Many trains operate like first-class mobile hotels, with room service, overnight shoeshines and mints left on your pillow by the sleeping-car attendant.

Conrail took over six bankrupt railroads in the northeast in 1976 and allowed Amtrak to acquire its first tracks (the electrified Boston–New York–Washington route). Despite cutbacks to the network by the Carter administration, employee numbers have risen from 1,200 in 1972 to approximately 24,000 today. Amtrak owns 436 locomotives (360 diesel, 76 electric), 2,188 passenger cars and 730 miles (1,168km) of track, mainly between Boston and Washington and in Michigan. In co-operation with contract railroads and local government, 30 new stations have been built and 35 others completely renovated.

If Amtrak was an airline it would be the country's third biggest. It serves more than 23 million passengers a year and clocks up a total of 5 billion passenger miles (a passenger mile is one person transported one mile). Each day, up to 265 trains use its 22,000-mile (35,200km) network, reaching most cities in 45 states and the District of Columbia. The states not served are Alaska, Hawaii, Maine, South Dakota and Wyoming, although Wyoming does have Amtrak Thruway buses and there will soon be a train service in Maine. There are plans also to serve such places as Las Vegas, Abilene, Louisville, Boise and Nashville, and for a luxury transcontinental route (60 hours from coast to coast). Other possibilities include more midwestern trains out of Chicago, an *Aztec Eagle* train from San Antonio to Monterey in Mexico, and the reintroduction of the *Pioneer* route between Chicago and Seattle.

More people each month are turning to trains as a convenient and enjoyable alternative to congested highways and crowded airports. Of the 510 communities currently served by Amtrak, 130 have no air service, 113 are without intercity buses and 35 have neither air nor bus services. Altogether, 65 million people a year in the USA travel by train and without them there would be 167,000 more cars on the road. Amtrak is a partner in some of America's largest commuter train services, including the Massachusetts Bay Transportation Authority (MBTA), Maryland Area Regional Commuter (MARC), Virginia Railway Express (VRE), Coasters (California), Metrolink (California), Caltrain (California) and Shoreline East (Connecticut). These services operate 708 trains daily, carrying 174,000 passengers, and the three services in the state of California alone carry 50,000 people every weekday. Other commuter services use Amtrak's tracks and facilities, carrying a further 357,000 passengers.

The future looks bright, with in excess of $10 billion investment in infrastructure expected to take place over the next ten years. Plans are already well under way for a $4 billion high-speed network over 3,000 miles of track with a hub in Chicago and reaching nine states. The first phase should be completed in 2003. Amtrak plans to profit from shipping refrigerated produce as an addition to its expanding mail and express business, especially for time-sensitive paper and food products. This should open up new markets for passenger service and provide the necessary financial support to build a commercially viable nationwide system.

Congress has authorised a bill giving Amtrak access to $2.3 billion of capital investment but the company must still be free of Federal support by the year 2003, at least so far as operating costs are concerned. Ticket revenue (over $1.8 billion a year) already covers more operating expenses than for any other national railway in the world. Monthly revenue passed $100 million a month for the first time during year 2000 as new records were set for ridership. Amtrak even has a new logo, replacing its 'pointless arrow' with the more dynamic 'travel mark'.

In efforts towards greater efficiency Amtrak has introduced many new locomotives and coaches, and a mobile satellite communications and tracking system now links trains and support facilities. Passenger numbers continue to increase and as part of its strategy to expand on a commercial basis, Amtrak has identified route changes and improved frequencies for 21 states, serving 975 new station pairs and increasing train miles by four million to 38 million.

Excellent newsletters about current Amtrak activities can be found on the websites of Friends of Amtrak (http://trainweb.com/crocon/amtrak.html) and the National Corridors Initiative (www.nationalcorridors.org). The magazine *Rail Travel News* is published twice a month and has information about Amtrak and commuter trains, including travelogues and photographs. For a subscription or sample copy contact Message Media, Box 9007, Berkeley, CA 94709; email: rtn@trainweb.com; web: www.railtravelnews.com.

# NON-AMTRAK SERVICES

Many cities have their own **suburban and commuter services**, either operating independently or in association with Amtrak, and these sometimes provide a more frequent or cheaper alternative for shorter journeys. The best metropolitan services operate out of Chicago, Houston, Denver and Seattle. Details can be obtained at the local Amtrak station or information bureau. City operated services often use locally the same routes served by Amtrak's longer distance trains, but the stops and timing may be different.

The **American Orient Express** is a privately-operated train which travels among some of North America's finest scenery, including the Grand Canyon and many miles of Pacific shoreline. Restored club cars, originally built for the Union Pacific Railroad in the 1940s and 50s, feature dark mahogany panels, polished brass, inlaid marble, gold leaf ceilings, armchairs, couches and baby grand pianos (complete with pianist). The *New York* observation car, with its plush seating and circular bay window, was dedicated in 1948 by Dwight Eisenhower and Beatrice Lillie and previously served on the famous *Twentieth Century Limited*.

The Pullman sleeping carriages were originally constructed in the 1940s and 50s for the Chesapeake & Ohio, Nickel Plate, Southern Pacific and Union Pacific Railroads. All have been rebuilt to modern standards, including showers at the end of each carriage, but retain their elegant style. The *Chicago* and *Zurich* dining cars have rich mahogany woodwork, fresh cut flowers and tables set with china, crystal, linen and silver. Meals and sightseeing are included in the ticket price, which varies between $2,590 and $7,290, depending on the length of tour and type of accommodation provided. Discounts are available for early bookings – at least six months ahead of departure date.

There are four categories of cabin, all with sleeping accommodation that includes a washbasin and toilet. Vintage Pullmans have upper and lower berths. Single sleepers have one lower berth. Parlour suites have two lower berths, an upper berth and a couch as well as a sofa seat. Presidential suites are double-sized cabins with two lower berths, two single sofa seats and a private shower. All come equipped with large windows, individually controlled air-conditioning and a courtesy phone to call the porter.

Tours include the Great Continental Rail Journey (Washington, DC–Los Angeles via the *Silver Star* and *Sunset Limited* routes), Antebellum South (Washington, DC–New Orleans via the *Silver Star* and *Sunset Limited* routes), Pacific Coast Explorer (Seattle–Los Angeles via the *Coast Starlight* route) and Northwest and Glacier (Seattle–Salt Lake City, partly on the *Empire Builder* route). Other journeys take you to the Rockies, Yellowstone National Park and across Canada (see *Chapter 31*, page 364). For more information about all American Orient Express operations contact 5100 Main Street, Suite 300, Downers Grove, IL 60515; tel: 630 663 4550 or 800 320 4206 (for reservations); web: www.americanorientexpress.com.

The **Alaska Railroad** operates from 411 W 1st Ave, Anchorage, to Denali, Seward and Fairbanks, using three large-windowed Vistadome cars, and is one of the few railroads in the USA to carry both freight and passengers. Trains travel through 350 miles of national park land with pristine mountain scenery and wildlife that includes moose, caribou, grizzly bear and beaver. You pass close to Bartlett Glacier (named in 1907 after Frank Bartlett, the Alaska Central Railroad's civil engineer at the time) and cross the continental divide at its lowest rail pass point (2,363ft) in the Rocky Mountains. You also cross the Mears Memorial Bridge, a 700ft steel structure which is one of the world's longest single-span bridges and which marked the completion of the Alaska Railroad in 1923.

Services operate daily from May to September, otherwise at weekends. A new Whittier trip follows the shore of Turnagain Arm, where you may be lucky enough to see beluga whales. For more information contact the Alaska Passenger Service, PO Box 107500, Anchorage, Alaska 99510-7500; tel: 907 265 2494 or 800 544 0552; web: www.akrr.com.

**American Spirit** trains tour the Rocky Mountains region and the Pacific Northwest, including Yellowstone, Grand Teton and Glacier National Parks, the Columbia River Gorge and along the Lewis & Clark Trail. The vintage cars reflect the 'golden age' of streamliner travel in the 1940s and 50s. Amtrak or Montana Rail Link provide the diesel locomotives and engineers, and American Spirit Rail Tours operate and staff the fleet of passenger cars and streamlined vista domes mostly built by the Budd Company. These art deco and art moderne carriages originally served on trains such as the Great Northern's *Empire Builder*, the Northern Pacific's *North Coast Limited* and the Denver & Rio Grande's *Rio Grande Zephyr*.

All have been fully restored with air conditioning, wide picture windows and large reclining seats. Up to 12 cars operate per train and there are beer and wine lounges as well as diners and domes. Trains run mostly between Portland, Whitefish and Bozeman from July to September, with motor coach trips to the national parks. For more information call **American Spirit Rail Tours** on 208 265 8618. For reservations call 800 519 7245, or visit the website: www.americanspiritrail.com.

## AMTRAK FACILITIES AND SERVICES
### Tickets
Coach class is the standard Amtrak ticket. Metroliner, Club or Custom Class (available mainly on *Acela/Northeast Corridor* routes) are First Class services with extra facilities (see *Equipment* later in this chapter). Sleeping car accommodation is also First Class. Since most long-distance trains require advance reservations you normally have to reserve and purchase separate tickets if you wish to break your journey en route. Business Class, available on some trains in the northeast, midwest and on Empire services, provides coaches with more room around the seats and extra facilities such as changing rooms and telephones.

Fares naturally depend on the distance travelled and standard of service provided, though special offers, seasonal rates and excursion deals often provide big reductions. Ticket prices are often 50% or 75% less than the equivalent air fare, especially if you travel off-peak. This may be influenced by the season, day of the week or time of day, depending on the route. Check Amtrak's website or your travel agent for news of the current special deals.

Sleeping accommodation is always charged for in addition to the journey fare.

Accompanied children aged 2–15 pay half fare (limited to two half fares per adult) and those aged under two travel free if they share an adult's seat. There are further reductions for group travel, a group being 15 people or more. You can buy one-way standard rate tickets on board but a penalty will be added if the ticket-office was open at the time of your departure. Where space is available you can upgrade accommodation on board, including sleepers, Business, Club and Custom Class, and sometimes obtain a discount on the usual rate. Ask the conductor or chief of on-board services. Tickets can be delivered by mail if paid for by credit card but Amtrak accepts no responsibility for lost, stolen or destroyed tickets.

Quik-Trak self-service machines with touch screen menus are now in use at almost half of Amtrak's stations. These accept credit and debit cards and enable you to purchase coach class tickets to any city listed on the machine. You can also pick up tickets for previously made reservations by entering your reservation number.

Ticket information can also be found on Amtrak's award-winning website: www.amtrak.com.

## Reservations

Coach seating on unreserved trains is not guaranteed and is allocated on a first-come, first-served basis. Coach Class and all First Class and sleeping accommodation on all-reserved trains should be booked well in advance, particularly during summer when some routes may be very busy. If travelling overnight through particularly scenic areas try to make your departure date just before a full moon.

Reservations can be obtained up to 11 months ahead via Amtrak's website, through any Amtrak station ticket-office (try to avoid busy times) or at designated travel agents, including those abroad. Many travel agents in North America are connected into the Amtrak computer booking system. Alternatively, you can call 800 USA RAIL or 1 800 872 7245. You will be given a reservation number and hold date by which time you must collect your tickets. Reservations will be cancelled if collection is not made by then. Telephone lines are open 24 hours a day, 365 days a year, but you may receive faster service by calling early in the morning or late at night.

A computerised voice response unit (VRU) provides schedule and fare information as well as reservations. For group reservations call 800 USA 1GRP. Tickets can be paid for when you make your reservations and picked up at any time prior to travel. A service charge is made for prepaid tickets. If you need to upgrade and find no sleeper is available try calling again at a later date, if possible early in the morning, as there are sometimes compartments and coach seats available as a result of cancellations or 'no-shows'.

## Explore America

This scheme allows you to make a one-way or round-trip journey during any 45 day period for a set fare in one of four regions – Central, Eastern, Western or Florida. For an additional fee you can make a trip in two adjacent regions or throughout the United States. Three stopovers are permitted and prices vary depending on season, with off-peak rates generally about $100 lower. Reservations should be made as far ahead as possible.

These fares are not valid on *Metroliners*, the *Auto Train*, some Thruway bus connections, or the Canadian portions of trains operated jointly by Amtrak and VIA Rail.

## Great American vacations

You can arrange a complete package to your own itinerary, including hotels, sightseeing, car rental and tours, by calling Amtrak on 1 800 321 8684. There are also inclusive deals to many big cities as well as to national parks and ski areas.

## Combined air and rail travel

The Air Rail Travel Plan allows you to travel by train to any destination in the US or Canada and fly home on United Airlines. Or you can fly out and return by train, making up to three Amtrak stopovers along the way. Call 1 800 437 3441.

## USA Rail Pass

Anyone not American or Canadian can purchase a 15- or 30-day pass giving unlimited coach travel on Amtrak trains, including a National Pass which covers the entire system. The Northeast Pass allows you to go from Virginia up to Montreal and across to Niagara Falls, while the Eastern Pass is for routes as far west as Chicago and down to New Orleans.

The Far West Pass covers trains from the Pacific inland to Denver, Albuquerque and El Paso, and the Western Pass allow you to explore from the Pacific across to Chicago and down to New Orleans. Western and Eastern Passes both permit travel on the *City of New Orleans* train. Coastal Passes allow 30 days travel in either the west (from Vancouver down to San Diego) or the east (from Montreal to Miami). Peak season runs from June to early September and the following prices currently apply:

| | | Off-peak | Peak |
|---|---|---|---|
| National | 15 days | $295 | $440 |
| | 30 days | $385 | $550 |
| Northeast | 5 days | $149 | $149 |
| | 15 days | $185 | $205 |
| | 30 days | $225 | $240 |
| Western | 15 days | $200 | $325 |
| | 30 days | $270 | $405 |
| Eastern | 15 days | $210 | $260 |
| | 30 days | $265 | $320 |
| Far West | 15 days | $190 | $245 |
| | 30 days | $250 | $320 |
| Coastal | 30 days | $235 | $285 |

In addition there are:

**California** The 7-in-21 Day Statewide Pass ($159) includes over 90 destinations throughout California. The 5-in-7 Day Northern California Pass and Southern California Passes (both $99) can be used for up to five days of travel in a seven day period.

**Florida** Valid for unlimited travel between 33 cities in Florida by train or via Thruway motorcoach connections ($249 for twelve months), the Florida Pass is available only to Florida residents who present a valid state ID (driver's license, state ID, or voter registration) at time of purchase. Not valid on Thruway coaches between DeLand and Daytona Beach or Miami and Key West, or on Coach USA Orlando shuttles. Advance reservations and ticketing are not permitted or required but the pass must be presented on board the train along with valid photo identification.

All passes allow unlimited stopovers but must be bought through Amtrak-appointed agents outside the United States or Canada (see *Appendix 3*, pages 377–9).

Passes are valid on most, although not all, Thruway buses. *Metroliner* services, the *Auto Train*, Business Class, Club Class, Custom Class and sleeping car accommodations require a supplementary charge. Rail pass tickets for children aged 2–15 are half the adult fare and children under two ride free.

## North America Rail Pass

North America Rail Passes include both Amtrak and the VIA Rail network of Canada. For details, see under VIA Rail (pages 342–3).

## Payment

You can pay for Amtrak tickets and dining car meals by cash or credit card or by travellers' cheques designated in US$. Personal cheques must be drawn on a US bank and be for a minimum of $25. Two pieces of identification are required, including one with your photograph or signature. Amtrak will not accept personal cheques in California, except from customers aged 62 or over.

## Refunds

If you change your plans you should apply for a refund as soon as possible to avoid penalties. In most cases a fee will be charged. Refunds can be made on the unused value of a coach ticket cancelled prior to departure (at least one hour before in the case of the *Auto Train* and Club Class). Refunds on sleeping accommodation cancelled less than 24 hours before the train's departure time will be assessed a penalty. Partly used special fare and excursion tickets may have limited refunds.

Reimbursement can be received at ticket-offices or by mail from Amtrak Customer Refunds, 30th Street Station, 30th and Market Streets, Philadelphia, PA 19104-2898. Send your ticket via certified mail. Travel agency-sold tickets must usually be refunded through the agent, although Amtrak will make refunds on the spot if this is due to service disruption or downgrading.

## Timetables

Amtrak ticket-offices and travel agents can provide free timetables for individual routes, the Northeast and for the National network. Up-to-date timetables can also be found on the Amtrak website. Times shown are local, taking into account any zone changes en route. You should confirm your departure time the day before travelling, especially if the tickets were bought several weeks in advance. In the autumn, on the day clocks go back, trains may be deferred for an hour in order to arrive 'on time'. On the day clocks go forward in spring a new timetable comes into effect and trains attempt to make up time lost before reaching subsequent stations. Arizona and parts of Indiana do not observe daylight saving time.

Generally speaking, Amtrak's timekeeping performance in recent years has compared favourably with that of airlines, although circumstances beyond the corporation's control can lead to delays. Freight trains sometimes have to take precedence and Amtrak trains crossing into Canada may be held up by customs and immigration inspections. Connections of less than 60 minutes are not guaranteed (90 minutes between arriving long-distance trains and local trains in the Northeast Corridor) so you should allow at least an hour between trains. Even a guaranteed connection may sometimes be missed. If this happens, alternative transport on Amtrak or another carrier will usually be provided and, in exceptional circumstances, overnight accommodation arranged.

If you have limited time to change trains ask the conductor on the train where you should go to get your next one when you reach the depot. This will save you having to hunt for signs or wait in an information line. Note that some cities have more than one station. Trains may not pause for as long as the timetable indicates at scheduled stops, so listen to the announcements or ask an attendant before deciding to stretch your legs on the platform. Stay within sight and hearing of the train and be prepared to reboard at a moment's notice or you may be left behind. Anyone intending to meet a train can check times of arrival and departure by calling 1 800 USA RAIL and listening to the automated information.

## Thruway buses

Amtrak's Thruway bus service provides coordinated train/bus connections with through fares and ticketing. Where a Thruway bus is necessary to complete your journey the cost is included in the rail fare.

Timetables show some of the connecting services provided by other carriers to destinations not served by Amtrak or Thruway buses. Reservations and tickets for these services can be obtained from Amtrak but you should note that they may leave from another terminal.

## Boarding

You should arrive at least half an hour before departure time (or two hours for the *Auto Train*). It is important that you go to the right coach, so tell the gate attendant your destination and he will direct you. Red Caps (porters) are there to assist with luggage if required. Choose a window seat for a better view of the scenery, a little more privacy and a corner to lean against when sleeping. An aisle seat will give you more freedom to move without disturbing other passengers. Try not to sit too near the front as the view there may be more restricted.

## Metropolitan Lounge

New York, Washington, DC, Philadelphia, Miami, New Orleans, Portland and Chicago have Metropolitan waiting rooms located away from the crowds. Another is under construction in Boston and the one in New Orleans is called the Magnolia Lounge. All provide a staffed reception desk, comfortable chairs, television, telephones, fax machines, computer links, a conference area, rest-rooms, newspapers, luggage stores and a superior class of muzak. They also offer complimentary coffee, soft drinks and doughnuts. Metropolitan lounges are only available (on arrival or departure) to Club Class, sleeping car and some *Acela* and *Metroliner* passengers.

## Equipment
### Superliner

Manufactured by the Pullman-Standard Company for Amtrak between 1979 and 1981, these spacious, twin-decked coaches operate on all long-distance routes west of the Mississippi as well as on some in the east. Designed to be 'the finest trains anywhere in the world', they have air-cushioned suspension and were built with extra sound-absorbing materials. Each Superliner car measures 85ft (26m) long and 16ft (5m) high, weighs 75 US tons (68 tonnes) and has large windows with excellent views, especially from the upper level. The reclining seats, about equivalent to flying First Class, provide leg- and foot-rests, folding trays and personal reading lights.

A new generation of Superliner II cars, built by the Bombardier company, has been introduced on the *Auto Train* and several western routes. These have bigger windows and larger compartments than the first range of Superliners.

Dining cars cater for up to 72 people and are on the upper level above the kitchen. Sightseer lounge cars and most kinds of sleeping accommodation are also usually available. Rest-rooms (toilets) are mostly on the lower level, with at least one accessible to disabled passengers. Facilities include toilet, washbasin, mirror, infant changing table, soap, tissues and a 120V AC electric point. Luggage may be left at the lower level on entry or stored in overhead racks.

### Amfleet

Designed for short and medium journeys and operating mostly in the east, Amfleet coaches were built by the Budd Company of Philadelphia. They offer reclining seats, fold-down trays, overhead luggage racks and personal reading lights. Amfleet II coaches, intended for longer journeys, provide leg rests and more space. At least one rest-room caters for disabled passengers. Dinette and lounge cars serve light meals which you can take to a table or back to your seat.

Club Class cars have a double seat on one side of the aisle and a single on the other, with complimentary at-your-seat food and drinks service, including wine, as well as free newspapers and hot towels. Custom Class includes a newspaper and complimentary coffee, plus tea or juice in a café car shared only with Club Class passengers.

## Metroliner

Introduced by the Penn Central on the profitable route between New York City and Washington, DC, Metroliners are sleek electric trains capable of up to 160mph (250km/h), although top speed is usually restricted to 125mph (200km/h). They carry over two million passengers a year and the latest models have bright interiors, halogen reading lights and a computer hook-up at each seat. Café cars provide large tables on which to work. For the Metrophone information and reservations line call 1 800 523 8720.

## Heritage

Predating Amtrak, these refurbished coaches have reclining seats, leg rests and overhead luggage racks. Rest-rooms are located at one end of each coach. Full dining car service is normally available, together with lounge and sometimes dome cars. Sleeping accommodation consists of bedrooms and roomettes.

## Horizon Fleet

These short-distance coaches built by Bombardier operate out of Chicago or in the San Joaquin Valley. Horizon cars have similar facilities to Amfleet coaches but provide easier access for disabled passengers.

## California Fleet

Bi-level coaches feature large picture windows and headphone connections for recorded music. There are telephone and fax facilities as well as electrical outlets for laptop computers and handheld games. These coaches operate on the *San Joaquins* route and elsewhere in southern California. They were purchased by the state and are operated by Amtrak in partnership with the California Department of Transportation.

## Pacific Surfliner

With aerodynamic styling and ultra-efficient engineering, these latest bi-level trains are operated in partnership with Caltrans in southern California. Each five-car train has 422 seats and includes one Business Class car with personal audio and visual systems. Coach Class cars have wide reclining seats, panoramic windows, electrical outlets for laptop computers, Railfone and a digital information display showing station arrivals. Surfliner trains are designed to be easily accessible, especially for mobility-impaired passengers.

## Acela

Pronounced 'Ah-cell-ah', the name combines the words 'excellence' and 'acceleration'. *Acela Express* trains have replaced some *Metroliner* services in the Northeast Corridor, using all new equipment and making fewer stops. The sleek trains, built by Bombardier and Alstom in Vermont, New York and Quebec, use tilt technology to achieve speeds of up to 150mph and cut the time between New York City and Washington, DC, to two and three-quarter hours. *Acela Regional* trains will serve more destinations, while *Acela Commuter* trains will replace *Clockers*. *Metroliner* equipment is being refurbished for use on *Acela Regional* and *Commuter* routes.

## Cascades Service

Sporting distinctive, seven foot tall tail fins, Amtrak's sleek Cascades trains were built in Spain by Talgo and in Seattle by General Motors. They incorporate tilt technology and consist of 12 cars, each half the length of a normal Amtrak car, including a bistro and a dining car. They were bought in partnership with the Washington State Department of Transportation to operate along the Northwest Corridor. For safety reasons they are currently limited to 79mph but improvements to the track will eventually allow them to reach speeds of up to 110mph.

The comfortable coaches are painted in bold colours, officially known as Double Latte and Evergreen, and feature plush seats and Railfone as well as video and stereo services. Business Class includes wider seats, more leg room, TV screens and laptop computer outlets, plus complimentary snacks, drinks and newspapers.

For more information write to WSDOT Rail Office, PO Box 47387, Olympia, WA 98504, or call 1 800 822 2015 (705 7901 in Olympia).

## Sleeping

Reclining seats, dimmed lights and a free pillow from the attendant complement a gentle rocking and the hypnotic rumble of the wheels: obtaining a comfortable night's sleep is easy even when travelling Coach Class given a certain amount of practice. You also save money on hotels. For the best results you should choose a seat in the middle of the car away from the noise of sliding doors, and take a coat or blanket to ward off sometimes over-enthusiastic air conditioning. Souvenir blankets are sold on most long-distance trains. The pillows provided by Amtrak are fairly small so you may wish to take a larger one of your own. Alternatively, you could take a pillow case and ask the attendant for two pillows to put inside.

All sleeping car accommodation is designated First Class. Compartments are ingenious but small, and become no bigger as your journey progresses, so it helps if you enjoy camping. You do get extra privacy and there is a strange pleasure to be had from hurtling through the night in your personal travelling capsule. Try to obtain a compartment in the centre of the coach away from the vibration of the wheels. You can either make up your own bed or let the attendant do it for you, and he may even leave a goodnight sweet on your pillow. Towels, soap and bed linen are provided. Remember that sleeping car walls are usually thin so keep the noise down at night.

Complimentary tea, coffee or fruit juice (plus a newspaper) are served 06.30–09.30 to passengers in sleeping accommodation and your fare includes all meals in the dining car. Sleeping car passengers are entitled to make use of Amtrak's Metropolitan lounge waiting rooms both before and after their journey.

## Superliner bedrooms

All Superliner bedrooms have adjustable climate controls, individual reading lights, a fold-down table, garment rack and an electrical outlet.

### Standard bedroom

Ten standard bedrooms on the upper level and four on the lower level each accommodate two adults. Two reclining seats face each other or slide together to form the lower berth, and a second berth folds out from the wall. Features include a picture window, narrow closet (wardrobe) and an aisle window with curtains. Rooms are compact so it pays to leave most of your luggage in the lower storage area and take only a small bag into your bedroom. Room dimensions: 3ft 7in by 6ft 6in. Rest-rooms are provided on the lower or upper level.

### Deluxe bedroom

Five deluxe bedrooms are located on the upper level, each sleeping two adults in berths which fold down. Daytime seating consists of a large sofa and an armchair. Adjoining rooms can sometimes be combined into a suite for up to four people. Features include a closet and an aisle window with curtains. Space for two medium-sized suitcases. Room dimensions: 6ft 6in by 7ft 6in. Rest-room facilities include a shower, washbasin and toilet.

### Family bedroom

One family bedroom on the lower level sleeps two adults and two children, with daytime seating consisting of two chairs and a long sofa. Only a few family rooms are available on each trip so book well in advance if possible. Upper and lower berths are for adults, with two short berths for children. Family bedrooms extend the full width of the car, giving windows on each side. The windows are smaller, though, which makes watching the scenery less easy. Being on the lower level puts you closer to the wheels so you may find travelling slightly noisier, although this should not affect sleeping. Room dimensions: 5ft 3in by 9ft 6in. There is space for up to three suitcases and a rest-room is provided on the lower level.

### Accessible bedroom

Each sleeping car has a bedroom on the lower level intended for up to two people, including one passenger with special mobility requirements. Features include an attendant call button. Two berths fold down for sleeping and for daytime use there are two reclining seats. Space for two suitcases. The accommodation includes meals and drinks served in your room by the car attendant. Room dimensions: 6ft 6in by 9ft 6in. Rest-room facilities (which are curtained off) include a toilet, washbasin and hand grips.

## Heritage coaches
### Bedroom

Designed for two adults or for one adult and two children. Daytime accommodation consists of a long couch or two seats, and two berths fold down for sleeping. Space for three medium suitcases. Rest-room facilities include toilet, washbasin and 120V AC electric point.

### Roomette
For use by one adult, with a single seat for daytime use. A short berth folds down for sleeping. Individual controls regulate heating and air conditioning. There is also a shoe locker, a narrow closet and space for two medium suitcases. Rest-room facilities include toilet, washbasin, drinking water and 120V AC electric point. The toilet cannot be used when the bed is in position.

### Special roomette
For use by a disabled passenger, with an attendant call button provided. A single berth folds down for sleeping. Individual controls regulate heating and air conditioner and there is space for two suitcases. Accommodation includes all meals and drinks served in your room by the attendant. Rest-room facilities (curtained off) include a toilet, washbasin, hand grips, mirror and 120V AC electric point.

### Viewliners
These Amtrak-designed cars were the first single-level sleepers to be manufactured in the US for 40 years. Introduced on routes in the east and midwest they have largely replaced Heritage sleepers, which are now mostly used on the *Three Rivers* train or as crew dorms. Viewliners are larger and give a smoother ride. Their modular design means that each bedroom is a separate structure, making them quieter, and there are more windows so that upper berth passengers can have a view. All Viewliner bedrooms have adjustable climate controls, an electrical outlet, reading lights, built-in audio and a video screen for movies.

### Standard bedroom
Designed for one or two people. Two reclining seats convert into a bed at night and an upper berth drops down from the ceiling. There is a picture window and another window above for extra light. Rest-room facilities include a toilet, mirror and washbasin, and a shower is located nearby. If you are in a Viewliner by yourself, sleep in the top bunk, leaving more room to store your belongings below and have access to the toilet. Room dimensions: 3ft 7in by 6ft 6in.

### Deluxe bedroom
Extra space is provided for two people, with an armchair and a sofa. The sofa converts into a wide berth below an upper berth. Rest-room facilities include a private shower, toilet, mirror and washbasin. Two deluxe bedrooms can be combined into a suite for four people. Room dimensions: 6ft 6in by 7ft 3in.

### Accessible bedroom
This is a deluxe bedroom equipped for passengers with special mobility requirements, with all facilities accessible by wheelchair. There is a reclining

seat and upper and lower berths. Meals and drinks can be served to those with disabilities. Rest-room facilities include a private shower, toilet, mirror and washbasin. Room dimensions: 6ft 6in by 7ft 3in.

## Dining

Most long-distance trains have a complete dining car service, providing breakfast (06.30–10.30), lunch (11.30–14.30) and dinner (16.30–21.00). Meal service is generally available for passengers boarding 30 minutes before the end of each meal period.

Regional specialities such as barbecued spare ribs or fresh salmon are often added to the standard steak, chicken and lasagne menu, and there are special meals for vegetarians and children. Dessert is usually a choice of fruit pie (à la mode if you wish), cake or cheesecake. Breakfast is likely to consist of fresh fruit, cereal, bagels and muffins with cream cheese, jelly and butter. For kosher, low sodium or low cholesterol food you should let Amtrak know your requirements at least 72 hours before travelling. Call 1 800 USA RAIL and ask for the Special Services desk.

Advance dinner reservations are normally taken by the chief of on-board services or dining car attendant moving through the train. This minimises waiting time, since on arrival you can be seated straight away by the steward. The tables usually seat four so you may find yourself eating with strangers, which can be an entertaining and revealing experience. Amtrak uses china dishes and linen tablecloths on the *Capitol Limited*, *Coast Starlight* and *Southwest Chief*, and has plans to extend these civilised touches to other trains. *Auto Train* passengers receive a full dining car service but buffet-style dining cars operate on most Florida routes.

Lunch is usually better value than dinner for those keeping to a tight budget. Entrées range from about $8 to $14 and anything alcoholic tends to be expensive. Many people bring their own supplies of food and drink on board, but this is not encouraged and may be impractical for longer journeys. You can buy snacks such as sandwiches, pizza, soup, salad, drinks and sweets to take back to your seat or consume in the dinette or café car, which usually opens from 06.00 to midnight. Club Class provides a meal service to your seat.

## Lounge and dome cars

Superliners have a Sightseer lounge car, giving views through huge windows that extend part way over the roof. Here you can mingle with fellow passengers, watch a video movie (most likely a comedy or light drama) on the TV monitor in the evening, get a drink at the bar, buy a sandwich or coffee, and watch the changing landscape pass by outside. Movies and sometimes cartoons or travelogues are also occasionally shown during the afternoon. The films are about what you would expect to see on a 'pay per view' channel. You can also buy souvenir blankets, playing cards and postcards. Seating is on a first-come, first-served basis but it is good manners not to monopolise a seat all day.

Hospitality hour in the lounge is an excellent opportunity to sample exotic drinks, snack on hors d'oeuvres and break the ice by meeting new people. The relaxed atmosphere on board seems to encourage Americans in particular to tell their life stories to a complete stranger. This special kind of friendliness is encouraged by the thought that, unless you make a considerable effort, you are unlikely ever to see them again.

Amfleet and Heritage lounge and dome cars offer similar services to Superliners, with more 'land cruise' experience and wide-angle viewing on eastern and midwestern routes.

## Baggage

Trains can accommodate up to two items of carry-on luggage (maximum weight 50lb/22.7kg each) per passenger, but Amtrak encourages you to use its checked baggage service whenever possible. Carry-on bags with shoulder straps are easier to handle. There is storage space in overhead racks and at the end of the car. When occupying sleeping accommodation you can bring on board as much as will safely fit into your bedroom, although sometimes this will not be much. Additional bags can be left in the storage area outside your room.

Amtrak usually accepts no liability for loss or damage to carry-on luggage but you should report any problems to the attendant as soon as possible. Although usually safe to leave things behind on your seat when you visit the diner or lounge car, you should take expensive cameras or other items of value with you just in case.

Where a check-in service is provided you are allowed to check up to three items of baggage weighing no more than 50lb (22.7kg) each or 150lb (68kg) altogether. You pay a surcharge if this is exceeded but items slightly over the limit are usually permitted. Well-secured boxes or cartons weighing less than 50lb will also be accepted. If you require special assistance with your bags you should let Amtrak know when making reservations. Many stations provide free luggage trolleys. Others have handcarts for which a small charge is made, partly refunded when you return the cart to a vending machine.

Bags should be labelled with your name and address and checked in at least half an hour before departure. Checked baggage may be sent by a different route and get to your destination before you do. It will be held for up to five days without charge following your arrival. Amtrak's liability for checked baggage is limited to $500 per passenger, but you can purchase additional insurance up to $2,500. Claims for loss or damage must be submitted within 30 days. For more details ask for a copy of *Checked Baggage Service*, available at most stations or by mail.

An increasing number of trains now offer bicycle and ski racks. Space for bikes remains limited, though, so you should make reservations well ahead of your journey.

### Red Caps

Assistance with baggage is provided free of charge by uniformed Red Cap porters at most large stations. Items handled by Red Caps are not checked baggage and are your responsibility once loaded on to the train. Make sure you obtain a claim check for each bag in case anything is mislaid. Amtrak recommends you accept help only from a Red Cap.

## Safety

Try to arrive early in order to avoid rushing for your train. Don't leave luggage in the aisle or in the vestibules between cars. Always wear shoes when moving about the train and use handrails when boarding or climbing stairs. Only touch connecting doors on the 'press' plate to open them.

## Smoking

Smoking is prohibited on all short- and medium-distance trains as well as on the *Coast Starlight* and *Twilight Shoreliner*. For other long-distance overnight trains cigarette smoking is usually allowed only in a designated section of the lounge car or in a separate smoking room. No smoking is allowed in sleeping cars, dining cars or lounge cars on trains with a smoking room. Pipes and cigars are prohibited and cigarettes are not sold on trains that do not allow smoking.

Some long-distance trains provide semi-official smoking stops at certain stations along the way. Metropolitan lounges are non-smoking, as are all except the largest stations. If you smoke on a non-smoking train you may, without a warning, be asked to get off at the next stop.

## Tipping

You do not have to tip Amtrak personnel, although most people reward bar staff, waiters and sleeping car attendants, especially after a long trip. Some of the older, more wily attendants can judge how many dollar bills you have in your roll just by looking at it. The IRS taxes Amtrak officials based on what they expect the crew to receive in tips, so a dollar at breakfast is usual and a few dollars at dinner. Red Caps should be tipped one dollar per bag, or more where extra help has been provided. Train operating personnel such as conductors are never tipped.

## Alcohol

Except in sleeping cars you are not officially supposed to consume your own supplies of alcoholic drinks.

## Radios

Earphones or headphones must be used when listening to radios, personal stereos or portable TVs. Keep the volume down to prevent 'leakage'.

## Laptop computers

Electrical outlets for use with computers are available in Metropolitan lounges. Some trains also provide electrical sockets for use with laptops but train power current is not always stable so a surge protector should be used.

## Pets
Only certified guide or service animals accompanying passengers with disabilities are permitted on board. Documentation is required.

## Children
When travelling with children you should take a good supply of books, games and other amusements, such as quiet toys. Children must always be supervised by an adult while in the lounge car and should never be left unattended. Most trains have rest-rooms with infant changing facilities. Chicago's Union Station and the *Auto Train* have special play rooms and a private area for nursing mothers.

Even more than adults, children love to travel by train, especially since this is often a rare treat. Those aged under eight are not allowed to travel unaccompanied. Children aged between eight and eleven can do so during daylight hours, provided there are no transfers and both boarding and detraining stations are staffed. Prior written permission is required from the person in charge at the boarding station. Full adult fare will be charged. Call 1 800 USA RAIL for more information.

## Senior citizens
Those aged over 62 get a 15% discount off most coach fares. Some blackout dates apply and discounts are not available on *Metroliners*, the *Auto Train* or sleepers. For information on discounts for accommodation and other matters of interest contact the National Council of Senior Citizens, 8403 Colesville Road, Suite 1200, Silver Spring, MD 20910-3314; tel: 301 578 8800; fax: 301 578 8999; web: www.ncscinc.org.

## Students
Those with a Student Advantage card can get 15% off most Amtrak fares as well as reductions for hotels, car hire and theatres. Call 1 800 96 AMTRAK if you are a university or secondary school student, or visit www.studentadvantage.com.

## Group and convention travel
Generous extra discounts are available if you can rustle up a group of 20 or more people to travel (contact Amtrak for details).

## Passengers with disabilities
Except for the *Auto Train* and *Metroliners*, disabled passengers are entitled to 25% off regular one-way coach fares. Personal companions do not qualify for this discount. Disabled children pay half the disabled adult fare and guide dogs accompanying blind or deaf passengers travel free.

Wheelchair lifts are available at most stations. Passengers can receive special assistance at a station or on board provided 24 hours' notice is given. Most trains have special rest-rooms and sleeping accommodation, and meals can usually be served at your seat by the attendant. Call 1 800 USA RAIL for details and ask for a copy of *Access Amtrak*, a guide to services for the elderly or disabled. Explain your needs when making reservations and remember to bring any medication you require.

Amtrak Thruway and other bus connections are not accessible by wheelchair, although folding chairs can be stored. Disabled passengers must occupy a standard seat and be able to board the bus unassisted.

Hearing-impaired people can obtain information or make reservations by teletypewriter (1 800 523 6590). The service operates nationwide 24 hours a day, seven days a week. Many states supply access details in their brochures and a wide range of materials for people with disabilities, including information sheets, are available from the Society for the Advancement of Travel for the Handicapped (SATH), 347 Fifth Ave, Suite 610, New York, NY 10016; tel: 212 447 7284; web: www.sath.org.

## Railfone

An on-board telephone service is available on *Metroliners* and most other trains between Boston and Washington, DC, as well as on some trains in California and the midwest. You can make a call to anywhere in the world from a private booth, charging directly by credit card.

## Entertainment

Video movies, travelogues and card games are often a feature in the lounge car, as are games of trivia and scavenger hunts where you win a modest prize by giving the correct answers to a quiz or coming up with a specific object. Desperately competitive types should carry their birth certificate, a two dollar bill and a photograph of their pet. Games of bingo are sometimes organised in the dining-car.

On some routes an official guide will board the train to describe the history and wildlife of the landscape through which you are travelling.

## Photography

Seeing the country by train provides passengers with almost too many photo-opportunities. For best results a medium-speed film (ASA 64 or above) is recommended for shooting scenery through the windows. If your camera's shutter speed is adjustable (and light conditions permit) set it at 1/125sec or 1/250sec. Keeping the lens close to the window will help eliminate glare and reflections, or you can use a polarising filter. For interior shots using flash you can avoid reflections by not pointing directly at the windows.

## Things to take

Pack as lightly as possible, especially the bags you carry on board. You may find it useful to take a pair of binoculars, a good book, a deck of cards, maps (preferably showing rail lines), a light blanket, a pillow or large pillow case, earplugs or an eyeshade if you are a light sleeper, bathing and grooming items, a pocket torch, sunglasses, a cheap digital watch with an alarm, a small first-aid kit, bottled mineral or spring water (which will probably taste better than that provided at the drinking fountain), fresh fruit, nuts and other snacks. Wear comfortable clothes, especially shoes. There are no places on board to get cash, except by cashing a travellers' cheque, so take enough money to last the journey. A neck wallet or money belt will allow you to keep money hidden safely beneath your clothes.

## On-board service

The conductor is in charge of the train's crew and responsible for collecting tickets, identifying stops and ensuring the safety of the train. The chief of on-board services supervises the attendants on overnight long-distance trains.

Each coach attendant looks after a particular car and is a good person to make your friend. He or she will help with boarding, detraining, arranging seats, answering questions, bringing pillows and generally making your journey more agreeable. You are assigned a seat when you board and should not change it without consulting the attendant.

The sleeping-car attendant will help with your luggage, make up rooms for day or night use and bring your orders from the lounge car. In the morning he will provide complimentary tea, coffee or fruit juice and deliver a copy of the latest local newspaper to your room.

Service crew members such as car attendants, waiters and chefs ride the train all the way (except on the *Sunset Limited*) and have their own sleeping accommodation. Train personnel, such as conductors and engine crew, change every six or eight hours on long-distance routes.

## Crossing borders

US and Canadian citizens must have a passport, birth certificate, citizenship certificate or naturalisation certificate – a driver's license is not sufficient. Non-US citizens permanently or temporarily residing in the US must have an Alien Registration Card (I-551, or I-688 bearing proper endorsement on the reverse). Citizens of other countries not listed above must have a passport. Citizens of many countries must also have a visa, a US Employment Authorisation Card showing 210 as a section of law, or a Canadian Form IMM 1000. Passengers under 18 years old who are not accompanied by an adult must bring a letter from a parent or guardian giving them permission to enter Canada. Except for citizens of the USA and Canada, a valid visa is required for return to the United States after visiting Mexico, even after a one day trip.

See also *Chapter 3, Documents* (page 33). If in doubt check with your US embassy or contact the Immigration and Naturalisation Service in Washington, DC (see *Chapter 3* and *Appendix 2*). Passengers without proper documentation are prohibited from entering the US or Canada and will be detrained before reaching the US/Canadian border.

## Charter services

An entire train, or an exclusive Amtrak coach attached to a regular scheduled service, can be hired for group travel. Handsomely furnished, privately-owned cars are also available, offering the chance to experience a different type of train travel. The *Overland Trail* uses a 1949 lounge car restored to its former glory, making monthly trips between Los Angeles and San Diego. For information call 1 800 539 7245. To find a private railcar available for charter near you, contact the American Association of Private Railroad Car Owners on 202 547 5696.

## Complaints and suggestions

If you have any comments, compliments or suggestions regarding Amtrak services you can write to the Amtrak Customer Satisfaction Center, Washington Union Station, 60 Massachusetts Avenue, NE, Washington, DC 20002-4285 (enclosing your ticket receipt). Or contact the website: www.amtrak.com.

In July 2000, on the same day it unveiled its new logo, Amtrak introduced a guarantee of commitment to passenger satisfaction by promising to compensate for unsatisfactory experiences. If you did not receive a safe, comfortable and enjoyable trip you will be entitled to a certificate good for future Amtrak travel at equal cost. To encourage employees to 'take personal initiative and do what is necessary to solve guest problems' they will be offered a bonus equal to the average Amtrak ticket price (about $50) every month that 99.9% of customers are satisfied.

# For the Visitor from Overseas

## DOCUMENTS

Travellers to the USA should have a full passport valid for at least six months after the intended date of return, although the US has an agreement with most countries, including the UK, automatically to extend the validity of a passport for six months past its expiration date. A British passport therefore needs to be valid only for the duration of your stay. Passport information (for the UK) is available on the web: www.open.gov.uk/ukpass.

Children should have their own passport or be included in that of a parent or guardian. Canadians and permanent legal residents of the USA do not require a visa, nor do citizens of the UK, Australia, New Zealand, Argentina, Uruguay, Singapore, Brunei, Japan and most countries in western Europe, provided you intend to stay for no more than 90 days. You must have an unexpired passport, a return or onward ticket and a completed form I-94W, obtainable from airline and shipping companies en route. UK travellers to Canada planning to cross the land border into the USA no longer require a visa.

British passports must state that the holder is a British Citizen. If the passport states British Subject the holder must apply for a visa, and visa-free travel does not apply if you intend to work, study or stay in the US for more than 90 days. You may then require either a B-1 visa (for business) or a B-2 (pleasure). Application forms are available from travel agents, airlines, US embassies and consulates. Applications must be made by post or through a travel agent or courier two weeks (preferably a month) before your departure date. No charge is made to UK citizens.

Indefinite visas are no longer provided (the maximum is now ten years) but those in existence remain valid for ten years from the date they were issued. A visa is still valid in an expired passport if you also have a current passport. Make sure that when your expired passport was cancelled it was not clipped by the authority in such a way as to damage the visa and thereby make it invalid. If you are travelling visa-free and your passport is valid for less than 90 days you will only be admitted until the date your passport expires. If you hold a visa of any classification you are not required to hold a return ticket and may enter the US on a one-way ticket.

If in doubt, contact your US embassy for the latest requirements (in the UK call the premium rate number 09061 500 599 or 09068 200 290). Visa information is also available on the web: www.travel.state.gov/visa_services.html.

Where appropriate you should obtain in advance an International Student Identification Card, an American Youth Hostel card and an International Driver's Licence.

## Immigration

Before passing through immigration control you are given a form to complete, asking where you will be staying and the date you intend to leave. This is attached to your passport and must be shown on your departure. If you lose the certificate or wish to extend your stay you should contact the nearest Immigration and Naturalisation office. For more details contact US Immigration and Naturalisation (INS), 425 Eye Street NW, Washington, DC 20536; tel: 1 800 375 5283; web: www.ins.usdoj.gov.

Immigration officers may ask for some evidence that you can support yourself during your visit, usually reckoned on the basis of a minimum $150 per week. Take plenty of travellers' cheques and perhaps a copy of your latest bank statement or evidence of current employment. Resist any temptation to test the officers' sense of humour.

## Customs

As well as personal belongings you can bring in 200 cigarettes and 100 cigars. If aged over 21 you can also import one litre of wine, beer or spirits for your own use or as a gift. Food, illegal drugs, firearms and endangered species products such as ivory are forbidden. If carrying prescribed drugs, only take the quantity a person in your condition would normally require, and keep them in their original containers. You are allowed to take in or bring out any amount of currency but if it comes to more than $10,000, including travellers' cheques, you should report it to the Customs. The penalty for not doing so could be severe.

For more information contact the Customs Office of your US embassy or the Director, Passenger Programs, US Customs Service, 1300 Pennsylvania Ave NW, Room 5.4D, Washington, DC 20229; tel: 202 927 5580; web: www.customs.ustreas.gov.

Write to PO Box 7407, Washington, DC 20044 for a copy of *Know Before You Go* or check the website: www.customs.treas.gov/travel/know.htm.

## Health regulations

No inoculations are required for visitors from Europe. Visitors from elsewhere should check with their US embassy.

## Student card

Students can claim discounts ranging from air fares to accommodation to sightseeing. An International Student Identity Card (ISIC) gives generous deductions for VIA Rail train travel in Canada and for hotel chains such as Travel Lodge and Howard Johnson throughout North America. Discounts are available on airlines and for airport shuttle services in New York, Boston, San Francisco and Washington, DC, as well as at Busch Gardens, Sea World, Elvis Presley's Graceland, and the Rock and Roll Hall of Fame and Museum in

Cleveland. There is a 24-hour emergency assistance service which card holders can call toll-free from anywhere in the world.

Cards can be bought at Council Travel and STA Travel (see Appendix 1) or on the ISTC website. To be eligible you must be a full-time student. Ask for a directory when buying your card or look for current discounts on the International Student Travel Confederation website: www.istc.org.

## WHEN TO VISIT

Most people choose summer, when days are warmer and longer and most of the attractions will be open, but this can create problems. Hotels are more expensive, restaurants crowded and train reservations harder to come by. Large numbers of people, many as foreign as yourself, crowd around the very things you have come to see, and sometimes it can be too hot for comfort. Usually the weather is fine, though, and it can be exciting to travel when half the country seems on the move.

Train reservations, flights and accommodation are more readily available in winter, often at reduced prices. You see fewer tourists and more of the real America, with only an hour's wait for the Washington Monument elevator. The sun still often shines, at least in the south, and the skiing season is open. Landscapes, especially the Rocky Mountains, can look even more spectacular when sprinkled with snow.

For many people, spring and autumn (known as 'fall' to Americans) are probably the best times to visit. During spring, flowers bloom in the mountains and the countryside is at its greenest. New England's forests always put on a dazzling show for autumn 'leaf peepers'.

### Weather

The United States is a huge country with a diverse geography so the climate varies accordingly. Temperatures in some places can go well above 100°F (38°C) or as cold as minus 40°F (-4°C). Some places see dramatic differences between seasons; others scarcely change at all.

The north experiences European-type summers, but other regions, especially the southwest, become considerably hotter. The south and midwest are often humid. In winter the northwest continues to follow a European pattern, while the northeast and midwest become much colder. Florida, southern California and the southwest stay mostly warm throughout the year.

Although spring and fall are good times to visit, these seasons can be quite short. In the midwest summer and winter sometimes swap places within a few days. Autumn is the hurricane season along the Gulf of Mexico and tornadoes can occur in central regions during the spring.

## GETTING THERE

Competition has reduced the cost of flights, particularly over the North Atlantic, but fares vary tremendously according to date and season. Low season generally runs from November to March, excluding Christmas. Midweek flights tend to be cheaper and it usually pays to fly into a gateway airport such as Boston, Los Angeles or New York (John F Kennedy and Newark), though places such as Cincinnati, served by Delta (tel: 0800 414767; web: www.delta.com) and Charlotte, served by BA (tel: 0345 222111) are worth considering.

The main airlines flying from Europe include American (web: www.americanair.com), British Airways (web: www.britishairways.com), United Airlines (web: www.uk.ual.com) and Virgin Atlantic (web: www.fly.virgin.com). Air India, El Al and Kuwait Airlines may be cheaper to book through agents such as Trailfinders in the UK (tel: 020 7937 5400).

Charter flights are not necessarily less expensive but may offer a greater choice of departure airports, especially to Florida. British operators include Airtours (tel: 01706 260000) and Thomson (tel: 0990 133 122). Globespan, 10 West Mill Road, Colinton, Edinburgh EH13 0NX; tel: 0990 561522 operates mainly to Canada. For the latest deals check the national press or teletext for flight-only advertisements.

Council Travel sells Amtrak passes and specialises in student and budget travel. It offers flights to all the major North American cities and has offices world-wide, including 28A Poland Street, London W1V 3DB; tel: 020 7437 7767 and 205 East 42nd Street, New York, NY 10017; tel: 212 822 2700; web: www.counciltravel.com.

## MONEY

The American dollar (or buck) is worth 100 cents. Coins are one cent (penny), five cents (nickel), 10 cents (dime), 25 cents (quarter), 50 cents (half dollar) and one dollar. Dollar and half dollar coins seem almost as scarce as two dollar bills (now no longer printed). The most common denomination banknotes, all confusingly similar in size and colour, are for 1, 5, 10, 20 and 50 dollars. You need plenty of coins for telephones, buses, vending machines and tips so carry enough cash on arrival to last for two or three days. US dollars are widely accepted in Canada.

US dollar travellers' cheques are the safest and most convenient currency, with American Express and Thomas Cook the most widely recognised varieties. You can use them as cash in hotels, restaurants and shops (take your passport for identification). Signs saying 'no checks' generally refer to personal cheques. Lost or stolen cheques can be replaced by contacting the issuing company by phone (American Express: 1 800 221 7282; Thomas Cook: 1 800 223 7373). Keep a note of your cheque numbers separately from the cheques.

Charge and credit cards such as American Express, Visa and Access (usually known as Master Card in the US) are accepted throughout the USA. Handy when paying a deposit for hotels, car hire or tickets by phone, they can also be used to obtain cash at banks and bureaux de change. Always make a note of the card number and keep it separately. In case of loss or theft you should notify the police and call the card company's emergency number immediately. It pays to take two credit cards with you because hotels and car hire companies often 'block' an amount for themselves as a deposit and do not release it for some time after you have paid the bill. A second card helps in emergencies or if your first card balance gets too low. You could also ask your card company for a higher limit before you travel.

Banks generally open at 09.00 on weekdays, closing at 15.00 (Mon–Thur) or 17.00 (Fri). Not all of them will change foreign currency or travellers' cheques and, even if they do, the commission may be high. In an emergency you can have money transferred from your bank account at home to an associated US bank, or to an office of Thomas Cook. International money orders take about a week to arrive by airmail. If you become desperate, consulates will reluctantly help you obtain money from home.

## Prices

Unless you are rich or feeling extravagant you should reserve the uptown streets for window-shopping, looking for bargains where tourists are less in evidence. Books and records are particularly good value and are often found at a discount. Video tapes and computer games may not be compatible with your equipment at home but music cassettes and CDs should be fine. Clothing is also a good buy and New York's garment district has many bargain stores. American clothing and shoe sizes are different from British or European, so try things on before you buy.

Car hire, gas (petrol) and cigarettes are often only a third the price of their European equivalents. You can save even more on gas by using a self-service station and paying with cash. US gallons (3.8 litres) are five-sixths the volume of Imperial gallons (4.5 litres).

Local buses and subways provide excellent value, especially with a travel pass. Tourist bureaux should have the details. Taxis, on the other hand, can be expensive, although occasionally there is no safe or reliable alternative.

In most states a sales tax ranging from 3% to 9% is added to retail prices except on some foods and other goods, and these taxes may also apply to hotel rooms, airline tickets and car rental. Municipalities often impose their own taxes, too, so prices shown are usually less than you actually have to pay.

## FOOD

Americans dine out more than most people so finding somewhere to eat is rarely a problem. New York City alone boasts 15,000 places, from unpretentious cafés and hamburger bars to some of the finest restaurants in the world. Hot dogs, burgers, pizzas, Kentucky Chicken and McDonalds are sure to make you feel at home, although American versions are likely to be superior.

You may be lucky enough to find one of the few remaining 1940s-style diners. An authentic place should have chrome fittings, a juke box, ornate mirrors, counter seats and booths. Like coffee shops, diners are great for sampling the traditional American breakfast of eggs (cooked your way), crispy bacon, pancakes (with maple syrup), sausage, buttered toast and hash browns (fried grated potato). All washed down with coffee, tea (for the adventurous) or the ubiquitous Pepsi and Coca-Cola. Some places serve breakfast 24 hours a day.

Puddings are a major temptation, from home-made apple pie to chocolate fudge. No country has fancier doughnuts or better Danish pastries, not to mention chocolate-covered, peanut-filled pretzel nugget ice-cream. Other ice-cream varieties you may meet include garlic, lobster and many more.

America's diverse population produces a formidable range of cuisines. Some of the world's best Chinese food can be found in the Chinatowns of cities such as San Francisco and Los Angeles. You can sample black-eyed peas and grits in the south, steaks in Texas, and lobster, crabs or clam chowder in New England. Chicago invented the deep pan pizza and in New Orleans eating is a way of life.

Some restaurants offer all you can eat for a fixed charge or have two for the price of one deals. Lunch is usually better value than dinner, but look for early bird specials where evening meals are discounted until five or six pm. Mexican food is tasty and cheap and salad bars, delis and supermarkets provide the basis for an inexpensive picnic. Sandwich bars sell any filling or bread you can think of, including the famous bagels with cream cheese.

## DRINK

The water is safe to drink and Americans prefer it iced. If a glass is not delivered with your meal you only have to ask. Any soft drink is a soda. Pepsi and Coke come in small, medium (meaning large) and large (meaning gigantic) sizes. Sprite and 7-Up may be familiar but root-beer is definitely an acquired taste.

Bars range from the seedy to the glamorous and from cheerful to film-noir gloomy. The clientele may consist of businessmen, sports fans, gays, singles, TV addicts or any other all-American type. Look for cut-price drinks during happy hour, which sometimes stretches much further than 60 minutes. Arrive looking respectable between five and seven in the evening and you can often fill up on free hors d'oeuvres as you sample a margarita or mint julep.

Drinks served 'on the rocks' have ice added while those 'straight up' do not. If you fail to specify you will usually get the ice. Measures are generous and spirits often 90° proof so don't underestimate your consumption. Draught, canned and bottled beer will most likely be served well chilled, with brands such as Budweiser familiar to many non-Americans. Canadian or Mexican brands can also often be found. Various low-alcohol and alcohol-free 'Lite' beers are widely available. Groups can save money by ordering draught beer in a (usually half-gallon/2 litre) jug or pitcher. American wines, especially those from California, can be excellent.

Some states, including Utah, have laws restricting the sale of alcohol in various ways or in certain areas. All states have a minimum legal age for the purchase of alcohol (usually 21) so if you look young enough you may be asked for identification. It is an offence in most cities to consume alcohol in a public place.

## ACCOMMODATION

All big cities have international-style hotels such as Hiltons and Hyatts where you can expect first class service. Many of these have a toll-free reservation number available by calling 1 800 555 1212. Prices vary with the season but a double room is likely to cost upwards of $100 per night. Single rooms cost almost as much as doubles or triples so it pays to travel in company. Hotels may offer American plan (meals included) or European (without meals). Rates are lower if you book for a week or more and some chains offer discounts with prepaid vouchers.

Smaller hotels are more individual and charge $25-$75 per night for a single room. The local tourist bureau will help you choose a place in a safe area convenient for sightseeing. Bed & breakfast is becoming easier to find, especially in rural areas. Standards are high and prices start at around $35. Check with the tourist bureau or contact one of the agencies or directories for details. Those covering the whole country include BedandBreakfast.com, 1855 Blake Street, Suite 201, Denver, CO 80202; tel: 1 800 462 2632 or 303 274 2800; web: www.bedandbreakfast.com. Bed & Breakfast Inns ONLINE, PO Box 829, Madison, TN 37116; tel: 615 868 1946; email: info@bbonline.com; web: www.bbonline.com. BnBFinder, 355 South End Avenue 4th Floor, New York, NY 10280; tel: 212 432 7693; email: info@bnbfinder.com; web: www.bnbfinder.com/USA. Bed & Breakfast Inns of North America, 4516 Lovers Lane, Suite 204, Dallas, Texas 75225; web: www.inntravels.com.

Motels can cost as little as $25 a night but vary greatly in quality and service. Ask to see the room before accepting. The best motels will have a restaurant, a shop and possibly a swimming pool. Major chains include Holiday Inn, Travelodge, Marriott, Ramada and Best Western, all of which provide toll-free reservation numbers (1 800 555 1212). Econo Lodge (tel: 0800 444444) and Super 8 (tel: 1 800 889 9698; fax: 605 229 8907; web: www.super8.com/super8.html) are among the most economical places to stay. Unfortunately, motels tend to be a long way from downtown, making them less convenient for rail travellers.

An alternative, particularly for young people, are the YMCAs (2,400 altogether) found in most large cities in the USA. Many have swimming pools, cafés, a library and sports facilities. Single and double rooms are usually available to men and women. For information contact YMCA of the USA, 101 North Wacker Drive, Chicago, IL 60606; tel: 800 872 9622; email: info@ymcaworldservice.org; web: www.ymca.net

America also has more than 300 YWCA centres, for women only. Contact YWCA of the USA, Empire State Building, 350 Fifth Avenue, Suite 301, New York, NY 10118; tel: 212 273 7800; fax: 212 273 7939; web: www.ywca.org.

Hundreds of youth hostels provide some of the best value and friendliest accommodation, often located in a historic building. Some have family rooms. *The Hostel Handbook* written by Jim Williams gives details of over 700 hostels in the USA and Canada. The listings include the 200 hostels affiliated with Hostelling International and the almost 500 hostels not affiliated with HI. To obtain a copy write to The Hostel Handbook, 722 Saint Nicholas Avenue, New York, NY 10031, enclosing a cheque or money order for US$6 ($5 in the USA) made payable to Jim Williams. The book is also available from Amazon. Contact information: Tel: 212 926 7030; email: editor@hostelhandbook.com; web: www.hostelhandbook.com.

Most hostels close during the day and operate a midnight curfew. Cooking facilities are provided but alcohol and drugs are forbidden. For about $10 a night you get a bed in a dormitory (segregated by sex) but must supply your own sleeping bag. Although no age restrictions apply you are more likely to enjoy your stay if you remain young at least in spirit. International Youth Hostel membership can be taken out before travelling or guest membership purchased on arrival.

For more information contact American Youth Hostels, 733 15th Street NW, Suite 840, Washington, DC 2005; tel: 202 783 6161; fax: 202 783 6171; email: hostels@hiayh.org; web: www.hiayh.org.

For Canada contact Hostelling International-Canada, 400-205 Catherine Street, Ottawa, Ontario K2P 1C3; tel: 613 237 7884 or 1 800 663 57777 (for reservations); fax: 613 237 7868; email: Info@hostellingintl.ca; web: www.hostellingintl.ca.

Camping sites, public and private, can be found in most parts of the country. Unrestricted camping is still possible in wilderness areas (with a permit from the nearest park rangers' office) and some youth hostels permit camping. Reservations are recommended for state sites and those in national parks. For information contact the Director, National Park Service, 1849 C Street NW, Washington, DC 20240; tel: 202 208 6843; web: www.nps.gov.

Kampgrounds of America is a private organisation with 75,000 campsites throughout North America. Contact KOA, PO Box 30558, Billings, MT 59114; tel: 406 248 7444; web www.koakampgrounds.com.

If staying in one place for a few weeks it might be worth checking the price of apartments and rooms. Usually you need to rent for at least a month. Ask around and check in local newspapers under 'furnished rooms'. For college rooms available for let during summer you should enquire at the university housing office or local visitors' bureau.

## SIGHTSEEING

CityPasses are available for visitors to New York, Boston, Philadelphia, Chicago, Seattle, Hollywood and San Francisco. The San Francisco programme includes unlimited rides aboard cable cars and all other MUNI transportation. Each booklet contains actual tickets, not vouchers, to six of the most popular attractions and cultural institutions (except Hollywood, which includes eight), together with information about the best times to visit. Tickets are valid for nine days once the booklet has been presented to the first attraction.

Passes can be purchased at any CityPass attraction as well as many US travel agencies, visitor centres and at the website. Tel: 888 330 5008 or 707 256 0490 (for recorded information); email: info@citypass.net; web: www.citypass.net.

## TELEPHONES

The US telephone system is famous for its efficiency and economy. Public phones are found in train and bus stations as well as in stores, hotels, restaurants and bars. You don't have to be a customer to use one. Read the instructions before making your call and have lots of change handy, or pay with a credit card by calling 1 800 CALL ATT. Local calls usually cost 25 cents. Press '1' before the area code when calling from out of town, and for operator assistance press '0'.

If you need to find a local number and have no directory call 1 555 1212. For long-distance information call 1 (area code) 555 1212. Directory inquiries are free from pay phones. The international dialling code for the USA and Canada is 1. No international code is required for calls from the US to Canada and vice versa. Simply use the area code in the usual way.

Calls prefixed 800 or 1 800 are toll-free and any toll-free number can be obtained by calling 1 800 555 1212. Toll-free numbers can be dialled from outside the US but in that case they are charged at the same rate as any other international call. Use only the 800 part of the prefix, not the whole 1 800.

Calling home is cheaper from a public telephone than from a hotel, which may add a surcharge. It is easiest to call collect (reverse charges) and the international operator can be contacted on 1 800 874 4000. The international prefix for calls from the USA is 011, which must be followed by the relevant country code (44 for the UK). Use a private telephone and dial direct between 23.00 and 08.00 for the lowest call rates.

In most places the emergency number for police, fire or ambulance is 911. No coin is required. If in difficulty call the operator on 0 or 01.

## ON-LINE COMMUNICATIONS

Electronic mail (email) can be sent or received immediately by those with access to the internet and there is no need to lug around a notebook computer or modem. Instead, look for cybercafés, web terminals, libraries or arrange to meet friends with internet connections along the way. You may also gain brief access to the Web in computer/Internet company showrooms (ask the salesperson nicely) or at universities and colleges. If this is not possible they may be able to recommend somewhere suitable.

With an email account through an Internet Service Provider, or if you sign up for a free POP mail account, you can access your mailbox using a Web-based POP mail interface such as Hotmail. You will need to know your email server name as well as your username and password. Write these down and test the system before leaving home. Your server name will most likely be the information after the '@' mark in your email address and your username is usually the information before the mark.

If you want to keep the messages in your mailbox to read again when you get home, leave them on the server. Otherwise, make sure you select the 'Delete' option. Free email providers include USA-NET (web: www.usa.net), Hotmail (web: www.hotmail.com) and Mail2Web (web: www.mail2web.com). Do not leave your email account unused for more than two or three months or it may be closed.

## POSTAL SERVICE

The US Mail service is less wonderful than America's telephones, so when sending postcards home you should allow at least a week for delivery. Either put them in the appropriate box or hand them over the counter at a post office, where you will find information on mailing rates. Post offices open 09.00–17.00 on weekdays and 09.00–12.00 on Saturdays. Large cities often have one branch that opens 24 hours a day. You can also buy stamps (at 25% extra cost) from shops or vending machines.

Street corner mail boxes are dark blue and may be mistaken by the unwary for litter bins. Allow between two and four days for letters to be delivered within the US, or a day more without the Zip (area) code. The correct code can be obtained from the telephone directory or at a post office or by calling 1 800 ASK USPS (1 800 275 8777). This toll-free number also has details of mailing costs, post office hours and other information.

Packets or parcels weighing 16 ounces (half a kilogram) or more must be presented to a postal clerk or mailing agent. This is an anti-terrorist policy designed to eliminate the risk of terrorism on aircraft.

Mail can be delivered c/o General Delivery at any main US Post Office, which will keep it for up to a month. To collect your letters you will need a passport or other identification.

## NEWSPAPERS

America has more daily newspapers than any other country in the world. There is no national press apart from the *Wall Street Journal* and *USA Today*, but the *Los Angeles Times* and *New York Times* are widely distributed outside their own cities. Local papers are inexpensive (some only 25 cents), heavy (especially at weekends) and great value for the funny pages alone. You can buy them from station shops and street corner vending machines. A local paper gives you insight into a town's character and provides up-to-date information about clubs, hotels, shops and theatres. Look for restaurant and cinema advertisements offering special deals.

Foreign newspapers are hard to find even in big cities, although public libraries should be able to track down a week-old copy of something reassuring.

## TIPPING

You may think that tipping is a class-conscious anachronism inappropriate for a country where everyone has been proclaimed equal. This is not a good line to adopt with the average cab driver. He expects 10% or 15%, as do bartenders and hairdressers, and in restaurants 20% is more usual. Follow the practice of other customers or you may notice an abrupt change in the standard of service. Tipping is not necessary in self-service cafés or fast food restaurants.

Most hotels don't include a service charge so a tip is expected. Hotel, airport and railway porters receive one dollar per bag. Of course, you don't have to tip anyone who is rude or unhelpful. Amtrak service is free but attendants should be rewarded for exceptional assistance.

## CAR TRAVEL

Trains and buses may not take you everywhere you wish to go so you may need to hire a car. You are allowed to drive for up to a year in the USA provided you hold a valid licence in a country (such as the UK) which has ratified the Geneva Road Traffic Convention. An international driving licence is not essential but will be more readily accepted by a traffic cop than the home country version. The speed limit is mostly 25 mph (40km/h) in towns, 55mph (88km/h) outside towns (65mph; 105km/h on some interstates) and strictly enforced. Always carry your licence when driving – it is a legal requirement.

Rental companies have a minimum age restriction (usually 21) and sometimes a maximum. Check the limits when booking and take your passport as proof. National firms have offices in most cities and can be reached on the following toll-free numbers or websites – Hertz (tel: 1 800 654 3131; web: www.hertz.com); Avis (tel: 1 800 230 4898; web: www.avis.com); Budget (tel: 1 800 527 0700; web: www.drivebudget.com); Dollar (tel: 1 800 800 3665; web: www.dollar.com); Thrifty (tel: 1 800 847 4389; web: www.thrifty.com). For cheap transport, companies with names like Rent-A-Wreck (tel: 1 800 944 7501; web: www.rent-a-wreck.com) hire out battered but roadworthy cars past their prime.

Local companies may be less expensive but national ones allow you to rent a car in one place and leave it in another, though this may be expensive. Prices depend on location, size of vehicle and rental period. Economy cars are smallest, followed by compact and standard (the normal American size). Virtually all have automatic gears. The cheapest rates are obtained if you book well ahead, especially online.

Make sure you obtain third party insurance of at least half a million dollars, and ask for a collision damage waiver (CDW) or loss damage waiver (LDW) that includes protection against vandalism and theft. Avoid 'fuel purchase plans' where you have to prepay for a full tank of gas or pay for what you have used when you return the car with a part-filled tank. The hire company will charge an exorbitant amount (by US standards) for the refill fuel.

If you plan to drive extensively you may find it more economical to take out car insurance before leaving home. American policies don't always include third party protection and in some states insurance is voluntary – two good reasons for having full medical cover (see next section). Members of affiliated organisations can obtain free assistance and route maps from the American Automobile Association, 1050 Hingham Street, Rocklin, MA 02370; tel: 1 800 222 4357; web: www.aaa.com.

### Cars for the disabled

Some rental companies provide hand-controlled cars (call their toll-free numbers to check). For further information contact the Society for the Advancement of Travel for the Handicapped (SATH), 347 Fifth Ave, Suite 610, New York, NY 10016; tel: 212 447 7284; web: www.sath.org.

## MEDICAL INSURANCE

The USA has no free health service available to overseas visitors. A hospital room alone can cost $300 per night so horror stories about people being financially ruined by illness or accident are not apocryphal. Make sure you take out sufficient insurance cover for your entire stay, including provision to be flown home for treatment if necessary ($5 million is recommended). Airlines and travel agents usually try to sell you their own policies but check the small print and compare prices. If you plan a long stay it may be cheaper to buy annual cover.

Hospital clinics will often provide simple treatments and some have a 24-hour emergency room. Most towns have a late-opening pharmacy. If you need regular medication you should be sure to take sufficient to last for your visit. For prescribed drugs you should obtain a letter from your doctor explaining why you need them. If you wear glasses, carry an extra pair.

## Other insurance

Make sure your policy protects against cancellation or delays, loss of baggage or passport, and claims for negligence. LIS (personal liability insurance) will protect you if you are sued by third parties in the event of an accident. PAI (personal accident insurance) provides a one-off payment in the case of death or serious injury. PEC (personal effects coverage) will pay for lost or stolen items, including those stolen from a car. If you plan to indulge in adventurous sports such as skiing or white-water rafting you may have to pay an extra premium. For motor insurance, see *Car travel*.

Take copies of all your insurance policies with you and make a separate note of their numbers and any emergency phone numbers.

## CRIME

Most people survive a visit to the United States without being mugged, assaulted or robbed, but sensible precautions should always be taken. Don't keep all your valuables in one place, then if some are stolen you still have an emergency fund. Keep to downtown or well-lighted areas at night and avoid going to secluded places alone. Your hotel desk clerk will advise on safety for the part of town in which you are staying.

Try to be inconspicuous. Don't flash money around in public but carry a small amount to surrender if threatened. Carry your camera in a bag, use the hotel safe for valuables and always lock your hotel door. Watch over your belongings and be wary of pickpockets or bag snatchers in crowded places such as train and bus stations. Don't ask strangers to keep an eye on your things. At stations, only trust your bags to a uniformed member of staff. Report any theft to the police and ask for a reference number to show to your insurance company.

When driving, don't stop if flagged down by anyone other than the police, and keep all windows and doors locked. If you get lost, drive to a well-lit area before asking directions. When leaving your car, lock any bags and packages in the boot and park in a busy place. Never hitch-hike or pick up hitch-hikers.

Many cities have residential areas which are effectively segregated by race so ask advice before venturing where your presence might be too distinctive. All policemen and some security guards carry guns. Do not run away if challenged.

## DRUGS

The authorities take a dim view of illegal drug use even in California, where possession of small amounts of cannabis may be overlooked. Apart from the dangers inherent in dealing with shifty characters on street corners you are more than likely to be ripped off. If caught with drugs the best you can hope for is to be put on the next flight home, and you will find it less easy to get into

America another time. If you do run into trouble you should contact your nearest consulate, which will recommend a lawyer.

## SEX
The dangers of casual sex are well known. AIDS is a serious problem in the USA, where upwards of 1.5 million people are thought to be HIV-positive. In many cities a majority of prostitutes carry the virus and Nevada is the only state where prostitution is legal. Enjoy the bars and night life but save your affections for those you can trust.

Some states, particularly in the south and midwest, have laws restricting certain types of sexual behaviour that may be permitted where you come from. In most places the age of consent is 16, although it may be up to 18. Statutory rape (consensual sex with a minor) is treated legally in the same way as any other rape.

## TIME ZONES
Mainland USA has four time zones. Seattle (Pacific Time) is an hour behind Denver (Mountain Time), two hours behind Chicago (Central Time) and three hours behind New York (Eastern Time). Amtrak schedules take account of this and show local times for arrival and departure.

Canada and most of the USA, apart from Arizona and some of Indiana, observe Summer Time (Daylight Saving Time). Clocks are set ahead an hour at 02.00 on the last Sunday in April. Standard Time returns when clocks go back an hour on the last Sunday in October.

## PUBLIC HOLIDAYS
Banks, post offices, businesses, museums and government agencies are likely to be closed on the following dates:

## USA
| | |
|---|---|
| New Year's Day | January 1 |
| Martin Luther King's Birthday | Third Monday in January |
| Lincoln's Birthday | First Monday in February |
| Presidents' Day | Third Monday in February |
| St Patrick's Day | March 17 |
| Memorial Day | Last Monday in May |
| Independence Day | July 4 |
| Labor Day | First Monday in September |
| Columbus Day | Second Monday in October |
| Election Day | November 4 |
| Veteran's Day | November 11 |
| Thanksgiving | Fourth Thursday in November (the day after Thanksgiving is also effectively, if not officially, a holiday) |
| Christmas Day | December 25 |

Some states celebrate George Washington's Birthday (February 22) instead of Presidents' Day or make October 12 Columbus Day.

## Canada

Public holidays in Canada include the following:

| | |
|---|---|
| New Year | January 1 |
| Good Friday | |
| Easter Sunday | |
| Easter Monday | |
| Victoria Day | Next to last Monday in May |
| Canada Day | July 1 |
| Labour Day | First Monday in September |
| Thanksgiving Day | Second Monday in October |
| Christmas | December 25 |
| Boxing Day | December 26 |

Travelling on holidays, even when possible, is sure to be crowded. However, if it is unavoidable, remember to book tickets and accommodation well ahead.

## WORKING

Working illegally can result in stiff penalties, including being deported and banned from re-entering the USA for up to five years. To work legally you must obtain a special visa (J-1 or H-2) prior to departure. Forms are available from US employer sponsors. For more information contact the Consumer Center, Department 455W, Pueblo, CO 81009; tel: 1 888 878 3256.

If you get on well with children and are aged 18 or over you can apply to work at one of America's 12,000 summer camps. Most are in the northeast but some can be found as far west as California and Oregon. Work starts in June and lasts for about nine weeks. You can also be employed as a family companion – providing child care and doing light household duties. You receive a return flight, the necessary work permit, pocket money, board and lodging, plus two months free time for independent travel. Contact Camp America, 37a Queens Gate, London SW7 5HR; tel: 020 7581 7373; email: equiries@campamerica.co.uk; web: campamerica.co.uk.

BUNAC (the British Universities North America Club) has summer camp and other work programmes in the US and Canada. Jobs last for up to 12 months and are for students only. Early application is strongly advised. Visas are usually valid from June to October and support is provided from a New York office. There are good travel deals, loan plans and free job directories. BUNAC is at 16 Bowling Green Lane, London EC1R 0QH; tel 020 7251 3472; fax: 020 7251 0215; email: enquiries@bunac.org.uk; web: www.bunac.org/uk.

In the USA, contact PO BOX 430, Southbury, CT 06488; tel: 203 264 0901; fax: 203 264 0251; email: info@bunacusa.org; web: www.bunac.org/usa.

# Part Two

# Trains and Routes in the United States

## HOW TO USE PART TWO OF THIS BOOK

Each of the following sections gives details of a different long-distance Amtrak train. Scheduled stops are those shown in **ALL CAPITALS**. These and other places en route are followed by figures in parentheses, eg: **Kent (20/32)**. This shows that when you are travelling in the direction described in the text you will pass through Kent 20 minutes after departing from the previous scheduled stopping station, **SEATTLE**. Going on from Kent it will be 32 minutes to the next stop at **TACOMA** (see page 52 for this example). Routes can therefore be read in either direction, changing left for right and arrival for departure as appropriate. However, you should note that the timetable means that some places can only be seen by day when you are travelling in one direction.

### Accommodation

Accommodation has been selected wherever possible for easy access from the rail station or from the downtown area. Consideration is also given to safety and value for money, hotels being listed in descending order of price per room.

### Telephone codes

Where a telephone code is separately listed in the information given for a town or city, unless otherwise noted, it applies to all visitor attractions, places to stay etc included within that town's entry, whether these are actually situated within the city limits or some distance away.

### The maps

The strip maps that illustrate the routes are inevitably schematic. They are not to scale and curves have been straightened, although the North indicators will show you roughly which direction you are travelling in. Please refer to the Area Maps (inside front cover) for a more accurate impression of the routes.

# The *Coast Starlight*
# Seattle–Los Angeles

## General route information

One of Amtrak's most popular and scenic routes, this is a particular favourite with young people. Not surprisingly, a party atmosphere often develops, starting in the lounge car and spreading throughout the train. On the 35-hour journey you can see snow-covered mountains, deep forest valleys and long stretches of Pacific shoreline. When travelling south, choose a seat on the right of the train for the best views.

Between San Francisco and Los Angeles the *Coast Starlight* follows tracks formerly used by the Southern Pacific Railroad's *Daylight Express*, and one of the *Express*'s last steam engines was brought out of retirement to haul the American Bicentennial Freedom Train.

As on some other routes, first class passengers on the *Coast Starlight* may be presented with a gift, such as a glass mug or an umbrella decorated with the train's logo.

**Frequency** Daily.

The southbound service leaves Seattle mid-morning to arrive in Portland by early afternoon, Emeryville (for San Francisco) early next morning, Santa Barbara by early evening and Los Angeles mid-evening.

Travelling north, trains leave Los Angeles mid-morning to reach Santa Barbara just after midday and Emeryville by mid-evening. You arrive in Portland the following afternoon and Seattle by mid-evening.

**Reservations** All reserved.

Book well ahead during summer and at weekends. Passengers for San Francisco have bus transport from Emeryville included.

**Equipment** Superliner coaches.

**Sleeping** Superliner bedrooms.

**Food** Complete meals, snacks, sandwiches and drinks.

**Lounge Car** Video movies, games, hospitality hour. A children's playroom on some trains provides games, movies and other activities (parental supervision required). The Parlor Car (for first class passengers) has a library, large-screen movies, wine tastings, fresh flowers and candle-lit evenings. Parlor Cars are refurbished Santa Fe Heritage coaches with polished wood panelling.

**Baggage** Check-in service at most stations.

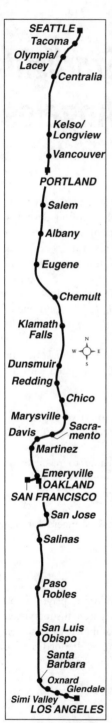

SEATTLE
Tacoma
Olympia/
Lacey
Centralia

Kelso/
Longview
Vancouver
PORTLAND
Salem

Albany

Eugene

Chemult

Klamath
Falls

N
W ─◇─ E
S

Dunsmuir
Redding
Chico
Marysville
Sacra-
Davis ─ mento
Martinez

Emeryville
OAKLAND
SAN FRANCISCO

San Jose

Salinas

Paso
Robles

San Luis
Obispo
Santa
Barbara
Oxnard
Glendale
Simi Valley
LOS ANGELES

# Joining the train
## SEATTLE
Surrounded by mountains, Lake Washington and Puget Sound, the Emerald City was named after Chief Sealth of the Damish and Suquamish tribes. Seattle sees only 56 days of sun a year but has less rainfall than New York or Atlanta, so the city is not quite so wet as outsiders may imagine. Water provides an important leisure resource, however, and countless marinas provide enough space for two boats to every three people.

Seattle was the birthplace of Jimi Hendrix (buried in Greenwood Cemetery in the suburb of Renton), Starbucks coffee, grunge rock and the Microsoft company owned by Bill Gates, America's richest man. Lately one of America's most fashionable cities, famous for its coffee houses, Seattle has been the setting for movies such as *The Fabulous Baker Boys*, *Sleepless In Seattle* and *Singles*, as well as television's *Frasier*. A month-long film festival is held each spring and the Folklife music festival takes place around Memorial Day.

### Seattle basics
**Telephone code** 206.
**Station** Handsome King Street Station at 303 S Jackson, with its distinctive clock tower, was built by the Great Northern Railway in 1905. Ticket-office open 06.15–20.00. Waiting-room 06.00–22.00. Lockers, vending machines, newspapers, handcarts, Red Caps, ATM banking, taxi stand.
**Connections** Amtrak trains operate daily into Canada and Thruway buses (tel: 604 875 1307) connect incoming and outgoing *Coast Starlight* trains with Vancouver, BC.
**Local transport** Metro buses (tel: 553 3000) are free in the downtown area. Seattle has some of the worst traffic problems in the USA and so it pays to use public transport. The monorail (tel: 905 2600) operates a startling 90 second service between the downtown Westlake shopping mall and the Seattle Center.
**Taxis** Yellow; tel: 622 7395. Farwest; tel: 622 1717.
**Car rental** Budget 19030 28th Ave S; tel: 800 527 0700.
**Greyhound** 8th Ave and Stewart; tel: 628 5555.
**Seattle-Tacoma Airport** Located 14 miles south and accessible by Airport Express (tel: 626 6088) and Metro bus #174.
**Tours** Gray Line (tel: 624 5077) has coach and boat excursions. Sunset trips over Puget Sound from Sound Flight; tel: 255 6500. Spirit of Washington Dinner Train; tel:

425 227 7245 or 1 800 876 7245; fax: 425 277 8839; web:
www.SpiritofWashingtonDinnerTrain.com.

**Visitors bureau** Open weekdays, daily in summer, at 8th and Pike; tel: 461 5840;
email: visinfo@seeseattle.org; web: www.seeseattle.org.

**Accommodation** Contact Pacific Bed & Breakfast, 701 NW 60th; tel: 784 0539 or
the B & B Inn Association, Box 95853, Seattle, WA 98145 (tel: 547 1020).

YMCA, 909 4th Ave; tel: 382 5000. Incorporates the Traveller's Aid office. Over
200 rooms for men or women. Single $30, double $35. YWCA, 1118 5th Ave; tel:
461 4888. Women over 18 only. Single $30, double $42, weekly $185. AYH Youth
Hostel, 84 Union; tel: 622 5443; web: www.hiseattle.org. Free lockers and storage.
Dormitory rooms. Members $16, non-members $19. Bigfoot Backpackers Hostel,
126 Broadway E; tel: 720 2965; web: www.bigfootbphostel.com. Free coffee,
breakfast and pick-up service from anywhere downtown. Single $35, double $40,
shared rooms $15.

Hotels include the Four Seasons Olympic at 411 University; tel: 621 1700;
Sorrento, 900 Madison; tel: 622 6400; Sixth Avenue Inn, 2000 6th Ave; tel: 441 8300;
Town Center Inn, 2205 7th Ave; tel: 622 3434; Hotel Seattle, 315 Seneca; tel: 206 623
5110; Inn at Queen Anne, 505 First Ave N; tel: 206 282 7357.

## Recommended in Seattle

**Seattle Center** 305 Harrison; tel: 684 7200 or 684 7100; web:
www.seattlecenter.com. This legacy of the 1962 World's Fair, a minute or so from
downtown by monorail, has over 70 acres (28ha) of parkland and entertainments,
dominated by the 605ft (198m) Space Needle (tel: 443 2111; web:
www.spaceneedle.com). Take an elevator to the observation deck for lofty views of
the city, Puget Sound and Mount Rainier.

**The Waterfront** Where gold arrived during the 1897 Klondike rush, ex-
Australian streetcars now run along waterfront tracks. Ferries to Canada and
Alaska go from Pier 48, and to Bremerton and Bainbridge Island from Pier 52,
giving wealthy island commuters inspiring views of snow-capped mountains and
an occasional whale.

**Ye Olde Curiosity Shop** at Pier 54 sells souvenirs and has a museum of bizarre
relics (tel: 682 5844). Pier 55 has Argosy Cruises (tel: 623 1445) and excursions from
Pier 56 go to Tillicum Village on Blake Island (tel: 933 8600). The **Seattle
Aquarium** is at Pier 59 with its coral reef and underwater dome; tel: 386 4320; web:
www.seattleaquarium.org.

**Pike Place Market** Between downtown and the Waterfront at 1st and Pike; web:
www.pikeplacemarket.org. This 1907 market is a warren of shops, restaurants,
galleries and stalls selling every kind of fish, fruit and vegetable. Great for street
entertainment, people-watching and dodging the flying salmon. Open daily, free.

**Pioneer Square** Covering 12 blocks from 2nd Ave to the Waterfront. The square is
where Seattle began in the 1850s with the setting up of a sawmill and where logs were
skimmed along Skid Road. During the gold rush this became a dangerous place and
in the Depression it was a refuge for down-and-outs (the original 'Skid Row'). Art
galleries, restaurants and shops now occupy restored buildings and daily
**Underground Tours** (tel: 682 4646) explore the basements of old Seattle.

**Klondike Gold Rush National Historic Park** 117 S Main; tel: 553 7220.
Depicting the excitement and hardship, with old mining photographs and clothes.
Chaplin's *The Gold Rush* is shown on weekend afternoons. Open daily, free.
**Museum of Flight** 9404 E Marginal Way S; tel: 764 5720; web:
www.museumofflight.org. Chronicles the history of flying from the Wright Brothers
up to the space age. Open daily, admission charge.
**Northwest Railway Museum** 38625 SE King in Snoqualmie; tel: 425 888 3030;
web: www.trainmuseum.org . One of the largest displays in the country, with steam
locomotives, passenger and freight cars, and specialised railway equipment that built
and maintained the right-of-way. **Snoqualmie Depot**, built in 1890, has been fully
restored and there are train rides through the upper Snoqualmie Valley. Open daily,
admission charge.
**Seattle Art Museum** 100 University; tel: 654 3100; web: www.seattleartmuseum.org.
The largest art museum in the region, with Native American paintings, African masks,
old masters and contemporary works. Open daily, admission charge.
**Pacific Science Center** 200 2nd Ave N; tel: 443 2001; web: www.pacsi.org. Explore
the tropical butterfly house and see robotic dinosaurs. IMAX films in 3D. Open daily,
admission charge.

# All aboard!

The *Coast Starlight* leaves King Street Station with Smith Tower, once one of
the city's tallest buildings, on your right. You pass the Kingdome sports
stadium, also on the right, and for the next few miles travel through
industrial scenes where factories are owned by the likes of Westinghouse,
Nabisco and Ford.

**Boeing Field (7/45)** Seattle's largest manufacturing company is on your
right. The airport is used for testing and sometimes by private planes. Boeing's
original factory, a redbrick building seen across the runway, is now the
Museum of Flight.

The *Coast Starlight* continues through residential areas, with the Green River
on your right.

**Kent (20/32)** Look left for an interesting old train station and Longacres
racetrack.

After the train crosses the Green River, half an hour from Seattle, the urban
landscape begins to give way to small farms and dairies. The train crosses the
White River and makes a long right turn towards the east, crossing the
Puyallup River.

**Puyallup (40/12)** This town, like the river, was named after a Native
American tribe. A pioneer named Ezra Meeker who had crossed the plains
with an ox team in 1882 to set up home here returned to New York in 1906,
marking the Oregon Trail with many monuments.

You go through downtown and attractive western suburbs then cross

Clark's Creek, travelling southwest through tall pine forest. Look for the bright, dandelion-like flowers of gosmore, or 'cat's ear'.

**TACOMA (52/42)** Note the eccentric domed Transit Center building. Tacoma was chosen as the terminus of the North Pacific Railroad in 1873 and soon became known as 'the city of destiny', where much of the state's lumber reached the sawmills. The old Milwaukee, St Paul & Pacific Railroad freighthouse, located a few blocks south of Amtrak's station, has found a new life as Tacoma's public market. Timber is still an important industry here, along with shipbuilding. The **visitors bureau** is at 1001 Pacific Ave; tel: 800 272 2662; email: info@traveltacoma.com; web: www.tpctourism.org.

Tacoma overlooks Commencement Bay in the east and the Tacoma Narrows highway bridge to the west. Point Defiance Park, zoo and aquarium is famous for its octopuses (tel: 253 591 5337; web: www.pdza.org). The State History Museum can be found at 1911 Pacific Ave; tel: 253 272 3500; web: www.wshs.org.

The *Coast Starlight* leaves Tacoma alongside the City Waterway. Old City Hall, with its elaborate clock tower, can be seen perched beside the North Pacific Railroad building on cliffs to your left.

A few minutes later the train goes through a tunnel and turns due south, emerging on the shoreline of Puget Sound with the Olympic Mountains beyond. This idyllic coast has dozens of coves and piers, with pleasure boats coming and going. Look also for herons and bald eagles gliding above the rivers, which have names such as Nisqually, Nooksack and Skookumchuck.

**Stellacoom (26/16)** A ferry terminal serves Anderson and McNeal Islands, visible across Henderson Bay to your right. Brilliant yellow broom grows beside the track.

**OLYMPIA/LACEY (42/20)** Olympia is Washington's state capital, with a Capitol dome that claims to be the largest domed masonry building in the country. Amtrak's station is at 6600 Yelm Hwy SE. The 900,000 acres (360,000ha) Olympic National Park is accessible along US 101.

Soon after pulling out of Olympia, the *Coast Starlight* crosses the Skookumchuck River.

**CENTRALIA (20/45)** This food processing and logging town was founded in 1875 by a former slave from Virginia called George Washington. Early settlers built the blockhouse in Fort Borst Park as a defence against marauding Indians. Amtrak's picturesque brick station is at 210 Railroad Ave. Ticket-office open 09.30–18.00.

As the train departs you glimpse the Mount St Helens volcano across fields to your left. A massive eruption in 1980 killed 57 people, together with thousands of birds, animals and fish. Traces of grey ash can still be seen, although grass and a few trees now grow on 'pumice plain'.

The train continues south through Chehalis then crosses the Newaukum River.

**Winlock (18/27)** 'The egg capital of the world', where the planet's largest egg nestles in a monument to your right. Winlock's mighty chicken industry is celebrated with an annual festival.

**Castle Rock (35/10)** You cross the Toutle River, with the Cowlitz River on your right. Mud was pushed this far from the St Helens' explosion 40 miles away. The volcano is now a 110,000-acre (45,000ha) park where you can take a flight over the summit and buy souvenirs sculpted from the debris.

**KELSO/LONGVIEW (45/40)** 'The smelt capital of the world', where vast numbers of these small fish swim up the Cowlitz River each year to spawn. Kelso also has a major lumber industry and deep water port. The Cowlitz County Historical Museum is at 405 Allen; tel: 360 425 1297.

On a clear day, three of America's most impressive mountains can be seen as you leave. Mount St Helens (8,400ft/2,560m) and Mount Adams (12,307ft/3,750m) are to your left, and Mount Rainier (14,410ft/4,390m) to your right. Between May and October, Gray Line tour buses operate from Seattle to Rainier National Park.

**Columbia River (8/32)** To your right, the train joins the river which used to represent the border between the United States and Canada. The *Coast Starlight* route follows the Columbia River as far as Vancouver, Washington, with Oregon on the opposite shore. Look for gigantic rafts of logs being transported downstream.

**Trojan Power Plant (12/28)** This nuclear energy plant stands on the Oregon side of the river.

**Kalama (15/25)** Look right for a giant totem pole. The landscape begins to turn into marsh as you approach Lake Vancouver, meeting its shoreline on the right.

**VANCOUVER (40/25)** Not to be confused with Vancouver, Canada. The Hudson's Bay Company built Fort Vancouver as a trading post in 1824, making this the oldest non-Indian settlement in the northwest USA. Amtrak's station is at 1301 W 11th; tel: 360 694 7307. Ticket-office open 08.30–20.30. Waiting-room 08.30–21.30.

The *Coast Starlight* leaves Vancouver and soon afterwards crosses the Columbia into Oregon by way of Hayden Island. You then cross the Willamette River near Portland before crawling among freight yards, industrial plants and ocean-going ships being loaded. Look for the *River Queen*, an old steamboat now converted into a restaurant.

# PORTLAND (25/65)

Spread along the Columbia River between the Cascade Mountains and the Pacific, Oregon's only metropolis is a seaport famous for its many gardens, fountains and parks, and for having one of the country's largest bookstores, which covers an entire city block. The 'City of the Roses' considers itself a rival to Seattle for the accolade of 'America's most liveable city'.

## Portland basics

**Telephone code** 503.

**Station** Union Station is at 800 NW 6th Ave; tel: 273 4864. Built in 1896 on what had been a lake in an old part of town, the large echoing building boasts chandeliers, ceiling fans, evocative pictures and an antique weighing machine. Ticket-office open 07.45–21.30. Waiting-room 07.30–21.30. Metropolitan lounge, vending machines, newspapers, handcarts, Red Caps, café/shop, restaurant, left luggage room, taxi stand.

**Local transport** Portland is well served by Tri-Met buses (tel: 238 7433) and the MAX light railway. Both are free downtown.

**Taxis** Green Cab; tel: 234 1414. Broadway; tel: 727 6159.

**Car rental** Enterprise, 452 SW Pine; tel: 275 5359.

**Greyhound** 550 NW 6th Ave, close to Union Station; tel: 243 2357.

**Portland International Airport** is eight miles (13km) northeast by Raz Tranz bus (tel: 246 3301) or Tri-Met bus #12. A MAX service also opened in the fall of 2001.

**Tours** Gray Line; tel: 285 9845 and Rose-Smith; tel: 201 1921. Columbia and Willamette River cruises from Cascade; tel: 223 3928 and whale watching with Marine Discovery; tel: 800 903 2628; web: www.marinediscovery.com.

**Visitors bureau** Open daily (Mon–Sat in winter) at 701 SW Sixth Ave; tel: 275 8335; email: info@pova.com; web: www.pova.com.

**Accommodation** Contact MacMaster House Bed and Breakfast Inn, 1041 SW Vista (tel: 223 7362 or 800 774 9523; email innkeeper@macmaster.com; web: www.macmaster.com) or White House Bed and Breakfast, 1914 NE 22nd Ave (tel: 800 272 7131 or 287 7131; email: pdxwhi@portlandswhitehouse.com; web: www.portlandswhitehouse.com.

YMCA, 2831 S.W. Barbur Blvd; tel: 294 3366; web: www.ymca-portland.org. YWCA, 1111 SW 10th; tel: 223 6281. Women only. Single $20. AYH Youth Hostel, 3031 SE Hawthorne Blvd; tel: 236 3380. Members $15, non-members $18.

Hotels include the Imperial at 400 SW Broadway; tel: 228 7221 – single $70, double $80; Caravan, 2401 SW 4th; tel: 226 1121; Saharan, 1889 SW 4th; tel: 226 7646; Cabana, 1707 NE 82nd; tel: 252 0224; Days Inn City Center, 1414 W Sixth Ave; tel: 221 1611; Mark Spencer, 409 SW 11th Ave; tel: 224 3293; web: markspencer.com.

## Recommended in Portland

**Rose Festival** A week of mostly free parades, concerts, sporting events and bands honour the city's favourite flower in early June; tel: 227 2681; web: www.rosefestival.org.

**Washington Park** 4001 Canyon Rd; tel: 823 3636. Douglas firs, a Japanese garden and statues can be found here, along with 400 varieties of rose.

**Oregon Zoo** Two miles from downtown by Tri-Met bus #63 or the Westside MAX; tel: 226 1561; web: oregonzoo.org. Beavers, otters and nocturnal cats live in natural settings. Steam and diesel trains operate around the zoo and through the forested hills to Washington Park. Open daily, admission charge. Free on the second Tuesday of each month.

**Portland Art Museum** 1219 SW Park Ave; tel: 226 2811; web: www.portlandartmuseum.org. Featuring works by Renoir and Monet as well as Native American art and English silver. Open daily, admission charge.

**Pioneer Courthouse** 5th Ave and Morrison; tel: 221 0282. The oldest public building in the northwest dates from the 1870s. You can tour the historic courtroom and judge's quarters. Open daily, free.

**Classical Chinese Garden** NW 3rd Ave and Everett; tel: 228 8131; web: www.portlandchinesegarden.org. Located in the middle of Portland, this is the largest urban Suzhou-style garden outside China. Rugged rocks and serpentine walkways are reflected in the lake.

**Oregon History Center** 1200 SW Park Ave; tel: 222 1741; web: www.ohs.org. State history comes to life in this spectacular building with interactive exhibits. Closed Mon, admission charge.

**Oregon Museum of Science and Industry** 1945 SE Water Ave; tel: 797 4000 or 1 800 992 8499; web: www.omsi.edu. Hands-on fun, with live demonstrations, a planetarium and laser shows. Visit the *USS Blueback* submarine, see the OMNIMAX cinema and check out the latest touring exhibitions. Open daily, admission charge.

# All aboard!

Departing Portland, the *Coast Starlight* quits the Burlington Northern route followed so far and travels a Southern Pacific line all the way to Los Angeles. You cross the Willamette River on a steel bridge then pass through Milwaukie, Gladstone and Chackamas suburbs. As the train heads into the flat Willamette Valley, the Cascades and Mount Hood (11,235ft/3,425m) can be seen to your left. The Coast Range is on the right.

**Oregon City (30/35)** The original capital of Oregon Territory, this was the end of the Oregon Trail. More than 200,000 people travelled the 2,000 mile trail when 'Oregon fever' swept the country over 150 years ago. The first protestant church and first masonic lodge west of the Rockies were built here. An Interpretive Center at 1726 Washington (tel: 503 657 9336) has films, exhibits and a multimedia show which explain the famous pioneer route.

Waterfalls appear on your right, with lumber factories and giant logs next to the river. In springtime, look for fields of daffodils and tulips near the city of Canby.

**Aurora (45/20)** Reached after the train crosses the Pudding River, Aurora was founded by Germans in the 19th century as America's first commune.

**Woodburn (50/15)** A nostalgic Southern Pacific steam engine stands on the left. As the train continues, you travel among fields of strawberries, raspberries, blackberries and loganberries.

**SALEM (65/28)** Oregon's capital is the home of Willamette University, the oldest in the west, and it can be seen to your right as the train arrives. Look right also for the white marble Capitol topped by a gold-plated statue of a man with an axe (the 'spirit of Oregon'). The beautiful 1919 station building has been fully restored, with hanging light globes in the lobby recast according to the original designs.

The *Coast Starlight* pulls out of Salem past the city airport to your left. Between the towns of Turner and Marion, 15 minutes later, look for a llama farm on your right. Formerly kept for their wool, the llamas are now used as pack animals on expeditions into the mountains.

**Jefferson (20/8)** You cross the Santiam River.

**ALBANY (28/40)** Founded in 1845, Albany was connected by railroad in 1870 after citizens paid the O & C company $50,000 to be included in the line. This agriculture and lumber town now supplies almost all the grass seed sold in America. It also hosts the world championship timber carnival, with everything from tree climbing to axe throwing. Amtrak's station is at 110 W 10th.

The **visitors bureau** is at 435 W First Ave; tel: 1 800 526 2256; email: albanyorvisit@proaxis.com; web: www.albanyvisitors.com.

The *Starlight* leaves Albany and crosses the Calapooia River, entering a region known as 'the plains of Lebanon'.

**Tangent (15/25)** The town was named after the long, straight stretch of track here. The buttes seen on the left, created by prehistoric volcanoes, contain fossils and mammoth bones. To your left are some of the fields producing grass seed. Between here and Eugene look out also for farms growing mint, another local speciality.

**Harrisburg (25/15)** The snow-covered Three Sisters Mountains appear in the left distance before the train crosses the Willamette River. Southern Pacific rail yards and Lane County jail are seen to your right as you near Eugene and travel through Junction City.

**EUGENE (40/165)** 'The lumber capital of the USA' is the most western city served by Amtrak. Look for huge stacks of timber being sprayed with water to reduce the fire risk. Named after a settler called Eugene Franklin Skinner, who built the first cabin here in 1846, Eugene is now the second largest city in Oregon and the 'running capital of the universe' (home town of Mary Decker Slaney). This region is famous for its mild climate and for fishing and boating on the McKenzie River. The ticket-office of Amtrak's green and white station at 433 Willamette opens 05.30–19.00.

The *Coast Starlight* leaves past the University of Oregon campus on the right before crossing a tree-lined Willamette River into Springfield, the sister city to Eugene.

Tracks curve right as the train climbs slowly for 70 miles into the Cascade Mountains, winding through 22 tunnels and several snow-sheds towards the source of the Willamette. Snow-sheds are wooden or concrete structures built over the track to protect it from avalanches and accumulating snow. Spectacular waterfalls, wild flowers, rhododendrons and dense vegetation feature in the alpine scenery of Willamette National Forest on both sides.

**Lookout Point Reservoir (30/135)** The dam and reservoir are on your left, with Diamond Peak (8,750ft/2,670m) to the south. The Three Sisters Mountains appear in the left distance.

**Westfir (60/105)** Spanning the Willamette River to your right is one of the many covered bridges in this region.

**Oakridge (65/100)** The train starts climbing 'the hill' to Cascade Summit, an ascent of 3,600ft in 44 miles (1,100m in 70km). You cross Salmon Creek then follow Salt Creek on the right.

**Salt Creek Canyon (80/60)** Views of the tracks above and below dramatically demonstrate the steepness of your climb. There are another 2,700ft/800m to go from the health resort of McCredie Springs to the summit along 30 more miles (48km) of track. The tops of tall trees appear beside the train windows and dense, dark evergreens cover the mountains to your right. In autumn, the occasional maple makes a spectacular splash of crimson or yellow.

**Willamette Pass (120/45)** Source of the Willamette River, with the slopes of Willamette Path ski resort visible ahead.

**Cascade Summit (140/25)** The line is 4,800ft (1,460m) above sea level here. Maiden Peak (7,811ft/2,380m) overlooks the deep blue water of Odell Lake to your left. The purple and green Cascade Mountains are all around, giving breathtaking views as the train gently descends among Douglas firs, waterfalls and wild flowers towards the Oregon/California border. Look for quail creeping in the grass banks between tunnels.

**CHEMULT (165/70)** Diamond Peak (8,750ft/2,670m) can be seen on your right. Buses connect Chemult with Bend, a resort 60 miles (96km) to the northeast.

After Chemult you pass Mount Thielsen and Mount Scott (both over 9,000ft/2,750m) to your right. Diamond Lake is also on the right a few minutes later as you enter the Winema National Forest. Logging operations appear on both sides as you continue towards Klamath Marsh. Half an hour from Chemult the train joins the Williamson River on the right, following it intermittently through a canyon for the next 15 miles (24km) after crossing at Kirk.

**Chiloquin (55/15)** America's largest museum of logging is in nearby Collier State Park. The train continues down Calimus Hill to Modoc Point.

**Upper Klamath Lake (60/10)** One of the country's largest freshwater lakes, where in summer you may see white pelicans. You follow the eastern shore of the lake for 18 miles, with Mount McLaughlin (9,760ft/2,975m) to your right.

**KLAMATH FALLS (70/160)** Sawmills appear on your left near the station. Geothermal springs once used by Klamath Indians for cooking are now harnessed to heat homes, and the Klamath County Museum explains this underground activity along with pioneer history. Amtrak's station is at 1600 Oak.

The *Coast Starlight* departs with the Klamath River to your right then travels via two short tunnels and crosses the state line, 20 miles (32km) south, into California. You may catch a first glimpse of the Cascades' highest peak, Mount Shasta (14,160ft/4,453m), snow-clad and ethereal by moonlight as the train speeds through the small Butte Valley communities of Dorris and Mount Hebron.

**Grass Lake (80/80)** This is the highest point on the route and from here the *Coast Starlight* descends around the base of Mount Shasta, cutting through solidified lava flows. Black Butte is seen on the left before you travel down via the alpine town of Mount Shasta City into the Sacramento River Canyon. The train follows this winding canyon for 32 miles (51km) and passes a spectacular waterfall.

**DUNSMUIR (160/100)** A base for the Southern Pacific railway, Dunsmuir is also an all-year recreation centre. The train departs and continues its slow descent from the high tableland. The grey granite spires of Castle Crags appear to the right.

**REDDING (100/70)** Located at the north end of the Sacramento Valley, close to Lake Shasta and Lassen National Park. Shasta Dam, three times the height of Niagara Falls, backs up the Sacramento, McLoud and Pit Rivers. Amtrak's station is at 1620 Yuba.

Look left as the train continues to see the Sierra Nevada, and right for views of the Coast Range.

**CHICO (70/40)** Home of one of California State University's campuses, Chico was originally settled by gold miners. Fortunes were later made by those who came to farm, since most things seem able to grow here, including rice, peaches and olives. General John Bidwell established the town and his mansion now forms part of a state park. Nearby is Oroville Dam, the largest earth-filled dam in America.

**MARYSVILLE (40/70)** Another former gold prospectors' town and centre for agriculture, with Yuba City adjacent to the west. Marysville is an important railroad town, with classification yards and locomotive workshops.

**Roseville (50/20)** The train turns southwest here, crossing the American River just before Sacramento.

**SACRAMENTO (70/20)** California's capital since 1854, to the scorn of some who live in glitzier cities further south. The 1849 gold rush started nearby at Sutter's Mill (gold was actually first found in 1848) and the Pony Express ended its inaugural run here in 1860. A rail link over the Sierra Nevada soon afterwards brought the first trains.

Many 19th century houses have been preserved and a reconstructed **Fort Sutter** stands on the east side of town. The 1869 **State Capitol** features ornate plaster and splendid oak staircases. Sacramento is the hub of a food producing area specialising in almonds, peaches and pears, and the **visitors bureau** is at 1303 J; tel: 916 264 7777; web: www.discovergold.org.

Amtrak operates from the historic renovated station at 401 I. Close by is the **California State Railroad Museum**, seen to your left at 125 I; tel: 916 445 7387 and 916 445 6645 (for recorded information); web: www.csrmf.org. The Transcontinental and Sacramento Valley Railroads began in Old Sacramento and this massive museum on an 11-acre (4.5ha) site displays 21 restored locomotives, railroad cars and 46 exhibits, including a 1929 St Hyacinthe Pullman sleeper. The Central Pacific depot at 1st and J is a reconstruction of Sacramento's 1876 depot and shows bustling train travel in the late 19th century. Open daily, admission charge.

Steam trains travel on holidays and at weekends (April–September) on the **Sacramento Southern Railroad** for a six-mile round-trip through the Feather River Canyon; tel: 916 445 7387. Another train through the Nevada desert is pulled by the Union Pacific engine *Challenger*, the world's heaviest locomotive still in working order. More nostalgia is on hand at the hardware store where the Central Pacific and Southern Pacific were planned by the Big Four – Leland Stanford, Charles Crocker, Mark Hopkins and Collis Huntington. Together with designer Theodore Judah, these financiers and merchants had the idea for a transcontinental route which would make it easier to trade with the east coast and would encourage more trade with Asia. The store museum recreates the boardroom and has much archive material. The Southern Pacific Railroad eventually came to own a fifth of California's land.

The Capitol's gilded dome can be seen to your left as the train leaves, crossing the Sacramento River with a drawbridge on the left. As you travel through the flat landscape of the Sacramento Valley look for fields which are sometimes flooded to grow rice. The Coastal Range is to your right and the attractive Sierra foothills away to your left as you cross the Yolo Bypass on a long low trestle.

**DAVIS (20/40)** Part of the University of California is based here and Davis has enlightened policies promoting recycling and energy conservation. Bicycle pathways exist throughout the city to discourage car use. Amtrak's Spanish adobe-style station on the right dates from 1913 and carries a Southern Pacific logo.

As the *Coast Starlight* leaves past the university campus look right to see some of the research animals, including llamas and pygmy goats. You also pass fields of sunflowers.

**Suisun-Fairfield (25/15)** Note the pretty pink and cream station building on your left, a scheduled stop for the *California Zephyr*. The white pillars of Solano County courthouse are to your right at the end of Union Avenue. Large military transport aircraft can be seen at the Travis Air Force base on your left.

The train races on over flat agricultural land past a ridge on the right, beyond which is the Napa Valley. As you cross Suisun Marsh at up to 79mph (130km/h) look for ducks, herons and cattle. Boeing's experimental wind farm generates electricity on your right.

**Mothball Fleet (30/10)** To your left, near the shoreline of Suisun Bay, floats a large fleet of transport ships kept neatly lined up in 'mothballs'. Many date from the Second World War but some saw action in Vietnam and the Gulf War of 1991. Also to your left are docks packed with imported Japanese cars. In the left distance is Mount Diablo (3,849ft/1,170m). The beacon on top of the mountain was extinguished after Pearl Harbor but is lit once a year by war veterans.

You cross the impressive Benicia-Martinez Bridge spanning the Carquinez Strait. Before the double-track steel bridge opened in 1930 trains had to be ferried across the water in sections. Benicia, on your right, was the state capital from 1853 to 1854. Look for oil tankers in the harbour as you near Martinez.

**MARTINEZ (40/40)** Named after a Spanish governor, Martinez was the birthplace of baseball star Joe DiMaggio. It was also the home of John Muir, an early environmentalist and father of the modern conservation movement. Amtrak's station at 401 Ferry is the connecting point for services along the San Joaquin Valley. The city's museum occupies an old house to the left of the station building.

Amtrak Thruway shuttle buses make a 20 minute journey from Martinez to **Six Flags Marine World** at 2001 Marine World Pkwy, Vallejo; tel: 707 643 ORCA (6722); web: www.sixflags.com.

Marine World is home to thousands of animals, including tigers, sharks, dolphins, walruses, killer whales and a herd of elephants. Among the thrill rides is Medusa – the tallest, fastest and longest roller-coaster in Northern California.

The *Coast Starlight* continues along the rocky shore of Pablo Bay and Carquinez Strait to the right, with gulls, yachts and fishing boats. You go through Crockett and pass the California & Hawaii Sugar factory and several large oil refineries. Mare Island Shipyard and California's Maritime Academy are on the far side of the strait. To the right also are the Marin County Hills and Mount Tamalpais (2,604ft/791m).

**Richmond (25/15)** Over 100,000 people worked at Richmond's Kaiser Shipyards during the Second World War. The town is now a San Francisco suburb, its modern station on the right linked to the Bay Area Rapid Transit system. Look for BART trains lined up on the left.

San Francisco's skyline appears across the bay to your right as you leave and speed through Berkeley. The Golden Gate Bridge is to the north and Oakland Bay Bridge (eight miles/13km long) to the south.

**Golden Gate Racetrack (5/35)** Look for the racecourse on your right, next to an aquatic park.

**EMERYVILLE (40/5)** Passengers for San Francisco disembark at Amtrak's new station for transfer by shuttle bus into San Francisco's downtown area, connecting via the Oakland Bay Bridge with the Ferry Building at 425 Mission, Pier 39 on Fisherman's Wharf and the San Francisco Shopping Center at 835 Market.

## SAN FRANCISCO
'Baghdad by the bay' is famous for its Golden Gate Bridge, fog in the morning, vertiginous streets, elegant houses and Alcatraz. Home of Dashiell Hammett and Sam Spade, San Francisco was the birthplace of beatniks, hippies and the topless bar. Finance, industry and a large gay community coexist in the cosmopolitan atmosphere. With 'silicon valley' to the south, the city has lately become home to some of the world's most successful dot.com companies, creating hundreds of 25 year old millionaires.

Spaniards arrived here in 1776 but the city prospered only after it became a part of the United States. When gold was discovered in 1848, ships and wagon trains, then the railroads, began bringing thousands of settlers across the Sierra Nevada. San Francisco's Chinatown was founded (like the one in Vancouver, Canada) by immigrants who worked on the transcontinental railroad. Neither the 1906 earthquake nor the tremors of 1989 have dissuaded a million people from making the city their home.

### San Francisco basics
**Telephone code** 415.
**Weather** Daytime temperatures average in the mid-50s to mid-60s Fahrenheit (12°C–18°C) so a sweater can sometimes be necessary, especially when fog blankets the city.
**Station** Amtrak's handsomely refurbished Ferry Building terminal at 31 The Embarcadero is close to downtown. Open 06.45–22.45 (ticket-office) and 06.45–23.00 (waiting-room). Ferries cross at hourly intervals between here and Oakland's Jack London Square, calling at Alameda and passing under the Bay Bridge.
**Connections** CalTrain services operate to San Jose and Santa Cruz; tel: 1 800 660 4287. Futuristic BART trains leave from Market Street and are a fast and inexpensive

way to explore Oakland, Berkeley, Fremont and Concord; tel: 992 2278. Alameda-Contra Costa Transit District buses serve the East Bay area; tel: 510 477 0192.

**Local transport** San Francisco can best be seen on foot or by cable car. Or you can use buses and the MUNI Metro, a light railway running partly underground. For information on buses, cable cars and Muni trains call 673 6864.

**Taxis** Luxor; tel: 282 4141. De Soto; tel: 673 1414.

**Car rental** Rent-A-Wreck, 295 Third; tel: 282 6293.

**Greyhound** Transbay Terminal, 425 Mission; tel: 495 1575.

**San Francisco International Airport** (SFO) is 14 miles (22km) south on US 101. Airporter buses connect to a downtown terminal at Taylor and Ellis; tel: 495 8404, or you can take SamTrans bus #7F; tel: 800 660 4287.

**Tours** Super Sightseeing, Pier 9; tel: 777 2288. Bay cruises from the Blue and Gold Fleet at Pier 39; tel: 705 5555. Air tours from Commodore Helicopters (tel: 332 4482) and Skycruise (tel: 568 4101).

**Visitors bureau** Open daily at Hallidie Plaza, Market and Powell; tel: 391 2000 or 391 2001 (for the latest events); email: visitor-info@sfcvb.org; www.sfvisitor.org.

**Accommodation** Everything from expensive, classic hotels to downbeat rooming houses can be found, with budget accommodation in Japantown and Oakland. Contact Bed and Breakfast San Francisco (tel: 415 899 0060; email: bbsf@linex.com; web: www.bbsf.com) or Red Victorian Bed & Breakfast, 1665 Haight (tel: 864 1978; web: www.redvic.com).

Central YMCA, 220 Golden Gate Ave; tel: 885 0460. A short bus ride from Amtrak's Ferry Building and the best value in town. Single $28, double $38. Hostel accommodation $15 (for students with valid IYH ID). Friendly staff, complimentary breakfast, swimming pool, sauna, restaurant. For men and women. Embarcadero YMCA, 169 Steuart; tel: 957 9622. Single $25, double $35. International (IYHF) Hostel, Building 240, Fort Mason; tel: 771 7277. Overlooks the Golden Gate bridge. Mostly dormitory rooms, $16. Central (IYHF) Hostel, 312 Mason; tel: 788 5604. Double $18.

For the latest accommodation offers contact the Visitors Bureau hotel reservation service on 1 888 782 9673 (1 888 STAY N SF). Hotels include the Allison, 417 Stockton; tel: 986 8737 – single and double $50; Essex, 684 Ellis; tel: 474 4664 – single $59, double $69; Sheehan, 620 Sutter; tel: 775 6500 – single $45, double $55; Amsterdam, 749 Taylor; tel: 673 3277 – single $45, double $50; Grant Plaza, 465 Grant Ave; tel: 434 3883 – single $40, double $45; Ansonia, 711 Post; tel: 673 2670 – single $46, double $54.

## Recommended in San Francisco

**Golden Gate Bridge** Linking the city with Marin County to the north is one of the world's best known and most impressive landmarks. Two miles (3.2km) long – seven miles (11km) including approaches – it incorporates 80,000 miles (128,000km) of cable and is painted orange rather than gold. Magical views of San Francisco from the Marin County side.

**Golden Gate Park** Between Fulton and Lincoln Way is one of the world's largest man-made parks, where many museums and the odd buffalo can be found among 1,000 acres (400ha) of lakes, redwoods and eucalyptus. Information from the office at Fell and Stanyan; tel: 831 2700.

**Maritime Museum** At the foot of Polk Street; tel: 561 7100; web: www.maritime.org. Photographs, models and relics showing west coast seafaring life from sail to steam are located in a building shaped like a 1930s liner. Excellent ranger-guided tours of the historic ships moored at nearby Hyde Street Pier. Open daily. Museum free, admission charge to the pier.

**Cable Car Barn and Museum** Washington and Mason; tel: 474 1887; web: www.cablecarmuseum.com. Cable cars travel nine miles (14.5km) of track at up to nine miles an hour and are America's only historic landmarks with wheels. Observe this unique system in operation and see old cable cars (including the first, built in 1873) along with other exhibits and films. Open daily, museum free.

**Fisherman's Wharf** On the waterfront between Taylor and the Embarcadero, the Wharf has gift shops, salt air, cruise boats and hordes of tourists. Open-air stalls sell freshly cooked seafood while sealions bark for fish and gulls glide above the water. Down-market pleasures include a wax museum, the **Guinness World of Records** and **Ripley's 'Believe It Or Not!'**.

**The Cannery** 2801 Leavenworth; tel: 771 3112; web: www.thecannery.com. Built in 1894 as a fruit-canning factory, the Cannery has been converted into a mall with dozens of shops, a comedy club, restaurants and art galleries. **Jack's Cannery Bar** boasts more beers on tap than almost anywhere in the country. There are stalls and cafés among century-old olive trees in the courtyard and street performers entertain on summer weekends.

**Coit Tower** Located on top of Telegraph Hill, just east of North Beach; tel: 362 0808. The wealthy eccentric Lillie Hitchcock Coit left San Francisco $125,000 to build this memorial to volunteer firemen. Completed in 1933, the tower has great views and impressive murals depicting California during the 1930s. Open daily, admission charge.

**Ansel Adams Center for Photography** 250 Fourth; tel: 495 7000. The museum features five galleries with exhibitions of contemporary and historical photography. One is dedicated solely to the work of Ansel Adams. Closed Mon, admission charge.

**Wells Fargo Museum** 420 Montgomery; tel: 396 2619. A history museum for one of California's largest banks. Among the hundreds of relics are pistols, photographs, early posters and mining equipment. Open weekdays, free.

**Alcatraz** A million visitors every year come on boats from Pier 41 to the isle of pelicans, former residence of Al Capone, 'Machine Gun' Kelly and the 'Birdman'. Call 705 5555 for ferry information and tickets; web: http://alcatraz.san-francisco.ca.us. The prison's first 53 inmates, including Capone, were brought on a thousand mile journey in a train equipped with barred windows and reinforced doors. Each man was clamped in leg irons and chained to his seat. The rock closed as a federal penitentiary in 1963 but still has the power to freeze your spirit. Make reservations early (at least one week ahead during summer) and dress warmly for the excellent tours led by national park rangers.

# All aboard!

Buses leave from the Ferry Building and cross the Oakland Bay Bridge, with great views to your left of the city, Alcatraz and the Golden Gate Bridge. To your right are Oakland and the tall Gothic tower of the University of California at Berkeley. The *Coast Starlight* continues south from Emeryville to Oakland.

**OAKLAND (5/70)** Known as 'the place where the trains stopped', Oakland lacks San Francisco's glamour but does have inexpensive accommodation less readily found on the other side of the bay. A pedestrian bridge takes you across from Amtrak's new glass and steel station to Jack London Square, named after Oakland's former resident and author of *The Call of the Wild*. Other notable citizens have included Gertrude Stein, Jessica Mitford and the Black Panthers. The **visitors bureau** is at 475-14th; tel: 510 839 9000; web: www.oaklandcvb.com.

The **Oakland Museum**, 1000 Oak (tel 510 238 2200; web: www.museumca.org) features Californian art and a simulated journey from sea level to the Sierra Nevada. Nearby are the Victorian houses of Old Oakland and the **Pardee Museum**, once the home of Governor George Pardee. **Lake Merritt**, close to the city centre, has a wildlife refuge and boating.

The train leaves and gathers speed through industrial suburbs with the Bay Bridge still visible to your right.

**Jack London Square (5/65)** Oakland's main tourist attraction on your right features the Jack London Museum, the *USS Potomac*, Franklin Roosevelt's yacht and dozens of waterfront restaurants. Also on your right is the Alameda naval base.

**Oakland Coliseum (20/50)** This massive circular construction on your right is home to the Oakland A's baseball team. The BART train line is to your left.

**Alameda Stadium (25/45)** The Alameda County stadium can be seen on your right before you continue across mud flats via Drawbridge, an officially certified 'ghost town' which was formerly the home of railroad workers, bootleggers and duck-hunters.

**Moffett Field (50/20)** Beyond the lower end of San Francisco Bay are the giant hangars of this naval air station.

**Marriott's Great America Park (60/10)** Look right for roller-coasters and other amusement rides as the mud flats are left behind.

**Santa Clara (65/5)** The enclosed sports stadium of Santa Clara University can be seen to your right in this computer industry centre of 'Silicon Valley'. Just south of town you travel among extensive Southern Pacific rail yards and pass a historic brick roundhouse.

**SAN JOSE (70/70)** California's oldest city and first capital was founded in 1777 as Pueblo de San Jose de Guadalupe. Larger than San Francisco in area and population, San Jose has fruit and wine industries as well as many companies specialising in aerospace and computer technology. The **Mission of Santa Clara de Assisi** is a reminder of earlier days. Amtrak's recently restored station is at 65 Cahill and CalTrain commuter services operate between here and San Francisco.

The *Coast Starlight* travels on through the Santa Clara Valley, one of the richest farming regions in America. To your left are Mount Hamilton (4,430ft/1,350m) and the Diablo Mountains, with the beautiful Santa Cruz Range to your right.

**Gilroy (30/40)** 'The garlic capital of the world', where tons of garlic-laden food are cooked and eaten by devotees at an August festival. You can see and sometimes smell these plants growing near the tracks. Marilyn Monroe was once crowned as Gilroy's 'garlic queen'. To your right are St Mary's church (with its gold bell) and the City Hall clock tower.

**Pajaro Gap (40/30)** You cross the Santa Cruz Mountains, via Chittenden Pass and the San Andreas Fault on a bridge near Logan, into the Pajaro Valley – 'the valley of the birds'. Look for herons, divers and buzzards, as well as more of the Santa Cruz Range to your right. Exotic eucalyptus trees flourish beside the tracks.

**Watsonville (45/25)** First settled during the 18th century gold rush, Watsonville has many attractive Victorian houses. This area specialises in growing apples, lettuces and strawberries. Spanish explorer Don Gaspar de Portola was the first European to discover the nearby redwoods.

**Castroville (60/10)** 'The artichoke capital of the world', where tall, bushy plants grow in fields of black earth to your right. In 1949 an unknown Marilyn Monroe was named the town's first 'artichoke queen'.

**SALINAS (70/110)** The centre of America's salad bowl, where huge crops of lettuce, sugar beet and other vegetables fatten beneath a benevolent sun. Salinas was the birthplace of John Steinbeck, who described his home town in *East of Eden*. His house at 132 Central Ave is now a restaurant and museum, and the public library owns a collection of his manuscripts. Amtrak's station is at Railroad Ave.

Monterey (immortalised by Steinbeck in *Cannery Row*) and Big Sur (where Jack Kerouac, Henry Miller and Orson Welles lived) are 15 miles (24km) to the west.

You leave Salinas past an incongruous Firestone factory standing in fields to your right then travel a hundred miles along the Salinas River Valley. San Benito Mountain (5,258ft/1,600m) is the highest peak of the Diablo Range to your left. The rugged Santa Lucia Mountains are on your right.

**Soledad (20/90)** The large, modern prison to your left once held the Black Panther leader, Eldridge Cleaver. Soledad was originally a mission town, its name being Spanish for 'solitude'.

The *Starlight* continues along the Salinas Valley with the river to your right and Pinnacles National Monument on the left. Just before Rocky Point tunnel

(1,305ft/400m long) look left for an airfield where light planes used for crop-spraying are based.

**King City (45/65)** 'The most metropolitan cow town in the west', where many crates of agricultural produce await transportation on your right. John Steinbeck's father was the town's first railroad agent.

**San Lucas (65/45)** A statue of Christ protects the cemetery seen to your right.

**Camp Roberts (85/25)** The camp is the headquarters of California's National Guard.

**San Miguel (95/15)** On your right is the 18th century Mission San Miguel Arcangel, its two-storey adobe structure enclosing the best-preserved interior of all California's missions. *Coast Starlight* tracks from Oakland to Los Angeles closely follow the Spanish mission path, *El Camino Real*, 'the Royal Road', founded between 1769 and 1823 by Franciscan Father Junipero Serra. The 21 missions and four chapels along the *Camino Real* from San Diego to Sonoma were each a day's journey apart.

**PASO ROBLES (110/60)** A new station has been built beside the old, burned down Southern Pacific depot.

**Atascadero (15/45)** The golf course on your right is bounded by the Santa Lucia foothills. Atascadero's redbrick City Hall houses a history museum.

**Cuesta Pass (40/20)** A quintessential railroad experience begins as the train climbs into the Santa Margarita Mountains, negotiating five tunnels and giving magnificent views of the Santa Lucias. Los Osos Valley is below and Highway 101 opposite. Look for rocky outcrops, adventurous sheep, pine trees, eucalyptus and scrub oak. Splendid white oaks can be seen in the valley below.

The descent from Cuesta Grade represents a fall of more than 1,000 feet in 11 miles (300m in 18km), with the old wooden trestle over Stenner Creek visible ahead.

**Horseshoe Curve (55/5)** The *Starlight* winds down to San Luis Obispo, taking two spectacular sweeping curves that bring the entire train into view. On your right is the California Men's Colony, a state penitentiary from which Timothy Leary once made his escape. As the train crosses Stenner Creek, look left for California's Polytechnic State University.

**SAN LUIS OBISPO (165/125)** This oasis of palm trees, sunshine and Spanish architecture began in 1772 as the Mission San Luis Obispo de Tolosa. Many of the buildings on Marsh Street were built for rail workers' families when it was an important railroad town. **San Luis Obispo County Historical Museum** at 696 Monterey (tel: 805 543 0638) explores the history of the county. Open Wed–Sun, free. The **visitors bureau** is at 1039 Chorro; tel: 805 781 2777; email: slocvcb@slonet.org; web: www.sanluisobispocounty.com.

Amtrak's station is at 1011 Railroad Ave, from where buses leave for the amazing **Hearst Castle**, open daily at 750 Hearst Castle Road in nearby San Simeon; tel: 1 800 444 4445; web: www.hearst-castle.org. California's main tourist attraction after Disneyland was the home of William Randolph Hearst, the real life entrepreneur and newspaper tycoon who became Orson Welles' inspiration for *Citizen Kane*. The 'Mediterranean Revival' mansion boasts 130 telephones and is crammed with baths, swimming pools, marble statues, armour, Persian rugs and flamboyant furniture from around the world. Former guests have included Charlie Chaplin, George Bernard Shaw, Buster Keaton, Cary Grant and Winston Churchill.

As the train leaves San Luis Obispo note the historic locomotive turntable on your right.

**Grover City (15/110)** Obsolete rail coaches to the right now house a restaurant. The *Coast Starlight* continues south, crossing the Santa Maria River.

**Pismo Beach (20/105)** Eucalyptus trees and dunes to your right conceal the resort of Pismo Beach, famous for its clams.

The train climbs Callendar Hill then travels through Guadalupe and the Santa Maria Valley before emerging from the Schuman Canyon.

**Vandenberg Air Force Base (50/75)** For half an hour the train proceeds through the Strategic Air Command western missile test range, home of B-52 planes and firing site for Minuteman missile tests. Minuteman Beach is to your right. Further south, at Purisma Point, several satellite launch pads can be seen on the right and Vandenberg airfield to your left. The base is military territory so no photography is allowed.

**Pacific Ocean (51/74)** More peaceful scenes appear on your right as the train travels for over a hundred miles through heather moorland with splendid views out across the Pacific Ocean.

**Surf (60/65)** You cross the Santa Ynez River with more launch pads on your right and oil rigs out to sea.

**Space Shuttle (65/60)** The big white buildings on your left were used during the Space Shuttle development programme and are now abandoned.

**Point Arguello (70/55)** This has been the site of many wrecks and an automatic lighthouse on the cliffs warns passing ships of the danger. Look out for dolphins and migrating grey whales in spring and autumn. The train's tracks run over a trestle above Jalama Beach Park at the southern end of Vandenberg Base.

**Point Conception (80/45)** Note the historic lighthouse still in use on the bluff as you continue south along the cliff tops. Ocean views here are shared only with grazing cattle since this area is inaccessible to the public except by train. The Santa Ynez Mountains begin in the left distance and extend south beyond Santa Barbara.

**Gaviota (95/30)** The name is Spanish for 'seagull'. You cross on high trestles above Gaviota Pass and Tajiguas Creek.

**Refugio State Beach (100/25)** Picnic tables dot the beach to your right. Oil rigs and production platforms then come into view as the train accompanies the Santa Barbara Channel, discovered in 1542 by the Portuguese explorer Juan Cabrillo. He was buried on San Miguel Island, seen out to your right, after he died there the following year.

The *Coast Starlight* temporarily leaves the coast and goes inland towards Santa Barbara, passing on the right the bell tower of the University of California at Santa Barbara.

**Santa Barbara Mission (123/2)** The 'Queen of the Missions' on your left was founded in 1786 and has been in use ever since. The only mission with twin towers, its fountain is fed by an aqueduct.

**SANTA BARBARA (125/45)** Originally the home of Chumash Indians, this resort and retirement area is located invitingly between a palm-lined beach and the Santa Ynez foothills. Santa Barbara was discovered by Sebastian Vizcaino on St Barbara's Day in 1602 and it was here in 1782 that Spain built its last New World fortress, the Presidio Real. Spanish influence continues in the white adobe and red-tiled architecture, much of which had to be reconstructed after a 1925 earthquake.

The **visitors bureau** is at 1 Santa Barbara; tel: 805 965 3021; web: www.santabarbaraca.com.

Amtrak's station is at 209 State, an unsafe area at night. To the left of the station is the Moreton Bay fig tree, planted in 1877 and the largest of its kind in America. Branches spread more than 160ft (50m) to provide welcome shade. The **Museum of Art** at 1130 State (tel: 805 963 4364; web: www.sbmuseart.org) has American and Impressionist works as well as art from Asia and a children's gallery.

The **South Coast Railroad Museum** is seven miles (11km) west at 300 N Carneros Rd, Goleta (tel: 805 964 3540; web: www.goletadepot.org). A 1901 Southern Pacific depot has been relocated in Lake Los Carneros Park and restored to house model trains, rare photographs and miniature train rides. Open Wed–Sun, donation.

The *Coast Starlight* leaves Santa Barbara among some of the city's finest residential areas.

**Andree Clark Bird Refuge (4/41)** The wildlife sanctuary next to a freshwater lagoon on your right is home to herons, egrets, cormorants and many migrating birds.

**Miramar (5/40)** The old station house to your left has been converted into a restaurant.

**Summerland Beach (6/39)** Nude bathers are sometimes seen frolicking to your right. Bates Beach, a similar venue to watch for or recoil from, is passed 15 minutes further on. From here to Ventura the train, like Highway 101, travels directly along the shoreline.

Look for surfers at Carpintera Beach and Emma Woods Beach, where on a clear day you can see out to the Channel Islands. At Mussel Shoals a causeway leads to the island on which oil production began in 1964. More oil platforms appear in the channel before you cross the Ventura River and again head inland.

**Ventura (30/15)** The county fairgrounds are to your right and the 1809 San Buenaventura Mission to your left. The mission's unique wooden bells are preserved in a museum.

A Spanish expedition of 1542 was the first to discover Ventura, now a scheduled stop for some *Pacific Surfliner* trains. Nearby is the Ojai Farm Hostel (tel: 805 646 0311) with free pickup from Amtrak's station.

The *Coast Starlight* continues south, crossing the Santa Clara River on a long low trestle.

**OXNARD (45/20)** Founded in 1897 by the Oxnard brothers, who made their fortune out of raising sugar beet. Now a centre for citrus and other fruit production, Oxnard is the home of California's strawberry festival.

The train travels east into the beautiful Simi Valley with the Simi Hills to your right. The Santa Susanna Mountains are to your left.

**Camarillo (10/10)** A mission-type church stands on the hill to your left.

**SIMI VALLEY (20/45)** Ronald Reagan's Presidential Library is located in this predominantly white suburb of Los Angeles. In 1992 a local jury acquitted four white policemen of using excessive force to arrest a black motorist, Rodney King, and the verdict led to riots in cities across America.

After Simi Valley the *Starlight* tackles the imposing Santa Susanna hills, where tunnels and passes take you through a stark landscape of rocks and cacti. This was a film location for the *Lone Ranger* TV series, James Cagney's *White Heat* and Alfred Hitchcock's *North by Northwest*.

**Chatsworth (20/25)** On the border of Los Angeles County, this is the San Fernando Valley – land of the swimming pool. Millions of Angelinos live the suburban life in an area the size of Chicago.

**Van Nuys (30/15)** The recently built station is a stop for Amtrak's *Pacific Surfliner* trains. Look for factories belonging to General Motors and Schlitz as the scenery becomes industrial. Van Nuys Airport appears to your right before the train passes beneath the San Diego Freeway.

**Hollywood-Burbank Airport (35/10)** The airport is a test area for the Lockheed factory seen beyond runways to your left.

**Burbank (40/5)** The city of Burbank is to the left. Disney, Warners and Columbia film studios, as well as NBC Television, have facilities among the Santa Monica hills on your right. This is where the helicopter scenes for TV's *MASH* were shot.

**GLENDALE (45/15)** The ornamental Spanish-style 1920s station has starred in many movies and has recently been renovated.

Soon after Glendale you see Forest Lawn Memorial Park next to Griffith Park on your right. Made famous as Whispering Glades in Evelyn Waugh's novel *The Loved One*, Forest Lawn is the burial place of Clark Gable, Carole Lombard, Jean Harlow and Errol Flynn. Tasteful highlights include a stained glass version of Leonardo's 'Last Supper'. The *Coast Starlight* travels on deeper into the city of Los Angeles.

**Los Angeles River (8/7)** The concrete channel to your right is another favourite film location, notably for *Point Blank*, *Chinatown* and *Repo Man*. The channel stays dry most of the year but at times of flooding becomes a river. The train crosses the channel then passes beneath the Golden State and Pasadena Freeways before winding slowly towards Union Station.

**Dodger Stadium (10/5)** Perched on a bluff to your right is the home of epic baseball. Look right also for Elysian Park and the impressive Los Angeles skyline. Los Angeles County jail is on your left.

## LOS ANGELES
Palm trees, beaches, blondes, surfing, freeways, smog and David Hockney swimming pools: Los Angeles is a sprawling place with an atmosphere all its own. Founded by the Spanish in the 18th century as El Pueblo de Nuestra Señora de la Reina de Los Angeles (the City of Our Lady, Queen of the Angels) its name grew shorter as the town became bigger. Completion of the transcontinental railroad in 1869, together with oil, Hollywood and a near perfect climate, brought millions of settlers in search of the good life.

America's second largest city now spreads 10 million people over an area as big as Rhode Island and true Angelinos would never live anywhere else. The sun really does shine 90% of the year, although smog can be a problem in summer.

### *Los Angeles basics*
Telephone code 213.

**Station** The renovated Union Passenger Terminal at 800 N Alameda is one of the world's prettiest railway stations, built in Spanish mission and art deco styles with gardens shaded by palm trees. It was constructed in the 1930s on part of the original Chinatown and has starred in many movies, including *Bugsy*. For information call 624 0171. Ticket-office and waiting-room open 24 hours. Vending machines, ATM banking, newspapers, handcarts, Red Caps, restaurant, left luggage room, shop, taxi stand.

**Connections** Thruway buses go to Santa Barbara, Long Beach and Bakersfield and there are plans for a daily train service between Los Angeles and Las Vegas, Nevada, using Talgo equipment. This would restore part of the route once used by Amtrak's *Desert Wind* train.

**Local transport** Los Angeles used to boast the largest electric railway in the world, its *Pacific Red* streetcars often appearing in early silent films. As in other cities, the oil, tyre and car companies bought up the railway in order to close it down. City-sponsored Blue Line trains (tel: 626 4455) have lately begun to travel again on tracks built along old Red Line routes, including one between Union Station and Westlake.

MTA buses take in most city attractions, with free maps from the customer service centre at 5301 Wilshire Blvd; tel: 1 800 COMMUTE. MTA bus #1 leaves from the corner of Broadway and Arcadia for Hollywood. DASH shuttle buses operate Mon–Sat, connecting Union Station with Chinatown and the downtown area; tel: 808 2273.

For Metrolink commuter trains serving southern California call 1 800 371 LINK (or 213 347 2800 from outside the area).

**Taxis** LA Taxi; tel: 627 7000. Yellow; tel: 481 2345.

**Car rental** Budget, at the terminal; tel: 617 2977 and Avon at 8459 Sunset Blvd; tel: 654 5533. LA is the ultimate city of the automobile, with 6,500 miles (10,000km) of road and freeway and 24 million vehicle trips on an average day. Renting a car is no problem but finding your way around is more tricky. If you have the time and inclination, the Automobile Club will supply maps and advice.

**Greyhound** 1716 E 7th; tel: 629 8536. Also at 1715 Cahuenga Blvd, Hollywood; tel: 466 1249.

**LAX Airport** is 16 miles (26km) southwest of downtown by the Super Shuttle; tel: 310 782 6600 and MTA bus # 439.

**Tours** Gray Line, 6541 Hollywood Blvd (tel: 856 5900) goes to Hollywood, Beverly Hills and the film studios. Other companies include Starline; tel: 463 3131 and Hollywood Fantasy; tel: 469 8184. The Los Angeles Conservancy at 849 S Broadway; tel: 623 2489 offers walking tours and Grave Line; tel: 469 4149 provides morbid and sometimes irreverent tours by chauffeur-driven hearse to places where famous people have died. These include the Highland Gardens/Landmark Hotel (Janis Joplin), the Knickerbocker Hotel (D W Griffith) and the Hollywood sign (where a failed English actress, Peg Entwistle, was the first person to commit suicide).

**Visitors bureau** 685 S Figueroa; tel: 689 8822; web: www.lacvb.com.

**Accommodation** Los Angeles has 12 million visitors a year so there are plenty of rooms to choose from. Consult the local press for weekend rates and special offers. For bed and breakfast contact Baywood Inn B&B, 1370 2nd St, Baywood Park, CA 93402-1112; tel 805 528 8888; email: innkeeper@baywoodinn.com; web: www.baywoodinn.com.

International (IYHF) Hostel, 3601 S Gaffey; tel: 310 831 8109. Members $12, non-members $14. Banana Bungalow-Hollywood, 5533 Hollywood Blvd; tel: 800 4 HOSTEL. Dormitory rooms, $12. Free pick-ups from the airport and Amtrak's station. Hollywood YMCA, 1553 North Schrader Blvd (formerly Hudson Avenue); tel: 467 4161. Dormitory rooms for men or women $11. Single $30, double $40. Hollywood International Hostel, 6561 Franklin Ave; tel: 850 6287. Rooms $12. Santa Monica AYH Hostel, 1436 2nd; tel: 310 393 9913. Dormitory rooms $16, double $45. Take MTA bus #33.

Hotels include the Doubletree, 10740 Wilshire Blvd; tel: 475 8711; www.doubletree.com; Figueroa, 939 S Figueroa; tel: 627 8971 – rooms $75; Brady Acres, 649 Jones; tel: 929 8033; Park Plaza, 607 S Park View; tel: 384 5281 – single $57, double $63; Orchid, 819 S Flower; tel: 624 5855 – rooms $40; Milner, 813 S Flower; tel: 627 6981 – single $50, double $60; Stillwell, 838 S Grand Ave; tel: 627 1151 – single $40, double $45.

## Recommended in Los Angeles

**El Pueblo de Los Angeles State Park** Opposite Amtrak's station. Los Angeles began here in 1781 and the city's oldest house, the Avila Adobe, which dates from 1818 is at 10 E Olvera. This street also features Mexican restaurants and cheerfully tacky souvenir shops. Look also for the Masonic Hall (1858), Old Plaza Church (1822), Old Plaza Firehouse (1884) and Sepulveda House (1884). Free film and walking tours from the **visitor centre** at 622 Main; tel: 680 2381; web: www.cityofla.org/elp.

**Natural History Museum** 900 Exposition Blvd; tel: 763 DINO; web: www.nhm.org. Two world-famous habitat halls show African and North American mammals in their natural environments, and the museum is home to Megamouth, the world's rarest shark. The Lando Hall of California History has fascinating exhibits showing the Southwest from the 1500s through to downtown Los Angeles in 1940.

**Mann's Chinese Theater** 6925 Hollywood Blvd; tel: 323 464 8111. Match your favourite actor's cement prints in front of this outlandish pagoda. Nearby, 2,500 bronze stars in the **Walk of Fame** celebrate the great and not so great of Tinseltown.

**LA County Museum of Art** 5905 Wilshire Blvd; tel: 323 857 6000 or 323 857 0098 (TDD); web: www.lacma.org. LACMA is one of the finest art museums in the country, with more than 150,000 works spanning the history of art from ancient times to the present and major special exhibitions. Closed Wed, admission charge.

**J Paul Getty Museum** 1200 Getty Center Dr, in Brentwood; tel: 310 440 7300; web: www.getty.edu. With panoramic views of Los Angeles and the Pacific Ocean, the museum has 54 galleries to display one of the richest collections in the world, including medieval manuscripts and 65,000 photographs, as well as paintings by Cézanne, Goya, Leonardo, Michelangelo, Monet, Titian, Turner and Van Gogh. Closed Mon, free.

**La Brea Tar Pits** 5801 Wilshire Blvd; tel: 934 7243. Bubbling black deposits contain hundreds of fossilised mammals, seen at the museum and observation pit. The fossils are up to 40,000 years old and include camels, mammoths and mastodons. Open daily, admission charge.

**Griffith Park** Los Feliz Blvd; tel: 485 5501. This 4,107-acre (1650ha) city park is the largest in the country and incorporates a planetarium, bird sanctuary, miniature railway, carousel and zoo (tel: 323 644 6400). Open daily, admission charge to the zoo and some other attractions. Take bus #97.

**Universal Studios** 100 Universal City Plaza, Universal City; tel: 1 800 UNIVERSAL; web: www.universalstudios.com. The second biggest tourist attraction in southern California has spectacular rides such as Jurassic Park and The Terminator as well as other movie-themed entertainments. You can be attacked by Jaws and experience a flood, an earthquake and the parting of the Red Sea. Open daily, admission charge.

**Travel Town** 5200 Zoo Dr, in the northwest corner of Griffith Park; tel: 662 5874; web: steamlocomotive.com. The museum has 14 steam locomotives, including one of the oldest in the United States, built for the original Western Pacific Railroad in 1864 and used by the Central Pacific during construction of the Transcontinental Railroad. There are also many passenger cars, freight wagons and cabooses (brake cars). Trains ride for one mile along a 16-inch (42cm) gauge track, crossing several bridges and an 80ft (27m) tunnel. Open daily, free.

**Forest Lawn Memorial Park** 1712 S Glendale Ave, near Griffith Park; tel: 323 254 3131 or 1 800 204 3131; web: www.forestlawn.com. This is the last resting place of Buster Keaton, Stan Laurel, Clara Bow, W C Fields, Alan Ladd and Charles Laughton. Open daily.

**Lomita Railroad Museum** Just south of Los Angeles at 2137 W 250th, Lomita; tel: 310 326 6255; web: www.lomita-rr.org. Includes live steam engines, memorabilia and a replica of the Boston & Maine's Greenwood station at Wakefield, Massachusetts. On display is a Southern Pacific Railroad steam locomotive and tender, a 1910 Union Pacific caboose and a 1913 Southern Pacific wood box car. Open Wed–Sun, admission charge.

# The *California Zephyr*
# Chicago–Emeryville
## (for San Francisco)

## General route information

One of the world's great trains, the *California Zephyr* travels for two days and nights over farmland, prairie, deserts, rivers and mountains. Western pioneers came this way, as did gold prospectors, the Pony Express and the first long-distance telegraph line. The *Zephyr* follows America's earliest transcontinental rail route for much of its 2,420-mile (3,900km) journey, and many people take this train just to explore the Rocky Mountains.

**Frequency** Daily.

The westbound service leaves Chicago mid-afternoon to arrive in Omaha at midnight and Denver by early next morning. You reach Salt Lake City at midnight on the second evening, Reno the following morning and Emeryville (for San Francisco) early in the evening.

Travelling east, you leave San Francisco early in the morning to arrive in Reno by late afternoon and Salt Lake City early next morning. You reach Denver by mid-evening and Omaha early on the second day, arriving in Chicago late afternoon.

**Reservations** All reserved.

**Equipment** Superliner coaches.

**Sleeping** Superliner bedrooms.

**Food** Complete meals, snacks, sandwiches, drinks.

**Lounge car** Video movies, games. A California State Railway Museum history guide provides a commentary between Reno and Sacramento.

**Baggage** Check-in service at major cities.

## Joining the train

### CHICAGO

The proclaimed capital of America's third coast is one of the country's largest and most ethnically diverse cities. Writers such as Saul Bellow, Nelson Algren and Sara Paretsky have lived in 'the city of big shoulders', as have Al Capone (gangster) and Mother Cabrini (first American saint). Harrison Ford and Raymond Chandler, whose father was a railway engineer, were born here, and Ernest Hemingway grew up in the middle-class suburb of Oak Park. Muddy Waters, Howlin' Wolf and John Lee Hooker made blues history on the South Side.

CHICAGO
Naperville
Princeton
Galesburg
Burlington
Mount
Pleasant
Ottumwa
Osceola
Creston
OMAHA
Lincoln
Hastings
Holdrege
McCook
Fort Morgan
DENVER
Winter Park
Granby
Glenwood Springs
Grand Junction
Green River
Helper
SALT   Provo
LAKE
CITY
Elko
Winnemucca
Sparks
Truckee   Reno
Colfax
Roseville
SACRAMENTO

For Sacramento to
San Francisco, see
The Coast Starlight

SAN FRANCISCO

Chicago began in 1833 but stayed a village until railways connected it to the east coast in 1852. Destroyed by fire in 1871 soon after the rail link with San Francisco was completed, the city rebuilt itself as a centre for industry, finance and the arts. The Junction Railway's stock yards were where cowboys brought their cattle, and although these have long closed down Chicago retains a hard-headed commercial spirit. More workable and less pretentious than New York or Los Angeles, the city has become the fashionable home of television's *ER* and *Oprah*.

The first 11-storey skyscrapers were erected here, leading to the Chicago school of architecture and subsequently Frank Lloyd Wright and Mies van der Rohe. You can see three of the world's ten tallest buildings and superb architecture in every modern style, as well as outdoor sculpture, an elevated railway and the brooding Chicago River. Chicago boasts 29 miles (46km) of beaches but it can be bitingly cold in winter, when ice sometimes floats on Lake Michigan.

## Chicago basics

**Telephone code** 312 downtown, 773 for the rest of the city.
**Station** Chicago has long been a port for ships arriving on Lake Michigan via the St Lawrence Seaway. It has also been called the railroad hub of the world, with Union Station at 225 S Canal (tel: 558 1075) the centre of America's rail network. The cathedral-like Great Hall features huge marble columns, statues, sweeping staircases, balconies, original wooden benches and a soaring, arched ceiling. This magnificent waiting-room has appeared in many films, including Brian de Palma's *The Untouchables*. *The Narrow Margin*, set mostly on board the Central Pacific's *Golden West Limited*, has intriguing shots of how the station looked in 1951.

Amtrak operates from a more modern part of the building, with a fountain into which you can throw pennies for luck. A separate waiting-room is reserved for Amtrak passengers, and the Metropolitan lounge opens 08.30–20.00. Ticket-office opens 06.15–21.00. The Great Hall waiting-room opens 06.15–22.00. Lockers, vending machines, ATM banking, newspapers, handcarts, Red Caps, restaurants, shops, taxi stand. Amtrak has other offices in Chicago at 203 N LaSalle and 500 N Michigan Ave.
**Local transport** METRA runs commuter trains out of Union Station and City Transit Authority buses cover the whole city, with a stop outside the Adams Street exit. CTA

buses and a subway augment the El railway; tel: 836 7000; web: www.yourcta.com.
PACE buses operate to the suburbs; tel: 847 364 7223; web: www.pacebus.com. Free
maps from the tourist bureau and the METRA information window at Union Station.

Chicago also has an underground Pedway system of pedestrian walkways that
makes navigation easy even in bad weather. From the Illinois Center at Michigan
Avenue and the Michigan Avenue Bridge a network of walkways lead to stores in
the Loop area and to major train stations, with an entrance elevator in Loop
buildings and subway stations. Maps of the Pedway are available in hotels and at the
Illinois Center.

**Taxis** Flash; tel: 773 561 1444. Checker; tel: 243 2537

**Car rental** Thrifty, 5552 S Archer Ave; tel: 1 800 847 4389.

**Greyhound** 630 W Harrison; tel: 408 5800.

**O'Hare Airport**, the world's busiest, is 20 miles northwest by coach or El train.
Continental Air Transport buses (tel: 454 7800) run every few minutes between
downtown and the airport. CTA trains are just as frequent and much cheaper ($1.50).

**Tours** Gray Line; tel: 251 3107. Chicago Motor Coach; tel: 922 8919. Untouchable
Tours visits infamous gangster scenes; tel: 881 1195. For views of the city from Lake
Michigan call Mercury; tel: 332 1353 or Chicago From the Lake; tel: 527 1977.
 From May to September the Loop Train offers free 40-minute tours of downtown
attractions. Tours are conducted each Saturday afternoon by guides from the Chicago
Architecture Foundation (tel: 922 TOUR) and tickets can be obtained at the Chicago
Cultural Center on the morning of the tour.

**Visitors bureau** The Cultural Center opens daily in what was once Chicago's first
central library building at 77 E Randolph; tel: 744 2400; web: www.ci.chi.il.us/Tourism.
The Visitor Center, also open daily, is located on N Michigan Ave in the pumping
station adjacent to the Water Tower, sole survivors of Chicago's great fire.

**Accommodation** Contact Chicago Bed & Breakfast, PO Box 14088, Chicago, IL
60614; tel: 951 0085.

YMCA and YWCA, 33 W Chicago Ave; tel: 944 6211. Over 18s only. Single $30,
double $35. Arlington House IYH Hostel, 616 W Arlington Place; tel: 929 5380.
Private and dormitory rooms. Members $15, non-members $18.   International
Hostel, 6318 N Winthrop Ave; tel: 773 262 1011. Members $10, non-members $13.
Family rooms available. Take bus #151.   Some hotels offer weekend and summer
packages. Call the Tourist Council (tel: 793 2094) or the Hotel Association (tel: 346
3135). For discount hotel rates call Hot Rooms; tel: 1 800 468 3500 or 773 468 7666;
email: hotrooms@hotrooms.com; web: www.hotrooms.com.

Hotels include the Drake at 140 E Walton Place; tel: 787 2200; Blackstone, 636 S
Michigan Ave; tel: 427 4300; Bismarck, 171 W Randolph; tel: 236 0123 – double $89;
Cass, 640 N Wabash Ave; tel: 787 4030 – single and double $59; Harrison, 65 E
Harrison; tel: 427 8000 – single $42, double $52; Allegro, 171 W Randolph; tel: 236
0123.

## Recommended in Chicago

**Sears Tower** 233 S Wacker and Jackson, near the station; tel: 875 9696. Edward
Sears, a former railway clerk, founded Sears, Roebuck, the world's largest mail order
company. Railways proved ideal for distributing the catalogue and its goods, including

entire houses. The Sears Tower is the second tallest building on earth, reaching 110 storeys and 1,454ft/443m (1,707ft/520m including antennae). Ear-popping elevators shoot you to the 103rd floor Skydeck for views of the city, Lake Michigan and four states. Go before sunset and watch the city come alight. Open daily, admission charge.

**John Hancock Observatory** 875 N. Michigan Ave; tel: 751 3681; web: www.hancock-observatory.com. Even at 327ft lower than the Sears Tower, the John Hancock Center observation deck gives wonderful views of Lake Michigan and the city. The 94th floor observatory is more than 1,000 feet (300m) above Chicago and features an outside Skywalk, a virtual reality tour of more than 80 city sites, 3D 'talking' telescopes and a Chicago history wall. Open daily, admission charge.

**John Shedd Aquarium** 1200 Lake Shore Drive; tel: 939 2438; web: www.sheddnet.org. This splendid building holds thousands of fish as well as the largest indoor collection of marine mammals in the world, including beluga whales, seals, sea otters and dolphins. Don't miss the penguins and the amazing alligator snapping turtle. Open daily, half price Thu.

**Art Institute** 111 S Michigan Ave; tel: 443 3600; web: www.artic.edu/aic. One of the world's top galleries features Impressionist, American and Renaissance works alongside major exhibitions. Crowded at weekends. Open daily, free Tue.

**Museum of Science and Industry** 57th and Lake Shore Drive; tel: 773 684 1414; web: www.msichicago.org. Includes a German U-Boat, a British Spitfire, the Apollo 8 spacecraft and many automobiles, plus Omnimax film shows. Among the railroad engines is the New York Central's *No. 999*, which in 1893 was the first locomotive to exceed 100mph (160km/h). A Santa Fe miniature railroad operates model trains over 1,000ft (300m) of track. Open daily, free Thu.

**Navy Pier** 600 E Grand Ave; tel: 595 PIER or 800 595 PIER (outside Chicago); web: www.navypier.com. A city landmark with 50 acres of parks, gardens, shops, restaurants and attractions, including a Ferris wheel, carousel and children's museum. The 3,000ft pier was one of several planned for the city but the only actually to be constructed (in 1916).

**Robie House** 5757 S Woodlawn; tel: 773 834 1847; web: www.wrightplus.org. Designed by Frank Lloyd Wright, this spectacular building features 174 art glass windows and doors. Daily tours and special events. The house is managed by the Frank Lloyd Wright Foundation.

**Pullman Community** 11111 Forestville Ave; tel: 785 8181. America's earliest railway sleeping cars were made here by the businessman and inventor George Mortimer Pullman's Palace Company. They were the first to have electric lights and folding berths. Pullman's company town was designed in 1885 by an English architect, Solon Beman, as a model community for 12,000 workers. Some were expert carriage makers who had arrived from Germany. The majority of the town was built around the factory between 1880 and 1884, and included a church, school and library but no saloon. Workers lived in houses which reflected their level of skills.

Pullman is a designated landmark district and most of the original buildings in the town are still standing. The **Hotel Florence**, built in 1881, is the community's showpiece but  hundreds of homes are undergoing restoration. Pullman is located about 14 miles south of downtown but can easily be reached by Metra train on the Illinois Central Gulf Railroad.

The Historic Pullman Foundation visitor center occupies part of the former American Legion Building and opens on Saturday (11.00–14.00) and Sunday (12.00–15.00). Guided walking tours leave from the visitor center on the first Sunday of the month between May and October. For group tours (20 or more people) call 773 785 3828.
**A Philip Randolph/Pullman Porter Museum** 10406 S Maryland; tel: 773 928 3935; web: www.aphiliprandolphmuseum.com. Located in the Pullman district, this museum gallery is named after Asa Philip Randolph, chief organiser of the Brotherhood of the Sleeping Car Porters (BSCP) and regarded by some people in government as 'one of the most dangerous Negroes in America'. Wonderful photographs and memorabilia show the struggle between corporate power and disenfranchised workers in 1937, when Randolph chartered the first African-American labour union. Open Thu, Fri and Sat.

# All aboard!

The *California Zephyr* departs Chicago with the city skyline diminishing to your right. You should pass the eastbound *Zephyr* a few minutes out of Union Station. The westbound train continues at a modest pace through industrial scenes followed by many miles of suburbs such as Hinsdale, Westmont and Downer's Grove.

**NAPERVILLE (30/60)** Chicago's main western suburb has attractive restored buildings and a river walk. Commuter trains provide connections to La Grange, Cicero and Aurora.

**Aurora (10/50)** A stone roundhouse and other early railway buildings can be seen to your right. Double-decked commuter trains wait on your left. Aurora has been a transport junction since stage-coach days and was the first American city to have electric street lights. The Chicago, Burlington & Quincy Railroad was formed here in 1849. Not just a place but a state of mind, Aurora was the setting for the excellent *Wayne's World*.
    Look right as the train leaves to see the Caterpillar Tractor company's water-tower and factory. You then cross the Fox River before travelling among corn fields and the small communities of Plano, Sandwich, Somonauk and Mendota.

**PRINCETON (60/60)** 'The pig capital of the world' began as a New Englander settlement in 1833. It was the home of John Bryant, a founder of the Republican party, and the anti-slavery Underground Railroad had a 'station' here. An old caboose from the Burlington Railway can be seen to your left just before the train station.

**Wyanet (15/45)** Look for some of the large local population of pigs and cattle.

**Kewanee (30/30)** Located next to the Spoon River, this was another early New Englander settlement.

**Galva (40/20)** Swedish dissidents set up the utopian community of Bishop's Hill among these wooden houses in the 19th century.

**GALESBURG (60/50)** Former home town of George Washington Ferris, creator of the original Ferris wheel, and Olmsted Ferris, who invented popcorn. To your right is the copper spire of Knox College. Galesburg was another station on the secret Underground Railroad for escaped slaves. A 1930s' Hudson engine with its coach and caboose stands to the right of Amtrak's attractive canopied station. Thruway buses connect with *Texas Eagle* trains stopping at Springfield.

**Monmouth (20/30)** Wyatt Earp was born here and the railway brought a large block of granite to Monmouth to build a monument in his honour. You travel on through a region of cattle farms and corn fields. Nearing the Mississippi River you start to see woodland, marshes and wildfowl.

**Mississippi River (45/5)** The train crosses on a 2,000ft-long (600m) steel bridge, giving wonderful views of the river and its forested banks. A graceful highway bridge reflects in the water to your right. The Mississippi is the world's third largest river, stretching 2,350 miles (3,780km) to the Gulf of Mexico and draining a third of the United States. Before the railway bridge opened in 1868, passengers crossed here by ferry. During winter they sometimes went over the ice on foot. Crossing the river takes you from Illinois into Iowa.

**BURLINGTON (50/30)** The nearby Shoquoquon hills were one of the few places in this area where flint could be found, so Native Americans came to regard them as neutral territory. Strategically placed next to the river, Burlington became a natural railroad centre and capital of both Wisconsin and Iowa. Look for the steam locomotive to the left of Amtrak's station at 300 S Main. This location played an important part in the history of rail technology when George Westinghouse developed the air brake on adjacent Burlington Hill from 1863 onwards.

The *California Zephyr* passes slowly through an older part of town, with warehouses and an ammunition factory on the left, before travelling among wide fields of maize and oats.

**Danville (15/15)** Trees surround a town once used by stage-coaches and the Pony Express.

**MOUNT PLEASANT (30/40)** The Old Settlers & Threshers Reunion celebrates America's frontier heritage each September in this typical midwestern town. Vintage steam locomotives pull wooden coaches and cabooses on the **Midwest Central Railroad** (319 385 2912). The red building to your right is Iowa's Wesleyan College, dating from 1842. America's first toll roads with plank surfaces were laid between here and Burlington.

Soon after leaving Mount Pleasant the train crosses the Skunk River. Note the dilapidated Rock Island Line building on your right as you approach Ottumwa. Celebrated by Leadbelly and other balladeers, the Rock Island Line had a colourful history, beginning in 1852 when the first train out of Chicago sported a rainbow-painted locomotive and six bright yellow coaches. Jesse James and his gang carried out their first hold-up on a Rock Island train, derailing its locomotive and killing the engineer. The railroad faced bankruptcy several times but somehow managed to struggle on over its weather-beaten tracks until the 1970s.

**OTTUMWA (40/70)** Named after a Native American tribe when this was a trading post on banks above the Des Moines River. Ottumwa subsequently became a business centre and 'home town' to *MASH's* Radar O'Reilly.

You leave Ottumwa and cross the Des Moines River on its way to join the Mississippi.

**OSCEOLA (70/30)** Settlers in the 19th century discovered the first 'Delicious' apple tree 30 miles (48km) to the north of here at Winterset, where John Wayne was born and christened Marion Morrison. Osceola was named after a Seminole warrior chief whose wooden statue stands on your left beyond the station. Des Moines is 50 miles (80km) to the north.

As the train travels east look for some of the covered wooden bridges made famous by Robert Waller's book *The Bridges of Madison County*, and by the subsequent film starring Clint Eastwood. The story takes place in Winterset and this small town has been invaded by romantics attempting to trace the steps of the star-crossed lovers.

**CRESTON (30/105)** This railroad town set on a ridge between the Des Moines and Missouri Valleys is the *Zephyr's* highest point east of the Missouri River. The beautiful yellow-brick rail depot to your right is a national landmark. Farmers' co-operatives' silos, also on your right, provide the town's best viewing platform.

The train continues among corn fields, neat towns, woods, quiet rivers, cattle and horse farms. Sometimes you may catch sight of a roving coyote.

**Stanton (40/65)** Look right for the famous water-tower shaped like a coffee pot, complete with handle. Also to your right is the town's courthouse building.

**Council Bluffs (75/30)** This pioneer trading post became the eastern end of the Union Pacific Railroad leading to California. A former Rock Island depot at 1512 Main houses the **Railswest Railroad Museum** and model railroad (tel: 712 323 5182).

**Missouri River (80/25)** From its source in the Montana Mountains (where the Gallatin, Jefferson and Madison Rivers converge) the Missouri River comes through here to join the Mississippi at St Louis. Crossing the river takes you from Iowa into Nebraska.

**Offutt Air Force Base (90/15)** The airfield and Strategic Air Command museum are seen to your left before you approach Omaha through extensive freight yards.

## OMAHA (105/60)

This was the birthplace of Fred Astaire, Marlon Brando, Montgomery Clift, Malcolm X and Henry Fonda, and Mormons wintered here in 1846 on their way to Utah. Omaha played an important part in the great days of westward migration, being a stop on the first transcontinental railroad. The Union Stockyards have been in business since 1884 and the city deals mostly in grain and cattle raised on the prairies.

### Omaha basics

**Telephone code** 402.

**Station** Amtrak's modest brick station is a mile from downtown at 1003 S 9th; tel: 342 1501. Open 22.30–11.15 and 12.30–16.00. Vending machines, handcarts, taxi stand. Next to the Amtrak station is a massive old Burlington Northern building.

**Connections** Thruway buses connect with Kansas City and St Joseph.

**Local transport** MAT bus information and maps are available at the Park Fair Mall, 16th and Douglas; tel: 341 0800.

**Taxis** Happy Cab; tel: 339 8249. Checker; tel: 339 8294.

**Car rental** Rent-A-Wreck, 501 N 17th; tel: 344 2001.

**Greyhound** 1601 Jackson; tel: 800 312 2222.

**Eppley Airport** can be reached by MAT bus #28 from 10th Street.

**Visitors bureau** 6800 Mercy Road; tel: 800 332 1819; email: info@visitomaha.com; web: www.visitomaha.com. Open weekdays. For the events hot line call 444 6800.

**Accommodation** For bed & breakfast contact the Offutt Mansion, 140 N 39th; tel: 553 0951.

YMCA, 430 S 20th; tel: 341 1600. For men and women. Single $10.

Hotels include the Red Lion Inn at 1616 Dodge; tel: 346 7600; Oak Creek Inn, 2808 S 72nd; tel: 397 7137; Crowne Plaza 655 N 108th Ave; tel: 496 0850 or 800 227 6963; Thrifty Scot, 7101 Grover; tel: 391 5757; Super 8, 7111 Spring; tel: 390 0700 – single $32, double $37; Excel Inn, 2211 Douglas; tel: 345 9565 – single $25, double $35.

### Recommended in Omaha

**Durham Western Heritage Museum** 801 South 10th; tel: 444 5071; web: www.dwhm.org. The Union Pacific collection, formerly housed in the UP headquarters building at 12th and Dodge, is now located here.

The museum describes the railroad's long and sometimes controversial history, and includes an auditor's office, Abraham Lincoln's funeral car with its original furnishings, and the surveying instruments of General Grenville M Dodge, who was the Union Pacific's chief engineer and responsible for constructing some of America's most vital early routes. There is also a research facility and library.

*Above* South rim of the Grand Canyon at sunset (DG)
*Below* American Falls at Niagara (SC)

*Above* Cable car, San Francisco (GR)

*Below left California Zephyr* (Amtrak)

*Below right Coast Starlight* (Amtrak)

The photograph collection contains an estimated 590,000 images, some of which can be viewed in the UPRR Photo Gallery (web: www.uprr.com/aboutup/photos). The famous picture of the Golden Spike ceremony shows General Dodge shaking hands with Samuel S Montague of the Central Pacific. The Western Heritage Museum opens daily, admission charge.

**Old Market** Farnam to Jackson Sts, 10th to 13th; tel; 341 7151 or 346 4445; web: www.omahaoldmarket.com. Bookstores, art galleries, antique shops, pubs and more than 30 restaurants populate this historic neighbourhood.

**Murdock Historical Society** 9014 310th; tel: 867 3331. The settlement of Murdock began in 1890 when it was a water stop on the Rock Island Railroad. Many German settlers moved to this area and the Historical Society tells their story.

**Joslyn Art Museum** 2200 Dodge; tel 402 342 3300; web: www.joslyn.org. Nebraska's only fine arts museum opened in 1931. The encyclopedic collection features works from antiquity to the present with a special emphasis on 19th- and 20th-century art from Europe and America. Designed as a cultural centre for the community, the museum was built as a gift to Omaha from Sarah Joslyn in memory of her husband George, a prominent Omaha businessman and community leader. Closed Mon, admission charge.

**Greenwood Depot Museum** 340 N Broad, in Greenwood; tel: 789 2232. Cass County's only preserved depot is almost 130 years old and contains history of the town and surrounding area.

**Malcolm X Birthsite** 3448 Pinkney; tel: 444 5955. Visit the house where the 1960s civil rights' activist Malcom X was born on May 19 1925. Open weekdays.

**Henry Doorly Zoo** 10th and Deer Park Blvd; tel: 733 8401; web: omahazoo.com. Gorillas, orang-utans and white tigers live beside the Missouri River in Omaha's greatest tourist attraction, which has the largest indoor rainforest in the world. The aquarium features sharks and king penguins. Union Pacific has funded a new engine house from where steam trains chug through the grounds on a 30-inch gauge line. Open daily, admission charge.

**Girls and Boys Town** Located 10 miles west of the city at 138th & W Dodge Rd; tel: 1 800 625 1400; web: boysandgirlstown.org. Boys Town was founded in 1917 as a home for underprivileged youngsters by Father Flanagan, played in the *Boys Town* film by Spencer Tracy. Boys Town is now a National Historic Landmark with attractions that include Father Flanagan's House, a working farm and two Gothic chapels. Open daily, free.

**Strategic Air and Space Museum** 28210 W Park Hwy in Ashland; tel: 800 358 5029; web: www.strategicairandspace.com. The museum includes a flight simulator and has many aircraft and missiles to show the entire development of military aviation. Open daily, admission charge.

# All aboard!

The *Zephyr* leaves past high-rises to the right and rolls on across Nebraska, crossing the Platte River midway between Omaha and Lincoln. The course of this river was followed west by Mormons, then by the Pony Express and settlers on the Oregon Trail.

**LINCOLN (60/90)** Nebraska University appears to your left as the train approaches the station with the state fairgrounds to your right. Amtrak occupies the north end of an old Burlington & Northern building, using a renovated waiting-room called the Great Hall. Lincoln's 400ft (120m) high State Capitol, known as the 'tower of the plains', can be seen on your left and is the only unicameral (single house) state legislature in the country. The statue on its gold dome represents a man broadcasting seed. Lincoln's **visitors bureau** is at 1135 M; tel: 402 434 5335 or 800 423 8212; web: www.lincoln.org/cvb.

**HASTINGS (90/50)** The town is a centre for trade and manufacturing, especially of farm machinery. The House of Yesterday Museum portrays the life and times of pioneers.

Grand Island, 30 miles (48km) north, is home to the **Stuhr Museum of the Prairie Pioneer** at 3133 W Hwy 34 (tel: 308 385 5316; web: www.stuhrmuseum.org). The cottage where Henry Fonda was born is one of 60 authentic buildings in Railroad Town, which recreates a prairie community of the late 19th century. The rail-yard includes an 1890 depot, turntable, steam locomotives and rolling stock. Open daily, admission charge.

The countryside becomes progressively dryer as the *California Zephyr* pulls out of Hastings and travels west, moving from farmland into predominantly cattle country.

**Kenesaw (15/35)** You cross the Oregon Trail once used by wagon trains.

**HOLDREGE (50/70)** Named after George Holdrege, a former manager of the Chicago, Burlington & Quincy Railroad.

**McCOOK (70/115)** This was a division point on the railroad before becoming an oil town.

**Nebraska/Colorado State Line (70/45)** As you change from Central to Mountain Time, watches go back an hour (forward when travelling east). The *California Zephyr* leaves Nebraska and travels towards Denver over the high plains of eastern Colorado, which used to be buffalo territory.

**FORT MORGAN (115/80)** The fort dates from 1864, since when the town has grown rich on oil and cattle.

**Pike's Peak (60/20)** This 14,110ft (4,300m) mountain is just visible on the far left horizon. It was on top of Pike's Peak in 1893 that Katherine Lee Bates was inspired to write the words to *America the Beautiful*. The Rockies are 80 miles (130km) away to your right.

**Commerce City (65/15)** Denver's chief industrial suburb boasts America's busiest sheep market and largest sugar beet factories. Look for extensive cattle yards beside the track.

**Riverside Cemetery (70/10)** The pioneer graveyard to your right dates from 1876. As the train passes beneath Interstate 70 look for Denver's skyline on your left. The front of the train comes into view on the right, turning north before reversing into the station.

## DENVER (80/120)

'The mile high city' was a gold rush town founded in 1858 when flakes of gold were discovered at nearby Cherry Creek. Many narrow gauge railroads were built to serve the camps and in 1876 a route was opened via the steep black rock walls of Clear Creek Canyon to the town of Central City. It was here that George Pullman was working as a miner when he thought of the idea for his sleeping car.

The Union Pacific bypassed Denver on its transcontinental route but citizens built their own railroad to meet it at Cheyenne, Wyoming. This line and the Kansas City railroad helped transform Denver from a frontier town (where Bat Masterson patrolled the saloons) into one of the fastest growing cities in the United States, with a population of over two million (not counting the Carringtons). Skyscrapers glitter in the brilliant light and older parts of the city have been restored.

Denver invented the cheeseburger and brews more beer than anywhere else in the world, yet still claims to have America's thinnest residents. The dry climate and high altitude make this city unique, so treat its pure sunlight with respect and allow a few days to become acclimatised before undertaking anything too strenuous. Many ski resorts are close by and equipment can easily be hired.

### Denver basics

**Telephone code** 303.

**Station** When Union Station at 1701 Wynkoop opened in 1881 it was the biggest train station in the west and the largest building in Colorado. Built in Italian Romanesque style with neo-classical additions, it received 80 trains a day and served one million passengers a year. Information tel: 534 2812. Ticket-office and waiting-room open 07.00–21.00. Lockers, ATM banking, Red Caps, newspapers, handcarts, snack bar, shop, taxi stand.

**Connections** Thruway buses connect with Boulder, Cheyenne and Laramie, as well as Colorado Springs and Pueblo. The *Rio Grande Ski Train* (tel: 296 4754) leaves Union Station each weekend morning during December and January (Fri–Sun from February to March) for a two-hour journey via the Moffatt Tunnel and 27 others to Winter Park in the Rockies. The train is pulled by two locomotives and uses ex-Canadian Pacific cars.

**Local transport** RTD light rail trains and buses (tel: 299 6000) serve downtown and the suburbs, with maps and schedules from the station. A free shuttle service runs along 16th Street.

**Taxis** Yellow; tel: 777 7777.

**Car rental** Thrifty; tel: 342 9400.

**Greyhound** 1055 19th; tel: 293 6555.

**Denver International Airport** cost $4.3 billion, covers an area twice the size of Manhattan and has its own underground railway. It can be reached from downtown by Super Shuttle bus; tel: 800 525 3177.

**Tours** Gray Line city and mountain excursions leave from the Greyhound depot; tel: 289 2841. The Culture Trolley goes from the visitors bureau to most of the main attractions. Walking tours can be taken with Historic Denver, 1330 17th; tel: 866 3682.

**Visitors bureau** 1668 Larimer; tel: 892 1112; web: www.denver.org. Closed Sun and holidays. For a free guide to Denver call 800 393 8559 or visit the website.

**Accommodation** A Touch of Heaven Bed & Breakfast is at 16720 W 63rd Pl in Golden; tel: 279 4133; email: Talmar5000@aol.com; web: www.coloradovacation.com/bed/talmar.

YMCA, 25 E 16th; tel: 860 9622. For both men and women. Single $28, double $44. International Youth Hostel, 630 E 16th Ave; tel: 832 9996. Dormitory rooms $10.

Hotels include the Brown Palace at 321 17th; tel: 800 321 2599; Broadway Plaza, 1111 Broadway; tel: 893 0303; Fairfield Inn, 1680 S Colorado Blvd; tel: 691 2223; Residence Inn, 2777 Zuni; tel: 458 5318; Regal 8, 12033 E 38th; tel: 371 0740; Standish, 1530 California; tel: 534 3231 – single $14, double $16.

## Recommended in Denver

**Larimer Square** This historic part of the city, once the haunt of outlaws, has Victorian houses, courtyards, gaslights, craft shops, restaurants and nightclubs.

**US Mint** 320 W Colfax; tel: 405 4761; web: www.usmint.gov. The mint, located in an Italian Renaissance style building, produces ten billion coins a year and boasts more gold bullion (an estimated $100 billion worth) than anywhere outside Fort Knox. Souvenir coins are on sale. Open weekdays, free tours but no free samples!

**Denver Art Museum** 13th and Acoma; tel: 720 865 5000; web: www.denverartmuseum.org. The spectacular 28-sided museum building houses over 40,000 works, including the world's finest Native American art collection. The New World gallery has 5,000 pre-Columbian and Spanish Colonial works, and there are pictures by Georgia O'Keeffe, Degas, Matisse, Monet, Picasso and Renoir. The spirit of the American West is captured by artists such as Frederic Remington and Norman Rockwell. Closed Mon, admission charge.

**State Capitol** 200 E Colfax; tel: 866 2604. Murals, unique Colorado onyx and a dome covered with gold leaf, plus balcony views towards the Rockies and north to the Wyoming border. The 15th step on the west side is exactly one mile above sea level. Open Mon–Fri, free tours.

**Black American West Museum & Heritage Center** 3901 California, opposite Amtrak's station; tel: 292 2566; web: www.coax.net/people/lwf/bawmus.html. A third of working cowboys in the Old West were African Americans, often freed slaves who travelled west after the Civil War. This museum uses photographs, personal belongings, clothing and oral histories to tell the story of Black pioneers, Buffalo Soldiers, African American cowboys and businessmen who helped settle the west. Open Wed–Sun.

**Coors Brewery** 13th and Ford Street in Golden; tel: 277 2552; web: www.coors.com. The Coors Brewery has been in business since 1873 and this is the largest single brewing site in the world. Over 10 million people have taken the free tour, which takes you through the entire brewing process and lets you sample the products in the hospitality lounge. Closed Sun.

**Colorado Railroad Museum** 17155 W 44th Ave in Golden, 12 miles west of Denver; tel: 279 4591; web: www.crrm.org. The 1880s-style masonry depot has 50,000 rare photographs and artifacts. The sprawling grounds contain more than 50 narrow and standard gauge locomotives, cars and other rolling stock, including some of the oldest in the state. A large model railroad recreates local lines such as those at Cripple Creek, Telluride and Tennessee Pass. Over 2,000 miles of tracks once probed the local mountain canyons, and there are short steam train rides at weekends. Open daily, admission charge.

**Forney Transportation Museum** 4303 Brighton Blvd; tel: 297 1113; web: www.forneymuseum.com. The museum features locomotives, including a 1941 Union Pacific 'Big Boy', as well as horse-drawn vehicles and antique cars such as Amelia Earhart's *Kissel Kar* and a Mercedes belonging to Hitler's US ambassador. Closed Sun, admission charge.

# All aboard!

The *California Zephyr* departs on Rio Grande Railroad tracks, having arrived on the Burlington Northern line from Chicago. Look back to your right for terrific views of Denver.

**Arvada (20/100)** You pass through another major suburb with the Front Range of the Rockies ahead. Mount Evans (14,264ft/4,350m) is on your left and Long's Peak (14,255ft/4,345m) on your right. The road up to Mount Evans is the highest paved road in North America.

**Rocky (40/80)** The train takes an S-shaped curve to gain height among the foothills. Winds can reach 100mph (160km/h) here so the track is protected at Big 10 Curve by railroad cars anchored with sand. The *Zephyr* climbs a 2% gradient and enters the first of 29 tunnels, with Coal Creek Canyon on your left.

**Plainview (50/70)** Look for spectacular sightings of the barren Colorado plains 1,500ft (450m) below and the whole city of Denver back to your right. Rocky Flats nuclear weapons factory can be seen in the foreground. To your right are Colorado University and the city of Boulder. The train rumbles on into the Rockies through South Boulder Canyon.

**Gross Reservoir (60/60)** A 340ft-high (100m) dam provides Denver with 14 billion gallons (62 billion litres) of water. Look out for deer and elk as you enter the Roosevelt National Forest with the continental divide ahead.

**Moffat Tunnel (105/15)** The tunnel is over six miles (10km) long and is the highest point (9,239ft/2,820m) on Amtrak's network. Before the tunnel opened in 1928, reducing the distance between Denver and Salt Lake City by

65 miles (100km), trains took five hours to cross the continental divide around James Peak (13,260ft/4,040m). Now the journey takes only 10 minutes before you emerge from darkness into dazzling light.

**Winter Park Ski Resort (115/5)** Ski slopes appear close by on your left.

**WINTER PARK (120/20)** One of many mountain parks in a densely wooded region which is famous for pine trees, tourists and ranching. The train station is actually in Fraser – called 'the icebox of America' because temperatures sometimes get as low as minus 50°F (-46°C). Look on a ridge to your right to see the Devil's Thumb rock formation.

**Tabernash (5/15)** Named after a Native American chief. Before the Moffat Tunnel opened, helper (pusher) locomotives would be added here to enable trains to climb the pass.

**Fraser Canyon (10/5)** The *Zephyr* accompanies the clear, trout-laden Fraser River, which President Eisenhower often came here to fish.

**GRANBY (20/180)** This area of meadow lands is known as Middle Park. Trail Ridge Road (the world's highest car road) runs through Rocky Mountain National Park to your right. Evidence has been found locally of people who predate all known Native American tribes.

After Granby the train joins the Colorado River near its source and accompanies it for more than 200 miles (320km), making this one of the longest stretches of river followed by a train route anywhere in the world.

**Hot Sulphur Springs (15/165)** Thermal springs heat the indoor swimming pool to your right.

**Byers Canyon (16/164)** Spiky rock formations tower above the track and Highway 40 can be seen on your left. Watch for herds of deer and the occasional buffalo as the train picks up speed through prime cattle country.

**Kremmling (35/145)** The town is on your right and Mount Powell (13,534ft/4,125m) to your left.

**Gore Canyon (40/85)** Sheer rock walls reach 1,500ft (450m) and make the canyon accessible only by train. The Gore Range to your left touches 13,000ft (4,000m). Coming out of the canyon you travel through meadows and ranch land. Just before Bond you see the old State Bridge to your left.

**Bond (100/80)** A historic railroad town where the Rio Grande branch line to Steamboat Springs can be seen above on the right. The cut-off line between Bond and Dotsero was built by the Denver & Salt Lake Railroad.

**Red Canyon (110/65)** Spaniards called this place Colorado (meaning red) after seeing the vivid colours of these strange rock formations.

**Dotsero (140/40)** An 1885 survey of the Colorado River marked this point '.0' or 'dot-zero' on its maps and it represents the midpoint of the *California Zephyr*'s journey. The Eagle River joins the Colorado on your left.

**Glenwood Canyon (155/10)** Brightly coloured rocks, cliffs, aspen trees and evergreens proliferate as you follow beside the river. Interstate 70, one of the longest highways ever built, is on the far shore.

**GLENWOOD SPRINGS (180/100)** A centre for fishing, hiking and white-water rafters who come to dice among the rapids. The ski resorts of Snowmass and Aspen, where you might bump into Jack Nicholson or Martina Navratilova, can be reached by bus. On your right is one of the world's largest outdoor swimming pools, heated all year round by Yampa Hot Springs. Beyond the pool is Theodore Roosevelt's favourite Colorado Hotel. John Henry 'Doc' Holliday, the gambler, gunfighter and part-time dentist, lived and was buried here when he died at the age of 35. Sheriff Pat Garrett was also buried nearby. Amtrak's attractive stone and red tile station to your left has unusual square Chinese-style towers.

As the train leaves along a typical Rocky Mountain valley look for rafters riding on the Roaring Fork River joining the Colorado to your left.

**New Castle (30/70)** Massive oil shale deposits have been discovered in this area and some of them are visible in the cliffs to your right. Also to your right is Mount Baxter (11,188ft/3,410m). In 1896, 54 workers died in a local mine explosion and a second disaster in 1931 killed 37 more. The mine continues to burn.

**Grand Valley (70/30)** The aptly named Parachute Mountains can be seen to your right.

**De Beque-Palisade (80/20)** The beautiful and majestic Grand Mesa on your left is the world's largest flat-top mountain (over 10,000ft/3,000m). This region produces great quantities of fruit, especially peaches and apricots. As you approach Grand Junction among fruit fields and orchards look for a goat farm on your right.

**GRAND JUNCTION (100/155)** Where the Gunnison and Colorado Rivers meet the Denver and Rio Grande Railroads. Amtrak's station is on the left at 337 S 1st. Grand Junction is a centre for agriculture and the coal industry, as well as a base for visitors travelling to Mesa Verde National Park, Grand Mesa Forest and Colorado National Monument. The latter's red cliffs are visible to your left as you leave.

**Ruby Canyon (20/135)** Another splendid photo-opportunity as the train winds through beautifully coloured rocks carved by the Colorado River out of the Uncompahgre Plateau. Bald and golden eagles ride currents of air along the canyon walls and above the river. Several sets of *moki* steps on your right show where Anastosia Indians used to climb, and a mark signifies the Colorado/Utah border.

At Westwater the Colorado goes south and enters a quite different landscape, travelling 150 miles (240km) through sandy desert. Watch for antelope as you cross the dried river beds of this arid region, which used to be below sea level. The massive eroding mesas to your right are the intricately carved Book Cliffs, made from sandstone and shale. La Sal Mountains can be seen in the left distance.

**Thompson (60/25)** The white and green station on the left is a flag stop, so trains halt only on request. Look beyond the station for the Sweet Grills café featured in the film *Thelma and Louise*.

Rich in uranium, this part of Utah has dramatic and sometimes desolate scenery. Nearby are Arches National Monument, Dead Horse Point, Canyonlands National Park and Monument Valley (star of many John Ford westerns, including *Stagecoach*).

**GREEN RIVER (85/70)** Look for fields of cantaloupes and watermelons before you cross the Green River and enter a town of the same name. Green River Bible Church is to your right. An altitude of 4,075ft (1,240m) makes this the lowest point on the line between Denver and Salt Lake City. To your left are Mount Marvine (11,600ft/3,540m) and Thousand Lake Mountain (11,306ft/3,450m).

**HELPER (70/120)** Named after the extra locomotives once attached here to westbound freight trains to enable them to climb the mountains. Burlington Northern freight wagons stand on your right and Helper remains a busy centre for shipping coal, of which this region has enough to supply America for hundreds of years.

You leave past a western downtown district to your left, where a large brick building on the hillside belongs to the Utah Railway. As the train heads into the Wasatch Mountains by way of Soldier Summit it is joined on the left by the Price River. The conglomeration of machinery to your right, 10 minutes from Helper, is a coal-processing plant.

**Castle Gate (15/105)** So called because the rock walls resemble a castle. Also high up on the right is Balancing Rock, topped by a flying flag. The train robber Butch Cassidy lived in this area.

**Soldier Summit (60/60)** The 7,440ft (2,270m) peak's name commemorates US Army soldiers who were buried here in 1860. Look for the abandoned mine to your right. The train descends sharply from this summit of the snow-capped

Wasatch Mountains by a series of horseshoe curves into the Spanish Fork River Canyon. You may catch sight of deer and elk as you travel between the rusty red and white canyon walls.

**Thistle (100/20)** Heavy rains caused a mud slide in 1983 which deluged the village of Thistle along with the river and parts of the Rio Grande tracks. The route had to be closed for three months while a 3,000ft (910m) tunnel was constructed beneath Billy's Mountain. Old tracks can be seen below to your left and remnants of the village are visible just before the tunnel.

Look for llamas and horses in fields to your right as the train approaches Springville.

**Springville (115/5)** The colonial building on the right was once a school.

**PROVO (120/55)** Founded by Mormons in 1849, Utah's third biggest city is the headquarters of Brigham Young University (America's largest private college) as well as the Osmond family. Provo's nondescript industrial buildings and car-wrecking yards are set among beautiful mountain ranges, with the Uinta and Manti La Sal National Forests close by.

The *Zephyr* crosses the Provo River with US Steel's Geneva Works to the right. Mount Timpanogos (11,750ft/3,575m) is also to the right and Mount Nebo on your left.

**Utah Lake (15/40)** The lake is to your left with the Tintic Mountains in the distance.

**Riverton (25/30)** Kennecott copper mine, once the largest in the world, is among the hills to your left. Nearing Salt Lake City look right for the Salt Lake Temple and domed State Capitol.

## SALT LAKE CITY (55/250)

Founded in 1847 by Brigham Young and other pioneers seeking to practise their beliefs in freedom, Mormon influence still dominates this pretty valley between the Wasatch Mountains and the Oquirrh Range. The Golden Spike ceremony which completed the first transcontinental rail route took place 40 miles (60km) north of here at Promontory Summit.

Salt Lake City is an attractive place with clean air, wide streets and downtown crossing signals that chirrup endearingly. Nearby ski resorts include Alta (America's second oldest) and Sundance (proprietor Robert Redford). Five national parks with dramatic rock scenery are within a single day's drive.

### Salt Lake City basics

**Telephone code** 801.

**Station** The station used by Amtrak is at 340 S 300 West. Information: 531 0188. Ticket-office open 04.00–12.30 and 16.15–01.00 (Mon–Sat) and 16.00–01.00 (Sun).

Waiting-room open 24 hours (weekdays) and 23.00–14.30 (weekends). Lockers, vending machines, handcarts, restaurant, taxi stand.

**Local transport** Utah Transit Authority buses (tel: 743 3882; web: rideuta.com) visit most tourist attractions. UTA also provides an extensive bus and light rail (TRAX) service to the ski resorts and Provo as well as throughout the valley.

**Taxis** City; tel: 363 8400. Yellow; tel: 521 2100.

**Car rental** Advantage, 460 S Redwood Rd; tel: 266 5579.

**Greyhound** 160 W South Temple; tel: 355 9579.

**Salt Lake City International Airport** is five miles west by UTA bus #50.

**Tours** Brigham City; tel: 800 837 7229. Adven; tel: 288 2118. For a free 15-minute guided tour on the open-air trolley (Mon–Sat) giving an overview of the Mormon sites call 240 6279.

**Visitors bureau** 90 S West Temple; tel: 521 2822; web: www.visitsaltlake.com. Open daily. Free guide.

**Accommodation** For bed & breakfast contact Alpine, 4235 S Lynne Lane, Salt Lake City, UT 84124; tel: 277 9300.

Avenues (AYH) Youth Hostel, 107 F; tel: 359 3855; email: hostel@sisna.com. Free pick-up from Amtrak's station. Members $14, non-members $16. Single $22, double $32. Ute Hostel, 21 E Kelsey Ave; tel: 595 1645; web: www.infobytes.com/utehostel. Free transport to and from the airport and train station. Some private rooms. Dormitory rooms $13.

Hotels include the Brigham Street Inn at 1135 E South Temple; tel: 364 4461; Crystal Inn-Downtown, 230 W 500 South; tel: 328 4466; Desert, 50 W 5th South; tel: 532 2900; Days Inn Central, 315 W 3300 South; tel: 486 8780; Regal, 1025 N 900 West; tel: 364 6591; Carlton, 140 E South Temple; tel: 355 3418 – single $20, double $30.

## Recommended in Salt Lake City

**Temple Square** 50 W South Temple; tel: 240 4872. The heart of the Church of Jesus Christ of Latter-day Saints is a six-spired Temple which can only be entered by Mormon church members. Film shows and tours take place elsewhere. The Mormon Tabernacle Choir (tel: 240 3221) broadcasts a television and radio programme each Sunday morning (free admission) and there are daily recitals on the Temple's 11,623-pipe organ, complete with light effects. Free concerts takes place in summer on Tuesday and Friday evenings in Brigham Young Historic Park (tel: 240 3323). Buildings of interest within walking distance include the **Lion House** at 63 E South Temple, named after the stone lion sculpted for the front porch, and the 1847 **Deuel Log Home**, one of the first log homes built in the Salt Lake Valley. Brigham Young's **Beehive House** at 67 E South Temple (tel: 240 2571) provides free tours and traditional candy.

**The Church Office Building** 50 E North Temple; tel: 240 2190. The tallest structure in Salt Lake City is this world headquarters of The Church of Jesus Christ of Latter-day Saints. Two observation decks on the 26th floor are open free to the public to give spectacular views of the valley and surrounding mountains.

**Family History Library** 35 N West Temple; tel: 240 2331. Trace your family line among two million rolls of microfilm, 278,000 books and several electronic data files in the largest library of its kind in the world. Closed Sun, free tours Mon–Sat.

**Family Search Center** In the Joseph Smith Memorial Building at 15 E South Temple; tel: 240 4085; web: www.familysearch.org. Another likely place to check out your ancestors, with a collection of compiled genealogical data on 150 computers and the aid of helpful staff. Open Mon–Sat, free.

**The Capitol** At the north end of State Street; tel: 538 3000. This impressive state house was constructed from marble and granite beneath a copper dome. Closed Sun.

**Pioneer Memorial Museum** 300 N Main; tel: 538 1050. Pioneer artifacts including clothes and vehicles are looked after by ladies every bit as formidable as those in the photographs. Open daily, free.

**Trolley Square** At Sixth S and Seventh E; tel: 521 9877. Originally a fairground, this city block was the site of the Utah Light and Railway Company's trolley system carbarn complex. Now a registered historic place, it has been carefully converted into a shopping and entertainment centre. Walking tour highlights include the original 97ft high water tower and a stained glass dome from the First Methodist Church in Long Beach, California. Open daily, free.

**Gardner Mill** 1100 W 7800 South; tel: 566 8903; web: www.gardnervillage.com. Scottish immigrant Archibald Gardner was one of the original settlers with Brigham Young and he set up mills here in the 19th century. His main mill is now a restaurant and many historic buildings have been moved here to recreate a village, complete with a stream winding among connecting pathways and covered bridges. Closed Sun, free.

**Hansen Planetarium** 15 South State, between South Temple and Social Hall Ave; tel: 538 2104; web: www.hansenplanetarium.net. Built in 1904, this planetarium is the place to watch Utah skies. Star shows, laser/music concerts and science exhibits, including the International Space Station (ISS) project. Open daily, admission charge.

**Great Salt Lake State Park** PO Box 16658, Salt Lake City, Utah 84116-0658; tel: 250 1898; web: http://parks.state.ut.us. Located about 16 miles west on Interstate 80, the lake was once part of Lake Bonneville and the water's high salt content makes swimming here a buoyant experience. The park is open all year round for picnics, boating and wildlife-watching.

## All aboard!

The *California Zephyr* makes a long service stop before leaving on Union Pacific tracks, touching the edge of the Great Salt Lake before crossing Bonneville Salt Flats. The run between here and Elko is Amtrak's longest without a scheduled halt. As you pass from Mountain to Pacific Time, watches should go back an hour (forward when travelling east).

**ELKO (250/120)** The name is a Native American word for 'white woman'. Elko was a stop for wagon trains on the Humboldt River Overland Trail and is now a base for the region's sheep and cattle ranches. Each spring the town holds the world chariot race championships.

As the train travels west look for the Ruby Mountains to your left and the Independence Range on your right.

**WINNEMUCCA (120/165)** The town changed its name from French Ford to that of a Paiute Indian chief. In 1900 Butch Cassidy's gang robbed the town's First National Bank, brimming with cash for local gold and silver mines. Formerly a trading post where wagons crossed the Humboldt River, Winnemucca is now a distribution point for agriculture and livestock.

The *California Zephyr* changes to Southern Pacific tracks before following the Humboldt River.

**Lovelock (80/85)** The Trinity Range is to your right and the Humboldt Mountains to your left. You cross the Humboldt Sink, a muddy region located in the middle of a desert.

**Fernley (140/25)** The Truckee River joins on the right and the train begins to trace it back to the High Sierras as far as Truckee.

**Mustang Ranch (145/20)** The red-tiled building to your left was Nevada's best-known little whorehouse.

**SPARKS (165/10)** The *Zephyr* makes a service stop at the old wooden station with its canopy, tower and peeling cream paint. Sparks has long been a railroad town and has become a major distribution centre since the introduction of Nevada's tax-free warehousing scheme. Southern Pacific freight wagons stand on the left and the Nugget Casino on the right. Pyramid Lake's bird sanctuary, famous for pelicans, is 30 miles to the north.

As you leave Sparks and approach Reno look left to see MGM's massive Grand Hotel casino.

**RENO (10/55)** 'The biggest little city in the world' tries hard to be Las Vegas but still retains its charm. What started as a Mormon settlement became more riotous once silver was discovered. Gambling was legalised in 1931, after which Reno began accumulating the neon-clad casinos which draw fun-seekers to Virginia Street, located on either side of Amtrak's Spanish-style station. The **visitors bureau** is at 4590 S. Virginia; tel: 775 827 RENO or 888 HIT RENO; web: www.renolaketahoe.

If you plan to gamble, or just want to know what goes on behind the mirrors, you can take a Behind the Scenes tour. **Harrah's Hotel** has a collection of antique cars and the **Liberty Belle Saloon** features old slot machines. *Bonanza*'s Ponderosa Ranch is nearby and Lake Tahoe, North America's largest alpine lake, 35 miles (56km) southwest.

The *Zephyr* departs with the dome of St Thomas Aquinas Church a calming presence on your left. You travel through ranch country into Tahoe National Forest then cross the Sierra Nevada range, which climbs to over 7,000ft (2,100m). Gold prospectors were the first white men to follow this route, which later became a heroic challenge to pioneer railroad constructors.

The train accompanies the fast running Truckee River most of the way to the town of Truckee. On weekends (daily during summer) a guide from the

California Railroad Museum joins the train across the Sierras to describe the line's history and places of interest.

**Verdi (15/35)** A hydroelectric generator on the far side of the Truckee River is powered by water brought along wooden flumes from the mountains. The first train robbery took place here on November 4 1870, less than 18 months after the railroad arrived. The same *Atlantic Express* was robbed again less than 24 hours later in Independence, Nevada, and some of the loot is said to be still buried locally.

**Nevada/California State Line (20/350)** Look right for the border mark. Wooden flumes on the cliffs to your left are relics of the mining industry.

**Floriston (30/20)** A splendid yellow mansion stands on the left.

**Boca (40/10)** The small dam to your right is all that remains of a town drowned beneath the reservoir. Boca formerly earned a living by supplying ice packed in sawdust to San Francisco. It once registered California's lowest ever temperature (-45F/-42C) and became known as 'the coldest place in the nation'.

**TRUCKEE (50/125)** Named after Paiute Winnemucca's father, Chief Tro-Kay, and located on the banks of the Truckee River, the town had 14 lumber mills by the time the railroad arrived. Truckee managed to burn down six times between 1871 and 1882, but Chaplin filmed some of the remaining wooden buildings on Main Street for *The Gold Rush*.

Truckee is a gateway to Lake Tahoe and the ski resorts of Squaw Valley and Sugar Bowl. Pullman railway cars used to run from Oakland to Lake Tahoe but the branch line, abandoned in the 1940s, is now a cycle track. Amtrak's long, low station is on the right. For **tourist information** call 530 587 0476 or 800 548 8388.

After leaving town the train starts to ascend the Donner Pass in a sequence of horseshoe curves, providing fine views of the Truckee River basin below. All the trees are less than a hundred years old because the original forest was demolished to feed wood-burning locomotives.

**Donner Lake (15/110)** Blizzards in 1846 trapped 87 Illinois settlers who had been travelling to California. By the time a relief party arrived here on February 19 1847 nearly half the settlers, including five women and 14 children, had frozen to death or died from starvation. Others were reduced to cannibalism or had gone mad in the greatest single natural disaster of America's westward expansion. The place became known as Donner Pass after the Donner family, who were among the settlers. A museum on Donner Pass Road depicts their ordeal and describes the building of the Central Pacific Railroad.

**Mount Judah (25/100)** Nearing Judah's summit the slopes of Sugar Bowl ski resort can be seen on both sides of the track, joined by an overhead trestle.

The train then enters a tunnel through the mountain named after the Central Pacific's designer, Theodore Judah.

**Norden (35/90)** Snowfall averages 34ft (10m) a year so building and maintaining this track is a remarkable achievement. The *City of San Francisco* was once snowbound here for four days but today's trains are often able to run when the nearby highway becomes impassable.

There used to be 37 miles (60km) of snow-sheds between Truckee and Sacramento, leading some to describe the route as 'like railroading in a barn'. Sheds were usually made from wood and often caught fire during the days of steam power. Special fire trains had to be kept in readiness and only four miles (6.5km) of sheds now remain. On a mountain to your left is the small box which was once a fire lookout point.

**Soda Springs (40/85)** Lake Van Norden and the Soda Springs ski resort are to your left. On the other side of the valley to your right is Castle Peak, shaped like a fortress. Beside it is Black Butte Mountain (8,030ft/2,450m).

**Emigrant Gap (65/60)** Lake Spalding's irregular outline appears to your right as the train crosses Interstate 80. Trees sometimes grow almost horizontally in the alpine scenery. Pioneers used to lower wagons by rope into the beautiful Bear Valley on your right after travelling through Emigrant Gap.

**Blue Canyon (70/55)** Named after the blue haze produced by sawmills, this was a gold rush town and a servicing stop for steam trains.

**American River Canyon (90/35)** Astonishing views appear to your left as the train inches along evergreen-covered cliffs 1,800ft (550m) above the North Fork of the American River. The remains of gold mine workings can be seen opposite in a valley that stretches all the way to Sacramento.

**Alta (100/25)** A red fire station stands on the right. Among the hills are flumes originally constructed by gold miners and which are now used to carry water to the farms below.

**Gold Run (105/20)** Note the old post office building to your left. Until it became illegal in 1884, hydraulic gold mining washed away huge sections of the hillside. The *California Zephyr*'s tracks run alongside the old mine site.

**Cape Horn (118/7)** This is the steepest slope on the *Zephyr*'s entire journey. Chinese labourers constructing the route were lowered on ropes to hack out a rocky ledge for the track. Lewis Metzler Clement was hired by Theodore Judah as one of the Central Pacific's chief assistant engineers and was primarily responsible for designing and building the section of the line between Truckee and Colfax, including Cape Horn, all the tunnels and the snow-sheds. Although not present at the Golden Spike ceremony he is shown in the famous Thomas Hill painting standing behind Judah (who was by then dead) and Charles Crocker. Clement later worked on constructing the cable car system in San Francisco.

Colfax can be seen ahead to your left as the train curves left over a highway.

**COLFAX (125/60)** Look left for a flea market and an ancient Southern Pacific railroad car housing a bank. During the gold rush, goods were brought to Colfax by mule for transfer into the mountains. The town became the Central Pacific's 'end of track' in 1865. Pears, grapes and prunes are now grown around the former 'mother lode' town.

As the *Zephyr* eases down the western side of the Sierra Nevada (the snowy mountains) look for drifts of wild lupins and red and yellow poppies.

**Auburn (25/35)** When gold was discovered at Coloma, just south of here, Auburn supplied the camps and administered claims. Among several preserved buildings is the 1893 fire-house on your left, which boasted the first volunteer fire department west of Boston. Outlaws were publicly hanged in the grounds of the gold-domed Placer County courthouse, also on your left.

As you leave, the town cemetery can be seen on a hill to your right before the train descends through less mountainous terrain and enters the fields, ranches and orchards of the Sacramento Valley.

**Rockville (45/15)** Local granite was used as ballast (for laying railroad tracks) but only one quarry remains open.

**ROSEVILLE (60/25)** The *California Zephyr* picks its way carefully among the complexities of Southern Pacific's rail yards. Note the large locomotive maintenance shop next to a wooden station building to your left.

**McClellan Air Force Base (10/15)** The airfield and depots can be seen on your right. Approaching Sacramento, both sides of the track are engulfed by the Blue Diamond Company – the largest almond-processing plant on earth. Most of California's yearly crop of one million pounds (450 tonnes) find their way here and groves of almond trees can often be seen.

## SACRAMENTO (25/20)
For Sacramento and the rest of the *California Zephyr* route to San Francisco, see *The Coast Starlight* (pages 60–74). The *Zephyr* makes a scheduled stop at Suisun-Fairfield.

# The *San Joaquins*
# San Francisco–Bakersfield
### (via Emeryville/Oakland)

## General route information

With fig trees, vineyards, date palms, orchards and oil wells, the San Joaquin Valley is definitive California: a heady blend of warmth and almond blossom. *San Joaquin* trains travel more than 300 miles (480km) between Emeryville/ Oakland and Bakersfield, giving access to several national parks and some of the richest farm country in America.

**Frequency** Four trains operate daily in each direction.

Departure times are early morning, mid-morning, afternoon and late afternoon for a trip lasting six hours.

**Connections** Connecting buses link Emeryville with San Francisco, and Bakersfield with Los Angeles and San Diego. An extensive Amtrak Thruway bus system operates in the Bay Area and throughout the Sacramento Valley. Trains and buses are funded by Amtrak and Caltrans (the California Department of Transportation) and are a good way to explore some of the less well known parts of the state. Schedules are available from Amtrak agents or by post from Timetable, c/o Caltrans, Rail Program, PO Box 942874, Sacramento, CA 94274-0001. Information about Amtrak services in California can also be found on the website: www.dot.ca.gov/hq/rail.

**Reservations** All reserved.

**Equipment** Bi-level California coaches. Railfone.

**Food** Complete meals, snacks, sandwiches, drinks.

**Baggage** Check-in service on all trains. Bicycle racks.

## Joining the train

### SAN FRANCISCO
For San Francisco, Emeryville/Oakland and the route to Martinez, see *The Coast Starlight* (pages 61–2). *San Joaquin* trains initially travel north from Oakland towards Martinez, stopping en route at Richmond (described in the *Coast Starlight* section).

## All aboard!

**MARTINEZ (25/22)** As the train leaves Martinez it parts company with the *California Zephyr* and *Coast Starlight* tracks, which continue over the bridge to your left. Storage tanks and a Shell oil refinery appear on the right.

**Mothball Fleet (12/10)** Across the bay to your left lies a fleet of transport ships kept in 'mothballs'. Many date from as long ago as the Second World War but some saw action in Vietnam and as recently as the Gulf War in 1991.

Between here and Antioch-Pittsburg, *San Joaquin* trains change from Southern Pacific tracks to those of the Santa Fe Railroad.

**ANTIOCH-PITTSBURG (22/35)** You begin to escape the Bay Area's influence as the Sacramento and San Joaquin Rivers converge to your left. Look for the deep-water channel linking Stockton, 80 miles (128km) from the sea, with San Francisco.

**STOCKTON (35/25)** The Magnolia District has 19th century houses and this inland port and distribution centre was the location for John Huston's *Fat City*. Amtrak's station is at 735 S San Joaquin, from where Thruway buses go north to Sacramento. The Stockton **visitors bureau** is at 46 W Fremont; tel: 209 943 1987; web: www.ssjcvb.org.

After leaving town the train travels through a landscape where hundreds of vineyards supply local wineries. You cross the Stanislaus River.

**MODESTO (25/15)** Served by ferries during the 1880s gold rush, further development came to neighbouring Riverbank with the arrival of the Santa Fe Railway.

**Hetch Hetchy Aqueduct (3/12)** The train crosses the concrete-lined aqueduct which supplies the Bay Area with water from the Sierra Nevada. A few minutes later you cross the Tuolumne River.

**TURLOCK-DENAIR (15/22)** The station is at Santa Fe Ave in Denair, although adjacent Turlock is much larger. The Diablo Mountains can be seen in the right distance.

As the *San Joaquin* crosses the Merced River look for the numerous almond trees growing on both sides – an especially wonderful sight when they blossom in late winter.

**Atwater (15/7)** Note the preserved Second World War planes at the air base to your left. As you approach Merced the town's 1875 courthouse can be seen on your right.

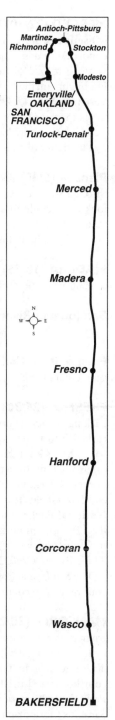

**MERCED (22/30)** Built in Renaissance style and restored, the **Courthouse Museum** dominates the main square with a figure of Justice perched on its cupola. Amtrak's station is at 324 W 24th, from where Thruway buses will take you east to one of America's finest experiences, **Yosemite National Park**. Highlights include El Capitan (a granite dome twice as tall as Gibraltar) and Yosemite Falls (2,425ft/740m). Late spring and early summer are the best times to visit. A visitor centre opens daily in the park or you can contact PO Box 577, Yosemite NP, CA 95389; tel: 209 372 4726; web: www.nps.gov/yose.

The train pulls out of Merced past a Goodyear factory on the right.

**Planada (5/25)** Kadota fig trees grow raggedly on your left as you continue through some of America's most productive land. Other local specialities to look for include pistachio nuts, rice, tomatoes, peaches and grapes. Back to your left before the train crosses the Fresno River you can see the Sierra Nevada's Cathedral Mountains (13,000ft/4,000m).

**MADERA (30/25)** A busy farming town, located in the geographical centre of California and famous for its wines and olives.

**San Joaquin River (10/15)** A golf course is on your right as you cross the river.

**Fresno State College (20/5)** The campus is seen to your right before the train enters Fresno, passing a water-tower and the Santa Fe Railway offices.

**FRESNO (25/30)** 'The raisin capital of the world', where Sunmaid's packing facility covers 73 acres (30ha). Grapes grown south of here are mostly turned into raisins while those produced further north become wine. The Meux Mansion, located a block from the station, is an ornate Victorian house originally built for a doctor.

Fresno's station at 2650 Tulare is Amtrak's busiest stop between Emeryville and Bakersfield. It is also the nearest station to **Sequoia** and **Kings Canyon National Parks** in southern Nevada. These are quieter than Yosemite but still have fantastic mountains, caves, meadows and sequoia trees (the largest living things in the world). For **information** contact 47050 Generals Highway Three Rivers, CA 93271-9651; tel: 559 565 3341; web: www.nps.gov/seki.

The *San Joaquin* leaves Fresno with the water-tower of Sunmaid's old plant on your right. You continue among sun-baked vineyards and cross the Kings River.

**HANFORD (30/20)** Named after James Hanford, a Southern Pacific paymaster who sometimes paid his company's employees in gold. Hundreds of Chinese came to work on constructing the railroad and left behind the Taoist temple in China Alley. You can also visit Hanford's neo-classical courthouse and the Courthouse Square jail, which resembles the Bastille in Paris. Amtrak's station is at 432 W 7th, from where Thruway buses connect to San Luis Obispo and Visalia, the central valley's first settlement.

The train travels on, making good time through the flat landscape of orchards, vineyards and alfalfa fields. Irrigation means prolific crops can be grown over an area the size of the Netherlands.

**CORCORAN (20/25)** Note the grain elevators and cotton gin to your right beyond Amtrak's unstaffed station at the corner of Whitley and Otis Ave. Corcoran is the home of a California State Prison built on what was once Tulare Lake, home of the Tachi Indians.

**Allensworth Park (10/15)** The park on the right is in the middle of the Tulare Lake region.

**WASCO (25/22)** This is another predominantly agricultural town, this one famous for growing roses. Amtrak's stop is at 700 G and Hwy 43.

**Shafter (2/20)** Look for more grapes and almond trees before the *San Joaquin* passes through Kern County oil field, where pumps can be seen working on both sides of the track. The area's largest refinery is to your left as you near Bakersfield. A few minutes from town the train crosses a canal then enters the Santa Fe yards with an old roundhouse to your right.

## BAKERSFIELD
Home of country music's Merle Haggard and Glen Campbell, Bakersfield rapidly expanded when oil was discovered at the turn of the century. **Kern County Museum and Pioneer Village** at 3801 Chester Ave (tel: 661 852 5000; web: kcmuseum.org) has more than 50 buildings dating from 1865 to the Second World War.

The station is at 1501 F, from where Amtrak buses link with many places in the Los Angeles area, as well as with trains from Los Angeles to San Diego.

# The *Pacific Surfliner*
# Los Angeles–San Diego

## General route information

*Pacific Surfliner* (formerly *San Diegan*) trains travel one of Amtrak's busiest routes, serving two major cities and a growing population. For part of their journey the *Pacific Surfliner* hugs the Pacific shoreline and other pleasures include Disneyland, San Juan Capistrano and the Tijuana Trolley.

**Frequency** Departures are approximately every two hours in both directions from early morning until late evening (a total of 12 daily round-trips, with four trains continuing to Santa Barbara or San Luis Obispo). The journey between Los Angeles and San Diego takes just under three hours (half an hour less on the *Pacific Surfliner Express*).

**Connections** Amtrak Thruway buses and some local trains, as well as the *Coast Starlight*, connect Los Angeles with Santa Barbara along the San Fernando Valley.

**Reservations** Unreserved except for Pacific Business Class.

**Equipment** Bi-level Surfliner coaches. Business Class. Railfone.

**Food** Snacks, sandwiches, drinks.

**Baggage** Check-in service on most trains. Bicycle and surfboard racks.

## Joining the train

### LOS ANGELES

For Los Angeles city information, see *The Coast Starlight* (pages 71–4).

## All aboard!

As the *Pacific Surfliner* leaves Los Angeles look for City Hall's white tower dominating the skyline to your left. Between here and Fullerton the train passes through the residential and industrial suburbs of Los Angeles County.

**Los Angeles River (5/10)** The train accompanies a concrete channel to your left. Designed for flood control and usually dry, the channel has been a location for dozens of movie chases.

**Redondo Junction (10/5)** Amtrak superliners for the *Coast Starlight*, *Sunset Limited* and *Southwest Chief* are set up in the yards and roundhouse to your right.

**COMMERCE (15/17)** This is a stop for two trains a day in each direction.

**Santa Fe Springs (7/10)** Oil wells, tanks and derricks gradually accumulate on both sides.

**FULLERTON (17/9)** An attractive restored Santa Fe station with pink stucco and red tiles stands on your left next to the grand Union Pacific depot, which was moved to this site and is now a restaurant. The Donald Duck citrus juice plant also features on your left. Fullerton is a suburban stop as well as the station for three of the state's most popular venues.

### Recommended near Fullerton

**Disneyland** 1313 Harbor Blvd, Anaheim; tel: 714 999 4565; web: http://disney.go.com/Disneyland. Opened in 1955, the original fun park has been added to ever since. California's largest tourist attraction features Tomorrowland, the Indiana Jones Adventure, Splash Mountain (the world's longest flume ride) and a twice nightly Fantasmic! light show. Disneyland's Railroad train circles the park every few minutes. Open daily, admission charge.

**Knott's Berry Farm** 8039 Beach Blvd, Buena Park; tel: 714 220 5200; web: www.knotts.com. This recreated ghost town comes with shops, restaurants and a hundred rides, including Montezooma's Revenge (0–55mph/88km/h in 5 seconds) and the Corkscrew (first upside-down roller-coaster). Steam engines and equipment formerly owned by the Denver & Rio Grande Western and Rio Grande Southern operate over a 36-inch gauge track. Train rides are included in the admission charge. Open daily.

**Movieland Wax Museum** 7711 Beach Blvd, to the north of Knott's Berry Farm; tel: 714 522 1155; web: www.movielandwaxmuseum.com. The museum has almost 300 wax images of such disparate characters as Clint Eastwood and George Burns. The Black Box allows you to participate in creepy scenes from *Halloween* and *Alien*. Open daily, admission charge.

## All aboard!

As the *Pacific Surfliner* pulls out of Fullerton you can just make out Disneyland's replica Matterhorn to your right. Approaching Anaheim, look right also for the enormous sports stadium located beyond the station.

**ANAHEIM (9/9)** One of the country's fastest-growing cities, this was the birthplace of Leo Fender, pioneer of the electric guitar. Founded by German settlers and former gold miners from San Francisco, Anaheim's name combines the nearby Santa Ana River with *heim* (German for home). The Rams (football) and Angels (baseball) perform in the stadium next to an ultra-modern railway station at 2150 E Katella Ave.

The train leaves for another brief run to Santa Ana through Orange County, famous for Valencia oranges.

**Orange (4/5)** Seen away to your right with an old station building on the left.

**SANTA ANA (9/10)** This was the birthplace of Michelle Pfeiffer. The restored downtown area and more recent developments feature traditional Spanish architecture. Amtrak's station is at 1000 E Santa Ana Blvd.

As the train leaves, look right for the two giant hangars which accommodated Second World War air balloons and now house US Marine helicopters. The Santa Ana Mountains are to your left.

**US Marine Corps (8/2)** The air base is on the left.

**IRVINE (10/10)** You continue south from here through a land of orange groves interspersed with the occasional small town.

**SAN JUAN CAPISTRANO (10/30)** Amtrak's station at 26701 Verdugo features a restaurant and live jazz performances. The 1776 mission where Juanero Indians converted to Christianity was damaged by earthquake but part of the adobe building still stands in neatly kept grounds to your left. The famous San Juan Capistrano swallows leave in October, returning (fairly) punctually on March 19 each year.

Soon after leaving town the train joins the Pacific Ocean on your right, staying in touch with its shoreline until Del Mar. Enviable houses cling to cliffs on your left.

**San Clemente (10/20)** Two trains a day stop in San Clemente, where Richard Nixon lived at Casa Pacifica for some of his time as president. The beach is one of the prettiest in California.

**San Onofre Nuclear Plant (16/14)** Look right for this ominous presence next to the beach, where the extra-warm water attracts heedless surfers.

**Camp Pendleton (25/5)** One of many naval facilities to be found in this part of the state. Yachts and pleasure boats bob in the busy marina to the right.

**OCEANSIDE (30/17)** Amtrak and Greyhound share the transit centre at 235 S Tremont. Mission San Luis Rey is on nearby Mission Ave. Oceanside is the home of the Legoland Museum, featuring a castle, miniature lego cities and a safari adventure complete with lego animals.

**Carlsbad (5/12)** Look out for a military boys' school to your right before the train passes a gigantic power plant, also to the right.

**Del Mar Racetrack (15/2)** The racetrack is immediately to your left.

**SOLANA BEACH (17/30)** The nearby town of Del Mar is famed for its conservatism and exclusive beach apartments. A hundred annual events take place at the Del Mar fairgrounds, where Thoroughbred Club meetings are a regular meeting place for Hollywood names.

The *Pacific Surfliner* shifts away from the ocean at this point and travels inland through rugged country towards its final destination. Look for the celebrated Torrey Pines on both sides as you descend through Soledad and Rose Canyons.

**University of San Diego (20/10)** The campus is to your left.

**Lindbergh Airport (25/5)** Runways and buildings appear on the right.

## SAN DIEGO
The state's oldest city has smog-free sunshine, Spanish architecture and an easy-going atmosphere. Portuguese explorer Juan Cabrillo discovered this bay in 1542 but settlement began much later when a garrison and California's first Spanish mission were built. San Diego became part of the United States in 1847, after which the Santa Fe Railway brought rapid expansion to a city which continues to grow. It is now the seventh biggest city in the country and has the world's largest military complex (125,000 acres).

### San Diego basics
**Telephone code** 619.
**Transport** Amtrak's station at 1050 Kettner Blvd is a beautiful, spacious building close to the waterfront in an older part of downtown. The Spanish mission-colonial revival style depot was originally built by the Atchison, Topeka & Santa Fe Railway for passengers arriving at the 1915 Panama-California Exposition, replacing the California Southern Railway's 1887 Victorian depot. From 1916–51, the depot also served the San Diego & Arizona Railway (later SD&AE) as the Union Depot.
**Information** tel: 239 9021. Ticket-office open 05.30–21.00. Waiting-room 04.30–00.15. Luggage store, ATM, Red Caps, taxi stand. The station is the home of the research library of the San Diego Railroad Museum and the Santa Fe Historical Society library.
**Local transport** The city is easy to negotiate on foot or by bicycle. San Diego Transit buses (tel: 238 0100) operate a comprehensive service. Passes can be used on all SDT routes as well as the San Diego Trolley (downtown and from the station to San Ysidro on the Mexican border) and the Bay Ferry from Broadway Pier to Coronado. Coaster runs commuter rail services to Oceanside.
**Taxis** Yellow; tel: 234 6161. Checker; tel: 234 4477.
**Car rental** Avis, 3180 N Harbor Drive; tel: 688 5062.
**Greyhound** 120 W Broadway; tel: 239 3266.
**Lindbergh Airport** is three miles (5km) north of downtown by SDT bus #2.

**Tours** Harbour cruises from Hornblower; tel: 686 8700 and trips to Santa Catalina Island with California Cruising; tel: 296 800.

**Visitors bureau** Open daily at 11 Horton Plaza; tel: 236 1212 or 234 2787 (for the latest events); email: sdinfo@sandiego.org; web: www.sandiego.com/visitor.

**Accommodation** The San Diego Bed & Breakfast Guild is at 3829 Albatross; tel: 523 1300; web: bandbguildsandiego.org.

Grand Pacific Hostel, 726 5th Ave; tel: 232 3100. Dormitory $15, single $35. Armed Services YMCA, 500 W Broadway; tel: 232 1133. Dormitory and other rooms, not restricted to the military. Single $25, double $35. YWCA, 1012 C; tel: 239 0355. Women only. Single $20, double $35. Elliott AYH Hostel, 3790 Udall, Point Loma; tel: 223 4778. Members $12, non-members $15. Take bus #35. The nearest campsite is Campland On The Bay, 2211 Pacific Beach Dr; tel: 858 581 4200. Take bus #30.

Hotels include the Churchill, 827 C; tel: 234 5186; Pickwick, 132 W Broadway; tel: 234 9200; Golden West, 720 Fourth Ave; tel: 233 7596; Clarke's Flamingo Lodge, 1765 Union; tel: 234 6787 – single $33, double $43; Villager Lodge, 660 G; tel: 238 4100 – single and double $27; Baltic Inn, 521 6th Ave; tel: 237 0687 – single $20, double $28.

## Recommended in San Diego

**Balboa Park** 2125 Park Blvd. The park information centre is at 1549 El Prado; tel: 239 0512; web: www.balboapark.org. The park has over 1,000 acres (400ha) of gardens, trees and lawns, as well as the world's largest outdoor pipe organ. The California-Pacific Exposition succeeded the Panama-California Expo here in 1935, and Spanish-style buildings house 14 excellent art galleries, museums and theatres. A pass gives access to all the museums, most of which are free on the first Tuesday in the month; a free tram service operates around the park.

**San Diego Historical Society** The Prado in Balboa Park; tel: 232 6203; web: www.sandiegohistory.org. Changing exhibits and lectures are used imaginatively to interpret San Diego's regional history. Open Tue–Sun, admission charge.

**Aerospace Museum** 2001 Pan American Plaza in Balboa Park; tel: 234 8291; web: www.aerospacemuseum.org. Aviation history from the Wright Brothers to the space age is brought to life with over 65 aircraft, including a replica of the *Spirit of St Louis* monoplane in which Charles Lindbergh made his first flight in 1927 from a San Diego airfield. The first transcontinental flight, from New York to San Diego, took place in 1923. Open daily, admission charge.

**Museum of Contemporary Art** 1001 Kettner Blvd; tel: 234 1001; web: www.mcasandiego.org. The museum has two distinct, complementary locations and includes collections, exhibitions and programmes that focus on present day art and artists. Another part of the museum is located next to the ocean at 700 Prospect in La Jolla; tel: 858 454 3541 (for 24-hour recorded information).

**Model Railroad Museum** 1649 El Prado, on the lower level of the Casa De Balboa on the Prado in Balboa Park; tel: 696 0199; web: www.sdmodelrailroadm.com. The largest of its kind in the world, with four gigantic layouts. Open daily. Admission charge, but children under 15 enter free.

**San Diego Zoo** At Balboa Park, north of the museums; tel: 231 1515; web: www.sandiegozoo.org. Koalas, tigers, giant pandas, rhinos and gorillas are among the 4,000 creatures (over 800 species) living in the world's best zoo. Children's area, tours and an aerial tramway. Open daily, admission charge.

**Old Town Historic Park** The information centre is at 4002 Wallace; tel: 469 3174; web: www.ot-boot.com. Restored buildings, galleries and restaurants occupy the site of the first (1769) Spanish settlement. Highlights include the **Machado y Silvas Adobe**, San Diego's first schoolhouse and **the Casa de Estudillo**, built in 1827 by a presidio commander who would watch bull and bear fights from its cupola.

The **Whaley House**, built in 1856 on a former gallows site, was the first two-storey brick building in southern California and has been officially designated as a haunted house by the US Department of Commerce. Free walking tours leave daily from the information centre. For Old Town trolley tours call 298 8687.

**The Gaslamp Quarter** 614 Fifth Ave; tel: 233 5227; web: www.gaslamp.org. Many of the buildings in this area from Broadway to the waterfront were erected in the late 19th century and have been returned to their former glory, serving now as shops, restaurants and nightclubs. You can take a walking tour narrated by the former Gaslamp Quarter saloon owner and gunslinger, Wyatt Earp. Call the Gaslamp Quarter Foundation (tel: 233 4692) for information and reservations.

**La Jolla** This affluent northern suburb is famous for its beaches, scuba-diving and chic residents. Raymond Chandler used La Jolla as the setting, renamed *Poodle Springs*, for his last novel *Playback*. Chandler's former home can be seen at 6005 Camino de la Costa. La Jolla's racetrack also features in the film of Jim Thompson's *The Grifters*, along with several shots of *San Diegan* trains.

**San Diego Railroad Museum** Located at the Campo Depot, 31123-1/2 Highway 94 in Campo, 50 miles (80km) to the east; mail address: 1050 Kettner Boulevard, #5, San Diego, California 92101-3339; tel: 478 9937 (weekends) or 595 3030 (weekdays); web: www.sdrm.org. Over 80 pieces of railroad equipment, including steam and diesel locomotives of the Southern Pacific and California Western railroads, passenger cars, freight cars and cabooses can be seen at the restored depots at La Mesa and Campo.

Steam train excursions using vintage equipment over parts of the San Diego & Arizona Railway take place on weekends, and diesel-powered trains travel to Tecate in Mexico. Admission charge.

## Tijuana

Not classic Mexico, and less wild than it used to be, but 'the world's most visited city' is an easy trip from San Diego. The trolley and bus #932 will take you the 17 miles to the border, although beggars and the concrete walkway make crossing on foot a bleak experience. San Ysidro is the world's busiest international border crossing, with 60 million people a year passing through.

Tijuana offers cheap drinks, accommodation, food, shopping and bullfights. US dollars are welcome as you shop for blankets, leather goods, jewellery and tequila. For youth hostel rooms call 52 (the international country code for Mexico) +66 (Mexican area code) 842523 or 832680.

*Note* Except for citizens of the USA and Canada, a valid visa is required for return to the United States even after a one day visit.

# The *Empire Builder*
# Chicago–Seattle

## General route information

The *Empire Builder* crosses the Mississippi River and travels more than 2,200 miles (3,500km) past wheat fields, cattle ranges, forests, mountains and glacial lakes. America's northern plains were mostly wilderness until the freewheeling tycoon James J Hill built his Great Northern Railway between St Paul, Minnesota, and Seattle. Amtrak's *Empire Builder* takes its name from the train called after him, which ran on this route during the heyday of rail travel.
**Frequency** Daily.

The westbound service leaves Chicago mid-afternoon to arrive in Milwaukee by late afternoon and St Paul/Minneapolis late in the evening. You reach Havre on the second afternoon, West Glacier by mid-evening and Spokane during the night, arriving in Seattle or Portland by mid-morning.

Travelling east, trains leave Seattle or Portland late in the afternoon to reach Spokane at midnight and West Glacier early next morning. You reach Havre by early afternoon and St Paul/Minneapolis early the following morning, arriving in Milwaukee early afternoon and Chicago by late afternoon.

**Reservations** All reserved.

**Equipment** Superliner coaches.

**Sleeping** Superliner bedrooms.

**Food** Complete meals, snacks, sandwiches, drinks.

**Lounge car** Video movies, games, hospitality hour.

**Baggage** Check-in service at most stations.

## Joining the train

### CHICAGO

For Chicago city information, see The *California Zephyr* (pages 75–9). The *Empire Builder* leaves on complex tracks of the Chicago, Milwaukee, St Paul & Pacific Railroad (also known as the Soo Line or Milwaukee Road), following what was a plank road in the days of horse-drawn wagons.

Some of the fastest ever trains, capable of well over 100mph (160km/h), ran between Chicago and Milwaukee in the 1930s when this route was known as 'the world's greatest steam railroad speedway'.

# All aboard!

On your right as the train pulls out of Chicago is the Chicago River, with the Merchandise Mart building and the cylindrical towers of Marina City. Also to your right are a Rock-Ola Jukebox factory and the tapered Hancock Building. Sears Tower is to your left. You continue among the older buildings and spired churches of Chicago's northside.

**Niles (4/20)** The Niles version of Pisa's leaning tower appears on your left.

**GLENVIEW (24/60)** The train pauses at this busy suburban station before continuing north through residential areas, farms and industrial plants owned by the likes of Fiat. Look for the patriotic water-tower to your left.

**Glenview Naval Station (2/58)** This air base is visible on the left.

**Gurnee (15/45)** Look right for Marriott's Great American Amusement Park.

**Wadsworth (20/40)** The Des Plaines River comes into view on your left, and a few minutes later the *Empire Builder* crosses the Illinois/Wisconsin state line into 'America's dairyland'.

**Franksville (40/20)** Named after the Frank Pure Food Company on the left, proudly keeping old country traditions alive.

**Mitchell Field (50/10)** The international airport can be seen to your right. As the train nears Milwaukee and crosses the Monomonee River look left for two of the city's finest churches. **St Josaphat's**, with its distinctive dome, was North America's first Polish basilica, built in 1901 by immigrants using material salvaged from the post office building in Chicago. Next to it are the gold spires of **St Stanislaus Cathedral**.

Also on your left as the train snakes into the station are the octagonal dials and square tower of the **Allen Bradley clock**, an enduring local landmark.

CHICAGO
Glenview
MILWAUKEE
Columbus
Portage
Wisconsin
Dells
Tomah
La Crosse
Winona
Red Wing
ST PAUL/
MINNEAPOLIS
St Cloud
Staples
Detroit
Lakes
Fargo
Grand Forks
Devil's Lake
Rugby
Minot
Stanley
Williston
Wolf Point
Glasgow
Malta
Havre
Shelby
Cut Bank
Browning
East Glacier
Park
Essex
West Glacier
Whitefish
Libby
Sandpoint
Spokane
Ephrata
Wenatchee
Everett
Edmonds
SEATTLE

## MILWAUKEE (60/70)

'The Genuine American City' is Wisconsin's largest and is famous for *Happy Days*, Miller beer and Harley-Davidsons. Milwaukee stands on a Lake Michigan bay which Potawatomi Native Americans called 'Millioki' or 'the gathering place by the waters'. In the 19th century many thousands of immigrants came from Italy, Ireland, Poland, Scandinavia and especially Germany. One of them was the future Israeli premier, Golda Meir. Milwaukee's different ethnic groups give the city a lively cultural atmosphere and its annual Summerfest on the lakefront is the largest music festival in the world.

### Milwaukee basics

**Telephone code** 414.

**Station** Union Station is at 433 W St Paul Ave, not a safe area by night. Ticket-office open 05.30–21.00. Waiting-room 05.30–22.00. Lockers, newspapers, Red Caps, restaurant, taxi stand.

**Local transport** Many attractions are within walking distance of the Milwaukee River and a skywalk system means you can get around easily without going outdoors. Milwaukee County Transport at 1942 N 17th (tel: 344 6711) operates a near 24-hour bus service.

**Taxis** Yellow; tel: 271 1800. American United; tel: 220 5000.

**Car rental** Avis, 916 E State; tel: 272 0892. Budget, 550 W Grange Ave; tel: 481 1424.

**Greyhound** 606 N James Lovell; tel: 272 9949.

**General Mitchell Airport** is six miles (10km) from downtown by bus #80.

**Tours** MCT has summer excursions to historic sights and the lake shore. Walking tours are available from Historic Milwaukee; tel: 277 7795 and boat trips from Iroquois Boat Line; tel: 384 8606.

**Visitors bureau** Open weekdays at 400 W Wisconsin Ave; tel: 908 6205 or 800 554 1448; email: visitor@milwaukee.org; web: www.milwaukee.org.

**Accommodation** Contact Little Red House Bed & Breakfast, 9212 Jackson Park Blvd, Wauwatosa, WI 53226; tel: 479 0646; email: mjwey@earthlink.net.

Hostelling International, 5900 N Port Washington Rd; tel: 961 2525; email: info@hostellingwisconsin.org; web: www.hostellingwisconsin.org.

Hotels include the Wyndham at 139 E Kilbourn Ave; tel: 276 8686; Astor, 924 E Juneau Ave; tel: 271 4220; Sheraton Mayfair, 2303 N Mayfair Rd; tel: 257 3400; Wisconsin, 720 N 3rd; tel: 271 4900 – double $89; Leilani, 18615 W Bluemand Rd; tel: 786 7100; Metro, 411 E Mason; tel: 272 1937; Belmont, 751 N 4th; tel: 271 5880 – single and double $26.

### Recommended in Milwaukee

**Milwaukee Art Museum** 700 N Art Museum Drive; tel 224 3200; web: www.mam.org. More than 20,000 works of art from ancient to contemporary are housed in the city's 'masterpiece on the lakefront', designed by Eero Saarinen. A $63 million expansion with its wing-like design gave the city skyline a new profile when it opened in May 2001. Closed Mon, admission charge.

**Milwaukee Public Museum** 800 W Wells; tel: 278 2722; web: www.mpm.edu. A recreation of old Milwaukee, a tropical rain forest and the first known total habitat diorama are included among five million objects and specimens. Open daily, admission charge.

**Mitchell Park Conservatory** 524 S Layton Blvd; tel: 649 9800. Three giant glass domes, each 85ft high and 140ft wide (26m by 43m), house collections of plants in desert, tropical and temperate environments. Brightly coloured birds and iguanas live among the exotic rainforest flowers of the tropical dome. Open daily, admission charge.

**Milwaukee County Zoo** 10001 W Blue Mound Rd; tel: 771 3040; web: www.milwaukeezoo.org. Around 2500 creatures, including endangered trumpeter swans and black rhino, live among 200 wooded acres. There are 300 species of mammals, birds, reptiles, fish and invertebrates plus a children's zoo, guided tours and a miniature train ride (from mid-April to mid-October). Open daily, admission charge. Take #10 bus.

**Pabst Mansion** 2000 W Wisconsin Ave; tel: 931 0808; web: www.pabstmansion.com. Built by the sea captain, beer baron and philanthropist Frederick Pabst in 1892, the mansion boasts 37 rooms, 14 fireplaces and 12 baths as well as stained glass, carved woodwork and ornamental iron. The mansion was the home of Roman Catholic archbishops for 67 years and is now being restored to its original splendour. Guided tours. Closed Mon, mid January–March, admission charge.

**Old World Wisconsin** Off Highway 67 at nearby Eagle; tel: 262 594 6300; web: www.wisconsinhistory.org. This open-air museum captures the lifestyles, ideas and challenges of 19th and early 20th century rural immigrants. Open daily from May to October, admission charge.

**Historic Cedarburg** Located 20 minutes north of Milwaukee at Washington Ave and Spring in Cedarburg; tel: 262 377 9620; web: www.cedarburg.org. First settled by Irish immigrants in the 1840s, Cedarburg prospered with the coming of the railroad in 1870 and German families who built dams and mills along the fast-running Cedar Creek. Over a hundred main street businesses, many of them antique shops, occupy registered historic buildings surrounded by attractive limestone houses. Special events and festivals take place all year round.

# All aboard!

As the *Empire Builder* departs Milwaukee, look for the Mitchell Park Conservatory's three graceful domes. The County Stadium is to your left and the Miller Brewery, which made Milwaukee famous, on your right. The train travels through city suburbs for 20 minutes towards America's heartland of lakes and farms.

**Pewaukee Lake (30/40)** The shoreline and town are visible to your left before you cross the Rock River three times. Lake Oconomowoc also comes into view on the left, with Pine and Okauchee Lakes to your right. Look for wheat fields, silos, cattle and horse-drawn farm wagons.

**Watertown (50/20)** The steeple of St Bernard's Church pokes above trees on your right just before the campus of Marantha College. The train then crosses the Crawfish River.

**COLUMBUS (70/30)** Zion Evangelical Lutheran Church is to the left of Ludington Street station. The steeple bell, presented by Germany's emperor, was cast from pieces of French cannon captured during the Franco-Prussian War. Beside the church stands the 1892 City Hall.

**Wyocena (25/5)** Santa's rocket stays grounded in a salvage yard to your right. Wyocena Lake is famous for angling and commercial fishing.

**PORTAGE (30/20)** The town was founded as a stopover between the Fox and Wisconsin Rivers to serve traders and settlers. They had to *portage* (carry) goods across this strip of land when going from Lake Michigan to the Mississippi. Milwaukee Road freight cars gather on the left of Amtrak's station at 400 W Oneida. Madison is 25 miles (40km) to the south.

**Wisconsin River (15/5)** The river on your left cuts through many miles of finely streaked rock. A Baptist Indian church and cemetery can be seen high up to your right.

**WISCONSIN DELLS (20/45)** Situated in a sandstone canyon created by the winding Wisconsin River, natural beauty and an amusement park combine to make this one of the state's chief attractions. Rafting and boat trips are popular pastimes along the river.

Amtrak's station is at Lacrosse Street, and the **Park Lane Model Railroad Museum** in nearby Reedsburg features 2,000 model trains of various vintages (tel: 608 254 8050).

The *Empire Builder* continues northwest and crosses the Wisconsin River.

**Mauston (20/25)** The spire of St Patrick's Church is to your right. Lake Decorah, to your left, was formed by a dam built across the Lemonweir River.

**Camp Douglas (30/15)** The flow of the Wisconsin River over centuries has produced the splendid red sandstone rock formations seen in Mill Bluff State Park to your left.

**TOMAH (45/40)** Tomah's chamber of commerce occupies a Milwaukee Road Pullman car on the left, its sign supported by characters from the comic strip *Gasoline Alley*. The strip's creator, Frank King, grew up in Tomah. Wisconsin's annual dairyland tractor pull brings competitors to the city from the whole Midwest.

Tomah Lake is to your left as the *Empire Builder* leaves town and suddenly enters a landscape of steep hills.

**Tunnel City (5/35)** The train runs along a single track through the 1,350ft (410m) tunnel.

**Sparta (15/25)** Look right for the airport. You join the La Crosse River on your right and follow it for the next 25 miles (40km) until it joins the Mississippi.

**Bangor (25/15)** An imposing village hall appears on your right before the train crosses the river.

**LA CROSSE (40/40)** Situated at the junction of the Mississippi, Black and La Crosse Rivers, the town was named after a term French trappers gave to a game they saw being played by Native Americans. Amtrak's station is at 601 St Andrew.

After leaving La Crosse the *Empire Builder* crosses the Mississippi River for the first time, going from Wisconsin into Minnesota. Islands in midstream divide the Mississippi into three channels. Once across the river you enter one of the route's most attractive stretches, accompanying the Mississippi into Richard J Dover hardwood forest. The train bowls along for 40 miles (64km) past farmland and riverboat towns, with the river at times becoming as wide as a lake.

**Number 7 Dam (5/35)** The dam and lock system on your right is one of several built in attempts to tame the river.

**Number 6 Dam (20/20)** Another dam appears on the right.

**WINONA (40/60)** The city's name is a Sioux word for 'first-born daughter'. Sugar Loaf Mountain, rising 500ft (150m) to your left, was a ceremonial meeting place for the Sioux. Chief Wa-Pa-Sha's outline could be seen there before quarrying altered the mountain's shape. Winona has grown from its early sawmill days to become a centre for shipping and manufacturing.

Look for large grain elevators standing on your right as the train leaves the station.

**Number 5 Dam (10/50)** Another dam built in the federally-financed series.

**Weaver (15/45)** This is 'the white bass capital of the world', with many fishing camps located in the area. The *Empire Builder* crosses the Zumbro River.

**Wabasha (30/30)** At the 1856 Anderson House (the oldest hotel in the state) services include free shoe shines, hot bricks to warm your bed and pet cats to keep you company.

**Lake Pepin (35/25)** Where the Chippewa River joins the Mississippi. Lake Pepin is home to eagles and claims to be the place where water-skiing was invented. Watch out for the romantic riverboat steamer.

**Frontenac (50/10)** The small town dates back to a French fort built in 1723. Mount Frontenac ski resort is to your left. As the train nears Red Wing look left for the 1891 Minnesota State Training School, resembling a German castle.

**RED WING (60/65)** The name came from a Dakota chief whose emblem was a swan's wing dyed scarlet. Red Wing today is famous for shoes and pottery. In 1905 the Milwaukee Road built a station which the city acquired from the Milwaukee's successor, the Soo Line, and Amtrak leases a waiting-room restored to its original condition. The St James Hotel is to your left.

**Cannon River (5/60)** Look right to see the Prairie Island nuclear power station before you cross the Vermillion River.

**Hastings (20/45)** A domed 1871 courthouse stands on your left, with another lock and dam system to your right. The *Empire Builder* continues north, again crossing the Mississippi River.

**St Paul Airport (45/20)** The airport appears across the river to your left, with the city skyline on palisades to the right.

**Harriet Island (50/15)** During summer, picturesque riverboats go from the island on your right to Fort Snelling. As you approach St Paul, look right for the cathedral and left for a castle-like Schmidt brewery.

## ST PAUL/MINNEAPOLIS (65/80)
The 'Twin Cities' began as frontier towns on the banks of the Mississippi, settled by immigrants from Scandinavia, Germany and Great Britain. Two million people now live in the metropolitan area.

Minneapolis, home of the artist formerly known as Prince, is brasher and noisier. The state capital, St Paul, was the birthplace of F Scott Fitzgerald. Some of the world's most powerful computers are built in St Paul, and there are hundreds of lakes and parks.

### Twin City basics
**Telephone codes** 612 in Minneapolis, 651 in St Paul.
**Station** Amtrak's modern Midway Station at 730 Transfer Rd, St Paul, serves both cities. Ticket-office and waiting-room open 07.15–22.30. Lockers, vending machines, handcarts, taxi stand. Take bus #7 to the downtown areas.
**Connections** Amtrak Thruway buses connect with Duluth, birthplace of Robert Allen Zimmerman (better known as Bob Dylan). Duluth also has the **Lake Superior Museum of Transportation**, where lovingly restored steam engines and coaches, including the *Gallery Car* exhibit with its works of art rescued from the ashes of a fire that destroyed the old Union Depot in Ashland, Wisconsin, are housed in an old railway depot at 506 W Michigan; tel: 218 733 7590; web: www.lsrm.org. There are also regular trips on the **North Shore Scenic Railroad**; tel: 218 722 1273.
**Local transport** Minneapolis and St Paul have glass-covered skyways which make it easy to get about on foot, even in winter. MTC bus maps and timetables are available from 560 6th Ave N; tel: 373 3333.
**Taxis** (St Paul) Diamond; tel: 642 1188. Yellow; tel: 222 4433.
**Taxis** (Minneapolis) Town; tel: 331 8294. Yellow; tel: 824 4444.

**Car rental** Thrifty, 160 E 5th; tel: 800 367 2277.

**Greyhound** (St Paul) 166 W University Ave; tel: 222 0507.

**Greyhound** (Minneapolis) 950 Hawthorn Ave; tel: 371 3325.

**Twin Cities International Airport** is eight miles (13km) from downtown by Airport Express (tel: 726 6400) and MTC bus #35.

**Tours** Metro Connections, 1219 Marquette Ave, Minneapolis; tel: 333 8687 or 800 747 8687. Gray Line, 21160 Holyoke Ave N, Lakeville; tel: 952 469 5020. Mississippi stern wheel riverboats leave from Harriet Island (tel: 651 227 1100).

**Visitors bureau** 40 S 7th in Minneapolis; tel: 335 5827. Also at 175 W Kellogg Blvd in St Paul; tel: 651 265 4900 or 800 627 6101; email: btoll@stpaulcvb.org; web: www.stpaulcvb.org. Open weekdays. The Capitol and IDS Center also have information booths. For the latest events call 922 9000 or 645 6060.

**Accommodation** For Bed & Breakfast contact Nan's Bed and Breakfast, 2304 Fremont Ave South, Minneapolis, Minnesota 55405; tel: 377 5118; email: zosel@mcad.edu. Or contact Chatsworth Bed & Breakfast, 984 Ashland Ave, Saint Paul 55104; tel: 227 4288. The University of Minnesota housing office often has inexpensive rooms; tel: 624 2994. City of Lakes Hostel, 2400 Stevens Ave; tel: 871 3210. From $14.

Minneapolis hotels include the Whitney at 150 Portland Ave; tel: 339 9300; Northstar, 618 2nd Ave S; tel: 338 2288; Luxeford, 1101 La Salle Ave; tel: 332 6800. St Paul hotels include the St Paul at 350 Market; tel: 292 9292; Radisson, 11 E Kellogg Blvd; tel: 292 1900; Excel Inn, 1739 Old Hudson Rd; tel: 771 5566.

## Recommended in the Twin Cities

**Minneapolis Institute of Arts** 2400 3rd Ave S; tel: 870 3131; web: www.artsmia.org. Among 100,000 exhibits spanning 5,000 years are Rembrandts, Chinese jade, Roman sculptures and an Egyptian mummy. Tours, films and lectures. Closed Mon, free.

**American Swedish Institute** 2600 Park Ave, Minneapolis; tel: 871 4907; web: www.americanswedishinst.org. This chateauesque mansion, built in 1908 for the newspaper publisher Swan J Turnblad, has wooden panels and carvings, Swedish art, glassware, furniture and a reference library. Closed Mon, admission charge. The *Svenskarnas Dag* festival takes place each May in Minnehaha Park.

**Landmark Center** 75 W 5th; tel: 292 3225. St Paul's 1902 Federal Court building has been restored to its Romanesque splendour, with guided tours of the chambers and courtrooms. Open daily, free. The building also houses the Minnesota Museum of Art (closed Mon).

**James Hill House** 240 Summit Ave, St Paul; tel: 297 2555; web: www.mnhs.org. Canadian-born James Jerome Hill owned the St Paul-Pacific Railroad and was closely involved with the building of the Canadian Pacific. He gained control of the Great Northern Railroad (later to become the Burlington Northern) after a stock exchange battle, and no expense was spared when he constructed this mansion in 1891. Open Wed–Sat, admission charge. The house is one of many fine residences on Summit Ave, where Scott Fitzgerald lived.

The James J Hill Library owns a vast and complete collection of Hill's business and private papers, including thousands of letters. As well as financing and constructing railroads, he ran experimental farms, helping to improve livestock and crop yields for those who came to settle along the line. In 1915 the Panama-Pacific Exposition in San Francisco named him 'Minnesota's greatest living citizen'.

Hill retired in 1907, handing over the Great Northern to his son, Louis W Hill, but he continued to go into the office to supervise business until his death in 1916. Every train and steamship on the Great Northern came to a stop for five minutes in his honour on the day of his funeral.

**Twin City Model Railroad** Club 1021 Bandana Blvd E, St Paul; tel: 647 9628; web: www.tcmrm.org/index.html. Three thousand square feet (280m²) of O-gauge railroad are located in former Northern Pacific maintenance shops. On display outside are locomotives from the Grand Trunk Western and Northern Pacific Railways, as well as passenger and box cars. Closed Mon, admission charge.

**Minnesota Transportation Museum** 193 Pennsylvania Ave E, St Paul; tel: 228 0263 or 800 711 2591; web: www.mtmuseum.org. The museum operates the Jackson Street Roundhouse in Saint Paul, the Como Harriet Streetcar line in Minneapolis and the Steamboat *Minnehaha*.

The museum also operates the **Osceola & St Croix Valley Railway**, PO Box 176, Osceola, WI 54020 (tel: 715 755 3570; web: www.mtmuseum.org/railroad). The railway is located east of the St Croix River, about an hour's drive from the Twin Cities, and has steam and diesel train rides.

# All aboard!

After a service stop, the *Empire Builder* leaves St Paul on the Burlington Northern line. Minneapolis can be seen in the left distance, dominated by the 57-storey IDS Tower.

**ST CLOUD (80/60)** Located on the shores of the Mississippi, St Cloud ships granite from local mines. To your right is the largest granite wall in the world, surrounding the St Cloud Reformatory completed in 1889.

**STAPLES (60/60)** This former railroad town became run down but has lately attracted new industries.

**DETROIT LAKES (60/55)** The 400 lakes nearby are a popular venue for fishing and other outdoor pursuits. Amtrak's station is at 116 Pioneer.

**Red River (53/2)** You cross the river and go from Minnesota into North Dakota, the Sioux State.

**FARGO (55/60)** Named after William Fargo of the Wells Fargo Express Company, North Dakota's largest city is at the heart of the Red River Valley. In the late 19th century this was the main hub of the North Pacific Railroad. Amtrak's station at 420 4th Street N also serves Moorhead in Minnesota. **Bonanzaville USA**, in West Fargo, relives pioneer days with a village reconstructed from original buildings, including two rail depots.

**GRAND FORKS (60/80)** Located where the Red Lake River meets the Red River, Grand Forks is the home of North Dakota University. Buses connect downtown with Amtrak's station at 5555 DeMers Ave and Thruway buses go north to Winnipeg in Canada.

**DEVIL'S LAKE (80/60)** Catchily nicknamed 'the goose and duck hunting capital of America', the town stands next to North Dakota's largest lake. Sioux and Chippewa Indians called this the Evil Spirit Lake, telling of water monsters, thunderbirds and overturned canoes.

The *Empire Builder* continues across the vast yellow and gold expanses of the northern plains, above which can often be seen eagles and huge flocks of wild geese.

**RUGBY (60/65)** The geographical centre of North America boasts a stone monument and museum to support its claim. The Canadian border is less than 50 miles (80km) from Amtrak's redbrick station on your left.

Look for crops of sunflowers and fields of ploughed black earth as the train travels on over the plains. Near Minot look left for the converted green railroad car used as part of a plant nursery. Also to your left are several picturesque railway buildings and a large letter M.

**MINOT (65/50)** Located on the Souris River, this service stop was called the Magic City when it seemed to grow overnight after the Great Northern Railroad arrived. Minot remains an important divisional point with extensive marshalling yards, and the city prospers thanks to oil and the military. Amtrak's utilitarian station is on your left.

The landscape opens out dramatically as large, flat fields of wheat stretch to the horizon on all sides.

**STANLEY (50/65)** This small town's economy is based mainly on grain and livestock production. Mountrail County courthouse can be seen to the right of the single-storey station with its fading green sign.

**WILLISTON (65/80)** Oil discoveries at the western edge of Lake Sakakawea during the 1950s turned Williston into a boom town. Several wells with patiently nodding pumps can be seen along the train's route. Look also for the steam locomotive to your right just before the station.

The *Empire Builder* joins the Missouri River on the left and follows it along the Missouri Breaks for the next 60 miles (96km). Garrison Dam on the Missouri greatly increased this region's farming activity and rows of tall grain elevators stand next to many small stations along the way.

**Fort Buford (15/65)** Where Chief Sitting Bull surrendered after the battle of the Little Big Horn in Montana (1876). The army officers' quarters, a cemetery and other relics can be seen at the fort.

**Fort Union (20/60)** On your left is one of the 19th century's liveliest fur trading posts. Wild West excitement returns each June with the Fort Union Rendezvous.

**North Dakota/Montana State Line (22/58)** You officially enter big sky country and change from Central to Mountain Time. Watches go back an hour (forward when travelling east).

For most of the next 700 miles (1,100km) the train rolls across the grassland plains of northern Montana, where cattle are more frequent than people and sheep more frequent than cattle. Watch also for woodchuck, wolverine and herds of antelope.

**Culbertson (50/30)** Just west of town the *Empire Builder* crosses Big Muddy Creek into Fort Peck Indian Reservation, where Sitting Bull lived after surrendering. The train then crosses the Poplar River.

**WOLF POINT (80/45)** This small town is set among hundreds of thousands of acres of Montana's high plains. Note the wolf silhouette on the welcome sign, recalling frontier days when this was a wolf-trappers' trading post. Each July, Wolf Point hosts the Wild Horse Stampede – 'the granddaddy of Montana rodeos'.

**Fort Peck Dam (30/15)** Built in 1940, the earth-filled dam is 250ft (75m) tall and forms a 383 square mile (990km²) lake. As the train leaves Fort Peck Reservation and approaches Glasgow look right for a large letter G on the hillside.

**GLASGOW (45/55)** The neat station stands to your left and a church to your right. Fossils and dinosaur bones discovered nearby are displayed at the Fort Peck Museum.

The train accompanies the Milk River west to Havre (pronounced Have-er) and somewhere between here and Malta, assuming both trains are on time, you should pass the eastbound *Empire Builder*.

**Tampico (15/40)** The small town is visible to your right.

**Saco Hot Springs (35/20)** A large bell hangs on the Methodist church to your right. The train passes Nelson Reservoir and part of Lake Bowdoin, also to your right. The wildlife refuge on the left is a resort for water birds.

**MALTA (55/70)** Local cattle empires inspired the western artist Charles Russell and ranching is still big business.

The *Empire Builder* makes a fast run from Malta to Havre, passing many more grain elevators alongside the track.

**Wagner (10/60)** Butch Cassidy and the Sundance Kid (Harry Longbaugh) robbed the Great Northern's *Oriental Limited* of $68,000 here in 1901.

You travel beside the northern edge of Fort Belknap Indian Reservation, with the Bear Paw Mountains ahead to your left. In 1877, Chief Joseph of the Nez Perce Indians surrendered to the US Army after a 1,700-mile (2,700km) retreat with the words 'From where the sun now stands I will fight no more forever.' On your left beyond the highway are the Little Rocky Mountains.

**HAVRE (70/95)** This is an Amtrak service stop so you should have plenty of time to detrain and inspect the S-2 locomotive standing on a pedestal to the left of the station. It was one of the last 14 steam engines acquired from the Baldwin works for main line service by the Great Northern in 1930. They were the most powerful steam locomotives built until then. Some continued in freight service after the previous *Empire Builder* was streamlined and switched to diesel power in 1947.

Native Americans used to hunt buffalo by driving them over nearby cliffs, and a museum at the site shows some of the animals' skeleton remains. Havre has expanded greatly since the discovery of natural gas in this area.

**Milk River (5/90)** The river departs to the north, entering Canada before finding its source in Montana's Glacier National Park.

**SHELBY (95/30)** Look for freight wagons and grain elevators standing beside the track. This characteristic prairie town is located at the heart of Montana's oil region. Rimrock Stages buses (tel: 406 453 1541) connect the station on your right with Great Falls, Helena and Butte. A railway branch line goes north through the Crowsnest Pass to Lethbridge in Alberta.

Shelby was the unlikely venue in 1923 for a heavyweight boxing championship fight between Jack Dempsey and Tom Gibbons. Chaos ensued when the match was cancelled before being reconvened in front of 7,000 fans and 17,000 gatecrashers, many of whom arrived by chartered train. Dempsey won but received no prize money after his manager vanished with $300,000. Several banks failed and the city never hosted another fight.

**CUT BANK (30/32)** Winter temperatures in this small, oil-producing town are among the nation's coldest. Sweetgrass Hills and the Canadian border are only 25 miles (40km) away to your right.

The *Empire Builder* departs on tracks supported by a trestle across Cut Bank Creek and you get your first views ahead of the Rocky Mountains. This horizon becomes increasingly impressive as you near Glacier National Park, but if you wish to be sure of seeing this section of the route by daylight you should travel during summer or take an eastbound train.

**Lewis and Clark Monument (20/12)** An obelisk on your left commemorates Lewis and Clark's search for a pass through the mountains when they made the first overland journey across North America in 1804–06.

**BROWNING (32/20)** The train stops here when East Glacier Park Station is closed during winter. Browning is at the heart of the Blackfeet Indian Reservation and a good place to shop for Native American goods. The **Museum of the Plains Indians** features the art of many tribes.

The train continues towards the Rockies, approaching Glacier Park Station on a high trestle over Two Medicine River.

**EAST GLACIER PARK (20/60)** The station opens in summer to provide a gateway into one of America's most stunning national parks, featuring 200 lakes, 10,000ft (3,000m) mountains and 50 living glaciers. For **information** on boating, hiking and skiing call 406 888 7800.

Timber was brought from Oregon and Washington by the Great Northern to build Glacier Park Lodge, seen to your right beside the 1913 station. When the station closes out of season, access to the park may still be possible via Browning or Essex. Having enjoyed relatively easy conditions so far the *Empire Builder* now has to tackle the jagged barrier ahead.

**Maria's Pass (15/45)** The continental divide at this point is lower (5,216ft/1,590m) than anywhere else between Canada and New Mexico. Native Americans may have crossed Mystery Pass but Meriwether Lewis and William Clark were unable to chart an accurate route. It was John Stevens, working as a surveyor for the Great Northern, who finally discovered a passage in 1889. Almost freezing to death in temperatures of minus 40°F (−4°C), he fully earned the statue dedicated to him on your right.

Look right also for a fence constructed to keep out grizzly bears. The monument to your left honours President Theodore Roosevelt, after whom the adjacent highway was named.

As the train descends the western side of the pass the scenery becomes even more breathtaking, with waterfalls and deep gorges cutting through the rugged mountains.

**Flathead River (45/15)** Joining from your left, the river is crossed on another trestle.

**ESSEX (60/25)** A flag stop, so trains only halt at this village if requested. The Izaak Walton Inn to your right was named after the English writer and angler.

**WEST GLACIER (25/35)** Entrance to the western part of **Glacier National Park**, where yearly snowfall can reach over 200 inches (500cm). The *Empire Builder* again crosses the Flathead River.

**Columbia Falls (20/15)** Look for the preserved steam engine on your left and an Anaconda aluminium plant to your right.

**WHITEFISH (35/110)** A German-style station on the left complements the alpine-style scenery. Whitefish is located in a valley of the Flathead

National Forest close to the resorts of Whitefish Lake and Big Mountain. Flathead Lake, the greatest expanse of water west of the Mississippi, is 25 miles (40km) to the south.

**Flathead Tunnel (40/70)** You travel seven miles (11km) through one of the longest tunnels in the world.

**LIBBY (110/55)** The town is in the middle of **Kootenai National Forest**, popular with hunters and fishermen. Libby's sawmills and log processing plants are sometimes open to visitors.

Between here and Sandpoint the train goes from Montana into Idaho, changing from Mountain to Pacific Time. Watches go back an hour (forward when travelling east).

**SANDPOINT (55/80)** Sandpoint stands next to Lake Pend Oreille and close to the Schweitzer ski area.

Travelling on through the night, the *Empire Builder* leaves Idaho for Washington, the Evergreen State.

**SPOKANE (80/120)** 'The monarch of the inland empire' stands next to the Spokane River and is surrounded by farmland. An important railroad junction, this is where the Great Northern route meets the Spokane, Portland & Seattle line. The old Great Northern clock tower remains a prominent downtown landmark and Amtrak's station is at W 221 1st.

Bing Crosby attended Spokane's Gonzaga University and the library owns photographs, memorabilia and a bronze statue. The **Museum of Native American Cultures** is at E 200 Cataldo. Empire Lines (tel: 624 4116) runs a bus service to the **Grand Coulee Dam**, 80 miles (128km) east. Famously sung about by Woody Guthrie, the dam was begun in 1933 as part of President Roosevelt's New Deal.

The *Empire Builder* divides into two trains at Spokane, and what follows in this chapter is the continuation to Seattle. For the route to Portland, see the next chapter (pages 124–6).

**EPHRATA (120/65)** The town is set among fertile land irrigated by water from the Columbia River project.

**Rock Island Dam (35/30)** The dam to your left holds back the Columbia River, which the *Empire Builder* crosses five minutes later.

**WENATCHEE (65/175)** Wenatchee is one of the apple capitals of the world. Orchards in the Cascades foothills have perfect weather conditions for producing a seventh of the country's crop. **North Central Washington Museum** offers spirited demonstrations of apple sorting.

The train pulls out past warehouses and lumber yards then accompanies the Wenatchee River to your left. To enjoy the best scenery for the next hour or so you should stay on this side of the train. This region is one of the last refuges for the spotted owl, a consequent source of conflict between conservationists and loggers.

**Cashmere (15/160)** Look for more apple warehouses. Turkish delight-type sweets called aplets (made from apples) and cotlets (from apricots) are local specialities.

The train crosses the Wenatchee River several times as it approaches the Cascade Mountains.

**Leavenworth (25/150)** Bavarian-style buildings appear among the orchards as the *Empire Builder* starts a long, steep climb, entering the first of many tunnels before again crossing the river.

**Merritt (60/115)** The train slows further as it gains height among streams, mountains and marshland.

**Icicle Canyon (65/110)** The best views are now to your right. Keep a look out for goats, elk, deer and perhaps beaver.

**Cascade Tunnel (75/100)** Completed in 1929, the tunnel is another of the world's longest (7.79 miles/12.53km). It helped replace 43 miles (69km) of stiff grades with an easier 34-mile (54km) route. Stevens Pass is 500ft (150m) higher at 4,061ft (1,225m). The tunnel lasts 15 minutes before the train emerges to begin a 65-mile (105km) descent to Everett, giving delightful views of the Cascades and Puget Sound.

The *Empire Builder* crosses the Skyomish River, which it follows to Everett. A waterfall appears on the left but the best scenery remains to your right. This is *Twin Peaks* country, with wooden houses, cloud-topped mountains, pine forests, fast-running streams and huge logging trucks. The modest towns look as if they belong in a Norman Rockwell painting.

You cross the Skyomish River on another dramatic high trestle, with the Mount Baker-Snoqualmie National Forest ranger station to your right.

**Skyomish (100/75)** A logging town which has an interesting historic Burlington Northern station.

**Sunset Falls (115/60)** The falls are to your left before you again cross the river. Look also for Indian Falls, Table Rock and Index Mountain.

**Grotto (117/58)** A small village stands among the mountains to your right. The train crosses the river twice more, leaving the Cascades for less demanding terrain.

**Monroe (150/25)** Note the old station building away from the tracks to your right.

**EVERETT (175/25)** Thanks to its being a natural inland port, Everett was a focal point for the fishing and lumber industries even before the railroad came. Boeing's 747/767 assembly plant is contained here in what may be the world's largest building. Trailways Northwest buses connect with Vancouver, British Columbia.

South of the city you join Puget Sound on your right for the next 15 miles (24km), with the Olympic Mountains in the distance. Islands in the sound include Bainbridge and Whidbey, linked to the mainland by ferry.

**EDMONDS (25/30)** 'The gem of the Puget Sound', Edmonds is mostly residential and its Old Milltown shopping arcade was developed inside an old Ford garage. The *Empire Builder* stops at 211 Railroad Ave, near the dock where ferries leave for Kingston and the Olympic Peninsula.

**Shilshole Bay (15/15)** Innumerable boats are moored in the marina to your right. Bainbridge Island, where Michael Douglas lived in the movie *Disclosure*, is across the water. You cross Salmon Bay inlet then travel briefly inland past Chittenden Locks to your left, part of a waterway system linking the bay with Lake Washington. On your right is a statue of the Norwegian explorer Leif Ericsson.

The train returns to the shoreline by way of a US Navy reservation then travels along Seattle's waterfront. Pier 70 to your right is America's largest restored wooden building. The former warehouse has 40 shops and restaurants and is connected to downtown by a trolley running on tracks beside the train. Seattle's Space Needle comes into view on your left before the *Empire Builder* passes through a mile long (1.6km) tunnel to complete its journey at King Street Station.

### SEATTLE

For Seattle city information, see *The Coast Starlight* (pages 50–52).

# The *Empire Builder*
# Spokane–Portland

## Joining the train

### SPOKANE (80/150)

For Spokane, the route from Chicago and onward to Seattle, see the previous chapter (pages 109–123).

## All aboard!

Through coaches for this branch of the *Empire Builder* service to Portland continue via Pasco.

**PASCO (150/115)** The Columbia and Snake Rivers meet in this territory, which was claimed by the British before it became part of the United States in 1846. Pasco is the furthest seagoing vessels can voyage up the Columbia, and the town's name derives from a shortening of Pacific Steamship Company. The station at Clark and Tacoma also serves Kennewick and Richland.

**North McNary (30/85)** Named after Charles McNary, who was a long-serving US Senator from Oregon.

**Columbia River (75/40)** The state of Oregon can be seen on the opposite side as you travel the water level route through the Columbia River Gorge – a land of stone cliffs, lakes, streams, meadows and woods.

**Roosevelt (80/35)** Barges shipping grain are a common sight on the river between here and Vancouver.

**John Day Dam (100/15)** The dam is 5,900ft (1,800m) long and was completed in 1968 at a cost of $487 million. Masses of pylons take away enough electricity to supply Portland three times over. The locks carry eight million tons of shipping a year and incorporate one of the highest (113ft/35m) single lifts in the world.

**Maryhill (105/10)** Just past an emu and ostrich farm to your left, look right for a glimpse of the Maryhill Castle Art Museum. Also on the hill to your right is a concrete replica of Stonehenge, built to honour troops who died in the First World War.

**WISHRAM (115/30)** Named after a Native American settlement known to Lewis and Clark, Wishram is the site of a legendary 'beanery' – one of the cheap restaurants built and operated by the railway for its workers.

On the far side of the Columbia are the Union Pacific tracks used until 1997 by Amtrak's *Pioneer* train from Seattle and Salt Lake City. A bridge ahead takes the Burlington Northern line south to Klamath Falls.

**Avery (2/28)** The pyramid of Mount Hood can be seen to the south as you continue through the Columbia Gorge.

**Dalles Dam (10/20)** Dalles is French for 'trough' and describes the narrow channel formed by the river. The 8,700ft (2,650m) zigzag shaped dam provides irrigation and power, and created Horsethief Lake. The town of Dalles is on the opposite shore.

**Mount Hood (15/15)** Look left for another view of Oregon's tallest mountain, 11,235ft (3,425m) and permanently snow-capped.

**Lyle (25/5)** The train crosses the Klickitat River, with the Native American burial ground of Memaloose Island to your left.

**BINGEN-WHITE SALMON (30/80)** Jointly named after the White Salmon River and a German town called Bingen. The city of Hood River can be seen on the far shore.

For the next 55 miles (88km) the landscape changes from near desert to rain forest as the *Empire Builder* travels through the Columbia Gorge, carved into ancient rocks by the river. Lewis and Clark were the first white people to venture this far and settlers on the Oregon Trail would often refuse to risk crossing the powerful river.

**Cooks (15/65)** Wind Mountain (2,500ft/760m) is to your right. One of this region's few remaining log flumes transports lumber to a sawmill beside the river.

**Stevenson (30/50)** Amtrak's *Pioneer* formerly stopped at Cascade Locks across the water.

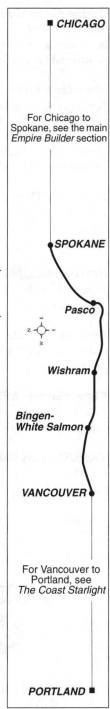

■ *CHICAGO*

For Chicago to Spokane, see the main *Empire Builder* section

● *SPOKANE*

● *Pasco*

*Wishram* ●

*Bingen-White Salmon* ●

*VANCOUVER* ●

For Vancouver to Portland, see *The Coast Starlight*

*PORTLAND* ■

**Bridge of the Gods (33/47)** The bridge ahead to your left replaced a stone bridge which Native Americans say their god destroyed when he was angered by his sons arguing over a maiden. The sons became Mount Hood and Mount Adams and the maiden was transformed into Mount St Helens.

**Sheridan's Point (35/45)** Philip Sheridan, a cavalry officer and later a Civil War general, defended settlers from Indian marauders here in 1855 when he was a young officer. He notoriously remarked that the only good Indians he ever saw were dead ones. The final spike was driven nearby in 1908 to complete the Spokane, Portland & Seattle route between Pasco and Vancouver.

**Bonneville Dam (36/44)** This was the Columbia's first great dam, worked on by Woody Guthrie. The half-mile (0.8km) feat of engineering created Lake Bonneville. Look for the fish ladder which allows migrating salmon to swim upstream.

**Beacon Rock (40/40)** The 840ft (255m) rock on your right is second in magnitude only to Gibraltar. Named by Lewis and Clark, it was an unmistakable guide for travellers.

**Multnomah Falls (42/38)** The second-highest waterfall in the country cascades 620ft (190m) on the Oregon side. Look also for rafts of logs, paper mills and sawmills.

**Cape Horn (48/32)** The train leaves the Columbia Gorge by way of a 2,369ft (720m) tunnel through the western Cascades. Just before Vancouver you can glimpse a smart Spokane, Portland & Seattle railroad car to your left.

### VANCOUVER (80/22)

For Vancouver and the rest of the *Empire Builder* route to Portland, see *The Coast Starlight* (pages 54–6).

# The *Southwest Chief* Chicago–Los Angeles

## General route information

Amtrak's fastest trip from Chicago to the Pacific is along part of the Santa Fe Trail first used by Native Americans and Spanish *conquistadores*, then by mule caravans, wagon trains, stage-coaches and gold prospectors. The train travels 2,256 miles (3,609km) through eight states, passing wheat fields, ranches, missions, pueblos, mountains and deserts. Sometimes the canyons you go through are only a few feet wider than the train. Close by this route are Santa Fe, Taos and the Grand Canyon.

The *Southwest Chief* follows a Santa Fe Railway line which the *Super Chief* first took in 1937, cutting 15 hours from the time of its predecessor, the *Chief*. The *Chief* in turn had succeeded two other luxury trains, the *Southwest Limited* and the *Santa Fe De Luxe*. Even as late as the 1970s, Frank Sinatra was inclined to hire a luxury private car to travel with his friends between San Bernadino and Chicago.

**Frequency** Daily.

The westbound service leaves Chicago mid-afternoon to arrive in Kansas City late in the evening and Dodge City early next morning. You reach Albuquerque late in the afternoon, Flagstaff (for the Grand Canyon) by mid-evening and Los Angeles early on the third day.

Travelling east, trains leave Los Angeles early in the evening to reach Flagstaff early next morning, Albuquerque by early afternoon and Dodge City about midnight. You arrive in Kansas City early on the third day and Chicago by mid-afternoon.

**Reservations** All reserved.

**Equipment** Superliner coaches.

**Sleeping** Superliner bedrooms.

**Food** Complete meals, snacks, sandwiches, drinks.

**Lounge car** Video movies, travelogues, hospitality hour. A Native American guide provides commentary between Albuquerque and Gallup.

**Baggage** Check-in service at most stations.

## Joining the train

### CHICAGO

For Chicago city information and the route as far as Galesburg, see *The California Zephyr* (pages 75–80). In addition to the stops made by the *California Zephyr*, the

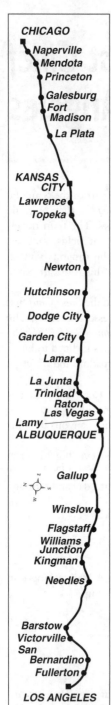

CHICAGO
Naperville
Mendota
Princeton
Galesburg
Fort Madison
La Plata
KANSAS CITY
Lawrence
Topeka
Newton
Hutchinson
Dodge City
Garden City
Lamar
La Junta
Trinidad
Raton
Las Vegas
Lamy
ALBUQUERQUE
Gallup
Winslow
Flagstaff
Williams Junction
Kingman
Needles
Barstow
Victorville
San Bernardino
Fullerton
LOS ANGELES

*Southwest Chief* serves the renovated station in Mendota – the first long-distance train to stop there in 26 years.

**GALESBURG (42/45)** Settled by Presbyterians from Oneida, New York, Galesburg was the scene of a Lincoln-Douglas debate in 1858. It was also the home of George Washington Ferris (creator of the first Ferris wheel) and Olmsted Ferris (inventor of popcorn). Amtrak's station is at 184 N Broad.

**Mississippi River (35/10)** North America's greatest waterway appears to your right. A few minutes later the train crosses the river from Illinois into Iowa by means of the longest (3,347ft/1,020m) double-track, double-decked bridge on earth. The structure pivots to allow larger boats to pass beneath.

Approaching Fort Madison, note the Santa Fe steam engine on your left. The old Santa Fe station is a museum.

**FORT MADISON (45/65)** The train's only stop on its brief passage through Iowa is this industrial city. US soldiers set fire to the original fort in 1813 to divert attacking Indians while settlers escaped through a tunnel to the Mississippi. This event is commemorated by One Chimney Monument to your right.

Fort Madison is Amtrak's closest stop to Keokuk, five miles south along the river.

**Nauvoo (10/55)** The old Mormon town seen across the Des Moines River is being restored as a monument. Soon after Nauvoo you cross the river from Iowa into Missouri.

**LA PLATA (65/130)** A small farming town in a region famous for deer, pheasant and turkey hunting. La Plata Lake is on your left and Kirksville, home of Northeast Missouri University, 10 miles (16km) to the north.

**Marceline (35/95)** Childhood home of Walt Disney, who invented Mickey Mouse while riding on the *Southwest Chief*. Walt Disney Park to your right features a steam locomotive from the Santa Fe Railway.

**Mendon (45/85)** Waterfowl migrate to Canada from Swan Lake game reserve, seen on your right. Hunters account for several hundred thousand birds each year.

**Bosworth (50/80)** You cross the Grand River, bordered by pecan trees.

**Missouri River (105/25)** The train crosses on a 135ft-high (40m) bridge. To your right are the remains of Fort Osage, built in 1808.

**Sugar Creek (120/10)** The town was a haunt of the outlaw Jesse James, who died in 1882 at nearby St Joseph.

## KANSAS CITY (130/50)
Birthplace of Harry S Truman, Jean Harlow and Charlie Parker, the larger and better-known Kansas City is in Missouri rather than Kansas. Kansas City, Kansas, is immediately across the Missouri River but is politically separate. 'The heart of America' was named after Kanza Indians who traded with the city's founder, John Calvin McCoy. A settlement on a bend in the river later became the place where wagon trains were equipped for the Santa Fe, California and Oregon Trails. After the Civil War, with the coming of the railroad, Kansas City turned to agriculture and transport for a living.

The stockyard district reflects Cowtown history and the Royal Livestock Show has been held here every year since 1899. Around the turn of the century the architect George Kessler set out to create 'one of the loveliest cities on earth'. Today's Kansas City rivals Paris for boulevards and claims to have more fountains than Rome. Kansas City has been 'the home of the barbecue' since the 1920s and has more than 60 barbecue restaurants. The city is also famous for its jazz tradition, which flourished in the 1930s Prohibition era when the authorities still allowed alcohol to be served in this 'wide-open town'.

### Kansas City basics
**Telephone code** 816, for Kansas City, Missouri; 913 for Kansas City, Kansas. All numbers given in this section are 816 code unless otherwise noted.
**Station** Amtrak is currently based at 2200 Main, and the station also serves Kansas City, Kansas. Information tel: 421 3622. Ticket-office and waiting-room open 24 hours. Lockers, newspapers, Red Caps, shops, taxi stand.

The adjacent Union Station is a grandiose stone building notorious for the 1933 'Pretty Boy' Floyd massacre in which five people died. Built in 1914, this 'Great Gateway to the West' featured ornate oak leaf clusters, a 95ft ceiling in its Grand Hall, three huge chandeliers and a clock over 6ft (2m) in diameter. Marble decorated separate male and female lounges and the north waiting room measured longer than a football field.

Almost 80,000 trains visited Union Station in 1917 and during the Second World War half of all military personnel passed through, but with decreasing traffic the station building fell into disrepair. An expensive renovation has restored the station to its original glory and it is hoped that Amtrak and commuter rail services will soon return.
**Local transport** Kansas City covers 300 square miles (770km²), so most people get around by car. Metro buses; tel: 221 0660 and the Kansas City Trolley; tel: 221 3399 operate downtown. Kansas City, Kansas, buses are run by the Transportation Department; tel: 913 371 6402.

**Taxis** Yellow; tel: 471 5000. Economy; tel: 621 3436.
**Car rental** Thrifty, 2001 Baltimore; tel: 842 8550.
**Greyhound** 1101 N Troost; tel: 221 2885.
**Kansas City International Airport** is 20 miles (32km) northwest by KCI Express bus (tel: 243 5000).
**Tours** Self-guided walking tours from the Historic Kansas City Foundation, 20 W 9th (tel: 471 3391) and Plaza Merchants Association, 4625 Wornall (tel: 753 0100).
**Visitors bureau** Open weekdays at 1100 Main; tel: 221 5242 or 800 767 7700; email: info@visitkc.com; web: www.visitkc.com.
**Accommodation** Contact Bed & Breakfast in Kansas City (tel: 913 888 3636). Downtown hotel rates can be expensive but look for weekend deals. Hotels include the Raphael at 325 Ward Pkwy; tel: 756 3800; Westin Crown Center, 1 Pershing Rd; tel: 474 4400; Best Western Inn, 1315 North State; tel: 620 365 5161; Travelodge, 1600 Parvin Rd; tel: 453 5210; Belton Inn, 155 S 71 Hwy; tel: 331 6300; Drury Inn-KC Stadium, 3830 Blue Ridge Cut-off; tel: 923 3000.

## Recommended in Kansas City

**The Parks** Among the city's 300 parks is America's second largest, Swope Park, with its Starlight Theatre, the Kansas City Zoo and two golf courses. Others include Loose Park (famous for its roses) and Shawnee Mission Park.
**Crown Center** 2450 Grand Ave, opposite the station; tel: 274 8444; web: www.crowncenter.com. This complex of shops, offices and hotels incorporates an indoor waterfall and the headquarters of Hallmark Cards. Open daily. Free concerts in summer.
**Country Club Plaza** Two miles south of Crown Center at 450 Ward Pky; tel: 753 0100; web: www.countryclubplaza.com. This was America's first (1922) shopping precinct and has pretty Spanish-style architecture, fountains and sculpture. The Plaza Art Fair takes place each September.
**Kansas City Museum** 3218 Gladstone Blvd; tel: 483 8300; web: www.kcmuseum.com. Housed in the mansion of lumber tycoon R A Long, the museum includes a replica trading post. Closed Mon, donation.
**Science City** Union Station 30 W Pershing Rd; tel: 460 2020; web: sciencecity.com. This beautiful, restored 1914 train station features an interactive science museum, restaurants, shops and theatres. Take a behind-the-scenes tour with characters from the station's past.
**American Jazz Museum** 18th and Vine; tel 474 8463; web: www.americanjazzmuseum.com. The story of jazz and performers such as Louis Armstrong, Charlie 'Bird' Parker, Duke Ellington and Ella Fitzgerald is celebrated in one the country's most interactive museums. This ultra-modern building is shared by a visitors centre, a theatre and the
**Negro Leagues Baseball Museum**, 1616 E 18th; tel: 221 1920. The museum opened in 1991 and is located in the historic Lincoln Building. Closed Mon, admission charge.
**1859 Jail Museum** 217 N Main, Independence; tel: 252 1892; web: www.crn.org/jchs/jail/museum.html. Frank James was a resident within the massive, limestone walls of the jail during Wild West days. As well as the two-storey County Jail, with its barred windows and double iron doors, the museum features a schoolhouse and marshal's office. Open Tue–Sat, admission charge.

*Above* Skyline looking east from the Empire State Building, New York City (NS)

*Left* Royal Café, Royal Street, New Orleans, (NS)

*Below* Central clock at Grand Central Terminal, New York City (GE)

*Above* Mammoth Springs, Yellowstone Park, Wyoming (GR)

*Below left* The spectacular Spiral Tunnels were built beneath Cathedral Mountain and Mount Ogden in the Rocky Mountains. (SR)

*Below right* Maroon Bells, Aspen, Colorado (GE)

# All aboard!

The *Southwest Chief* departs Kansas City, Missouri, and crosses the state line into Kansas City, Kansas.

**LAWRENCE (50/32)** This was a 'station' on the Underground Railroad founded by abolitionists before the Civil War. In 1863, Quantrill's pro-Confederate guerrillas attacked the peaceful town, killing 150 of its citizens. Kansas University began here in 1866.

The 1906 Santa Fe depot at Baldwin, 12 miles (19km) south, has vintage equipment, memorabilia and diesel-powered trips from May to October on the historic **Midland Railway**; tel: 800 651 0388; web: www.midland-ry.org/midland.

**TOPEKA (32/130)** The capital of Kansas is home to the Menninger Foundation, a world leader in the treatment of mental illness, and the clinic owns an important collection of Sigmund Freud's papers.

**Emporia (65/65)** Home of Emporia State University and the *Emporia Gazette*. The newspaper's editor, William White, gave the city its Peter Pan Park.

**NEWTON (130/35)** One of America's largest Mennonite settlements, Newton was founded in 1872 by immigrants from Russia. Seed they brought for winter wheat helped Kansas become 'the world's breadbasket'. Amtrak's station also serves Wichita, 20 miles (32km) further south.

**HUTCHINSON (35/95)** The largest wheat market anywhere on earth, boasting 50 massive grain elevators. Nearby is one of the world's biggest salt mines.

Between here and Dodge City the train travels through oil country, with nodding pumps seen on both sides of the track.

**Kinsley (65/30)** A sign to your right states that Kinsley is exactly 1,561 miles (2,510km) from both San Francisco and New York.

**DODGE CITY (95/42)** This former trading post and army fort began to prosper when the Santa Fe Railway arrived in 1872. Dodge soon became the cowboy capital of the world, shipping longhorn steers brought on cattle drives from Texas and the south. Lawlessness took hold of 'the wickedest little city in America' until Bat Masterson, Wyatt Earp and Doc Holliday restored order. The hangman's tree still survives and many gunfighters and outlaws who died were buried on Boot Hill to your left. The rail yards still ship great quantities of cattle and wheat. Front Street, to your right, looks much as it always did, although calmer these days.

The **tourist bureau** is at 4th and W Spruce; tel: 620 227 3119. Amtrak's Santa Fe station, a national historic landmark, is at Central and Wyatt Earp.

Two sundials on your right signify a change of time zone which actually takes place further west.

**Cimarron (15/27)** Where the Santa Fe Trail crosses the Arkansas River, seen to your left.

**GARDEN CITY (42/75)** Apparently named by a passing hobo who admired the garden of its founder's wife, the city claims to have the world's largest swimming pool and most capacious grain elevator. Nearby are the world's biggest buffalo herd and a massive natural gas field.

**Holcomb (5/70)** The murders described in Truman Capote's *In Cold Blood* took place here. This part of the Sunflower State has many fields filled with these impressive plants, grown for their oil and as cattle feed.

**Coolidge (50/25)** The train leaves Kansas and enters Colorado, changing from Central to Mountain time, so watches go back an hour (forward when travelling east).

The *Southwest Chief* crosses the Arkansas River, which it then follows west to La Junta. The valley is famous for vegetables and fruit, especially cantaloupe melons.

**LAMAR (75/45)** As the train nears the station in 'the goose hunting capital of America', look left to see the Madonna of the Trails statue erected by the Daughters of the Revolution.

**John Martin Dam (10/35)** The dam forms a reservoir frequented by herons and cranes.

**Las Animas (25/20)** Named after the Rio de las Animas Perdidas (the river of lost souls) where a wagon train of settlers camped and disappeared overnight, presumably having been attacked by Native Americans.

**Bent's Old Fort (35/10)** The settlement seen among the trees to your right was built in the 1840s to protect fur traders and service wagon trains on the Santa Fe Trail. Kit Carson worked at the adobe fort, which has been restored.

**LA JUNTA (45/75)** The Santa Fe Trail meets the Cimarron Cut-off here and La Junta is the Santa Fe Railway's divisional headquarters. Outlaws such as Belle Star inscribed their names on nearby rocks. On a clear day you can see Pike's Peak on your right even though it stands a hundred miles north.

After La Junta the *Southwest Chief* leaves the valley and swings south to make a fast run across the Commanche National Grassland.

**Sunflower Valley (50/25)** Farms in this region produce enormous crops of wheat, corn and sugar beet. As the train approaches Trinidad, look right for the snow-covered Sangre de Cristo Range and the twin Spanish Peaks of the Colorado Rockies. Native Americans called these mountains 'the breasts of mother earth'.

**TRINIDAD (75/65)** The name (meaning 'trinity') appears to your left on the hill known as Simpson's Rest, after the pioneer who was buried there. Fisher's Peak (10,000ft/3,038m) is also to your left.

Trinidad became known for the battle fought between Spanish and US settlers on Christmas Day in 1867, and the town's **Pioneer Museum** reveals the struggles of early settlement life. Amtrak's station is on Pine Street.

**Purgatoire River (5/60)** The *Southwest Chief* crosses the river and begins the steep climb to Raton Pass.

**Morley (20/45)** Look for an old coal mine and the ruins of a Spanish mission on the hill to your right.

**Wootton Ranch (35/30)** On your right is the ranch owned by Dick Wootton, a noted frontier scout and Indian fighter, paid for by the Raton Pass toll road he established. The road became obsolete when the railway was built. The original Santa Fe Trail can be seen to your right and Interstate 25, which the train accompanies most of the way to Albuquerque, is off to your left.

**Raton Pass (40/25)** Highest point (7,588ft/2,310m) on the *Southwest Chief's* journey, the ascent to this pass is the steepest on the route. Entering a half-mile (0.8km) long tunnel, you go from Colorado into New Mexico.

**RATON (65/105)** Thruway buses connect with Colorado Springs and Denver's Union Station. A railroad and mining town nestled in the foothills of the Sangre de Cristo Mountains, Raton is Amtrak's nearest stop to the Philmont Ranch, a 137,441-acre (55,600ha) estate owned by the Boy Scouts of America.

**Clifton House Ruins (5/100)** The house to your left was a resting place on the Santa Fe Trail.

**Maxwell (20/85)** The 1.75 million-acre Maxwell wildlife refuge belonged to Lucien Maxwell – hunter, trapper and a friend of Kit Carson.

**Springer (35/70)** After following the Canadian River the train crosses the Cimarron River with Baldy Peak (12,441ft/3,795m) on the far right. Keep a look out for antelope.

**Wagon Mound (60/45)** The butte to your left, shaped like a wagon and horses, was one of many landmarks on the Santa Fe Trail.

**Shoemaker Canyon (80/25)** The train crosses then follows the Mora River. Pines and cottonwoods flourish in what was once a trade route for Plains and Texas Indians.

**Watrous (85/20)** To your left are the ruins of Fort Union, founded in 1851 as one of the largest forts in the southwest. Ahead to your right are the higher Sangre de Cristo Mountains, called 'the blood of Christ' by Spanish settlers because of the hardships suffered crossing them.

**LAS VEGAS (105/100)** Not to be confused with any other Las Vegas. Look right just before the station to see La Castenada Hotel, a former Harvey House. The first of Englishman Fred Harvey's dining rooms opened at Topeka, Kansas, in the spring of 1876 on the Atchison, Topeka & Santa Fe line. Orders taken on the train were ready to be served as soon as passengers arrived. Theodore Roosevelt joined his Rough Riders at La Castenada for a reunion in 1899 following their exploits on Cuba during the Spanish-American War of the previous year.

Native Americans knew this region for thousands of years before Coronado discovered it in 1541. White settlers began to arrive in the 1830s and the town grew faster when the railroad came in 1879. Prosperity also attracted outlaws such as Billy the Kid.

As the train pulls out look for an old railway roundhouse to your right. The letter H on the hill to your left signifies New Mexico Highlands University.

**Bernal (20/80)** The ruins of a Las Vegas–Santa Fe stage-coach relay station can be seen off to your right. Martinez Canyon is to your left.

**Starvation Peak (30/70)** A band of 30 early 19th century Spanish settlers are said to have climbed the small, flat-topped mesa ahead to your left. They defended themselves from Navajo Indians by throwing rocks but were eventually starved to death.

**S-Curve (35/65)** The *Southwest Chief* descends a zig-zag sequence of curves. Both ends of the train come into view as you travel through a wild landscape of dry river beds and pink earth.

**Pecos River (45/55)** The 1775 Mission of San Miguel is to your left.

**Rowe (65/35)** Pecos Indians lived here in New Mexico's largest pueblo. After conversion to Christianity by the Spanish in 1617 they built the adobe mission seen in ruins across the valley to your right. Known as the **Pecos National Monument**, it rests on land donated by the actress Greer Garson. The pink pillars on the right mark the entrance to her Forked Lightning ranch.

The *Southwest Chief* travels on past Glorieta Mesa to your left, with Santa Fe National Forest on your right.

**Glorieta (80/20)** One of the Civil War's most westerly battles took place here in 1862 when a Texan supply train was destroyed by Union forces. A Baptist retreat centre can be seen to the right.

Between Glorieta and Lamy the train descends Glorieta Pass – a 1,000-foot drop over 10 miles (300m in 16km). The route twists through dry, red-rock canyons and hills thick with juniper, tamarisk, scrub oak and ponderosa pine.

**Apache Canyon (95/5)** A narrow granite gorge cuts into one of the oldest parts of the Rocky Mountains, where the rock face is sometimes only inches from the train as it snakes through the canyon.

**LAMY (100/65)** Named after Jean Baptiste Lamy, a 19th century missionary. The ruins of his school can be seen to your left as the train arrives. To your right is the Legal Tender saloon.

Lamy Shuttle buses connect with the *Southwest Chief* and you can book through tickets (tel: 505 982 8829). Amtrak's adobe-style station is at County Road 41.

### Connections from Lamy

**Santa Fe** is the southwest's oldest city, founded in 1610, and the country's highest (7,000ft/2,100m) state capital. Crooked streets follow the contours of the earth and the flat-roofed buildings come in every shade of adobe. Formerly the royal city of the *conquistadores*, known as La Villa Real de Santa Fe de San Francisco de Asis, Santa Fe still has fine Spanish architecture, along with opera, art galleries, restaurants and probably too many tourists.

Handmade silver jewellery is sold by Native Americans on the pavement outside the Palace of the Governors and you can visit San Miguel Mission, the oldest house in the United States. The Loretto Chapel's Miraculous Staircase was built by a mysterious man who arrived from nowhere and left without payment after completing his task. Santa Fe's **visitor centre** is at 201 W Marcy; tel: 505 955 6200 or 800 777 2489; web: www.santafe.org

The **Santa Fe Southern Railway** is at 410 S Guadalupe; tel 1 888 989 8600; web: http://www.sfsr.com. You can ride in vintage passenger cars along a working freight line through high desert scenery on a four hour round-trip from the historic depot in Santa Fe to Lamy. Construction difficulties prevented the Santa Fe Railway's tracks reaching Santa Fe until 1880, when this line and the beautiful adobe-style station were built by the Atchison, Topeka & Santa Fe Railway. Trains operate on Tuesday, Thursday, Saturday and Sunday (year round) or on every day except Friday (from April to October).

**Taos** 75 miles (120km) further north, has an adobe pueblo culture going back at least 900 years, and it was here that DH Lawrence and his wife Frieda came in the 1920s to seek mystical enlightenment. His ashes are buried in a shrine on their former ranch, which has spectacular views across the desert to distant mountains. For **visitor information** about Taos call 1 800 732 8267 or 505 758 3873.

# All aboard!

As the *Southwest Chief* leaves Lamy and travels through tracts of barren countryside you begin to lose sight of the Sangre de Cristo Mountains back to your right.

**Los Cerrillos (15/50)** The Ortiz Mountains are in the left distance. This area is rich in minerals, including silver and turquoise, and was the site of the earliest (1830s) US gold mine. Amtrak scenes for the first *Superman* film were shot here on one of the network's fastest sections of track.

**Santo Domingo (30/35)** The settlement on your right dates from 1598. Look for the beehive-shaped *hornos* – ovens used for baking bread.

**San Felipe (35/30)** This pueblo was established more than 500 years ago. A Catholic church and a Native American *kiva* (religious council chamber) can be seen to your right.

**Sandia Crest (55/10)** The mountain over on your left in the **Cibola National Forest** is 10,678ft (3,250m) high. These 'watermelon mountains' go bright red at sunset, when trees on the slopes resemble seeds.

As the train nears Albuquerque look right to see the tower and gold globe of the Federal Office building.

## ALBUQUERQUE (65/140)

A centre for business, government and the military, Albuquerque is sought after for its dry, invigorating climate. Named after a Portuguese duke, the city was ruled by Spain and Mexico before being won for the United States in 1846. The railroad arrived in 1880, after which Albuquerque became the site of the main locomotive works of the Santa Fe Railway. Today's population of 400,000 represents a quarter of the total for the entire state.

### Albuquerque basics

**Telephone code** 505.

**Station** Amtrak's attractive Spanish-style station at 214 First SW is five blocks from downtown. Tiwa Indians sell pretty silver and turquoise jewellery on the platform. Ticket-office and waiting-room open 09.30–18.00. Information tel: 842 9650. Free baggage store, vending machines, handcarts, taxi stand.

**Connections** Thruway buses travel to Truth or Consequences and El Paso.

**Local transport** Sun-Tran buses (tel: 843 9200) will take you to most places, Mon-Sat.

**Taxis** Yellow; tel: 842 5292. Albuquerque; tel: 883 4888.

**Car rental** In a city 20 miles long by 25 miles wide (32km by 40km) a car can be essential. Alamo is at 3400 University Blvd NE; tel: 842 4057.

**Greyhound** 300 Second SW; tel: 243 4435.

**Albuquerque International Airport** is five miles (8km) from downtown by bus #50 or the Airport Shuttle; tel: 765 1234 or 800 395 7680.

**Tours** Grayline; tel: 242 3880. The Albuquerque Trolley; tel: 242 1407 has a commentary guide. Walking tours of the Old Town start from the Albuquerque Museum (Wed–Sun from April till October, free).

**Visitors bureau** Open weekdays at 20 First Plaza; tel: 800 284 2282; email: info@abqcvb.org; web: www.abqcvb.org.

**Accommodation** Contact Adobe & Roses Bed & Breakfast at 1011 Ortega NW, Albuquerque, NM 87114 (tel: 898 0654) or the Mauger Estate, 701 Roma; tel: 242 8755.

KOA's nearest campsite is at 12400 Skyline NE; tel: 296 2729. Route 66 Hostel, 1012 Central Ave SW; tel: 247 1813. Single $20, double $25. The hostel is within walking distance of the train station, and there are free pick-ups from Albuquerque and El Paso.

Hotels include the Sheraton Old Town Inn at 800 Rio Grande; tel: 843 6300; Hotel Blue, 717 Central NW; tel: 924 2400; La Posada, 125 2nd; tel: 242 9090; Holiday Inn Mountain View, 2020 Menaul; tel: 884 2511; Rodeway Inn, 2108 Menaul; tel: 884 2480; Rio Grande Inn, 1015 Rio Grande Blvd NW; tel: 843 9500 – single $30, double $35.

## Recommended in Albuquerque

**Old Town** Off Central Ave and Rio Grande Blvd; tel: 243 3215. Colourful activity around the plaza with artists, craft shops, good food and adobe architecture. The most impressive building is the 1706 San Felipe de Neri Church.

**Albuquerque Museum** 2000 Mountain Rd, in Old Town; tel: 243 7255; web: www.cabq.gov/museum. Over 400 years of New Mexican art and history, exploring the culture of the Rio Grande Valley. Closed Mon, free.

**Indian Pueblo Cultural Center** 2401 12th NW; tel: 843 7270; web: www.indianpueblo.com. Traditional food, crafts, fetishes, carvings and dancing. The shop has a wide range of posters, music and books relating to Native American culture. Open daily, admission charge. Take bus #36.

**Sandia Peak** East of Albuquerque off Interstate 25. As well as mountains and desert you can see the impressive lights of night-time Albuquerque and Santa Fe. Look too for wildlife such as mule deer, black bear, racoons, bobcats and various types of squirrels. Birds include golden eagles, hawks, jays, ravens and canyon wrens.

The Sandia Peak Tram (tel: 856 7325) travels up the longest (14,657ft) tramway in the world, rising 4,000ft (1,200m) in 15 minutes. Sandia Crest (10,680ft/3,255m) is 300ft/90m higher and can be reached by road from the east. The tramway closes for two weeks each spring for maintenance.

**National Atomic Museum** 1905 Mountain Rd; tel: 284 3243; web: www.atomicmuseum.com. Documentary film and exhibitions reveal how atomic bombs were developed for use at Hiroshima and Nagasaki. Much of the early atom research was carried out at Los Alamos, 60 miles (96km) north of Albuquerque.

The museum incorporates robotics and nuclear medicine exhibits as well as information about atomic time keeping, micro worlds, nuclear arms control and renewable energy. Open daily, admission charge.

**New Mexico Museum of Natural History and Science** 1801 Mountain Rd; tel: 841 2800; web: www.museums.state.nm.us/nmmnh. Includes footprint fossils dating back to animals that lived in New Mexico 280 million years ago – 60 million years before dinosaurs. Dynamax movies. Open daily except Christmas and non-holiday Mondays in January and September.

## All aboard!

The *Southwest Chief* departs this service stop past the University of New Mexico's sports stadium on the left. Rio Grande Park and Zoo are to your right.

As the train starts to leave the Rio Grande Valley behind and enters New Mexico's desert country a guide from the Inter-Tribal Indian Ceremonial Association describes some of the route's highlights. The Ladron Mountains are to your right and the Manzano Range on the far left horizon. As you cross the Rio Grande, look for lavender-coloured tamarisk trees (salt cedars).

**Isleta Indian Reservation (15/125)** St Augustine Church to your left dates from 1613 and is still in use. Away to your right is an extinct volcano, Mount Taylor (11,301ft/3,445m).

The train crosses the River Puerco, a tributary of the Rio Grande, and begins a 3,000ft (900m) climb to the continental divide.

**Kneeling Nuns (48/92)** The distinctive rock formation on your right resembles two nuns praying at an altar.

**Route 66 (50/90)** Crossing the track on a wooden bridge is the road which ran for 2,000 miles (3,200km) between Chicago and Los Angeles. The last official Route 66 marker was taken down in 1977 but the highway lives on in Bobby Troup's song and Jack Kerouac's *On The Road*.

**Mesita Pueblo (55/85)** The pueblo to your left is one of several seen as you cross the Laguna Indian Reservation. Gypsum cliffs on the right reveal local uranium workings. The *Southwest Chief* joins the San Jose River on the left before crossing it several times ahead.

**Laguna Pueblo (60/80)** This is the youngest and largest of the pueblos on this route.

**Paraje Pueblo (63/77)** Look for the mission building to your left.

**Acomita (65/75)** An adobe church stands on the left. Just to the south of here, 850 years ago, Acoma Indians built a pueblo on top of a 365ft (110m) mesa.

**McCarty's Pueblo (68/72)** The stone built pueblo is part of an Acoma Indian Reservation to your left, where a 200-year-old church dominates the bluff.

**Anzac (75/65)** Mount Taylor produced the black lava beds to your left, much favoured by warmth-loving rattlesnakes.

From here to Gallup the *Southwest Chief* travels among the Red Cliffs, some of which are 7,000ft (2,100m) high. The desert sun can produce spectacular changes of colour. Native Americans say that the hills became red after a wounded stag shed blood while escaping from hunters.

**Grants (90/50)** An Anaconda uranium smelter appears to your right.

**Bluewater (100/40)** Mount Taylor is on the right.

**Continental Divide (110/30)** The train crosses at Campbell's Pass.

**Fort Wingate Depot (124/16)** Army ammunition bunkers are securely hidden in the hillside to your right.

**Pyramid Rock (130/10)** Behind this landmark on your right is the spire of Church Rock, where a jilted Indian maiden is said to have jumped to her death.

**Red Rock State Park (132/8)** Each August, 50 tribes gather on the right for ceremonial dancing and games.

**GALLUP (140/90)** 'The Indian capital of the world', where half the population are Native Americans, is a good place to buy silver jewellery, baskets, pottery, rugs and blankets. The tribes include Acoma, Zuni, Hopi, Navajo and Apache.

Amtrak's station at 210 E Highway 66 gives access to the Four Corners region comprising the Painted Desert, Petrified Forest, Mesa Verde National Park and South Colorado Mountains.

**New Mexico/Arizona State Line (10/80)** Arizona does not observe Daylight Saving Time, so watches go back an hour (forward when travelling east) only from November to April.

The train continues through a stark desert country of mystical beauty, the wide plains interrupted by mesas and buttes. Sharp winds have carved the red and yellow sandstone into wonderful spires and caves. Part of the Painted Desert and Petrified Forest can be seen to your left.

**Holbrook (70/20)** The train makes a street crossing at Holbrook, trading place for Hopi, Navajo and Apache. To your right is the Blevins House where in 1887 Perry Owens, sheriff of Apache County, shot a horse thief and three other men. The flamboyant Owens later became a US deputy marshal and businessman in Seligman.

The *Southwest Chief* accompanies the Little Colorado River for the next few minutes. The giant electricity generating plant you see on your right consumes four million tons of coal a year.

**WINSLOW (90/60)** About 20,000 years ago a meteor hit the earth 23 miles (37km) west of here, causing a crater 600ft deep and 4,000ft wide (180m by 1,200m). 'Meteor city' is another trading post for Hopi and Navajo. Amtrak's pink stucco station at E 2nd Street is a fine example of Spanish-style architecture.

**Canyon Diablo (25/30)** The train crosses on a 544ft/165m-high bridge, with a trading post and store ruins to your right, then continues through further canyons and high desert country. In the days of steam power, tank cars of water had to be hauled into this arid region to feed the locomotives.

You continue through Canyon Padre. Approaching Flagstaff, look right among the San Francisco Peaks for Mount Agassiz (12,340ft/3,760m) and the highest mountain in Arizona, Humphrey's Peak (12,670ft/3,860m).

**FLAGSTAFF (60/35)** Situated almost 7,000ft/2,100m above sea level, the town was named after local settlers who celebrated America's 100th birthday by making a flag staff out of a pine tree stripped of branches. Amtrak's picturesque station is at 1 E Santa Fe Ave, where Thruway buses connect with Sedona, Williams and the Grand Canyon. Open Road/Gray Line Tours (tel: 602 997 6474 or 800 766 7117; web: www.openroadtours.com) offers a Colorado River Float Trip, a Grand Canyon Railroad excursion that includes a 23-mile east rim tour, travel through the Painted Desert and a stop at the Cameron Trading Post on the Navajo Indian Reservation. You can also take a 30-minute helicoptor ride (optional) as an inclusion to the Grand Canyon tour. Additional services include shuttles between Phoenix Sky Harbor Airport and Flagstaff Amtrak Station.

The Colorado River, which from the rim of the **Grand Canyon** looks little more than a thin green thread of water, created this 277 river miles (443km) long phenomenon revealing two billion years of geological history. The canyon is about 190 air miles long and ranges between 600 yards (549m) and 18 miles (29km) wide, averaging 10 miles. This 1,900 square miles (4,921km²) phenomenon is actually 600 interlinked smaller canyons and much of the rain which falls here has evaporated in the heat before it reaches the bottom.

The best way to appreciate the Grand Canyon is to walk one of its trails, that on the south rim being easiest. You can also go down into the canyon itself, but temperatures often reach 100°F (38°C) in summer and fall below freezing in winter, so take sensible precautions.

Five million people visit the canyon each year. Mule-back rides need to be booked well in advance and flights are available from Grand Canyon Airlines; tel: 520 638 2407; web: grandcanyonairlines.com. For tours and lodge accommodation contact the Reservations Department, Grand Canyon National Park, PO Box 129, AZ 86023; tel: 928 638 7888; web: www.nps.gov/gnca.

The *Southwest Chief* leaves Flagstaff to travel among some of the Coconino Forest's many ponderosa pines. Lowell Observatory, from where the planet Pluto was discovered, stands on a hill to your right.

**WILLIAMS (35/120)** The Grand Canyon Railway operates steam trains from the 1908 depot at nearby Bill Williams Ave to the edge of the canyon on a line built by the Atchison Topeka & Santa Fe Railway (see *US Steam Today*, page 325).

**Seligman (45/75)** This mining and cattle-trading town was founded by the railroad in 1882 at the junction of the Santa Fe line and a route south to Prescott.

**KINGMAN (120/64)** Another historic railroad town.

**Arizona/California State Line (50/14)** As the train crosses the Colorado River near Lake Havasu you change from Mountain to Pacific Time. Since Arizona does not observe Daylight Saving Time, watches go back an hour (forward when travelling east) only from November to April.

**NEEDLES (64/160)** California's most eastern city was named after neighbouring rock pinnacles and this part of the Mojave Desert often registers the country's hottest temperatures. Connecting Thruway buses link Needles with Las Vegas and Lake Havasu City.

**BARSTOW (160/35)** Capital of the Mojave, Barstow began as a station on the Santa Fe Trail before becoming a railroad town. To your right, set among cypress trees, is one of the few surviving Harvey House buildings, Casa del Desierto (house of the desert).

Fred Harvey built 47 restaurants and hotels in the 19th century to service the railways and help civilise the west. Hundreds of people would leave the train, enjoy 'the best food and lodging anywhere', and be back on board inside an hour. Waitresses wore immaculate black dresses and lived in dormitories guarded by matrons. They had to forgo half their salary if they married in the first year of employment but 5,000 still found western husbands. Judy Garland made the waitresses immortal in *The Harvey Girls*. Barstow is now a tourist centre, with military bases and NASA's Goldstone satellite station close by.

Leaving North Street station, the train manoeuvres through a complex of Santa Fe marshalling yards before setting out towards the San Bernardino Mountains.

**Edwards Air Force Base (15/20)** Beyond the Kramer Mountains to your right is the landing site for NASA's Space Shuttle. Craig Breedlove chose this six-mile runway in 1996 to test his *Spirit of America* vehicle for an attempt at the land speed record and sound barrier. The late Francis Vincent Zappa was born in nearby Lancaster.

**Oro Grande (25/10)** Wrightwood Mountain is to your left, along with several cement mines and processing plants.

**VICTORVILLE (35/65)** You cross the Mojave River, which runs 20ft (6m) below ground and forms dangerous quicksand. Another cement plant appears on the right.

The *Southwest Chief* starts a long climb among spectacular rocks and Joshua trees to Cajon Pass (Spanish for 'box canyon'). The Union Pacific and Southern Pacific Railroads also use this route to approach Los Angeles from the east. At their highest point the tracks reach more than 3,800ft (1,160m) as they travel the border between the San Bernardino and San Gabriel Mountains. The San Andreas fault is seen as a raised blue line along the hills.

Stunning rock formations feature on both sides as the train begins a slow, twisting 2,743ft (835m) descent towards San Bernardino. Desert scenes give way to a greener country of jacarandas, palm trees and bougainvillaea.

**SAN BERNARDINO (65/70)** Note the handsome grounds and Spanish mission-style station to your right. Other Spanish buildings blend with modern architecture and the heritage of Mormon settlers who came here from Salt Lake City 100 years ago. A citrus fruit industry has existed since the first navel orange crop was grown locally in 1873, and the McDonald brothers opened their first hamburger stand in San Bernardino during the 1930s. The **visitors bureau** is at 201 North E Street; tel: 1 800 867 8366 or 909 889 3980; web: www.san-bernardino.org.

To your left as the train leaves is southern California's highest peak, Mount San Gorgonio (11,502ft/3,500m).

**Riverside (20/50)** The March Air Force Base is in Riverside, now part of the inexorable Los Angeles expansion.

**Santa Ana Mountains (45/25)** You travel through a canyon formed by the Santa Ana River on your left. Prado Dam was built at the head of the canyon to control flooding.

**Yorba Linda (50/20)** Birthplace of Richard Nixon, where the modest house constructed by his Quaker father stands next to the $21 million presidential library. Despite Watergate, Orange County still celebrates Richard Nixon Day.

**FULLERTON (70/35)** A restored Santa Fe station with pink stucco and red tiles can be seen on the right, next to a grand Union Pacific depot which was moved to this site and converted into a restaurant. A Donald Duck citrus juice plant is also on the right. Fullerton is a suburban stop as well as being the station for **Disneyland**, the **Movieland Wax Museum** and **Knott's Berry Farm**. For details of these attractions, see the Fullerton entry in *The Pacific Surfliner* (page 103).

From here to Los Angeles the train passes through residential and industrial suburbs of Los Angeles County.

**Santa Fe Springs (10/25)** Oil wells, tanks and derricks accumulate on both sides.

**Redondo Junction (25/10)** Amtrak superliners are set up for the *Coast Starlight*, *Sunset Limited* and *Southwest Chief* in the yards and roundhouse to your left.

**Los Angeles River (30/5)** The train accompanies a concrete channel on your right. Designed for flood control and normally dry, the channel has been a location for dozens of movie chases. As the *Southwest Chief* nears Los Angeles look for City Hall's white tower dominating the skyline to your right.

## LOS ANGELES

For Los Angeles city information, see *The Coast Starlight* (pages 71–4).

# The *Sunset Limited*
# Orlando–Los Angeles

## General route information

The *Sunset Limited* is the only way to travel from coast to coast on a single train and it takes almost three days to make the 2,764-mile (4,472km) journey. After going north from Orlando to Jacksonville the train heads west into two sunsets. You visit the swamps of bayou country, flirt with the Mexican border and cross Texas range lands before seeing mountains, deserts and the orange groves of California.

The original *Sunset Limited* began in 1895 as an all-Pullman service, complete with silver finger-bowls, operating between San Francisco and New Orleans. Passengers could continue to New York by steamship.

**Frequency** Three trains a week in each direction.

The westbound service leaves Orlando early on Tuesday, Thursday and Sunday afternoons to reach Jacksonville by early evening. You arrive in New Orleans mid-morning on the second day, Houston by late evening and San Antonio during the night. You reach El Paso by mid-afternoon, Tucson mid-evening and Los Angeles early on Friday, Sunday or Wednesday morning.

Travelling east, trains leave Los Angeles late on Sunday, Wednesday and Friday evenings, reaching Tucson early next morning and El Paso by mid-afternoon. You arrive in San Antonio by early morning, Houston mid-morning and New Orleans mid-evening, reaching Jacksonville late afternoon and Orlando mid-evening on Wednesday, Saturday or Monday evening.

**Reservations** All reserved.

**Equipment** Superliner coaches.

**Sleeping** Superliner bedrooms.

**Food** Complete meals, snacks, sandwiches, drinks.

**Lounge car** Movies, games, hospitality hour. National Park Service guide.

**Baggage** Check-in service at main stations.

## Joining the train

### ORLANDO

For Orlando city information and the route to Jacksonville, see *The Silver Star* (pages 227–31).

**JACKSONVILLE (60/50)** The *Sunset Limited* begins its long journey west by crossing the cattle ranches and farms of northern Florida – a land of twisted cypress trees, oaks, swamps and lakes, with birds such as herons, egrets and flamingos.

## LAKE CITY (50/50) Suwannee State Park can

be seen on both sides of the track. Lake City used to be known as Alligator, after a Seminole Indian chief, and is located on the banks of the graceful Suwannee River. A museum honours Stephen Foster, the composer of *Swannee River* and *Camptown Races*. The only significant Civil War battle fought in Florida took place at nearby Olustee.

As the train travels among more cypress trees and cattle ranches, look for the attractive lake to your right just before Madison.

## MADISON (50/65) In the 19th century this was one

of the world's great centres for processing cotton. The *Sunset Limited* pauses at a modest platform building on the right, beyond which can be seen an impressive example of mechanical engineering.

You continue through farms and woodland where alligators lurk beneath gnarled trees. Approaching Tallahassee, the train passes through Chaires then crosses US Highway 27. Look right for the old Capitol building and the clean, white high-rises of downtown.

## TALLAHASSEE (65/120) You pass a redundant

platform to your right before the train stops at Tallahassee's station. This former freight depot is one of the oldest station buildings in Florida. Florida A & M University can be seen on the hill to your right.

Tallahassee was named by Apalachee Indians from their words for town (*talwa*) and old (*ahasee*). It became Florida's capital as a compromise between the previous capitals of St Augustine and Pensacola. The 'canopy roads' at the centre of the town are cool, lush tunnels formed beneath oak trees dripping with Spanish moss.

The city is home to **Wakulla Springs**, one of the deepest natural springs in the world, where several *Tarzan* movies and *The Creature from the Black Lagoon* were made. Wildlife areas include **Falling Waters State Park** with its forests, lakes, mysterious caverns and waterfalls, and the **Apalachicola National Forest** where you may see bald eagles or even black bears. For more information about Tallahassee and the surrounding region call the **visitors bureau** (tel 850 413 9200).

**ORLANDO**

For Orlando to Jacksonville, see *The Silver Star*

Jacksonville
Lake City
Madison
Tallahassee
Chipley
Crestview
Atmore
Mobile
Pensacola
Pascagoula
Biloxi
Gulfport
Bay St Louis
NEW ORLEANS
Schriever
New Iberia
Lafayette
Lake Charles
Beaumont
HOUSTON

SAN ANTONIO
Del Rio
Sanderson
Alpine
El Paso
Deming
Lordsburg
Benson
PHOENIX
TUCSON
Yuma
Palm Springs
Ontario
Pomona
LOS ANGELES

As the *Sunset Limited* pulls out, look in the right distance for the stadium of Florida State University. The train continues through a landscape scarcely populated except for an occasional small house or village. Between here and Chipley you change from Eastern to Central Time, so watches go back an hour (forward when travelling east).

**CHIPLEY (120/70)** Named after Colonel William Chipley, responsible for building the Louisville & Nashville Railroad between Tallahassee and Pensacola in 1883. Chipley is Amtrak's nearest stop to the resort of Panama City.

The white building with a red roof to your left is Washington County's Agricultural Center. As the train continues west through the 17th century resort of De Funiak Springs look for azaleas, magnolia trees and Victorian houses.

**CRESTVIEW (70/60)** The town is situated on the Old Spanish Trail, a historic trade route between Jacksonville in Florida and El Paso, Texas. This is Amtrak's nearest stop to Fort Walton Beach and Destin on the Gulf of Mexico. Crestview's Eglin Air Force Base is one of the largest (724 square miles/1,875 km$^2$) in the world.

The *Sunset Limited* travels on across Florida's panhandle. Approaching Pensacola look left for glimpses of Escambia Bay.

**PENSACOLA (60/65)** The city's name derives from the local Pansfalaya tribe. To your left, beyond the site of an old railway station, is the Grand Pensacola hotel. This area was occupied by Spanish conquistador Don Tristan DeLuna in 1559 but his settlement was later abandoned. Fort San Carlos was built in 1698 as the region went through Spanish, French and British ownership before being ceded to the US in 1821. A US Navy base was established in 1825.

Pensacola also has splendid white beaches, historic houses and the **National Museum of Naval Aviation**. Apache leader Geronimo and some of his followers were held for several years at Fort Pickens after being brought here by train. Fort Pickens, Fort McRee and Fort Barrancas now form part of the **Gulf Islands National Seashore Park**, which stretches for 150 miles (240km) to Gulfport. This is one of the world's best fishing areas and the Barrier Islands are home to rare brown pelicans. It was the dredging of channels around the islands which inspired John Grisham's novel *The Pelican Brief*.

The train continues among fields growing watermelons, strawberries, sweet potatoes and corn. The Gulf Breeze region between Pensacola and Biloxi is famous for UFO sightings, perhaps because there are so many local military bases.

**Florida/Alabama State Line (25/40)** Look for scrub oaks, cypresses and pine trees, often half smothered by kudzu vines.

**ATMORE (65/80)** Originally called Williams Station, the town was a small supply stop on the Mobile & Great Northern Railroad. In 1880 the Louisville & Nashville Railroad took over and extended the line to Mobile. The town was renamed after Charles Pawson Atmore, chief ticket agent on the Louisville & Nashville.

To your right as you leave is Atmore's fire station, beside which is parked an old US Air Force plane. Between here and Mobile the train crosses the Alabama and Tombigbee Rivers.

**MOBILE (80/35)** Founded by the French in 1704, Mobile has become a modern industrial city. Look for the new convention centre building next to Amtrak's station. On your left is Mobile Bay, one of the largest ports in the world, where a great Civil War naval battle took place. The battleship *USS Alabama* is preserved as a memorial to those who fought in the Second World War.

As you leave, look left for Mobile's international speedway track. You can also see Fort Condé, which was once the French headquarters in Louisiana Territory.

**Alabama/Mississippi State line (25/10)** The *Sunset Limited* crosses into the Magnolia State.

**PASCAGOULA (35/24)** Industrial scenes dominate as you cross the Singing River, which can sometimes be heard making strange humming sounds. Legend says that a group of Pascagoula Indians committed suicide by walking into its waters singing because they feared being massacred by the Biloxi tribe.

Industrial buildings appear on both sides and the Ingles Shipyard is to your left. The train departs and crosses the Pascagoula River Swamp, rich in birds and animals. In the left distance you can see trees on the island of Petit Bois.

**Ocean Springs (20/4)** A white gazebo to your left marks where Ocean Springs was briefly the capital of Louisiana. The healing springs which made this area famous were known to Native Americans, who often came to drink from the water of the Great Spirit.

As you near Biloxi look left for Biloxi Bay, with Deer Island in the distance. The big white building to your left houses Mississippi's largest aquarium.

**BILOXI (24/15)** Note the interesting old train station on the left. Pierre Le Moyne d'Iberville claimed Biloxi Bay for the French in 1699 and a settlement at Fort Maurepas became the original capital of Louisiana Territory. Biloxi has existed under six flags, including that of the West Florida Republic. Some of the town's famous shrimp boats and canning factories can be seen to your left.

Also to your left as you leave are the extensive Keesler Air Force Base and Barq's root-beer plant. The train then passes Beauvoir, where Confederate President Jefferson Davis spent the last 12 years of his life.

**GULFPORT (15/28)** Founded in 1887 by William F Hardy as the terminal for his Gulf & Ship Island Railroad, this is Mississippi's largest port and the home of the **Marine Life Oceanarium**. Gulfport became a seaside resort during the 1920s when the rail line was purchased by the Illinois Central. The town's beaches and sailing waters are protected by islands, including Ship Island, which form the western end of the **Gulf Islands National Seashore Park**.

**Pass Christian (18/10)** One of the world's longest man-made beaches was built from Pass Christian to Biloxi after the Second World War. 'The Pass' also has the oldest yacht club in the south.

Approaching Bay St Louis the train crosses St Louis Bay. US 90 is to your right and the Gulf of Mexico to your left.

**BAY ST LOUIS (28/70)** This became a tourist resort after the New Orleans, Mobile & Chattanooga Railroad arrived in 1869. Look for some of the city's fine trees, including oaks, magnolias, azaleas and bald cypresses. Wonderful views can be had of the bay and Mississippi Sound from this coast's only bluff, shared by pelicans and blue herons.

The *Sunset Limited* continues through swamp country – the haunt of alligators and wild boar.

**Mississippi/Louisiana State line (25/45)** You cross into the Pelican State and ahead to your right is Lake Catherine. Lake Pontchartrain lies beyond.

A few minutes before New Orleans the city skyline appears to your left, together with Lake Borgne and a NASA space facility. Also to your left is the Rosedale Cemetery with its above-the-ground tombs. The New Orleans population was formerly plagued by yellow fever and high infant mortality, with more than 8,000 people dying in 1853 alone. Many turned to voodoo for comfort or decided to live it up, believing they might not be around tomorrow.

## NEW ORLEANS (70/70)

The 'Big Easy' features jazz, blues, Mardi Gras, voodoo and Creole cooking, and more churches per person than anywhere else in the country. Immortalised by Tennessee Williams and William Faulkner, New Orleans was founded by the French in 1718, taken over by the Spanish, then bought by the US for $15 million in 1803. Settlers from France, Spain, England, Germany and the Caribbean have given it a uniquely cosmopolitan atmosphere.

Relaxed charm and a ragged beauty make New Orleans the perfect place for letting *le bon temps* roll. Apart from Las Vegas, this is one of the few places in America without a closing time law and where you can legally buy a drink in a bar if you are under 21. Louis Armstrong and Fats Domino were born here and blues, soul and Cajun music are played in hundreds of music clubs. **Jazz venues** include Mahogany Hall at 309 Bourbon Street and Preservation Hall at 726 St Peter.

New Orleans becomes humid during summer and like Florida it has the occasional hurricane.

## New Orleans basics

**Telephone code** 504.

**Station** Amtrak shares with Greyhound the modern Union Passenger Terminal at 1001 Loyola Ave. Information: 528 1612. Ticket-office open 05.45–23.00 (Tue, Thu and Sun) and 05.45–20.00 (Mon, Wed, Fri and Sat). Waiting-room 24 hours. Metropolitan lounge. Lockers, vending machines, handcarts, restaurant, shop, taxi stand.

**Connections** Thruway buses go to Baton Rouge.

**Local transport** The RTA (tel: 827 2600) operates buses throughout the city, as well as streetcars along the Riverfront and St Charles Ave.

**Taxis** Checker; tel: 943 2411. United; tel: 522 9771.

**Car rental** Budget, 1317 Canal; tel: 467 2277.

**Greyhound** 1001 Loyola Ave; tel: 524 7571.

**Airport** Louisiana Transit (tel: 737 9611) and Airport Shuttle (tel: 592 0555) buses go to Moisant Airport at Kenner, 15 miles (24km) west of downtown.

**Tours** City and plantation tours from Gray Line (tel: 569 1401) and Dixie (tel: 522 9422). Steamboat river cruises on the *Creole Queen* (tel: 529 4567) and *Natchez* (tel: 586 8777). Free walking tours leave from Jean Lafitte Historical Park, 916 N Peters; tel: 589 2636.

**Visitors bureau** Open daily at 1520 Sugar Bowl Dr; tel: 566 5011; web: www.neworleanscvb.com.

**Accommodation** A wide range of hotels is available, from ultra-modern to historic. Call the Tourist Commission (tel: 566 5011), or contact New Orleans Bed & Breakfast, 671 Rosa Ave, Suite 208, Metairie, LA 70005; tel: 838 0071 or 1 888 240 0070; web: www.neworleansbandb.com.

YMCA, 920 St Charles Ave; tel: 568 9622. In the heart of downtown, a few minutes' walk from Amtrak's station and directly on the streetcar line to the French Quarter. Air conditioning, television, swimming pool, fitness facility and restaurant. Single $29, double $35, weekly from $175. Marquette House AYH Hostel, 2253 Carondelet; tel: 523 3014. Members $12, non-members $15. India House Hostel, 124 S Lopez; tel: 821 1904. Dormitory $12, double $30.

Hotels include the Fairmont at 123 Baronne; tel: 529 7111; Bourbon Orleans, 717 Orleans; tel: 800 521 5338; Cornstalk, 915 Royal; tel: 523 1515; Landmark French Quarter, 920 N Rampart; tel: 800 535 7862; Old World Inn, 1330 Prytania; tel: 566 1330 – single $30, double $45; LaSalle, 1113 Canal; tel: 523 5831 – single $30, double $35.

## Recommended in New Orleans

**French Quarter** The Vieux Carré (Old Square) centres on Jackson Square, where the first settlers arrived in 1718. The finely decorated wrought-iron on the houses was made in Birmingham, England. You can soak up the atmosphere best at the French Market and along Bourbon Street.

**Jackson Square** Originally the Place d'Armes, where soldiers marched and public executions took place. Later it became a park and was renamed after General Andrew

Jackson, whose statue stands opposite the cathedral. See artists, street musicians and entertainers free and have your future told by tarot cards.

**Pontalba Apartments** Constructed on two sides of Jackson Square over 100 years ago for the Baroness Micaela Pontalba, these buildings have handsome balconies and ironwork. The 1850 House at 523 St Ann (tel: 568 6968) opens Tue–Sun, admission charge.

**Louisiana State Museum** 751 Chartres; tel: 568 6968; web: http://lsm.crt.state.la.us. The museum oversees a complex of five national landmarks reflecting Louisiana's history and culture. The properties, all located in the French Quarter, are the Cabildo, Presbytère, 1850 House, Old U.S. Mint and Madame John's Legacy.

The museum also maintains the **Wedell-Williams Memorial Aviation Museum** in Patterson and the Old Courthouse in Natchitoches. Two hour walking tours through the Vieux Carré start at the 1850 House Museum Store on Jackson Square at 523 St Ann.

**Old US Mint** 400 Esplanade Ave; tel: 1 800 568 6968; web: http://lsm.crt.state.la.us/mintex.htm. This 1835 building is the only one to have served as both a Confederate and a US mint. It now houses carnival exhibits and the **New Orleans Jazz Collection**, including Louis Armstrong's first trumpet, as well as a history of coins. Closed Mon, admission charge.

**The Cabildo** 701 Chartres; tel: 568 6968; web: http://lsm.crt.state.la.us/cabex.htm. This was the site of the Louisiana Purchase Transfer and was built in 1795–99 as the seat of the Spanish city council in New Orleans. The building has also served as the Louisiana Supreme Court and became part of the Louisiana State Museum in 1911. Reopened in 1994 after being damaged by fire, the Cabildo focuses on Louisiana's early history. Closed Mon, admission charge.

**Mardi Gras** The greatest free show on earth takes place during the month before Lent, with parades, bands and every kind of revelry. Book your accommodation in good time. **Mardi Gras World** has a collection that includes thousands of carnival props and giant figures at 233 Newton; tel: 361 7821 or 1 800 362 8213; web: www.mardigrasworld.com.

**Confederate Civil War Museum** 929 Camp; tel: 523 4522; web: www.confederatemuseum.com. The second largest collection of Confederate memorabilia in the world, and the oldest continually operating museum in Louisiana, housed in Memorial Hall. The collection includes uniforms, guns, swords, photographs, paintings and 125 battle flags. Open daily, admission charge.

**Louisiana Railroad Museum** 739 3rd Street, Gretna, just across the river; tel: 283 3091; web: www.railroadmuseum.org. Located in a restored Illinois Central caboose and a former Southern Pacific freight depot near the Texas & Pacific station are 9-inch gauge steam trains and many evocative photographs. The little station was built in 1905 to replace a pre-Civil War wood structure and was the starting point of all Texas-Pacific rails going north and west of the Mississippi.

After passengers boarded in New Orleans, the cars were ferried across the river and assembled into a train in front of Gretna Station. It became redundant once a rail bridge was opened in 1935 but has been restored as a museum. Open Mon–Sat, admission charge.

# All aboard!

As the *Sunset Limited* departs after a lengthy service stop look right for the Superdome sports complex – four times larger than Houston's Astrodome. The buildings on your left belong to the *Picayune States-Item Times* and Xavier University.

**Huey P Long Bridge (20/50)** Seen ahead to your left, the bridge was named after a state governor and US senator prominent in Louisiana and national politics during the 1930s. Before the 4.4-mile (7.1km) bridge opened, trains had to cross the river on barges. The *Sunset Limited* inches carefully over the Mississippi with views of the Avondale shipyard and other industrial plants to your right. The New Orleans skyline becomes visible as the river curves away to your left, showing how the Crescent City earned its name.

The train slowly descends from the bridge and enters a bayou country of swamps, forests, mansions and Spanish moss. 'Bayou' comes from a Choctaw word meaning sluggish stretch of water. The French-born pirate and smuggler Jean Lafitte hid in this region during the early 19th century. In summer, Jean Lafitte National Park Service guides join the train between here and Lafayette.

**Harahan (30/40)** The cemetery to your right has graves above the ground to accommodate the swampy conditions.

**Mississippi River (40/30)** Look for grain loading facilities next to the river as you travel beside the levees.

**Highway 90 (45/25)** To your left is the highway which the train will accompany for 1,100 miles to El Paso. You pass an oil refinery on the right then lose sight of the Mississippi to the north.

**Des Allemands (50/20)** The name is French for 'of the Germans'. The bayou is on your right, and to your left are the first of many sugar cane fields. The land is so wet that much of this line had to be constructed on pilings.

**Bayou LaFourche (65/5)** You cross the bayou at the town of the same name.

**Bayou Blue (67/3)** The train crosses just before Schriever.

**SCHRIEVER (70/80)** An industrial town which serves as a base for off-shore oil drilling.

The *Sunset Limited* crosses Chacahoula Swamp, its graceful cypress trees decorated with Spanish moss.

**Bayou Boeuf (15/65)** To your left is more evidence of the oil industry as the McDermott plant assembles giant rigs. The pontoon helicopters service platforms in the Gulf of Mexico. A few minutes after leaving Bayou Boeuf you cross Bayou Chene.

**Morgan City (25/55)** Named after Charles Morgan, who built this section of the line when it belonged to the Louisiana & Texas Railroad. The Intercoastal Waterway to your left stretches from Brownsville, Texas, to New York, giving inland industries access to the Gulf.

**Atchafalaya River (26/54)** Over 200ft (60m) deep, the river has busy embankments on both sides.

**Garden City (40/40)** Look for a plantation house and estate to your right.

**Jeanerette (65/15)** A church and another above-the-ground cemetery (city of the dead) can be seen on the right. As the train approaches New Iberia several mansions and the towers of St Peter's Church appear to your right.

**NEW IBERIA (80/22)** Commercial activity coexists with French and Spanish heritage among the town's ante-bellum homes. Edward McIllhenny, founder of the Tabasco Sauce Company, created Avery Island as a sanctuary for egrets, herons and ibises.

Between here and Lafayette you travel through typical southern Louisiana countryside, with more mansions and sugar cane fields in evidence after you cross the Vermillion River.

**LAFAYETTE (22/80)** Henry Longfellow called these bayous, forests and flowers the Eden of Louisiana. The French-speaking locals arrived when the British took over Nova Scotia, then called Acadia, from France during the colonial wars of the 18th century, and Cajuns are their descendants.

Lafayette is 'the capital of Acadiana' and home to many oil companies, as well as the University of Southwestern Louisiana. Amtrak's stop is at 133 E Grant, where buses connect with Baton Rouge. The station building has been destroyed by fire and replaced by a small, temporary-looking structure.

**Rayne (15/65)** 'The frog capital of the world' holds jumping contests at its annual frog festival.

**Mermenteau River (40/40)** You cross the river connecting Lake Charles with the Intercoastal Waterway. Between here and the lake look for rice paddies and the flooded cages of crayfish farms.

**LAKE CHARLES (80/80)** A small, attractive brick-built station with a gabled roof stands next to the old station. Although barely 16ft (5m) above sea level the deep water port at Lake Charles ships vast quantities of oil, chemicals and cement.

**Calcasieu River (5/75)** As the *Sunset Limited* crosses the river note the duelling-pistol design on the highway bridge to your left, a reminder that pirates once operated here.

**Orange (40/40)** You cross the Sabine River and enter the Lone Star State of Texas. The landscape remains Louisiana-like for a while, with cypresses, rice fields and the odd alligator. Between Orange and El Paso the train travels for 941 miles (1,500km) across Texas.

**BEAUMONT (80/100)** The town produces many professional footballers and was the home of Mildred 'Babe' Didrikson-Zaharias. When 18 years old this remarkable athlete won six events in three hours during trials for the 1932 Los Angeles Olympics, subsequently setting two world records in the Olympics. In the 1940s and 50s she was the world's top woman golfer, winning 17 tournaments in a row.

Nearby, the Lucas Gusher began delivering 75,000 barrels of oil a day in 1901 at Spindletop Field. Port Arthur, birthplace of Janis Joplin, is five miles southeast. Look for irrigated rice fields to your right half an hour after the train leaves Beaumont.

**Trinity River (50/50)** You cross as the train approaches the small town of Liberty.

**San Jacinto River (70/30)** You cross the river (on its way to Galveston Bay) and see in the far left distance the 570ft (170m) San Jacinto Monument.

Approaching Houston the train passes Santa Fe rail yards to the left, busy with long lines of freight wagons. As the city skyline comes into view note the Allied Bank spires and the chisel-shaped towers of the Pennzoil building.

## HOUSTON (100/250)

The largest city in Texas covers more than 500 square miles (1,300km²) and is a brash, bustling place where both international banker and redneck can feel at home. Houston was founded in 1836 by New York property developers who called their creation 'Baghdad on the bayou'. The boom in oil subsequently brought prosperity and many tall buildings.

A 50-mile (80km) ship canal links 'Bayou City' to Galveston on the coast. The oil business has its ups and downs but Houston remains hot in more ways than one, sharing the same latitude as the Sahara. For most of the year the weather is subtropical, but air conditioning prevails.

### Houston basics

**Telephone code** 713.

**Station** Amtrak's insignificant station is at 902 Washington Ave, near downtown but not in a safe area. It was built by the Southern Pacific Railroad in 1959 to replace a much more attractive one. The benches in the present waiting-room were salvaged from the original station. Information: 224 1577. Ticket-office and waiting-room open 07.00–16.30 (Mon, Tue, Thu); 07.00–00.30 (Sun, Wed); 15.00–00.30 (Fri); 11.00–20.00 (Sat). Lockers, vending machines, handcarts, taxi stand.

**Connections** Thruway buses connect to Galveston and with Amtrak's station in Dallas.

**Local transport** Metro buses (tel: 635 4000) operate throughout the city and to outlying places. A large fleet of Metro trolleys provide free services downtown. Maps and schedules from 813 Dallas.

**Taxis** Yellow; tel: 236 1111. Liberty; tel: 695 6700.

**Car rental** Budget, 450 N Sam Houston Parkway E; tel: 445 3700.

**Greyhound** 2121 S Main; tel: 759 6565.

**Airport** Bush Intercontinental Airport is 25 miles (40km) north by Airport Express (tel: 523 8888). Hobby Airport (for domestic flights) is eight miles (13km) southeast.

**Tours** Gray Line; tel: 671 3250. Houston Excursions; tel: 408 0638.

**Visitors' bureau** Open weekdays at 901 Bagby; tel: 437 5200; email: houtour@ghcvb.org; web: www.houston-guide.com.

**Accommodation** Contact Angel Arbor Bed & Breakfast, 848 Heights Blvd; tel: 868 4654.

YMCA, 1600 Louisiana; tel: 659 8501. For men and women, $18. International AYH Hostel, 5302 Crawford; tel: 523 1009. Members $12, non-members $14.

For the free hotel reservations service call 1 800 964 6835. Hotels include the Westin Galleria at 5060 W Alabama; tel: 960 8100; Holiday Inn Downtown, 801 Calhoun; tel: 659 2222; Doubletree, 2001 Post Oak Blvd; tel: 961 9300; La Quinta Inn, 1625 W Loop S; tel: 355 3440; Brookhollow Hilton, 2404 North Loop West; tel: 688 7711; Grant, 8200 S Main; tel: 668 8000 – single $32, double $42.

## Recommended in Houston

**Port of Houston** Contact PO Box 2562, Houston, TX 77252; tel: 670 2400; web: www.portofhouston.com. The Houston Ship Channel has been a catalyst for growth ever since the first journey of a steamship up Buffalo Bayou in 1837. You can watch the non-stop activity in America's second largest and rather polluted port from a platform on Kirby Drive. Boat trips are available as well as free tours of the *MV Sam Houston*, for which you require reservations.

**Houston Astrodome** 8400 Kirby Dr; tel: 799 9595. Called the eighth wonder of the world when it opened in 1965, the 'Dome' was the world's first large (45,000 seats) indoor venue for a major league field sport. Open daily for tours, admission charge.

**Gulf Coast Railroad Museum** 7390 Mesa Drive; tel: 631 6612. Historic engines, passenger coaches and freight cars are on display with a visitor centre housed in a former Santa Fe baggage car. Occasional steam and diesel excursions operate. Open Sat, April–October, admission charge.

**Sam Houston Park** 1100 Bagby and Lamar; tel: 655 1912. A green space in the midst of downtown, with historic buildings such as the 1847 Kellum-Noble House (the oldest brick house in Houston) and an 1891 Lutheran Church. The Texas History Museum features items from the 16th century to the present. Open daily, free.

**Space Center Houston** 20 miles (32km) south at 1601 Nasa Road 1 off I-45 in Clear Lake; tel: 281 224 2100; web: www.spacecenter.org. Better known as the headquarters of the manned space programme, the Center has rockets, lunar vehicles, moon samples and training simulators. Film shows and tours daily. Open daily, admission charge. Take bus #246.

**San Jacinto Battleground** 20 miles (32km) southeast on TX 225; tel: 281 479 2421; web: www.tpwd.state.tx.us/park/battlesh/battlesh.htm. Sam Houston defeated General Antonio Lopez de Santa Anna here in 1836 to create an independent Texas. Great views from the 570ft/170m monument (elevator admission charge). You can also take a tour of the First and Second World War battleship *USS Texas*, commissioned in 1914. The museum is open daily, free. Admission charge to film shows.

# All aboard!

After Houston the *Sunset Limited* embarks on its longest run without a scheduled stop. The landscape changes as you begin to leave the Gulf Coast's green humidity for drier conditions. Cacti replace live oaks and Spanish moss, and there are fields of soya beans and cotton. Look also for some of this region's many birds, including flocks of delicate white egrets.

**Sugarland (50/200)** A large Imperial Sugar processing plant appears to your right just before you cross the Brazos River.

**Richmond and Rosenberg (60/190)** These towns were infamous in prohibition days for their brazen gambling and fast women. A brick courthouse stands on the right. Soon after Richmond, look right for rice elevators storing some of the local crop.

**Colorado River (110/140)** The train crosses the Texas Colorado River – no relation of its larger namesake.

**Columbus (111/139)** The dome and clock of an historic courthouse can be seen to your left. Approaching the station, look left also for the ancient live oak which was once the town's hanging tree.

**Weimar (125/125)** The old train depot on your left is now a library.

**Randolph Air Force Base (220/30)** Look for runways on your left and a mission-style tower to your right.

## SAN ANTONIO (250/185)

This modern, relaxed city is the place where tourists (including other Texans) come to unwind. Only 160 miles (250km) from the border, it has sometimes been called the northernmost town in Mexico.

Named by explorer Domingo Teran when he arrived on St Anthony's Day in 1691, San Antonio has lived under six flags. Influences are evident in the Spanish missions, Mexican ambience, fiestas and cattle stockyards – not forgetting the Alamo. April's Fiesta is a Mexican Mardi Gras featuring a river parade, rodeos and a 'night in Old San Antonio'.

## San Antonio basics

**Telephone code** 210.

**Station** Amtrak's station at 224 Hoefgen is an elegant Spanish-style building with a vaulted ceiling, colourful stained glass and an imposing black marble staircase. Information tel: 223 3226. Ticket-office and waiting-room open 22.30–18.00. Lockers, vending machines, handcarts. A major development in the station area, called Sunset Station, includes nightclubs, an outdoor dance hall and scores of shops.

**Connections** Thruway buses connect with Laredo.

**Local transport** VIA buses (tel: 362 2020) serve the metropolitan area. You can see downtown on foot or by VIA's replica 1907 Trolley; tel: 438 3846.

**Taxis** Checker; tel: 222 2151. Yellow; tel: 226 4242.

**Car rental** Budget, 430 Sandau Rd; tel: 828 8888.

**Greyhound** 500 N St Mary's; tel: 270 5824.

**San Antonio International Airport** is eight miles (13km) north by bus #2.

**Tours** Alamo (tel: 228 9776) and San Antonio City (tel: 212 5395) tour the Alamo and missions. The trolley makes a 45-minute circuit of downtown. Riverboats leave from the Paseo del Rio dock on Commerce; tel: 244 5700.

**Visitors bureau** Open daily at 317 Alamo Plaza; tel: 207 6700; email: sacvb@SanAntonioVisit.com; web: www.SanAntonioVisit.com.

**Accommodation** Contact Contact Joske House Bed & Breakfast, 241 King William; tel: 271 0706. AYH Hostel, 621 Pierce; tel: 223 9426. Members $14, non-members $16. Take bus #11.

Hotels include Riverwalk Inn, 329 Old Guilbeau; tel: 212 8300; Menger, 204 Alamo Pl; tel: 223 4361; Rodeway Inn Downtown, 900 N Main; tel: 223 2951; Seven Oaks, 1400 Austin Hwy; tel: 824 5371 – single $70, double $75; Westpoint Inn, 2434 S W Loop; tel: 673 7490 – single $30, double $45; Navarro, 116 Navarro; tel: 223 8453 – single $28, double $32; Traveler's, 220 N Broadway; tel: 226 4381 – single $20, double $30.

## Recommended in San Antonio

**Paseo Del Rio** 554 Soledad; web: thesanantonioriverwalk.com. A two-mile (3.2km) downtown walk through parkland beside canals and the meandering river, with music, bars, floating restaurants, boat rides and a cosmopolitan parade of people. At twilight, fireflies and lanterns glow while cicadas hum among the pecan trees and palms.

**The Alamo** 300 Alamo Plaza; tel: 225 1391; web: www.thealamo.org. Mission San Antonio de Valero (The Alamo) is one of the city's oldest buildings and the most visited attraction in Texas. In 1836, 189 defenders (including Davy Crockett and Jim Bowie) died fighting General Santa Anna's overwhelming forces after a 13-day siege which came to symbolise the Texan battle for independence.

The cool rectangular chapel is set among subtropical gardens surrounded by high stone walls. Museum and guided tours by the doughty Daughters of the Republic of Texas, who rescued the mission from dereliction in 1905 and have looked after it ever since. Open daily, donation.

**King William District** These imposing Victorian houses on the southern edge of downtown were built for German merchants. The Steves Homestead, built in 1876, is at 509 King William (tel: 227 9160) and open daily, admission charge. The Guenther House at 205 E Guenther was built for the founder of Pioneer Flour Mills and is open daily, free.

**Spanish Governor's Palace** 105 Plaza De Armas; 224 0601. 'The most beautiful building in San Antonio' once housed officials of the Spanish Province of Texas. It was completed in 1749 and features period furnishings, a cobblestone patio and a fountain. Open daily, admission charge.

**Botanical Gardens** 555 Funston Place; 207 3255; web: www.sabot.org. A miniature representation of the Texas landscape, from Hill Country wild flowers to formal rose gardens. Includes an exhibition hall, tropical house, desert house, palm house, fern room and orangery. Open daily, admission.

**Tower of the Americas** 600 HemisFair Park; tel 207 8615. This 750 ft tower, built for the HemisFair in 1968, symbolises progress made by Western civilisations. Glass-walled elevators take you over 500ft to the restaurant and observation level for panoramic views of the city and surrounding area. Open daily, admission charge.

**Texas Transportation Museum** 11731 Wetmore Road, McAllister Park; tel: 490 3554; web: www.txtransportationmuseum.org. Featuring locomotives, rolling stock, a Southern Pacific station and a model railroad. Steam train rides operate on the first Sunday in each month. Open Thursday and weekends, admission charge.

**The Missions** Apart from the Alamo, four others can be seen on the Mission Trail starting at S Alamo and Market; tel: 534 8833; web: www.nps.gov/saan. All missions are open daily, free. The **visitor centre** (tel: 932 1001) is next to Mission San José and has a free film showing early life at the mission.

Mission Concepción, 807 Mission Rd; tel: 534 1540. The oldest unrestored mission, dating from 1731, still has original frescoes.

Mission San José, Roosevelt Ave and Mission; tel: 932 1001. Largest and most impressive, with a church, granary and aqueduct. *Mariachi* mass on Sundays. The 'Queen of the Missions' also has impressive carvings and the famous Rose Window.

Mission San Juan, 9107 Graf; tel: 534 0749. Quiet, with a pretty bell tower and guided nature trail.

Mission San Francisco de la Espada, 10040 Espada; tel: 627 2021. The dam and aqueduct built in the 1730s between this remote mission and Mission San José are still in working order.

# All aboard!

The *Sunset Limited*, accompanied by through cars of the *Texas Eagle*, continues from San Antonio into prairie country. Cactus plants, sage and yuccas thrive in these arid conditions as the train descends from the Anacacho Mountains to the Rio Grande Valley. Native Americans used the spiked leaves of yucca plants to make shoes and baskets.

**Laughlin Air Force Base (175/10)** The base can be seen away to your left across the flatlands.

**DEL RIO (185/160)** The Queen City of the Rio Grande, otherwise known as 'the wool and mohair capital of the world', Del Rio is famous for sheep, goats and the Val Verde winery (oldest in Texas). Immediately to the south is the Mexican town of Ciudad Acuna, visible on bluffs across the river.

The train is joined on the left by the Rio Grande, the 'big river' separating the United States from Mexico.

**Amistad Reservoir (15/145)** *Amistad* is Spanish for friendship, and the reservoir was a joint project between the US and Mexican governments. About 30 miles long and 20 miles wide (48km by 32km), it dams the Rio Grande near its junction with the Devil River.

As the *Sunset Limited* climbs 3,500ft/1,000m over the next 200 miles (320km) watch for prickly pear cacti, more yuccas and the woolly grandpa's beard. Between April and June prickly pears produce bright magenta flowers. Persimmons, mesquite and greasewood (the creosote bush) also grow here.

**Pecos River (50/110)** The train crosses a dramatic river canyon on the state's highest railroad bridge (321ft/98m tall and 1,390ft/420m long).

**Eagle Rock Canyon (70/90)** In 1883 the last spike was driven nearby to complete the nation's second transcontinental railway. Look for strange rock formations jutting from the canyon wall.

**Langtry (71/89)** Where 'Judge' Roy Bean ran the saloon and dispensed his version of justice west of the Pecos. Reverence for the actress Lily Langtry caused him to change the town's name from Vinegaroon.

**Dryden (140/20)** Look for parts of a wall that was built to keep out Pancho Villa's raiders.

**SANDERSON (160/100)** Roy Bean owned another saloon here when the town had a wild and woolly reputation, and outlaws and rustlers mingled with cattle ranchers and sheep men. Amtrak's station at 201 Downey is a flag stop.

The train leaves with the ruined brick walls of Sanderson's Wool Commission to your right. Wool remains an important industry, but sheep and goat ranching become impractical further west because of predators such as coyotes, pumas, bobcats and eagles. An Apache cave and cooking mound can be seen away to your right.

**Haymond (60/40)** The former cow camp is now a ghost town, with its cemetery and deserted buildings on your right.

**Warwick Flat (65/35)** A crossing place on the Comanche War Trail, which ran for 1,000 miles (1,600km) from upper Texas to Chihuahua. As the train travels among the Glass and Del Norte Mountains look for deer, pronghorn antelope, jackrabbits and javalina (wild pigs). Mount Ord (6,814ft/2,075m) is to your left and Altveda Mountain (6,860ft/2,090m) on your right.

Approaching Alpine you see the town's rodeo grounds to your right. The letters SR engraved on a hill signify Sul Ross University.

**ALPINE (100/220)** Capital of Texas's largest county, Brewster, with Mitre Peak (6,100ft/1,860m) on your right. The Spanish-style station at 101 W Holland is used by tourists visiting **Big Bend National Park**.

The *Sunset Limited* continues through colourful canyon lands to Paisano Pass, the highest point (5,074ft/1,550m) on this journey. Chinati Peak (7,730ft/2,350m) is ahead to your left.

**Marfa Ghost Lights (20/200)** For many years mysterious lights have appeared among the Chinati Mountains and across the desert to your left. The lights were even seen by pioneers on wagon trains during the 1840s.

**Marfa (25/195)** The domed, stone building to your right is a Presidio County courthouse dating from 1886. The adobe walls of a Second World War POW camp can be seen to your left. Also on your left, a few minutes west of Marfa, is the wooden windmill that was used as a location in the James Dean film, *Giant*.

**Valentine (60/160)** Bear Mountain and Mount Livermore (8,332ft/2,540m) are to your right. As the train descends further from the high plains, fields begin to appear and Van Horn is ahead in the right distance.

**Quitman Mountains (90/130)** You change from Central to Mountain Time, so watches go back an hour (forward when travelling east). For the first time in 24 hours the train parts company with Highway 90, which continues further north.

**Hot Wells (100/120)** A ruined adobe school appears on the right and the Eagle Mountains to your left.

**Sierra Blanca (120/100)** Look for the last adobe courthouse still functioning in Texas. The Sierra Blanca Peak (6,970ft/2,070m), located among mountains to your right, looks lighter because it contains soapstone.

**Fort Hancock (150/70)** The fort's remains are to your right. Beyond them can be seen the Finlay Mountains.

As the train approaches Fabens look right for cheerful decorations displayed on the graves in a Mexican cemetery.

**Fabens (180/40)** A splendid mission-style church stands on the left next to a cotton gin.

**Ysleta (190/30)** Texas's longest-surviving ethnic group, the Tigua Indians, live in Ysleta, which has the second-oldest (1682) church in the country.

The train travels through industrial scenes towards El Paso, with oil and copper refineries on both sides. The building to your left, shaped like a shell, is the civic auditorium.

**EL PASO (220/85)** Encircled by the mile-high (1,600m) Franklin Mountains, this laid-back city was named after a pass (El Paso del Rio del Norte) formed by the Rio Grande. Nearby are **Carlsbad Canyon National Park**, Las Cruces and Cloudcroft ski resort. Amtrak's renovated station at 700 San Francisco dates from 1904–05 and was designed by Daniel Burnham, the architect for Washington's Union Station. The **tourist bureau** is at 1 Civic Center Pl; tel: 915 534 0600 or 1 800 351 6024; web www.elpasocvb.com.

El Paso maintains close links with Ciudad Juarez in Chihuahua, Mexico, seen above palisades to your left as the train departs. To your right are the campus and stadium of the University of Texas. On top of the Sierra de Cristo Rey ahead to your left is a 33ft (10m) statue of the crucifixion known as the Christ of the Rockies. Pilgrims climb four miles to the 4,576ft (1,390m) summit to celebrate the Feast of Cristo Rey at this meeting place of Texas, Mexico and New Mexico.

**Rio Grande (5/80)** A cement plant appears to your right and a mineral refinery to your left before the train crosses the river and enters New Mexico.

**Sunland Park (7/78)** The race track is on your right.

**US/Mexico Border (10/75)** A white post 30ft (10m) to the left of the tracks indicates the border line. The mountains on both sides are the Portillos. It was just to the north of here that the infamous Lincoln County cattle wars were fought in 1881, resulting in the shooting of Billy the Kid by Pat Garrett at Mesilla.

In 1916 this barren land witnessed the passage of Pancho Villa's marauders on their way to attack the town of Columbus and provoke a brief US–Mexico conflict.

**Florida Mountains (75/10)** Florida Peak is prominent close by to your left. A hole in the ridge at 7,300ft (2,200m) is known as the Window Peak. On your right the Cooke's Peak Range rises to 8,408ft (2,560m). The train crosses the Mimbres River near Deming, with the clock tower of Luna County courthouse to your left.

**DEMING (85/50)** Deming is the venue each August of the world's only duck races. Over 70,000 irrigated acres (28,000ha) nearby produce wine, peanuts, pecans, beans, cotton and grain sorghum. A mild climate among the Cooke's and Florida Mountains makes this a popular retirement town. Similar secluded resorts can be found further north near Silver City, where Billy the Kid grew up. Amtrak's station in Deming is at 301 E Railroad Ave, close to Rock Hound State Park.

**Continental Divide (25/25)** The lowest elevation (4,587ft/1,400m) for any rail crossing of America's divide, where water falling to the west flows into the Pacific and to the east into the Atlantic.

**LORDSBURG (50/110)** Lordsburg began as a railroad town in a hollow between the Burro and Pyramid Mountains. The US Government bought this land from Mexico in 1854 to enable the rail line to be built to California.

On your right soon after Lordsburg you pass a dry lake where mirages transform the sand into sheets of water.

**Steins (20/90)** The final battle between Apache chief Cochise and the US Army took place here.

**New Mexico/Arizona State Line (25/85)** Arizona does not observe Daylight Saving Time, so watches go back an hour (forward when travelling east) only between April and October.

**Cochise's Face (35/75)** On a ridge of the tawny Chiricahua Mountains rising 9,795ft (2,985m) to your left is the commanding outline of Cochise, gazing at the sky. The Peloncillo Mountains away to your right are rich in gold, silver and copper.

**Dos Cabezas (60/50)** Look in the Sulphur Hills to your left for this 'two heads' rock formation, named after Cochise and the Indian agent Thomas Jeffords.

**Wilcox (65/45)** From this altitude of 4,167ft (1,270m) the *Sunset Limited* will descend 3,000ft (900m).

**Wilcox Playa (70/40)** A dry lake creates convincing mirages, even reflecting the mountains to your left.

**Dragoon (95/15)** During wars with the US Army between 1861 and 1872, Cochise and the Chiricahuas occupied the Dragoon Mountains to your left. The train crosses the San Pedro River.

**BENSON (110/55)** Formerly a stop on the Butterfield stage-coach run from St Louis to San Francisco, a 2,800-mile (4,500km) journey which took 55 days. When the railway came in 1880 Benson developed as a shipping point for mines around Tombstone, 25 miles (40km) to the south.

The *Sunset Limited* leaves past the Rincon Mountains on the right and travels through a series of canyons down the Pantano Wash. The buildings away to your right, 15 minutes from Benson, were a TV film set for *Little House on the Prairie*.

East and westbound trains proceed on different lines for part of the way between Benson and Tucson, allowing the eastbound *Sunset Limited* an easier climb. Tracks are sometimes half a mile (0.8km) apart.

**Durant Castle (25/30)** Look for this large house situated high up on your right.

**Vail (27/28)** You travel the higher of two overlapping bridges – eastbound trains use the one below – and catch sight of the train ahead as you continue down into the rose-coloured Texas Canyon.

**Santa Rita Shrine (37/18)** A pink Catholic church is surrounded by desert to your right.

**Davis Monthan Air Force Base (47/8)** Thousands of planes stand mothballed in the aircraft 'boneyard' to your right, preserved by dry desert air. Beside the track is the **Pima Air Museum** featuring Second World War bombers.

As the train nears Tucson it enters the rail yards of the Santa Fe Pacific (formerly the Southern Pacific).

**University of Arizona (50/5)** Look for the stadium and campus to your right. Low down on the southern horizon is the Santa Rita Range.

## TUCSON (55/60)

The city began in 1776 as a supply station for the Mission San Xavier del Bac, located on the banks of the Santa Cruz River. The city today is a centre for farming, government and high-tech industry. It was capital of Arizona from 1867 to 1877 and Spanish, Mexican and Confederate flags have flown here at various times.

Tucson is 60 miles (96km) from the Mexican border and surrounded by mountains – the Santa Ritas to the south, Santa Catalinas to the north, Rincons in the east and Tucsons to the west. Being a thousand feet (300m) higher than Phoenix, temperatures are slightly cooler.

### Tucson basics

**Telephone code** 520.

**Station** The mission-style station is at 400 E Toole. Information: 623 4442. Ticket-office and waiting-room open 06.15–13.45 and 15.45–23.15 (Sat–Mon); 06.15–13.45 (Tue, Wed); 15.45–23.15 (Thu, Fri).

**Connections** Thruway buses connect with Phoenix.

**Local transport** Sun Tran operates buses and the 4th Ave trolley; tel: 623 4301.

**Taxis** Yellow; tel: 624 6611. Arizona Stagecoach; tel: 889 9681.

**Car rental** Budget, 401 E Orange; tel: 742 6171.

**Greyhound** 2 S 4th Ave; tel: 892 3475.
**Tucson International Airport** is six miles (10km) south by bus #16.
**Tours** Gray Line; tel: 622 8881. Lost Souls visits haunted downtown Tucson; tel: 795 1117.
**Visitors bureau** Open daily at 100 S Church Ave; tel: 624 1817; email: visitorinfo@mtcvb.com; web: www.visittucson.org.
**Accommodation** Contact Cactus Quail Bed & Breakfast, 14000 N Dust Devil Drive, Tucson, AZ 85739; tel:825 6767. Congress Hostel, 311 E Congress; tel: 622 8848. Members $12, non-members $15. Single rooms $35, double $40.

Hotels include the Doubletree Reid Park at 445 S Alvernon Way; tel: 881 4200; Continental Inn, 750 W 22nd; tel: 624 4455; Big House, 629 N 7th Ave; tel: 623 1907; Motel 6, 1031 E Benson Hwy; tel: 628 1264; Franciscan Inn, 1165 N Stone Ave; tel: 622 7763; Desert Inn, I-10 at Congress; tel: 624 8151 – single $25, double $35.

## Recommended in Tucson

**Presidio Historic Park** 1 Burruel; tel: 398 2252; web: www.pr.state.az.us/parkhtml/tubac.html. Tucson became a walled city (or presidio) when the Spanish built a barrier against Native Americans. Many places are within walking distance of the station, including the Pima County courthouse which preserves a small part of the wall. It also has a mosaic-tiled dome and a courtyard fountain. El Tiradito (the wishing shrine) makes dreams come true for believers who light a candle.
**Arizona State Museum** 1013 E University Blvd; tel:621 6302; web: www.statemuseum.arizona.edu. The oldest and largest anthropological museum in the Southwest features the history of the American Southwest and northern Mexico. Combines prehistoric, historic and contemporary items with high-tech displays. Open daily, donation.
**Arizona Historical Society Museum** 151 S Granada Ave; tel 622 0956; web: http://w3.arizona.edu/~azhist/general.htm. Featuring Spanish and Native American exhibits, a replica copper mine, vintage cars and a stage-coach. Open daily, donation.
**Saguaro National Monument** 3693 S Old Spanish Trail; tel: 733 5153; web: www.nps.gov/sagu. Located in two sections, east and west of the city; tel: 733 5100. The eastern section has older and taller stands of the giant saguaro cactus, which can live for 200 years and only grows in two states. White saguaro blossom, the state flower, appears in May and June. Open daily, admission charge.
**Mission San Xavier del Bac** Nine miles (15km) southwest of Tucson at 1950 W San Xavier Road; tel: 294 2624. Father Kino arrived in 1692 and built a church two miles (3km) to the north. This mission, the most elaborate and beautiful in America, was completed a hundred years later. Sometimes called 'The White Dove of the Desert', the mission is located on the Tohono O'dham Indian Reservation, where you can also sample Indian fry bread. Open daily, donation.
**Pima Air and Space Museum** 6000 E Valencia Road; tel: 574 0462; web: www.pimaair.org. Five hangars contain 250 military, civilian and commercial aircraft, including a replica Wright Brothers *Flyer*. Experience simulated space flights and a full motion simulator. Walking and tram tours. Open daily, admission charge.

**Tombstone** 65 miles (105km) southeast on Route 80. The **Old Courthouse State Historic Park** is at 219 Toughnut; tel: 457 3311; web: www.pr.state.az.us/parkhtml/tombstone.html. 'The town too tough to die' began as a mining settlement and was the scene of the 1881 OK Corral shootout between Wyatt Earp, 'Doc' Holliday and the Clantons. Tombstone is quieter now but looks little different from when it was 'the next best thing to hell on earth'. Big Nose Kate's saloon, the church, Boot Hill cemetery and the Epitaph building are intact, and the OK Corral appears much as it did on the day of the gunfight. The **Tourist Association** is at 9 S 5th; tel: 888 457 3929.

## PHOENIX

The *Sunset Limited* does not currently stop in Phoenix but Thruway buses connect the city with Amtrak's Tucson station in about two hours.

Arizona's capital sprawls over 393 square miles (1,020km²), surrounded by impressive mountains. The original settlement was made on the ruined villages of Anasazi and Mogollon Indians, who lived here from before the time of Christ until the 15th century and used irrigation to tame the desert. The Anasazi grew maize, made fine art pottery and constructed sophisticated architecture but their civilisation was mysteriously destroyed. Settlers prophesied that a city would rise again like the legendary phoenix bird. Roosevelt Dam, 75 miles (112km) to the north, harnessed the Salt River in 1911 and helped fulfil the prophecy.

Phoenix boasts the highest (560ft/171m) water fountain in the world. The city has 300 days of sunshine a year and only seven inches (17cm) of rain, with summer temperatures sometimes up to 120°F (49°C).

### Phoenix basics

**Telephone code** 602.

**Connections** Thruway buses still use the renovated station at 401 W Harrison, not a safe area at night. Information tel: 253 0121. Lockers, taxi stand.

**Local transport** Metro buses operate from the City Bus Terminal; tel: 253 5000.

**Taxis** Yellow; tel: 252 5252. Ace; tel: 254 1999.

**Car rental** Rent-a-Wreck, 1202 S 24th; tel: 254 1000.

**Greyhound** 2115 E Buckeye Rd; tel: 389 4200.

**Sky Harbor International Airport** is four miles (6.5km) southeast by bus #13.

**Tours** Gray Line; tel: 495 9100. The Capitol walking tour includes the Capitol Museum and Confederate Monument; tel: 255 3618. Desert excursions from Arizona Awareness; tel: 947 7852.

**Visitors bureau** Open weekdays at 50 N Second; tel: 254 6500; web: www.phoenixcvb.com.

**Accommodation** For Bed & breakfast contact Maricopa Manor, 15 W Pasadena Ave, Phoenix, Arizona 85013; tel: 274 6302 or 1 800 292 6403.

AYH Youth Hostel, 1026 N 9th; tel: 254 9803. Dormitory rooms $12, non-members $15. YMCA, 350 N 1st Ave; tel: 253 6181. Single $20, weekly $80.

Hotels often have low rate specials during summer, if you can take the heat. They include the Executive Park at 1100 N Central Ave; tel: 252 2100; Ramada Inn, 401 N

1st; tel: 258 3411; Crescent, 2620 Dunlop Ave; tel: 943 8200; San Carlos, 202 North Central Ave; tel: 253 4121; Hyatt Regency, 122 North Second; tel: 252 1234.

## Recommended in Phoenix

**Heritage Square** 6th and Monroe; tel: 262 5071. Restored 19th century houses give an idea how old Phoenix looked. The 1895 Rosson House opens Wed–Sat, admission charge.

**Encanto Park** An oasis in the middle of the city at 15th Ave and Encanto, featuring a lake, nature trails and a swimming pool. Open daily.

**Desert Botanical Garden** 1201 N Galvin Pkwy in Papago Park; tel: 941 1225; web: www.dbg.org. The garden is an important conservation institution with 169 rare, threatened or endangered plant species from the world's deserts, especially the southwestern US and northern Mexico. Over 1,350 varieties of cactus are among the 20,000 plants located in 145 acres, five miles east of downtown. Open daily, admission charge. Take bus #3.

**Phoenix Art Museum** Located on the northeast corner of McDowell Road and Central Ave; tel: 307 2020; web: www.phxart.org. The largest visual arts museum between Denver and Los Angeles features 14,000 exhibits, including art from Asia, the Americas and Europe to 1900, along with contemporary works. Closed Monday, admission charge.

**Heard Museum** 2301 N Central Ave; tel: 252 8840; web: www.heard.org. One of the best places to experience the cultures and art of Native Americans of the southwest. Ten galleries and outdoor courtyards feature traditional and contemporary Native American art. Open daily, admission charge. Free tours.

**Phoenix Zoo** Near the Botanical Garden; tel: 273 1341; web: www.phoenixzoo.org. A thousand species of birds and animals live here, including rare Arabian oryx. Open daily, admission charge.

**Arizona Railway Museum** 399 N. Delaware in Chandler, 20 miles (32km) southeast; tel: 480 821 1108; web: www.siege.net/~arm/index.html. Located in a building resembling a train depot, the museum tells the history of southwestern railways. Open weekends from Labor Day to Memorial Day, donation.

**Verde Canyon Railroad** North of Phoenix at 300 N Broadway in Clarkdale; tel: 1 800 293 7245; web: www.verdecanyonrr.com. A 20-mile (32km) round-trip takes you to the ghost town depot at Perkinsville over a line built in 1911 for the United Verde Copper Company. You travel through North Verde River Canyon and the Sycamore Wilderness area, which can only be visited by train. You cross the SOB Canyon on a 175ft-high (50m) trestle then go through a 680ft/200m tunnel blasted with 20,000 pounds (9,000kg) of dynamite.

Parts of *How The West Was Won* were filmed among the canyon's Sinagua ruins and abandoned gold mines. You can see cacti, wild flowers, bald eagles, javalinas, blue herons and deer, as well as sometimes beavers, mountain lions and black bears. The line was formerly operated by the Santa Fe, Prescott & Phoenix Railroad, which hauled freight until 1988. Open Wed–Sun, plus Mon in peak season, admission charge.

# All aboard!

To your right as the *Sunset Limited* pulls out of Tucson are the Santa Catalina Mountains, including Mount Lemmon (9,157ft/2,790m). The train begins a journey of more than four hours to Yuma, although a stop is planned for Maricopa.

**Pima Air Park (30/210)** The base on your left refurbishes jets for sale around the world. The Little Owl Head Mountains are to your left and the Tortolita Range directly ahead. In this fertile country you see fields of cotton, pecans, cabbage and broccoli.

**Picacho Pass (40/200)** Picacho Peak (3,382ft/1,030m) is to your left and the Picacho Range to your right.

Look for stands of candelabra-like saguaro cactus on both sides of the track for the next few miles as desert predominates. A saguaro can grow to 50ft/15m and store 2,000 gallons (9,100 litres) of water. Look also for the portly barrel cactus, prickly pears, tangling chollas and the spindly ocotillo shrub. The latter acquired its name (Spanish for 'little torch') because of the bright red flowers it sprouts after winter rain.

**Maricopa (60/180)** Nearby Superstition Mountains were sacred to the Apache thunder god and a search for Apache gold has been going on here ever since. Hundreds of miners and their guards were massacred in the 1860s after being sent to look for the treasure by a Mexican cattle rancher. The Lost Dutchman mine, believed to be located somewhere in the canyons to your right, was never found again after its German prospector was shot trying to return to his find. An Apache girl reputedly had her tongue cut out for showing him the gold.

Amtrak is building a new station in Maricopa to serve Phoenix, 25 miles to the north, as well as the surrounding area. An old round tail observation car is being brought from Los Angeles Union Station to serve as a ticket office and waiting room.

As the *Sunset Limited* continues across the Sonoran Desert, home of the gila monster lizard, look for distant rocks eroded into natural sculptures. The flat rectangular ones are known as mesas. Others have been carved into recognisable figures, such as a praying monk and a weeping Apache.

**YUMA (240/135)** A resort set in farmland which is irrigated from the Colorado River. The former Yuma Prison is now a state park.

**Colorado River (20/115)** Crossing the river takes you from Arizona into California. Since Arizona does not observe Daylight Saving Time, watches go back an hour (forward when travelling east) only from October to April.

**Indio (110/25)** 'The date capital of the world' hosts a date festival each February.

**PALM SPRINGS (135/75)** Half of Palm Springs is owned by the Cahuilla tribe, who were given a vast area of desert by the US Government in return for the right to build a railroad. The Cahuillas thought they already owned the land, which subsequently became some of the world's most exclusive real estate and made them America's richest Native Americans.

**Colton (65/10)** The train crosses the Santa Ana River, with the San Gabriel Mountains to your right.

**ONTARIO (75/10)** Look left for the international airport.

**POMONA (10/45)** Named after the Roman goddess of fruit, although residential development has mostly replaced orchards and vineyards. Singer Tom Waits was born in the back of a taxi just outside the hospital here in 1949. Los Angeles County Fair, held in September, attracts more people than any other similar event in the country. Amtrak uses the Southern Pacific station at 156 W Commercial.

The train leaves with St Joseph's Church to your left and St Paul's mission-style church on the right, next to the California Polytechnic.

**San Gabriel River (15/30)** You cross this often dried out river bed.

**El Monte Airport (17/28)** The airport to your right was named after nearby Mount Wilson (5,700ft/1,730m).

The train crosses the concrete-lined Rio Hondo then enters a short tunnel to Temple City, dramatically emerging along the centre strip of the San Bernadino Freeway.

**California State University (33/12)** The campus is to your right as you part company with the freeway.

**LA County Hospital (37/8)** Look right for the hospital's tall buildings. On your left is the concrete channel of the Los Angeles River, with Dodger Stadium visible ahead on a hill. The *Sunset Limited* crosses the river then passes the Post Office building's twin domes and the tower of City Hall on the right. LA's county jail is to your left just before the station.

## LOS ANGELES
For Los Angeles city information, see *The Coast Starlight* (pages 71–4).

# The *Texas Eagle* Chicago–San Antonio
## (for San Francisco)

## General route information

From Lake Michigan to the Alamo, the *Texas Eagle* makes a 1,308-mile (2,100km) journey down the centre of America, travelling through Lincoln land then crossing the Mississippi before continuing through the Ozarks to Arkansas and Texas. Pine forest and lakes north of Dallas give way to cattle country as you approach San Antonio, where through coaches to Los Angeles join the *Sunset Limited*. The *Texas Eagle* is Amtrak's fastest growing train, with growth in ridership increasing faster than on any other long-distance route.
**Frequency** Daily.

The southbound *Texas Eagle* leaves Chicago mid-afternoon to reach St Louis by mid-evening and Little Rock early next morning. You arrive in Dallas early in the afternoon and San Antonio by late evening. On Tuesday, Thursday and Saturday, coaches continue to Los Angeles by joining the *Sunset Limited* (see page 144).

Travelling north, trains leave San Antonio early in the morning to reach Dallas by late afternoon and Little Rock during the night. You arrive in St Louis early next morning and Chicago by mid-afternoon. On Sunday, Wednesday and Friday, coaches leave from Los Angeles with the *Sunset Limited* to join the *Texas Eagle* in San Antonio.
**Reservations** All reserved.
**Equipment** Superliner coaches.
**Sleeping** Superliner bedrooms.
**Food** Complete meals, snacks, sandwiches, drinks.
**Lounge car** Movies, games, hospitality hour. National Park Service guide in summer.
**Baggage** Check-in service available at main cities.

## Joining the train
### CHICAGO
For Chicago city information, see the *California Zephyr* (pages 75–9). On the first part of its journey as far as St Louis, the *Texas Eagle* uses tracks belonging to the Illinois Central Gulf Railroad (ICG), travelling initially through industrial suburbs.

# All aboard!

Look back for fine views of the city as you cross the Chicago River, which provided French explorers with a passage from Lake Michigan almost as far as the Mississippi River. A few minutes out of Union Station the *Texas Eagle* crosses the Chicago Sanitary Ship Canal, a waterway which reverses the Chicago River's flow. The canal forms part of an inland system which runs 30 miles (48km) from Chicago to Lockport, linking the Great Lakes with the Mississippi.

**Bridgeport (15/30)** First settled by Irish immigrants who built the Illinois & Michigan (I & M) Canal, Bridgeport was the home of Chicago's influential former mayor, Richard J Daley.

**Willow Springs (30/15)** Look left for deer hiding in a wooded enclave.

**Lambert (32/13)** The train crosses the Calumet Sag Channel joining Lake Michigan with the Sanitary Ship Canal. You then continue to Joliet through the urban park land of the I & M National Corridor.

**Lockport (38/7)** Restored buildings can be seen to your right as the *Texas Eagle* accompanies a towpath.

**Illinois State Prison (41/4)** Joliet's notorious correctional centre is to your right.

**JOLIET (45/35)** Named after the 17th century French-Canadian explorer Louis Jolliet, this manufacturing town has busy rail and water connections, including four riverboat casinos. Amtrak's station is at 50 E Jefferson.

You continue with the Des Plaines River and conservation area to your right, next to the I & M Canal. To your left is a limestone quarry and a US Army arsenal where munitions are stored underground.

**Kankakee River (15/20)** The train crosses this tributary of the Illinois River.

**Braidwood (20/15)** The tall towers on your left are part of a Con-Edison nuclear energy plant.

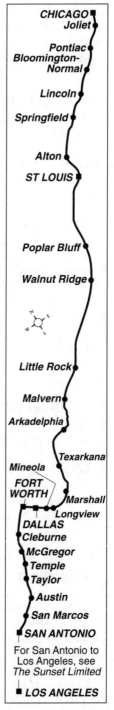

CHICAGO
Joliet
Pontiac
Bloomington-
Normal
Lincoln
Springfield
Alton
ST LOUIS
Poplar Bluff
Walnut Ridge
Little Rock
Malvern
Arkadelphia
Texarkana
Mineola
FORT
WORTH
Marshall
Longview
DALLAS
Cleburne
McGregor
Temple
Taylor
Austin
San Marcos
SAN ANTONIO
For San Antonio to
Los Angeles, see
*The Sunset Limited*
LOS ANGELES

**Dwight (35/17)** In 1860 the then Prince of Wales attended Dwight's small, white pioneer Gothic church. The station to your right dates from 1892. Beyond it is a brick building with a clock – the only one of three banks designed by Frank Lloyd Wright still in existence. An impressive windmill can be seen to the left before the train crosses the Vermillion River.

**PONTIAC (17/30)** The town was named after a Native American chief of the 18th century. Part of the original Route 66 was constructed right next to the tracks here.

**Normal (25/5)** Illinois Normal School was a teacher's college which became the State University. Dormitories and other campus buildings appear to your right.

**BLOOMINGTON-NORMAL (30/33)** Abraham Lincoln delivered his final speech here on his way to becoming president in 1860. This was the birthplace of Adlai Stevenson and George Pullman also lived here. Pullman's luxury Pioneer car proved too wide for some railroads until Mrs Lincoln used one following her husband's assassination in 1865. Alterations were made so that his body could be transported across country to Springfield. The journey took two weeks in order to let the nation pay its respects along the route. A reconstruction of the Washington *Night Flyer* train of 1861 can be seen in a Dick Powell film called *The Tall Target*, where Lincoln is saved from assassination by 'John Kennedy' during a fraught journey.

**Funk's Grove (8/25)** Illinois' only tract of virgin timber, mostly maple, was donated to the state by Eugene Funk of Funk Seeds. Just before Lincoln you cross Kickapoo Creek.

**LINCOLN (33/30)** The only town named after Lincoln before he became president, and he christened it in 1853 using melon juice. A 'slice of watermelon' statue stands to the left of the station. Also to your left is the domed Logan County courthouse where Lincoln practised law.

The *Texas Eagle* crosses the Sangamon River near Springfield, with the Illinois Fairgrounds to your right.

**SPRINGFIELD (30/40)** Lincoln spent 25 years in Springfield before becoming president. You can visit the only house he ever owned, the place where he was married and the grave in which he and his family are buried. He made his farewell address on leaving town in 1861 at a rail depot a short distance from the present station and gave his 'house divided' speech at the Old State Capitol. The present Capitol and Supreme Court can be seen to your right.

Amtrak's station is at Washington and 3rd and the **visitors bureau** at 109 N 7th; tel: 217 789 2360; web: www.springfield.il.us.

**Lake Springfield (10/30)** The *Texas Eagle* crosses the western tip of the lake.

**Carlinville (40/30)** The spired Macoupin County courthouse on your left dates from when Carlinville hoped to become the state capital. When Standard Oil operated local coal mines the company's workers lived in Sears, Roebuck houses which arrived in sections by train. The mines are closed but some of the prefabricated houses remain.

**Macoupin Creek (5/25)** The *Texas Eagle* crosses at Beaver Dam State Park.

**ALTON (30/40)** Birthplace of Miles Davis. This Mississippi River port's newspaper editor, Elijah Lovejoy, was lynched in 1838 by a mob opposing his anti-slavery views. The town later became a supply point for the Union Army.

Unseen to your right as you cross the Wood River is Lewis and Clark State Park, where the Missouri and Mississippi Rivers meet. Lewis and Clark's expedition wintered here before beginning their explorations west.

**Cahokia Diversion Canal (10/30)** Levees on both sides try to prevent flooding when the Mississippi rises. During the summer of 1993 the worst floods in history brought chaos to this region, covering 16,000 square miles (41,000km$^2$) of crops in eight states and killing at least 40 people.

The Native American city of Cahokia stretched across 2,200 acres here and was inhabited from around 700 to 1400AD. The inhabitants, known as Mississippians, had a culture based on cosmology and built sacred ritual mounds as large as Egypt's Great Pyramid. It is thought that deforestation caused devastating floods which ruined crops and made the population flee their 'Native American Jerusalem'.

**Lenox (11/29)** The train travels next to tracks which run between St Louis and Detroit and were used by the celebrated *Wabash Cannonball* train.

**Granite City (14/26)** Steel and other heavy industries accumulate as you approach St Louis. The *Texas Eagle* leaves the ICG, changing to tracks belonging to the Terminal Railroad Association (TRRA).

**Mississippi River (22/18)** You cross high above the river on the Merchants Railroad bridge, leaving Illinois for Missouri. Look for barges on the river and the St Louis skyline to your left.

**Eads Bridge (30/10)** The train passes beneath the city's oldest bridge, which had the longest steel spans anywhere when it was completed in 1874.

**Gateway Arch (35/5)** The landmark to your right is America's tallest (630ft/192m) monument, with a cathedral at its base. Old riverboats can be seen moored on your left.

**Busch Memorial Stadium (38/2)** The St Louis Cardinals' baseball ground is to your right.

## ST LOUIS (40/240)

This gateway to the west was founded by Pierre Laclede in 1764 on high ground where the Mississippi River joins the Missouri. Named after King Louis IX of France, St Louis was acquired by President Jefferson as part of the 1803 Louisiana Purchase. The original fur-trading post became a place for wagon trains to gather before heading west, so the massive 630ft stainless steel Gateway Arch designed by Eero Saarinen makes an appropriate symbol.

Scott Joplin invented ragtime when he lived here and W C Handy's *St Louis Blues*, the most recorded song of all time, also helped put the city on the music map. Jazz musicians came by riverboat and train from New Orleans to join blues artists from the Mississippi delta to create new musical styles. Their influence can still be heard in the many live music clubs and bars.

### St Louis basics

**Telephone code** 314.

**Station** Amtrak's modern station at 550 S 16th replaces the famous old Union Station. **Information** tel: 331 3300. Ticket-office open 06.00–20.00, 20.30–01.00 and 03.30–04.30. Lockers, vending machines, taxi stand.

**Local transport** Bi-State Transit (tel: 231 2345) operates buses, with free travel on the Levee Line between Union Station and the river.

**Taxis** Yellow; tel: 991 1200.

**Car rental** Enterprise, 29 Hunter Ave; tel: 863 0110 or 800 227 9449.

**Greyhound** 1450 N 13th; tel: 231 4485.

**Lambert-St Louis International Airport** is 14 miles (22km) northwest by Greyhound or bus #104.

**Tours Gray** Line/Vandalia; tel: 800 542 4287. During summer you can take the downtown St Louis Tram tour. Open-air cars pause at the major attractions and a pass permits unlimited stops. The *Tom Sawyer* and *Becky Thatcher* offer cruises on the river; tel: 621 4040.

**Visitors bureau** Open daily at 308 Washington Ave; tel: 421 1023 or 800 325 7962; email: visitorinfo@explorestlouis.com; web: www.st-louis-cvc.com.

**Accommodation** Contact Central West End Bed & Breakfast, 4045 Washington Blvd, St Louis, MO 63108; tel: 535 7900 or 866 535 7900. Huckleberry Finn AYH Hostel, 1904 S 12th; tel: 241 0076. Members $15. Take bus #73.

Hotels include Best Western, 4630 Lindell Blvd; tel: 367 7500; Marriott Pavilion, 1 Broadway; tel: 421 1776; Best Western St Louisian, 1133 Washington Ave; tel: 421 4727; Comfort Inn, 3730 S Lindbergh Blvd; tel: 1 800 228 5150; Quality Inn, 7350 Hanley Rd; tel: 1 800 228 5151.

### Recommended in St Louis

**City Museum** 701 N 15th; tel: 231 2489; web: www.citymuseum.org. Located in a factory built in 1909 for the International Shoe Company, the museum features history, science and architecture. Includes working glass studio, a giant fish tank and Art City – where artists can be seen at work. Open Wed–Sun, admission charge.

**National Museum of Transportation** 3015 Barrett Station Road; tel: 965 7998; web: www.museumoftransport.org. America's greatest collection of railway engines and equipment, including 70 locomotives, plus streetcars, buses and aircraft. Open daily, admission charge.

**Union Station** 18th and Market; tel: 421 6655. Opened in 1894, this splendid building with its great clock tower was once the world's largest and busiest train station. Now a National Historic Landmark, the station has been transformed into a shopping mall and entertainment venue with paddle boats, a Ferris wheel and a carousel.

**Museum of Westward Expansion** Next to the Gateway Arch, 702 N 1st; tel: 982 1410. The museum depicts wagon trains and pioneer life, with clothing, tools, weapons, household goods and personal items. The Saarinen Arch's observation deck (twice the height of the Statue of Liberty) gives unbeatable views of the city. Open daily. Museum free, admission charge to the observation deck.

**Laclede's Landing** On the riverfront, between the Eads and Martin Luther King Bridges; tel: 241 5860. This historic district stands next to the site of Pierre Laclede's original encampment. Dozens of shops and restaurants line 19th century cobblestone streets decorated with cast-iron lamps.

**Cupples House** 221 N Grand Blvd; tel: 977 3025; web: www.slu.edu/the_arts/cupples. This restored Romanesque mansion dates from 1888 and has 42 rooms, wooden floors, 22 fireplaces, gargoyles and elegant stone carvings, as well as an art gallery. Closed Sun, admission charge.

**Missouri History Museum** In the Jefferson Memorial Building, Forest Park; tel: 746 4599; web: www.mohistory.org. Missouri Historical Society displays include Charles Lindbergh's flight suit and items from the 1904 World's Fair. Open daily, admission charge.

**Scott Joplin State House** 2658 Delmar Blvd; tel: 340 5790. Dating from just after the Civil War, this was the home of the composer Scott Joplin in the early 1900s. Open daily, admission charge.

**Anheuser-Busch Brewery** 1127 Pestalozzi; tel: 577 2626; web: www.budweisertours.com. Tour the world's largest brewery, admire the Clydesdale horses and sample a free beer. Open daily, free. Take bus #40.

# All aboard!

The *Texas Eagle* departs on the Missouri Pacific section of the Union Pacific Railroad for a run of almost four hours through Mark Twain country to Poplar Bluff.

**Mississippi River (30/210)** The shipyard to your left constructs boats for use on the river.

**Jefferson Barracks (35/205)** Chief Blackhawk of the Sac Indians was imprisoned at this 18th century military post.

**Pevely (70/170)** The *Texas Eagle* parts company with the Mississippi River.

**Big River (120/120)** You cross to the north of Ironton in an area that has some of the world's largest lead and iron ore mines.

**POPLAR BLUFF (240/50)** Winner of the 'all American city' award, Poplar Bluff is a manufacturing centre located among farmland. Amtrak is at 400 S Main. Nearby are the Ozark Mountains and Wappapello Lake.

**Missouri/Arkansas State Line (20/30)** You cross into the smallest state west of the Mississippi.

**WALNUT RIDGE (50/106)** Close by are Lake Charles State Park and one of Arkansas's first settlements, Old Davidsonville. Walnut Ridge is Amtrak's nearest stop to Jonesboro.

**Newport (26/80)** Newport prospered after the Cairo & Fulton Railroad arrived. At neighbouring Jacksonport, Confederate troops massed beside the White River during the Civil War.

**Arkansas River (105/1)** You cross the river dividing North Little Rock from Little Rock then see the Capitol dome and city skyline to your left.

**LITTLE ROCK (80/45)** French explorers called this La Petite Roche but Arkansas's biggest city has been the state capital since 1821. Until Governor Bill Clinton ran for President, Little Rock was best known for its strict 1950s' segregationism.

The present Capitol is a smaller version of the one in Washington, DC. An older, Greek-style **state house** at 300 W Markham features Arkansas history and a display in honour of President Clinton. Little Rock is dominated by the TCBY tower (named after The Country's Best Yogurt) and hosts the annual autumn State Fair. Amtrak's depot is at Union Station Square and the **visitors bureau** at 615 E Capitol Ave; tel: 501 370 3290 or 1 877 220 2568; web: www.littlerock.com.

The *Texas Eagle* leaves with the Capitol again to your left. The train eases through suburbs before entering hillier country covered with forests of pine and hardwood.

**Benton (30/15)** Most of America's aluminium comes from the local bauxite mines. You cross the Saline River soon after leaving Benton.

**MALVERN (45/21)** The original town of Rockport, located on the Ouachita River, transferred here and changed its name to Malvern Station. Amtrak's stop at 200 E 1st also serves **Hot Springs National Park**, established in 1832. The Hot Springs **visitors bureau** can be found at can be found at 134 Convention Blvd; tel: 1 800 543 2284 or 501 321 2277; web: www.hotsprings.org.

**Ouachita River (20/1)** You cross the river, with Arkadelphia to your right.

**ARKADELPHIA (21/80)** The former steamboat landing stage is famed for its colleges and aluminium plants. A few minutes before reaching Prescott the *Texas Eagle* crosses the Little Missouri River.

**Prescott (25/55)** Note the red-roofed station on your right. To the west is the 'Trail of Tears' travelled by Cherokee Indians. Forced by the US Army to move to Oklahoma reservations, a quarter of the Cherokee nation died from inadequate food and clothing in the winter of 1838.

**Hope (40/40)** Look right for an old brick kiln chimney. 'The watermelon capital of the world' claims the all-time record (265lbs/120kg) and was the birthplace of Bill Clinton. Richard Ford, author of *Independence Day*, lived here while working on the Louisiana-Pacific Railroad.

Between Hope and the Red River you can see boisdarc trees, often with enormous green seed pods. Their exceptionally hard wood was used for horse-drawn farm implements.

**Red River Valley (55/25)** You cross the river on its way south, eventually to join the Mississippi. The valley's red earth washes into the water and gives the river its name. Soya beans and grain grow on land which once raised cotton.

**Homan (65/15)** Pecan trees on both sides of the track prove this really is the south.

**Texarkana Airport (70/10)** Runways and buildings appear to your left.

**TEXARKANA (80/75)** When the train stops, its front end is in Texas while the rear remains in Arkansas. Texarkana's unique position calls for two mayors and two police departments, and the post office is the only Federal building to straddle a state line. Texarkana was the birthplace of one-time presidential candidate Henry Ross Perot, whose medals are displayed at the local Boy Scout Center. Amtrak's station is at 100 E Front.

The *Texas Eagle* departs on Texas & Pacific tracks associated with the Missouri Pacific, travelling south along the Texas border.

**Sulphur River (20/55)** Look left for a paper mill as you cross.

**Atlanta (30/45)** Prehistoric Native American settlements have been found nearby.

**Jefferson (50/25)** One of the state's earliest ports, where an old cemetery can be seen on the right.

**MARSHALL (75/25)** Travelling south, the *Texas Eagle* no longer stops in Marshall or Longview. Instead the train goes from Texarkana to Mineola by way of Big Sandy and Gilmer, the first time passenger trains have stopped there since the 1950s. Passengers for Marshall or Longview can disembark at Gilmer and continue the journey by bus. This change has been brought about by conflicting freight schedules on the Union Pacific tracks.

Marshall was the birthplace of Lady Bird Johnson. When Texas seceded from the Union in 1861 this became one of its largest cities, making ammunition and saddles for the Confederate Army. After the fall of Vicksburg, Marshall became the Missouri governor's capital. Shreveport, Louisiana, is 25 miles (40km) to the west. The fine Texas & Pacific depot museum and station have lately been renovated.

**LONGVIEW (25/45)** The *Texas Eagle* stops in Longview and Marshall only when travelling north. Longview is the home of the Schlitz brewery, which produces four million barrels of beer a year. Amtrak Thruway buses connect with Houston and the casinos at Boissier City and Shreveport.

**Gladwater (20/25)** Located in the middle of east Texas oil country, where the industry has expanded since the first major discovery of 1931. Production fields can be seen on both sides of the track and a Texaco refinery is to your left.

**MINEOLA (45/95)** The train's route follows the Sabine River for the next 50 miles (80km) through country famous for beef cattle and quarter-horses.

**Big Sandy (10/85)** Garner Ted Armstrong's Ambassador College is bounded by white-fenced fields on your right.

**Grand Saline (20/75)** Named after the 700ft/210m-deep salt mine seen to your left.

**Mesquite (45/50)** A large building to your left houses the Mesquite Rodeo. Thorny mesquite scrub trees are a common sight throughout the southwest. As the Dallas skyline appears to your right, look for the Texas Fairgrounds' Ferris wheel in the distance.

## DALLAS (95/65)

The train halts opposite the Hyatt Hotel, mesmerised by its reflection in the glass façade familiar from TV's *Dallas*. 'The city that should never have been' had few natural resources and no proper transport links until the railway arrived. Founded as a log cabin trading post in 1841, it became a utopian colony of artists and scientists.

Today's Dallas specialises in banking, oil and transport. The city has more shops, Cadillacs and divorces than anywhere else, as well as the world's largest computer centre. Neighbouring Fort Worth is more relaxed.

## Dallas basics

**Telephone code** 214.

**Station** Union Station at 400 S Houston is a splendid renovated building decorated with white marble. Information tel: 653 1101. Ticket-office and waiting-room open 09.30–19.00. Lockers, vending machines, newspapers, handcarts, restaurant, shops, information centre, taxi stand. A walkway leads to the Hyatt Regency Hotel and Reunion Tower.

**Connections** Thruway buses link with Abilene, Big Spring and Odessa.

**Local transport** Dallas is primarily designed for cars but DART commuter rail, light rail and bus services (tel: 979 1111) operate downtown and to the suburbs. The McKinney Ave heritage streetcar operates daily; tel: 855 0006.

**Taxis** Yellow; tel: 426 6262 and Terminal; tel: 350 4590.

**Car rental** All-State, 3206 Live Oak; tel: 741 3118.

**Greyhound** S Lamar; tel: 655 7082.

**Dallas/Fort Worth Airport** (larger than Manhattan) is 16 miles (25km) west, with bus connections to both downtown areas. Take the Super Shuttle from 729 E Dallas Rd; tel: 817 329 2000.

**Tours** Kaleidoscope; tel: 522 5930. Gray Line (tel: 972 263 0294) has tours around Dallas, Fort Worth and to the Southfork Ranch.

**Visitors bureau** Open weekdays at 100 South Houston; tel: 571 1301; web: www.dallascvb.com.

**Accommodation** Contact Southern House Bed & Breakfast, 2625 Thomas Ave; tel: 720 0845; web: www.southernhouse.com.

Downtown YMCA, 601 N Akard; tel: 954 0500.

Hotels include the Hyatt Regency at 300 Reunion Blvd; tel: 651 1234; Stoneleigh, 2827 Maple Ave; tel: 871 7111; Colony Park, 6060 N Central Expressway; tel: 750 6060; Holiday Inn-Downtown, 1015 Elm; tel: 747 9951; Holiday Inn, 10650 N Park Pl; tel: 373 6000; Park Cities Inn, 6101 Hillcrest Ave; tel: 521 0330.

## Recommended in Dallas

**Reunion Tower** 300 Reunion Blvd; tel: 651 1234. The best views of Dallas are from the observation deck of this 50-storey building next to Union Station. Spectacular light displays from the high geodesic dome after dark. Open daily, admission charge.

**Old City Park** 1717 Gano; tel: 421 5141. Historic buildings relocated from the surrounding area include a blacksmith's shop, general store, railway depot, church and pre-Civil War mansion. Closed Mon, admission charge.

**State Fair Park** Two miles east of downtown on 1st and Grand Ave; tel: 421 9600. Art deco Texas Centennial buildings date from 1936. The park has been the site of the annual Texas State Fair since 1887 and has symphony concerts, opera, roller-coaster rides and eight museums.

**Age of Steam Railroad Museum** Located in State Fair Park; tel: 428 0101. Features locomotives, passenger cars, freight wagons and Dallas's oldest train station. Open Thursday to Friday and weekends (daily during October's State Fair), admission charge.

**Museum of Natural History** Also in State Fair Park, at 3535 Grand Ave; tel: 421 3466; web: www.dallasdino.org. Authentic environments have been recreated, with the first mounted Texas dinosaur and a chance to handle some of the exhibits. Open daily, admission charge. Free Mon morning.

**South Fork Ranch** About half an hour's drive north of Dallas at 3700 Hogge Drive, Parker; tel: 972 442 7800; web: www.southfork.com. Tour the ranch where TV's *Dallas* was filmed and see the gun that shot JR Ewing. Lucy's flamboyant wedding dress is among the other memorabilia. Guided tours. Open daily, admission charge.

**World Aquarium** 1801 N Griffin; tel: 720 2224; web: www.dwazoo.com. Wander safely through a jungle filled with rare plants, monkeys, toucans, crocodiles, jaguars and piranhas. The aquarium features a 22,000 gallon walk-through tunnel with views of giant catfish, cichlids, huge turtles, stingrays and sea dragons. Open daily, admission charge.

**Dallas Zoo** 650 South R L Thornton Frwy; tel: 670 5656; web: www.dallas-zoo.org. View more than 1,400 animals from a monorail train as you travel through the wilds of Africa. Open daily, admission charge.

**The Sixth Floor Museum at Dealey Plaza** 411 Elm; tel: 747 6660; web: www.jfk.org. The old Texas School Book Depository now contains a museum which recreates the southeast window area as it looked on November 22 1963 when President John F Kennedy was assassinated. The museum uses films, photographs, radio broadcasts and reconstructions to tell the story, including numerous conspiracy theories. Dramatic views of Dealey Plaza and tours. Open daily, admission charge.

# All aboard!

You leave Dallas with Dealey Plaza to your right. President Kennedy was shot here and the familiar scene still provokes a shiver. The train goes over the overpass that JFK's motorcade sped under after he was shot.

The *Texas Eagle* crosses the Trinity River with the massive white Texas Stadium to your right.

**Grand Prairie (25/40)** Dallas naval air station and the Ling-Tempco-Vought aircraft factory are on your left.

**Arlington (35/30)** Part of the University of Texas can be seen to your right, with Six Flags Over Texas amusement park in the distance.

**Handley (45/20)** Look left for the man-made Arlington Lake. Lee Harvey Oswald, John Kennedy's alleged assassin, was buried in Rose Hill Cemetery to your right.

**FORT WORTH (65/40)** The sister city of Dallas became a shipping point for cattle when citizens financed a 26-mile (42km) link to the Texas & Pacific Railroad in 1876. After this line opened, cattle no longer had to be driven north to Kansas. Fort Worth has acquired other industries since but an old cowtown flavour still persists. Amtrak's modest station is at 1501 Jones and the **visitors bureau** is at 415 Throckmorton; tel: 800 433 5747 or 817 336 8791; web: www.fortworth.com.

The **Tarantula** steam train operates from Wednesday to Saturday over the **Fort Worth & Western Railroad**, going through the centre of town with excellent views of the skyline as it crosses the Trinity River on massive trestles. The Tarantula also follows part of the Chisholm Trail between 2318 Eighth Ave and 140 E Exchange Ave in the stockyards, the largest train station in the southwest. For information tel: 817 625 RAIL; web: http://www.tarantulatrain.com

The *Texas Eagle* goes south from Fort Worth on a Santa Fe line towards the small towns and villages of Texas hill country. This area has an exciting history of Comanche raids and cattle drives.

**CLEBURNE (40/60)** The town was named after Confederate General Pat Cleburne in 1867, having previously been known as Camp Henderson. Cleburne deals in agricultural crops and livestock, especially longhorn cattle.

**Balcones Fault (15/45)** Limestone hills suddenly rise out of the prairie as the train follows this fault line to San Antonio.

**Brazos River (17/43)** After crossing the Noland River you cross the Brazos, which runs to your left into Lake Whitney (15,000 acres/6,000ha of water created by a dam).

**Meridian (28/32)** Watch for Angora goats being raised for their mohair. Look also for fields of cotton, still a commonplace sight in the south.

**Bosque River (30/30)** You cross the river then accompany it for the next 30 miles (48km).

**Clifton (40/20)** Founded by Swedish and Norwegian settlers. To your right is one of the region's many limestone quarries.

**Middle Bosque River (55/5)** The *Texas Eagle* crosses the river shortly before Crawford.

**McGREGOR (60/32)** Amtrak's stop for McGregor's bigger neighbour Waco, 20 miles (32km) to the east. David Koresh and his henchmen allegedly shot dozens of Branch Davidian cult members in 1993 during a siege by federal agents at nearby Mount Carmel. Many members died as fire swept through their ranch.

**Moody (10/22)** A small town which boasts a very large (2,200ft/670m) TV antenna.

**TEMPLE (32/55)** The Gulf, Colorado & Santa Fe Railroad connects with the Missouri, Kansas & Texas here, making this a key junction. The town was named after a Santa Fe surveyor in 1880 and the **Temple Depot** has vintage furniture and equipment, including a working telegraph machine (tel: 817 778 6873). Amtrak's station is at 315 W Ave B. Close by are Fort Hood and Killeen.

The *Texas Eagle* continues on the M-K-T line through ranch land and tree-covered hills.

**Little River (25/30)** You cross the river near the town of the same name.

**San Gabriel River (40/15)** As you cross look right for pecan trees growing on the river's banks.

**TAYLOR (55/42)** A rail town which ships much of the prairie's ranch and farm produce. The *Texas Eagle* changes from M-K-T tracks back to the Union Pacific.

**Round Rock (22/20)** A residential town for many who commute to Austin.

**Camp Mabry (35/7)** The US Army base can be seen to your right.

**AUSTIN (42/40)** Capital of Texas and a former capital of the Texas Republic, Austin was founded in 1839 on hills beside the Colorado River. The 1991 film *Slacker* was set among Texas University at Austin's 49,000 students. The city is also home to the Lyndon Johnson Library and the Harry Ransom Center, where among nine million manuscripts are three versions of *Lady Chatterley's Lover*.

This being Texas, the Capitol building is seven feet taller than the one in Washington, DC. Amtrak's station is at 250 N Lamar Blvd, and **tourist centers** can be found in the Capitol and at 201 E 2nd; tel: 1 800 926 2282; web: www.austintexas.org.

**Colorado River (2/38)** Look back to your left as you cross for views of Austin's skyline, dominated by the Capitol's ornate pink dome.

**Aquarina Springs (37/3)** The clear springs to your right are the source of the San Marcos River, which you cross as you enter San Marcos.

**SAN MARCOS (40/85)** Home of Southwest Texas State University, alma mater of Lyndon Johnson, the town hosts an annual cooking contest for chilli aficionados. The train crosses the Guadalupe River.

**New Braunfels (20/65)** This town was founded in 1845 by a German prince called Carl von Solms-Braunfels.

**San Antonio International (50/35)** The airport can be seen to your right.

**Olmos Park (52/33)** The train travels through the middle of a golf course with Trinity University away to your left.

As San Antonio comes into view on the left look for the InterFirst building, the 750ft/225m Tower of the Americas and the green-roofed Tower Life building (San Antonio's oldest skyscraper).

**King William District (75/10)** Victorian houses appear to your left beyond the Pioneer flour mill.

**Lone Star Brewery (78/7)** The brewery museum is seen on your right just before you cross the San Antonio River.

## SAN ANTONIO

For San Antonio city information and through travel on Thursday, Friday, Saturday and Monday to Los Angeles, see *The Sunset Limited* (pages 155–67).

# The *City of New Orleans*
# Chicago–New Orleans

## General route information

The *City of New Orleans* train divides the United States neatly into two as it travels more than 900 miles (1,450km) from the Great Lakes to the Gulf of Mexico. Between Chicago and New Orleans are prairies, farms, plantations and the Mississippi basin where Civil War history was made. You also visit Memphis, birthplace of the blues and rock and roll.

A previous daytime train on this route was the Illinois Central's *Panama Limited*, so called because hundreds of construction workers came this way to build the Panama Canal. Amtrak changed the name after Arlo Guthrie's song became popular.

**Frequency** Daily.

The southbound service leaves Chicago mid-evening to reach Memphis early next morning and New Orleans by mid-afternoon.

Travelling north, the train leaves New Orleans mid-afternoon to reach Memphis by late evening and Chicago by early morning.

**Reservations** All reserved.

**Equipment** Superliner coaches.

**Sleeping** Superliner bedrooms.

**Food** Complete meals, snacks, sandwiches, drinks.

**Lounge car** Movies, games, hospitality hour. A National Park Service guide provides commentary along part of the route.

**Baggage** Check-in service available at main stations.

## Joining the train

### CHICAGO
For Chicago city information, see the *California Zephyr* (pages 75–9).

## All aboard!

The *City of New Orleans* leaves Union Station then reverses for a few minutes before continuing forward with the city's skyline to your left. After crossing the Chicago River look left for Soldier Field and a view of Lake Michigan.

**Chicago State University (20/25)** Campus buildings appear on your right just before you cross the Calumet River.

**HOMEWOOD (45/30)** A leafy suburb served by the Metra/IC commuter rail line, with its neat red-tiled station building seen to your right.

You continue through several more attractive suburbs interspersed with stretches of farmland.

**KANKAKEE (30/65)** The town stands next to the Kankakee River. Chicago's best known architect, Frank Lloyd Wright, once lived here and many of the houses feature elaborate stonework, domes and spires.

You travel on through an increasingly rural landscape. Look for farmhouses and gently rolling fields of mostly cotton and soya beans.

**Gilman (20/45)** An agriculture and railroad town which used to be a scheduled stop for *City of New Orleans* trains travelling north.

**Rantoul (45/20)** Originally known as Neipswah, an Illiniwek Indian word for 'where the minks are'. This used to be a scheduled stop for *City of New Orleans* trains.

**Chanute Field (47/18)** The large US Air Force training base has an aviation museum.

**CHAMPAIGN-URBANA (65/35)** Champaign is a commercial and manufacturing centre and the inspiration for an obscure Bob Dylan song. Less industrial Urbana has been home to the University of Illinois since 1867. Amtrak's station is at 116 N Chestnut.

**MATTOON (35/22)** Another manufacturing town set among Illinois farm country. Lincoln Log Cabin State Park is close by and Eastern Illinois University 12 miles (19km) east at Charleston.

The train continues among more fields, trees, farmhouses and barns.

**EFFINGHAM (22/45)** Grain elevators and industrial scenes dominate both sides of the track.

**Little Wabash River (8/37)** You cross this tributary of the Ohio.

**CENTRALIA (45/50)** Amtrak's station is at 100 E Broadway. Founded by the Illinois Central Gulf Railroad in 1854, Centralia's busy yards are among this region's most impressive.

**CARBONDALE (50/105)** Home of Southern Illinois University, Carbondale is in the Shawnee Hills region. The town acquired its name as the centre of a coal mining area. Amtrak's station is at 401 South Illinois, where Thruway buses connect for passengers coming to join the train from Kansas City via St Louis. Nearby Crab Orchard wildlife refuge is a sanctuary for wintering birds such as Canada geese.

**Cairo (60/45)** 'Little Egypt' stands where the Mississippi and Ohio Rivers meet at the borders of three states – Illinois, Missouri and Kentucky. General Grant occupied this commanding position during the Civil War. Before that the Illinois Central line ended in Cairo and passengers had to continue their journey to New Orleans by Mississippi steamboat. One of the river pilots then was Samuel Clemens, later to become known as Mark Twain.

**Illinois/Kentucky State Line (62/43)** You cross the border southeast of Cairo by crossing the Ohio River.

**FULTON (105/50)** The city stands directly beside Fulton, Tennessee. Huge south and central American banana cargoes used to be distributed by refrigerated rail car from this 'banana crossroads of the USA'.

**Kentucky/Tennessee State Line (2/48)** The *City of New Orleans* crosses into the Volunteer State just south of Fulton.

**NEWBERN-DYERSBURG (50/90)** Named after William Dyer, a colonel in the War of 1812, Dyersburg processes cotton and other farm produce. It was once one of Tennessee's largest ports.

After travelling most of the way from Chicago in darkness the train nears Memphis around dawn. As you travel beside the Mississippi River look right for the shiny 32-storey Great American Pyramid which connects to Festival Island.

On your left is Confederate Park and beyond that the old Cotton Row market. Immediately before the station, look left to see the Beale Street district.

## MEMPHIS (90/120)

The train trundles through a nondescript part of the city before making a service stop at Amtrak's Main Street station. Set on bluffs overlooking the Mississippi, Memphis was named by Andrew Jackson in 1819 after the capital of ancient Egypt. It soon became a port and the largest city in Tennessee, with the world's biggest mule-trading market.

Memphis's railroads and a strategic position on the river made it an ideal supply base during the Civil War. The Memphis to Charleston Railroad was taken over by Union forces after victories at Fort Pillow and Shiloh. In 1862, eight Confederate steamers were sunk here within an hour on the Mississippi River.

The city remains a major port but hardwoods, soya and other agricultural products have replaced cotton as the chief cargo. Memphis was recently officially named by *American Heritage* magazine as a 'Great American Place', only the second US destination to be given this award. The **visitors bureau** is at 119 N Riverside Drive; tel: 901 543 5333; web:www.memphistravel.com.

A free shuttle bus service runs every hour between Graceland, the Sun Studios and Beale Street. **Tours** can be had from Blues City (tel: 901 522 9229) and riverboat cruises from *Memphis Queen* (tel: 901 527 5694). The room and balcony where Martin Luther King was killed at the Lorraine Motel in 1968 are kept as a memorial.

Blues and Dixieland jazz feature in the handsomely restored Victorian **Beale Street** buildings (web: www.bealestreet.com) of WC Handy's home town, which was also the birthplace of Stax Records. Elvis Presley, Roy Orbison, Johnny Cash, the Everly Brothers, Dolly Parton and many others made their earliest recordings at Sam Phillips' **Sun Records** studio, a brownstone building preserved in its original state at 706 Union Avenue; tel: 901 521 0664; web: www.sunstudio.com.

**Graceland**, where 'The King' died in August 1977, is 10 miles to the south at 3734 Elvis Presley Blvd; tel: 901 332 3322 or 1 800 238 2000; web: www.elvis.com.

This is the country's second most visited residence (after the White House). Go early and avoid a grilling wait in summer humidity for a tour of the mansion's surprisingly modest rooms, admire Elvis's 1955 pink Cadillac and put flowers beside his bronze gravestone.

The **Peabody Hotel**, where Tom Cruise made *The Firm*, has been restored to its original ornate splendour at 149 Union Ave; tel: 901 529 4000. Live ducks fed on strawberries and lettuce leaves are paraded from their rooftop home each day to splash in the lobby's marble fountain.

The train pulls out of Memphis among freight and storage facilities then travels through wooded, undulating country. Between here and New Orleans you mostly accompany the route of Interstate 55.

After 25 minutes the Mississippi River appears again to your right beyond a line of trees as the train enters delta country – a flat land of cotton fields, woods and small towns with dirt roads and Baptist churches. It was here that early blues singers such as Charley Patton and Robert Johnson played and made their first recordings. Others later took the train and their music north to Chicago.

You pass through Marks, a likely future stop for this train, and North Money. Extensive cotton fields can be seen on both sides. As you approach Greenwood look left to see a lake and church among the trees.

**GREENWOOD (120/55)** The *City of New Orleans* holds up traffic as it pauses across the town's main street. Amtrak's neat brick station is to your right, with the town beyond.

You leave past a decaying railway building to your left then pass modern houses before seeing more cotton fields, processing plants and mansions. The train moves deeper into the south, passing small towns with white clapboard churches. There are houses with verandas, dusty roads, abandoned shacks and muddy, meandering rivers lined with trees. Woods and green fields start to predominate as you near Yazoo City.

**YAZOO CITY (55/60)** Note the impressive church to your left and an abandoned station building to your right.

The train departs through attractive forest and crosses several narrow, almost dry streams. You see cypress trees, sleepy towns and sun-bleached barns. Look also for log stacks being sprayed with water to keep them cool.

One of America's most famous train wrecks occurred just east of here on a rainy night in April 1900. The *Cannonball Express*, speeding to make up time between Memphis and Canton, ploughed into the back of a stationary freight train at Vaughan. The train's headstrong engineer, John Luther 'Casey' Jones, died on board *No. 382* but his skill saved others' lives. A friend of his wrote the well-known song and sold it for a case of gin. Vaughan's depot has a museum in Casey Jones' honour.

**JACKSON (60/28)** Named after Andrew Jackson, Mississippi's capital and largest city began as a trading post beside the Pearl River and had to survive being burned down during the Civil War. You can tour the gold-domed Capitol and Greek-style Governor's Mansion. Amtrak's station is at 300 W Capitol and the **visitors bureau** at 921 N President; tel: 601 960 1891; web: www.visitjackson.com.

As you depart, look left for the old 1840 Capitol (now a history museum) and the Arts Center Planetarium.

**Crystal Springs (24/4)** 'The tomato capital of the world' is famed for its bumper crops. This is also a well known turkey hunting area.

**HAZLEHURST (28/19)** Named after George Hazlehurst, who was chief engineer for the railroad. Lumber and other freight wagons gather to your left with the station and town to your right.

You leave among pine forests, massive lumber yards and processing plants. As well as timber, this region produces pine oil and turpentine.

**Wesson (13/6)** The preserved Old Wesson Hotel on your left once had a casino where passengers could while away their time and money between trains.

**BROOKHAVEN (19/22)** A recruiting town during the Civil War, Brookhaven deals in oil, timber and farm produce. The red brick and tile station seen among magnolias to your right is Amtrak's nearest stop to **Natchez**, home of 'King Cotton'. Natchez is considered the prettiest town on the Mississippi, with many of its ante-bellum homes furnished in authentic style. Visitors are escorted around by brisk society matrons during the Natchez Pilgrimage (four weeks in March/April, three weeks in October).

You leave Brookhaven among the town's older residential suburbs, with the Bogue Chitto River to your left.

**McCOMB (22/50)** Named after Colonel Henry McComb, who took charge of rebuilding the New Orleans, Jackson & Great Northern Railroad after the Civil War. The town's camellias and azaleas are especially fine during spring. Illinois Central freight yards appear to your left as the train travels past lines of wagons loaded with logs.

**Magnolia (10/40)** Named after the state's official flower, the giant magnolia. Look right for colonial mansions hiding among the trees.

**Tangipahoa River (12/38)** You cross the river, which continues to your left.

**Mississippi/Louisiana State Line (20/30)** The border is crossed just south of the small town of Osyka. You travel among beautiful ranches and pine trees, with modest houses fronted by porches and rocking chairs.

**Kentwood (27/23)** Look left soon after Kentwood for the Camp Moore cemetery and museum. The camp was a training ground for Confederate troops during the Civil War.

**Amite (36/14)** New Orleans-type ironwork decorates some of the houses. This area, known as the Florida Parishes, belonged to Florida until 1810. Strawberry plantations appear on both sides until the train approaches Hammond through thick forest.

**Independence (45/5)** On your right are Southeastern Louisiana College and an above-the-ground cemetery, or 'city of the dead'.

**HAMMOND (50/60)** 'The strawberry capital of the world', from where vast quantities of fruit used to be sent by train to Chicago and New York. The pointed roof of Amtrak's station can be seen to your right. Hammond's **Railroad Museum** has steam engines, rolling stock and a well-preserved depot.

You depart past warehouses, a flea market and freight cars loaded with wood chippings. Note the rusting Illinois Central caboose to your left just before Ponchatoula.

**Ponchatoula (6/54)** A *Louisiana Express* locomotive stands on the left at a picturesque station building. You pass three large greenhouses and, a few minutes later, enter Cajun country. In this eerily beautiful land of forests, swamps and water hyacinths, egrets fly among the evergreen live-oaks and cypress trees are draped with Spanish moss. During earlier days, trains sometimes had to stop for the engineer to remove an occasional alligator sunning itself on the rails.

**Interstate 55 (7/53)** The highway to your right strides across the wet wilderness on two arched bridges supported by concrete pillars. Look right also for water lilies among the reeds, rushes and trees. You may spot alligators and such exotic birds as pelicans, black herons and egrets.

The *City of New Orleans* curves left around an oceanic Lake Pontchartrain, the state's largest expanse of water, as the train travels the longest continuous railway curve in the world.

**Pass-Manchac (10/50)** You cross the waterway linking Lake Pontchartrain with Lake Maurepas to your right.

**Moisant Field (33/27)** New Orleans' international airport appears on the left beyond factories and warehouses.

**Xavier University (51/9)** Look right for campus buildings as you approach New Orleans with the skyline ahead to your left featuring the massive Superdome. The train continues to crawl towards the city before making a safety stop and reversing into the station.

## NEW ORLEANS

Thruway buses connect with Baton Rouge and Mobile. For New Orleans city information, see *The Sunset Limited* (pages 148–50).

# The Northeast Corridor Boston–Washington

## General route information

This is Amtrak's busiest route and the only one where it owns both track and stations. Since 1986 Amtrak has been the dominant carrier, moving more passengers between New York and Washington than any airline. It would require 10,000 packed DC-9s to carry the same number of passengers each year between these cities. *Acela* trains capable of 150mph (240km/h) have been introduced on Amtrak's 'main street' to replace *Metroliners* but services are already frequent and fast. En route you encounter cities, rural scenery and splendid seascapes.

Some trains go all the way between Boston and Washington while others, such as *Metroliners*, operate over just part of the line. Non-*Metroliner* or *Clocker* services are designated as *NortheastDirect* trains. They used to rejoice in names such as *Foggy Bottom*, *Nutmeg State*, *Mayflower* and *Liberty Bell* but are now usually given mere numbers. All trains may not stop at every station indicated, so check when buying your ticket.

*Acela Regional* trains have reduced the time between Boston and New York by as much as 90 minutes, with a corresponding 40% increase in passengers. *Acela Regional* trains now make the journey in four hours and the *Acela Express* will cut this by another hour. There will eventually be ten *Acela Express* round-trip trains daily (Boston–New York) and seven *Acela Regional* trains serving more stations. *Acela Commuter* trains will replace *Clockers*.

*Acela Regional* coaches have been refurbished with improved seats and overhead lights and have a more modern colour scheme. They also give a much smoother ride. The motive power will be provided by new Bombardier/Alstom 8,000 horsepower locomotives capable of up to 125mph (200km/h).

*Acela Express* trains consist of one First Class and four Business Class cars, with a total seating of 304 passengers. First and Business Class are more comfortable, with lumbar support, moveable armrests and headrests, laptop computer outlets, conference tables, extra telephones, deluxe rest-rooms and personal controls for lights and audio.

**Frequency** Over 40 trains daily, running almost 24 hours a day out of New York. *Metroliners* operate hourly between New York and Washington, taking three hours for the journey. *Clockers* are commuter trains between New York and Philadelphia and make many local stops on their two-hour trips.

**Reservations** About half the trains are reserved, including *Metroliners* and the *Twilight Shoreliner*.

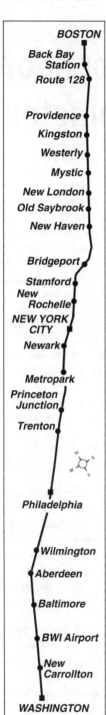

BOSTON
Back Bay Station
Route 128
Providence
Kingston
Westerly
Mystic
New London
Old Saybrook
New Haven
Bridgeport
Stamford
New Rochelle
NEW YORK CITY
Newark
Metropark
Princeton Junction
Trenton
Philadelphia
Wilmington
Aberdeen
Baltimore
BWI Airport
New Carrollton
WASHINGTON

**Equipment** Amfleet coaches. Through trains from Boston to Washington have Club cars. Railfone.

**Sleeping** Viewliner bedrooms on the *Twilight Shoreliner*.

**Food** Most trains except *Clockers* provide snacks, sandwiches and drinks. The *Twilight Shoreliner* sleeper includes free breakfast.

**Baggage** No check-in service.

# Joining the train

## BOSTON

English Puritans arrived in the 17th century and the Revolution began here when British troops fired on colonists during the 'Boston Massacre' of 1770. New England's largest city became the hub of the solar system, where 'the Lowells spoke only to Cabots and the Cabots spoke only to God'.

Today's Boston is one of America's most sophisticated and attractive cities. Modern buildings, green spaces and the *Cheers* bar mingle successfully with older parts of the city.

### Boston basics

**Telephone code** 617.

**Station** Amtrak's restored South Station at Atlantic Ave and Summer was Boston's first beaux arts building. Information tel: 345 7442. Ticket-office open 05.45–21.30. Waiting-room 05.30–03.00. Lockers, newspapers, Red Caps, restaurants, shops, ATM banking, taxi stand.

**Local transport** MBTA operates commuter trains from South Station to points south and west, and to points north and northwest from North Station, 126 Causeway; tel: 222 3200.

You can see the city best on foot, with help from an MBTA system (tel: 222 3200) that includes bus, trolley and subway (the 'T'). A subway stop is located in the station and a 'T passport' offers unlimited travel on buses and subway as well as discounts at various attractions.

**Taxis** Red Cab; tel: 734 5000.

**Car rental** Thrifty; tel: 1 800 367 2277. Budget; tel: 1 800 527 0700.

**Greyhound** South Station; tel: 526 1801.

**Logan Airport** is in East Boston, accessible by subway or bus.

**Tours** Gray Line, 275 Tremont; tel: 720 6342. National Park Rangers lead Black Heritage Trail walking tours, beginning at the Robert Gould Shaw and 54th Regiment Memorial on the corner of Park and Beacon; tel: 617 742 5415. Harbour and island trips from Bay State Cruises; tel: 748 1428.

**Visitors bureau** 2 Copley Place (tel: 888 733 2678; web: www.bostonusa.com). An information booth opens daily on Boston Common at Tremont and Park, and the National Historical Park Service is at 15 State; tel: 242 5642; web: www.nps.gov/bost/home.htm.

**Accommodation** Contact the B & B Agency of Boston (tel: 0800 248 9262) or Host Homes of Boston PO Box 117, Boston 02468; tel: 800 600 1308; web: www.hosthomesofboston.com.

International (IYHF) Hostel, 12 Hemenway; tel: 536 9455. Members $14, non-members $19. Irish Embassy Hostel, 232 Friend; tel: 973 4841. Beds from $15. Free barbecues. YMCA, 316 Huntington Ave; tel: 927 4653. Swimming pool, gym, restaurant, complimentary breakfast. For men and women. Single $36, double $54. Berkeley Residence Club (YWCA), 40 Berkeley; tel: 375 2524. Women only. Members $42, non-members $54.

For discount rates contact Citywide Reservation Services Inc; tel: 800 468 3593; web: www.cityres.com. Hotels include the Park Plaza in Park Sq; tel: 426 2000; Lenox, 710 Boylston; tel: 536 5300; Eliot, 370 Commonwealth Ave; tel: 267 1607; Copley Square, 47 Huntington Ave; tel: 536 9000; Ramada, 800 Morrissey Blvd; tel: 287 9100; Quality Inn, 275 Tremont; tel: 426 1400.

## Recommended in Boston

**John Hancock Building** 200 Clarendon; tel: 572 6429. Great views can be had from the 60th floor of New England's tallest (740ft/220m) building. Open daily, admission charge.

**Museum of Fine Arts** 465 Huntington Ave; tel: 267 9300; web: www.mfa.org. Includes art from Egypt, Asia and Europe, including more than 40 works by Monet, as well as portraits of eminent Americans such as George Washington. Open daily, admission charge.

**Museum of Science** Science Park; tel: 723 2500; web: www.mos.org. The museum has a planetarium with laser displays and a theatre showing films on a giant screen. Open daily, admission charge.

**Freedom Trail** Most of Boston's historic buildings can be explored by following the Freedom Trail, marked somewhat erratically in red on the sidewalks. Tel: 227 8800; web: www.thefreedomtrail.org. Information and a free map are available from the booth on Boston Common. Highlights include the Old State House, the Old South Meeting House, Paul Revere's House and the *USS Constitution* from the War of 1812.

**Bunker Hill Monument** is a 221ft (67m) granite memorial to the battle fought nearby during the War of Independence. The monument's staircase leads to excellent views of the city and harbour. Most places on the Trail are open daily, free.

**Museum of Afro-American History** 46 Joy; tel: 725 0022. Located in what was once the first publicly funded school for African-Americans, the museum has many exhibits showing their contribution to the city's history. Open daily, free.

**John F Kennedy Library and Museum** Near the University of Massachusetts in Dorchester; tel: 929 4500; web: www.cs.umb.edu/jfklibrary/museum.htm.

Photographs, films and memorabilia trace the Kennedy family history. You can listen to JFK's speeches and review the Nixon-Kennedy debates in an impressive building designed by I M Pei. Open daily, admission charge.

**Isabella Stewart Gardner Museum** 280 The Fenway; tel: 566 1401; web: www.gardnermuseum.org. Built in 1903 around a courtyard in the style of a 15th century Italian palace, the museum's art collection includes Renoirs and many Renaissance works. Closed Mon, admission charge.

**Harvard University Art Museums** 32 Quincy in Cambridge; tel: 495 9400. The Sackler has Roman, Egyptian and Islamic antiquities. The adjacent Fogg Museum features European, Asian and American art, and the Busch-Reisinger Museum specialises in art from Germany. Open daily, admission charge (one admission covers all museums). Free on Sat before noon.

# All aboard!

The Capitol, seen high above the city as the train departs, is topped by a marble dome and a statue of 'the independent man'. For the best coastal views choose a seat on the left of the train when travelling south.

**BACK BAY STATION (5/10)** A subterranean station serves Copley Square and the downtown hotels. This is also a stop for commuter trains, which pause only to receive passengers (or discharge them if travelling north).

You leave and continue for several minutes below ground, occasionally surfacing amid concrete car parks for glimpses of Boston's skyline back to your right.

**ROUTE 128 (10/28)** A south suburban halt where trains pause only to receive passengers (or discharge them if travelling north). Route 28 is one of Amtrak's main weapons in its battle with the airline shuttle services, being closer to New York and more convenient than Logan Airport for most people in southern and western Boston. The new station is a bright and spacious building with a glass-fronted waiting-room facing the tracks and new platforms.

You pass freight and warehouse facilities on your right then travel through suburbs interspersed with woodland before entering the flat landscape of eastern Massachusetts.

**Attleboro (20/8)** The **Branson Museum** has numerous locally discovered prehistoric exhibits. Look left as you depart to see an imposing white church and steeple.

Approaching Providence you cross the border into Rhode Island. The city's green-domed Capitol and skyscrapers are ahead with freight yards to the right.

**PROVIDENCE (28/22)** The capital of America's smallest state has many interesting 18th and 19th century buildings. The 1786 John Brown House at Benefit and Power is furnished in period style. The Roger Williams Memorial is located on the site of the original 1636 settlement. Other highlights include the Capitol and the Athenaeum Library where Edgar Allan Poe courted Sarah Whitman (his inspiration for Annabel Lee). The **visitors bureau** is at 1 W Exchange; tel: 401 274 1636 or 1 800 233 1636; web: www.providencecvb.com.

Amtrak trains stop at 100 Gaspee, a new building next to the Capitol. Note the impressive post-modern apartment block to your left as the train pulls out.

**East Greenwich (12/10)** The old seaport's 1773 General Varnum House and garden are preserved in their original condition. Narragansett Bay and its colourful yachts come in view to your left before the train departs temporarily inland through wooded countryside.

**KINGSTON (22/10)** Some of the buildings in this quiet town date from when it was an 18th century trading centre for plantation owners. The George Fayerweather House was built by the blacksmith son of a slave. Look for the lumber company mural to the right of a picturesque grey station flanked by evergreens. Located in West Kingston, this is Amtrak's nearest stop to Newport, famous for its naval base, mansions and jazz festival. Other sights in this former colonial seaport include the Friends Meeting House (1699) and the Old Colony House (1739).

You continue west among woods, streams and marshes.

**WESTERLY (10/10)** An 18th century town situated on the border between Rhode Island and Connecticut. Ancient industrial buildings stand on the opposite side of the track from the solid brick and red tile station. Between here and New Haven the train accompanies an attractive shoreline to your left.

**Stonington (5/5)** This well-preserved coastal town boasts Connecticut's first lighthouse (now a museum). You can tour vineyards in summer and take boat trips to the Isle au Haut.

As you depart past a marina and dry dock look right for a Christmas tree plantation and several old railroad cars converted into unusual homes.

**MYSTIC (10/10)** Built in 1905, the wooden station on your right has been restored to its pink and yellow glory. The town is on the banks of the Mystic River and owes its existence to the sea and shipbuilding. Vessels constructed here include America's first ironclad (the *Galena*) and the clipper *Andrew Jackson*, which sailed to San Francisco round Cape Horn in a record 89 days. **Mystic Seaport Museum** (tel: 888 973 2767; web: www.mysticseaport.org) owns one of the largest outdoor displays in the country, with a 19th century whaling ship, the *Charles Morgan*, moored in a recreated New England village. This was the last wooden whaler ever built (in 1841) and you can tour its cramped conditions and ghoulish vats.

You pass another marina then continue along an embankment where water and pleasure craft can be seen on both sides. The pretty shoreline ahead features many inlets, trees and herons.

**NEW LONDON (10/20)** Trains cross the River Thames (rhymes with 'shames') on a steel bridge before entering a large Romanesque station designed by Henry Hobson Richardson. Over 100 years old, this brick and granite building was one of Amtrak's first major restoration projects. Thruway buses connect with the Foxwoods Casino. The Cross Sound Ferry is based adjacent to Amtrak's station and travels to Orient Point on Long Island.

New London was among North America's earliest settlements and grew rich on whaling. The **Lyman Allyn Museum** (tel: 860 443 2545; web: http://lymanallyn.conncoll.edu) is dedicated to a whaling captain and seagoing tradition continues at the US Coastguard Academy. The training vessel *Eagle* can usually be seen either moored to your left or in full sail on the river. New London's shipyards launched the world's first nuclear submarine, *Nautilus*.

From here to Old Saybrook trains run mostly alongside the beach, with the waters of Niantic Bay just a few feet from the track. Look for sunbathers, fishing boats and enviable homes.

**Connecticut River (14/6)** You cross the river on a drawbridge then continue among marshes.

**OLD SAYBROOK (20/30)** The blue and white station dates from 1873. Long Island Sound and some of its small islands can be seen to your left as the train speeds along this coastal stretch. Approaching New Haven you see a power plant and docks to your left before the train crawls through rail yards into the station.

**NEW HAVEN (30/25)** The first planned city in the USA, this is where the first sulphur matches and Colt revolvers were made. Other firsts claimed are the hamburger, pizza and frisbee, named after apple pie plates from the Frisbie Baking company. Founded in 1638 as Quinnipiac and renamed two years later, New Haven became one of the strictest Puritan towns. Dr Benjamin Spock was brought up here, where his father was a lawyer with the New Haven Railroad. The **visitors bureau** is at 59 Elm (tel: 203 777 8550; web: www.newhavencvb.org).

Amtrak's restored Union Station is at 50 Union Ave. Look right for Amtrak trains from Springfield and Hartford joining the main *Northeast Corridor* line as Metro-North trains wait on your left.

New Haven surrounds a green with three historic churches and you can take a cruise on the sound from Long Wharf Dock. Nearby are Fort Nathan Hale, the Pardee-Morris House and **Yale University**, named after its early benefactor, Elihu Yale. Bill and Hillary Clinton first met here at Law School. Free guided tours of Yale include the 1752 Connecticut Hall, the Harkness Tower (221ft/66m tall) and the Center for British Art. A Gutenberg Bible is one of 400,000 books in the Beinecke Library.

You leave among rail yards, houses and factories to continue through southern Connecticut.

**Milford (5/20)** Milford is the scene of an annual oyster festival. As you travel southwest you cross the Housatonic and Pequonnock Rivers.

**BRIDGEPORT (25/24)** Connecticut's largest city contains 1,300 acres (525ha) of park land and the state's largest zoo. City Hall was named after a socialist mayor, Jasper McLevy (in office 1933-57). Amtrak is at 525 Water.

To your right as you leave is the **Barnum Museum** (tel: 203 331 1104; web: www.barnum-museum.org), containing an Egyptian mummy and the clothes worn by General Tom Thumb. Showman Phineas Taylor Barnum (also a Bridgeport mayor) was buried in Mountain Grove Cemetery, where Tom Thumb's grave is marked by a supposedly life-size 2ft/60cm statue. Ocean-going ships can be seen in the harbour to your left.

**Westport (10/14)** A handful of New Yorkers commute further north but this is as far as most will travel. Houses here and along the coast to Stamford are among this area's most expensive and fashionable. Nearby Sherwood Island is popular for swimming and boating on Long Island Sound.

As the train nears Stamford look ahead to your right for the most modern part of the city.

**STAMFORD (24/18)** Research City claims to have more international corporations than anywhere except New York or Chicago. Smart new office blocks and malls have transformed the downtown skyline.

Amtrak shares the glass and concrete Transportation Center on Washington Blvd with Metro-North trains, seen to your left, and a walkway links the platforms.

**Greenwich (6/12)** First settled by the Dutch, Greenwich is the home of many film and TV stars and is possibly the richest town in Connecticut. Places of interest include the Bush-Holley House (of colonial 'saltbox' design) and the US Tobacco Museum.

From here the train loses touch with Long Island Sound and travels through an increasingly urban and bleak landscape towards New York City.

**NEW ROCHELLE (18/30)** Amtrak trains part company with Metro services, which operate out of New York's Grand Central.

**Pelham Bay (4/26)** Massive Co-op City apartment blocks appear to your right as you cross the bridge. Calvary Hospital is to your left.

The train crosses the Hutchinson River then slows down as it passes through a deprived South Bronx before entering Hell Gate Viaduct. The Hell Gate Bridge, 320ft (96m) above the East River, was the world's largest steel arch bridge when it was completed in 1917, and served as a model for the bridge across Sydney harbour in Australia. The Hell Gate Route (or New York Connecting Railroad) was built to link the New York, New Haven & Hartford line with the Pennsylvania Railroad.

**Manhattan State Hospital (10/20)** Look right for this sombre 1930s' building and your first views of Manhattan. The train crosses Randalls and Wards Islands before going through Astoria. Rail yards and commuter trains extend on both sides as you enter a tunnel on Long Island, burrowing beneath the East River and Manhattan to reach Pennsylvania Station.

## NEW YORK CITY (30/15)

*Manhattan, Wall Street, 42nd Street, West Side Story* and *Breakfast at Tiffany's* – everyone has visited New York in the movies. The birthplace of Bogart and Bacall is a world leader in fashion, finance and the arts, inspiring admen and bankers as much as painters, writers and musicians.

Niew Amsterdam began in 1625, and the following year Peter Minuit bought Manhattan Island from the Indians for $24. Today its population is three million, plus 11 million commuters.

Nowhere else has such energy and style, although homelessness and urban decay seem as much part of the fabric as Fifth Avenue and the St Patrick's Day parade. Not everyone loves New York, but no-one forgets the experience.

### New York City basics

**Telephone codes** 212 for Manhattan; 718 for Queens, Brooklyn, the Bronx and Staten Island. All numbers given in this section have Manhattan codes unless otherwise stated.

**Station** Amtrak uses **Pennsylvania Station** at 7th Ave and 32nd, beneath Madison Square Garden. It has been made cleaner and safer lately but remains a poor substitute for the building it replaced in the 1960s, built by McKim, Mead and White. Thomas Wolfe described the original Penn Station as 'vast enough to hold the sound of time' and it can be seen in the 1942 film *The Palm Beach Story*.

As part of Amtrak's high speed service development, a special annex to Penn station is being constructed at a cost of $484 million in the historic Farley Post Office building, restoring its original glass-covered atrium and creating a new concourse for *Acela* trains.

**Information** tel: 582 6875. *Metroliner* information tel: 736 3967. Ticket-office open 05.10–22.00. Waiting-room open 24 hours. The Metropolitan lounge opens 05.15–02.00 (weekdays) and 07.00–02.00 (weekends) and is particularly swish – a welcome respite from the busy waiting-room outside. Baggage room, newspapers, restaurants, snack bars, shops, ATM banking, taxi stand, subway.

**Connections** The Long Island Railroad (tel: 718 217 5477) and New Jersey Transit (tel: 201 762 5100) also operate from Penn Station.

The magnificent, atmospheric **Grand Central Terminal** at 89 E 42nd and Park Ave is where John Barrymore won Carole Lombard after their cross-country train journey in the 1934 film *Twentieth Century*. Completed in 1913 by Cornelius Vanderbilt, the largest train station in the world replaced a smaller 1898 station which had proved to be unable to cope with increased traffic. In 1902 an explosion in the open rail yards had killed 15 people with fumes, smoke and steam. It was decided therefore to electrify the trains and construct a roof over the entire complex, excavating 48ft (14m) into Manhattan Island to create three separate levels. Eight underground tracks carried 700 trains per day while above ground a new New York grew, including all the buildings on Park Avenue. The $180 million station had been financed by selling air space above.

A 'city within a city', Grand Central originally had tennis courts, an art gallery, a bakery, a betting parlour and a hospital. Restored in magnificent style and rededicated in 1998, the station has five brass chandeliers (each with a hundred lights), Tennessee marble floors, frescoes, grand balustraded staircases and triumphant arched windows where people walk in a wall of glass. Look for the Vanderbilt family's oak leaves emblem incorporated into the vaulted ceiling of the main concourse. The Oyster Bar, located in the bowels of the station, continues to serve shellfish stew, pan roasts and oysters across splendid marble counters and a new steak house occupies the north balcony. A murmur from the 'whispering gallery' outside the Oyster Bar's entrance can be heard clearly in the far corners of the cavernous hall.

By 1946 more than 65 million passengers a year were using Grand Central and rush hour can still be frantic. Metro-North (tel: 532 4900) operates over 500 commuter trains daily to the suburbs and Connecticut. Sadly, Amtrak stopped using Grand Central in April 1991. Despite attempts to deal the building a similar fate to the old Penn Station, campaigners such as Jackie Kennedy kept this spectacular building safe. The Municipal Art Society (tel: 935 3960) gives free tours each Wednesday afternoon.

**Local transport** Manhattan's logical grid of streets and avenues makes it easy to find your way around, although driving or finding a place to park can be a nightmare.

The visitors bureau has maps and schedules for public transport and more details are available from the NYC Transit Authority, 370 Jay Street, Room 875, Brooklyn, NY 11201. A MetroCard provides a week's unlimited travel on the subway and buses throughout the city for only $17. Call 718 330 1234 for all bus and subway information. The **NY Transit Museum** is located in an authentic 1930s' subway station at the corner of Boerum Place and Schermerhorn Street in downtown Brooklyn; tel: 718 694 5139.

**Taxis** A taxi stand is located on 31st Street between 7th and 8th Avenues. Otherwise look for a yellow cab with a lighted sign and hail it by raising your arm. In case of complaints or lost property contact the Taxi Commission; tel: 221 8294.

**Car rental** National, 252 W 40th; tel: 1 800 227 8368. Budget, 333 E 34th; tel: 1 800 527 0700.

**Greyhound** Port Authority Terminal, 8th Ave; tel: 271 6300.

**Airports** New York is served by three airports, the largest being **John F Kennedy** in Queens. Access is by taxi, bus and limousine. The JFK Express (tel: 718 330 1234) is a subway and bus line connecting with Brooklyn and Manhattan. Thruway buses operated by Carey Express (tel: 718 632 0500 or 1 800 678 1569) travel at half-hourly intervals between JFK, La Guardia, the Port Authority Terminal and Grand Central Station. Amtrak passes are not valid on this service. JFK is currently undergoing a $9 billion redevelopment programme which includes $1.5 billion for AirTrain, the New York Port Authority's rail line which should provide a service linking midtown Manhattan and the airport in half an hour by 2003.

**La Guardia Airport** in Queens is also served by Carey buses. A planned extension of the subway system should soon allow a 'one seat' ride to La Guardia from Manhattan.

**Newark Airport** is 14 miles (22km) southwest and was briefly, in the 1930s, the world's busiest airport. New Jersey Transit buses (tel: 201 762 5100) connect to the Port Authority Terminal and Olympia Trails buses (tel: 201 964 6233) run from Newark to Grand Central. A monorail links Manhattan with Newark and operates three times an hour during daytime. The journey is 25 minutes instead of 90 minutes by road.

**Tours** Gray Line; tel: 397 2620. Apple; tel: 1 800 876 9868. Three-hour boat cruises around Manhattan from Circle Line at Pier 83, W 42nd at the Hudson River; tel: 563 3200. Helicopter flights from Liberty; tel: 967 6464. The Staten Island ferry (tel: 718 815 2628) chugs around the harbour and Statue of Liberty, making 50 crossings each way on weekdays between the Whitehall Ferry Terminal in Lower Manhattan and St George Ferry Terminal on the island. The five mile journey takes 25 minutes and is free to foot passengers, including Melanie Griffiths in *Working Girl*.

The **Jazz Trail** takes place about once a month around Queens, visiting the former houses of musicians such as Louis Armstrong, Dizzy Gillespie, Lena Horne and James Brown. Take the subway from Times Square or the Long Island Railroad from Penn Station to Flushing Town Hall, 137–35, Northern Blvd; tel: 718 463 7700.

**Visitors bureau** 810 Seventh Ave, between 52nd and 53rd; tel: 484 1222; web: www.nycvisit.com.

**Accommodation** Contact Bed & Breakfast Network of New York at 134 W 32nd, Suite 602, New York, NY 10001 (tel: 645 8134).

AYH Hostel, 891 Amsterdam Ave; tel: 932 2300. The world's largest hostel, with 624 beds. Members $22, non-members $28. McBurney YMCA, 206 W 24th; tel: 741 9226. Near to Penn Station and located in the attractive Chelsea district. Safe, comfortable rooms for men and women. Television and café. Free use of swimming pool, sauna and sports facilities in an adjacent building. Single $40, double $55. Vanderbilt YMCA, 224 E 47th; tel: 756 9600. A classic-style building on the fashionable East Side. Television, air conditioning, swimming pool, gym and restaurant (with room service). For men and women. Single $46, double $57. West Side YMCA, 5 W 63rd; tel: 875 4273. Located off Central Park West in a European-style building close to Upper West Side attractions. Television, air conditioning, swimming pool, fitness facilities, restaurant. Single $44, double $54.

Hotel room prices are often very high apart from some weekend rates. Hotels include the Algonquin, 59 W 44th; tel: 840 6800; Salisbury, 123 W 57th; tel: 246 1300; Novotel, 226 W 52nd; tel: 315 0100 – single $149, double $229; Chelsea, 222 W 23rd; tel: 243 3700; Gorham, 136 W 55th; tel: 245 1800; Grand Union, 34 E 32nd; tel: 683 5890 – single $70, double $90; Hotel 17, 225 E 17th; tel: 475 2845 – double $75; Carlton Arms, 160 E 25th; tel: 679 0680 – single $50; Pickwick Arms, 230 E 51st; tel:355 0300 – single $45, double $105.

## Recommended in New York City

**Statue of Liberty** On Liberty Island, reached by Circle Line ferry from Battery Park; tel: 363 3180; web: www.nps.gov/stli/mainmenu.htm. 'Liberty enlightening the world' was designed by Frederic Bartholdi and paid for by the French. See Manhattan from the observation deck or climb 171 steps for views from The Lady's crown. The

**Immigration Museum** on nearby Ellis Island occupies the building which 12 million immigrants passed through between 1892 and 1954. Open daily, admission charge.

**The Frick Collection** 1 East 70th; tel: 288 0700; web: www.frick.org. The collection, housed in an elegant mansion built by Henry Clay Frick, one of America's most successful steel and railroad tycoons, includes masterpieces of Western painting, sculpture and decorative art, displayed in a serene and intimate setting. Among the sixteen galleries are the Fragonard Room and the Living Hall, with works by Holbein, Titian, El Greco and Bellini. Closed Monday, admission charge.

**Empire State Building** 350 5th Ave; tel: 736 3100; web: www.esbnyc.com. The people's favourite skyscraper was the world's tallest building when completed in 1931 and kept the record for 40 years. The 86th and 102nd floor observation decks still give great views of New York but arrive early to miss the crush. Open daily, admission charge.

**St Patrick's Cathedral** 5th Ave and 50th; tel: 753 2261. The Gothic towers of New York's Roman Catholic cathedral contrast with the adjacent Rockefeller Center's art deco. Open daily, free.

**Central Park** Bounded by 59th and 110th Streets, and by 5th Ave and Central Park West; web: www.centralparknyc.org. Watch New York at play, listen to concerts and enjoy free Shakespeare performances. The park has America's oldest carousel, a zoo and Strawberry Fields, dedicated to John Lennon. Open daily. Free maps and details of latest events from the **Mid-Park Visitor Center** at 65th (tel: 794 6564). Open Tue–Sun. For guided walks call the Park Rangers at 800 201 7275.

**Metropolitan Museum of Art** 5th Ave at E 82nd; tel: 879 5500; web: www.metmuseum.org. More than four million people each year visit this vast Victorian Gothic building to see the largest art collection in the USA. More like a dozen museums in one, with great works by Picasso, Rembrandt and Vermeer along with French Impressionists, Egyptian art, a Chinese Ming-period courtyard, the Frank Lloyd Wright room and a terrific sculpture garden on the roof. For concerts and lecture tours call 570 3949. The Met is always busy so go early, although some galleries do not open until late on Sunday morning. Closed Monday, admission charge.

**Museum of Modern Art** 11 W 53rd, between Fifth and Sixth Avenues; tel: 708 9400. One of the world's finest collections includes Monet's Water Lily room and works by Picasso, Matisse, Miro and Jackson Pollock. Open daily, admission charge.

**United Nations** First Ave and 46th, overlooking the East River; tel: 963 7713. Take a guided tour of the Secretariat Building, General Assembly Hall and Hammarskjold Library. Free tickets to observe meetings. Open daily, admission charge for tours.

**Stock Exchange** 20 Broad; tel: 656 5165. Formed in 1792 when a group of brokers met at the junction of Wall and William Streets, where kerbside brokers sold railroad stocks in the 1860s. Free film and tours. Open weekdays.

# All aboard!

The train pulls out of Pennsylvania Station by way of a 2.5-mile (4km) tunnel beneath the Hudson River, surfacing three minutes later in New Jersey. The

Hudson tunnels were the first structural links across the river between New Jersey and New York City. Train services began when Penn Station opened in 1910.

The city's outline on the far left features the Empire State Building and the Giants Stadium is beyond a New Jersey Turnpike bridge to your right.

**Hackensack River (10/5)** You cross with an impressive bridge to your left and lose sight of New York. The train follows then crosses the Passaic River before going through a New Jersey Transit depot at Harrison.

**NEWARK (15/14)** New Jersey's largest city is one of the country's great manufacturing centres. It was the birthplace of the novelist Stephen Crane, author of *The Red Badge of Courage*. The Thomas Edison Historic Site in the suburb of West Orange preserves Edison's laboratory, his early gramophone and the first movie camera. Edison was once a newsboy on the Grand Trunk Railway.

Amtrak's echoing art deco Pennsylvania Station in Newark is at Raymond Plaza W and has a beautifully restored waiting-room. The train leaves past PATH trains, warehouses and brick-built factories, picking up speed as it travels through commuter stops such as Lincoln.

**Elizabeth (6/8)** The former New Jersey capital, an influential town during the American Revolution, is bound to Newark by continuous suburbs. Look right for a General Motors factory.

**Rahway (10/4)** Interesting old brownstone buildings appear on both sides.

**METROPARK (14/15)** Amtrak's station is at 100 Middlesex-Essex Turnpike. You cross the Garden State Parkway and continue among industrial plants owned by some of America's biggest companies. The scene is occasionally brightened by a stretch of farmland and near New Brunswick you cross the Rariton River.

**New Brunswick (7/8)** A scheduled stop for some Amtrak trains, New Brunswick has frequent New Jersey Transit services to Newark and Trenton. Look right for Rutgers University (founded in 1776) and the headquarters of Johnson & Johnson.

The train continues through semi-rural scenes until factories, chemical plants and warehouses take over again on the approach to Trenton.

**Princeton Junction (10/5)** The University's ivy-clad campus to your right features Albert Einstein's house. Other inhabitants have included future presidents Woodrow Wilson and Aaron Burr. The art museum features pictures by Cézanne, Van Gogh and Picasso, and panels in University Chapel are carved from Sherwood Forest wood. For **visitor information** call 258 6115. A few Amtrak trains stop at Princeton Junction and New Jersey Transit trains go to Princeton from Penn Station in New York.

**TRENTON (15/32)** Home of New Jersey's State Museum and the 1792 Capitol building. Amtrak's rather lived-in station with open platforms is at 72 S Clinton Ave.

Look right for the Capitol's gold dome as you leave among older parts of the city. The train slows down to cross the Delaware River near where Washington crossed in 1776 to attack a garrison of British-financed mercenaries. The bridge to your right proclaims that 'Trenton makes, the world takes'. Crossing the river transports you from New Jersey into Pennsylvania.

**Holmesburg Junction (20/12)** Holmesburg Prison is to your right and the Tacony-Palmyra bridge arches across the Delaware River, seen beyond trees to your left.

**Schuylkill River (30/2)** You pass two spired churches then cross the river and enter Philadelphia through Fairmount Park. The zoo is on your left.

An old signal box mural announces 'the city of brotherly love' as the train crawls among freight yards and half-derelict buildings, with Philadelphia's skyline in the left distance. Nearing the station, look left for Boathouse Row and the Parthenon-style Museum of Art with its famous *Rocky* steps.

## PHILADELPHIA (32/22)

'On the whole I'd rather be in Philadelphia' was W C Fields' malign epitaph on his birthplace when he thought he was dying. The city has also been the home of Benjamin Franklin, Sammy Davis Jr, Dizzy Gillespie and Live Aid. Elfreth's Alley, occupied since 1772, is America's oldest street.

William Penn founded Philadelphia on a peninsula between the Schuylkill and Delaware Rivers in 1682 and it became America's capital from Independence until 1800. By then it was the world's second-largest English-speaking city. Apart from historic buildings and museums, Philly is known for its cheesesteaks, pretzels and alarming crime rate.

### Philadelphia basics

**Telephone code** 215.

**Station** Stately 30th Street Station at 30th and Market is one of Amtrak's busiest terminals, restored at great expense. Information tel: 824 1600. *Metroliner* information tel: 824 4224. Ticket-office open 05.00–22.30 (weekdays) or 06.00–22.30 (weekends). Waiting-room open 24 hours. Metropolitan lounge open 06.30–21.30. Electronic train information, newspapers, Red Caps, restaurants, shops, ATM banking, taxi stand.

**Connections** SEPTA trains operate to the suburbs and Philadelphia airport; tel: 580 7800. PATCO high speed trains to New Jersey leave from 8th and Market; tel: 856 772 6900. For New Jersey Transit trains to Atlantic City and southern New Jersey call 569 3752 (or 1 800 228 7246 in New Jersey).

Amtrak ticket-holders can travel free by commuter train between 30th Street and the downtown Penn Center station at 1617 John F Kennedy Blvd. Ticket-office 09.10–14.00 and 15.00–17.30 Mon–Fri.

**Local transport** The historic district is best explored on foot, using maps from the tourist bureau, and SEPTA operates buses, trolleys and the subway (tel: 580 7800).
**Taxis** Yellow; tel: 922 8400. Quaker City; tel: 728 8000.
**Car rental** National (tel: 492 2760) and Budget (tel: 1 800 824 7088) are located in 30th Street Station.
**Greyhound** 10th and Filbert; tel: 931 4075.
**Airport** The airport is eight miles (13km) southwest by Boston Coach (tel: 800 672 7676) and Airport Express trains (call SEPTA for times).
**Tours** Gray Line; tel: 569 3666. Philadelphia on Foot; tel: 800 340 9869. The Fairmont Park Trolley (tel: 925 TOUR) takes in most sights and allows unlimited stops. Water cruises on the *Spirit of Philadelphia*; tel: 923 1419 and the riverboat *Liberty Belle*; tel: 629 1131.
**Visitors bureau** 16th and JFK Blvd; tel: 636 1666; email: info@pcvb.org; web: www.pcvb.org.
**Accommodation** Contact Philadelphia Bed & Breakfast City Center, 1804 Pine, Philadelphia, PA 19103; tel: 735 1137.

AYH Hostel, Chamounix Mansion, a historic building in Fairmount Park; tel: 878 3676. Some family rooms. Closed December. Members $11, non-members $14. YWCA, 1315 Walnut; tel: 790 9006.

Hotels include the Four Seasons at 1 Logan Sq; tel: 963 1500; Holiday Inn Midtown, 1305 Walnut; tel: 735 9300; Quality Inn Center City, 501 N 22nd; tel: 568 8300; Alexander Inn, 12th and Spruce; tel: 923 3535; Chestnut Hill, 8229 Germantown Ave; tel: 242 5905; Apollo, 1918 Arch; tel: 567 8925.

## Recommended in Philadelphia

**Museum of Art** 26th and Benjamin Franklin Pkwy; tel: 763 8100; web: www.philamuseum.org. Three hundred thousand works, including Van Gogh (*Sunflowers*), Picasso, Renoir, Rubens and Cézanne (*Bathers*), plus American crafts, a Japanese tea house and an Indian temple. Guided tours. Closed Mon, free Sun morning.
**Fairmount Park** Covering 4,500 acres (1,800ha) from downtown to the city's northwest boundary, the park features forests, waterways, sports fields and museums. Highlights include Boathouse Row (19th century buildings used by rowing clubs), Strawberry Mansion and Memorial Hall (dating from the 1876 Centennial).
**City Hall** Broad and Market; tel: 686 9074. Completed in 1900 and topped by a 37ft/11m bronze statue of William Penn, this 548ft/166m tower is the tallest masonry structure in the world. Open weekdays. Free tours and observation deck.
**Franklin Institute Science Museum** 20th and Benjamin Franklin Pkwy; tel: 448 1200; web: www.fi.edu. Includes a science centre, planetarium and theatre. The museum has many hands-on and walk-through exhibits, and the garden features high-tech displays and a maze. Open daily, admission charge.
**Rodin Museum** 22nd and Benjamin Franklin Pkwy; tel: 763 8100. The largest collection of Rodin drawings and sculptures (including *The Thinker*) outside Paris. Closed Mon, donation.
**Independence Park** The national park centre opens daily at 6th and Market; tel: 965 7676; web: www.independencevisitorcenter.com. This historic square mile draws five

million tourists every year and most buildings are open daily, free, including the following:

**Independence Hall** Chestnut Street. Opened in 1732, this is where the Declaration of Independence (1776) and Constitution (1787) were adopted. You can tour the Assembly Room and Old City Hall, where the US Supreme Court held sessions from 1791 to 1800.

**Liberty Bell Pavilion** Market Street. Cast in England in 1751, the State House Bell hung in Independence Hall for 200 years before moving to its new glass-walled home.

**Old City Hall** On Chestnut at 5th. This was the home of the US Supreme Court between 1791 and 1800. See the prisoner's dock and jury box as well as restored furniture.

**Christ Church** Beyond Franklin Court to Market. The pews in this church have been occupied by such luminaries as George Washington and Benjamin Franklin. Services are held on Sundays.

# All aboard!

The train departs Philadelphia past the National Publishing Company building to your left and the ivy-league university's Franklin Field to your right, next to the Convention Hall. You continue among residential suburbs and smokestack industry, with the tall cranes of the Pennsylvania Shipbuilding yard on your left.

**Commodore Barry Bridge (11/11)** The imposing steel structure to your left spans the Delaware River between Chester, PA, and New Jersey. Look for ships being loaded below.

**Pennsylvania/Delaware State Line (15/7)** The Delaware River is to your left as you enter the Small Wonder State at Marcus Hook. A Phoenix Steel factory stands to your right, with chemical plants and Sun Oil refineries on both sides. Chimneys burn off waste in dramatic bursts of flame.

**Brandywine Creek (18/4)** You cross the creek, flowing into the Christina River to your left. The Christina eventually joins the Delaware.

From here to Wilmington the train progresses through Fort Christina Park, site of the first (1638) Swedish settlement. The **Holy Trinity (Old Swede's) Church** and graveyard on your right date from 1698 and are still in use. As you travel among more factories look right near Wilmington for the station's decorative clock tower.

**WILMINGTON (22/25)** 'The chemical capital of the world', where Eleuthère du Pont founded a gunpowder mill in 1802. The site is now occupied by the **Hagley Museum of Industrial History**. Wilmington's 1871 Opera House boasts a splendid cast-iron façade. Look left for the cutter *Mohawk*, retained as a memorial to the Second World War Battle of the

Atlantic. Amtrak's large, refurbished Victorian-style station at Martin Luther King Blvd and French was designed in 1907 by Frank Furness. It boasts terracotta window arches, marble steps and a clay-tiled roof.

The train leaves past freight yards and a Berger Brothers factory before travelling beneath a highway bridge with a twin-spired church to your right.

**Newark (8/17)** A scheduled stop for some trains but not to be confused with Newark, New Jersey. The University of Delaware appears to your right. To your left is a vast Chrysler plant which originally manufactured tanks.

**Delaware/Maryland State Line (14/11)** You cross into Maryland, exotically sculpted by Chesapeake Bay and the Potomac River. At the town of Hancock the state is only five miles wide. Stone markers (one white, one black) in a field to your right indicate the state boundary, which is also the Mason-Dixon line. This divided, and some say still divides, north and south.

**Elkton (15/10)** Wedding chapels here witnessed thousands of quickie marriages during the 1930s. You pass a quarry to your right before continuing through a colonial countryside of streams, woods and traditional buildings.

**Northeast River (16/9)** The tree-lined river to your left flows towards Chesapeake Bay.

**Perryville (20/5)** The train slows down to cross the Susquehanna River. Look left for a marina and Chesapeake Bay, with sailboats and the supports of a former bridge. Three more bridges span the river upstream to your right.

**Havre de Grace (23/2)** This neat town on the south shore of the bay was burned by the British during the War of 1812.

**ABERDEEN (25/22)** Home of Aberdeen Proving Grounds and the US Army Ordnance Museum, this is a stop for a few Amtrak trains.

The train gathers speed as it travels southwest and crosses the mile-wide (1.6km) Bush River, with attractive houses and boat jetties ranged along the banks. **Susquehanna Wildlife Refuge** can be seen to your left as green fields, forests and grain silos appear.

**Edgewood (9/13)** William Paca, one of the signatories to the Declaration of Independence, was born near this prosperous small town. You cross the Gunpowder River, also a mile (1.6km) wide, and pass the Maryland National Guard headquarters on your left.

Industrial scenes return as the train nears Baltimore and travels beneath Interstate 40. Look for an old brownstone district to your right and Baltimore's downtown skyline ahead to your left before the train curves left into a tunnel.

## BALTIMORE (22/12)

Birthplace of the American railroad and one of the country's busiest ports, Baltimore has been the home of Billie Holliday, F Scott Fitzgerald, Babe Ruth and *Homicide – Life on the Street*. During the 1830s, Edgar Allan Poe lived in poverty at 203 N Amity. When he died in 1849 he was buried in the grounds of Westminster Church.

Amtrak's renovated station stands on your left at 1500 N Charles. MTA light rail connections are available to the harbour and elsewhere (tel: 410 539 5000) and you can experience panoramic views of the revived city and its harbour from the World Trade Center. The **Visitors Center** is at 451 Light; tel: 410 837 4636 or 1 800 282 6632; web: www.baltimore.org.

The **B & O Railroad Museum** at 901 W Pratt (tel: 410 752 2490; web: www.borail.org) occupies an 1884 roundhouse and features engines, rolling stock, replicas and model trains. It also has the nation's earliest passenger and freight station. Train rides take place along America's first main line railroad at weekends. Open daily, admission charge.

The train continues through a tunnel to another district of traditional brownstones. Look for the pretty Renaissance-style church to your left and a Calvert whiskey distillery to your right before the train speeds up through a more wooded landscape. The water-tower at Piney Orchard is balanced on stilts.

## BALTIMORE/WASHINGTON INTERNATIONAL (12/10) Concrete

platforms and an overhead walkway are set among attractive trees. This international airport is one of several serving Washington, DC, but is not a stop for all trains.

## NEW CARROLLTON (10/10) A key transport junction in Washington's

northern suburbs, where the station and yards of Metro Rail can be seen beside Amtrak's depot.

After New Carrollton you enter the District of Columbia across the narrow Anacostia River and see the 555ft (170m) **Washington Monument** to your right. Also on your right, beyond Amtrak's maintenance facility, are the dome and tower of the **Shrine of the Immaculate Conception**. The train creeps among extensive rail yards before finally entering Union Station.

## WASHINGTON

'Southern efficiency and northern charm' was President Kennedy's mischievous description of Washington, an elegant neo-classical city designed by Pierre Charles L'Enfant on what had been a swamp. The architecture, boulevards and green spaces provide a fine setting for Washington's main business – government.

Events include the cherry blossom festival in April and an Independence Day parade in July. Tourist areas are clean and impressive but the nation's capital has a darker side. Drugs and other crime make parts of the city unsafe, so stay on the beaten track. Summer can be oppressively humid.

## Washington basics

**Telephone code** 202.

**Station** Union Station is at 50 Massachusetts Ave; tel: 289 1908 or 1 800 527 2554; web: www.unionstationdc.com. The station is as grand as Washington's other public buildings and is one of Amtrak's showpieces. The most visited destination in the city, with almost 24 million visitors a year, is also downtown's most impressive shopping centre. Ancient Rome's Baths of Diocletian inspired Daniel Burnham's waiting-room design, the 96ft/29m ceiling of which was decorated with 70 pounds (32kg) of gold leaf. The main concourse, with its marble floor and glazed terracotta columns, is long enough (750ft/225m) to hold the Washington Monument horizontally.

The station, built in 1907 at a cost of $125 million, originally included a bakery, butcher's shop, bowling alley, YMCA, hotel, ice house, liquor store, Turkish baths, nursery, police station and mortuary. The dining-room could handle a thousand people at one sitting and there were separate men's and women's waiting rooms, each with heavy mahogany benches and built-in steam heaters. Union Station employed 5,000 people and became known as the 'crossroads of America'. It was made a national historic landmark in 1964 but, as the railroads declined, the building fell into decay. It was reopened in 1988 after America's largest ever restoration project, which took two years and cost $160 million.

Train information tel: 484 7540. *Metroliner* information tel: 484 5580. Ticket-office open 05.15–23.00. Waiting-room open 24 hours for Amtrak ticket holders. Metropolitan Lounge open 06.30–22.30. Dozens of shops and restaurants, nine movie theatres, a post office, lockers, vending machines, ATM banking, newspapers, handcarts, Red Caps, taxi stand, subway. Amtrak also has ticket offices at 1721 K Street and in the Capitol Building.

**Local transport** Washington is best appreciated on foot, most places of interest being within walking distance of the station, although the length of the Mall can be deceptive. Metrobus (tel: 637 7000) operates throughout the city as well as into Maryland and northern Virginia. The expanding Metrorail subway has a stop at the station and services as far as northern Virginia and Maryland. MARC commuter trains (tel: 1 800 325 7245) and the Virginia Railway Express (tel: 703 497 7777 or 1 800 RIDE VRE) operate from Union Station.

**Taxis** Diamond; tel: 387 6200. Yellow; tel: 544 1212.

**Car rental** National (tel: 842 7454) and Budget (tel: 289 5374) are located in Union Station.

**Greyhound** 1005 1st NE; tel: 289 5154.

**Airports** Dulles Airport, 25 miles (40km) west, is the main international flight centre. Washington National is in Arlington, Virginia, four miles (6.5km) from downtown by subway. Baltimore/Washington International (BWI) is 30 miles (48km) northeast by bus, Amtrak and MARC trains. Call 703 417 8471 for Washington Flyer buses to all airports.

**Tours** The Old Town Trolley (tel: 832 9800) visits the main attractions, including Arlington Cemetery and Union Station. Unlimited stops are permitted en route. Gold Line/Gray Line coaches (tel: 800 862 1400) operate from the station.

**Visitors bureau** 1212 New York Ave (tel: 724 5644; web: www.washington.org) and at Union Station.

**Accommodation** Contact the Bed & Breakfast League, PO Box 9490, Washington, DC 20005 (tel: 363 7767) or Bed & Breakfast Accommodations, PO Box 12011, Washington, DC 20005 (tel: 328 3510).

AYH Hostel, 1009 11th NW; tel: 737 2333. Dormitory rooms, free tours and movies. Members $18, non-members $20. Washington has no YMCA but the Hotel Harrington at 436 11th and E (tel: 628 8140 or 800 424 8532) offers discounts for students and YMCA members. Handily located for the museums and monuments, it has air conditioning, a restaurant and cable TV with HBO. Singles and doubles from $55. Large family rooms are also available.

The Capitol Reservations Service (tel: 800 847 4832) has special rates and package deals among the 40,000 hotel rooms. Hotels include the Hampshire, 1310 New Hampshire Ave; tel: 296 7600; Holiday Inn, 415 New Jersey Ave; tel: 800 638 1116; Four Point Sheraton, 1201 K St NW; tel: 289 7600; Phoenix Park, 520 N Capitol NW; tel: 638 6900; Center City, 1201 13th NW; tel: 682 5300 – single $59, double $75; Allen Lee, 2224 F; tel: 331 1224 – single $33, double $43.

## Recommended in Washington

**The Capitol** At the east end of the Mall; tel: 225 6827. The nation's most important building was completed in 1800, when the Senate and House of Representatives met in joint session on November 22. The familiar white dome is a later addition. Open daily, free tours.

**Supreme Court** 1st and Maryland Ave; tel: 479 3211. Housed in a white marble building, the court sits for two weeks each month from October to June (you are invited to watch). At other times, members of staff give free lectures on weekdays.

**White House** 1600 Pennsylvania Ave; tel: 456 7041; web: www.nps.gov/whho. This official residence has been occupied by every US president since George Washington. A million tourists come each year (open Tue–Sat mornings, free) but the tour of rather plain reception rooms is underwhelming. You obtain tickets from a booth on the Ellipse at Constitution Ave or from the visitors centre at the Department of Commerce Building, 1450 Pennsylvania Ave (tel: 208 1631).

**Washington Monument** On the Mall at 15th and Constitution Ave; tel: 426 6841; web: www.nps.gov/wamo. The tallest (555ft/170m) structure in the city and the highest free-standing masonry edifice in the world. A line in the marble a quarter of the way up shows where building work stopped during the Civil War. Finally completed in 1888, the monument provides stunning views from narrow slits in the observation deck. Expect a long wait for the elevator. Open daily, free.

**Lincoln Memorial** At the west end of the Mall; tel: 426 6842; web: www.nps.gov/linc. A classical Greek temple overlooks a reflecting pool. The walls around Abraham Lincoln's 19ft (5.8m) statue are inscribed with the words of his Gettysburg Address. Appropriately, this is where Martin Luther King made his 'I have a dream' speech. Open daily, free.

**National Archives** 7th and Constitution Ave; tel: 501 5000. A classical-style building which contains over three billion items, including the Declaration of Independence, the Constitution and the Bill of Rights. Open daily, free.

**Smithsonian Institution** The Castle visitor centre is at 1000 Jefferson Drive; tel: 357 2700; web: www.si.edu. This complex of 14 museums and galleries, mostly located between 6th and 14th, is open daily, free, and includes the following:

**National Postal Museum** 2 Massachusetts Ave, next to Union Station. The story of the US Mail service is entertainingly demonstrated with motor vehicles, aircraft, a stage-coach and a reproduction railroad mail car (the last one was retired in 1977). You can print and mail a free personalised postcard.

**Air and Space Museum** Independence Ave and 6th; web: www.nasm.si.edu. The most visited museum in the world features the Wright Brothers' *Flyer*, Lindbergh's *Spirit of St Louis*, the Apollo 11 command module and a piece of moon rock billions of years old. Film shows, planetarium and tours.

**Museum of American History** 14th and Constitution Ave; web: www.americanhistory.si.edu. Includes pieces of the original *Stourbridge Lion* and *DeWitt Clinton* locomotives. Look for a gold crescent moon on the cylinder of a 1926 Pacific engine from the Southern Railway's *Crescent Limited*. The museum also has Henry Ford's Model T, Edison's phonograph, Washington's false teeth, Mohammed Ali's gloves, and the flag which inspired the national anthem.

**Museum of Natural History** 10th and Constitution Ave; web: www.mnh.si.edu. The 45.5-carat Hope Diamond (biggest blue diamond in the world) and the Fenkovi African elephant (largest ever recorded) are among 60 million exhibits.

# The Northeast Corridor
# New Haven–Springfield
## (for Boston)

## Joining the train

Several *Northeast Corridor* trains branch north at New Haven to travel inland through some of Connecticut's most appealing countryside.

## All aboard!

### NEW HAVEN (30/17)
For New Haven city information and the main *Northeast Corridor* route, see the preceding section (pages 189–208).

**WALLINGFORD (17/7)** Look for a spired church to your right.

**MERIDEN (7/10)** Located between Mount Beseck and the Hanging Hills. **Meriden's Heritage Museum** recreates life in the 1700s and you can see Long Island Sound from the tower of **Castle Craig**, accessible through Hubbard Park. Amtrak's station is at 60 State.

**Beaver Pond (4/6)** The pond is to your left and Silver Lake to your right.

**BERLIN (10/10)** Berlin was famous in the 18th century for manufacturing tinware. Amtrak's station also serves nearby New Britain.

**HARTFORD (10/8)** Birthplace of Katharine Hepburn. Founded in 1633, the former landing post known as Sucking became Connecticut's capital in 1875. Look for the Capitol's gold-plated dome high up to your right as the train arrives. The white-domed **Old State House**, designed by Charles Bulfinch, is now a museum. Hartford's Library and Supreme Court are opposite the Capitol building and contain the table where Abraham Lincoln signed the emancipation document. Amtrak's small station is at Union Place and the **tourist bureau** is at 234 Murphy Road; tel: 860 244 8181 or 1 800 793 4480; web: www.enjoyhartford.com.

When Hartford's English colonists displaced the Dutch, the latter called them *jankes* (thieves), so inventing the word Yankee. Around 50 companies now make this the 'insurance capital of the world' and the Travelers Insurance skyscraper on the site of the Charter Oak is one of America's tallest buildings

BOSTON ■

For Springfield to
Boston, see
*The Lake Shore Limited*

SPRINGFIELD ●

Windsor Locks ●

Windsor ●

Hartford ●

Berlin ●

Meriden ●

Wallingford ●

NEW HAVEN ●

(527ft/160m). The homes of Mark Twain (*Tom Sawyer*) and Harriet Beecher Stowe (*Uncle Tom's Cabin*) are preserved at Nook Farm.

**Connecticut River (5/3)** The river is to your right. Between here and Old Saybrook it runs through one of America's prettiest valleys.

**WINDSOR (8/5)** The town was originally settled in 1663 among colonial tobacco farms. You continue north across the Farmington River.

**WINDSOR LOCKS (5/20)** The 19th century canal to your right supplies water for Dexter and Sons, a paper products manufacturer. Windsor Locks' **Bradley Air Museum** owns more than 50 aircraft, including a 1909 Bleriot. The train crosses the Connecticut River.

**Enfield (10/10)** A future president of New Jersey College, Jonathan Edwards, preached here in colonial days.

**Connecticut/Massachusetts State Line (15/5)** You leave the Constitution State for the Bay State.

**SPRINGFIELD** A 17th century trading post on the banks of the Quinnitukqut (Native American for 'long tidal') River has become an industrial city and host to the Eastern States Exposition. Springfield's **Armory** contains a huge military collection and the **Basketball Hall of Fame** honours the sport's inventor, James Naismith. Free sights downtown include the **Natural History Museum** and the **Connecticut Valley Historical Museum**. The **visitors bureau** is at 1441 Main (tel: 413 787 1548) and Amtrak's station at 66 Lyman.

Some trains continue from Springfield to Boston. For this part of the route, see *The Lake Shore Limited* (pages 275–7).

# The *Crescent* New York–New Orleans

## General route information

The *Crescent* makes a 1,380-mile (2,200km) journey between New York and the more relaxed city of New Orleans. Southern hospitality envelops staff and passengers as Amtrak's friendliest train travels the *Northeast Corridor* route then passes through Civil War country to Atlanta, Birmingham and the south. You pass through 12 states and the District of Columbia. A National Park Service guide accompanies the train to provide passengers with a commentary along part of the route.

The *Crescent* began in 1891 as the Washington & Southwestern *Vestibule Limited*, an overnight train between Washington and Atlanta. Operated by the Richmond & Danville Railroad, the predecessor of the Norfolk Southern (whose line the present train uses south of Washington), the *Vestibule Limited* offered luxurious staterooms, a library and an observation car. It became a through train from New York City to New Orleans in 1906 and was later renamed the *Crescent City Limited*. The Southern Railway continued this service until Amtrak took over in 1979.

**Frequency** Daily.

The southbound train leaves New York early in the afternoon, reaching Washington by early evening and Greensboro just after midnight. You arrive in Atlanta early next morning, Birmingham by late morning and New Orleans mid-evening.

Travelling north, trains leave New Orleans early in the morning to reach Birmingham by early afternoon, Atlanta mid-evening and Greensboro during the night. You arrive in Washington early on the second day and New York by early afternoon.

**Reservations** All reserved.

**Equipment** Heritage coaches.

**Sleeping** Viewliner bedrooms.

**Food** Complete meals, snacks, sandwiches, drinks.

**Baggage** Check-in service at most stations.

## Joining the train

### NEW YORK

For New York City information and the route to Washington, see *The Northeast Corridor* (pages 196–208).

NEW YORK CITY

For New York City to
Washington, see
*The Northeast Corridor*

WASHINGTON

Alexandria

Manassas
Culpeper

Charlottesville
Lynchburg

Danville
Greensboro

High Point
Salisbury

Charlotte
Gastonia
Spartan-
burg
Greenville
Clemson
Toccoa
Gainesville
ATLANTA

Anniston
Birmingham
Tuscaloosa

Meridian
Laurel
Hattiesburg
Picayune
Slidell

NEW ORLEANS

## WASHINGTON

The *Crescent* departs by way of a tunnel, emerging with the Capitol Building to your right. Also to your right are the Bureau of Engraving, the Washington Monument and the Jefferson Memorial. To your right as you cross the Potomac River is the 14th Street road bridge.

**The Pentagon (5/10)** The nerve centre of America's military network, with 23,000 personnel occupying the world's largest office building (3.7 million square feet or 340,000m²). Nearby Arlington Cemetery was the last resting place for General Pershing, Admiral Byrd and the boxer Joe Louis. President John Kennedy's grave is marked by an eternal flame.

You pass the National Airport to your left then a huge Crystal City hotel and office development to your right, built on former railroad property. As the train approaches Alexandria, look left for long lines of Metro trains.

**ALEXANDRIA (15/30)** The massive grey stone building to your right is the George Washington Memorial Masonic Temple. Amtrak's attractive station at 110 Callahan Drive is one of many on this line which have been renovated.

Alexandria, 'the cradle of history', began in the 1740s as a port on the Potomac River. A million visitors each year now come to see the hundreds of restored buildings, a cobblestone waterfront and the nation's second-oldest apothecary shop. Gadsby's Tavern in Market Square was the traditional focus for business and social gatherings. Tours of **Old Town Alexandria** start at the Ramsay House, 221 King (tel: 703 549 0205). The *Spirit of Mount Vernon* travels along the Potomac River to George Washington's colonial estate, where you can visit his grand farmhouse, smokehouses and slave quarters.

**MANASSAS (30/30)** The town was fiercely fought over during the Civil War, when two battles around a strategic rail junction in 1861 cost 24,000 lives and earned Thomas 'Stonewall' Jackson his nickname. The present brick station on your right at 9500 West dates from 1915 and has original wood panelling in the waiting-room. Bristow Air Park is to your left.

The *Crescent* passes a cemetery and grain elevators on the right before travelling among forests and farms.

**Remington (20/10)** Look right for a farmers' market before you cross the Rappahannock River. Factories and warehouses accumulate on the right as you approach Culpeper.

**CULPEPER (30/60)** The Union Army had a headquarters here during the Civil War and the **Cavalry Museum** features weaponry and other equipment from that time. The attractive downtown area of Culpeper can be seen beyond the redbrick station to your right.

The *Crescent* continues southwest, accompanying the Blue Ridge Mountains and Shenandoah National Park to your right.

**Rapidan River (15/45)** More Civil War battles were fought at nearby Cedar Mountain, Port Republic and the Wilderness. You travel through lush farmland adorned with dogwoods and apple trees.

**Orange (30/30)** The James Madison Law Office appears to your left just before the town. Look left also for Montpelier Station and President Madison's estate.

**CHARLOTTESVILLE (60/65)** Named after King George III's wife, Charlotte, this is where Thomas Jefferson founded the University of Virginia and created his Monticello home on a nearby hill. Other residents have included Meriwether Lewis, William Faulkner and President James Monroe, whose **Ash Lawn Estate** is open to the public. Amtrak's new station is next to Union Station at 810 W Main, where Thruway buses connect with Warrenton and Dulles International Airport. The **visitors bureau** is at 108 Second; tel: 434 977 6100 or 877 386 1102; web: www.charlottesvilletourism.org.

To your right as you leave town is the University of Virginia Medical Center, then other academic buildings and the distinctive rotunda.

**Monroe (55/10)** Sweet Briar College is across the highway to your right as the train continues past rolling green fields with hedgerows, cattle, barns and streams. You cross the James River on a high trestle then enter Rivermont Tunnel.

**LYNCHBURG (65/65)** Named after John Lynch, who founded a ferry service here after the town grew rich on tobacco. Lynchburg has many Victorian houses and is one of Virginia's chief industrial and education centres. Amtrak's station is at Kemper and Park Ave. Appomattox Court House, where Robert E Lee surrendered to General Grant, is 21 miles (33km) east. Kemper Street Station, built in 1912 by the Southern Railway, has been handsomely restored as a modern bus and rail terminal with antique charm.

The *Crescent* continues through mellow Piedmont countryside and the forests of the Blue Ridge Mountains, which extend from Pennsylvania down to Georgia as part of the Appalachian range.

**DANVILLE (65/60)** Located beside the Dan River, Danville boasts 'the world's best tobacco market' and the largest textile mill on earth. The town became (briefly, in 1865) the Confederate capital, and was later the birthplace of Lady Astor. A marker on Riverside Drive commemorates the 'wreck of the old 97' in 1903, when a mail train crashed at 90mph on the grade between Lynchburg and Danville. Thirteen people were killed, including engineer Joseph Broady. Three crates of canaries escaped and were found flying surreally in the wreck's smoky aftermath.

**Virginia/North Carolina State Line (5/55)** The train crosses the border as it continues into the night.

**GREENSBORO (60/25)** Famous for an annual golf tournament and a Revolutionary War battle where British General Cornwallis defeated General Greene at Guilford Courthouse.

**HIGH POINT (25/40)** So named because it represents the highest point on the route between Charlotte and Goldsboro.

**SALISBURY (40/50)** Daniel Boone grew up in this colonial town set among pretty hills and lakes. Amtrak's station is at Depot and Liberty.

A short distance to the north, at 411 S Salisbury Ave in Spencer, is the **North Carolina Transport Museum**; tel: 704 636 2889; web: www.ci.salisbury.nc.us/nctrans/index.htm.

Located on the site of the Southern Railway's largest repair plant, the museum has historic locomotives, railroad equipment, antique cars and memorabilia from Native American times to the present. Open daily, free. Steam and diesel rides take place from April to December, admission charge.

**CHARLOTTE (50/25)** Another city named after George III's wife, Charlotte became the first place in America where gold was found. Railroads converged on what is now the largest city in the Carolinas. An important financial centre, this is also America's main producer of cotton cloth. Each May the **World 600 Auto Races** take place at the motor speedway.

Charlotte was the birthplace, in a log cabin, of President James Polk, and you can take a self-guided tour of the Old City from the **information center** at 122E Stonewall; tel: 704 331 2700 or 1 800 231 4636; web: www.charlottecvb.org/info.

Highlights include a settlers' cemetery and the blushing pink splendour of Overcarsh House. Latta Plantation Park has costumed guides and a 19th century merchant's house.

**GASTONIA (25/55)** The *Crescent* makes a slight detour west to take in this industrial town, near where a Revolutionary War battle was fought at Kings Mountain.

**North Carolina/South Carolina State Line (5/50)** You cross between the two Carolinas and enter the Palmetto State, travelling through countryside famous for peaches.

**SPARTANBURG (55/40)** A manufacturing town which was named after the Spartan regiment of the South Carolina militia.

**GREENVILLE (40/35)** Another major textile town, where inexpensive clothes can be bought at many factory outlets. Bob Jones University became established here in 1827 and Greenville was the birthplace of Joanne Woodward and Jesse Jackson. The small modern station is part of a large building containing offices of the Norfolk Southern Railroad.

**CLEMSON (35/35)** A university town which until 1943 was called Calhoun, after the 19th century politician John Calhoun.

**South Carolina/Georgia State Line (20/15)** As the *Crescent* travels deeper into the south through wooded countryside look for examples of the fast-growing kudzu vines. These were imported from Japan to combat soil erosion but have become a menace throughout the south, spreading over the ground to smother all in their path.

**TOCCOA (35/40)** Home of Toccoa Falls (186ft/56m) and a college of the same name. Note the traditional station building to your right and an impressive spired church on your left.

The *Crescent* departs past warehouses and freight trains to travel among tree-covered hills, lumber yards, orchards and occasional fields. Near Gainesville, factories and freight trains gather on both sides.

**GAINESVILLE (40/55)** The town is on the eastern edge of Lake Sidney Lanier, Georgia's largest lake. The Lake Lanier Islands are a popular recreation area with beaches, camp-sites, fishing and boating. Amtrak's charming brick station at 116 Industrial Blvd also serves Athens, home of the University of Georgia (America's oldest state college).

The train pauses across a barriered road junction before continuing among more factories, lumber yards and freight wagons. Look right for a flea market after you pass beneath a highway bridge.

As the day becomes lighter you begin to travel through less mountainous scenery, with cattle, horses and dark ploughed fields.

**Norcross (35/20)** Industry returns as MARTA commuter trains assemble. Look for the old green Pullman car sidelined to your left.

**Oglethorpe University (40/15)** The campus is to your right. As you near Atlanta the city's imposing skyscrapers can be seen ahead to your left.

## ATLANTA (55/130)

Birthplace of Spike Lee and venue for the 1996 Olympic Games, Atlanta is America's fastest growing city. The unofficial capital of the south has the most affluent black middle class in the country and one of America's highest crime rates. Magnolias still bloom along the older streets and spring fills Atlanta's parks with flowering azaleas and dogwoods.

The city began in 1837 as a railroad town called Terminus but was renamed after the Western Atlantic Railroad. By the time of the Civil War more rail lines converged here than anywhere else in the south and the city became a prime target for General Sherman's Union forces. The war's destruction failed to halt growth for long and many large corporations are now resident, including Coca-Cola and CNN. The glass building to the left of the station belongs to AT&T.

### Atlanta basics

**Telephone code** 404.

**Station** Amtrak's renovated Brookwood (Peachtree) station is at 1688 Peachtree, three miles (5km) north of downtown (take bus #23). Built by the Southern Railway in 1918 as a small suburban halt, the station is barely adequate today even though slightly expanded. Information tel: 881 3061. Ticket-office and waiting-room open 06.30–21.45. Lockers, vending machines, handcarts. Connections: Thruway buses connect with Montgomery and Mobile, Alabama. Others go to Chattanooga and Nashville, Tennessee, or to Columbus and Macon, Georgia.

**Local transport** MARTA operates buses and subway trains; tel: 848 5501.

**Taxis** London; tel: 688 5658. Checker; tel: 351 1111.

**Car rental** Avis, 143 Courtland; tel: 800 331 1212.

**Greyhound** 232 Forsyth; tel: 584 1728.

**Hartsfield Airport** is 10 miles (16km) south by MARTA train, Shuttle Tran (tel: 800 556 5466) and Airport Express bus (tel: 800 842 2770).

**Tours** American Coach/Gray Line; tel: 800 593 1818. Walking tours from the Preservation Center, 327 St Paul Ave; tel: 876 2041.

**Visitors bureau** 233 Peachtree; tel: 521 6600; web: www.atlanta.net.

**Other information centres** can be found at 3393 Peachtree (tel: 266 1398), 231 Peachtree (tel: 654 1296) and 65 Upper Alabama (tel: 577 2148).

**Accommodation** Contact Bed & Breakfast Atlanta, 101 St Charles Ave NE, Atlanta, GA 30306; tel: 875 0525.

Youth Hostel, 223 Ponce De Leon Ave; tel: 872 1042. Beds from $12. YMCA, 22 Butler; tel: 659 8085. Men only. Single $22.

Hotels include the Holiday Inn, 101 International Blvd; tel: 800 535 0707; Terrace Garden Inn, 3405 Lenox Rd; tel: 800 241 8260; Quality Inn, 89 Luckie; tel: 424 7991; Howard Johnson, 330 W Peachtree; tel: 577 6970; Travelodge, 1641 Peachtree; tel: 873 5731 – single $45, double $54; Midtown Manor, 811 Piedmont Ave; tel: 872 5846 – single $35, double $45.

### Recommended in Atlanta

**State Capitol** 206 Washington; tel: 656 2844. Topped by a dome of gold leaf mined in north Georgia, the 1889 building houses state offices, Confederate flags and the

**Georgia History Museum**. Open weekdays, free tours.

**Stone Mountain Park and Village** 16 miles east of Atlanta on US 78; tel 498 5600; web: www.stonemountainpark.com. This 3,200-acre (1,296ha) park attracts six million visitors a year, giving it the third-largest attendance in the USA (after the Disney parks). The site includes the world's largest granite outcrop, where you can see carved figures of Jefferson Davis, Robert E Lee and Stonewall Jackson on horseback. The **Antebellum Plantation Village** features 19 restored historic buildings and you can take a paddlewheel riverboat cruise on the lake.

The **Stone Mountain Scenic Railroad** takes visitors on a five-mile excursion around the mountain's base aboard a full size locomotive. Opened in 1962, the railroad features diesel engines, built in 1950 and 1956, pulling newly renovated open-air train cars. The train departs from a scale replica of the Main Train Depot from late 19th century downtown Atlanta. Open daily, admission charge.

**New Georgia Railroad** 10 Central Ave; tel: 656 0769. On most Saturdays a steam engine takes vintage passenger cars on an 18-mile (29km) tour of the city. On one Saturday a month, trains go to Stone Mountain Park, leaving from Milepost Station close to the 1869 Georgia Railroad freight depot (Atlanta's oldest building).

**Governor's Mansion** 391 W Paces Ferry Rd; tel 261 1776. Built in Greek Revival style, the mansion has a fine collection of federal period furnishings. Open Tue–Thu, free.

**Martin Luther King Historic District** The Center for Nonviolent Social Change at 449 Auburn Avenue has a library, films and museum; tel: 526 8900; web: www.thekingcenter.org.

Atlanta was a focal point for the 1960s' civil rights movement. You can visit Dr King's birthplace and see the Ebenezer Baptist Church where he preached. Open daily, donation.

**Carter Library** 441 Freedom Pkwy; tel: 331 3942; web: www.jimmycarterlibrary.org. The Jimmy Carter Library is the only Presidential library in the southeastern United States. Documents and memorabilia, including some of the nation's historic treasures, are on exhibit. Open daily, admission charge.

**Southeastern Railway Museum** 3966 Buford Hwy in Duluth, 20 miles (32 km) northeast of Atlanta; tel: 770 476 2013; web: www.srmduluth.org. Among the rolling stock are vintage steam engines, wooden cars and Pullmans such as the 1911 car *Superb* used by President Harding. Train rides in restored coaches. Open Thu–Sat, admission charge.

**Big Shanty Museum** At 2829 Cherokee in Kennesaw, 25 miles north of Atlanta, the only town in America where it is illegal for citizens not to own a gun; tel: 427 2117. The museum, also known as the Kennesaw Civil War Museum, is housed in a former cotton gin and features *The General*. This 1855 Rogers steam engine was stolen at Big Shanty by Northern soldiers in 1862, along with two cars of a Western & Atlantic passenger train. It was captured half way to Chattanooga after being pursued at 60 mph by southern troops aboard the locomotive *Texas*. The 'great locomotive chase' inspired a classic 1926 film *The General* starring Buster Keaton, who was born close to the sounds of a rail junction and had a lifelong obsession with trains. Open daily, admission charge.

**Chattanooga** Located 110 miles (176km) northwest of Atlanta; web: www.choochoo.com. Chattanooga is dominated by Lookout Mountain, the top of which can be reached on the world's steepest passenger railway line. The 1909

Southern Railway terminal has been renovated, its magnificent 85ft/24m dome becoming the lobby of a hotel where you can spend the night in restored Victorian passenger cars and eat in an original dining car (tel: 423 266 5000). The station also holds the largest HO gauge model railway in the world.

The original 'Chattanooga Choo-Choo' was a passenger train which first operated from Cincinnati in 1880. Almost all trains going south passed through Chattanooga then, and this one later encouraged Glenn Miller to make a million-selling record. A vintage wood-burner locomotive resembling *The General* used on that first run is displayed at the terminal. The state has plans to reopen a regular train route between Chattanooga and Atlanta.

# All aboard!

The *Crescent* leaves Atlanta through western industrial suburbs. Extensive freight yards sprawl to your right and the Chattahoochee Brick Company is to your left. The train crosses Interstate 75 and the Chattahoochee River before re-entering a landscape of tree-covered hills and ridges.

**Douglasville (35/95)** One of many quiet towns encountered on this section of the route. An imposing Commercial Bank and the Young Refining Corporation building are to your right.

**Villa Rica (50/80)** Look right for the Golden Hosiery Mills factory set among pine trees and dogwoods.

**Bremen (65/65)** The Hubbard Slacks Company is seen to your right before the *Crescent* moves slowly out of Bremen. You pass a church on your left then start climbing a series of S-shaped curves into the hills.

**Tallapoosa (75/55)** Note one of Georgia's finest golf courses on your left as you approach town. The American Thread Company is to your right. The *Crescent*'s tracks run on an island along the centre of main street and an ancient steam engine can be seen on display.

The train picks up speed as it crosses the attractive Tall River then climbs further into forested hills. Look for logs being loaded aboard railway wagons on your left before you cross the Tallapoosa River.

**Georgia/Alabama State Line (90/40)** You pass from Eastern to Central Time, so watches go back an hour (forward when travelling east). The landscape becomes ever more densely wooded as you enter Talladega National Forest at the southern end of the Appalachian Mountains.

**Heflin (105/25)** This was once a gold rush town. In the left distance is Alabama's highest mountain, Mount Cheaha (2,407ft/735m).

**ANNISTON (130/90)** One of the state's main manufacturing centres, with an old brick station building on the right.

**Anniston Depot (10/80)** Second World War Sherman tanks guard silos at the US Army's largest military depot, stretching away to your right.

**Lincoln (15/75)** Look for a modest blue railroad building on your right.

**Pell City (30/60)** A Chrysler factory appears to your right before the train enters Chula Vista Mountain Tunnel, the only tunnel on this line.

**Gahaba River (65/25)** You cross by means of two high bridges. The river continues on your left as undulating, forest-covered hills give way to industrial scenes near Birmingham.

**Irondale (70/20)** Freight wagons assemble on the right. Look right also for the Sloss Furnace, dating from 1890. The Dr Pepper company appears to your left.

**Red Mountain (85/5)** A 55ft (17m) statue on the mountain to your left represents Vulcan, the Roman god of fire and forge. Made for the 1904 St Louis World's Fair, this is the largest (60 tons; 54,000kg) cast-iron statue ever constructed. A stairway inside leads to an observation deck at the top.

**BIRMINGHAM (90/60)** Alabama's biggest city has been the home of Willie Mays, Nat King Cole and Hank Williams Jr. Amtrak's stop at 1819 Morris Ave stands opposite a cluster of dismal factories with tall brick chimneys. To your left is the University of Alabama Medical School.

Named after its English equivalent, Birmingham is also an industrial city but has parks and gardens filled with roses and dogwood trees. The zoo features Siberian tigers and golden spider monkeys. Birmingham's **visitors bureau** is at 2200 9th Ave; tel: 205 458 8000; web: www.birminghamal.org.

The *Crescent* departs among rail yards, with Vulcan still dominating the skyline to your left.

**Bessemer (22/38)** To your right are the Royster Guano Company and a former Pullman-Standard factory. Assuming both trains are on time you should soon be passing the northbound *Crescent*.

**TUSCALOOSA (60/90)** The University of Alabama, home of the 'Crimson Tide' football team, is to your right as you approach the beautiful brick and stucco station. Named after a Choctaw chief, Tuscaloosa used to be Alabama's capital.

The train skirts a golf course to your left then travels southwest through swamp country. Sleepy towns, sunburned houses and characterful general stores appear between the forest plantations and logging sites.

**Mound State Monument (15/75)** Prehistoric mounds to your right were used by Native Americans for ceremonial purposes, although the temple on the highest one is more recent.

**Black Warrior River (35/55)** The *Crescent* slows down to clank across a steel drawbridge into further swamp country. Another track runs along the raised bed to your left.

**Tombigbee River (45/45)** Note the white cliffs as you cross this part of the Tenn-Tom project which links the Tennessee, Ohio and Upper Mississippi Rivers with the Gulf of Mexico.

**Livingston (70/20)** Named after Robert Livingston, who negotiated the Louisiana Territory purchase in 1803.

**York (75/15)** Look for picturesque stores to your right and a sawmill to your left.

**Alabama/Mississippi State Line (80/10)** The train continues south among cotton fields and magnolias.

**MERIDIAN (90/60)** Birthplace of delta country blues artist Jimmie Rodgers, the 'singing brakeman' whose memory lives on at a museum and the town's music festival. Rodgers worked on the railroad and wrote many songs about his experiences. *Waiting For A Train* told the story of a hobo who jumped freights to look for work during the 1930s' Depression.

Meridian is an important rail junction, where tracks radiate in six directions. In the shunting yards beyond the remodelled station you can see rolling stock from many lines, including the Southern Railway, the Delaware & Hudson and the Illinois Central Gulf. The splendid station was built in traditional style and is remarkably large, since it sees only two Amtrak trains a day (one in each direction).

As the *Crescent* leaves, look for a faded Gulf Mobile Sohio Railroad building falling apart to your left.

**Key Field (8/52)** Light aircraft are housed in the hangars to your right and other planes belong to the Mississippi National Guard. You cross Chunky Creek and pass a natural gas facility to your left.

**LAUREL (60/30)** This is a crew change point for the *Crescent*. Laurel is a trading centre for farmers, with a fire station on the left and disused tracks that run into the trees. Amtrak has a waiting-room set aside at the north end of the large brick station building, which has been restored as a community centre.

The *Crescent* crosses the Leaf River just before Hattiesburg station, where an old baggage car can be seen confined between two steam locomotives.

**HATTIESBURG (30/60)** Home of Southern Mississippi University and the Magnolia Classic golf tournament, Hattiesburg was founded on the railroad and lumber industries. The old red-tiled station at 308 Newman is mostly boarded up. To the right of its wide platform and large wooden canopy stands a futuristic coal-fired electricity generating plant.

You leave past a square-towered church on your left.

**Poplarville (40/20)** Birthplace of Theodore Bilbo, a US senator and segregationist who was governor of Mississippi in the 1920s–40s.

**PICAYUNE (60/15)** This is the *Crescent*'s final stop in the state of Mississippi. Note the short platform and an open wooden pavilion to provide shelter for waiting passengers.

**Pearl River (5/10)** Crossing the river takes you into the flat, subtropical landscape of southern Louisiana.

**SLIDELL (15/55)** A residential town for many who commute into New Orleans. Main Street is to your left beyond the station.

**Lake Pontchartrain (10/45)** Taking the *Crescent* is worthwhile just to experience this spectacular six-mile (10km) crossing of Lake Pontchartrain's eastern tip. The train runs along a causeway immediately above the lake's surface, giving sensational views across 630 square miles (1,630km$^2$) of water. The scene is especially wonderful at sunset (or sunrise if travelling east). Look for fishing shanties on stilts and a road bridge to your left.

Soon after leaving Lake Pontchartrain you glimpse the New Orleans skyline ahead to your left. Look also for Tulane University and the Greenwood Cemetery with above-the-ground graves. On arrival in New Orleans the *Crescent* pauses before reversing into the station.

## NEW ORLEANS
For New Orleans city information, see *The Sunset Limited* (pages 148–50).

# The *Silver Star* New York–Miami

## General route information

Another train with a party atmosphere, the *Silver Star* travels between the great northeastern cities and Florida's subtropical resorts, passing through historic Virginia, tracts of pine forest and Old Savannah. Beyond Lake Okeechobee you visit many of the beach communities leading to Miami.

**Frequency** Daily.

The southbound service leaves New York late in the morning to reach Washington by late afternoon, Richmond early evening and Raleigh late evening. You arrive in Savannah and Jacksonville early next morning, Orlando by late morning and Miami late in the afternoon.

Travelling north, trains leave Miami at mid-morning to reach Orlando by late afternoon, Jacksonville mid-evening and Savannah late evening. You arrive in Richmond next morning, Washington by midday and New York late in the afternoon.

**Reservations** All reserved.

**Equipment** Amfleet coaches. Movies are shown in coaches, with headphones available for purchase.

**Sleeping** Viewliner bedrooms.

**Food** Complete meals, snacks, sandwiches, drinks.

**Baggage** Check-in service at most stations.

## Joining the train

### NEW YORK

For New York City and the *Silver Star* route to Washington, see *The Northeast Corridor* (pages 196–208). For the route from Washington to Alexandria, see *The Crescent* (page 212).

## All aboard!

**ALEXANDRIA (15/90)** Soon after leaving Alexandria the *Silver Star* crosses the first of several inlets leading to the Potomac River.

**Lorton (14/76)** Amtrak's new northern *Auto Train* depot is to your right. The *Silver Star* crosses the Occoquan River and Neabsco Creek.

**Possum Point (20/70)** A huge Virginia Power electricity generating plant appears to your left.

**Quantico Base (30/60)** Amtrak's *Carolinian* train makes a stop inside this 60,000-acre (24,000ha) US Marine Corps base, where the museum features Second World War tanks and aircraft. Look left for the airfield and assault course.

You continue with the Potomac away to your left and travel south among forests and rivers.

**Falmouth (36/54)** Soon after this small residential and manufacturing town you cross the muddy Rappahannock River, across which George Washington famously threw a silver dollar. A highway bridge is to your right.

**Fredericksburg (40/50)** Another stop for the *Carolinian*. Washington lived in Fredericksburg as a boy and Mary Washington's garden at 1200 Charles still has the box hedges she planted. George's brother, Charles, owned the Rising Sun Tavern. The **visitors bureau** is at 706 Caroline (tel: 540 373 1776) and Amtrak's station at Caroline and Lafayette Blvd. Nearby Fredericksburg and Spotsylvania Military Park explains events at four Civil War battlefields.

The train leaves with Fredericksburg's airport and runways to your left.

**Meade Pyramid (45/45)** This memorial to the Civil War General George G Meade can be seen to your left.

**Jackson Shrine (55/35)** Stonewall Jackson died in the modest white house to your left at Guinea. You cross the Mattaponi and Pamunkey Rivers as the train travels through pleasant countryside. Logging operations and marshes are often close to the sides of the track.

**Ashland (80/10)** As the train runs carefully beside the town's main street look left for picturesque Randolph-Macon College. Dating from 1830, it was originally for women only.

**RICHMOND (90/30)** State capital since 1779, Richmond was the Confederate capital for much of the Civil War. The old tobacco town has recently revived

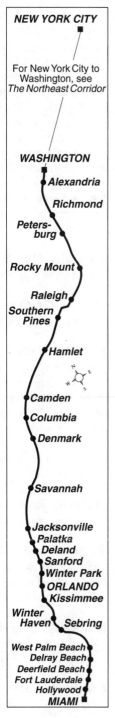

NEW YORK CITY

For New York City to Washington, see *The Northeast Corridor*

WASHINGTON
Alexandria
Richmond
Petersburg
Rocky Mount
Raleigh
Southern Pines
Hamlet
Camden
Columbia
Denmark
Savannah
Jacksonville
Palatka
Deland
Sanford
Winter Park
ORLANDO
Kissimmee
Winter Haven  Sebring
West Palm Beach
Delray Beach
Deerfield Beach
Fort Lauderdale
Hollywood
MIAMI

after a period of decline, and the Cultural Link trolley runs from the Science Museum at 2500 W Broad to take in 35 historic landmarks. Richmond's **tourist bureau** is located in an old railway depot at 405 N Third; tel: 804 783 7450; web: www.richmondva.org.

The **Confederate Museum** owns the world's largest collection of Civil War memorabilia, including General Lee's sword. There are free tours of the Capitol, which Thomas Jefferson helped design, and of the Philip Morris plant (largest cigarette factory on earth). Amtrak's impressive modern station on your right is some way from downtown but is open 24 hours a day.

The train curves right through massive yards bustling with goods traffic. As you near the James River the University of Richmond can be seen to your left.

**James River (14/16)** You cross the rock-strewn waterway with an Interstate 95 highway bridge to your right. As you approach Petersburg, houses begin to replace the trees.

**Centralia (20/10)** Centralia is the headquarters of the main US Army clothing supply depot.

**Chester (24/6)** Several battles were fought here during the Civil War. Look for the remains of an 1863 campsite to your left.

**PETERSBURG (30/80)** The *Silver Star* stops at South Street Station on your right at Ettrick. The Civil War ended 75 miles (128km) west of here when Grant accepted Lee's surrender at Appomattox Court House.

Virginia University appears high up to your left as the train departs Ettrick on Seaboard Coast Line tracks. You cross another muddy river, the Appomattox, into Petersburg proper. Just to the south is Fort Hell, a large Civil War fort.

The train continues through Carson and Stoney Creek then crosses the Nottoway River.

**Meherrin River (30/50)** After you cross the river near Emporia look for fields producing prolific crops of peanuts.

**Virginia/North Carolina State Line (35/45)** The Georgia Pacific Plywood factory straddles the border to your right. The train enters the Tar Heel State, so named after a promise Jefferson Davis made to tar the heels of soldiers to make them stand their ground.

**Roanoke River (45/35)** You cross the river on its way from the Blue Ridge Mountains to the Atlantic. This area around Weldon was the setting for the Sally Field film *Norma Rae*.

**Enfield (65/15)** Peanut storage warehouses appear on both sides before the train travels through a region of swamps renowned for their outsize crocodiles. North Carolina Wesleyan College can be seen to your right at Battleboro. Approaching Rocky Mount you cross over the Tar River.

**ROCKY MOUNT (80/80)** North Carolina grows the largest tobacco crop in America and much of it comes here to be marketed, along with cotton and other produce. In the old days most of the tobacco was transported from here by rail. Amtrak's station is at 101 Hammond.

**Wilson (20/60)** Wilson is a scheduled stop for *Silver Palm* and *Carolinian* trains. Local manufacturing companies include Levi Strauss (jeans) and Ralston Purina (pet food). An annual tobacco auction brings people from all over the country, and warehouses and curing facilities feature on both sides of the track.

**Selma (45/35)** A modest town serving adjacent farm communities, this is another stop for the *Carolinian*. Several houses have pictures of locomotives painted on their sides.

The *Silver Star* travels on past oil storage tanks then crosses the Neuse River before going through Wilson Mills. Look for more tobacco plants and peanut fields. Fox-hunters can sometimes be seen during spring and fall.

**RALEIGH (80/65)** The 'city of oaks' was named after its founder, Sir Walter Raleigh, and proclaimed North Carolina's unalterable seat of government. Raleigh's statue takes pride of place near the Capitol, completed in 1840 and restored for the US bicentennial. Beautifully preserved Victorian houses stand on streets lined with oak trees, magnolias and dogwoods. Raleigh has many educational establishments and high-tech industries, and *Money* magazine voted it the best place to live in America.

The **North Carolina Museum** depicts life from the first settlements through Revolutionary days to the Civil War. Amtrak is at 320 W Cabarrus. For information on the Victorian neighbourhoods contact the **visitor centre** at 301 N Blount; tel: 919 733 3456; web: www.raleighcvb.org.

**North Carolina Central Prison (5/60)** The jail's forbidding walls are to your left.

**North Carolina State University (7/58)** Seen to your right before the train continues among lakes, streams and hills thick with pine trees. You pass through the small communities of Cary, Merry Oaks and Moncure. On the approach to Southern Pines look left for the corrals where racehorses are prepared.

**SOUTHERN PINES (65/30)** The train holds up traffic among manicured bushes at a road junction. The large building beyond the station is an arts centre.

**HAMLET (30/70)** A proud sign proclaims this 'the all-American city'. Log trains are set up in rail yards to the right of canopied Main Street station, which is a registered historic building and houses the **National Railroad Museum** (tel: 919 582 3337).

After Hamlet, industry gives way again to forests, fields and white-spired churches.

**Carolinas State Line (7/63)** You move from North into South Carolina then cross the Pee Dee River north of Cherub and enter the Sand Hills.

**Bethune (50/20)** Located just south of the Lynches River, Bethune is one of the country's chief egg producers.

**CAMDEN (70/30)** Home of three racetracks and the Colonial Cup steeplechase, Camden is among South Carolina's oldest cities, often fought over during the Revolution.

**COLUMBIA (30/55)** The state capital since 1786, when government moved to the banks of the Congaree River from Charleston. The Hampton-Preston Mansion shows how Confederate general and statesman Wade Hampton lived in the 19th century. The **visitors bureau** is at 1012 Gervais (tel: 803 254 0479) and Amtrak's station at 850 Pulaski. Nearby are Fort Jackson and the state fairgrounds.

The **South Carolina Railroad Museum** is 25 miles (40km) to the north at Rockton (tel: 803 635 9893; web: www.scrm.org). Locomotives and rolling stock include a Seaboard office car and a hospital/command car. The museum's railroad, known today as the Rockton, Rion & Western, began life in 1883 as the Rock City Railway. Some of America's last steam trains ran between Rockton and Greenbrier, and on first and third Saturdays from June to October you can take a ride along the restored line.

**DENMARK (55/80)** A railroad town which is situated in the middle of swamp land.

**South Carolina/Georgia State Line (55/25)** You enter what was once Great Britain's 13th colony.

**SAVANNAH (80/130)** General James Oglethorpe and a group of English colonists founded Savannah on a bluff next to the river in 1733. Tobacco and cotton wealth soon resulted in great warehouses, mansions and a booming cotton exchange. America's first planned city was designed by Oglethorpe, who laid out a grid of streets and filled the squares with mountain laurel, oaks, azaleas and dogwoods. In *Treasure Island*, Robert Louis Stevenson refers to Savannah as a place of beauty and style. It was here, despite the rarity of snow, that James L Pierpoint composed *Jingle Bells*.

The cotton market and prosperity suffered after the Civil War but 1,000 buildings have been restored. Savannah has lately become better known by appearing as the setting for movies such as *Midnight in the Garden of Good and*

*Evil* and *Forrest Gump*. Bus and carriage tours are available from the **Historic Savannah Foundation** at 321 E York (tel: 912 233 7787). The **visitor centre** is in a former Central of Georgia railway station at 301 Martin Luther King Blvd; tel: 912 944 0455; web: www.savannahvisit.com.

The history museum next to the visitor centre occupies a railway shed on the site of the Siege of Savannah in 1779. There are presentations of the siege as well as displays of historic train engines and dining cars. Amtrak's station is a handsome old building four miles (6.5km) from downtown at 2611 Seaboard Coastline Drive.

The *Silver Star* departs through freight yards and travels among swamp land, trees, farms and villages. Watch for egrets and anglers along the banks of the many streams.

**Hunter Airfield (5/125)** A US Army establishment is seen to your left just before you cross the Ogeechee River.

**Richmond Hill (10/120)** The car magnate Henry Ford once owned a plantation here.

**Altamaha River (45/85)** You cross a river which flows into the Intracoastal Waterway.

**Jesup (50/80)** Named after Morris Jesup, who financed the line which is now part of the Seaboard Coast Railroad. Jesup is a scheduled stop for *Silver Meteor* trains. Nearby are Brunswick and St Simons Island. Look for the Jesup Shrimp Inc. building to your right and a very old freight wagon to your left as you pass through town.

After Jesup the train travels inland through eastern Georgia among more logging operations.

**Big Satilla Creek (70/60)** You cross the creek and a few minutes later cross the Satilla River.

**Folkston (85/45)** West and south of here is the 650 square mile Okefenokee Swamp and wildlife refuge. Its beguiling scenery and animal life can best be seen from a canoe or by walking the canal trails. Camp sites are raised on platforms to outwit alligators.

**Georgia/Florida State Line (95/35)** The *Silver Star* crosses high above the St Mary's River into the Sunshine State, which grows by around 1,000 people a day.

**JACKSONVILLE (130/60)** An industrial centre that is the second-largest US city by area, reaching from the St John's River to the Atlantic, Jacksonville has inexpensive accommodation but is not a tourist resort. The most attractive part of the city is down by the river, with its boardwalk and park. The

**Cummer Art Gallery** is in a former lumber baron's mansion and **Jessie Ball du Pont Park** features the 800-year-old Treaty Oak tree under which settlers and Native Americans concluded a truce. The **visitors bureau** is at 201 E Adams; tel: 800 733 2668 or 904 798 9111; web: www.jaxcvb.com.

*Sunset Limited* trains travel west from Amtrak's station at 3570 Clifford Lane to New Orleans and Los Angeles, as well as south to Orlando. Greyhound buses connect with Tallahassee. The *Silver Star* crawls out of Jacksonville among rail yards, crossovers, warehouses and loading facilities. The St John's River to your left is one of the few which flow 'up' from south to north.

You continue past Doctor's Inlet and Black Creek then travel through a constantly changing countryside of hardwood forests, lakes and rivers. Palm trees start to appear among the hills.

**Ortega River (16/44)** You cross with the St John's River still to your left and a marina to your right. Beyond the river you can see the extent of Jacksonville.

**US Naval Air Station (20/40)** The base is across the highway to your left, alongside an armed forces' reserve centre.

**St John's River (35/25)** The river appears again among trees to your left as the train goes through a land of woods, Spanish moss, small lakes and alligators. More than 300 species of birds live in this area, including bald eagles, black rails, bridled terns and yellow-breasted chats. Just before Palatka you cross a tributary of the St John's River.

**PALATKA (60/52)** The name is a Native American word for 'forbidding place'. Exotic palm trees grace the station to your left as the *Silver Star* stops twice to accommodate the train's length. Thruway buses connect with Ocala and Gainesville. Palatka is Amtrak's closest station to St Augustine, the oldest European settlement in the United States.

The train leaves past azalea bushes and holds up traffic at a road crossing – something which happens often on this part of the route. As you cross the St John's River, dairy farms and orchards begin to appear.

**Pierson (35/17)** 'The fern capital of the world' grows most of America's crop.

**DeLeon Springs (46/6)** The town was named after Juan Ponce de Leon, a Spanish explorer who discovered Florida in 1512 while on a quest for the fountain of perpetual youth.

**DELAND (52/20)** Founded by Henry Deland in 1876 and the home of Stetson University (named after the hat maker). A ferry goes from 2309 Riverride Rd to Hontoon Island, famous for Timucuan Indian settlements. The Amtrak station is at 2491 Old New York Ave. Thruway buses go to Daytona Beach, 25 miles (40km) east, where the 500 auto races are held each January and February and draw countless fans to the international speedway.

**St John's River (12/8)** The *Silver Star* crosses on a steel bridge.

**SANFORD (20/20)** After the South Florida Railroad arrived in 1884, joining Sanford to Jacksonville, this became a steamboat port and shipping point for the produce of central Florida. Amtrak's station is at 800 Persimmon Ave. The *Auto Train* terminates at 600 Persimmon Ave, where sidings for dealing with cars can be seen to your left.

You travel on among factories and housing estates with a large cement plant to your left. Urban scenes persist most of the way to Winter Park.

**WINTER PARK (20/15)** The train trundles through the streets of one of Winter Park's quiet, leafy neighbourhoods. The park itself is to your left. Rollins College, the oldest in the state, has a Spanish-style campus and the Cornell Fine Arts Centre. You continue through more suburbs to Orlando.

**Florida Hospital (5/10)** The imposing structure stands on both sides of the track and is connected by an overhead walkway.

**Church Street Station (11/4)** The old train station on your left has become part of an entertainment complex, complete with 19th century steam engine and street parties. Other delights include the Cheyenne Saloon and can-can dancing waitresses at Rosie O'Grady's Bar. Tours feature the history of the original rail depot (tel: 407 422 2434). Look for the high-rise buildings of Orlando ahead.

## ORLANDO (15/20)

Tourism has turned a modest agricultural town set among lakes and citrus groves into a 400 square mile city of a million people. Millions more visitors arrive throughout the year. Don't stray too far from the searchlights of the major attractions or you are almost certain to become lost.

Try to get to the theme parks early – at least half an hour before opening time – when the weather is cooler and fewer people are around. Queues for rides are usually shorter when a parade is on. Take snacks and plastic bottles to fill at the water fountains. Make sure you have a good breakfast before you go to give you energy, and alternate days at the parks with trips to the beach or you may find things too exhausting.

Orlando's daytime temperatures often reach 90°F (32°C) and even the coldest months rarely get below 50°F (10°C). As elsewhere in Florida, humidity can be high.

### Orlando basics

**Telephone code** 407.

**Station** Amtrak's cheerful whitewashed station is at 1400 Sligh Blvd. The splendid mission-style building, lately refurbished, has beautiful columns supporting the platform canopy. Information tel: 423 4882. Ticket-office open 07.00–18.45. Waiting-room 07.00–18.45. Baggage store, vending machines, newspapers, handcarts, Red Caps, taxi stand.

**Connections** Shuttle buses link to all the Disney resorts and the fare is half that of a taxi.

**Local transport** Most hotels are some distance from downtown, and the big attractions further still, but there is plenty of scheduled transport. The main companies are Phoenix Tours (tel: 859 4211) and Gray Line (tel: 422 0744). LYNX buses operate in Orlando and to the airport (tel: 841 8240).

**Taxis** Mears Transportation; tel: 839 1570. Yellow; tel: 422 4455.

**Car rental** Orlando Dodge, 4101 W Colonial Drive; tel: 800 342 1120.

**Greyhound** 555 N John Young Pkwy; tel: 292 3440.

**Orlando International Airport** is a few miles south of downtown by bus #8 and the Mears Shuttle (tel: 423 5566).

**Tours** Comet Bus Lines; tel: 240 3565. Gray Line; tel: 422 0744. Boat trips from Coastal Cruise Lines, 109 N Riverside Drive; tel: 1 800 881 2628.

**Visitors bureau** 8723 International Drive, Suite 100, Orlando, FL 32819; tel: 363 5872; web: www.orlandoinfo.com.

**Accommodation** Orlando has hundreds of hotels, especially around International Drive (known locally as 'I-Drive'). Rooms on Disney property tend to be more expensive but offer discounts off-season (September–December). Book well in advance at the Disney Central Reservations Office, Box 10,000, Lake Buena Vista, FL 32830-1000; tel: 934 7639.

Orlando/Kissimmee Hostel, 4840 W Irlo Hwy; tel: 396 8282. Young Women's Residential Center (AYH), 107 E Hillcrest; tel: 425 1076. Women only, $10.

Hotels in Orlando include the Peabody, 9801 International Dr; tel: 352 4000; Stouffer, 6677 Sea Harbour Dr; tel: 351 5555; Heritage Inn, 9861 International Dr; tel: 352 0008 – single and double $79; Radisson Barcelo, 8444 International Dr; tel: 345 0505 – single $59, double $89; Fairfield Inn, 8342 Jamaican Court; tel: 363 1944 – single $44, double $64.

## Recommended in Orlando

**Disney World** For information, advance tickets and a free guide contact Box 10,000, Lake Buena Vista, FL 32830; tel: 824 4321; web: http://disney.go.com/DisneyWorld. This 27,400-acre (11,000ha) complex opened in 1971 and is the world's most popular tourist attraction. Around 30 million visitors come each year and over 750 million passengers have ridden the world's largest monorail system. Other highlights include the Magic Kingdom (roller-coasters, Mickey Mouse and horrendous queues), the Epcot Center (cutting edge technology) and the MGM Studio (animation techniques, classic films and the Star Tours simulator). Admission is by day ticket or by 'passport' for several days.

The latest creation is Animal Kingdom, a fantasy zoo with an African savannah safari park conjured out of featureless farmland. Florida Oaks have been pruned to resemble acacias and forty thousand other trees planted. Among the animals are elephant, black rhino, cheetah and mhorr gazelle, which are extinct in the wild.

**Sea World** 7007 Sea World Dr, 20 miles (32km) southwest of Orlando; tel: 363 2200; web: www.seaworld.com. Features killer whales, stingrays, sea lions, penguins and some of Florida's few remaining manatees. You can hand-feed dolphins and enjoy close encounters with sharks from the safety of a glass tunnel. Open daily, admission charge. Take Greyhound or Tri-County bus #8.

**Universal Studios** 1000 Universal Studios Plaza; tel: 363 8000; web: www.uescape.com. The largest movie studio and theme park in the world has more than 40 rides, shows and film sets. The adjacent **Islands of Adventure** site lets you travel back to *Jurassic Park* and the *Lost Continent*. Open daily, admission charge. For VIP tours lasting four hours call 363 8295.

**Lake Eola Park** Rosalind and Central; tel: 246 2827. A favourite picnic and walking place in central Orlando, with swan-shaped paddle boats for hire on the lake. Open daily, free.

**Wekiwa Springs State Park** 1800 Wekiwa Circle, Apopka, 20 minutes northwest of downtown; tel: 884 2009; web: www.dep.state.fl.us/parks/wekiwa.html. A beautiful park with fishing, camping, swimming and canoeing on the St John's River. Open daily, free.

**Trainland of Orlando** 8990 International Drive; tel: 363 9002. Includes the world's largest model train layout and live steam passenger rides. Open daily, admission charge.

**Central Florida Railroad Museum** 101 South Boyd, Winter Garden; tel: 656 8749. Housed in a restored 1913 Tavares & Gulf Railroad depot, 15 minutes west of Orlando, are 3,000 antiques such as whistles and lights. Open Sun, free.

**The Kennedy Space Center** Located at Cape Kennedy (or Cape Canaveral), an hour's drive to the east; tel: 321 449 4444; web: www.kennedyspacecenter.com. Bus tours take in the museum, rocket garden and Shuttle launch site. Includes an IMAX film show, the Astronaut Hall of Fame and a 373ft (124m) Saturn V rocket saved by cancellation of the Apollo project. Open daily, admission charge.

# All aboard!

After suburban Orlando the *Silver Star* heads west among orange groves, lakes, trees and rivers. Florida has plans for a bullet train which would travel the 250 miles between Orlando and Miami in 90 minutes.

**KISSIMMEE (20/30)** Amtrak's nearest station to Disney World, but Orlando provides more hotels and better local transport connections. Kissimmee was originally built on reclaimed swampland late in the 19th century and this region is served by a network of rivers, canals and lakes. The oldest cattle auction in Florida takes place in Kissimmee each Wednesday. Amtrak's station is at 416 Pleasant and the **visitors bureau** at 1925 E Spacecoast Hwy; tel: 407 847 5000; web: www.floridakiss.com.

As the train pulls out note the **Monument of the States** among the downtown buildings to your left. This 70ft-high (21m) structure is made out of rocks from every state in the Union.

A few minutes later the *Silver Star* passes Lake Tohopekaliga before continuing among orange groves. Look for bald eagles and wading birds such as white ibis, blue herons and egrets.

**Auburndale (20/10)** The large citrus juice plants belong to Minute Maid and the Adams Company.

**WINTER HAVEN (30/45)** A Bordo Citrus plant stands opposite the station.

**West Lake Wales (8/37)** Beyond a disused station to your left is a 255ft-high (78m) stone and marble carillon called the **Bok Tower**. The tallest structure in Florida, it was named after E W Bok, the influential editor of *Ladies' Home Journal* around the turn of the century. The tower's 53 bronze bells weigh up to 12 tons each.

**Frostproof (25/20)** White beehives can be seen among the orange trees. The town failed to live up to its name in the winter of 1983, when the local crop was severely damaged.

**SEBRING (45/80)** Farming, packing and distribution were established here in the early 1900s. The famous international motor racing track is to your left.

**Lake Istokpoga (7/73)** The lake is visible among trees to your right before you cross the Kissimmee River, on course between Lake Kissimmee and Lake Okeechobee (the largest lake in the southern United States). On the far side is the swamp wilderness of **Everglades National Park**, where alligators lurk among floating islands of sawgrass and reed.

**Okeechobee (30/50)** The name is a Hitchiti Indian word for 'big water'. A few minutes later you pass the dikes restraining Lake Okeechobee on your right.

The *Silver Star* travels for the next 59 miles (95km) through cattle country at up to 79mph (127km/h) on the longest straight stretch of track east of the Mississippi. It takes an eight-car passenger train approximately 1.13 miles (1.8km) to stop when travelling at this speed. Look for a Florida Steel factory to your right.

**Indiantown (55/25)** The town was named after Seminole Indians. The train rattles across a bridge over the St Lucie Canal connecting Lake Okeechobee with the Atlantic.

**United (63/17)** The airfield is owned by Pratt and Whitney.

**WEST PALM BEACH (80/20)** This is the start of Florida's Gold Coast, with its mansions, condominiums, posh shops and polo fields. Three bridges link West Palm Beach with the island community of Palm Beach. Clear Lake is to your right and Amtrak's Spanish-style station on your left at 201 S Tamarind Ave.

The **Flagler Museum** in Palm Beach honours Henry Morrison Flagler, founder of the Florida East Coast Railway. When his line, some of which was built by slaves from the Bahamas, reached the island of Palm Beach he set about creating the most exclusive resort in the country by constructing the Breakers Hotel, where string orchestras and opera singers such as Dame

Nellie Melba were imported to entertain his rich friends. The present Renaissance-style hotel is a 'palace by the sea' built on the original site of Flagler's hotel in the 1920s. It boasts 567 rooms, 140 acres of gardens and two golf courses.

The opulent Flagler Museum is located in his stately Whitehall mansion on Cocoanut Row (tel: 561 655 2833) and features an Italian Renaissance library, Louis XIV music room, Elizabethan breakfast room, Swiss billiard room and a dining room imported from Warwick Castle in England. In Palm Beach you can also find the Estee Lauder mansion, the Kennedy compound and a former home of John and Yoko Lennon.

You leave West Palm Beach past the airport to your right. Plans to expand the runways were blocked when a population of rare gopher tortoises was discovered. The train continues among houses and waterways, interrupted by the occasional industrial scene.

**DELRAY BEACH (20/10)** An attractive, low-key resort which began as a settlement for artists. Delray Beach is the home of Florida's tennis championships and the **Morikami Museum of Japanese Art**.

**Boca Raton (4/6)** Another airport appears to your left. Boca Raton's dusty pink buildings were created by the architect Addison Mizner in a mixture of European styles and have an authentic 1920s atmosphere. Set among palm trees, shady cloisters and herb gardens, this is one of the few places on the coast where beaches and dunes remain in their natural state.

**DEERFIELD BEACH (10/15)** Palm trees line both sides of the track as you approach the station. The **South Florida Railway Museum** is located in the historic former Seaboard Air Line station at 1300 West Hillsboro Beach Blvd in Deerfield (tel: 954 698 6620; web: www.sfrm.org). The building is a fine example of Mediterranean-style architecture, with an arched entryway, stucco walls and a barrel tile roof. The museum preserves the history of railroads in southern Florida and has two impressive model railroad layouts.

**Pompano Beach Racetrack (5/10)** Harness racers and quarter horses use the track to your right.

**FORT LAUDERDALE (15/12)** One of Florida's main resorts, 'America's Venice' is also well known as a regular port of call for cruise ships. Named after the governor responsible for early Everglades drainage schemes, Fort Lauderdale has eight miles of beaches. An intricate system of waterways makes yachting a common mode of transport. **Ocean World** features sea lions and sharks.

The **visitors bureau** is at 1850 Eller Drive; tel: 954 765 4466. Amtrak's station at 200 SW 21st Terrace opens to the street, and is a busy stop during summer and in the spring break for colleges and universities. You leave past an airport to your left.

**HOLLYWOOD (12/20)** This eastern Hollywood was developed during the 1920s. Look for the colourful water-tower and a Hollywood Boulevard sign to your left. Tri-Rail commuter trains provide frequent services between Hollywood and Miami International Airport.

You continue past the Opa-Locka flea market and a racetrack at Hialeah. Approaching Miami, look for Miami Beach's hotels away to your left beyond an expanse of junked cars. Freight yards sprawl away complicatedly on the right of the line.

## MIAMI

America's Casablanca was founded for growing citrus fruits. Only a handful of people lived here when oil billionaire Henry Flagler's Central Florida railroad arrived in 1896 following a deal struck in a room above a pool hall between Flagler and the visionary Julia Tuttle, who owned the land. Tourism development in the 1920s and the pretty hotels of Miami Beach (10 miles/16km long and 300ft/90m wide) now attract ten million sun lovers and fashion victims every year and there is currently a $1.6 billion scramble to invest in new hotels on Miami beach. These will include the Four Seasons 67-storey tower, which will be the tallest building on the east coast south of New York City.

Greater Miami incorporates Key Biscayne (home of President Nixon's winter White House), upmarket Coral Gables, Hialeah and the elegant Coconut Grove. Half the city's two million population is of Spanish-American descent.

Temperatures can reach the high 70°F (over 30°C) even in winter, which is the peak season and avoids summer's humidity and showers. Spring and late autumn are the best times to visit.

### Miami basics

**Telephone code** 305.

**Station** Amtrak's station at 8303 NW 37th Ave in Hialeah has bus links to downtown (seven miles/12km south) and Miami Beach. Ticket-office and waiting-room open 06.15–24.00. Metropolitan lounge. Lockers, vending machines, newspapers, handcarts, Red Caps, taxi stand. Take bus L for Miami Beach.

**Connections** Tri-Rail trains (tel: 1 800 872 7245) go to Fort Lauderdale and West Palm Beach.

**Local transport** Metro-Dade buses run throughout Miami, with free maps and other information from 111 NW 1st; tel: 770 3131. Metrorail trains operate every day, with transfers to Metrobus, and its Northside station is close to Amtrak's depot.

**Taxis** Metro; tel: 888 8888. Aventura; tel: 599 9999.

**Car rental** Avis, 17760 Collins Ave; tel: 932 2350.

**Greyhound** 100 NW 6th; tel: 374 6160.

**Miami International Airport** is eight miles (13km) west by Metrobus #20 and Supershuttle vans; tel: 871 8488. Some hotels provide free taxis.

**Tours** American Sightseeing; tel: 688 7700. Boat cruises on the *Island Queen* start from Miamarina, 5th and Biscayne Bay; tel: 379 5119.

**Visitors bureau** 701 Brickell Ave; tel: 539 3000. Open weekdays. More information from the Chambers of Commerce at Key Biscayne (tel: 361 5207), Coconut Grove (tel: 444 7270), Miami Beach (tel: 604 2489) and the Everglades Visitor Association (tel: 245 9180).

**Accommodation** Miami has an abundance of rooms, from the economical to the ultra-luxurious. Top rates and biggest crowds are in winter, when prices can double. Contact the Miami Beach Hotel Association, 407 Lincoln Rd; tel: 531 3553. Miami Beach AYH Hostel, 1438 Washington Ave, in the historic district; tel: 534 2988. Members $13, non-members $15. Single $30, double $33. Take bus C from downtown.

Downtown hotels include the Hyatt Regency, 400 SE 2nd Ave; tel: 358 1234; Howard Johnson's, 1100 Biscayne Blvd; tel: 358 3080; Ramada Inn at Dupont Plaza, 300 Biscayne Blvd Way; tel: 358 2541.

Miami Beach hotels include the Alexander at 5225 Collins Ave; 865 6500; Seville Beach, 2901 Collins Ave; tel: 532 2511; Thunderbird, 18401 Collins Ave; tel: 931 7700; Tudor, 1111 Collins Ave; tel: 534 2934 – single and double $55; Sagamore, 1671, Collins Ave; tel: 538 7211; Adrian, 1060 Ocean Drive; 538 0007 – single $40.

## *Recommended in Miami*

**Art Deco District** From 6th to 23rd Streets, Miami Beach. Over 800 pastel-coloured buildings with 'eyebrow' balconies and Egyptian architraves make this the world's largest collection of art deco architecture. Walking tours start from the Art Deco Welcome Center at 1001 Ocean Drive (tel: 672 2014).

**Wolfsonian Foundation** 1001 Washington, in the Art Deco District; tel: 531 1001. The restored building contains 70,000 cultural items from the 1880s through the present, including furniture, murals and Second World War propaganda. Closed Mon, admission charge.

**Seaquarium** 4400 Rickenbacker Cswy, on Key Biscayne; tel: 361 5705; web: www.miamiseaquarium.com. The ocean aquarium stars alligators, dolphins, sharks, manatees, stingrays and killer whales. Nearby **Planet Ocean** provides a quieter look at underwater life. Open daily, admission charge.

**Vizcaya Museum and Gardens** 3251 S Miami Ave, in Coconut Grove; tel: 250 9133; web: www.vizcayamuseum.org. An Italianate palace built on the bay as a winter residence by the millionaire James Deering in 1916, with antique Renaissance furnishings brought from Europe. Formal gardens and fountains surround the house. Open daily, admission charge.

**Historical Museum of Southern Florida** 101 W Flagler; tel: 375 1492; web: www.historical-museum.org. Located in the Cultural Center, the museum shows Miami's past with hands-on displays and special exhibits. Walking and boat tours are available from September to June. Open daily, admission charge.

**Metrozoo** 12450 SW 152nd; tel: 251 0400 web: www.metro-dade.com/parks/metrozoo.htm. This 290-acre (117ha) zoo features 700 animals (240 species) including clouded leopards and Komodo dragons – the largest, most powerful lizards on earth. Most animals are uncaged on small islands made to resemble their natural habitats. The amphitheatre has wildlife shows throughout the day. Open daily, admission charge.

**Gold Coast Railroad Museum** Near the Metrozoo at 12450 Coral Reef Dr; tel: 253 0063; web: www.goldcoast-railroad.org. Among several Pullman cars displayed is the *Ferdinand Magellan*, used by presidents from Franklin Roosevelt to Ronald Reagan. The steam engines here once belonged to the Florida East Coast Railway. Half-hour train rides at weekends. Open daily, admission charge.

**Little Havana** Almost a tenth of Cuba's population has settled around Calle Ocho (SW 8th Street) after fleeing Fidel Castro's island, some braving the shark-infested Florida Straits on flimsy rafts. Family stores and cantinas are named after Havana streets and this is one of the few places in Miami where people still walk. Tours from the Development Authority, 970 SW 1st; tel: 324 8127. The Cuban Museum is at 1300 SW 12th Ave; tel: 858 8006. Open daily, donation.

**Key West** Henry Flagler set out to create modern Florida by constructing his East Coast Railway from Jacksonville to the end of the Keys, from where boats would continue to Havana and the Bahamas. He spent $18 million on the railroad, some $12 million on hotels and $10 million on the Key West extension. This continuation – 114 miles/182km long with 17 miles/27km of bridges – was completed in 1912 but a nameless hurricane destroyed the line in 1936.

The right of way now forms the base for a spectacular highway down which Greyhound buses travel from Miami to Ernest Hemingway's old haunts. For **visitor information** contact the Key West Chamber of Commerce, 402 Wall Street, Key West FL 33040; tel: 305 872 5988 or 800 LAST KEY.

# The *Silver Meteor*
# New York–Miami

## General route information

The *Silver Meteor* travels the eastern part of the United States between New York and Florida, visiting Charleston in South Carolina. Like the *Silver Star* and *Silver Palm*, it takes in the nation's capital, the Carolinas and Old Savannah.
**Frequency** Daily.

The southbound service leaves New York early in the evening to arrive in Washington by late evening and Charleston early next morning. You reach Jacksonville at midday, Orlando by mid-afternoon and Miami late evening.

Travelling north, trains leave Miami early in the morning to reach Orlando soon after midday and Jacksonville by mid-afternoon. You arrive in Charleston mid-evening, Washington early next morning and New York by mid-morning.

**Reservations** All reserved.

**Equipment** Amfleet coaches. Movies are shown in coaches, with headphones available for purchase.

**Sleeping** Viewliner bedrooms.

**Food** Complete meals, snacks, sandwiches, drinks.

**Baggage** Check-in service at most stations.

## Joining the train

### NEW YORK

For New York City and the route to Washington, see *The Northeast Corridor* (pages 196–208). For the route from Washington to Rocky Mount, see *The Silver Star* (pages 222–5).

**ROCKY MOUNT (80/80)** North Carolina grows the biggest tobacco crop in America and much of it comes here to be traded, along with cotton and other produce.

**Wilson (20/60)** Tobacco warehouses and curing facilities can be seen on both sides of the track.

**Selma (45/35)** The *Silver Meteor* continues on the Seaboard Line through tobacco, cotton and soya bean fields.

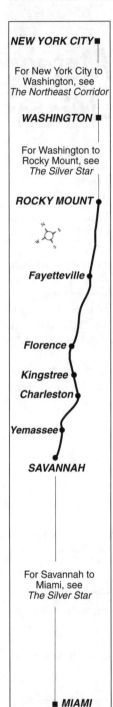

NEW YORK CITY ■

For New York City to
Washington, see
*The Northeast Corridor*

WASHINGTON ■

For Washington to
Rocky Mount, see
*The Silver Star*

ROCKY MOUNT ●

Fayetteville ●

Florence ●

Kingstree ●

Charleston ●

Yemassee ●

SAVANNAH

For Savannah to
Miami, see
*The Silver Star*

■ MIAMI

**Smithfield (60/20)** You travel past the birthplace of Ava Gardner then cross the Cape Fear River.

**FAYETTEVILLE (80/80)** The train crosses Hope Mill Lake at this farming town founded by 18th century Scottish immigrants. Nearby is Fort Bragg, home of the US Army's 82nd Airborne Division and Delta Force.

**Pembroke (25/55)** Home of Pembroke State University, the town is located on the banks of the Lumbee River.

**Carolinas State Line (35/45)** You cross from North to South Carolina just before the town of Hamer. You then cross the Little Pee Dee River.

**Dillon (45/35)** Dillon used to be a haunt of Francis Marion, 'the swamp fox' of the Revolutionary War. This is a scheduled stop for the *Silver Palm*.

The *Silver Meteor* crosses the Great Pee Dee River 20 minutes later and travels over an area of swamp land.

**FLORENCE (80/30)** Home of Francis Marion College and 'the denture capital of the world', Florence claims to make 1,000 sets of false teeth a week. The town originated with the coming of the railroad and has extensive Seaboard Coast Line yards handling mostly cotton, tobacco and corn. Thruway buses travel to Conway and Myrtle Beach.

Amtrak's modern building has been built in the same style as the old depot standing next to it. The old station was bought by the McLoud Regional Medical Center and has been returned to its former magnificence. Look for a steam locomotive parked to your right soon after you leave.

You cross the Lynches River 10 minutes from Florence and travel among the farms of the coastal plain. Note the distinctively shaped barns used for storing tobacco.

**KINGSTREE (30/45)** The rail depot also houses a restaurant. A few minutes later you cross the Black River close to where Robert Mitchum was born. Mitchum's father was a half Blackfoot Indian who died working as a train brakeman when two cars collided and crushed him.

**Santee River (10/35)** You cross the river then continue beside **Francis Marion Forest** to your left. Swamps, oak trees, pines and lakes cover an expanse of 250,000 acres (100,000ha). Marion earned his nickname by raiding from these marshlands. He was a master of the surprise attack, never camping in the same place for more than two nights.

**Lake Moultrie (20/25)** The lake is behind the levee to your left, with Lake Marion further inland. You cross the Cooper River on its way from Lake Moultrie to Charleston then pass a large Strawberry Corner shrubs nursery.

## CHARLESTON (45/45)

Founded in 1670 where the Cooper and Ashley Rivers meet on the Atlantic coast, Charleston's position made it one of the most prosperous early American ports and for a time the fourth-largest settlement in the American colonies. Further growth came with the start of America's first train service in 1830, which locals called 'the best friend of Charleston'.

Hundreds of merchants' houses survive and many can be visited during the spring festival. Down on the waterfront you can see spectacular sunsets and watch gulls glide over Battery Park. Charleston's brightly coloured mansions and cobblestone streets have recovered from the hurricane which devastated the city in 1989. For information contact the **Historic Foundation**, PO Box 1120, Charleston, SC 29402; tel: 723 1623; web: www.historiccharleston.org.

### Charleston basics

**Telephone code** 843.
**Station** Amtrak's station is at 4565 Gaynor Ave in North Charleston, seven miles (11km) from downtown (take the Durant Ave bus). Information tel: 744 8264. Ticket-office and waiting-room open 06.00–22.00.
**Local transport** SCE & G and DASH buses (tel: 724 7420) operate downtown, Mon–Sat.
**Taxis** Yellow; tel: 577 6565.
**Car rental** Thrifty, 3565 W Montague Ave; tel: 552 7531.
**Greyhound** 3610 Dorchester Rd; tel: 744 4247.
**Tours** Gray Line; tel: 722 1112. Talk of the Towne; tel: 888 795 8199. Carriage rides from Charleston Carriage; tel: 577 0042.
**Visitors bureau** Open daily, with film shows, at 375 Meeting; tel: 0 800 774 0006; web: www.charlestoncvb.com.
**Accommodation** Contact Historic Charleston Bed & Breakfast, 57 Broad Street, Charleston, SC 29401; tel: 722 6606.

Rutledge Victoria Inn, 114 Rutledge Ave; tel: 722 7551. Dormitory beds $15, single rooms $50.

Hotels are expensive downtown but reasonably priced motels can be found across the Ashley River on US 17. Downtown hotels include Best Western King Charles Inn, 237 Meeting; tel: 723 7451; Days Inn, 155 Meeting; tel: 722 8411 or 1 800 329

7466; Holiday Inn, 125 Calhoun; tel: 805 7900; Meeting Street Inn, 173 Meeting; tel:
723 1883 or 1 800 842 8022; Renaissance, 68 Wentworth; tel: 534 0300; Westin
Francis Marion, 387 King; tel: 722 0600 or 1 800 433 3733.

## Recommended in Charleston

**Charleston Museum** 360 Meeting; tel: 722 2996; web:
www.charlestonmuseum.com. America's first museum, begun in 1773, has snuff
boxes and silverware among its half a million items. Open daily, admission charge.
Tickets also give admission to the Joseph Manigault House (an Adam-style mansion)
and the 1772 Heyward-Washington House.

**St Michael's Church** At Broad and Meeting. The oldest of Charleston's 181
churches resembles St Martin-in-the-Fields, London. City Hall, the Federal Court,
the Post Office and the County Court House occupy the other 'four corners of
law'.

**Charles Towne Landing Park** 1500 Old Towne Rd, on the site of the first
settlement; tel: 852 4200. The park has trails, a reconstructed village, a sailing ship and
an enclosure with wolves and bears.

**Fort Sumter** A short boat ride from the municipal marina; tel: 883 3123. The Civil
War began here in 1861 when the garrison surrendered to Confederate General Pierre
Beauregard after two days of bombardment. Tours of the restored buildings.

**Gibbes Museum of Art** 135 Meeting; tel: 722 2706; web: www.Gibbes.com. The
collection includes American paintings, prints, and drawings from the 18th century to
the present, including views of Charleston and portraits of famous South Carolinian
citizens. The museum also has miniatures and Japanese prints. Closed Mon,
admission charge.

**The Best Friend Museum** Located on Ann Street, close to the Visitor Center; tel:
973 7269; web: www.charleston.net/org/railroad. The museum has a full-size replica
of the *Best Friend of Charleston* – the first (1830) US train to operate in regular
passenger service. The engine was constructed from the original plans in 1928 to
commemorate the 100th anniversary of the South Carolina Canal and Rail Road
Company. Open daily, free.

**Old Exchange and Provost Dungeon** 122 East Bay; tel: 727 2165; web:
www.oldexchange.com. Built in 1771 by the British as the Exchange and Customs
House, American Patriots were held prisoner here during the Revolutionary War. You
can see part of the Charles Towne Sea Wall built to defend the colony from pirates in
the 17th century. Open daily, admission charge.

**Drayton Hall** 3380 Ashley River Road; tel: 769 2600; web: www.draytonhall.org.
Completed in 1742, this is the only plantation house remaining on the Ashley river
that survived the Revolutionary and Civil Wars, and its Georgian Palladian
architecture contains much of the original 18th century craftsmanship. Guided tours
and nature walks. Open daily, admission charge.

**Magnolia Plantation** 3550 Ashley River Road; tel: 571 1266; web:
www.magnoliaplantation.com. This pre-Revolutionary War Plantation House has fine
American antiques and the estate boasts America's oldest gardens, dating from 1680
and featuring azaleas and camellias. Boat rides, wildlife observation tower, art gallery
and bird-watching walks. Open daily, admission charge.

## All aboard!

The *Silver Meteor* pulls out of Charleston among substantial rail yards. You cross the Ashley River before continuing south along the coastal plain.

**Jacksonboro (25/20)** The town was named after Andrew Jackson. You cross the Edisto River, then the Salkehatchie, Ashepoo and Combahee Rivers en route to Yemassee.

**YEMASSEE (45/45)** The town was named after Yemassee Indians and is a regular stop for marines returning from basic training at Parris Island.

**Interstate 95 (5/40)** The train passes under a highway which runs all the way down the east coast from Maine to Miami.

**Savannah River (30/15)** Look right for a concrete highway bridge as the train crosses the river into Georgia.

### SAVANNAH
For Savannah city information and the remainder of the route to Miami, see *The Silver Star* (pages 226–36).

# The *Palmetto* New York–Miami

## General route information

The *Palmetto* travels the eastern part of the United States between New York and Florida, following the *Silver Meteor* route to Jacksonville before travelling across central Florida to Tampa. This train rejoins the *Silver Star* and *Silver Meteor* route at Winter Haven.

**Frequency** Daily.

The southbound service leaves New York early in the morning to arrive in Washington by midday and Savannah late the same evening. You reach Jacksonville during the night, Tampa early next morning and Miami by midday.

Travelling north, trains leave Miami late in the afternoon to reach Tampa by late evening and Jacksonville during the night. You arrive in Savannah early next morning, Washington by late that afternoon and finally reach New York mid-evening.

**Reservations** All reserved.

**Equipment** Amfleet coaches. Movies are shown in coaches, with headphones available for purchase.

**Food** Complete meals, snacks, sandwiches, drinks.

**Baggage** Check-in service at most stations.

## Joining the train

### NEW YORK

For New York City and the route to Washington, see *The Northeast Corridor* (pages 196–208). For the route from Washington to Jacksonville, see *The Silver Star* and *The Silver Meteor* (pages 222–5 and 237–41).

### JACKSONVILLE (130/60)

You leave Jacksonville among rail yards, warehouses and loading facilities. The St John's River is to your left.

**WALDO (60/40)** Amtrak's stop for the nearby college town of Gainesville was a major rail junction until the workshops moved away in 1929. Look for the old Seaboard caboose to your right.

**Lake Lochloosa (20/20)** The lake on your right is where Burt Reynolds filmed *Gator*. Nearby is the home of Marjorie K Rawlings, author of *The*

*Yearling* and *Jacob's Ladder*. Most of her stories were set in this Florida hummock country.

**OCALA (40/25)** Ocala is one of the state's many centres for training and breeding thoroughbred horses. The **Appleton Museum** features Napoleon's sword and silver thrones from India.

About a mile to the east of Ocala is Florida's oldest tourist attraction, **Silver Springs**, with its glass-bottom boat rides and white alligators (tel: 1 800 234 7458). Nearby also is the 366,000-acre (148,000ha) **Ocala Forest Wilderness**.

**WILDWOOD (25/30)** A centre for phosphate mining, farming and distribution, Wildwood is also Amtrak's stop for the popular Lake Griffin recreation area.

**Center Hill (20/10)** Note the Spanish-style station buildings before you continue beside the Withlacoochee Forest. Florida was one of the first states to designate and protect its parks as a sanctuary for native plants and animals.

**DADE CITY (30/55)** Home of St Leo's College, this is Amtrak's stop for the winter resort of Zephyrhills.

**TAMPA (55/30)**
The name is a Seminole word for 'sticks of fire'. Settlement began when Fort Brooke was established in 1824, but most of Florida's early tourist development concentrated on the east coast. Henry Plant's railway reached Tampa late in the 19th century, when he built the 'world's most elegant' Tampa Bay Hotel. During the Spanish-American War this became a headquarters for Theodore Roosevelt. Florida's State Fair takes place in Tampa each February.

St Petersburg, adjacent to the south, is quieter and more residential. From the resorts along this coast you can see a variety of wildlife including cormorants, pelicans, dolphins and, if you are really lucky, a rare and charming manatee.

### Tampa basics
**Telephone code** 813.
**Station** Amtrak has an Italian-style station at 601 Nebraska

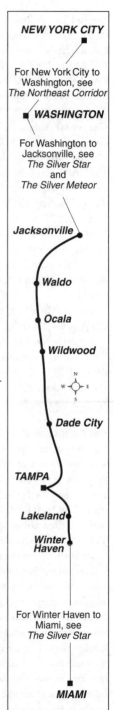

NEW YORK CITY

For New York City to Washington, see *The Northeast Corridor*

WASHINGTON

For Washington to Jacksonville, see *The Silver Star* and *The Silver Meteor*

Jacksonville

Waldo

Ocala

Wildwood

Dade City

TAMPA

Lakeland

Winter Haven

For Winter Haven to Miami, see *The Silver Star*

MIAMI

Ave and Twiggs. Information tel: 221 7600. Ticket-office and waiting-room open 05.30–23.00. Lockers, vending machines, handcarts, taxi stand.

**Connections** Thruway buses connect with Pinellas-St Petersburg, Orlando, Sarasota, Fort Myers, Naples and Clearwater Beach.

**Local transport** HART buses operate in the Tampa region (tel: 254 4278) and the Suncoast Transit Authority (tel: 727 530 9911) in St Petersburg.

**Taxis** Yellow; tel: 253 0121. United; tel: 253 2424.

**Car rental** Budget; tel: 800 527 0700.

**Greyhound** 610 E Polk; tel: 229 2174.

**Tampa International Airport** is six miles (10km) from downtown by limousine and HART bus #30. Contact The Limo (tel: 727 572 1111) for transport to St Petersburg's Clearwater Airport.

**Tours** Five Star; tel: 331 8232. Gray Line; tel: 727 592 0377. Boat trips on the *Spirit of Tampa*; tel: 273 9485.

**Visitors bureau** 400 N Tampa; tel: 223 2752 or 800 44 TAMPA; email: info@thcva.com; web: www.visittampabay.com.

Also at 100 2nd Ave N, St Petersburg (tel: 727 821 4715).

**Accommodation** Contact Ruskin House Bed & Breakfast, 120 Dickman Drive; tel: 645 3842.

YMCA, 110 E Oak; tel: 224 9622. Men only, $20. Gram's Place Hostel, 3109 N Ola Ave; tel: 221 0596.

Tampa hotels include the Radisson at 200 Ashley Dr; tel: 223 2222; Bay Harbor, 7700 Courtney Campbell Parkway; tel: 281 8900; Travelodge Resort, 820 E Busch Blvd; tel: 933 4011; Howard Johnson, 4139 E Busch Blvd; tel: 988 9191; Holiday Inn Busch Gardens, 2701 E Fowler Ave; tel: 971 4710; Red Roof Inn, 5001 US 301; tel: 727 623 5245.

## Recommended in Tampa

**Busch Gardens** 3605 Bougainvillea; tel: 987 5082; web: www.buschgardens.com. Take bus #5 to Florida's chief tourist attraction after Disney World. The gardens have more than 3,000 birds and animals, with a monorail to transport you among the lions and rhinos. Open daily, admission charge.

**Ybor City** 1600 E 8th Ave; tel 248 3712; web: www.ybor.org. Tampa's Cuban city-within-a-city features Spanish-style buildings, restaurants and shops. Many of Tampa's first residents were Cuban refugees from the Spanish-American War who brought with them their cigar-making skills.

You can see cigars being hand rolled at the Cigar Factory, 1901 13th (open daily, free). The **Ybor City Museum** is at 1818 9th Ave; tel: 247 6323. Open Tue–Sat, admission charge. For walking tours call 233 1111.

**Henry B Plant Museum** 401 West Kennedy Blvd; tel: 254 1891; web: www.plantmuseum.com. Housed in the 1891 Tampa Bay Hotel, a National Historic Landmark built by the railroad magnate, Henry Bradley Plant. This quintessential Victorian hotel was constructed in flamboyant Turkish and Moorish style with minarets, domes, cupolas, horseshoe arches and long verandas. Filled with opulent European furniture and art, the museum tells the story the hotel and of Florida's tourist industry. Closed Mon, donation.

**Tampa Bay History Center** Located in the Tampa Convention Center Annex at 225 S Franklin; tel: 228 0097; web: www.tampabayhistorycenter.org. This history and heritage museum preserves and teaches the history of the Tampa Bay area with exhibits showing the geographical, historical and cultural influences shaping the region from 12,000 years ago to the present. Open Tue–Sat, donation.

**Tampa Museum of Art** 600 N Ashley Dr; tel: 274 8130; web: www.tampamuseum.com. Located along the Hillsborough River downtown, the museum has 20th century and contemporary art as well as a famous collection of Greek and Roman antiquities. Lectures, walking tours and children's activities. Closed Mon, admission charge.

**Salvador Dali Museum** 1000 3rd S, St Petersburg; tel: 823 3767; web: www.salvadordalimuseum.org. The museum has the world's greatest collection of the eccentric Spanish surrealist's work. Open daily, admission charge.

## All aboard!

You travel west across central Florida and approach Lakeland past a huge Publix warehouse.

**LAKELAND (30/20)** The *Palmetto* stops at the attractive station in downtown which has replaced a larger station west of town. Lakeland's Civic Center is to your right and a power plant to your left. Home of Florida Southern College and centre of a vast citrus fruit region, the town boasts the state's main trading exchange and juice extraction plants. The largest phosphate mine on earth is nearby.

### WINTER HAVEN (20/45)

For Winter Haven and the remainder of the route to Miami, see *The Silver Star* (pages 232–6).

# The *Twilight Shoreliner*
# Boston–Newport News

## General route information

The *Twilight Shoreliner* is the *Northeast Corridor*'s premier overnight train, making a journey through time from Boston to Washington. It follows the *Northeast Corridor* route then travels through Virginia to the state capital. After Richmond the train turns east towards Newport News on the Atlantic coast, taking in historic Williamsburg and the tidewater region.

**Frequency** Daily.

The southbound service leaves Boston mid-evening to reach New York soon after midnight, Washington early next morning and Newport News by mid-morning.

Travelling north, trains leave Newport News mid-afternoon to reach Washington by mid-evening, New York late evening and Boston early next morning.

**Reservations** All reserved.

**Equipment** Amfleet coaches. Business Class.

**Sleeping** Viewliner bedrooms.

**Food** Tray meals, snacks, sandwiches, drinks.

**Lounge car** The Twilight Lounge (reserved for Business Class and sleeping car passengers) features speciality drinks and complimentary snacks.

**Baggage** No check-in service.

## Joining the train

### BOSTON

For Boston city information, the route to Washington and Washington city information, see *The Northeast Corridor* (pages 189–208). For the Washington to Richmond route, see *The Crescent* and *The Silver Star* (pages 212 and 222–4).

**RICHMOND (55/65)** The *Twilight Shoreliner* continues south from Richmond on the Seaboard Coast Line.

**Virginia Science Museum (10/55)** Look right for the museum's dome. Housed in the Seaboard Line's former Broad Street Station is a planetarium and space theatre.

The *Twilight Shoreliner* then progresses through a sequence of rail yards, transferring to the Chesapeake & Ohio line before heading southeast beside the James River.

**Main Street Station (15/50)** The railway building to your right is no longer in use.

**James River (17/48)** You glimpse the river to your right before the train crosses a canal and passes through more Chessie yards at Fulton.

**Byrd Airport (25/40)** Aircraft and runways can be seen to your left.

The landscape now becomes flatter as the *Twilight Shoreliner* continues on into Virginia's tidewater region. Elegant plantation mansions stand next to the river.

**New Kent (45/20)** The forestry establishment to your right produces thousands of fledgling pine trees.

**Chickahominy River (50/15)** Seen to your right, the Chickahominy flows towards the James River.

## WILLIAMSBURG (65/25)
America's largest restored town was named after King William III of Britain, and the Union Flag still flies on the Capitol building. The town became Virginia's capital in 1699. You can recapture colonial days in this reconstruction of 500 public buildings, taverns, gardens and houses. Costumed townspeople drive carriages, work as craftsmen and add appropriate atmosphere.

In summer it can be hot, humid and crowded, so visit during spring or autumn if possible.

### Williamsburg basics
**Telephone code** 757.
**Station** Amtrak uses the Transportation Center, 408 N Boundary. Information tel: 229 8750. Ticket-office and waiting-room open 08.00–21.30 Fri–Mon, 08.00–17.00 Tue–Thu. Lockers, vending machines, handcarts, taxi stand.
**Local transport** Buses from the visitor centre go to most parts of the historic area, best seen by strolling among the buildings.
**Greyhound** Located next to Amtrak's station; tel: 229 1460.
**Airport** The airport is 16 miles (26km) by bus or taxi from the station.
**Tours** Tickets are available at the Courthouse of 1770 for carriage rides and guided tours. Triangle Tours, 100 Workington (tel: 259 0697) has services throughout the historic triangle.

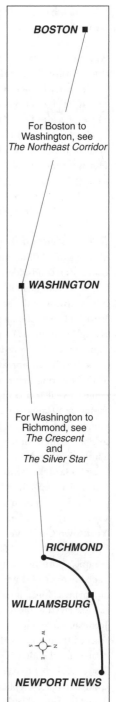

BOSTON ■

For Boston to Washington, see *The Northeast Corridor*

■ WASHINGTON

For Washington to Richmond, see *The Crescent* and *The Silver Star*

RICHMOND ●

WILLIAMSBURG ■

NEWPORT NEWS

**Visitors bureau** 421 N Boundary; tel: 253 0192; web: www.visitwilliamsburg.com or www.history.org. Open weekdays. Passes give admission to all the historic buildings as well as to Carter's Grove Plantation.

**Accommodation** Rooms are expensive and can be hard to find in summer. For up-to-date information, including guest houses, pick up a free guide from the visitor centre.

HJ Carter Hostel, 903 Lafayette; tel: 229 1117. Rooms from $20. Sangraal-by-the-Sea (AYH) Hostel, 30 miles (48km) away on Rte 626. Members $10, non-members $15. Contact PO Box 187, Urbanna, VA 23175; tel: 804 776 6500.

Hotel rooms in Williamsburg itself should be booked well in advance. Contact the Williamsburg Foundation, PO Box 1776, Williamsburg, VA 23187-1776; tel: 229 1000. Hotels include the Williamsburg Inn at 136 E Francis; tel: 229 1000; Fort Magruder Inn, 6945 Pocahontas Trail; tel: 220 2250; Quality Inn-Colony, 309 Page; tel: 229 1855; Holiday Inn, 814 Capitol Landing Rd; tel: 229 0200; Governor's Inn, 506 N Henry; tel: 229 1000; King William Inn, 824 Capitol Landing Rd; tel: 229 4933.

## Recommended in Williamsburg

**College of William and Mary** At the end of Duke of Gloucester Street is the country's second-oldest college, where Jefferson studied law and the Phi Beta Kappa Society began. Includes the Wren Building (1695) and the President's House (1734).

**The Capitol** At the other end of Duke of Gloucester Street is the place where Patrick Henry denounced King George III's stamp tax. Other buildings include the Raleigh Tavern, the Governor's Palace, the Magazine, Bruton Parish Church and the James Anderson House.

**US Army Transportation Museum** At Fort Eustis, 20 miles (32km) south; tel: 878 1115. Featuring a railroad ambulance car, a hospital kitchen car and an industrial crane, as well as aircraft and a marine park. Closed Monday, free.

**America's Railroads On Parade** 1915 Pocahontas Trail; tel: 220 TRAK. A wonderful collection with over 4,000 square feet of automated model trains, hands-on exhibits, train paintings, tinplate and classical porcelain buildings. Open daily, admission charge.

**Busch Gardens** 1 Busch Gardens Blvd; tel: 253 3350; web: www.buschgardens.com. Voted 'America's most beautiful theme park' for many years in succession, Busch gardens has also been called 'America's favourite theme park', edging out Disneyland. Open daily from March to October. Admission charge.

**Yorktown** On Route 31 S at the Colonial Pkwy, ten minutes from Williamsburg; tel: 253 4838 or 888 593 4682; web: www.historyisfun.org. Settled in 1630, Yorktown became a port and trading centre for the tobacco industry, and the Revolutionary War ended here in 1781 with the defeat of Lord Cornwallis. The battlefield is much visited and many colonial buildings survive or have been reconstructed. The **Victory Center** has displays and films. Open daily, admission charge.

**Jamestown** Part of the historic triangle, along with Yorktown and Williamsburg, and reached from Yorktown along the Colonial Parkway; tel: 898 2410. English settlers established the New World's first legislature here in 1619, although the Old Church Tower is all that remains standing. Also featured are the Tercentenary Monument, a Confederate fort, replicas of settlers' ships and the foundations of the first state house. Tours by national park rangers. Open daily, admission charge.

# All aboard!

You depart Williamsburg with the historic district to your right.

**Busch Gardens (5/20)** Look right also for this Old Country theme park, complete with steam train.

**Lee Hall (15/10)** Trains no longer stop at the restored station. Soon after passing through Lee Hall you cross a part of the local reservoir.

## NEWPORT NEWS

Founded in 1619 on a harbour shared with Norfolk, Portsmouth and Hampton Roads, where the James, York, Elizabeth and Nansemond Rivers flow into Chesapeake Bay (14 miles/22km long and 40ft/12m deep). Newport News boasts the world's largest shipbuilding yard and biggest naval base.

The **Mariners' Museum** features an outstanding nautical collection and the **War Museum** has weapons, uniforms and vehicles from the American Revolution to Vietnam. In Newport News Park you can enjoy boating, fishing and camping. Amtrak's station is at 9304 Warwick Blvd, from where Thruway buses link to Norfolk and Virginia Beach in Virginia. For information on attractions throughout the peninsula contact the **Visitor Center** at 13560 Jefferson Ave; tel: 757 886 7777 or 888 493 7386; web: www.newport-news.org.

# The *Cardinal*
# Washington–Chicago

## General route information

The *Cardinal*'s 929-mile (1,490km) journey takes you through some of America's finest scenery, going from Washington across Virginia to the Blue Ridge Mountains and Shenandoah Valley. You then travel west through the Appalachians, the Ohio River Valley and Cincinnati, before crossing the cornfields of central Indiana to Chicago.

**Frequency** Three trains a week in each direction.

The westbound service leaves Washington mid-morning on Sunday, Wednesday and Friday to reach Charlottesville by early afternoon and Charleston mid-evening. You arrive in Cincinnati during the night and Indianapolis early the next morning, reaching Chicago early on Monday, Thursday or Saturday morning.

Travelling east, trains leave Chicago mid-evening on Tuesday, Thursday and Saturday to reach Indianapolis soon after midnight and Cincinnati early next morning. You arrive in Charleston mid-morning, Charlottesville by late afternoon and Washington mid-evening on Wednesday, Friday or Sunday.

**Reservations** All reserved.

**Equipment** Superliner coaches.

**Sleeping** Superliner bedrooms.

**Lounge car** Video movies, hospitality hour. During summer months a CP Huntington Railroad Society guide joins the eastbound train between Charleston and White Sulphur Springs to provide a scenic commentary.

**Food** Complete meals, snacks, sandwiches, drinks.

**Baggage** Check-in service at main stations. Bicycle racks available (reservation required).

## Joining the train

### WASHINGTON

For Washington city information, see *The Northeast Corridor* (pages 205–8). For the route from Washington to Charlottesville, see *The Crescent* (pages 212–13).

**CHARLOTTESVILLE (60/55)** Note the colonnaded soccer ground to your right as the *Cardinal* leaves through residential and commercial suburbs, passing over main street on a trestle. You follow US 250 for some way through western Virginia, travelling among farms, orchards and forests and beginning a steep climb into the Blue Ridge Mountains. It was on this highly demanding route that the Chesapeake & Ohio Railway chose to introduce the first of its powerful American-type steam locomotives in 1911.

The idyllic Shenandoah Valley to your right is the home of bear, bobcat, fox and 200 species of birds. Skyline Drive goes along 100 miles (160km) of mountain ridge, where there are spectacular changes of colour during autumn.

The train passes through Crozet and East Braham then a long tunnel, the first of many on this route, climbing another stiff bank before beginning the descent towards Staunton.

**Waynesboro (35/20)** After passing this small town beside the river the *Cardinal* continues among cattle and sheep farms with pretty mountains to your right.

**Interstate 81 (52/3)** Look for a neo-classical building on your right as you pass beneath two highway bridges.

**STAUNTON (55/70)** This was the birthplace of President Woodrow Wilson. To your right when the train stops on a curve of the tracks beside the large passenger building you can see colourful Chessie System rail cars being used as station architecture. Staunton's altitude (1,359ft/414m) is inscribed on the station's canopy. The town's **Museum of American Frontier Culture** reveals farming life in the 18th and 19th centuries.

You leave among houses perched on hills, with Victorian buildings seen away to your left. As the train climbs, the tops of the tall trees to your left scarcely reach the tracks. Look also for horses, cattle, sheep and eagles.

**Elliott Knob (15/55)** This dark purple mountain (4,458ft/1,360m) is visible on the right. Near Clifton Forge the *Cardinal* passes through busy yards of the Chesapeake & Ohio, with freight trains to your left and a picturesque railway building to your right.

**CLIFTON FORGE (70/50)** This area was wilderness until the railroad arrived and enabled lumber and coal to be exploited. The Chesapeake & Ohio line was mostly

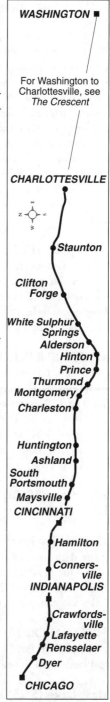

WASHINGTON ■

For Washington to Charlottesville, see *The Crescent*

CHARLOTTESVILLE

Staunton

Clifton Forge

White Sulphur Springs
Alderson
Hinton
Prince
Thurmond
Montgomery
Charleston

Huntington
Ashland
South Portsmouth
Maysville
CINCINNATI

Hamilton

Conners-ville
INDIANAPOLIS

Crawfords-ville
Lafayette
Rensselaer
Dyer

CHICAGO

built by former Virginia slaves supervised by ex-Confederate Army officers. One of the ex-slaves was John Henry, who worked on Big Bend Tunnel in the early 1870s. When a steam-powered drill was introduced he challenged it to a contest. With the help of a 'shaker' assistant to turn his drill, and swinging nine- or twelve-pound (4kg or 5.5kg) hammers in both hands, he made 15 feet to the steam drill's nine (4.5m/2.7m). He died of a heart attack soon afterwards but his exploits inspired songs such as *Take This Hammer* and *If I Had A Hammer*. A statue of John Henry, stripped to the waist, stands on the mountain above the tunnel.

Virginia's **Museum of Transportation** is housed in a 1917 Norfolk & Western freight depot at 303 Norfolk Ave in nearby Roanoke (tel: 703 342 5670; web: www.vmt.org). The museum features steam, diesel and electric engines, as well as passenger and freight cars, vintage automobiles, trucks and trolleys. Open daily, admission charge.

The *Cardinal* pulls out of Clifton Forge past a hospital and factories to your right.

**Covington (12/38)** Below the small town to your right is Highway 64.

The train ascends into the mountains through more tunnels, crossing the Virginia/West Virginia border just before White Sulphur Springs. Look right for a golf course and the immaculate grounds of Greenbrier Spa, where people have come to bathe in mineral waters since 1778. The Greenbrier Hotel was once owned by the Chesapeake & Ohio.

**WHITE SULPHUR SPRINGS (50/30)** Amtrak's unmanned station is at 315 Main. Greenbrier is a 2,600-acre resort with facilities for many sports, including ice-skating. The first 'horseless carriage' in these parts arrived in 1900 on a Chesapeake & Ohio freight car.

Somewhere in the surrounding hillside is a secret bunker built in 1958 for Congress to use in the event of a nuclear attack. You can look for this among the wooded mountains and waterfalls on both sides as the train pushes deeper into West Virginia.

**Alderson (30/30)** A flag stop where trains pause only on request. The building high up to your left is a women's prison.

**Greenbrier River (28/2)** The river on your right is often reduced to little more than a stream.

For the next 120 miles (192km) you follow the New River as it cuts a tree-lined gorge through America's oldest mountains, the Appalachians. Bluestone Lake and dam are to your left.

**HINTON (30/30)** Elegant houses stand on the hill. Hinton's busier past is revealed by its large brick station to your right, beside an open space where the rail yards used to be.

**Bass Lake (5/25)** Look for the ethnic cabins to your right.

**PRINCE (30/15)** A mountain village with another large depot, from which access to nearby Beckley is by Yellow Cab.

**THURMOND (15/45)** The line curves right into Thurmond, where the *Cardinal* stops only on request. Trains apparently go down main street, called Third Avenue.

**New River Gorge Bridge (20/25)** The world's longest (1,700ft/520m) and America's second-highest (876ft/267m) steel arch bridge carries Route 19 traffic across the valley.

The *Cardinal* continues through dramatically rugged scenery with waterfalls, mountains and a sheer drop to the boulder-strewn river. Approaching Montgomery the tracks diverge from the river and the town mayor's office is seen among houses to your left.

**MONTGOMERY (45/30)** West Virginia's Institute of Technology is on the left.

**Kanawha River (8/22)** The train joins the river to your right and pursues it most of the way to Charleston. Barges can be seen loading coal from a mine on the far side of the river.

You travel through semi-rural scenes, with wooded mountains on the opposite shore and industrial plants below. As you near Charleston the gold-domed Capitol building comes into view to your right.

**CHARLESTON (30/55)** Located on the Kanawha River and surrounded by mountains, Charleston is famous for white-water rafting. Apart from the domed Capitol, the most impressive buildings are the Cultural Center and the Governor's Mansion. Amtrak's stone and brick station is under a highway bridge at 350 McCorkle.

Chemical factories appear on both sides as you cross the river, passing rail yards to your right.

**Institute (10/45)** Where Union Carbide produces the chemical methyl isocyanate. In 1984, a leak at a similar factory in Bhopal, India, killed 3,800 people.

Approaching Huntington, you pass a large CSX yard on the left then a big shopping mall.

**HUNTINGTON (55/20)** To your right is the downtown area of Huntington, which ships enormous quantities of coal. **Heritage Village**, located in former Baltimore & Ohio yards, reveals this inland port's railway history. Amtrak's small brick station is to your left at 8th Ave and 10th.

**Big Sandy River (15/5)** Most of the train comes into view as it crosses the river and takes a long right curve. Look for a concrete highway bridge to your right, linking West Virginia with Kentucky.

**ASHLAND (20/55)** The historic industrial city to your left is noted for oil and steel. Look right for a major Armco plant. The station at 2001 Greenup Ave also serves Kenova, West Virginia.

The route between here and Cincinnati is on CSX tracks along the meandering southern shore of the Ohio River, which forms the Kentucky/Ohio border to your right, and the best views are on this side of the train. When travelling east you should have daylight to observe the river's houses, barges, locks, bridges and power stations. Ohio's bluffs are on the far side.

**Greenup Dam (40/15)** The lock on this side of the river was built in the 1950s.

**SOUTH PORTSMOUTH (55/50)** The modest Main Street station also serves Portsmouth, Ohio, across the river. Note the white Baptist church to your right as the train leaves and passes beneath a suspension bridge. A highway bridge also spans the river, usually busy with freight barges.

**Falls City (25/25)** The *Cardinal* makes slow progress through this small town before losing touch with the Ohio for a while, travelling among fields and tree-covered hills. The river and industry return near Maysville.

**MAYSVILLE (50/85)** This atmospheric river city on the edge of bluegrass country has tobacco auctions and New Orleans-style architecture. Amtrak's brick and tile station is on W Front.

**Augusta (20/65)** White houses and an imposing grammar school can be seen to your left but the best viewing remains on the right.

**Zimmer Nuclear Power Station (30/55)** A cooling tower and chimneys dominate the Ohio shore.

**Interstate 275 (50/35)** You travel under a highway crossing the river to your right then cross the Licking River as Cincinnati approaches.

**Covington (70/15)** At suburban Covington the train dramatically crosses the Ohio River, scene of an extravagant September festival. Other bridges cross the river on both sides and the Riverfront Stadium is to your right, along with the Cincinnati skyline. The suspension bridge on the right was built by John Augustus Roebling, designer of the Brooklyn Bridge in New York. The *Cardinal* skirts the west side of downtown before easing into Union Station.

## CINCINNATI (85/50)

The Queen City of the west was nicknamed 'Porkopolis' after its pork-packing industry. Another local speciality, Cincinnati chilli, contains not only pork and beans but also a choice of cheese, onions, spaghetti or even hot dog. Many parks, plazas and buildings were created to celebrate Cincinnati's 1988 bicentennial.

## Cincinnati basics

**Telephone code** 513.

**Station** Amtrak uses the old Union Terminal at 1301 Vine, a superb example of art deco design. Open 09.30–17.00 Mon–Fri, and 23.00–06.30 Tue–Sun. Information tel: 651 3337. Lockers, vending machines, handcarts, shops, cafés, museum, taxi stand.

**Connections** Thruway buses link with Indianapolis and Chicago.

**Local transport** Queen City Metro bus schedules and information are available from the downtown office at 122 W 5th; tel: 621 4455.

**Taxis** Yellow; tel: 241 2100.

**Greyhound** 1005 Gilbert Ave; tel: 352 6012.

**Tours** Ohio River excursions with Celebrations Riverboats, 7612 Hamilton Ave; tel: 931 6752.

**Greater Cincinnati International Airport** is 14 miles (22km) southwest across the river in Covington, Kentucky, reached by limousine and the Jetport Express; tel: 606 767 3702.

**Visitors bureau** Open weekdays at 300 W 6th; tel: 621 2142 or 421 4636 (for the information line); web: www.cincyusa.com.

**Accommodation** Contact the Empty Nest Bed & Breakfast, 2707 Ida Ave, Cincinnati, OH 45212; tel: 631 3494; web: http://home.fuse.net/EmptyNest.

Y2kBunkers Hostel, 3572 Lilac Ave; tel: 314 3149; web: www.y2kbunkers.com. $15 per night.

Hotels include the Holiday Inn-Downtown at 800 W 8th; tel: 241 8660; Crowne Plaza, 15 W 6th; tel: 381 4000; Blue Ash, 5901 Pfeiffer Road; tel: 793 4500; Cincinnatian, 601 Vine; tel: 381 3000; Symphony, 210 W 14th; tel: 721 3353; Red Roof Inn, 5300 Kennedy Ave; tel: 531 6589 – single $45, double $55.

## Recommended in Cincinnati

**Fountain Square** E 5th and Vine. Features interesting architecture, a historic fountain, gardens, shops and free concerts. Information from the Downtown Council at 441 Vine; tel: 579 3100.

**Contemporary Arts Center** 115 E 5th, near Fountain Square; tel: 721 0390; web: www.spiral.org. Includes music events, films and multimedia shows. Open daily, free Mon and Sun.

**Cincinnati History Museum** 1301 Western Ave; tel: 287 7000; web: www.cincymuseum.org. Walk through the city's streets as they used to be as costumed interpreters reveal the lives of early Cincinnatians, or take a ride on the sidewheel steamboat. Open daily, admission charge.

**Museum of Natural History & Science** 1301 Western Ave; tel: 287 7000; web: www.cincymuseum.org. Explore the Ohio Valley and learn how the natural world works as you travel through a Kentucky limestone cavern. Or visit Cincinnati's Ice Age and experience life 19,000 years ago. Open daily, admission charge.

**Union Terminal** 1301 Western Ave; tel: 800 733 2077; web: www.cincymuseum.org. Now partly a museum, this is one of the most opulent railway stations ever built. It has the highest unsupported masonry dome in the world and the interior of the rotunda (180ft/54m in diameter) features splendid mosaic murals. The ceiling has striking silver, yellow and orange plasterwork.

A co-operative project of seven railroad companies, Union Terminal opened in 1933 to centralise the freight and passenger operations of the Big Four (later the New York Central), Pennsylvania, Chesapeake & Ohio, Norfolk & Western, Southern, Louisville & Nashville, and the Baltimore & Ohio railroads.

**Taft Museum of Art** 316 Pike; tel: 241 0343; web: www.taftmuseum.org. Old Master paintings, Chinese porcelains, as well as European and American decorative arts, can be found in the restored interior of the former home of Anna and Charles Taft. Open daily, free on Wed and Sun.

**Cincinnati Zoo** 3400 Vine; tel: 281 4700; web: www.cincyzoo.org. The zoo breeds gorillas and rare white tigers. Open daily, admission charge.

# All aboard!

The *Cardinal* continues north from Cincinnati through scenes of heavy manufacturing.

**HAMILTON (50/50)** Close enough to Cincinnati still to be industrial, Hamilton! is spelled with an exclamation mark in the local telephone directory!

**Ohio/Indiana State Line (30/20)** You cross into the Hoosier State in darkness.

**CONNERSVILLE (50/80)** Founded on the Whitewater River in 1813, Connersville makes everything from auto parts to dishwashers.

## INDIANAPOLIS (80/65)

The birthplace of Kurt Vonnegut and former home town of Steve McQueen is Indiana's capital, located at the geographical centre of the state. The **Indy 500** motor race takes place each Memorial Sunday, drawing the world's largest sports crowd. For tickets and information call 636 4556.

### Indianapolis basics

**Telephone code** 317.

**Station** Amtrak operates from the Union Terminal at 350 S Illinois. Information tel: 263 0550. Ticket-office and waiting-room open 04.00–11.30 Mon; 08.30–12.30 & 23.00–24.00 Tue; 00.00–02.30 Wed, Fri & Sun; 04.00–08.00 & 23.00–24.00 Thu; 04.00–08.00 & 22.00–24.00 Sat.

**Connections** Thruway buses link with Nashville.

**Local transport** Metro buses (tel: 635 3344) operate throughout the city.

**Taxis** Yellow; tel: 247 6232.

**Car rental** Thrifty, 9445 Aronson Drive; tel: 844 3700.

**Greyhound** 350 S Illinois; tel: 800 231 2222.

**Airport** The airport is six miles (10km) southwest by bus #8.
**Visitors bureau** 1 RCA Dome, Suite 100, Indianapolis, IN 46225; tel: 639 4282;
web: www.indy.org.
**Accommodation** Fall Creek YMCA is at 860 W 10th; tel: 634 2478. Single $25,
weekly $75.

Hotels include the Holiday Inn Crowne Plaza at 123 W Louisiana; tel: 631 2221;
Canterbury, 123 S Illinois; tel: 634 3000; Stone Soup Inn, 1304 N Central Ave; tel: 639
9550; Tower Inn, 1633 N Capitol Ave; tel: 925 9831; Day's Inn, 401 E Washington; tel:
637 6464 – single $40, double $50; Embassy Suites, 110 W Washington; tel: 236 1800.

### Recommended in Indianapolis

**Children's Museum** 3000 N Meridian; tel: 921 4000; web:
www.childrensmuseum.org. Largest museum of its kind in the world, containing the
largest water clock in North America. The museum also features toy trains, rock
climbing, carousel rides and a petting zoo. Open daily (closed Mon from September
to February). Admission charge.
**Motor Speedway** 4790 W 16th; tel: 484 6784; web: www.brickyard.com. The 2.5-
mile (4km) track was built in 1909 and incorporates an entire golf course. Bus tours
except in May. The **Indy Hall of Fame** features historic cars (including more than
30 Indy '500' winners), films and memorabilia. Open daily, free if under 17.
**City Market** 222 E Market; tel: 634 9266. One of the few original city markets
remaining in the United States, this 19th century building contains 15 ethnic sections.
Closed Sun.
**Indianapolis Museum of Art** 1200 W 38th; tel: 923 1331; web: www.ima-art.org.
One of the oldest art museums in the country, located in a 52-acre park with gardens,
five pavilions, a theatre and a concert terrace. The collection includes ancient bronze
and masks. Paintings are by American and European masters, including Gauguin and
Post-Impressionist works. Open daily, admission charge.
**Indiana Historical Society** 450 W Ohio; tel: 232 1882; web: www.indianahistory.org.
Discover Indiana's past through exhibitions, a library, publications, educational
programmes and special events. Open daily, admission charge.
**Indiana Transportation Museum** At Forest Park, Noblesville, 20 miles (32km)
north; tel: 773 6000. Includes old vehicles from the Santa Fe, Burlington and
Louisville & Nashville Railroads, as well as locomotives and Henry Flagler's Florida
Coast Line business car. Museum and main line train rides. Closed Mon, admission
charge.

# All aboard!

The *Cardinal* departs Indianapolis past the massive RCA Dome, formerly the
Hoosier Dome sports arena, with the downtown area to your right.

**Brownsburg (25/40)** You pass through a less urban landscape as the train
makes for the corn and soya bean fields of central Indiana. You go through
several small towns and accompany Interstate 74 to your right. Just before
Crawfordsville the *Cardinal* transfers from former Conrail tracks to those of

the Seaboard System (formerly the Monon Railroad). All these tracks are now owned by CSX.

**CRAWFORDSVILLE (65/30)** Home of Wabash College, one of many educational establishments to be seen on this part of the journey. You cross Cherry Creek then pass beneath Interstate 74.

**Linden (10/20)** The train crosses tracks belonging to the Norfolk & Western line.

**LAFAYETTE (30/50)** You accompany a pretty valley with close-up views of this typical mid-American city, where the train used to run directly down main street and the old station was simply a storefront. The Big Four depot has been relocated underneath a bridge now used as a pedestrian walkway. Lafayette is the home of Purdue University and was the birthplace of Alvah Roebuck, founder of Sears Roebuck.

**Wabash River (10/40)** The train crosses the river then travels beneath Interstate 65 on its way to Chicago.

**Tippecanoe Battlefield (15/35)** On your left is the place where General Harrison defeated the Shawnee Indians in 1811.

You continue through the small communities of Brookston and Chalmers.

**Reynolds (35/15)** As you cross the former Toledo, Peoria & Western line you change from Eastern to Central Time, so watches go back an hour (forward when travelling east).

**RENSSELAER (50/40)** The *Cardinal* crosses the Kankakee River then proceeds through Shelby, Lowell and Creston as it crosses Indiana's plains.

**Cedar Lake (30/10)** The lake is visible to your left just before you reach a town of the same name.

**DYER (40/50)** The station is a tiny glass shack with a very short platform, requiring the train to stop several times.

You start to enter an industrial environment which will persist most of the way to Chicago as the *Cardinal* transfers back to former Conrail from former Seaboard track used since Crawfordsville.

**Eggers Woods Forest (24/26)** Look right for a rare splash of greenery.

**Hammond-Whiting (25/25)** Hammond-Whiting's modern, yellow-brick station on your right is Amtrak's usual stop for trains approaching Chicago from the east. Storage tanks belonging to the Standard Oil Company can be seen on both sides as you depart among freight yards.

Watch for grain elevators and ships being loaded as you cross the Calumet River on a steel lift bridge.

**Roby (35/15)** The New Regal Theater to your right was opened by Chicago's first black mayor as a centre for African-American culture. Mayor Washington was subsequently buried in the cemetery to your right. Interstate 90 (the Indiana Toll Road) is to your left.

The route crosses a now closed Rock Island Railroad track at Englewood then crosses the south branch of the Chicago River. Plans are in hand to turn the old depot and station buildings at Rock Island into a museum in honour of a mighty fine line.

Chicago's Skyway is to your left and the city skyline comes into view on the right, featuring the 110-storey Sears Tower. After crossing the Dan Ryan Expressway you see the El rail track overhead and Lake Michigan to your right.

**Comiskey Park (40/10)** The car park on the right is where White Sox baseball used to be played. A new Comiskey Park stadium, completed in 1991, has risen alongside.

Look for Conrail loading facilities to your left then Amtrak's extensive 21st Street yards on your right. Trains are set up here to travel to every corner of the land. The *Cardinal* lurches into Chicago, moving slowly from CSX tracks to a former Grand Trunk Western line, then on to tracks owned by Union Pacific and METRA, reversing into Union Station through a passage beneath the Post Office building.

### CHICAGO
For Chicago city information, see *The California Zephyr* (pages 75–9).

# The *Adirondack*
# New York–Montreal

## General route information

The *Adirondack* has been nominated by *National Geographic Traveler* magazine as one of the world's ten best rail trips. It goes from New York to the Gallic charms of Montreal by way of the beautiful Hudson River Valley, the Adirondack Mountains, Lake Champlain, Vermont and the St Lawrence River. This daytime journey is particularly wonderful during autumn.

**Immigration formalities** US and Canadian citizens must have a passport, birth certificate, citizenship certificate or naturalisation certificate – **a driver's license is not sufficient.** Non-US citizens permanently or temporarily residing in the US must have an Alien Registration Card (I-551, or I-688 bearing proper endorsement on the reverse). Citizens of other countries not listed above must have a passport.

Citizens of many countries must also have a visa, a US Employment Authorisation Card showing 210 as a section of law, or a Canadian Form IMM 1000. Passengers under 18 years old who are not accompanied by an adult must bring a letter from a parent or guardian giving them permission to enter Canada.

See under *Documents* in *Chapter 3* (page 33), check with your US embassy or contact the Immigration and Naturalisation Service in Washington, DC (see *Chapter 3* and *Appendix 2*). Passengers without proper documentation are prohibited from entering the US or Canada and will be detrained before reaching the US/Canadian border.

**Frequency** Daily.

The northbound service leaves New York early in the morning to reach Albany by late morning, Plattsburgh mid-afternoon and Montreal by early evening.

Travelling south, trains leave Montreal mid-morning to reach Plattsburgh just after midday, Albany by late afternoon and New York mid-evening.

**Reservations** All reserved.

**Equipment** Turboliner coaches. Custom Class.

**Food** Snacks, sandwiches, drinks. The lounge car serves specialities such as cheesecake baked by nuns of the Canadian New Skete Order.

**Baggage** No check-in service. Ski racks.

# Joining the train

## NEW YORK

For New York City information, see *The Northeast Corridor* (pages 196–9). Trains from Washington, DC connect with the *Adirondack*, which leaves Pennsylvania Station on *Empire Corridor* tracks. The first 10 miles were opened in 1991 at a cost of $89 million and this part of the route used to be the New York Central's west side freight line. Constructed by the Hudson River Railroad, passenger services had previously operated until 1872.

You emerge from a tunnel with the Jacob Javits convention centre (built on the site of the old 30th Street rail yards) to your left. You then continue through Riverside Tunnel, with Harlem's Cotton Club below to your right as the train exits. The Hudson River and Henry Hudson Parkway are to your left, followed by the North River Water Plant (world's largest sewage treatment works). You pass beneath the Hudson Parkway, which continues to your right.

**George Washington Bridge (8/12)** Spanning the river to your left is a suspension bridge which was the longest in the world when completed in 1931. Just before the bridge, look for the 'little red lighthouse' which featured in a well-known children's book and is now preserved.

Fort Tryon Park is to your right beyond the highway before you pass Inwood Hill Park. Among the high-rises on New Jersey's Palisades across the river is the cupola of St Michael Villa, run by the Sisters of St Joseph.

**Spuyten Duyvil Bridge (15/5)** The *Adirondack* crosses the Harlem River Ship Canal on a 610ft-long (185m) swing bridge, restored to accommodate this line. The Hudson Parkway bridge is to your right. Metro-North trains join on the right after travelling from Grand Central Station.

**YONKERS (20/20)** Where Elisha Otis invented the safety elevator and the **Hudson River Museum** occupies an 1876 mansion. Look for imposing houses among the hills.

**Hastings-on-Hudson (6/14)** To your left is the home of the promoter Florenz Ziegfeld, whose wife Billie Burke was the good witch in *The Wizard of Oz*.

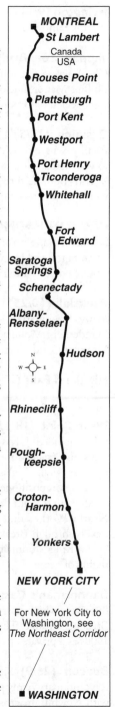

MONTREAL
St Lambert
Canada
USA
Rouses Point
Plattsburgh
Port Kent
Westport
Port Henry
Ticonderoga
Whitehall
Fort Edward
Saratoga Springs
Schenectady
Albany-Rensselaer
Hudson
N W–E S
Rhinecliff
Pough-keepsie
Croton-Harmon
Yonkers
NEW YORK CITY
For New York City to Washington, see *The Northeast Corridor*
WASHINGTON

**Irvington (9/11)** Named after Washington Irving, creator of *Rip Van Winkle*, and his Sunnyside home can be seen to your right past the station.

**Tappan Zee Bridge (10/10)** Carrying the NYS Thruway three miles (5km) across the Hudson River ahead to your left. Also to your left is the Phillips Manor, one of many estates in this region which have belonged to the well-heeled or famous.

**Ossining (15/5)** Look for the guard towers of Sing Sing Correctional Facility, where convicts were sent 'up the river' to do time. The main house is to your left and the annex to your right.

You continue through the most beautiful part of the Hudson River Valley, where maple trees flourish on steep river banks in a lush landscape.

**CROTON-HARMON (20/35)** The 18th century Van Cortlandt Manor belonged to New York's first lieutenant-governor and was visited by Generals Washington and Lafayette. Across the river are the twin towers of Indian Point atomic power station next to the town of Stony Point.

**Peekskill (10/25)** Once a frontier trading post, Peekskill was an American Army headquarters during the Revolutionary War. Across the river is Dunderberg Mountain, at the southern end of the Hudson Highlands. Bear Mountain Bridge carries the Appalachian Trail across the river.

**Highland Falls (17/18)** The falls cascade 100ft (30m) down cliffs on the far side.

**West Point (18/17)** The nation's oldest military academy, where cadets have included Ulysses S Grant, Robert E Lee, George Custer, Stonewall Jackson, Dwight Eisenhower and Norman Schwarzkopf. The Gothic chapel features stained glass windows and the world's largest church organ. Washington positioned troops here during the Revolutionary War.

After West Point the river narrows at the eastern end of Constitution Island. Nearby World's End is the river's deepest place (202ft/62m). The *Adirondack* travels through Breakneck Tunnel then alongside Sugarloaf Mountain, with Storm King Mountain across the river. Look for blue herons, cormorants and flights of geese.

**Bannerman's Castle (24/11)** Situated on Pollopel Island in the middle of the river, which narrows to a quarter of its width between Storm King and Breakneck Ridge. The mock medieval castle was constructed during the early 1900s as a private arsenal, complete with moat and drawbridge.

**Beacon (26/9)** Signal fires on the mountain to your right warned a Revolutionary Army post of approaching British troops. A bridge links Beacon with Newburgh across the river.

**Danskammer (28/7)** On the far side of the Hudson are the Roseton and Danskammer power plants, then the red buildings of the Royal Kedem Winery. As you approach Poughkeepsie look for rock quarries on the near shore.

**POUGHKEEPSIE (35/14)** Founded by the Dutch in 1683, this manufacturing city is famous for making cough drops and ball bearings. Interesting buildings include Clinton House and Glebe House on the corner of Main and N White. **Vassar College Art Gallery** has Rembrandt prints and Tiffany glass.

As the *Adirondack* pulls out of Amtrak's station at 41 Main, note the cantilever bridge spanning the river. This was the largest rail bridge in the world when completed in 1888 but has been out of use since a 1974 fire. To your right you pass Franklin D Roosevelt's home, where he was born and died, and the enormous mansion of Frederick Vanderbilt. The town of Hyde Park is on the near shore, with Fallkill Creek waterfall to the right.

An old lighthouse with a *trompe l'oeil* window can be seen at the south end of Esopus Meadows in mid-stream. German-style houses on the other side of the water demonstrate why this valley has been called 'the Rhine of America'. You travel through the neat village of Staatsburg.

**RHINECLIFF (14/20)** The station at Hutton and Charles is Amtrak's nearest stop for Rhinebeck and Kingston. Rhinebeck's historic buildings include America's oldest (1776) hotel, the **Beekman Arms**, which was a favourite with Franklin Roosevelt.

**Kingston Rhinecliff Bridge (4/16)** The bridge was built in 1957 and on both sides of the track is the marshland of Tivoli Bays, a haven for fish and birds. Across the river, at the mouth of the Esopus River, stands the oldest lighthouse on the Hudson, the Saugerties Light. Look also for the Carmelite Sisters' convent.

**Germantown (10/10)** First settled by Germans, this is now the centre of a fruit-growing region. Cement plants and barges appear across the river.

**Catskill (16/4)** Fine houses take advantage of dramatic riverbank locations as you enter a land dominated by the forests and gorges of the Catskills. This recreation area is bigger than Rhode Island and the mountains rise to more than 4,000ft (1,200m).

**Roeliff River (15/5)** Docks can be seen to your right as the train crosses the river and approaches Hudson. The 1872 Hudson-Athens lighthouse to your left is one of 13 coastguard lights on the river.

**HUDSON (20/15)** Dutch settlers called this Claverack Landing because of its luxuriant clover fields. The town was renamed after the explorer Henry

Hudson in 1785. Among the former whaling port's gardens and estates is the Persian-style Olana, a 37-room extravaganza designed by landscape artist Frederic Church. Hudson is also home to the **American Museum of Fire Fighting**. The railway station at 69 S Front is Amtrak's oldest on the line.

**Castleton-on-Hudson (11/4)** The Smith Memorial Bridge appears overhead, followed by a mile-long (1.6km) bridge connecting the New York State Thruway with the Massachusetts Turnpike. As the *Adirondack* nears Albany look left for the city skyline dominated by the Empire State Plaza. Glenmont Power Station is seen across the river.

**ALBANY-RENSSELAER (15/20)** The state capital's port prospered greatly with the arrival in 1825 of the Erie Canal, linking Lake Erie with the Atlantic. The railway came six years later when New York's first steam train, the *DeWitt Clinton*, ran on the Mohawk & Hudson line. Amtrak's East Street station is in adjacent Rensselaer.

Albany's sleek new buildings contrast with the Old State Capitol's Gothic architecture. The Schuyler Mansion is a Georgian house visited by George Washington and Benjamin Franklin. The **New York State Museum** (tel: 518 474 5843) is open daily at the Empire State Plaza. Nearby is 17th century **Fort Crailo**, America's oldest fortress, where tradition says a British surgeon wrote *Yankee Doodle Dandy*.

The *Adirondack* crosses the Hudson River after departing Rensselaer past extensive freight yards. The romantic buildings on your left once belonged to the Delaware & Hudson Railroad and now house State University headquarters. Albany city centre is to your left.

Approaching Schenectady through the environs of General Electric, look right for the gold dome of City Hall. The redbrick Van Curler Hotel to your left is part of a community college.

**SCHENECTADY (20/25)** 'The city that lights and hauls the world' began in 1661 as a fur trading station, its name being a Mohawk expression for 'through the open pines'. The Locomotive Works took care of haulage while Thomas Edison's Machine Works created the light. Edison's first job was selling sweets to railroad passengers, money from which he spent on chemistry sets and building a telegraph system out of scrap metal. He was dismissed from his job when he moved his chemistry lab into a baggage car and accidentally set fire to the train.

Apart from the electric light bulb and power stations, Edison developed or invented, amongst other things, the phonograph, motion picture camera, high-speed telegraph, typewriter, electric pen, copier and dictation machines, cement mixer and telephone, eventually holding a record 1,093 patents. The Edison factory eventually became General Electric, still one of the city's main employers.

Amtrak's station is at 332 Erie Blvd and you leave with the 17th century stockade district to your right. The train changes from *Empire Corridor* tracks to those of the Delaware & Hudson. After shaking off Schenectady's factories and power lines you begin to see logging and timber-processing plants among the wooded hills.

**SARATOGA SPRINGS (25/20)** Before the First World War the Vanderbilts and Whitneys came to Saratoga to drink the waters and take curative baths. Mixing only with their own kind, they enjoyed the best hotels, lavish casinos, gardens and America's oldest racetrack. Potato chips (crisps) were allegedly invented by a Native American chef called George Crum when Cornelius Vanderbilt asked for his potatoes to be sliced extra-thin.

No longer an exclusive resort of the rich, Saratoga Springs retains its bath-houses and you can still sample the waters. The 1777 Battle of Saratoga, a turning point in the Revolutionary War, took place 12 miles (19km) to the east and the site is now a military park. Amtrak's modern station is at West Ave and Station Lane.

After the *Adirondack* passes through a cutting lined with evergreens, look for a junkyard to your left then a field containing pheasants. You cross the river with a highway bridge to your left.

**FORT EDWARD (20/22)** The original fort was constructed during the French and Indian War (also known as the Seven Years War). A sequence of locks later linked the Hudson River to the Champlain Canal, creating a waterway through to the St Lawrence. Note the wood-framed houses on both sides. Amtrak's East Street station also serves neighbouring Glens Falls. Lake George, a few miles further north, has cruises, water-skiing and winter car races on the ice.

You continue through peaceful country into the heart of the Adirondacks, which were the tallest mountains in the world before the Ice Ages. Home to eagles, bobcat and deer, they became famous in 1869 when the Reverend William H H Murray published *Adventures in the Wilderness*. His book started a fashion for city dwellers to spend their summers in an area recently made accessible by railroads, and rail companies built many big hotels and lodges to accommodate them. Much of this region can still only be seen by train or on foot.

**Champlain Canal (10/12)** The canal is to your right behind a row of trees, and this is the best side of the train from which to see the scenery ahead.

**WHITEHALL (22/25)** A lock system connects the canal with Lake Champlain's South Bay. Rutland is five miles (8km) to the east in Vermont. You leave Whitehall by way of a short tunnel.

**Lake Champlain (5/20)** Seen to your right as you cross South Bay and enter the six million acres of the **Adirondack Forest Preserve**. These deep, rocky lakes and shallow-running rivers are favoured by hunters and fishermen.

A few minutes later you pass on your right a channel joining South Bay with Lake Champlain. America's sixth largest lake was named after its discoverer, Samuel de Champlain, and the *Adirondack* follows the clear waters of its shoreline for most of the next 100 miles (160km). In winter, look for ice fishermen fishing from ice houses on the lake. Vermont's tidy farmland is on the far side.

**TICONDEROGA (25/25)** The name is Iroquois for 'between two waters'. Amtrak's station consists of a small white box and a telephone on Route 9, some distance from both town and fort. Visible on bluffs ahead to your right, the fort was built by the French in 1775. This crucial position on the La Chute River between Lakes Champlain and George was constantly fought over during the Revolution, changing hands several times before the fort was abandoned, destroyed and lately restored.

You leave past the fort to your right and enter a tunnel before continuing among the mountains. Vermont's Green Mountains are across the lake.

**PORT HENRY (25/20)** Note the magnificent, ornate town hall to the left of the quaint chateau-style station. Abandoned railroad beds appear forlornly to your right before the train travels among hay fields, forests and hills. Lake Champlain's rocky shoreline continues on the right.

**WESTPORT (20/56)** A small fishing town where Thruway buses connect with Lake Placid, site of the 1932 and 1980 Winter Olympics.

The train keeps to a line between Lake Champlain on your right and mountains to your left, crossing high above the lovely Bouquet River. The tranquil lake boasts its own version of the Loch Ness monster called 'Champ', first seen by Samuel de Champlain in 1609.

**Willsboro (20/36)** Trout and salmon fishing are a major attraction on Lake Champlain and along the dammed Bouquet River. For 25 miles (40km) you travel a route hacked into cliffs 100ft above the lake, with wonderful views as the train negotiates hundreds of curves among birch trees, tunnels and houses.

**Port Kent (42/14)** Trains stop here from May to October, when ferries cross the water to downtown Burlington in Vermont. Nearby is Ausable Chasm – 'the Grand Canyon of the east'.

**Ausable River (45/11)** Watch for herons as you cross the tree-lined river, which has its source below the state's tallest mountain, Mount Marcy (5,344ft/1,629m).

**Valcour Island (49/7)** The *Adirondack* passes several Revolutionary War and French and Indian War battlefields. Benedict Arnold's ships were defeated by the British in 1776 near the island to your right as they competed for control of Lake Champlain.

At this point the train leaves **Adirondack State Park**, the largest in the United States.

**Plattsburgh Air Force Base (54/2)** Seen immediately to your left as you approach Plattsburgh, with yachts moored on your right.

**PLATTSBURGH (56/35)** To your left as the train enters this military and industrial city you can see a Delaware & Hudson Railroad turntable and the Thomas Macdonough Monument. The monument commemorates a victory in 1814 on Lake Champlain which foiled a British attempt to invade New York State from Canada. Amtrak's green-canopied station waiting-room is to your right.

The *Adirondack* finally parts company with Lake Champlain before travelling through corn fields and forests towards the Canadian border.

**ROUSES POINT (35/45)** The train's last stop before leaving the United States. A building to your right houses the US Customs checkpoint for those travelling south. In the days of Prohibition, trains crossing from Canada were known as 'bootleggers', since passengers often tried to sneak a few bottles past the border guards. Look for customs stickers adorning checked freight cars to your right.

You cross the US/Canada border and pass through St Jean, where a cannon on the right guards a military college.

**CANTIC (45/30)** The Canadian Customs checkpoint for people travelling north, this is not a passenger stop. After inspection the *Adirondack* proceeds over the flat, nondescript landscape of southern Quebec.

**ST LAMBERT (30/10)** Timber yards and city apartment blocks loom on the right as the train pauses briefly at a station operated by VIA Rail.

You cross the St Lawrence River on a long steel bridge, approaching Montreal through industrial scenes and Canadian National freight yards. The city's high-rise buildings are to your right.

## MONTREAL

Built on an island where the St Lawrence, Ottawa and Richelieu Rivers meet, Montreal hosted the 1967 Worlds Fair and 1976 Olympic Games. The French settled here in 1642 but explorers had arrived over a hundred years earlier. The British took over in 1760, then (for a short time) American revolutionaries.

Montreal today is the world's second-largest French-speaking city, although a third of its three million population have English as their first language. Like the rest of Quebec Province it can be cold in winter, with more snow than Moscow and temperatures well below zero into March, but the city is able to deal with the heaviest snowfall. Subterranean tunnels link 2,000 downtown stores. July highs can be in the 80's Fahrenheit (26°C–32°C).

## Montreal basics

**Telephone code** 514.

**Station** The excellent Gare Centrale (Central Station) at 895 rue de la Gauchetière Ouest is used by Amtrak, commuter trains and Canada's VIA Rail; tel: 800 561 9181. Amtrak reservations and information tel: 1 800 872 7245. Ticket-office open 08.00–17.00 (Amtrak) and 06.00–21.00 (VIA Rail). Waiting-room 06.00–21.00. Restaurants, shops, ATM banking, newspapers, Red Caps, taxi stand.

**Local transport** MUCTC runs an efficient bus and subway system throughout the city; tel: 288 6287. Le Métro operates 05.30–00.30.

**Taxis** Champlain; tel: 273 2435. Diamond; tel: 273 6331.

**Car rental** Budget, Central Station; tel: 866 7675.

**Greyhound** 505 Blvd de Maisonneuve; tel: 843 4231. The terminal is also used by Voyageur and Voyageur-Colonial; tel: 842 2281.

**Dorval Airport** is 12 miles (19km) from downtown by L'Aerobus; tel: 931 9002. Limousines include Montreal Dorval; tel: 990 7915. **Mirabel Airport** is 35 miles (56km) from downtown, with buses to Dorval and the city centre.

**Tours** Gray Line; tel: 934 1222. Old Montreal Ghost Trail, available in summer; tel: 868 0303. Boat trips on the St Lawrence River, May–October, from Harbor Cruises; tel: 842 3871.

**Visitors bureau** 1001 Dorchester Square, open daily; tel: 873 2015; web: www.tourism-montreal.org.

**Accommodation** Contact Bed & Breakfast City-wide, 422 Cherrier Street, Montreal, PQ H2L 1G9; tel: 738 9410 or 1 800 738 4338; web: www.bbmontreal.com.

International Youth Hostel, 1030 MacKay; tel: 843 3317; email: info@ajmontreal.qc.ca. Members $16, non-members $20. Auberge Youth Hostel, 901 rue Sherbrooke E; tel: 522 6861. Members $17. YMCA, 1440 rue Stanley; tel: 849 8393; web: www.ymcamontreal.qc.ca. Swimming pool, restaurant, gym. For men and women. Single $38, double $54. YWCA, 1355 Rene Levesque Blvd; tel: 866 9941; email: info@ywca-mtl.qc.ca. Women only. Single $44, double $59.

Hotels include Courtyard Marriott at 410 rue Sherbrooke; tel: 844 8851; Delta, 450 rue Sherbrooke; tel: 286 1986; Maritime, 1155 rue Guy; tel: 932 1411; Château de l'Argoat, 524 rue Sherbrooke; tel: 842 2046; Manoir Ambrose, 3422 rue Stanley; tel: 288 6922 – single $40, double $50; Americain, 1042 rue Saint-Denis; tel: 849 0616 – single $35, double $40; Kent, 1216 rue Saint-Hubert; tel: 845 9835 – single $30, double $40.

## Recommended in Montreal

**Mount-Royal Park** Reached via Camilien-Houde Pkwy or Remembrance Road; tel: 843 8240. Walk, picnic or take time to admire the views in this natural-looking park, dominated by the modest mountain which gave the city its name. The park was planned by Frederick Law Olmsted, designer of New York's Central Park. Winter activities include tubular slides and ice skating.

**Museum of Fine Arts** 1380 rue Sherbrooke; tel: 285 2000; web: www.mmfa.qc.ca. The museum has European and North American paintings as well as major international exhibitions. Closed Mon, free.

**Pepsi Forum Center** On the corner of Atwater and Sainte-Catherine; tel: 933 6786; web: www.forum-pepsi.com. This recently opened complex is the largest of its kind in the world, combining cinemas, restaurants, shops, high-tech games and free entertainment. Open daily.

**Canadian Centre for Architecture** 1920 Baile; tel: 939 7026; web: www.cca.qc.ca. Founded by the architect Phyllis Lambert, this museum and study-centre includes the (1874) Shaughnessy House and a splendid sculpture garden is part of the visit of this outstanding place. Guided tours on weekends. Closed Mon, admission charge.

**St Joseph's Oratory** 3800 rue Queen Mary; tel: 733 8211; web: www.saint-joseph.org. The world's largest church is dedicated to Canada's patron saint. Beneath a green copper dome is the original chapel founded by Brother André, said to have been able to cure the sick. Open daily, donation.

**St George's Anglican Church** Place du Canada, 1101 Stanley; tel: 866 7113; web: www.munica.com/stgeorges. Built in 1870, this beautiful neo-gothic church contains wonderful woodwork and a tapestry from Westminster Abbey. Open Tue–Sun, free.

**Canadian Railway Museum** 122 St Pierre in Saint Constant, one mile (1.6km) south of Montreal; tel: 632 2410; web: www.exporail.org. Canada's finest railway museum has over 130 examples of rolling stock, including the country's oldest surviving steam engines and the *Rocket* (Montreal's first electric streetcar). Train rides on Sundays and holidays. Open June–October, admission charge.

**McCord Museum** 690 rue Sherbrooke; tel: 398 7100; web: www.musee-mccord.qc.ca. An introduction to the history of Montreal and its citizens, including toys, photographs and splendid clothes. Open Tue–Sun and Mon (June to early September), admission charge.

**Botanical Garden** 4101 rue Sherbrooke E; tel: 872 1400; web: www.ville.montreal.qc.ca/jardin. One of the largest in the world, with over 300 outdoor gardens and ten exhibition houses, including a butterfly house and an insectarium. Open daily, admission charge.

# The *Vermonter*
# Washington–St Albans
## (for Montreal)

## General route information

Amtrak's alternative to the *Adirondack* travels from Washington via New York City to St Albans, Vermont, where a connecting bus service continues to Montreal, North America's most European city. The *Vermonter* follows the *Northeast Corridor* route before heading north at Amherst. This train replaces the previous night-time *Montrealer*, allowing you to travel through splendid New England scenery by day and see the sun set over the Green Mountains.

**Immigration formalities** US and Canadian citizens must have a passport, birth certificate, citizenship certificate or naturalisation certificate – **a driver's license is not sufficient.** Non-US citizens permanently or temporarily residing in the US must have an Alien Registration Card (I-551, or I-688 bearing proper endorsement on the reverse). Citizens of other countries not listed above must have a passport.

Citizens of many countries must also have a visa, a US Employment Authorisation Card showing 210 as a section of law, or a Canadian Form IMM 1000. Passengers under 18 years old who are not accompanied by an adult must bring a letter from a parent or guardian giving them permission to enter Canada.

See under *Documents* in *Chapter 3* (page 33), check with your US embassy or contact the Immigration and Naturalisation Service in Washington, DC (see *Chapter 3* and *Appendix 2*). Passengers without proper documentation are prohibited from entering the US or Canada and will be detrained before reaching the US/Canadian border.

**Frequency** Daily.

The northbound service leaves Washington early in the morning to arrive in Philadelphia by mid-morning and New York before noon. You reach Springfield mid-afternoon and St Albans by mid-evening, arriving in Montreal by Thruway bus towards midnight.

Travelling south, the bus leaves Montreal very early in the morning to connect with the train at St Albans. You leave St Albans early in the morning, arriving in Springfield by early afternoon and New York early in the evening. You reach Philadelphia mid-evening and Washington late in the evening.

**Reservations** All reserved.

**Equipment** Amfleet coaches. Custom Class.

**Food** Snacks, sandwiches and drinks.

**Baggage** Check-in service at most stations. Bicycle and ski racks are available (reservations required).

# Joining the train

For Washington, DC, and the route from Washington to Springfield, see *The Northeast Corridor* (pages 194–208 for Washington–New Haven & 209–10 for New Haven–Springfield). The *Vermonter* turns north from the *Northeast Corridor* route after Springfield and travels towards Amherst.

**AMHERST (60/45)** This is the home of the University of Massachusetts and a college founded in 1821 by Noah Webster (of dictionary fame). The poet Emily Dickinson was born and lived most of her life here, and her house at 280 Main is owned by the college. Another former Amherst poet was Robert Frost. The newspaper editor, Horace Greeley, who invented the slogan 'Go west, young man', was also born here.

Amherst is Amtrak's nearest stop to Northampton, where you can see the Cornet Joseph Parsons House (1658) and Wiggins Tavern (1786). The train leaves and continues north among farms and stately barns, crossing the Connecticut River and the Massachusetts/Vermont border.

**BRATTLEBORO (45/30)** Named after its original proprietor, William Brattle, the former mill town grew up around Fort Dummer, established by the British in 1724 as Vermont's first permanent settlement. Brattleboro's Museum and Art Center are in the old train depot, and Amtrak's present station is at Vernon Road. The **tourist bureau** is at 180 Main; tel: 802 254 4595; www.brattleboro.com.

**BELLOWS FALLS (30/22)** The first bridge across the Connecticut River was established here in 1785 and one of the country's first canals was built around the falls. A fish ladder allows Atlantic salmon to pass on their way upstream to spawn. The **Adams Old Stone Grist Mill Museum** (tel: 802 463 3706) features 19th century milling equipment, farm tools and machinery.

The **Green Mountain Railroad** at 54 Depot (tel: 802 463 3069 or 1 800 707 3530) operates diesel trains with vintage coaches from Union Station to Chester, with other trains going from North Bennington to Manchester or White River to Norwich . Trains use the Green Mountain freight line and tracks which belonged

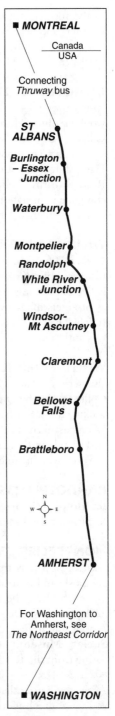

MONTREAL

Canada
USA

Connecting
Thruway bus

ST
ALBANS

Burlington
– Essex
Junction

Waterbury

Montpelier

Randolph

White River
Junction

Windsor-
Mt Ascutney

Claremont

Bellows
Falls

Brattleboro

AMHERST

For Washington to
Amherst, see
The Northeast Corridor

WASHINGTON

to the former Rutland Railroad. They run from June until September (to Chester) and September–October (to Ludlow).

Between Bellows Falls and White River Junction you fleetingly cross the border into New Hampshire before returning to Vermont.

**CLAREMONT (22/10)** The city was founded in 1762 on the Sugar River, which drops 300ft/90m and provided water power for the old cotton and woollen mills. Historic Mill District walking tours are organised by the Chamber of Commerce, Tremont Square (tel: 802 543 1296).

Among Claremont's other sights are a 19th century opera house and New Hampshire's oldest Catholic church, St Mary's. Amtrak's station is at Plains Road. Nearby Andover's **Historical Museum** features an 1874 depot complete with station master's office.

The train crosses the Connecticut River again into Vermont.

**WINDSOR-MT ASCUTNEY (10/20)** Home of Vermont's State Craft Center. **The American Precision Museum** (tel: 802 674 5781) is in a historic building originally built in 1846 as an armory. It has a large collection of tools from throughout the history of the United States, as well as products made by them. The **Old Constitution House and Museum** (tel: 802 672 3773) is located in the tavern where Vermont's first constitution was authored.

**WHITE RIVER JUNCTION (20/35)** Amtrak's station at Railroad Row also serves Lebanon (another mill city) and Hanover (home of Dartmouth College). Nearby **Quechee Gorge State Park** has excellent river fishing and walking trails. Further east is the New Hampshire lakes region, including Lake Winnipesaukee. The 30 mile (48km) long lake has hundreds of rocky, pine-clad islands and water is clean enough to drink.

You travel on amid Vermont's hilly forests towards the Green Mountains.

**RANDOLPH (35/30)** The Worcester Range is to your right. The **Randolph Historical Museum** on Salisbury (tel: 802 728 5398) features furnished period rooms and an antique drugstore.

**MONTPELIER (30/12)** Vermont's capital (population about 8,400) is located on a pass through the mountains along the wooded banks of the Winooski and North Branch Rivers. First settled in 1789, it was named after a French city. The 18th century Greek-style **State House** (tel: 802 828 2228) features a delicately beautiful gold dome as well as historic exhibits. Among the items in the redbrick pavilion housing **Vermont's Historical Society Museum** at 109 State (tel: 802 828 2291) is a hand-painted atlas dating from the Revolutionary War. The **tourist bureau** is at 134 State; tel: 802 223 3443.

Nearby Barre calls itself the granite centre of the world and at Granitesville you can tour a hundred-year-old quarry.

The *Vermonter* continues among green hills, pine trees, rivers and streams, with the graceful orange- and purple-shaded Green Mountains visible ahead as the train climbs.

**WATERBURY (12/27)** Amtrak's old redbrick station to your left also serves Stowe. Local ski resorts include Sugarbush and Jay Peak.

**Bolton Valley (10/17)** Another ski area appears to your right as you leave the attractively scattered small town and continue into the 266,000-acre (107,000ha) **Green Mountains National Forest**. Also to your right is the state's highest mountain, Mount Mansfield (4,393ft/1,340m). A toll road from Stowe leads to the summit, from where you can see across Lake Champlain.

**BURLINGTON-ESSEX JUNCTION (27/30)** Amtrak's station at 29 Railroad Ave is also the stop for Smugglers Notch ski resort. A white Vermont Federal Bank building features on your left and a graveyard to your right. It was the damming of the Winooski River in the late 18th century which led to the growth of Essex Junction. Six railroad lines converged on this small community by 1853, making it one of the most important rail junctions in the state.

Vermont's largest city, Burlington, is seven miles (11km) west, located on a hill above the shoreline of Lake Champlain. A resort and industrial centre as well as home to the University of Vermont and Trinity College, Burlington showed its maverick spirit by electing a socialist mayor in 1981 and keeping its old-fashioned downtown area, where you can see beautiful Italianate, Queen Anne and Colonial Revival-style houses. It has been voted 'Best small town for the arts' as well as 'Most liveable city in the USA'.

The Burlington jazz festival takes place each June. Except in winter, ferries operate across the lake to Port Kent, New York, served by Amtrak's *Adirondack*. For information throughout the Lake Champlain Valley contact the **visitors bureau** at 60 Main; tel: 802 863 3489; web: www.vermont.org.

Bed & breakfast accommodation can easily be found in this area but you should book early during the foliage season (peaking in mid-October). Contact the Howard Street Guest House, 153 Howard Street, Burlington; tel: 802 864 4668; Willard Street Inn, 349 Willard, Burlington; tel: 1 800 577 8712; web: www.willardstreetinn.com; Willey's Farm B & B, 74 Lincoln, Essex Junction; tel: 802 878 4666; Willow Pond Farm, 133 Cheesefactory Lane, Shelburne; tel: 802 985 8505.

The **Shelburne Museum**, seven miles (11km) to the south on Route 7, features the 1890 Shelburne railway depot (tel: 802 985 3346; web: www.shelburnemuseum.org). The station was originally located in central Shelburne to serve passengers of the Central Vermont and Rutland Railroads. Passenger service was discontinued in 1953 and the station was moved to its present site in 1959. Waiting rooms for men and women and the stationmaster's office were restored, and telegraphy systems, railroad memorabilia and maps complete a picture of late 19th and early 20th century rail travel. A small annex beside the station exhibits hand tools and equipment used by railroad workers and includes handcarts, picks and shovels, and signal lanterns from railroad lines around the country.

Other highlights at the museum include a Central Vermont steam locomotive, an inspection car from the Woodstock Railroad and the *Grand Isle*, a luxurious rail car built by the Wagner Palace Car Company for the Vermont Governor Edward C Smith. The *Grand Isle* features mahogany panels, an elegant dining room, staterooms and plush furnishings. The museum has a lighthouse, a 220ft Lake Champlain steamboat (the *Ticonderoga*) as well as 37 historic houses and exhibition buildings. The Impressionist paintings include works by Degas and Monet, and you can see one of the country's largest collections of Americana, including carriages, furniture, quilts, dolls and weathervanes. Open May–October, admission charge.

As the *Vermonter* leaves among wooden houses and travels for 30 miles (48km) along part of the Champlain Valley, look for dairy farms, hayfields and logging operations. Warehouses and factories start to intrude on the approach to St Albans.

## ST ALBANS

The station at Washington and 3rd is the *Vermonter's* final destination in the USA. St Albans is famous for its railroad shops and granite mills. During the Civil War it was raided by a party of Confederates who entered the town from Canada, killed several citizens and robbed the banks of $200,000. They failed in their attempt to burn the place down before fleeing back north of the border. **Franklin County Museum** at Taylor Park describes the raid and has a collection of railway exhibits.

Passengers for Canada continue to Montreal's Central Station on a one and a half hour journey aboard Amtrak's connecting Thruway bus.

## MONTREAL

For Montreal city information, see *The Adirondack* (pages 267–9).

*Above* New England's spectacular fall (autumn) foliage can be enjoyed on the Conway Scenic Railroad in New Hampshire. (CSR)

*Left* The Georgetown Loop Railroad twists and turns through mountain scenery, Colorado. (RR)

*Above* Amtrak's latest high-speed Acela train is capable of 150mph. (Amtrak)

*Right* Unit trains are used to carry products such as coal, minerals and grain across the Canadian prairies. (PC)

*Below* The Alaska Railroad operates through many miles of national park land. (KFT)

# The *Lake Shore Limited*
# Boston/New York–Chicago

## General route information

The *Lake Shore Limited* follows the water level route once travelled by the *Twentieth Century Limited*. Boston trains go through central Massachusetts before crossing the Berkshire Hills to Albany, where they are joined by New York trains which have travelled up the Hudson River Valley.

All coaches then accompany the Mohawk River and Erie Canal along a famous Native American highway. The *Lake Shore Limited* touches Lake Erie before hurrying across northern Indiana to Chicago.

**Frequency** Daily.

The westbound service leaves Boston early in the afternoon (or New York late afternoon) to reach Albany by early evening. You arrive in Cleveland early the following morning and Chicago by mid-morning.

Travelling east, trains leave Chicago mid-evening to reach Cleveland during the night. You arrive in Albany just after midday and Boston by early evening (or New York by mid-afternoon).

**Reservations** All reserved.

**Equipment** Amfleet coaches. Dome car.

**Sleeping** Viewliner bedrooms.

**Food** Tray meals, snacks, sandwiches, drinks. Complete meals on New York trains.

**Baggage** Check-in service at most stations.

## Joining the train

### NEW YORK

For New York City information, see *The Northeast Corridor* (pages 196–9). For the route from New York City to Albany, see *The Adirondack* (pages 261–4).

### BOSTON

For Boston city information, see *The Northeast Corridor* (pages 190–2).

## All aboard!

**BACK BAY STATION (5/27)** The *Lake Shore Limited* departs Boston's restored South Station to travel along the southern edge of the business

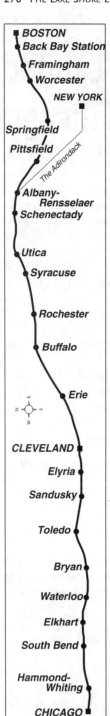

district, pausing to pick up passengers at Back Bay. This area was once covered by the Charles River and the railroad tracks had to be built on causeways.

As the train leaves Back Bay you glimpse the city skyline before heading into the wooded landscape of central Massachusetts. Fenway Park, home of baseball's Red Sox, is to your left.

**Newton (20/7)** You go through the suburb of Riverside then cross the Charles River.

**Wellesley (22/5)** Prestigious Wellesley College, formerly attended by Hillary Rodham Clinton, is to your right.

**FRAMINGHAM (27/30)** A study conducted here in the 1940s was the first to link heart disease with smoking. Framingham's old train station has become a fish restaurant.

The *Lake Shore Limited* continues through the small towns of Ashland, Cordaville, Southville and Westboro.

**Lake Quinsigamund (25/5)** The popular water sports area to your right is surrounded by attractive houses.

**WORCESTER (30/80)** Past residents have included the humorist Robert Benchley and Isaiah Thomas, publisher of one of America's first newspapers, the *Massachusetts Spy*. Blue and white Holy Cross College can be seen on the hillside to your left. Old Sturbridge village is located 20 miles (32km) southwest.

Worcester's industrial development began in 1828 when the Blackstone Canal linked the town to Providence. A railroad replaced the canal 20 years later. Worcester made America's first carpet loom, first liquid-fuel rocket and first calliope (a fairground music device using steam power to play a set of large whistles).

Amtrak is expected soon to move a hundred yards from its tiny depot at 45 Shrewsbury to take up residence in part of the grandly renovated Union Station, now owned by the MBTA. This impressive landmark, seen to your right as you leave, had been quietly decaying for decades before its magnificent twin towers and main hall were expensively restored.

**West Warren (45/35)** A miniature golf course features to your left.

**Quaboag River (50/30)** The *Lake Shore Limited* accompanies the river on the right for several miles.

**Chicopee River (60/20)** Look right for a waterfall.

**SPRINGFIELD (80/75)** Home of the Springfield rifle and Garand semi-automatic, used by US troops during the Second World War. Springfield began in the 17th century as a trading post on the banks of the Quinnitukqut River (the longest river in New England). When a railroad opened between here and Worcester in 1839 the city became industrialised.

Springfield is still an important gun-making town and its Armory has one of the world's best military collections. The Basketball Hall of Fame at 1150 W Columbus Avenue (tel: 413 781 6500) honours the game's inventor, James Naismith. The **visitors bureau** is at 1441 Main (tel: 413 787 1548) and Amtrak's station at 66 Lyman.

**Connecticut River (5/70)** You cross with the stone-arched Memorial Bridge to your left alongside the Eastern States Fairgrounds.

**Westfield River (7/68)** Look for sawmills and logging operations as the train follows the river through Oronoco, Russell, Huntington, Chester and Middlefield. You travel among some of the state's best scenery, including the Berkshire Mountains and **Chester Blanford State Forest**, where you may see deer, bobcat and wild turkey. Approaching Pittsfield you cross the Appalachian Trail.

**PITTSFIELD (75/65)** Capital of Berkshire County, surrounded by mountains, forest and lakes, this is where in 1851 Herman Melville wrote *Moby Dick*. His Arrowhead home is now a museum and the public library includes a room devoted to Melville. The **visitors bureau** is at Berkshire Common Pl (tel: 413 443 9186).

**Hancock Shaker Village** on the slopes of Lebanon Mountain is an open-air museum dedicated to one of the country's oldest religious sects. The **Berkshire Scenic Railway** offers weekend rides along part of the Housatonic Valley and its museum occupies the restored station at Housatonic and Willow Creek Road in nearby Lenox (tel: 413 637 2210).

**Richmond Pond (10/55)** The lake appears to your left. During summer the Boston Symphony Orchestra plays concerts at Tanglewood, the former home of Nathaniel West.

**Massachusetts/New York State Line (20/45)** The train enters the Empire State by way of the Taconic Mountains and State Line Tunnel. Look ahead for views of the Catskill Mountains and Hudson Valley.

**Chatham (55/10)** A wooden station stands on your right. The 'beefalo' farm on your left cross-breeds cows with buffalo to create a healthier alternative to beef.

The *Lake Shore Limited* rumbles on through such communities as Niverville, Post Road Crossing, Van Hoesen, Brookview and East Greenbush.

**ALBANY-RENSSELAER (65/24)** For Albany-Rensselaer city information, see *The Adirondack* (page 264).

**SCHENECTADY (24/75)** For Schenectady city information, see *The Adirondack* (page 264).

You cross the Mohawk River on a steel bridge then accompany the river to your left as far as Utica. The Mohawk Trail was the main colonial passage from the east to the Great Lakes. Mohawk Indians fought the Mohicans at Kinquariones, situated on the rocky cliff overhanging the tracks.

**Erie Canal (10/65)** The train accompanies the canal to your left for much of its route between here and Rochester. Look for the first in a series of locks.

**Amsterdam (25/50)** Home of Coleco, the company which created Cabbage Patch dolls. Among the town's buildings are several associated with Sir William Johnson and family, who joined with the Iroquois against the French and their Native American allies during the French and Indian Wars. Sir William built the mansion to your left for his daughter. Fort Johnson, seen to your right, dates from 1749. Eight missionaries who were killed attempting to convert Native Americans to Christianity are commemorated by a shrine.

You travel on through an attractive valley of woods, hills and dairy farms.

**Nelliston (35/40)** The stone depot with green shutters to your left is now an Elks Lodge. A marker on the other side of the river indicates the site of a Revolutionary Army base at Fort Plain.

**Palatine Bridge (40/35)** Home of Lifesavers candies and Beech-Nut Products, where the Old Palatine Church (1770) stands next to Caroga Creek on your right.

**Fonda (45/30)** Montgomery County court house is opposite the station, with the town's fairgrounds to your right.

**St Johnsville (48/27)** Famous for leather-tanning and dye factories, St Johnsville is the *Lake Shore Limited*'s halfway point along the Mohawk Valley.

**Herkimer (60/15)** The town featured in Walter Edmond's frontier novel *Drums Along the Mohawk*.

**Erie Canal (68/7)** You cross the canal above a sequence of locks. Constructed between 1817 and 1825, the waterway spans New York State from Albany on the Hudson to Buffalo on Lake Erie. It was later enlarged and partly relocated to incorporate Lake Oneida. You approach Utica among factories and junk yards.

**UTICA (75/45)** Located on the Mohawk River and New York State Barge Canal, Utica was called Old Fort Schuyler until it was renamed after a place in north Africa. Rapid development followed the arrival of the Erie Canal. Union Station on your left opened in 1914 and extensive rail yards stretch away to your right.

The train pulls out and continues its journey west. Look right as you near the town of Rome for the sculpture perched above the Paul Revere brass factory.

**Rome (15/30)** The Stars and Stripes first flew at the Battle of Oriskany in 1777, inspiring Francis Bellamy to compose the Pledge of Allegiance. Fort Stanwix battle site is now part of downtown. The Erie Canal began in Rome on July 4 1817 and you catch another glimpse of it off to your right as the train leaves for the northern highlands.

**SYRACUSE (45/80)** Salt City, where for many years the mines produced most of America's favourite seasoning. Extraction methods are demonstrated at the **Salt Museum** on the shore of Onondaga Lake (tel: 315 453 6767). The **Erie Canal Museum** is located in the 1850 weigh lock building at 318 Erie Blvd; tel: 315 471 0593; web: www.eriecanalmuseum.org.

Amtrak's station is among the rail yards of East Syracuse at Manlius Center Rd, more than 10 miles (16km) from downtown. Look for long Conrail trains being set up on your right as the train departs among factories and warehouses.

**LeMoyne College (4/76)** Seen high up to your left, the college was named after a French missionary.

**Onondaga Lake (8/72)** To your right is the place where Father LeMoyne discovered salt reserves.

**New York State Fairgrounds (13/67)** An annual state fair takes place from late August until early September. The racetrack is to your right.

**Erie Canal (32/48)** You rediscover the canal on your right soon after Weedsport then cross into a more rural landscape. For the next 40 minutes the train travels among orchards, farmhouses and fields of rich, dark earth.

**Clyde (38/42)** The town's colonial cemetery is to your left.

**East Palmyra (58/22)** Look left for a picturesque church standing on the hill. Nearer to Rochester the dairy farms and greenery dwindle, to be replaced by more factories and freight yards.

**Sibley Clock Tower (78/2)** Named after Hiram Sibley, who was the founder of Western Union.

**ROCHESTER (80/55)** The city's largest employer is Kodak (established in 1880) and a turreted Eastman Kodak building appears to your right. The Genessee Brewery is to your left. Rochester was 'the flour capital of the world' in the early 18th century, when the town grew along the upper falls of the Genessee River. It later became the northern terminal of the Underground Railroad, and has a spectacular lilac festival each May.

The **New York Museum of Transportation** on East River Road in nearby Rush includes a Philadelphia snow-sweeper and a Genessee & Wyoming caboose, along with buses, vintage cars and trolleys. Open Sun; tel: 716 533 1113; web: www.nymtmuseum.org.

The **Rochester & Genessee Valley Museum**, in a restored Erie Railroad station south of the city, has locomotives and cars from the New York Central, Baltimore & Ohio and Erie-Lackawanna Railroads; tel: 716 533 1431; web: www.rochnrhs.org. As the *Lake Shore Limited* crosses the Genessee River, look for a futuristic Times-Square building dominating the downtown area to your left.

**Erie Canal (5/50)** After you cross the canal for the last time, a massive limestone mine sprawls to your right.

**Bergen (20/35)** The train passes Bergen on the right as the rolling landscape gives way to flatter countryside approaching the Great Lakes.

**Lancaster (47/8)** Fences surround Alden Penitentiary to your left and Lancaster's air park is to your right.

**BUFFALO (55/90)** The city stands next to Lake Erie and is separated from Canada by the Niagara River. After the Civil War many railroads converged here to create important markets and a thriving railroad car industry. Buffalo remains a major rail centre and industrial city.

As the train pauses at Depew Station on Dick Road note the art deco clock tower of the old depot, which used to see 30,000 passengers a day. The Allentown area has Victorian buildings, shops and restaurants. For information contact the **visitor centre** at 617 Main (tel: 1 800 283 3256).

Between here and Toledo the train lives up to its name by skirting the southern shore of Lake Erie, sometimes visible to your right as you travel through a horizontal land of fields and low hedges.

**New York/Pennsylvania State Line (60/30)** You briefly enter the Keystone State, founded by William Penn in 1682.

**ERIE (90/90)** Pennsylvania's only port on the lake was named after Eriez Indians. During the War of 1812, Admiral Perry scored a vital victory over the British and the hull of his flagship *Niagara* is moored at the end of State Street. Dickson's Tavern, his base before the battle, became a station on the Underground Railroad and escaped slaves hid in its walls before continuing to Canada.

The **Lake Shore Railway Museum** is 15 miles (24km) away at North East; tel: 814 825 2724. Housed in a New York Central passenger station built for the Lake Shore & Michigan Southern Railway, its collection includes engines, sleepers, refrigerated freight wagons and a wooden business car. Open Wed–Sun from May to October, free.

**Pennsylvania/Ohio State Line (30/60)** Ohio's name comes from an Iroquois word for 'beautiful'. The *Lake Shore Limited* travels through the fishing village of Conneaut before passing the towns of Ashtabula and Mentor.

## CLEVELAND (90/28)

Founded in the 18th century by General Moses Cleaveland and misspelled by his men on the official document, Cleveland has been the home of President James Garfield, millionaire John D Rockefeller and Superman, created by Jerry Siegel and Joe Shuster. Ohio's largest industrial city has lately acquired a less sooty image, helped by cultural institutions such as its world famous symphony orchestra and the **Rock and Roll Hall of Fame**. In 1967 Cleveland elected Carl Stokes as the first black mayor of any major US city.

### *Cleveland basics*

**Telephone code** 216.

**Station** Amtrak's excellent modern lakefront station is at 200 Cleveland Memorial Shoreway, opposite the Municipal Stadium. Information tel: 696 5115. Ticket-office and waiting-room open 23.00–15.30. Lockers, vending machines, handcarts, taxi stand.

**Connections** Thruway buses go to Columbus and Cincinnati.

**Local transport** RTA buses operate downtown and to outlying areas; tel: 566 5100.

**Taxis** Yellow; tel: 623 1550. Americab; tel: 881 1111.

**Car rental** Hertz; tel: 267 8900.

**Greyhound** 1465 Chester Ave; tel: 781 0520.

**Hopkins International Airport** is 10 miles (16km) southwest by RTA train and bus #66X.

**Tours** North Coast Ghost Tour; tel: 330 225 1519. Trolley Tours from May to December; tel: 771 4484. The *Goodtime III* cruises Lake Erie and the Cuyahoga and Rocky Rivers; tel: 861 5110.

**Visitors bureau** Open daily at 3100 Tower City Center; tel: 621 7981; web: www.travelcleveland.com.

**Accommodation** For rooms in local homes call Cleveland Private Lodgings, PO Box 18590, Cleveland, OH 44118; tel: 321 3213.

Stanford House (AYH) Hostel, 6093 Stanford Rd, Peninsula; tel: 330 467 8711. A historic house 20 miles (32km) south of Cleveland (take #77F bus). Beds $10. YMCA, 2200 Prospect Ave; tel: 344 7700. Daily $28, weekly $95.

Hotels include the Renaissance Cleveland at 24 Public Square; tel: 696 5600; Bond Court, 777 St Clair Ave; tel: 771 7600; Clinic Center, 2065 E 96th; tel: 791 1900; Holiday Inn Lakeside, 1111 Lakeside Ave; tel: 241 5100.

### Recommended in Cleveland

**Museum of Art** 11150 East Blvd; tel: 421 7350; web: www.clemusart.com. An outstanding collection of more than 40,000 works of art, ranging over 5,000 years from ancient Egypt to the present. Includes Picassos, French Impressionists and Rodin's *Thinker*. Closed Mon, free.

**Tower City Center** An ultra-modern extravaganza of shops, offices and mall located in the Terminal Tower; tel: 771 0033.

**Rock and Roll Hall of Fame and Museum** 1 Key Plaza; tel: 781 ROCK; web: www.rockhall.com. From Muddy Waters and Little Richard to Bruce Springsteen and Neil Young, you can explore the past present and future of rock music. Open daily, admission charge.

**Health Museum** 8911 Euclid Ave; tel: 231 5010; web: www.healthmuseum.org. A hypochondriac's delight, with thousands of objects showing all aspects of medicine. See Juno the transparent talking woman and interact with an ingenious giant model of the brain. Open daily, free.

**Museum of Natural History** Wade Oval; tel: 231 4600; web: www.cmnh.org. Featuring rare prehistoric exhibits. Open daily, admission charge.

**Great Lakes Science Center** 601 Erieside Ave; tel: 694 2000; web: www.glsc.org. More than 330 interactive exhibits make this one of the largest science museums in the country. Permanent exhibits include Virtual Sports, the Indoor Tornado, giant outdoor mazes and one of the largest video walls east of the Rockies. Open daily, admission charge.

**Cleveland Metroparks Zoo** 3900 Wildlife Way; tel: 661 6500; web: www.clemetzoo.com. Thousands of animals roam 165 wooded acres and two indoor acres of tropics. Includes the Rain Forest, Wolf Wilderness, Birds of the World and Northern Trek, where cool weather-loving animals like bears, deer, tigers and wolves live. Open daily, admission charge.

## All aboard!

The train leaves with the Municipal Stadium on your right and a Goodyear plant to your left. You cross the Cuyahoga River.

**Hopkins Airport (10/18)** Cleveland's main airport is to your right.

**ELYRIA (28/32)** Named after Herman Ely, who founded this manufacturing city on the Black River in the 19th century. Oberlin College became the first in the USA to enrol African-Americans and women on equal terms with white males.

**Amherst (10/22)** The New York Central depot has been faithfully maintained and old rail cars stand proudly to the left of the tracks. On your right is a large Pillsbury factory.

**Vermillion River (15/17)** Look right for a sight of Lake Erie after you cross a river famous for its fishing fleet. You pass through the fishing towns of Vermillion (with its maritime museum) and Huron (where Thomas Edison was born).

**Hudson (24/8)** You cross the Huron River.

**SANDUSKY (32/45)** Once another stop on the Underground Railroad, Sandusky's busy port today ships coal and local wine. The city also has a museum devoted to merry-go-rounds. Nearby is the Cedar Point amusement park, America's fifth largest. Amtrak's modest station is on your left at N Depot and Hayes Ave, and the Lake Erie Islands can be reached by ferry from the waterfront.

The **Mad River & NKP Railroad Museum** at 253 Southwest in Bellevue (tel: 419 483 2222; web: www.onebellevue.com/madriver) features a Chicago, Burlington & Quincy dome car (the first in the country) as well US Army troop sleepers, uniforms, timetables, lanterns, china, locks and historic buildings. Henry Flagler, builder of the Florida East Coast Railroad, once lived on the property where the museum is located. Open daily, May–October.

You go through manufacturing districts then cross Sandusky Bay before veering east towards Toledo. To your right is the top of one of **Cedar Point's** 14 roller-coasters (tel: 419 627 2350; web: www.cedarpoint.com). The latest $25 million Millennium Force coaster is currently the tallest and fastest in the world.

**Lake Erie (12/33)** The lake is visible for the last time away to your right before you cross the Portage River at Port Clinton.

**Davis-Bessie Nuclear Plant (20/25)** Seen beneath a plume of steam in the right distance before you continue among vineyards, apple orchards and peach trees.

**Clay Center (27/18)** The town is surrounded by a limestone quarry.

**Maumee River (40/5)** Scenery becomes ever more industrial as you cross the river, with Toledo's outline to your right. The train curves left among some of the world's largest grain elevators while Conrail trains gather on both sides.

**TOLEDO (45/50)** Ohio and Michigan argued over this valuable harbour, where the Maumee River meets Lake Erie, until President Jackson settled the issue in Ohio's favour. The Toledo Museum of Art's crystal collection reflects the city's reputation as 'the glass capital of the world' and the Libbey Glass factory is to your left. Thruway buses connect with Detroit, Dearborn and Ann Arbor from Amtrak's terminal at 415 Emerald Ave.

The train pulls out on a 68.5-mile (110km) straight of track known as the air line route.

**Holland (12/38)** Neat farms start to replace industry again.

**BRYAN (50/25)** A distribution point for agricultural produce, the Fountain City is known for its artesian wells and the Ohio Art Company, maker of Etch-A-Sketch. To your right is WBNO, the first solar-powered radio station in the world.

You cross the St Joseph River and Ohio/Indiana State Line.

**WATERLOO (25/45)** Highest point on the route, situated 995ft/304m above sea level and 400ft/120m above the Great Lakes. Waterloo is the train's nearest stop to Fort Wayne.

**Elkhart River (25/20)** After crossing the river the train follows a leisurely course through rolling countryside.

**ELKHART (70/22)** Elkhart has been the world's largest producer of brass musical instruments and mobile homes and is the headquarters of Miles Laboratories, maker of Alka-Seltzer. The Michigan Southern Railroad built repair shops here and this was a division point on the New York Central (later the Penn Central). Amtrak's station is at 131 Tyler Ave, where shiny New York Central trains wait beside a steam engine across the tracks to your left. Amish and Mennonite Christian communities nearby include Goshen, located five miles (8km) southeast.

The *Lake Shore Limited* leaves among factories and warehouses, approaching South Bend past the old Studebaker car factory to your left. This plant closed in 1963 but classic Studebakers can be seen at the **Discovery Hall Museum**.

**SOUTH BEND (22/60)** Located on a bend of the St Joseph River where settlers negotiated a treaty with Native Americans under the Council Oak tree, which still stands in Highland Cemetery. Look right for the gold dome of Notre Dame University above the trees.

As you travel on you pass from Eastern to Central Time, so watches go back an hour (forward when travelling east).

**La Porte (20/40)** The town began in 1832 as a trading centre for farmers.

**Gary (45/15)** Long one of the nation's great steel producers, plants on both sides display a mass of complicated pipelines, pylons and storage tanks. Gary was the birthplace of Karl Malden, Michael Jackson and the astronaut Frank Borman.

The train continues sedately through the communities of Pine Junction and Indiana Harbor.

**Indiana Harbor Canal (50/10)** You cross on a drawbridge. The canal joins the Calumet River to Lake Michigan, seen a short distance away to your right. Look left for more steel mills and a Lever Brothers factory.

## HAMMOND-WHITING (60/25)

For Hammond-Whiting and the route to Chicago, see *The Cardinal* (pages 258–9).

## CHICAGO

Thruway buses connect with Madison, Wisconsin. For Chicago city information, see *The California Zephyr* (pages 75–9).

# The *Capitol Limited*
# Washington–Chicago

## General route information

The *Capitol Limited* takes you through West Virginia, Harper's Ferry and the beautiful Potomac and Shenandoah Valleys. You travel among the Allegheny Mountains, visit a revitalised Pittsburgh and see the corn fields of Ohio and Indiana.

Some of the splendid views experienced on this 780-mile (1,250km) journey are only available by train and for much of the way you follow the original Baltimore & Ohio line along which the very first *Capitol Limited* ran in 1925.

**Frequency** Daily.

The westbound train leaves Washington late in the afternoon, arriving in Cumberland by early evening and Pittsburgh late in the evening. You reach Toledo by early next morning and Chicago by mid-morning.

Travelling east, trains leave Chicago mid-evening to reach Toledo during the night and Pittsburgh by early morning. You arrive in Cumberland late morning and Washington by mid-afternoon.

**Reservations** All reserved.

**Equipment** Superliner coaches.

**Sleeping** Superliner bedrooms.

**Food** Complete meals, snacks, sandwiches, drinks. Exclusive First Class section in the dining-car.

**Lounge car** Video movies, hospitality hour.

**Baggage** Check-in service at most stations.

## Joining the train

### WASHINGTON

For Washington, DC city information, see *The Northeast Corridor* (pages 205–8). Thruway buses link with Dulles International Airport and Charlottesville, Virginia.

## All aboard!

As the *Capitol Limited* slowly departs Washington look left for the tiled blue and gold dome of the Shrine of the Immaculate Conception (America's largest Catholic church). You travel north through the suburbs of Takoma Park and Silver Spring then turn northwest to begin to follow Baltimore & Ohio tracks to Pittsburgh. Look left for the gold spires of a Mormon temple just before you cross the Beltway, often crammed with commuters' cars.

**Forest Glen (12/13)** The old building which looks like a castle was once a speakeasy and house of ill repute but is now a post office.

**Kensington (19/6)** As you cross Rock Creek Park look left for the 1891 train station standing beside a row of antique shops.

**Garrett Park (20/5)** Named after John B Garrett, president of the Baltimore & Ohio, this was a summer retreat for railway executives. Note the attractive Victorian houses among the trees to your left.

Approaching Rockville you see the town's original redbrick B & O station to your left, with beyond it the Rockville Courthouse. Like many others on this route the station was designed by Frances E Baldwin.

**ROCKVILLE (25/40)** An 18th century Maryland town which has become a Washington suburb. METRO commuter trains wait on the left beside a spartan station building.

After Rockville the *Capitol Limited* accompanies the METRO line for a few minutes to its final stop, Washington Grove.

**Gaithersburg (5/35)** The county fairgrounds and another Baldwin station can be seen to your right before the train crosses Interstate 270.

After passing through Germantown you begin to shake off suburbia, travelling instead among the farms and gently rolling hills of the Atlantic coastal plain. Ahead are the fertile farms of the Potomac Valley.

**Barnesville (10/30)** The station to your left is where the B & O began a new line in 1866. Look left also to see a steam locomotive stranded in the sidings.

**Dickerson (15/25)** Sugarloaf Mountain is to your right. Tall chimneys appear in the distance as the train eases over to accompany the Potomac along the Maryland/Virginia border. Between the tracks and the river you can see traces of a neglected section of the Chesapeake & Ohio (C & O) Canal. Trees grow in the

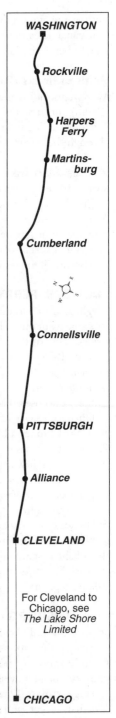

WASHINGTON

Rockville

Harpers Ferry

Martins-burg

Cumberland

Connellsville

PITTSBURGH

Alliance

CLEVELAND

For Cleveland to Chicago, see *The Lake Shore Limited*

CHICAGO

cutting and along a towpath which was formerly used by mules to haul barges. The canal dates from the mid-19th century, when it carried huge amounts of freight between Cumberland and Georgetown.

**Point of Rocks (23/17)** Another Baldwin depot stands where the line from Washington joins the original B & O line from Baltimore. You travel 800ft (240m) through Point of Rocks Tunnel, the first of 13 between here and Pittsburgh. The train then loses touch with the river for 15 minutes as it goes through the historic B & O town of Brunswick.

**Appalachian Trail (37/3)** The longest (2,050 miles/3,300km) footpath in the world crosses the tracks. Note the canal lock-keeper's red house to your left.

Just before Harper's Ferry you go through a tunnel beneath South Mountain and enter West Virginia's eastern panhandle. Watch for Seaboard trains to your left before you cross the canal then cross the rocky Potomac River on a spectacular long bridge. A second bridge can be seen to your left and beyond it the remains of a third. The Shenandoah River is also to your left.

**HARPERS FERRY (40/20)** A trading post was built in 1733 where Virginia, West Virginia and Maryland meet, but the ferry which gave the town its name went out of business in 1836 after the B & O Railroad built a wooden bridge. One of the most important events leading to the Civil War occurred here in 1859 when John Brown and his supporters seized the government arsenal. Federal troops led by Robert E Lee came by train to force Brown's surrender – the first time a railroad in North America had been used for military purposes. The arsenal ruins can be seen to your left.

During the war itself, nine bridges were built and destroyed here, and in June 1861 Stonewall Jackson set fire to 42 locomotives and 300 railroad cars. Harper's Ferry has museums, monuments and several buildings that date from before the Civil War. The **visitor centre** is at Shenandoah Street (tel: 304 535 6298) and Amtrak's station at Potomac Street, from where MARC commuter trains operate to Washington.

On your right as you leave are the remains of an early hydroelectric plant fed by water from a dam. Wind-powered irrigation pumps appear to your left.

Nearing Martinsburg look right for the two 1860s' roundhouses (one partly demolished) standing beside neglected railroad buildings. The stone mansion next to the tracks on your left once belonged to Revolutionary War General Adam Stephen.

**MARTINSBURG (20/85)** To your left is Martinsburg's original 1847 brick station, the only building in town to survive the Civil War and the oldest working train station in the country. Confederate forces stole 14 Baltimore & Ohio locomotives from Martinsburg during the Civil War and in 1877 the country's biggest ever rail strike began here.

**Hagerstown**, 12 miles to the north, was named after a German immigrant, Jonathan Hager, and became known as Hub City when six separate railways converged in the 19th century. Hagerstown still has four lines – Conrail, the Chessie-CSX, the Norfolk-Southern and the Winchester & Western – and rail infrastructure covers 228,000 square feet (21,000m²). It has two passenger stations, a roundhouse and the largest turntable in eastern America. The **National Railroad Historic Society** has developed a roundhouse museum and intends to make this a working centre for the restoration of steam engines. MARC commuter trains go to Hagerstown from Washington, DC.

The *Capitol Limited* pulls out of Martinsburg and continues past villages, farms, woods and orchards.

**Cherry Run (10/75)** Fort Frederick, seen across the Potomac to your right, dates from 1756 and was active during the Revolutionary, French and Indian, and Civil Wars. You follow the river for over an hour, with fine views apart from the few tunnels.

**Hancock (20/65)** The small town stands on both sides of the river in three states – West Virginia, Maryland and Pennsylvania. Potomac Park airport is to your right.

**Great Capcon (30/55)** You cross the Great Capcon River. Look right on the far side of the Potomac soon afterwards to see the remains of a C & O canal aqueduct.

**Orleans Road (35/50)** The *Capitol Limited* quits the old B & O main line at this point and enters the 1,592ft/485m Graham Tunnel. The tunnel is in Maryland but you emerge back in West Virginia and cross Kessler's Bridge.

Mountains and a tree-lined ravine appear to your right as the Potomac River runs through spectacular, sparsely populated country. Much of this region can only be seen from a raft or by travelling Amtrak. Look for deer among the wooded cliffs which sometimes rise sheer from the river. You cross the Potomac three times before leaving West Virginia.

**North Branch (80/5)** The C & O canal is visible for the last time before you pass under a highway bridge then under an old railroad bridge. On the approach to Cumberland, coal wagons and trailer trains gather to your left and the *Capitol Limited* leaves the Potomac Valley.

**CUMBERLAND (85/130)** Otherwise known as Washington Town or the 'Queen City of the Alleghenies'. Early coal, canal and railway barons built mansions here and many attractive houses can be seen on the hillside to your right. Cumberland was the eastern terminus of the Cumberland (National) Road and the western terminus of the Chesapeake & Ohio Canal. The Baltimore & Ohio Railroad arrived in 1842, construction having started in Baltimore in 1828.

The French and Indian War was sparked in 1755 when General Braddock led his forces 220 miles (350km) from Fort Cumberland towards Fort Duquesne. A thousand men died in the battle. George Washington also made expeditions from the fort, of which his log cabin is all that remains. Look left for a miniature fir plantation as the train departs.

**The Narrows (5/125)** This passage (the Cumberland Gap) through the Alleghenies provided a route for early traders and the military, becoming known as the Cumberland Trail. The railway came later, followed by America's earliest federal highway (US 40, seen to your left).

**Mount Savage (7/123)** America's first steel rails were produced at this junction of the B & O and Pennsylvania Railroads.

**Maryland/Pennsylvania State Line (10/120)** You cross the Mason-Dixon Line and enter the most central of the 13 original colonies. Look right for a large red barn.

The *Capitol Limited* climbs laboriously into the mountains, going through Hyndman station and Falls Cut Tunnel, constructed in 1897.

**Wills Creek (40/90)** Look right for anglers fishing a stream named after Indian Will, the last of the Shawnees. A flood here in 1984 damaged several small towns and 18 miles (28km) of track.

The train continues to climb a 2% grade, one of the steepest in these mountains. You go through the small communities of Mance and Manila by way of a series of curves.

**Sand Patch Tunnel (47/83)** Almost a mile (1.6km) from end to end, the tunnel is the longest and straightest on this route.

**Sand Patch (49/81)** This pinnacle of the Allegheny Mountains is the route's highest point (2,258ft/685m above sea level). The *Capitol Limited* passes beneath tracks of the Western Maryland Railroad, often busy with freight.

**Meyersdale (52/78)** Founded in the 18th century, Meyersdale is famous for maple sugar. Look left for Mount Davis (3,213ft/980m) before you continue through the towns of Salisbury Junction and Yoder.

**Garrett (60/70)** Another town named after the B & O boss, John Garrett. Helper locomotives were based here in the days of steam.

**Atlantic (65/65)** The remains of a millstone quarry are visible among the mountains on your right and two abandoned millstones lie in the Casselman River to your left.

As the train continues on a rightwards curve look left for the boulder called Saddle Rock, shaped like a western saddle.

**Markelton (80/50)** Situated on the banks of the Youghiogheny River, Markelton was a resort for Pittsburgh's elite at the beginning of the 20th century.

**Confluence (83/47)** The Casselman River is joined on the left by the Youghiogheny River and Laurel Hill Creek. A bicycle path runs to Connellsville along a former railroad bed beside the river.

**Sugar Loaf Mountain (90/40)** The mountain's distinctive shape is off to your right as you continue beside the river. Look for canoeists, fishermen, deer and possibly beaver.

**Ohiopyle (95/35)** Home of Ohiopyle Falls, out of sight to your left. Adjacent Laurel Highlands Park is especially beautiful in autumn and has the state's highest mountain, Mount Davis.

**Kaufman's Run (110/20)** Frank Lloyd Wright incorporated a small waterfall here inside the house he built and called Fallingwater. It was a weekend retreat for the Kaufman family, owners of a Pittsburgh department store.

**Indian Creek (120/10)** You cross the creek by an old stone bridge.

**CONNELLSVILLE (130/90)** Surrounded by coal fields producing the raw material for Connellsville Coke, this was an important railroad town. Service trains paused during the Second World War so that hundreds of female volunteers could serve food to the troops. Amtrak's station is at Front and Water.

Leaving town the train passes beneath a railway bridge which crosses the river to your left. You depart the Appalachian Mountains at Layton and descend towards the Allegheny Plateau via the attractive suburbs of Versailles and Smithton.

The *Capitol Limited* encounters heavy industrial scenes as it approaches Pittsburgh. The Duquesne Steel Works are to your left, followed by the J Edgar Thompson Works built by Andrew Carnegie, the Scottish-born rail and steel tycoon who became a philanthropist.

**Braddock (80/10)** Named after a British Army General, George Braddock, who died fighting the French in 1755. You pass through another tunnel into Pittsburgh.

## PITTSBURGH (90/100)

The birthplace of Gene Kelly and Perry Como is America's busiest inland port, where the Allegheny and Monongahela Rivers meet to become the Ohio. In the 1750s this strategic position led to the establishment of a fort named after the British Prime Minister, William Pitt (the Elder). Iron City eventually became so industrial it was known as 'hell with the lid off'. In 1877, 60 people died after soldiers fired on striking railroad workers.

The steel mills have lately been tamed and the slag heaps eliminated at a cost of $3 billion. Pittsburgh has instead acquired high-tech industry, smart skyscrapers and clean air. Now that the smoke has cleared, even outsiders are impressed by Renaissance City.

## Pittsburgh basics

**Telephone code** 412.

**Station** Amtrak's station is at Liberty and Grant Ave; tel: 471 6170. Ticket-office and waiting-room open 24 hours. Lockers, vending machines, ATM banking.

**Connections** Thruway buses link with Zanesville and Columbus, Ohio.

**Local transport** Port Authority light rail and bus services operate throughout the city. For details of routes, a free map and off-peak deals call 442 2000.

**Taxis** Checker; tel: 381 5600. Yellow; tel: 665 8100.

**Car rental** Budget, 700 5th Ave; tel: 261 3320.

**Greyhound** 55 11th and Liberty, near Amtrak's station; tel: 392 6513.

**Pittsburgh International Airport** is 15 miles (24km) west by Airline Transport; tel: 321 4990.

**Tours** Port Authority; tel: 231 5707. Lenzner; tel: 761 7000. River cruises (April–October) with the Gateway Clipper Fleet at Station Square Dock; tel: 355 7980. Cable railway inclines take you to an observation deck and restaurants on Mount Washington, from where you can see the Golden Triangle formed by the junction of three rivers. The Monongahela Incline (tel:442 2000) is near Smithfield Bridge and the Duquesne Inclined Plane (tel: 381 1665) at Fort Pitt Bridge.

**Visitors bureau** Open daily at 4 Gateway Center, Liberty Ave; tel: 1 800 366 0093 or 281 7711; web: www.visitpittsburgh.com.

**Accommodation** The (AYH) Hostel is close to downtown at 830 E Warrington Ave; tel: 431 1267. Family rooms $17.

Hotels include the Omni William Penn at 530 William Penn Way; tel: 281 7100; Hyatt Pittsburgh, 112 Washington Pl; tel: 471 1234; Hilton, Gateway Center; tel: 391 4600; Sheraton, 7 Station Square; tel: 261 2000; Parkway Center-Best Western, 875 Greentree Rd; tel: 922 7070; Red Roof Inn, 6404 Stubenville Pike; tel: 787 7870 – single $45, double $65.

## Recommended in Pittsburgh

**Andy Warhol Museum** 117 Sandusky; tel: 237 8300; web: www.warhol.org. Warhol was born in Pittsburgh and this collection (the world's largest devoted to a single artist) includes many films and paintings. Open Tue–Sun, admission charge.

**University of Pittsburgh** At Bigelow Blvd, Fifth Ave and Forbes Ave; tel: 624 4141; web: www.pitt.edu. The Cathedral of Learning tower (tel: 624 6000) has over 20 'nationality rooms' and a 36th floor observation area. Open daily, admission charge.

**Point State Park** Off Interstate 279, near Fort Pitt Bridge. Featuring the city's oldest building, Fort Pitt Blockhouse, built in 1764 by Colonel Henry Bouquet. **Fort Pitt Museum** (tel: 281 9285) shows the Point's history up to 1800. Fife and drum parades take place on summer Sundays. Open Wed–Sun, admission charge.

**Allegheny County Courthouse and Jail** 171 5th Ave and Grant; tel: 402 6703. This wonderful neo-Romanesque building was designed by Henry Hobson Richardson, with a dominating tower and a 'Bridge of Sighs' where convicts would cross the street from courthouse to prison. Tours by arrangement.

**Frick Art and Historical Center** 7227 Reynolds, in Point Breeze; tel: 371 0600; web: www.frickart.org. Includes the Frick Art Museum (mainly European works), the Car and Carriage Museum (historic automobiles from 1898–1940) and the Clayton Historical

House featuring Henry Frick's art collection. Closed Mon, admission charge for tours.
**Phipps Conservatory** Schenley Drive; tel: 622 6914; web:
www.phipps.conservatory.org. This huge and splendid Victorian conservatory features
tropical plants, cacti, orchids and bonsai. Closed Mon, admission charge.
**National Aviary** Arch Street and Ridge; tel: 323 7235; web: www.aviary.org. Opened
in 1952, the aviary contains more than 200 species, including many rare and
endangered ones. Open daily, admission charge.
**John Heinz Pittsburgh Regional History Center** 1212 Smallman; tel: 454 6000;
web: www.pghhistory.org. Housed in the former Chautauqua Lake Ice Company
building, this museum's Great Hall features a 1949 trolley, a Conestoga wagon and
the huge Pittsburgh city fire bell that was cast after the Great Fire of 1845. Life-sized
reconstructions show a log home, an immigrant worker courtyard house and a
suburban ranch home. Open daily, admission charge.
**Old Post Office Museum** 1 Landmarks Square, Allegheny Center; tel: 322 5058. Classic
clothes and toys in a domed building which used to be the North Side Post Office. Open
daily.
**Industrial Transportation Museum** In Station Square, across the Smithfield
Bridge. Includes steam engines, railroad cars and trolleys. The nearby P & L E
Railroad buildings house a restaurant.

# All aboard!

The train travels on through the night via Ambridge, Beaver Falls and Salem.

**Garfield (60/10)** Named after President James Garfield, who was
assassinated in 1881 in the old Washington, DC station.

**ALLIANCE (70/70)** An industrial city on the Mahoning River, Alliance
makes steel and electrical machinery and is the home of Mount Union
College. The station on the corner of Main and Webb is Amtrak's nearest stop
to Canton, seven miles southwest.

**Ravenna (30/40)** Founded in 1799, Ravenna has the Northeastern Ohio
University College of Medicine.

**Hudson (45/25)** The town dates from 1826 and was an important stop on
the stage-coach route between Pittsburgh and Cleveland.

## CLEVELAND (70/110)

For Cleveland city information and the rest of the route to Chicago, see *The
Lake Shore Limited* (pages 281–5). The *Capitol Limited* stops at Elyria, Toledo,
Waterloo, Elkhart, South Bend and Hammond-Whiting.

## CHICAGO

For Chicago city information, see *The California Zephyr* (pages 75–9).

# The *Three Rivers*
# New York–Chicago

## General route information

After travelling from New York through some of the country's most densely populated areas, the *Three Rivers* turns due west at Philadelphia into Pennsylvania Dutch country, home of the Amish people. You follow the Juanita River to the Allegheny Mountains then round spectacular Horseshoe Curve before reaching Pittsburgh. From there you accompany the Ohio River and cross Indiana farmlands to Chicago.

The *Broadway Limited*, which first ran in 1912, used this route until the mid 1990s. In 1938 the train was re-equipped as a streamliner which can be seen in action in a 1940 film called *Broadway Limited*.

**Frequency** Daily.

The westbound service leaves New York soon after midday to reach Philadelphia by mid-afternoon and Harrisburg late afternoon. Pittsburgh is reached late in the evening and Chicago early next morning.

Travelling east, trains leave Chicago mid-evening to reach Pittsburgh early next morning and Harrisburg by mid-afternoon. Philadelphia is reached late in the afternoon and New York by early evening.

**Reservations** All reserved.

**Equipment** Heritage coaches.

**Sleeping** Heritage roomettes and bedrooms refurbished with shower rooms.

**Food** Sandwiches, snacks, drinks.

**Baggage** Check-in service.

## Joining the train

### NEW YORK

For New York City, the route to Philadelphia and Philadelphia city information, see *The Northeast Corridor* (pages 196–203).

### PHILADELPHIA (10/26)

The *Three Rivers* leaves 30th Street Station between apartment buildings on the right and commuter trains to the left.

**Overbrook (10/16)** Look left for Victorian buildings beyond the wooden station.

**Ardmore (12/14)** One of several commuter stops occurring between Philadelphia and Paoli. Some stations have elaborately sculpted canopies.

**PAOLI (26/40)** Named after Pasquale Paoli, an 18th century Corsican revolutionary. Just to the north is Valley Forge, site of the base camp where George Washington's fledgling Continental Army spent a cold and hungry winter (1777–78) during the Revolutionary War. You can visit Washington's headquarters and the memorial chapel. Amtrak's utilitarian depot is located at Lancaster Pike and S Valley Rd.

The *Three Rivers* continues among residential areas and leafy hills which look especially attractive when dogwoods are in bloom during spring.

**Coatesville (10/30)** Industry sprawls to your left before the train enters fertile Pennsylvania Dutch country with its many wooden bell-towered churches. Dutch is a misnomer, since this area was largely settled by Germans whose nationality (*Deutsch*) was mispronounced by English colonists.

Many of those now known as Pennsylvania Dutch are members of the Amish church. Amish people adhere to strict religious beliefs and run their tidy farms much as they have done for 300 years, using mules and ploughs. The 1985 movie *Witness* was set among these white farmhouses, where Amish men dress in black and the women wear plain frocks and traditional bonnets. The Amish have no electricity or television, although mobile phones are allowed and they can drive but not own cars.

**LANCASTER (40/40)** America's oldest inland city was the nation's capital for a single day on September 27 1777. Founded in 1718 as Hickory Town before being renamed after a town in England, Lancaster is where the Amish come to market. You can find information on Amish life at the **Pennsylvania Dutch Visitors Center**, 501 Greenfield Rd; tel: 717 299 8901; web:www.padutchcountry.com.

Photographs are not allowed but you can visit several families, some of whom make a living selling woven baskets and cookies to 'the English'. For walking tours contact the Association of Commerce at 100 Queen.

The **Railroad Museum of Pennsylvania** in nearby Strasburg has one of the world's finest collections of

NEW YORK CITY

For New York City to Philadelphia, see *The Northeast Corridor*

PHILADELPHIA
Paoli
Lancaster
Harrisburg

Lewistown

Huntingdon

Altoona
Johnstown

Latrobe
Greensburg
PITTSBURGH
Youngstown

Fostoria

Nappanee

Hammond-Whiting

CHICAGO

locomotives, passenger cars and freight wagons dating from 1825 up to the present day (tel: 717 687 8628; web: www.rrmuseumpa.org). The Railroad Weekend in May is one of many special events organised by the museum and the Strasburg Rail Road runs daily steam train excursions from April until October. Open daily, admission charge.

You continue among factories and refineries, with a park to your left. Between here and Harrisburg the train follows the path of the first telegraph wires. A short distance to the north is Hershey, founded by Milton Hershey in 1903 and dedicated to all things chocolate.

**Three Mile Island (25/15)** Two of the power plant's four cooling towers puff plumes of white vapour away to your left. In 1979 this was the scene of America's worst nuclear accident, and the reactor which then suffered partial meltdown has been inoperative ever since.

**Harrisburg Airport (28/12)** The airport is to your left, with rolling hills beyond the Susquehanna River.

**HARRISBURG (40/65)** Pennsylvania's capital stands on the east bank of the Susquehanna where the Pennsylvania Canal arrived in 1834. The first trains came two years later and the main Pennsylvania Railroad linked the city with Pittsburgh in 1847.

Harrisburg's Capitol features bronze doors, stained glass windows and a marble staircase similar to one in the Paris Opera House. Its 272ft/83m dome resembles St Peter's in Rome. The **William Penn Museum** is next to the Archives Tower, which has records going back to 1681. The **visitors bureau** is at 114 Walnut; tel: 717 232 1377; web: www.visithhc.com.

Trailways buses connect Amtrak's atmospheric station at 4th and Chestnut with Scranton and Reading. The **Steamtown National Historic Site** at 150 S Washington Ave in Scranton (tel: 570 340 5200; web: www.nps.gov/stea) reveals early 20th century railroading in two museums, a theatre and a restored roundhouse. Steam trains travel between Scranton and Moscow, Pennsylvania.

As you depart Harrisburg look left for the Capitol's green dome beyond the office blocks and car parks.

**Susquehanna River (3/62)** The *Three Rivers* crosses on Rockville Bridge, the longest (3,820ft/1,165m) and widest (52ft/16m) stone-arch bridge in the world.

**Duncannon (20/45)** For the next 100 miles (160km) you accompany the Juanita River and ascend the Alleghenies. The Susquehanna River fades to your right as farmland gives way to mountains.

**LEWISTOWN (65/35)** A manufacturing town with a neglected-looking station building on the right.

As you move deeper into the Alleghenies, look right for Jack's Mountain and left for Blue Mountain.

**HUNTINGDON (35/45)** Another modest factory town situated next to the Juanita River.

**Spruce Creek (15/30)** You cross a creek which was fished by former President Jimmy Carter. After negotiating a short tunnel you continue among streams, hills, small towns and rivers. Wooded cliffs appear on both sides.

**ALTOONA (45/60)** Founded in 1849 by the Pennsylvania Railroad, Altoona was a supply base for railway construction over the mountains. The town still provides maintenance facilities and you travel through extensive yards to reach Amtrak's station at 1231 11th Ave.

The **Railroaders Memorial Museum** on your left has many engines, coaches and models associated with the Pennsylvania Railroad (tel: 814 946 0834; web: www.railroadcity.com). Exhibits include the *Loretto*, a private car that belonged to steel baron Charles M Schwab. Open daily, admission charge. Almost 7,000 steam locomotives were made in the adjacent shops, which now rebuild diesels.

Note the domed cathedral to your right as you go through the middle of Altoona.

**Horseshoe Curve (15/45)** A 2,355ft/718m landmark carved out of the Logan Valley hillside in 1854, its central curve measuring 220°. Horseshoe Curve was crucial during the early days of westward expansion since it enabled trains to cope with a demandingly steep gradient. A national park service guide is sometimes on board the *Three Rivers* to explain the line's history. Look out for an old Pennsylvania Railroad engine to your left next to the modern **visitor centre** (tel: 814 941 7960).

**Gallitzin Summit (25/35)** The train travels through a tunnel to the other side of the Alleghenies. Crossing these mountains was a much more laborious affair during the early 19th century, when the Allegheny Portage Railroad lifted canal boats 30 miles (48km) between the Juanita and Conemaugh Rivers. This unique engineering system is explained at Cresson's **Allegheny Portage Museum** with a full-size model and parts of the original stationary steam engine (tel: 814 886 6150; web: www.nps.gov/alpo/home.htm).

**JOHNSTOWN (60/45)** In 1889 a dam burst on the nearby Conemaugh River after heavy rain. John Hess, an engineer on board the Pennsylvania Railroad's *No. 1124*, warned the town of impending disaster by sounding the whistle as his train raced down the valley. He and his fireman jumped to safety just before the train was overtaken by the flood. Many lives were saved because of his warning but 2,200 people still died in the deluge. Before Prohibition, saloons would sometimes have signs reading 'Don't spit, remember the Johnstown flood'.

Further floods in 1936 and 1977 killed 25 and 85 people respectively. Since the steel industry's decline unlucky Johnstown has also been affected by high levels of unemployment.

You travel for 15 minutes through industrial scenes before forests and mountains return. A sinuously curving river follows below to your right.

**LATROBE (45/5)** A mostly residential town used as a training base by the Pittsburgh Steelers football team.

**GREENSBURG (5/42)** In 1763 Chief Pontiac and the Ottawa Indians were defeated by Henry Bouquet and the British at nearby Bushy Run. Fort Pitt was relieved four days later.

You continue among green hills with occasional houses and factories, including that of the Westinghouse Brake Company. The train slows down as it begins to approach Pittsburgh, seen ahead to your right.

## PITTSBURGH (42/110)

For Pittsburgh city information, see *The Capitol Limited* (pages 291–3). The Three Rivers travels on through the night across northeastern Ohio.

**YOUNGSTOWN (110/170)** Amtrak's recently restored station is at 528 Mahoning Ave. Youngstown is the seat of Mahoning County and in the 1920s it was one of America's largest steel-producing cities. Four main railroad lines and four branch lines were built to bring iron ore and coal.

**Akron (60/110)** German immigrant Ferdinand Schumacher began selling home-made oatmeal in 1854 and his business eventually became the Quaker Oats Company. Akron's Quaker Square features historic mills and silos. The National Football League was founded in nearby Canton, home of the **NFL Hall of Fame**.

The **Depot Restaurant and Museum** at 120 Mill (tel: 330 253 5970) has a solarium car from the Pennsylvania Railroad, along with semaphore signals and telegraph equipment. A 1940s *Broadway Limited* dining-car houses 800ft of model railway track.

**FOSTORIA (170/125)** Amtrak's station at 500 S Main also serves the city of Lima.

You cross the Ohio/Indiana state line an hour from Fostoria.

**Garrett (90/35)** Freight yards extend to the left of a two-storey red brick and tile station.

As the morning dawns you continue among fields, streams, trees, ponds and marshes. Look for cattle, mansard-roofed barns and a few small towns. The mobile home factory to your left signals the approach of Nappanee.

**NAPPANEE (125/70)** The train stops across a road, with Nappanee's neat station building to your right. You pass the Brunswick Marine plant to your left then re-enter farm country.

**Bremen (7/63)** Large factories accumulate to your left as you change from Eastern to Central Time. Watches go back an hour (forward when travelling east).

The train passes beneath a rare highway bridge just before Walkerton.

**Walkerton (22/48)** After passing through this small town look for giant irrigation machines as the fields become bigger. Pine trees are often grown here as windbreaks.

**Gary (65/5)** Freight yards, smoking chimneys and steel plants gather on both sides. Church spires feature to your left as you approach Hammond-Whiting through residential areas and glimpse Lake Michigan to your right.

**HAMMOND-WHITING (70/25)** For Hammond-Whiting and the route to Chicago, see *The Cardinal* (pages 258–9).

**CHICAGO**
For Chicago city information, see *The California Zephyr* (pages 75–9). Thruway buses connect with Rockford, Illinois, and Madison, Wisconsin.

# The *Maple Leaf* New York–Toronto

## General route information

The *Maple Leaf* starts in New York and travels more than 500 miles (800km) before reaching Canada's equivalent city, Toronto. The route takes in the Hudson River Valley, the Mohawk Valley, Niagara Falls and Lake Ontario. Travelling north by day gives you maximum viewing opportunities.

**Immigration formalities** US and Canadian citizens must have a passport, birth certificate, citizenship certificate or naturalisation certificate – **a driver's license is not sufficient.** Non-US citizens permanently or temporarily residing in the US must have an Alien Registration Card (I-551, or I-688 bearing proper endorsement on the reverse). Citizens of other countries not listed above must have a passport.

Citizens of many countries must also have a visa, a US Employment Authorisation Card showing 210 as a section of law, or a Canadian Form IMM 1000. Passengers under 18 years old who are not accompanied by an adult must bring a letter from a parent or guardian giving them permission to enter Canada.

See under *Documents* in *Chapter 3* (page 33), check with your US embassy or contact the Immigration and Naturalisation Service in Washington, DC (see *Chapter 3* and *Appendix 2*). Passengers without proper documentation are prohibited from entering the US or Canada and will be detrained before reaching the US/Canadian border.

**Frequency** Daily.

The northbound service leaves New York City early in the morning to reach Albany by mid-morning, Buffalo mid-afternoon and Niagara Falls late afternoon. You arrive in Toronto by mid-evening.

Travelling south, trains leave Toronto mid-morning to reach Niagara Falls (Ontario) by midday, Buffalo early afternoon and Albany early evening. You arrive in New York late in the evening.

**Reservations** Reserved except for travel locally between New York and Albany-Rensselaer.

**Equipment** Amfleet coaches.

**Food** Snacks, sandwiches, drinks.

**Baggage** No check-in service.

# Joining the train

## NEW YORK

For New York City and the route as far as Schenectady, see *The Adirondack* (pages 261–4); for the route from Schenectady to Depew station, Buffalo, see *The Lake Shore Limited* (pages 278–80).

**BUFFALO-DEPEW (55/10)** Leaving Depew station the *Maple Leaf* picks its way carefully through a mass of tracks. The clock tower of the New York Central station is to your right and a disused evangelical church home on your left. The city skyline appears ahead as you cross Highway 90 before continuing among industrial parks and residential areas. Near Exchange Street Station the eclectic buildings of downtown can be seen to your right.

**BUFFALO-EXCHANGE STREET (10/30)** Buffalo stands next to Lake Erie, separated from Canada by the Niagara River. After the Civil War many railroads converged, and this remains an important rail centre where freight trains gather on both sides of Amtrak's station.

Look for older, more elegant buildings in the Victorian Allentown district beyond a derelict factory to your right. The **visitors bureau** is at 617 Main; tel: 716 852 0511; web:www.buffalocvb.org.

You leave Buffalo between houses and high-rise apartments, travelling through several tunnels to emerge with Lake Erie on your left. The lake soon begins to narrow as it forms the Niagara River.

**Peace Bridge (8/22)** The bridge to your left connects the United States with Fort Erie in Canada.

**Squaw Island (13/17)** The island is linked to the mainland by a drawbridge. You lose touch with the river for a while as the train goes through Tonawanda and crosses the Erie Canal.

**Niagara (20/10)** The airport on your left lands thousands of honeymooners, as well as visitors to the new casino, from around the world.

As the *Maple Leaf* approaches Niagara Falls it curves right through ragged-looking yards. Unromantic pylons to your right indicate how much electricity the falls produce. Westinghouse built the world's first

NEW YORK CITY

For New York City to Schenectady, see
*The Adirondack*

● Schenectady

For Schenectady to Buffalo, see
*The Lake Shore Limited*

Buffalo ●

Niagara Falls, New York ●
USA
Canada
Niagara Falls, Ontario

St Catharines ●

Grimsby ●

Aldershot ●

TORONTO

Oakville

hydroelectric plant here in 1896, transmitting power to Buffalo. Nikolai Tesla, inventor of the alternating current, has a statue at the top of the falls.

**NIAGARA FALLS, NY (30/11)** Two cataracts pour 600,000 gallons (2.7 million litres) of water a second into the Niagara River below, creating awesome sights and sounds. The American Falls reach 167ft/51m. The Canadian (Horseshoe) Falls are a few feet lower but have a longer, sweeping crest of 2,600ft/790m. The **visitors bureau** is at 310 4th; tel: 716 285 2400 or 1 800 338 7890; web: www.nfcvb.com.

Previous visitors have crossed the falls on a high wire or gone over the rim in a barrel. Such stunts have now been made illegal but you can enjoy safe thrills on a *Maid of the Mist* cruise or tour caves under the falls (rented rain gear provided). Not so exciting, although less damp, is the observation tower above the falls.

Amtrak's station is at 27 Lockport Rd, some miles from downtown and the falls (take Metro bus #52). You can walk to Canada across the Rainbow Bridge.

**US/Canada Border (9/2)** The train crosses the Niagara River on a high bridge with the falls away to your left.

**NIAGARA FALLS, ONTARIO (11/20)** Before you are allowed to leave or continue your journey the train must pause for a customs check. A VIA Rail crew replaces Amtrak staff and even the napkins in the lounge car read 'VIA'.

Like its US counterpart, Canada's town of Niagara Falls makes it easy to see the main attraction. Most people prefer the view from this side, where the 520ft/158m Skylon tower offers a terrific vantage point and coloured lights create hypnotic effects on the water by night. The **information bureau** is at 5433 Victoria Ave; tel: 905 356 6061.

**Niagara Falls Museum** was established in 1827, making it the oldest in North America. The 700,000 artefacts include dinosaurs and Egyptian mummies.

After leaving Niagara through Canadian National rail yards the *Maple Leaf* continues on towards Lake Ontario, travelling among small farms and vineyards.

**Welland Canal (15/5)** You cross above one of the lock systems which enable ships to be lifted 326ft (almost 100m) between Lakes Erie and Ontario. Just before St Catharines you cross the Old Welland Canal, one of three which predated the present one. The previous canals took much longer for ships to negotiate.

**ST CATHARINES (20/15)** Garden City is surrounded by orchards, vineyards and wineries. From a viewing platform you can watch the ships of 30 countries pass through the locks. A museum at Lock 3 includes photographs and models explaining the Welland Canal's history.

More vineyards appear as you travel through pretty, rolling countryside and cross Sixteen Mile Creek.

**Jordan (4/11)** Lake Ontario is visible for the first time to your right. The train will stay in touch with the lake for most of the next 70 miles (112km) to Toronto.

**GRIMSBY (15/30)** Note the picturesque station building. In the late 18th century, Grimsby had Canada's first town government.

**ALDERSHOT (30/12)** Connecting VIA Rail trains link Aldershot with London and Windsor, Ontario. Reservations can be obtained through Amtrak.

The train passes through suburban districts until industry returns on the approach to Oakville. You again cross Sixteen Mile Creek.

**OAKVILLE (12/25)** Located at the mouth of the creek, Oakville grew as a harbour for exporting oak timber. It now manufactures cars, chemicals and machinery. Watch for the attractive Victorian houses before you leave past a Ford Motor factory and extensive rail yards to your left.

**Port Credit (10/15)** You cross the Credit River then the Etobicoke and Humber Rivers approaching Toronto. The skyline ahead to your right features the giant CN Tower.

**Ontario Place (15/10)** An amphitheatre and the world's largest movie screen appear to your right in a park built over part of Lake Ontario.

**Fort York Park (21/4)** The historic British garrison to your right is where Toronto was founded in 1793.

## TORONTO

Ontario's capital claims to be the most liveable big city in North America. Explored by the French in 1615, it became a trading post and later a British colonial town called York. In 1813, during the so-called War of 1812, York was attacked and burned by an American force commanded by Zebulon Pike, a noted western explorer.

Toronto officially began in 1834 when the town was named after an Algonkian word for 'a place of meetings', but it remained a small town until the railway arrived. Yonge Street, running north from Lake Ontario, is the longest street in the world.

Once scorned as infinitely boring, Canada's largest city has transformed itself into an exciting place of three million people, and among its 70 ethnic groups is the largest Italian community outside Italy. Toronto has acquired a reputation as the Hollywood of the north, with many television series filmed here as well as movies such as *Moonstruck*, *Sea of Love* and *The Fly*.

Freezing temperatures are likely from November to March and mid-winter can be very cold, although snow is actually less frequent than in many US cities.

## Toronto basics

**Telephone code** 416.

**Station** Clean, efficient and softly-lit Union Station at Front and York reflects Toronto's character. Opened by the Prince of Wales in 1927, this splendid structure has 40ft/12m stone pillars and an Italian tile ceiling. Part of the movie *Silver Streak*, starring Gene Wilder and a runaway train from Chicago, was filmed here.

Reservations and information tel: 1 800 872 7245. Ticket-office open 06.45–20.30 Mon–Sat; 08.00–20.30 Sun. Waiting-room 06.00–00.30. Lockers, newspapers, Red Caps, restaurants, shops, ATM banking, taxi stand, subway.

**Connections** Union Station is also used by VIA Rail (tel: 366 8411) and GO commuter trains to Hamilton, Oshawa, Richmond Hill and Georgetown (tel: 869 3200).

**Local transport** TTC buses and subway trains allow fast travel throughout the city, with day and monthly passes; tel: 393 6746.

**Taxis** Metro; tel: 363 5611. Diamond; tel: 366 6868.

**Car rental** Thrifty, 6040 Indian Line; tel: 1 800 367 2277.

**Greyhound** 610 Bay; tel: 367 8747. The terminal is also used by Voyageur Colonial and Gray Line.

**Pearson Airport** is 10 miles (16km) west of downtown by bus #58.

**Tours** Gray Line; tel: 594 0343. Olde Town Toronto; tel: 798 2425 offers sightseeing by trolley and double decker bus. Toronto Harbour tours (May–October) leave from 145 Queen's Quay Terminal; tel: 945 3431.

**Visitors bureau** 207 Queen's Quay W; tel: 203 2600 or 800 363 1990; email: toronto@torcvb.com; web: www.torontotourism.com.

**Accommodation** Contact Bed & Breakfast Homes of Toronto, PO Box 46093, College Park, 777 Bay St, Toronto, Ontario M5G 2P6; tel: 363 6362 or Toronto B&B Inc, Box 269, 253 College St, Toronto, Ontario M5T 1R5; tel: 705 738 9449.

International Youth Hostel, 76 Church; tel: 971 4440. Members $19, non-members $23. Leslieville Home Hostel, 185 Leslie; tel: 461 7258. Dormitory beds $15, singles $35. Central YMCA, 20 Grosvenor; tel: 921 5171. YWCA Woodlawn Residence, 80 Woodlawn Ave; tel: 923 8454. Single $45, double $60.

Hotels include the Sutton Place at 955 Bay; tel: 924 9221; Admiral, 249 Queen's Quay; tel: 203 3333; Holiday Inn, 370 King; tel: 599 4000; Ibis, 240 Jarvis; tel: 593 9400; Executive, 621 King St W; tel: 504 7441 – single $55; Selby, 592 Sherbourne; tel: 921 3142 – single $50, double $60.

## Recommended in Toronto

**CN Tower** 301 Front W; tel: 360 8500; web: www.cntower.ca. The western world's tallest free-standing structure (1,815ft 5in/553.3m) features outside elevators that rocket you to the Skypod two-thirds of the way up. Even better views can be achieved from the Space Deck, another 33 storeys above and the highest observation platform in the world. Given a clear day you can see as far as Niagara Falls. Open daily, admission charge. Try to avoid weekend queues. Next to the Tower is the SkyDome stadium, with its unique retractable roof and a hotel overlooking the pitch.

**Royal Ontario Museum** 100 Queen's Park; tel: 586 8000; web: www.rom.on.ca.

The collection of six million objects includes items from ancient Greece and Egypt, as well as giant totem poles and a dinosaur gallery. Open daily, admission charge. Free walking tours of the city on Wed and Sun (tel: 586 5797).

**Eaton Centre** On Yonge, from Queen to Dundas; tel: 598 8700; web: www.torontoeatoncentre.com. More than 300 stores and services operate inside this glittering building, with glass elevators and a 17-screen cinema. Open daily.

**New City Hall** Queen; tel: 392 7341. Curved towers enclose a circular council chamber completed in 1965. Free tours on weekdays. Next to City Hall is Nathan Phillips Square, a favourite meeting place for relaxing by the lake (in winter a skating rink).

**Art Gallery of Ontario** 317 Dundas W; tel: 979 6648; web: www.ago.on.ca. Includes special exhibitions by artists such as Matisse and Man Ray. Open daily, admission charge.

**First Post Office** 260 Adelaide E; tel: 865 1833. Dating from the 1830s and still in use. Costumed guides return you to a world of quill pens and sealing wax. Open daily.

**Spadina Historic House & Gardens** 285 Spadina Rd; tel: 392 6910. This elegant house has one of Toronto's finest restored gardens. Built by businessman James Austin in 1866, Spadina reflects the Toronto art scene of the late 19th and early 20th century and their Victorian, Edwardian and Art Nouveau influences. Guided tours. Open daily, admission.

**Toronto Aerospace Museum** Parc Downsview Park, 65 Carl Hall Road; tel: 638 6078; web: www.torontoaerospacemuseum.com. Aircraft important to the history of Toronto are on display, including planes manufactured by Avro Canada, de Havilland and Curtiss. Open Thu–Sat, admission charge.

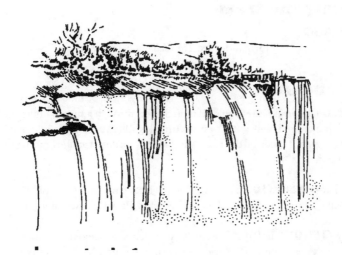

# The *Lake Cities*
# Chicago–Pontiac

## General route information

On a fast trip between Chicago and two of America's largest industrial cities, the *Lake Cities* train explores a section of middle America. En route are lakes, orchards and vineyards, together with manufacturing plants belonging to the likes of Kellogg and Ford. Infrastructure improvements are under way to reduce travel times between Chicago and Detroit by as much as two hours.
**Frequency** Daily.

The eastbound service leaves Chicago early in the afternoon, reaching Battle Creek by late afternoon, Detroit by early evening and Pontiac mid-evening.

Travelling west, trains leave Pontiac mid-morning to reach Detroit at midday, Battle Creek by mid-afternoon and Chicago late afternoon.
**Reservations** All reserved.
**Equipment** Amfleet coaches. Business Class.
**Food** Snacks, sandwiches, drinks.
**Baggage** No check-in service.

## Joining the train

### CHICAGO
For Chicago city information, see *The California Zephyr* (pages 75–9).

## All aboard!

The *Lake Cities* train eases out of Union Station through a tunnel under the Post Office building. Trains are set up in Amtrak's 21st Street yards on your left to travel to every corner of the land, and Conrail loading facilities can be seen to your right.

**Comiskey Park (10/15)** To your left is a car park where the old White Sox baseball stadium used to be. A new Comiskey Park has risen alongside.

**Roby (15/10)** The Regal Theater to your left was opened by Chicago's first black mayor as a centre for African-American culture. Mayor Washington was buried in the cemetery also seen to your left. Interstate 90 (the Indiana Toll Road) is on the right.

You see the El railway track overhead before you cross the Dan Ryan Expressway. Chicago's skyline back to your left features the 110-storey Sears Tower. The train crosses the south branch of the Chicago River and a defunct Rock Island line then crosses the Calumet River on a steel bridge. Look below for grain elevators and ships being loaded.

## HAMMOND-WHITING (25/35)
The modern yellow-brick station to your left at 1135 Calumet Ave is Amtrak's usual stop for trains approaching Chicago from the east. Oil storage tanks proliferate on both sides of the track before you travel east through the towns of Indiana Harbor and Pine Junction.

## Indiana Harbor Canal (10/25)
The train crosses the canal on a drawbridge. The canal links the Calumet River with Lake Michigan, a short distance away to your left. To your right are a Standard Oil refinery and a Lever Brothers factory.

## Gary (15/20)
Long one of the nation's great steel producers, with plants on both sides forming a mass of complicated pipelines, pylons and storage tanks. Gary was the birthplace of Karl Malden, Michael Jackson and astronaut Frank Borman.

## MICHIGAN CITY (35/30)
Look left for a colourful marina on Lake Michigan, seen just before you cross the Indiana/Michigan State Line.

The train moves inland through country famous for producing wine and fruit. You pass from Central to Eastern Time, so watches go forward an hour (backward when travelling west).

## NILES (30/40)
A small railway town which serves local farmers. Note the Michigan Central station and clock tower to your left.

As the *Lake Cities* travels on through grape country look also for cherry trees, strawberries, plums and cider-apple orchards.

## Dowagiac (12/28)
This is a scheduled stop for Amtrak's International train.

## KALAMAZOO (40/30)
The name is a Potawatomi word for 'place where the water boils' and the river has

PONTIAC
Birmingham
Royal Oak
DETROIT
Dearborn
Ann Arbor
Jackson
Albion
Battle Creek
Kalamazoo
Niles
Michigan City
Hammond-Whiting
CHICAGO

bubbling springs. Pretty 19th century houses can be seen to your right. Thruway buses connect with Amtrak's station in Grand Rapids and many other Michigan towns as far north as St Ignace.

The **Kalamazoo, Lake Shore & Chicago Railway** operates out of Paw Paw, 15 miles (24km) to the west (tel: 616 657 5963). Diesel-powered trains travel among orchards, woods and vineyards, running next to Lake Cora on a Pere Marquette/Chesapeake & Ohio branch line.

You cross the Kalamazoo River as the *Lake Cities* leaves town.

**BATTLE CREEK (30/25)** The Kellogg brothers invented flaked cereal in the 1890s and made Battle Creek's fortune. 'The cereal capital of the world' is home to the Kellogg Company, Post Cereals and a Ralston Purina plant, all of which can sometimes be smelt as well as seen. A three day festival in June features 'the world's longest breakfast table'.

Thruway buses connect with East Lansing and Flint from Amtrak's modern station on your left at 104 Capitol Ave, and the **tourist bureau** is at 77 E Michigan Ave; tel: 616 962 2240; web: www.battlecreekvisitors.org.

Among preserved buildings at the rail town of Coldwater, 40 miles (64km) southeast, are an 1883 depot, freight terminal and railroad granary. The **Little River Railroad's** 1911 engine *No. 110* makes steam train excursions from Coldwater to Batavia (tel: 219 825 9182).

You depart Battle Creek with Post and Kellogg plants to your right and left. You join the Kalamazoo River to your right and follow its meandering path through a waterlogged terrain.

**ALBION (25/22)** Albion College campus is to your right. Albion is a scheduled stop for the *Lake Cities* train before it pushes on among peaceful farming scenes beside the Kalamazoo River.

**Jackson Airport (18/4)** Runways appear to your left.

**JACKSON (22/35)** Look left to see an interesting old brick-built station at 501 E Michigan Ave. A stone tablet in Jackson marks the spot where in 1854 a meeting of Free Soilers, Democrats and Whigs founded the Republican Party. The 500ft/150m Cascade Falls, America's largest man-made falls, were constructed here in 1932.

The train pulls out among Conrail yards and travels east through the communities of Michigan Center and Leoni.

**Grass Lake (10/25)** Fire destroyed the station building to your right. You continue through Chelsea then cross the Huron River for the first of many times as it winds between here and Ypsilanti.

**ANN ARBOR (35/33)** In 1824 two settlers named the town after a grape arbor and their wives, Ann Rumsey and Ann Allen. The Michigan Central Railroad arrived in 1839, linking the town to Detroit. The **visitors bureau** is at 120 W Huron (tel: 734 995 7281) and Amtrak's station at 325 Depot.

The University of Michigan, one of the country's oldest and largest, moved here from Detroit in 1841. Located mostly downtown, it has America's biggest college football stadium and witnessed the first anti-Vietnam War teach-in. Note the fine 19th century Central Michigan building to your right as you leave and cross the Huron River.

**Ypsilanti (10/23)** Named after a Greek war hero, Ypsilanti is the home of Eastern Michigan University. **Depot Town** is a historic district preserving old railroad buildings and a large collection of antique cars (tel: 483 4444).

Look right just before crossing the River Rouge near Dearborn to see **Henry Ford's Museum** and **Greenfield Village** (tel: 313 271 1620). A million visitors a year come to look at historic cars, a letter from Clyde Barrow and the chair in which Abraham Lincoln was assassinated in 1865. Among 80 buildings are the Wright Brothers' workshop, Edison's laboratory and the courthouse where Lincoln practised law – all brought from their original sites and reconstructed. Also on show are a locomotive built by Ford in 1876 and an 1893 replica of the *DeWitt Clinton*. Steam trains operate from April to October. Take SMART bus #200 from Detroit.

**DEARBORN (33/25)** Originally a stop for stage-coaches travelling on the Sauk Trail. Amtrak's station is at 16121 Michigan Ave. Henry Ford built his modest **Fair Lane** mansion on 72 acres (29ha) next to the Rouge River at 4901 Evergreen Road; tel: 313 593 5590. He died there by candlelight after floods cut off the power to the house. Open daily, admission charge.

Soon after Dearborn you see a Ford Company factory to your right and from here to Detroit the *Lake Cities* travels through a landscape mostly dedicated to the automobile. Look for Chrysler and General Motors factories as well as many loading docks and rail yards.

## DETROIT (25/20)

The midwest's oldest city is the home of crime writer Elmore Leonard and has been the birthplace of Joe Louis, Motown Records and innumerable cars. Founded by the French in 1701 as Fort Pontchartrain d'Etroit ('of the strait'), Detroit stands between Lakes Erie and Huron. Fought over by French, British and US forces until 1813, it became a staging post on the Underground Railroad for slaves escaping to Canada.

The decline in local industries and the effect of 1960s race riots have drastically reduced the population, but great efforts have been made to repair the city's image. Among nearby scenic railway routes are the **Southern Michigan** at Clinton (tel: 517 423 7230), the **Coe Railway** at Walled Lake (tel: 248 960 9440) and the **Coopersville & Marne** (tel: 616 997 7000).

### Detroit basics

**Telephone code** 313.

**Station** Amtrak's station is at 11 W Baltimore; tel: 873 3442. Ticket-office and waiting-room open 05.00– 01.00. Lockers, newspapers, handcarts, taxi stand.

**Local transport** The 'people mover' monorail (tel: 224 2160) stops at many hotels and attractions. The Trolley and DOT buses (tel: 933 1300) operate downtown. SMART buses (tel: 962 5515) serve outlying regions.
**Taxis** Lorraine; tel: 582 6900. Checker; tel: 963 7000.
**Car rental** Thrifty, 29111 Wick Road; tel: 734 946 7830.
**Greyhound** 1001 Howard; tel: 961 8011.
**Detroit Metropolitan Airport** is 2 miles (3.2km) west by Commuter Transportation bus; tel: 941 3252.
**Tours** Kirby (tel: 963 8585) and Gray Line (tel: 833 0161) operate in summer. Cruises on the *Star of Detroit* (May–October) leave from 2 E Atwater.
**Visitors bureau** Open daily at 211 W Fort; tel: 800 DETROIT; web: www.visitdetroit.com.
**Accommodation** AYH Hostel, 2305 Park Ave; tel: 961 8310. Members $12, non-members $15.

Special rates are available for downtown hotels at weekends. Hotels include the Courtyard by Marriott at 333 E Jefferson Ave; tel: 222 7700; Pontchartrain, 2 Washington Blvd; tel: 965 0200; St Regis, 3071 W Grand Blvd; tel: 873 3000; Dearborn Inn, 20301 Oakwood Blvd; tel: 271 2700; Days Inn, 231 Michigan Ave; tel: 965 4646; Shorecrest, 1316 E Jefferson Ave; tel: 1 800 992 9616.

## Recommended in Detroit
**Rivertown** This area between Jefferson Ave and the river prospered in the 19th century as a centre for railroads, ship building and lumber yards. Historic warehouses have been transformed into restaurants, shops and nightclubs (tel: 567 8182). The **Woodbridge Tavern** is an enjoyable speakeasy at 289 St Aubin (tel: 259 0578).
**Detroit Historical Museum** At the corner of 5401 Woodward Ave and Kirby; tel: 833 1805; web: www.detroithistorical.org. Displays include the 'Streets of Old Detroit', a fashion library and an old automobile plant body 'drop'. Closed Mon, admission charge.
**Detroit Cultural Center** On Woodward Ave, two miles (3km) from downtown. Includes the Institute of Art, the Science Center (featuring spacecraft) and an Italianate Public Library, which has one million books and murals showing transport history. Closed Mon, Fri and Sun. Free.
**Detroit Institute of Arts** 5200 Woodward; tel: 833 7900; web: www.dia.org. The fifth-largest fine arts museum in the country houses Renaissance masterpieces in a building that resembles an Italian palace. The collection also includes Flemish and early American art as well as works by Van Gogh and Brueghel. Open Wed–Sun, admission charge.
**Museum of African-American History** 315 E Warren; tel: 494 5800. The country's largest museum of African-American history and culture includes documents from the Underground Railroad for escaping slaves. Open Wed–Sun, admision charge.
**Motown Historical Museum** 2648 W Grand Blvd; tel: 875 2264. Hitsville USA is the original home of Motown Records (derived from Detroit's nickname of Motor Town). Studio A is where Smokey Robinson and Stevie Wonder recorded their hits around the clock in the 1960s. Open daily, admission charge.
**Fort Wayne** 6325 W Jefferson Ave, at Livernois; tel: 297 9360. Built in 1843 to

protect the US border, the fort incorporates the **Great Lakes Indian Museum** and offers tours by costumed guides. Open Wed–Sun, May–Labor Day. Admission charge.

**Belle Isle** Reached via Grand River Blvd and the Douglas MacArthur Bridge; tel: 267 7121. An island park three miles (5km) from the city centre, granted to French settlers by Detroit's founder, Antoine de la Mothe Cadillac. The park has a half-mile (0.8km) beach, a zoo, an aquarium and a nature centre.

**Fisher Mansion** 383 Lenox; tel: 331 6740. This elegant Moorish/Spanish mission-style mansion belonged to the auto magnate Lawrence P Fisher and its interior has ornate stone and marble, rosewood parquet floors and gold-leaf decorations. Now known as the Bhaktivedanta Cultural Center and owned by the Hare Krishna community, it opens for tours Mon–Fri, admission charge.

# All aboard!

The *Lake Cities* train continues through Detroit's northern suburbs and industrial districts. Factories specialise in farm implements, electrical equipment and more automobile products.

**ROYAL OAK (20/5)** First settled in the 1820s, this mostly residential suburb is the home of Detroit's Zoological Park.

**BIRMINGHAM (5/12)** A small residential town on the banks of the River Rouge in Oakland County.

## PONTIAC

Located next to the Clinton River on the Saginaw Trail, Pontiac was named in 1818 after an Ottawa Indian chief who fought to hold back British forces and is thought to be buried locally.

Pontiac was one of America's earliest industrial cities and it expanded rapidly after the railroad arrived in the 1880s, making cars, trucks, buses and automotive parts. Motor-manufacturing has diminished greatly in recent years. The city is the home of the Silverdome sports arena, where the Detroit Lions play National League football, and many parks and lakes are nearby.

# Other Amtrak Trains

## GENERAL INFORMATION

No reservation or check-in baggage services operate except where stated, and trains run daily unless otherwise indicated.

## THE TRAINS
### The Auto Train

**Lorton–Sandford** This is perhaps the world's longest passenger train and is certainly one of Amtrak's finest, much favoured by 'snow birds' escaping the northern winter and by families travelling to Disney World. Being a major money-spinner, the *Auto Train* receives some of the best attendants and best-maintained cars as it operates daily at 70mph (122km/h) over 855 miles (1,376km) of track between Lorton in Virginia and Sanford, Florida. The train is for cars and their passengers only. Amtrak is considering introducing similar services between Chicago and Florida and along the Pacific coast.

The $25 million Lorton terminal (just off I-95, 25 miles (40km) south of Washington, DC) was opened early in 2000, with a larger waiting-room, snack bar and improved facilities. The new 1,500ft/457m platform enables an entire train to be accepted without having to be split as was previously the case. Sanford station (about a half hour drive north of Orlando in Florida) is fairly basic and dates from when the original, privately run, *Auto Train* began in the 1970s. Lorton is for *Auto Trains* only but the Sanford terminal is served by several other trains, including the *Sunset Limited*.

Cars are loaded by Amtrak staff between 14.30 and 15.30, when the train doors are closed and all passengers must be on board. Trains normally depart at 16.00 but if boarding is complete and the track ahead clear they may leave a little earlier. The only stop during the night is in Florence, South Carolina, where the engine is refuelled and the engineer crew and conductor changed. You arrive at 08.30 the next morning. The train is occasionally delayed by problems on CSX's main route along the eastern seaboard but if this happens to any extent there will be extra meals scheduled and movies shown. If the track has been clear and there have been no delays you may arrive up to an hour early – most likely to happen on weekends.

Boarding times are strictly enforced so it is important to allow for possible heavy traffic, especially on weekends and around Washington. All vehicles must be 65 inches/1.65m or lower and not have temporary luggage or bike racks. Remember to turn off any car alarms because if one goes off en route it could easily drain the battery. There is no check-in baggage except inside vehicles, where you can pack as much as can safely be carried. Personal property left inside your vehicle remains your responsibility. You do not have access to it during the journey so you need to take a small bag of necessities with you when you board.

Northbound fares are lowest between early January and mid-February and from mid-June to mid-December. Southbound fares are lowest between mid-February and late March and from May to December. Special deals are often available, including lodging and tickets to Orlando area attractions as well as your train fare. Amtrak uses Superliner II sleepers and specially designed bi-level lounge cars on this route. The lounge car features improved audio and video systems and booth seating. Complimentary dinner and breakfast in the dining-car are included.

Reservations are essential and you should allow at least one hour prior to departure (preferably two hours) for boarding. No pets are allowed and smoking is only permitted in designated areas of the lounge cars, no longer in private compartments. Railfone service is available. For directions and hours of operation there are recorded messages at Lorton (tel: 703 690 3355) and Sanford (tel: 407 323 4800). You can also call Amtrak's regular number (tel: 1 800 872 7245) or the special *Auto Train* toll free number (tel: 1 877 754 7495). *Auto Train* fans can join the VIP Club (tel: 1 800 836 6656) to receive newsletters and updates.

## The Downeaster
**Boston–Portland** Amtrak's Downeaster operates four times daily in both directions, travelling between North Station in Boston, Massachusetts, and Portland, Maine, along part of the former Boston & Maine Railroad. Famous trains such as the *Flying Yankee* used this route from the 1920s until the 1960s, taking passengers on overnight sleepers to New York or Montreal. Amtrak successfully re-introduced services by public demand in 2001 after a gap of 36 years and The Downeaster now attracts 20,000 passengers a month. On its 116-mile journey it stops at Haverhill, Exeter, Durham, Dover, Wells and Saco-Biddeford, as well as making seasonal stops at Old Orchard Beach (May 1 to October 31). There are plans also to extend services further north to Freeport, Brunswick and Lewiston/Auburn. The train is named after strong winds that used to blow ocean-going ships 'downeast' from Boston, and this route through woods, small towns and farmland is a great way to explore the unspoilt coastline.

All reserved. Coastal Club service available; web: www.thedowneaster.com

## The Cascades
**Seattle–Portland** Three European-style trains operate daily in each direction, following the *Coast Starlight* route (see pages 50–6). High-tech Spanish-built Talgo 200 equipment provides wider seats and a bistro dining-car. The new trains cut almost half an hour from the previous time on this

route. Since the introduction of the *Cascades* service, annual ridership has reached a record high of over half a million passenger trips and this has become Amtrak's most highly rated route for customer satisfaction.

Thruway buses connect Portland's Greyhound depot, opposite the Amtrak station, with other cities in Oregon and with Boise, Idaho.

All reserved. Checked baggage. Business Class. Bicycle racks. Railfone.

## The Pacific Northwest Service

**Seattle–Vancouver** One train a day follows the *Empire Builder* route (see pages 123) to Everett, then continues through north Washington via Mount Vernon and Bellingham before crossing the border into British Columbia. This train reopened the cross-border Seattle–Vancouver route in 1996 after a gap of 14 years. A second train operates between Seattle and Bellingham with through transport by bus to Vancouver, BC.

All reserved. Complete meals, snacks, sandwiches and drinks, including Red Hook beer and real coffee. Checked baggage. Business Class. Bicycle racks.

## The Capitols

**San Jose–Auburn** Eight trains a day in each direction follow parts of the *Coast Starlight* and *California Zephyr* routes (see pages 64–5 and 94–7). Most trains operate between Oakland and Sacramento. Many feeder buses link with places such as Reno, Santa Cruz and Santa Barbara.

Railfone. Bicycle racks.

## The Ethan Allen Express

**New York–Rutland** Follows the *Adirondack* route (see pages 260–5) from New York City to Fort Edward, then continues to Fairhaven and Rutland in Vermont. Buses provide connections from Rutland with Brandon, Middlebury, Vergennes and Burlington, as well as with ski resorts such as Killington.

Reservations required north of Albany. Business Class.

## The Keystone Service

**New York–Harrisburg** Eight trains a day (four at weekends) travel in each direction, following the *Three Rivers* route (see pages 294–6) as far as Harrisburg. *Keystone* trains are operated by Amtrak in partnership with the Pennsylvania Department of Transportation.

## The Carolinian

**New York–Charlotte** Follows the *Silver Star* route to Raleigh (see pages 222–5) then travels west through wooded hills to Charlotte in North Carolina via Greensboro.

Reservations required, except between New York and Washington. Carolina Business Class service offers complimentary drinks, newspapers, audio and movies between Washington and Charlotte. Check-in baggage. Railfone.

## The Empire Service
**Washington–Albany Rensselaer** Eight trains a day (four at weekends) travel in each direction, following part of the *Lake Shore Limited* route (see pages 275–8) as far as Harrisburg. A few trains also travel to Syracuse or from Schenectady.
   Business class. Railfone.

## The Piedmont
**Raleigh–Charlotte** Follows part of the *Carolinian* route (see this page) and serves fresh barbecued food in a refurbished dining car. Some trains operate between Charlotte and Wilson.
   All reserved. Complete meals service. Check-in baggage. Bicycle racks. Railfone.

## The Pennsylvanian
**Philadelphia–Chicago** Follows the same route as the *Three Rivers* to Pittsburgh (see pages 295–8) then the *Capitol Limited* route to Chicago (see pages 291–3). The *Pennsylvanian* makes more frequent stops, including Ardmore, Elizabethtown and Tyrone (a flag stop) in Pennsylvania.
   Reservations required except for local travel between Philadelphia and Harrisburg. Railfone.

## The Hiawatha Service
**Chicago–Milwaukee** Six trains daily (five at weekends) travel in each direction, stopping at Glenview and Sturtevant. From Milwaukee, Thruway buses link with Fond du Lac, Oshkosh, Wausau and other towns in Wisconsin.

## The Kentucky Cardinal
**Chicago–Louisville** Follows the *Cardinal* route (see pages 256–9) as far as Indianapolis then continues to Louisville, Kentucky.
   All reserved. Superliner sleeping cars. Full meal service available leaving Chicago on Tuesday, Thursday and Saturday. Breakfast available between Indianapolis and Chicago on Monday, Thursday and Saturday. Boxed meals are served on other days.

## The Lake Country Limited
**Chicago–Janesville** Departs early in the morning from Janesville, returning mid-evening from Chicago to arrive back in Janesville late evening. Travel is over rights of way belonging to Metra, the Wisconsin & Southern Railroad and the I & M Rail Link. There is an intermediate stop at Glenview and another stop is planned for either Walworth or Zenda, Wisconsin, to serve the Lake Geneva area.
   All reserved.

## The International
**Chicago–Toronto** Follows the *Lake Cities* route (see page 307) to Port Huron then continues across the Canadian border and southern Ontario. This

service is operated jointly by Amtrak and VIA Rail, so trains operating within Canada are subject to VIA Rail regulations.

All reserved. Superliner coaches.

## The Ann Rutledge

**Chicago–Kansas City** Travels via St Louis and connects at Kansas City with the *Southwest Chief* to Los Angeles (see page 129).

All reserved. Business Class.

## The State House

**Chicago–St Louis** Follows the *Texas Eagle* route (see pages 168–73) but also stops in Summit and Dwight, Illinois.

All reserved. Business Class.

## The Wolverine

**Chicago–Detroit** Follows part of the *Lake Cities* route (see pages 306–11) and stops at Greenfield Village for access to the Henry Ford Museum.

All reserved.

## The Twilight Limited

**Chicago-Pontiac** Follows part of the *Lake Cities* route (see pages 306–11), making an extra stop in Dowagiac, Michigan.

All reserved. Check-in baggage service when travelling east. Business Class.

## The Illinois Zephyr

**Chicago–Quincy** Follows the *California Zephyr* route to Galesburg (see pages 75–80) then continues south to Quincy, Illinois.

All reserved. Business Class.

## The Illini

**Chicago–Carbondale** Starts late in the afternoon and follows part of the *City of New Orleans* route (see pages 182–4).

All reserved. Business Class. Bicycle racks.

## The Kansas City/St Louis Mule

**Kansas City–St Louis** East and westbound services travel across Missouri via Jefferson City and Sedalia, with Thruway buses connecting to *City of New Orleans* trains at Carbondale (see page 184).

All reserved. Business Class.

## The Heartland Flyer

**Oklahoma City–Fort Worth** Travels between Oklahoma and Texas, making stops in Norman, Purcell, Pauls valley, Ardmore and Gainesville. This service is operated in partnership with the Oklahoma Department of transportation.

All reserved. Bicycle racks.

# US Steam Today

Steam locomotives have always been something special. They seem to possess a soul and to their operators often feel more like living creatures than machines. Early steam engines soon earned people's affection and were given nicknames such as calliope, hog, jack, mill, pig, pot or smoker. Smaller types were called coffee-pot, dinky, kettle or peanut-roaster. Their drivers, officially known as engineers, were hog-heads, hog-jockeys, grunts, eagle-eyes or dinkey skinners (if they worked for a logging railroad).

Other words to enter the language were highball (a hand or voice signal to move a train), hostler (someone who services locomotives), shoofly (a temporary bypass track around a damaged track or obstruction), torpedo (an explosive device put on the rail to warn an approaching train of danger ahead), varnish (a passenger train, from the days when coaches were made of wood and varnished) and gandy dancer (a track worker named after the Gandy company which made his tools).

To 'join the birds' was to jump from a moving engine or car, usually just before it ended up 'in the ditch' (wrecked). Picking up water from between the rails was 'jerking a drink' and a head-on collision was a 'cornfield meet'. Such train language, along with a host of stories, songs and legends, helped railroads become an integral part of American folklore. Even as late as the 1930s and 40s being an engineer was a much sought-after occupation and for some it ranked higher than becoming President.

An engineer earned good money, saw new and glamorous places, and was admired by small boys and women everywhere. It could be hard work, though, and getting the most out of a locomotive, often in difficult circumstances, required artistry as much as expertise. The engineer would use the throttle to 'beat on' the engine, making it run sweetly at maximum power. This was a considerable test of both his skill and the locomotive's strength. The fireman regulated the water and fire box to ensure that the engineer had the right amount of steam pressure to drive the engine.

Steam engine numbers peaked at 72,000 just after the First World War. Approximately 180,000 steam locomotives were built in the US altogether, culminating in the Union Pacific's 'Big Boys' of the 1940s. These (4-8-8-4) monsters weighed 600 tons, had a capacity of 7,000 horsepower and burned 20 tons of coal an hour. But as technology progressed, lower maintenance costs and safety considerations made the change to diesel increasingly inevitable and no new steam engines were put into service after 1953.

The Norfolk & Western Railroad, centred on Roanoke, was the last steam-powered Class One line. O Winston Link lovingly recorded its demise over a period of six years in the 1950s, making films and sound recordings as well as taking the extraordinary photographs published in *Steam, Steel and Stars*. He even bought his own locomotive, a 1911 Canadian Pacific 10-wheeler. The final Norfolk & Western steam trains ran on April 4 1960, after which most were scrapped and their metal exported to Japan. The Norfolk & Western merged with the Southern Railway in 1982 to form the massive Norfolk Southern system, with 17,000 miles (27,000km) of track in 20 states.

The age of steam still lives on around the USA though, thanks mainly to the efforts of 40,000 volunteer enthusiasts. It can take up to 30,000 hours of work to restore a single locomotive but more than 200 remain operational out of the 1,875 still in existence in the US and Canada. Most weigh between 100 and 150 tons, but the largest in working order is the Union Pacific *Challenger* (313 US tons/274 tonnes). Some modern reproduction engines have been imported from Europe and China.

Many 'steam chasers' continue to delight in the pungent smell of coal smoke, an echoing whistle and the clickety clack of the rails. Five million people each year take main line excursions or dinner trains, visit scenic railways or go to train museums. The magazine *Locomotive Quarterly* is published every three months and is available on subscription from Metaphor Inc, PO Box 383, Mount Vernon, NY 10552-0383; tel: 1 800 210 2211. The leading supplier of books, video tapes and vintage films is Pentrex, PO Box 94911, Pasadena, California 91109-4911; tel: 626 793 3400.

## TRAINS AND ROUTES

The following are among the most scenic and interesting railways still in regular operation. All are standard gauge except where indicated.

### Arcade & Attica

Steam trains travel over a historic route to Curriers from the depot in Arcade, New York, using coaches built around 1915. President Grover Cleveland's honeymoon car, complete with original dishes, is on show at the Arcade station along with other unique items from railroad history, including lanterns, an antique roll-top desk and two wooden telephones. The authentic ticket office has bars in the window.

Trains leave Arcade past the current station and pass a building which used to be a station of the Tonawanda Valley & Cuba Railroad, predecessor to the Arcade & Attica. You cross a bridge giving great views of Cattaraugus Creek and continue through an attractive wilderness area to Curriers. There the locomotive switches and pulls onto a siding to provide photo opportunities before returning to Arcade, pulling the train in reverse.

Steam trains operate mostly on weekends from Memorial Day until September, with foliage specials in October. Special event trains also operate in season and there are diesel-powered trips at other times. The nearest Amtrak stops are Buffalo and Rochester, served by the *Lake Shore Limited*.

Mail address: 278 Main, PO Box 246, Arcade, NY 14009-1223; tel: 585 492 3100 or 585 496 9777; web: http://welcome.to/arcade-n-attica.com.

## Austin & Texas Central Railroad

Located at 401 E Whitestone Blvd in Cedar Park, 20 miles north of Austin, Texas. A vintage Southern Pacific locomotive and period passenger cars make regular steam excursions into the hill country northwest of Austin, taking a scenic 33-mile route from Cedar Park through the cedar and oak woods of the South San Gabriel River valley. You cross the river on a spectacular trestle and climb 500 feet to the top of the valley before descending a steep grade to the town of Burnet.

The Austin Steam Train Association has trackage rights over this route under an agreement with the city and Capital Metro, which manages the line. The track is also used for weekday freight services and has recently been upgraded. Engine *No. 786* was built by the American Locomotive Company in 1916 and operated over the Southern Pacific's Texas and Louisiana lines until 1956. After more than 30 years on display in downtown Austin the 143-ton locomotive was restored to working order in record time to operate out of Cedar Park. Trains run mostly on weekends from March to December. Amtrak's *Texas Eagle* serves Austin.

Mail address: PO Box 1632, Austin, TX 78767-1632; tel:512 477 6377 or 512 477 8468; web: http://www.austinsteamtrain.org.

## Black Hills Central

Trains travel 20 miles (32km) through forests and mountains between Keystone and a former Chicago, Burlington & Quincy station at Hill City near Mount Rushmore, South Dakota. Vintage coaches and a 1919 Baldwin locomotive (star of TV's *Gunsmoke* and Disney's *Scandalous John*) run through the beautiful Black Hills of western South Dakota along part of what was once a Burlington Railroad line. You pass the Holy Terror mine, Old Baldy Mountain (5,605ft/1,545m) and Elkhorn Mountain (6,200ft/1,890m), climbing grades of up to 6% past the old tin mine route to Hill City.

Trains operate daily on a two hour round trip from May to September, with a reduced schedule at other times.

Mail address: PO Box 1880, Hill City, South Dakota 57745; tel: 605 574 2222; fax 605 574 4915; web: www.1880train.com/index.html.

## Boone & Scenic Valley

A 15-mile (24km) round-trip from Boone, Iowa, over the historic Dodge, Des Moines & Southern route, crossing the Des Moines River Valley on two great bridges, including the world's largest and highest double track rail bridge at 156ft (48m). The railroad was begun in the 1890s to transport coal from Fraser to another railroad at Fraser Junction, now called Wolf, before later extending north to Rockwell, Fort Dodge and Des Moines. Passenger cars operated on an hourly basis and freight business flourished. The Boone Railroad Historical Society purchased a section of the defunct line in 1983 for $50,000 and in 1989 the last commercially built steam locomotive made in China was bought for $350,000 to operate services with restored 1920s passenger cars.

For an additional fare you can travel first-class on the Wolf Train, making a 22-mile (36km) round trip to Wolf in an air-conditioned *City of San Francisco* Pullman lounge car with roomettes, an observation platform and free refreshments. The depot was built in 1985 in the style of the one in Rockwell, Iowa, using interior oak woodwork from the depot in Tama. The platform was constructed from bricks brought from several other old platforms. Boone also features **Iowa's Railway Museum**, with free displays and exhibits. Steam trains run on weekends and holidays from May to October, with diesels on weekdays. The nearest Amtrak stop is Osceola, served by the *California Zephyr*.

Mail address: 225 10th St, PO Box 603, Boone, IA 50036; tel: 515 432 4249 or 1 800 626 0319; web: www.scenic-valleyrr.com.

## California Western

The Skunk line runs 40 miles (64km) between Fort Bragg on the coast and Willits on US Highway 101. A variety of trains and schedules operate from both ends of the line, crossing up to 30 bridges and trestles. From Fort Bragg you can travel with an open observation car along Pudding Creek and the Noyo River, passing through a deep mountain tunnel and seeing splendid redwood trees, wildflowers, grazing cattle and apple orchards. At Northspur you have time to relax before returning to Fort Bragg or continuing to Willits.

The trip from Willits by vintage 1935 M-300 Motorcar begins with a climb into the rolling hills and through a tunnel at the 1,700ft (488m) summit before gently curving down the steep mountain to Northspur, from where you can continue to Fort Bragg or return to Willits. Steam trains operate daily (except Monday) in June and July, Saturdays in April and May. Diesel trains operate daily. Reservations are recommended. Amtrak Thruway buses link Oakland with Willits.

Mail address: PO Box 907, Fort Bragg, CA 95437; tel: 707 964 6371 (Fort Bragg) or 707 459 5248 (Willits); web: www.skunktrain.com.

## Cass

The Cass Scenic Railroad uses a splendid switchback route built in 1901 as a logging railroad to haul lumber to the mill in Cass. The locomotives are the same ones that were used in Cass and in the forests of British Columbia for more than 50 years. Old logging flat-cars have been refurbished and turned into passenger coaches, transporting you from the restored buildings of Cass into the mountains of West Virginia.

A 90-ton Shay locomotive hauls the train out of Cass past an old water tower from which its tanks are filled. The train then rounds the curve up Leatherbark Creek and chugs laboriously into the mountains, reversing up the steepest grades before reaching open fields. At times the train has to cope with a grade of 11% (11ft/3.6m in altitude for each 100ft/30m of track). A logging camp of the 1940s has been recreated at Whittaker Station, including a rare Lidgerwood tower skidder. You can continue from Whittaker to Bald Knob via a stop further up the mountain to take on more water at a spring. The train then climbs to the summit of Bald Knob, the second highest point (4,842ft/1,477m) in West Virginia, from where you can see across two states.

Trains travel either 8 miles/13km from Cass to Whittaker (half an hour) or 22 miles/35km on a round-trip lasting four and a half hours to the summit of Bald Knob. Daily from May to September; weekends in September and October. Amtrak's *Cardinal* stops at nearby White Sulphur Springs.

Mail address: PO Box 107, Cass, WV 24927; tel: 304 456 4300 or 1 800 225 5982; web: www.cassrailroad.com.

## Conway

Diesel and occasional steam trains operate from an imposing 1874 station built by the Portsmouth, Great Falls & Conway Railroad in North Conway, New Hampshire. Nathaniel J Bradlee of Boston designed this beautiful structure, housing separate men's and ladies' waiting-rooms, ticket-office, baggage room and rest rooms. Two curving mahogany staircases lead to offices in metal-sheathed domed towers and an eight-day clock was installed in the face of the building, opposite the park. The station has changed little since it was built, apart from the incorporation of a gift shop, and has been carefully restored in recent years.

Other buildings include a roundhouse, a free museum, a freight house and an original Boston & Maine crossing tender shanty. There is an outdoor display of restored railcars, operating turntable and roundhouse. The freight house is home to the North Conway Model Railroad Club, open on Tuesday and Saturday from July to September.

Some of the 41 railroad cars and locomotives are used to take passengers into the White Mountains over part of the Boston & Maine Conway branch line. The Valley train makes a 55-minute round-trip from North Conway to Conway (11 miles/17km) or a one and three quarter hour round-trip from North Conway to Bartlett (21 miles/34km). The Conway route takes you south through farmland, crossing Moat Brook and the Saco and Swift Rivers. The Bartlett train travels northwest through fields and woodlands, crossing the East Branch, Saco and Ellis Rivers. You can choose coach class, the elegant *Chocorua* dining-car or the first class *Gertrude Emma* Parlor-Observation car. The *Gertrude Emma* was built in 1898 for use on the *Pennsylvania Limited* and has been splendidly restored with wicker and rattan chairs, rich mahogany woodwork and an open observation platform.

The Notch train crosses two spectacular trestles and many streams, steep bluffs and ravines on its way to Crawford Depot (a five-hour round-trip) or Fabyan Station (five and a half hours). Live commentary includes history and folklore of the railroad and area as well as other points of interest. The open-air observation coach is available to coach and first class passengers.

Daily from June to mid-October.

Mail address: PO Box 1947, North Conway, NH 03860; tel: 603 356 5251 or 1 800 232 5251; web: www.conwayscenic.com.

## Cumbres & Toltec

This is the longest and highest narrow gauge steam railway in America and is one of the world's most scenic routes, taking you through the Rockies by way of tunnels and breathtaking trestles. There are snowdrifts in May, wildflowers in June and brilliant fall colours in September and October. The 64-mile (102km) Denver & Rio Grande Western track crosses the continental divide at Cumbres Pass (10,015ft/3,055m) then snakes through the Toltec Gorge of the Los Pinos River before making a precipitous descent towards Chama, New Mexico. Power is provided by Baldwin locomotives and trains sometimes have to use one of two preserved rotary snow ploughs to cope with the weather conditions.

The Cumbres & Toltec is one of the last remnants of a rail empire which began in 1871 with the construction of the Denver & Rio Grande Railroad. The original intention was to build a line from Denver to Mexico City via Santa Fe and El Paso. Financed mainly by British investors, this 'happy little railroad' was constructed to a three feet gauge to cope with the mountainous landscape, although standard gauge was already the norm. By 1876, it had changed its aim from Mexico to the prosperous silver mines of the San Juan Mountains in southwestern Colorado, reaching Silverton via Cumbres Pass and Durango in 1882. After 1955, only one section of narrow gauge line remained, running from Antonito through Chama to Durango and Silverton, Colorado, and to Farmington in New Mexico.

The states of Colorado and New Mexico purchased the Antonito–Chama section and created the Cumbres & Toltec Scenic Railroad in 1970. The Durango–Silverton line continued to operate and was sold to a private owner in 1981, becoming the Durango & Silverton Narrow Gauge Railroad (see below).

The *Colorado Limited* travels from Antonito to Osier, Colorado, through Toltec Gorge. The *New Mexico Express* leaves Chama, New Mexico, for Osier via Cumbres Pass. You can make through trips either way, returning by road, or make round-trips to and from Osier by train.

Trains run daily from late May to mid-October. Dress warmly.

Mail addresses: PO Box 668, Antonito, CO 81120 and PO Box 789, Chama, NM 87520; tel: 888 286 2737; web: www.cumbrestoltec.com.

## Durango & Silverton

Durango was founded by the Denver & Rio Grande Railway in 1880 and the 36-inch-gauge Durango to Silverton line was completed two years later at a cost of $100,000 per mile (see the previous Cumbres & Toltec Railroad section). The 500 construction workers were mostly Irish and Chinese

*Above* Golden Gate Bridge, San Francisco (GR)
*Below left* Hot-air balloon over vineyards, Napa Valley, California (GR)
*Below right* The Magic Kingdom at Disney World, Orlando (NS)

*Above* View of the city from Stanley Park, Vancouver (NS)
*Left* Totem pole in Stanley Park, Vancouver (NS)
*Below* View of Toronto from Lake Ontario (NS)

immigrants, earning an average $2.25 a day for often dangerous work as a ledge was blasted from solid granite above the Animas River. Some of them lived in caves dug out of the hillside near Rockwood in preference to the thin-walled railcars provided. This challenging project ranks with that of the Central Pacific Railroad's passage through the Sierra Nevada and the entire line has been designated a National Historic Civil Engineering Landmark.

The **D & SNGRR Museum** is housed in part of a renovated roundhouse and features full-size locomotives as well as elegant business class private cars, railroad paintings, lamps, photographs and books. The original bell from the Union Pacific locomotive *No. 119*, present at the Golden Spike ceremony of 1869, is also on display. The **Silverton Freight Yard Museum**, located in the 1882 depot, has more locomotive and freight equipment as well as the 'Casey Jones', a motorised vehicle powered by a 1915 Cadillac engine. Admission to both museums is included in the train ticket price.

Today's Durango & Silverton Railroad has been voted one of 'Top Ten Most Exciting Train Journeys in the World' by the Society of American Travel Writers. Trains run on a 45-mile (72km) spur of track using coal-fired locomotives built for the D&RGW by the American Locomotive Works (1923) and Baldwin (1925), one of which appeared in the film *Butch Cassidy and the Sundance Kid*. The train has appeared in many other movies, including *Viva Zapata*, *Around the World in 80 Days* and *How the West Was Won*. Robert Royem's book, *An American Classic: The Durango & Silverton Narrow Gauge Railroad*, contains hundreds of original photographs, including several from the 1880s, as well as a historical overview of the train.

Authentic 1880s coaches make a daily 90-mile (144km) round-trip from early May to mid-August among wonderful Rocky Mountain scenery, following the Animas River through the remote wilderness of the San Juan National Forest. The fireman shovels six tons of coal per day on the round-trip to Silverton, where there is a two hour layover. Open-sided gondola cars provide panoramic views. Cascade Canyon winter steam excursions operate daily from November 22 to early May. Reservations are recommended at least a month in advance.

The station is at 479 Main Ave, Durango, CO 81301; tel: 1 888 872 4607; web: www.durangotrain.com.

## Eureka Springs & North Arkansas

A four-mile (6.5km) journey through the Ozark Mountains, leaving from the 1913 Eureka Springs depot built from local limestone. The ES&NA collection of vintage rolling stock, including the elegant 1920s *Eurekan* dining car, is one of the Ozarks' largest. Authentic railroad memorabilia recreate a turn-of-the-century era when the railway first brought visitors to Eureka Springs.

Between trains you can check out exhibits such as the restored turntable, a handcar, vintage locomotives and rolling stock that includes an automobile fitted out to run on the rails.

Trains operate daily (except Sunday) from April to October. Sunday trains operate on Memorial Day, July 4 and Labor Day weekends.

Mail address: PO Box 310, 299 N Main Street, Highway 23 North, Eureka Springs, AR 72632; tel: 479 253 9623; web: www.esnarailway.com.

## Fillmore & Western

This 31-mile (50km) journey through the unspoilt Santa Clara Valley in southern California uses vintage equipment and the original 1887 station at 10th Street in Santa Paula is also a museum.

The Fillmore & Western Railway operates many excursions, dinner trains and other speciality trains. It is also engaged in the restoration of historic railroad cars and has recently bought a 1913 Baldwin steam engine originally owned by the Duluth & Northeastern Railroad. The railroad has begun restoring and expanding the track between Fillmore and Piru with a view to running excursions on this route. Steam trains operate mostly on weekends from March to December. Amtrak's nearest stop is Oxnard, served by the *Coast Starlight*.

Mail address: 351 Santa Clara Avenue, Fillmore, CA 93015; tel: 805 524 2546 or 1 800 773 8724; web: www.fwry.com.

## Georgetown Loop

The railroad is based at the old Georgetown station 42 miles west of Denver. Trains take a trip through spectacular mountain scenery, twisting and turning over part of the 36-inch-gauge former Colorado & Southern Railway built in 1884. Hailed as the 'far famed Loop', this marvel of engineering skill formed one of the most complex railroad loops in the world. The distance between Georgetown and Silver Plume is only two miles but the elevation difference is more than 600ft, so the rail line had to twist over four and a half miles of track to unite the two mining towns.

The 300ft long Devil's Gate Viaduct formed a spiral where the track actually crossed over itself, making the 'Loop' a popular tourist attraction, but with the end of mining it was dismantled and sold for scrap. The Colorado Historical Society (tel: 303 866 3678) rebuilt the railroad and Devil's Gate Viaduct in the 1970s. Today's route includes a crossing of the new viaduct (96ft/29m high) above Clear Creek and trains can be boarded in Silver Plume (two miles/3.2km west of Georgetown on I-70) or from Devil's Gate in Georgetown.

The daily round-trip between late May and early October takes 70 minutes. From May to early September you can also visit the Lebanon Silver Mine (accessible only by the Georgetown Loop Railroad, except on the last trip of the day). Historical Society guides will lead you through the mine on a tour lasting 80 minutes. Comfortable walking shoes are recommended and as the mine maintains a constant 44°F temperature a jacket or sweater is essential. The nearest Amtrak station is Denver, served by the *California Zephyr*.

Mail address: PO Box 217-1111 Rose Street, Georgetown, CO 80444; tel: 303 569 2403 or 1 800 691 4386; web: www.georgetownloop.com.

# Grand Canyon

The 1908 depot is at 518 E Bill Williams Ave, Williams, Arizona, from where trains travel 65 miles/104km through Ponderosa pine forest, small *arroyos* and high desert plains to the edge of the Grand Canyon. Watch out for the notorious Cataract Creek Gang and the Grand Canyon Railway Marshall. The line was built in 1901 by the Atchison Topeka & Santa Fe Railway and the canyon's 1910 South Rim station is one of only three log-built depots still in existence. The original Fray Marcos Hotel (a former Harvey House) in Williams is now occupied by the free **Grand Canyon Railway Museum**, with an authentic steam locomotive and caboose on display outside.

Notable passengers here have included Presidents Theodore Roosevelt, Taft, Franklin D Roosevelt and Eisenhower, as well as Clark Gable, Jimmy Durante and Doris Day. Today's restored 1920s Harriman coaches and vintage engines operate daily, with western entertainment and interpretive guides, and the five classes of service range from coach to Luxury Parlor class.

Steam trains run from the last weekend in May to the end of September and vintage 1950s diesel-powered trains in winter, carrying over 170,000 passengers a year. You can choose to stay overnight at the rim and return next day. The train stops in Grand Canyon Village and rooms can be booked at the Maswik Lodge, about a quarter mile from the rim and the Bright Angel trailhead. Amtrak's Southwest Chief serves Williams Junction, from where there are free shuttle buses to the Fray Marcos Hotel/Grand Canyon Railway depot.

Mail address: 233 N Grand Canyon Blvd, Williams, AZ 86046; tel: 1 800 843 8724 or 520 773 1976; web: www.thetrain.com.

# Heber Valley

This 32-mile (51km) journey is a three and a half hour round-trip, starting from the 1899 Denver & Rio Grande Western depot (now a museum) in Heber City, Utah. Trains cross farmlands of the Heber Valley, follow the shore of Deer Creek Lake and travel down into a majestic canyon, following the beautiful Provo River to Vivian Park. Look out for the abundant wildlife, including bald eagles, deer and elk.

The Denver & Rio Grande Western was built to serve the pioneers who first settled in this valley. The railroad served the people of this community by hauling freight in and livestock out, and in the 1930s and early 1940s more sheep were transported by rail from the Heber Valley than from anywhere else in the country. A new highway eventually took away traffic so in 1967 the line was abandoned, becoming a recreational railroad in 1970.

Today, 1920s coaches are pulled by two 1907 Baldwin steam locomotives and three vintage diesel-electrics. Utah's oldest steam railroad has featured in many TV shows, such as *Touched by an Angel* and *Promised Land*, and the engine, along with its 10 railroad cars, has appeared in more than 30 films over the past 20 years. Special events include Murder Mysteries, Blue Grass Music, Raft the River and the Vivian Park Dinner Train. The steam train service operates daily from May to September, otherwise on weekends.

Mail address: 450 South 600 West, Heber City, UT 84032; tel: 435 654 5601 or 801 581 9980; web: www.hebervalleyrr.org.

## Hocking Valley

Trains make a 12-mile (19km) round-trip to Haydenville or a 25-mile (40km) trip to Logan over a Chesapeake & Ohio route. This was part of the original Hocking Valley Railway and is now on the National Register of Historic Places. You leave from Nelsonville, Ohio, where 11 cabooses are on display, including an ex-Hocking Valley caboose. Trains make a stop at the 19th century settlers' village of Robbin's Crossing.

Mail address: PO Box 427, Nelsonville, OH 45764; tel: 740 753 9531 (at the depot), 614 470 1300 or 1 800 867 7834; web: www.hvsr.com.

## Huckleberry

Despite its name, the Huckleberry Railroad is not a toy ride. The name refers to the first Pere Marquette line trains which often travelled so slowly that passengers could hop off to pick huckleberries (wild blueberries) en route then reboard before the caboose reached them. Today's ride is somewhat faster as a historic Baldwin locomotive takes open and closed wooden coaches from the old Denver & Rio Grande Western and Rio Grande Southern for an eight-mile (13km) journey.

The Huckleberry Railroad operates in conjunction with Crossroads Village, a collection of 30 historic buildings that includes a working blacksmith's shop and the Davison depot from the Grand Trunk & Western Railroad. The train travels over a portion of the original Pere Marquette roadbed so you ride along the shores of Mott Lake, with great views and a good chance of seeing deer or other wildlife. During special event weekends such as those at Christmas and Halloween there are decorations along the track.

Trains operate daily from May to August and on weekends in September. Amtrak's *International* train stops in Flint.

Mail address: 5045 Stanley Road, Flint, MI 48506; tel: 810 736 7100 or 1 800 648 7275; web: www.geneseecountyparks.org/crossroadsvillage.htm.

## Kentucky Railway Museum

Located in the heartland of Kentucky, the Kentucky Railway Museum is one of the oldest rail museums in the United States. Founded in Louisville in 1954, the KRM now owns 17 miles (28km) of the ex-Louisville & Nashville Lebanon branch, with operating headquarters in New Haven and a passenger boarding area in Boston, Kentucky.

Steam and diesel trains operate on alternate weekends between New Haven and Boston, travelling through the Rolling Fork River Valley on a track built in 1857. A fine collection of Kentucky railway history has been assembled, including the only operating Louisville & Nashville steam locomotive and the largest set of L&N passenger equipment anywhere. A new museum building replicates the original New Haven depot.

The museum opens daily. Steam train and locomotive cab rides take place from late May to the end of October. Diesel trains operate at weekends until mid-December. Dining trips are available from the Louisville, Harrods Creek, & Westport Railroad Foundation on the third Saturday of each month except January.

Mail address: PO Box 240, New Haven, KY 40051-0240; tel: 502 549 5470 or 800 272 0152; web: www.kyrail.org.

## Kentucky Central

Trains operate from Paris, Kentucky, over part of the Central Kentucky Railway, later to become the Louisville & Nashville. The 50-mile (80km) route goes through wonderful bluegrass country where there are many thoroughbred horse farms.

Mail address: 1749 Bahama Road, Lexington, KY 40509; tel: 606 293 0807. Amtrak's *Cardinal* stops in Cincinnati, to the north.

## Kettle Moraine Railway

Located nine miles north of Interstate 94 on Highway 83 at North Lake, Wisconsin. A full size vintage steam engine takes passengers on nostalgic eight mile (12.8km), 50 minute round-trips on Sundays from June to September. More trains run at weekends in October, and the Santa Claus Express operates in November. Amtrak's *Empire Builder* stops in nearby Milwaukee.

Mail address: PO Box 247, North Lake, WI 53064; tel: 262 966 0516; email: info@kmry.org; web: www.kmry.org.

## Knox & Kane

An eight-hour journey from Marienville, Pennsylvania, taking you along a former Baltimore & Ohio line for a round-trip to Kane. Alternatively, you can board at Kane for a three and a half hour excursion. Trains cross the Kinzua Creek Valley by means of the Kinzua Bridge, which is on the register of Historic Places as well as a Historic Civil Engineering Landmark. Over 2,000ft (600m) long and 300ft (90m) high, the bridge was the world's tallest when it was completed in 1882. Trains operate mostly from Tuesday to Sunday between June and October.

Mail address: PO Box 422, Marienville, PA 16239; tel: 814 927 6621; web: www.knoxkanerr.com.

## Little River

From Coldwater, Michigan, trains travel 10 miles (16km) to Batavia (80 minutes) or 24 miles (40km) to White Pigeon (2½ hours) over tracks of the Michigan Southern Railroad. The engine used, *No 110*, was built in 1911 at the Baldwin Locomotive Works in Philadelphia. It was made specially for Colonel Townsend's Little River Railroad and is the smallest, standard gauge, Pacific type steam locomotive ever to be manufactured. Trains operate on Sundays from June to October.

Mail address: 13187 SR 120, Middlebury, IN 46540; tel: 219 825 9182.

## Mid-Continent

Trains make a seven-mile (11km), 50-minute journey from North Freedom, Wisconsin, along a former branch line of the Chicago & North Western Railroad. This was built in 1903 along the beautiful Baraboo River Valley to an old quartzite quarry. The **Mid-Continent Railway Museum** is today dedicated to preserving and interpreting railroad history, especially that of the Upper Midwest during its golden age (1880–1916).

The restored depot was built in 1894 by the Chicago & North Western Railway at Rock Springs, three miles west of North Freedom, and moved to the museum in 1965. Similar designs were used in small communities across the C&NW system in the 1890s, including those at Waunakee and Wonewoc. The interior has two waiting-rooms separated by the ticket office, with a freight room on the end, now occupied by the museum gift shop. The exterior has been painted in original C&NW colours. Next to the depot are a dozen steam engines, 33 vintage coaches, 19 cabooses and 33 freight cars, including a wooden tank car for transporting vinegar.

Other structures on site include a Soo Line watchman's tower which formerly stood in Neenah and a tool house for the section crew, moved here from Fond du Lac in 1981. The turntable was removed from an abandoned Milwaukee Road yard and roundhouse in Madison and brought to North Freedom in 1988 but is not yet installed.

Trains operate on weekends from May to September and daily from the end of May to Labor Day. There are also autumn and winter special excursions.

Mail address: PO Box 358, North Freedom, WI 53951-0358; tel: 608 522 4261 or 1 800 930 1385; web: www.mcrwy.com and www.midcontinent.org.

## Nevada State Railroad Museum

The museum houses over 60 pieces of railroad equipment from Nevada's past, including five steam locomotives and several restored coaches and freight cars. Most of this material is from the Virginia & Truckee Railroad, America's richest and most famous short line.

Museum activities include the operation of historic railroad equipment, lectures, an annual railroad history symposium and other special events. Free movies are shown every Wednesday in July and August in the park directly north of the museum. Steam trains operate on some weekends, May to October. The museum opens daily. Amtrak's *California Zephyr* stops at Reno and Truckee.

Mail address: 2180 South Carson Street, Carson City, NE 89701; tel: 775 687 6953; web: www.nsrm-friends.org/index.htm.

## Nevada Northern Railway Museum

The 'Best preserved shortline in America' was one of the last great mining railroads built in the early 20th century, carrying millions of tons of ore from the copper mines at Ely. Completed in 1906 by the Nevada Consolidated Copper Company (later the Kennecott Corporation), the Nevada Northern stretched from Ely to the Southern Pacific Railroad line at Cobre, located about 130 miles (209km) to the north. The rails were later extended west to

Lane City and Ruth. This railroad provided regular Pullman services until 1920 and carried passengers until 1938. It ceased regular freight operations in 1983 and that year the line was donated to the White Pine Historical Railroad Foundation to run as a working railroad museum.

Two classic steam locomotives are operated by the railway, pulling an original 1890 Pullman coach, a 1907 baggage/RPO and an open top flat car with benches. The 14-mile (22km) round-trip takes you around downtown Ely then past the ghost town of Lane City to the historic mining area of Keystone. You travel through one of the few curved tunnels in the world and along the scenic Robinson Canyon. Or you might take the 'Hiline' route above the Steptoe Valley, powered by a vintage Alco diesel engine.

You can visit the roundhouse, machine and blacksmith shops and view the historic rolling stock of steam, diesel and electric locomotives as well as turn-of-the-century passenger and freight cars.

The museum opens daily. Steam and diesel rides take place on weekends from mid-May to mid-September. There are guided tours daily from May to October and exhibitions include the general office, depot and dispatcher's office.

Mail address: 1100 Avenue A, East Ely, NV 89315-0040; tel: 775 289 2085; web: http://nevadanorthernrailway.net.

## New Hope & Ivyland

A vintage Baldwin Consolidation, coal-fired steam locomotive takes restored vintage coaches over a nine-mile/15km round-trip in about an hour, leaving New Hope's picturesque 1891 station at 32 West Bridge Street for Lahaska along a branch line of the old Reading Railroad. Steam passenger service between New Hope and Buckingham Valley began in 1966 and the New Hope & Ivyland Railroad ran one of the last regularly scheduled steam-powered mixed freights east of Mississippi. The NHIR became bankrupt in 1971 but the line was successfully operated by McHugh Brothers Heavy Hauling, Inc until 1989. From 1980, the volunteer New Hope Steam Railway (NHSR) operated weekend excursions.

The railroad was sold to the present owners, the Bucks County Railroad Preservation and Restoration Corporation, in 1990 and since then the New Hope & Ivyland has been completely restored to its original ambience at a cost of $2 million. The New Hope station, freight house and boarding platform were refurbished and tracks rebuilt before steam passenger services resumed in 1991. Freight services also continue to expand and prosper.

The Lahaska Station features a pretty picnic grove for the exclusive use of passengers and the freight house at New Hope has a gift shop. Narrated trips take you through attractive Pennsylvania countryside by way of Pauline's Trestle and part of the Underground Railroad route. Passenger steam trains operate daily from April to November, otherwise at weekends. A *Fireworks Express* runs on Independence Day and there are other special trains throughout the year.

Mail address: PO Box 634, New Hope, PA 18938; tel: 215 862 2332. The nearest Amtrak stops are New York, Philadelphia, Princeton and Trenton.

## New York, Susquehanna & Western

Trains travel 44 miles (70km) through attractive countryside over a former Lackawanna Railroad line between Syracuse and Tully, New York. Services operate from Thursday to Sunday between April and December.

Mail address: PO Box 1245, Syracuse, NY 13201; tel: 315 424 1212. Amtrak's *Lake Shore Limited* stops in Syracuse.

## Ohio Central

The Ohio Central Railroad is a system of seven railroads spanning over 400 miles (644km) of track throughout eastern and northeastern Ohio. The railroad's main business is freight but it also offers special excursions throughout the year. Trains are hauled by one of eight vintage steam locomotives or by one of several historic diesel engines, including F-units and Alco RS-3s.

Steam and diesel trains operate mainly along a former Wheeling & Lake Erie line out of the Ohio Central Station in Sugarcreek. This area, known as 'Ohio's Switzerland', is Amish country.

Hour-long trips (except on Sundays and holidays) are available from May to October.

Mail address: 111 Factory Street, Sugarcreek, OH 44681; tel: 216 852 4676; web: www.ohiocentral.com or www.amishsteamtrain.com.

## Railtown

This California State Historic Park is at 5th Ave and Reservoir Road, Jamestown. The Sierra Railway buildings include the only operating steam roundhouse in the west, dating from 1897 and still in original condition. As well as the Sierra's six-stall roundhouse, turntable and main yards, Railtown maintains four steam locomotives and a wide range of railroad equipment, making this one of the most comprehensive and best preserved steam railroad sites in the country. Railtown is managed by the **California State Railroad Museum** (CSRM), located in Sacramento.

The Sierra has appeared in more television shows, commercials and movies than any other railway. The first known filming was in 1919 for a silent serial called *The Red Glove* and the railroad has featured in *High Noon*, *Little House on the Prairie*, *Unforgiven* and *Back to the Future III*.

The museum opens daily. Among its exhibits is a classic Model T purchased in Sonora in 1919 and converted into a railcar for use by the Sierra Railway as a roadmaster's car. Steam trains operate along the central valley of California into the gold country of the Sierra Nevada foothills, travelling to the Jamestown-Rock siding and back among rolling hills, open pastures and beside a quiet creek. These six-mile (9.6km), 40 minute excursions take place on weekends from April to October and on Memorial Day, Independence Day and Labor Day.

Mail address: PO Box 1250, Jamestown, CA 95327; tel: 209 984 3953 and 916 445 6645 (recorded information); web: www.csmrf.org/railtown. The nearest Amtrak stops are Stockton and Riverbank.

## Roaring Camp & Big Trees

This is America's last steam-powered passenger railroad with a year-round passenger service. The Roaring Camp & Big Trees Narrow-Gauge Railroad was founded in 1857 when goldminers, lumberjacks and other pioneers arrived over the mountains of the American West in search of a new life. Today the Roaring Camp & Big Trees Narrow-Gauge Railroad still operates an old-fashioned steam passenger train service providing visitors with a rare opportunity to ride through some of the country's most beautiful and primitive scenery.

Trains leave the 1880 South Pacific Coast depot on Graham Hill Road at Felton, California, for a six-mile (10km) excursion lasting one and a quarter hours on a 36-inch-gauge track between Roaring Camp and the top of Bear Mountain. You travel among the earliest preserved redwoods then go through Spring Canyon into the Santa Cruz Mountains. On returning to the depot, you can explore an 1880s general store or visit the adjacent **Henry Cowell Redwoods State Park**.

Trains operate daily from April to September, otherwise on weekends only. A Steam Festival and Railroad Olympics are held in July and other special events take place throughout the year. The nearest Amtrak stop is San Jose.

Mail address: PO Box G-1, Felton, CA 95018; tel: 831 335 4484; web: www.roaringcamprr.com.

## St Louis, Iron Mountain & Southern

The route goes from Jackson, Missouri, along a Missouri Pacific branch line. Journeys last one and a half hours (to Gordonville), two hours (Dutchtown) or five hours (Delta). 'The most daring train robbery on record' took place here on the Mountain Railroad in 1874 when Jesse James and his gang held up the *Little Rock Express* at Gad's Hill. Trains operate on weekends from April to October, and Saturdays in November and March.

Mail address: PO Box 244, Jackson, MO 63755; tel: 314 243 1688; web: www.rosecity.net/trains.

## Silver Creek & Stephenson

Located at Walnut and Lamm Roads, Silver Creek, just south of the Stephenson County Fairgrounds. The Stephenson County Antique Engine Club purchased nearly two miles of right-of-way from the bankrupt Chicago, Milwaukee, St. Paul & Pacific Railroad in 1983 and volunteers from the club relaid the track. The shed which houses Heisler, Brookville and Plymouth locomotives and their maintenance facilities was erected in 1986. The Silver Creek depot, dedicated in 1993, was built from original plans for the Illinois Central depot in Elroy, Illinois. It contains a large collection of railroad memorabilia, including advertising signs and a working telegraph.

Trains leave the replica depot to travel through Illinois farmland, crossing Yellow Creek on a 30ft/9m-high stone pier bridge, operating mostly on weekends between May and October. Amtrak Thruway buses stop at Rockford, 15 miles (24km) east.

Mail address: SCAEC, PO Box 255, Freeport, IL 61032; tel: 815 235 2198 or 815 232 2306.

## Texas State

The railroad is located between Rusk and Palestine on part of the 1896 Texas State Railroad. This line was originally built and run by inmates from the East Texas State Penitentiary to transport iron ore to the prison's furnaces in Rusk. Prisoners were paid 50 cents a day and worked from sunrise to sundown, so the total cost to construct the 32 miles of track was only $573,724. Prison crews made up the train staff (except for the engineer) but when passenger service was extended to Palestine a crew of nine was employed. With the exception of the superintendent and engineer, staff members were paid $1.01 for each day they worked.

The iron furnace was dismantled in 1913 and the penitentiary converted into a state mental hospital. Regular train service was discontinued in 1921 and the line leased to the Texas & New Orleans (Southern Pacific Railroad Company). The Texas Southeastern Railroad leased the line in the early 1960s and continued operations until December 1969, after which it was conveyed to the Texas Parks and Wildlife Department. State inmates were again brought in to rebuild the track by clearing brush, building bridges and replacing ties and rails. The Texas State Railroad State Historical Park opened to the public on July 4 1976 as part of the nation's bicentennial celebrations.

Two of the railroad's four historic engines simultaneously depart from depots on each end of the shortline, giving passengers a rare chance to see steam locos switch and pass at the midpoint. You board at the historically accurate stations in either Rusk or Palestine for a four-hour, 50-mile (80km) round-trip among rolling hardwood creek bottoms and flowering dogwood trees. As well as train excursions, the park offers steam engine shop tours and tours of the 1927 Texas & Pacific *610* steam engine, plus train seminars and workshops.

Trains operate from Thursday to Sunday in June and July; on weekends from March to May and August to October, and on the first three Saturdays in November. Amtrak's nearest stop is Longview, served by the *Texas Eagle*.

Mail address: PO Box 39, Rusk, TX 75785; tel: 1 800 442 8951 (in Texas only) or 903 683 2561; web: www.tpwd.state.tx.us/park/railroad/railroad.htm.

## Tweetsie

The East Tennessee & Western North Carolina Railroad Company was given permission in 1866 for the construction of a railroad from Johnson City, Tennessee to the iron mines across the state line at Cranberry, North Carolina. The ET&WNC line (sometimes called the 'Eat Taters & Wear No Clothes' Railroad) began operations in 1881 over 50 miles (80km) of track through the Blue Ridge chain of the Appalachian Mountains. The line was extended to Boone, North Carolina, in 1916 to serve passengers and haul lumber.

The railroad was nicknamed the 'Tweetsie' because of the shrill 'tweet, tweet' of its train whistle echoing through the hills. Severe floods damaged sections of the line in 1940 and hastened its closure in 1950. Gene Autry, the movie cowboy, bought engine *No. 12*, the last remaining of 13 coal-fired ET&WNC steam engines, intending to use it out west in films. The locomotive was later bought by Grover Robbins, Jr for one dollar and returned to his home town of Blowing Rock to be restored, along with some of the original ET&WNC rail cars.

These are now used on the new Tweetsie Railroad, which had its first run in 1957. Trains follow a scenic three-mile loop through the mountains near Blowing Rock, not far from the original end of the line station in Boone. You can watch can-can girls at the Palace Saloon, chat with cowboys and gunslingers on main street, visit the deer park, or ride a chairlift to Miner's Mountain to pan for gold.

Trains operate daily from mid-May to late August, or on Fridays and weekends from late August to the end of October, plus Labor Day. Amtrak's nearest stop is Gastonia, NC, served by the *Crescent*.

Mail address: PO Box 388, Blowing Rock, NC 28605; tel: 828 264 9061 or 1 800 526 5740; web: www.tweetsie-railroad.com.

## Valley

A 10-mile (16km) trip through Connecticut countryside between Essex and Chester on a New Haven Railroad branch line, stopping at Deep River. Optional boat trips can be taken on the Connecticut River. Trains operate daily from May to October.

Mail address: PO Box 452, Essex, CT 06426; tel: 203 767 0103; web: www.valleyrr.com. The nearest Amtrak stop is Old Saybrook.

## Virginia & Truckee

The Virginia & Truckee Railroad was built in 1869 to connect Virginia City with the Carson River valley. By 1874, the 'Queen of the Short Lines' had been extended to Reno and as many as 50 trains a day carried passengers, supplies and silver ore through Virginia City.

Today you can take half-hour rides along part of the Virginia & Truckee line through the famous Comstock mining area, with the benefit of an informed commentary from the conductor riding in the caboose. Look for exposed silver ore along the track and occasional sightings of wild mustangs in the surrounding Flowery Mountains. The route takes you through Tunnel Number Four, one of six tunnels constructed to allow trains to descend nearly 1,600ft (488m) from Virginia City to the valley floor.

The station is at Washington and F, Virginia City, Nevada. Trains operate daily from May to September, or at weekends in October. Amtrak's nearest stop is Reno, served by the *California Zephyr*.

Mail address: PO Box 467, Virginia City, NV 89440; tel: 775 847 0380; web: www.roadtripamerica.com/wheels/vcrr.htm.

## Western Maryland

Trains leave Cumberland's 1913 station (now a museum) and travel west on Western Maryland and Cumberland & Pennsylvania tracks among the Allegheny Mountains, climbing grades of up to 2.8%. On the 32-mile (52km), three-hour round-trip you go through the Cumberland Narrows, negotiate the spectacular Helmstetter's Horseshoe Curve and travel through the 914ft (278km) long Brush Tunnel under Piney Mountain. You also pass the Castle at Mount Savage and make a stop at Frostburg's historic restored depot.

Steam trains run mostly from Tuesday to Sunday between June and mid-September, otherwise at weekends. Diesel trains also operate and special events are held for railfans. Amtrak's *Capitol Limited* stops at Cumberland.

Mail address: 13 Canal Street, Cumberland, MD 21502; tel: 301 759 4400 or 1 800 872 4650; web: www.wmsr.com.

## White Mountain Central

A half-hour journey among the attractive White Mountains begins at Clark's Trading Post depot near Lincoln, New Hampshire. Among the other entertainments are an 1890s replica railway station, freight car displays, a haunted house, trained bears, a Victorian style Main Street and a 1920s garage. The two and a half mile woodland ride takes you from the trading post up a 2% grade and across the Pemigewasset River through the Howe-Truss covered bridge, the only standing covered bridge still in use. In 1963–65 the bridge was dismantled at its location in East Montpelier, Vermont, before being transported and reassembled here across the river.

The railroad has been in operation for more than 40 years since the Clark brothers began to rescue steam locomotives from the cutting torch to create 'green pastures for iron horses'. Salvaged locos now include a 1927 Heisler once owned by the International Shoe Company as well as former Beebe River Railroad and East Branch & Lincoln engines. The restored wood-burning Climax locomotive weighs 42 tons and is one of only three in the world still in working order. The depot opens at weekends from May to mid-October and daily in July and August.

Mail address: PO Box 1, Lincoln, NH 03251; tel: 603 745 8913; web: www.clarkstradingpost.com/railroad.html.

## Whitewater Valley

Indiana's longest scenic railway runs between Connersville and the restored town of Metamora, next to the old Whitewater Canal. The Whitewater River formed a natural trade route for Native Americans and early settlers and a canal was built in the mid-19th century. In 1863, the Indianapolis & Cincinnati Railroad acquired the right to build on the old towpath and its subsidiary, the White Water Valley Railroad, reached Connersville in 1867. It continued on to Hagerstown in 1868 but passenger service ended in 1933 and freight traffic in 1972.

Today's Whitewater Valley Railroad operates along 18 miles (30km) of track purchased in 1983, plus an additional mile in Connersville. It uses historic diesel locomotives and open window coaches on a regular schedule from Connersville to Metamora. Another service, the Metamora Shuttle, carries passengers further South on a two-mile (3.2km) excursion along the restored canal, past the canal boat dock, a working aqueduct and a restored lock. The railroad's Baldwin Prairie locomotive is currently out of action whilst a new boiler is installed but it is hoped that steam train services will soon resume.

Trains operate on weekends and holidays from the first weekend in May to the last weekend in October, as well as at Christmas. Amtrak's *Cardinal* stops in Connersville.

Mail address: PO Box 406, Connersville, IN 47331; tel: 765 825 2054; web: www.whitewatervalleyrr.org.

## Wilmington & Western

The First State's oldest steam tourist railroad has been in continuous operation for more than 120 years. Starting from the impressive new Greenbank Station four miles (6.5km) southwest of Wilmington, trains travel to Mount Cuba over part of a Baltimore & Ohio Landenberg branch line (Sundays, May to November). Or you can travel past Mount Cuba along the Red Clay Creek Valley to Yorklyn or Hockessin (from June to October). There are special trains throughout the year, including dinner trains and the *Firework Express*. Amtrak's nearest stop is Wilmington.

Mail address: PO Box 5787, Wilmington, DE 19808-0787; tel: 302 998 1930; web: www.wwrr.com.

## Yosemite Mountain-Sugar Pine

Between 1899 and 1931, the Madera Sugar Pine Lumber Company operated many miles of narrow gauge railroad track. Almost one and a half billion board feet of lumber were harvested and transported to the mill on massive log trains by five wood-burning Shay locomotives.

Located south of Yosemite National Park among California's Sierra Nevada, today's Yosemite Mountain-Sugar Pine Railroad is a restoration of the old 36-inch-gauge line. A section of the railbed has been reconstructed using the same techniques used originally and two restored Shay steam locomotives were brought from the Westside Lumber company to provide authentic motive power. *Number 15* was built in 1913 and weighs 60 tons (54,000kg). *Number 10*, built in 1928, weighs 83 tons (75,000kg) and is the heaviest operating narrow gauge Shay engine in existence. Railcars which once provided transportation for logging and track repair crews have been refurbished for passenger use on narrated tours. The trains reach 5,000ft (1,800m) before descending through Lewis Creek Canyon and Cold Spring Crossing.

Logger steam trains operate daily from March to October. Antique Model A Ford gas engines power trolley-like 'Jenny' cars over the route every half hour, except when steam trains are in action. Amtrak's nearest stop is Merced, on the *San Joaquin* route.

Mail address: 56001 Yosemite Highway 41, Fish Camp, CA 93623; tel: 559 683 7273; web: www.ymsprr.com.

## Yreka Western

The *Blue Goose* makes a three-hour, 15-mile (24km) round-trip excursion between Yreka and the historic railroad and cattle town of Montague in California, travelling along the Yreka Railroad which in 1889 linked with the California & Oregon. You travel among lumber mills, cattle ranches and through the Shasta Valley, crossing the Shasta River with magnificent views of Mount Shasta (14,162ft/4.317m) to the south. The 1915 locomotive was built by Baldwin.

You have enough time to visit Montague's 1887 Depot Museum and other historic buildings before boarding the *Blue Goose* for the return trip to Yreka, where you can explore the historic district's attractive Victorian houses and the homes of such luminaries as Bret Harte, Zane Grey and Herbert Hoover.

Trains operate from Wednesday to Sunday between mid-June and early September, and on weekends in May and October. Amtrak's nearest stop is Dunsmuir, served by the *Coast Starlight*.

Mail address: PO Box 660, Yreka, CA 96097; tel: 530 842 4146 or 1 800 973 5277; web: www.yrekawesternrr.com.

# Part Three

## On Canadian Rails

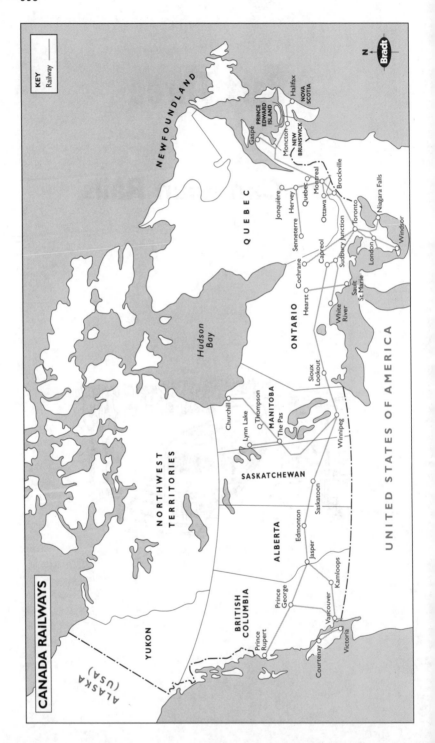

CANADA RAILWAYS

# Canada's Trains Today

Canada may be the only country in the world with a written constitution linking its formation to the building of a railway. British Columbia threatened to join the United States if it wasn't given its rail line, so a parliamentary act in 1867 proclaimed the construction of the Intercolonial Railway 'essential to the consolidation of the Union of British North America'. As a result, 4,000 miles (6,500km) of iron road were laid from the Atlantic to the Pacific. In 1871, British Columbia agreed to join the Confederation and trains have been a crucial part of Canada's history ever since.

A short tramway is thought to have been built in 1720 during the construction of a fort at Louisburg, Nova Scotia, and others later opened elsewhere to transport stone, coal and lumber. Canada's first public railway, the Champlain & St Lawrence, opened in 1836 as a 14-mile/22km route between Dorchester (now St-Jean), next to the Richelieu River, and La Prairie on the St Lawrence. The success of the Champlain & St Lawrence, and rail companies in the United States, encouraged further development, including the Grand Trunk Railway from Montreal to Toronto.

The Canadian Great Western Railway built the world's first sleeping car in 1857, inspiring the American Pullman design which came two years later. The Great Western originally operated between Windsor and Niagara Falls before extending to Hamilton and Toronto. An accident on the Grand Trunk Railway in Quebec in 1864 took 99 lives, making it Canada's worst ever railway disaster. The famous circus elephant, Jumbo (over 12ft/3.65km tall and weighing almost eight tons (8,000kg)), was killed on the track at St Thomas in 1885 when he was accidentally struck from behind while being loaded into a GTR freight train.

The great transcontinental Canadian Pacific route opened in 1885, having been blasted through some of the world's hardest rock in temperatures as low as minus 50°F (–45°C). Among the workers were more than 6,000 Chinese, some of whom had remained in California after building the Union Pacific Railway. Working for a dollar a day (which they considered good money) many died from hard labour, disease and careless use of explosives. Others survived to found the first permanent Chinese community in British Columbia.

Despite financial problems and the exceptionally difficult conditions the track was completed in only 54 months, almost six years ahead of schedule. The first train ran 3,000 miles (4,800km) from Montreal's Dalhousie Square Station to British Columbia in 1886, travelling 139 hours through a harshly beautiful landscape which was then almost uninhabited. The train arrived on November 9 at its final destination, Port Moody, only one minute late. The 1949 movie *Canadian Pacific* tells the story of the building of the railway rather fancifully but contains many shots of authentic locomotives and rolling stock.

The Canadian Northern line, later to become the Canadian National, reached Vancouver in 1915, going from Montreal via Hawkesbury, Ottawa, Capreol, Fort Frances, Winnipeg, Dauphin, North Battleford and Edmonton. The Grand Trunk Railway formed the Grand Trunk Pacific to run from Winnipeg to the west, reaching Prince Rupert on the Pacific by way of Yellowhead Pass. These railways and others began to open up the land to immigrants, farmers, mineral prospectors, wealthy travellers and land speculators. They created a crucial sense of nationhood in the world's second-largest country, bringing rapid development to what were otherwise isolated settlements along the way.

Sir William Van Horne, head of the Canadian Pacific, tempted passengers westward by creating a chain of luxurious château-style hotels in spectacular settings. The Banff Springs Hotel (half château, half Scottish baronial mansion) opened in Banff National Park in 1886 and was succeeded by the Hotel Vancouver, the Empress Hotel in Victoria and Chateau Lake Louise. A railway surveyor, Tom Wilson, had in 1882 been the first white man to see Lake Louise, which is now one of the country's most popular skiing and tourist destinations. Canadian Pacific remains the largest hotel company in Canada.

Canada's rail network was among the biggest in the world by the year 1900, and more than 40,000 miles (64,400km) of track were in place by the end of the First World War. The government took over the Canadian Northern company in 1917 and turned it into the Canadian National Railway, subsequently acquiring the Grand Trunk Pacific and other smaller operations. A transcontinental record was set on November 4 1925 by the Canadian National with a trip from Montreal to Vancouver in 67 hours, when the engine ran non-stop to average 45 mph. As in other countries, the 20th century brought increasing competition from airlines, highways and motor cars, but even in the 1950s more than 6,000 locomotives and 200,000 passenger and freight cars were in service.

In 1955, just at the time when air travel was taking over, the prestige *Canadian* train was equipped with glamorous, state-of-the-art stainless steel coaches. The last Canadian Pacific steam engines ran in 1960. Both CN and CP owned thousands of miles of track and had profitable freight operations, carrying cargoes such as wheat, coal and sulphur, but costs continued to mount for passenger trains. Annual passenger miles fell to around 20 million (one third of the peak figure) and, like its US counterpart, the Canadian government was compelled to act.

## VIA RAIL

Canada's equivalent to Amtrak began in 1977, when it took over most of the country's passenger services. VIA Rail has its own equipment and service personnel but uses tracks belonging to Canadian Pacific and Canadian

National. The company now employs 3,500 people and operates 429 trains weekly, using 8,750 miles (14,000km) of track to serve 450 communities.

Over four million passengers travel on VIA Rail each year and the company joins Amtrak to operate several trains (the *Adirondack*, *Maple Leaf* and *International*) connecting with cities in the United States. VIA Rail's equipment, although often older than Amtrak's, is comfortable and has usually been refurbished to a high standard.

## Arranging your trip
### Information
Information on VIA Rail is available from Amtrak at 400 N Capitol Street, Washington, DC 20001, or from the following in Canada:

**Alberta** VIA Rail, 10004 104 Ave, Edmonton, Alberta T5J 0K1.
**Manitoba** VIA Rail Travel Centre, Room 101, 123 Main Street, Winnipeg, Manitoba R3C 2P8.
**Quebec** VIA Rail Canada, Rail Travel Bureau, Central Station, Montreal, Quebec H3C 3N3.

For telephone information, reservations, special needs and tickets by mail, call the following numbers:

| | |
|---|---|
| Newfoundland | 1 800 561 3952 |
| Prince Edward Island | 1 800 561 3952 |
| Nova Scotia | 1 800 561 3952 |
| Moncton, NB | (506) 857 9830 |
| Elsewhere in New Brunswick | 1 800 561 3952 |
| Montreal, Que | (514) 989 2626 |
| Quebec City, Que | (418) 692 3940 |
| Elsewhere in Quebec | 1 800 361 5390 |
| Hamilton, Ont | (905) 522 7533 |
| Kingston, Ont | (613) 544 5600 |
| London, Ont | (519) 672 5722 |
| Ottawa, Ont | (613) 244 8289 |
| Toronto, Ont | (416) 366 8411 |
| Windsor, Ont | (519) 256 5511 |
| Elsewhere in Ontario | 1 800 361 1235 |
| Other provinces | 1 800 561 8630 |

People with hearing or speech problems can communicate through TDD (telecommunication devices for the deaf) on 416 368 6406 in Toronto and 1 800 268 9503 elsewhere.

For Amtrak train information or to make reservations when in Canada call 1 800 872 7245.

## Tickets
Information, reservations and tickets can be obtained through the VIA Rail website: www.viarail.ca or from authorised travel agents and VIA sales offices.

See *Appendix 3* (pages 379) for details of VIA agents abroad. Reservations may be made up to six months ahead and tickets can be ordered by mail and paid for by credit card at no extra cost. If you have not booked ahead, train conductors are able to issue a fare to a passenger not travelling beyond the end of the train run. Cash or credit cards are accepted for payment.

Although VIA does not normally accept responsibility for lost, stolen or destroyed tickets, you can apply for reimbursement by completing a lost ticket indemnity bond obtainable at VIA Rail offices.

## Canrail Pass

A Canrail Pass provides unlimited access to the VIA Rail system throughout Canada, giving 12 days coach travel within a 30-day period. Up to a maximum of three extra days may be purchased within the 30 days, either in advance or during the 30-day validity period. On payment of a supplement you have the option to upgrade to VIA 1 or sleeper class. You can start at any point on the network and make as many stops as you choose. The pass is also valid for buses between Moncton and Saint John, and for the ferry between Levis and Quebec City.

Canrail passes are available both inside and outside Canada but are not valid for other Canadian railways. Tickets must be obtained before boarding. The number of seats available to pass holders is limited so advance reservations are highly recommended.

Senior citizens (those aged 60 or more), students with an ISIC card and anyone aged up to 24 may qualify for Senior/Youth rates. The following pass prices (in Canadian dollars) currently apply, high season being from June to mid-October.

| | | |
|---|---|---|
| Adult Canrail Pass | $423 (low season) | $678 (high season) |
| Extra days | $37 | $58 |
| | | |
| Youth/Senior | $381 (low season) | $610 (high season) |
| Extra days | $34 | $50 |

### Corridor Pass

The Corridor Pass permits travel for up to ten days between Quebec City and Windsor, giving access also to cities such as Toronto, Ottawa, Montreal and Niagara Falls. Passes must be purchased at least five days in advance and are not transferable or refundable. Only one return journey between the same two cities is allowed.

### North America Rail Pass

This recently introduced pass includes both the Amtrak and VIA Rail networks, a total of 28,000 route miles (45,000km), the equivalent of a trip round the equator. Travel is limited to four one-way journeys over the same route and the pass is not valid for Amtrak's *Auto Train* or certain Thruway buses. Passes are available from travel agents in North America or from VIA Rail representatives abroad (see *Appendix 3*).

The North America pass covers 900 destinations and is valid for 30 days travel in economy class. Upgrades to sleeping car accommodation, Business and Club Class, *Metroliner* and VIA 1 Class may be purchased at the station. Prices are Cdn$1,029 (US$674) peak (June to mid-October) and Cdn$725 (US$475) off peak (mid-October to May). Youth/Senior prices are Cdn$926 (US$607) peak and Cdn$652 (US$427) off peak.

Travel must begin within one year of the date the pass is purchased and must be completed by midnight on the last day of travel for which the pass is valid. North America rail passes are only refundable if unused, with a cancellation fee of Cdn$30.

## Classes of travel
### Economy class
Economy or coach class provides adequate space, reclining seats and panoramic views, and is available on all trains except the *Bras d'Or*. You are allowed to make as many stopovers en route as you wish.

### Sleeper class
By day you have a comfortable armchair with a view of the passing landscape. At night your sleeping quarters are converted into a bedroom with facilities that include a private toilet, washbasin, mirror, razor outlet, small closet, reading lamp and optional table. Single, double and triple bedrooms are available as well as a combined bedroom – actually two double rooms separated by a retractable divider.

Berth seating consists of wide, sofa-style seats which convert at night into berths, with heavy curtains to ensure quiet and privacy. Passengers travelling alone can choose either an upper or lower berth. All necessary pillows and blankets are provided and sleeping class passengers have access to a shower room with complimentary soap, shampoo and towel.

### VIA 1
Except for short trips, VIA 1 is available on *Corridor* services between Windsor, Toronto, Ottawa, Montreal and Quebec City. This first class service offers pre-boarding privileges, meals served at your seat, complimentary drinks and a cellular telephone service. You also have access to private Panorama lounges in Toronto, Montreal and Ottawa.

### Silver & Blue
Elite Silver & Blue accommodation is available on the *Canadian* train to those who purchase sleeping accommodation. All meals are included and you get exclusive access to the Park Car and Skyline Dome Car. The *Canadian* has been restored to its sleek 1950s splendour and its Park Car, located at the rear of the train, comprises three separate saloons.

The Dome gives panoramic views from an observation deck, while the uniquely-shaped Bullet Lounge below features wrap-around windows, armchairs and a relaxed atmosphere. In the Mural Lounge you can admire

Canadian artworks or play games such as chess and backgammon. With the Silver & Blue service your private room converts into a bedroom at night.

### Totem
Available on the Skeena from mid-May to mid-October, Totem class includes meals served at your seat and exclusive use of the Park Car. All meals are included in the ticket price.

### Easterly
Easterly class takes its name from the refreshing breeze that wafts in from the sea. The service is available between Montreal and Halifax on the *Ocean* train and to the Gaspé region on the *Chaleur*, although Sleeper class on the *Chaleur* does not include Easterly class privileges.

Trains have art deco coaches and a Park Car with Skyline Dome. As well as your private bedroom you have privileged access to the Dome and Park Car plus complimentary breakfast, tea, coffee and magazines.

### LRC
Modern LRC (light, rapid, comfortable) equipment is mostly used on VIA's busiest route, the Windsor–Quebec City corridor. Trains travel at speeds of up to 95mph (152km/h).

## Reservations
Reservations are required for all first class seats and sleeping cars, as well as for certain trains between Ontario, Quebec and the Maritime Provinces. Economy class seats are automatically guaranteed on purchase of your ticket. You can obtain reservations up to six months ahead from most travel agents via computer or directly from VIA Rail's website.

## Discounts
A 38% discount applies (except during holiday periods) for local travel in eastern Canada. Similar reductions are available in the Quebec–Windsor corridor every day except Friday, Sunday and holidays (five days notice required). Between Toronto and Vancouver in off-peak periods there is a 25% reduction on economy and Silver & Blue classes, and during super-saver periods there are discounts of 38% (minimum seven days advance purchase). Reductions are also available on trains to Canada's more remote regions.

Seniors aged over 60 are entitled to a 10% discount on all classes throughout the VIA system, or up to 50% under certain conditions (advance purchase or restricted periods). Special rates apply for groups of 20 people or more.

## Children
Those under two years of age accompanied by an adult (one child per adult) travel free when not occupying a seat. Infants must occupy a seat in VIA 1 class but are entitled to a 25% discount. Children aged 2–15 pay half the adult fare in economy class and get a 25% discount in VIA 1 and sleepers. Those under

eight are not allowed to travel unaccompanied. Children aged 8–11 can travel with written permission from a parent or guardian provided certain other conditions are met, such as the signing of a liability waiver form (contact VIA Rail for details).

## Students

Full-time students holding an ISIC (International Student Identity Card) and people aged 12 to 17 receive a 40% discount in economy (coach) class and 50% in first class. You can also purchase a VIA 6 Pak of tickets at half price, receiving a free telephone card plus discount coupons for accommodation and car hire. VIA 6 Paks can be ordered on VIA's website for delivery by mail or for collection at a station or travel agent of your choice.

## Connections

Published connections with other trains, buses or ferries are not guaranteed and are subject to change without notice. VIA makes every effort to keep to schedules but does not accept responsibility for delays or inconvenience. You should allow at least an hour between trains when planning your itinerary. If a train is running late, its stopping time at stations may be reduced.

## Payment

Credit cards and travellers' cheques can be used for buying tickets and meals or to upgrade accommodation. Debit cards are accepted at most stations. Personal cheques must be drawn on a Canadian or US bank with your name and address printed on the cheque. Fares and accommodation prices are subject to a 7% goods and services tax.

## Refunds

If your travel plans alter you should notify VIA Rail as soon as possible. Refunds on most tickets, either unused or partially used, can be provided immediately at any VIA sales office or at the travel agency which issued the ticket. If a refund cannot be made straight away a refund application will be taken, and whatever adjustment is due forwarded by mail. Refunds of the Canrail pass and some reduced fare tickets may be subject to cancellation fees.

For refunds or credit by mail your original tickets and receipt coupon should be sent to VIA Rail Canada Inc, Ticket Refunds, 895 De La Gauchetière West, Montreal, Quebec H3B 4G1.

## VIA Preference

This is a frequent traveller programme which lets you earn points to spend on more rail travel, accommodation on the train, car rental and hotels. You only need to spend Cdn$500 (approximately US$350) to earn a free return trip over a section of the railway. Points can also be earned from certain car hire companies and hotels when making reservations or checking in. Preference Membership cards can be obtained at most VIA Rail stations or by calling 888 VIA PREFER (842 7733).

## Facilities and services

### Language

VIA Rail provides bi-lingual service in English and French.

### Baggage

Up to 300lb (135kg) of personal baggage may be checked in for each adult fare, the actual amount depending on the route. For Silver & Blue class the limits are higher. Each piece of checked baggage should not exceed 50lb (23kg) or measure more than 48in (120cm). Larger items will be counted as two articles and staff may refuse to handle baggage weighing more than 75lb (34kg). Bags should be labelled with your name and address and handed in at least half an hour before departure.

Extra baggage, such as sporting equipment, can be checked subject to a surcharge and you can even bring your canoe if it measures less than 18ft (5.4m). Free boxes are available for transporting bicycles and their use is mandatory where journeys involve a connection. VIA will adjust the price for carrying oversize items to make sure it does not exceed the fare you have paid for travel, except in the case of children's fares.

Carry-on luggage is limited to two items not exceeding 50lb (23kg) each in weight. VIA reserves the right to refuse carry-on baggage measuring more than 24in x 16in x 10in (61cm x 41cm x 25cm). No liability is accepted for loss or damage to carry-on luggage or for articles lost or left on the train, so take out insurance if necessary.

Many stations, including Halifax, Quebec City, Ottawa, Winnipeg, Edmonton and Vancouver, have free luggage carts. Red Caps operate in Montreal and Toronto.

### Lost property

No liability is accepted for items stolen or left behind in a train, although VIA personnel will make every effort to help you find your belongings.

### Boarding

The elderly, passengers with young children and those travelling VIA 1 class are encouraged to board trains early at major stations.

### Pets

With the exception of service animals for visually or hearing-impaired passengers, pets are not allowed in passenger cars. Caged pets such as dogs and cats can be transported in the baggage car on most trains but passengers are responsible for their feeding and exercise. Animals must be claimed immediately on arrival. Cages must be high enough to allow the animal to stand and VIA has the right to refuse cages it deems unsuitable (appropriate cages can be purchased at some stations).

### Radios

Headphones must always be used when listening to radios, tapes or CDs.

## Sleeping

Pillows and blankets are not provided for overnight travel in economy accommodation, except on the *Ocean* and *Chaleur* trains. All necessary bedding is supplied in sleeping cars. Roomettes (for one person) and bedrooms (for two people) have a hand-basin, mirror, electric razor socket, fold-down table and concealed or separate toilet. Easterly and Silver & Blue sleeping cars have showers.

Section accommodation offers two facing couch-style seats which convert at night into an upper and lower berth. Thick curtains provide privacy. A section can be bought separately for one person, either as an upper or lower berth. Washrooms are located in each coach.

## Smoking

Smoking is prohibited on all Windsor–Quebec City corridor trains. Elsewhere, smoking is allowed only in designated coaches or sections of coaches, enclosed sleeping cars and some parts of lounge cars. Pipes and cigars are prohibited and no smoking is allowed in dining cars. Smoking is permitted in designated areas at some stations. Cigarettes are not sold on trains.

## Alcohol

Alcoholic and other drinks purchased on board must be consumed where served. The law prohibits consumption of personal supplies other than by passengers travelling in enclosed sleeping accommodation.

## Special needs

Anyone with special needs will be given additional attention on request. Contact VIA in advance and ask for a copy of the brochure on special needs. You should give at least 48 hours notice for special meals (such as diabetic, kosher or low sodium) and 24 hours for a wheelchair. Special meals are not available in economy class.

With the exception of trains running between London and Sarnia in Ontario, all VIA trains are accessible to passengers in wheelchairs, and wheelchairs can be accepted as checked baggage. Passengers unable to care for themselves must travel with an escort, who will be offered free passage in economy class (subject to certain restrictions).

## Telephone

A credit card cellular phone service is available in VIA 1 cars and some LRC coaches. Personal mobile phones should be used with due consideration for other passengers.

## Service

If you have any comments or suggestions you should write to Customer Relations, VIA Rail Canada Inc, PO Box 8116, Station 'A', Montreal, Quebec H3C 3N3; fax: 514 871 6104; email: service@viarail.ca.

If you have a complaint or problem which cannot be resolved by discussion with VIA personnel on the spot you should call 1 800 681 2561 or write to

Customer Relations, enclosing ticket receipts if possible. You can also fill in a comments form on the VIA Rail website.

## THE ROUTES

Changes to VIA Rail operations and schedules may take place from time to time, so for the latest information call 1 800 561 0200. The following passenger services are among those currently operating.

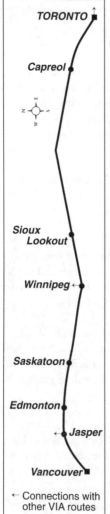

← Connections with other VIA routes

### The Canadian

This train was previously called the *Super Continental*. The government cut the southern transcontinental route through Banff, Calgary and Medicine Hat in 1990, transferring to a more northerly passage via Jasper. At the same time, a $200 million refurbishment of the *Canadian's* original 1950s equipment began. Modern comforts such as air conditioning and showers were added to the stainless steel coaches, and train staff were provided with smart new uniforms.

The *Canadian* now travels three times a week each way between Toronto and Vancouver, a journey of almost 2,765 miles (4,424km) taking three days and nights. Among its 69 stops are several which VIA calls 'dwell time' – brief pauses giving you a chance to stretch your legs on the platform. The train travels through southern Ontario then over the prairies of Saskatchewan, crossing the mountains and gorges of Jasper National Park before reaching British Columbia. In Jasper it connects with the *Skeena* to Prince Rupert.

The *Canadian* leaves Toronto just before midday on Tuesday, Thursday and Saturday to reach Capreol by mid-evening. You arrive in Winnipeg by early evening on the following day and Saskatoon during the second night. Edmonton is reached early on day three and Jasper by mid-afternoon. You arrive in Vancouver early on Friday, Sunday or Tuesday morning.

Travelling east, trains leave Vancouver mid-evening each Tuesday, Friday and Sunday, arriving in Jasper by mid-afternoon on the second day and Edmonton by late evening. You reach Saskatoon early in the morning and Winnipeg mid-afternoon on the third day, then Capreol on day four, arriving in Toronto mid-evening on Friday, Monday or Wednesday.

Check-in baggage is available at all major stations. Complete meals service, lounge car, bedrooms and roomettes. Economy and Silver & Blue class.

## Major stations

**Vancouver** 1150 Station Street. Information tel: 604 669 3050. Reservations tel: 1 800 561 8630. Ticket-office open 10.30–20.00 (Mon, Thu and Sat); 08.30–18.00 (Tue, Fri and Sun); 10.30–18.00 (Wed). Buses connect with the Amtrak network in Seattle, Washington. Amtrak's *Northwest Corridor* trains run between Vancouver and Seattle four times a day.

**Winnipeg** 123 Main Street. Reservations and information tel: 1 800 561 8630. Lockers, newspapers, handcarts, taxi stand. VIA Rail Headquarters West is at 123 Main Street, Room 104, Winnipeg, MN R3C 2P8; tel: 204 949 7400.

**Saskatoon** 11th and Chappel Drive, four miles/6.5km west of downtown. Reservations and information tel: 1 800 561 8630. Lockers, vending machines, taxi stand.

**Edmonton** 104th Ave at 10th; tel: 422 6032. Reservations and information 1 800 561 8630. Ticket-office and waiting-room open 07.00–15.30, Mon, Thu, Sat; 08.30–21.00, Tue, Fri; 08.30–16.00 Wed; and 10.30–21.00, Sun. Lockers, newspapers, taxi stand.

**Jasper** 400 Connaught Drive. Reservations and information tel: 1 800 561 8630. Ticket-office and waiting-room 07.30–22.30. Lockers, newspapers, Red Caps, restaurant, shop, taxis. For Jasper National Park contact the information centre at 500 Connaught Drive; tel: 403 852 6176.

## The Skeena

A 725-mile (1,160km) journey among British Columbia's spectacular mountains and snow-filled valleys, starting from Jasper in Alberta and following a route formerly used by Indians, trappers and gold prospectors. You accompany the Fraser River to Prince George then the Skeena River to Prince Rupert, only 40 miles (64km) south of Alaska. Prince Rupert is proud claimant to the title of 'halibut capital of the world'.

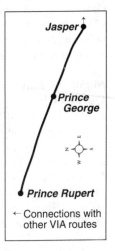

En route are glaciers, forests, salmon rivers, fishing villages and deserted gold rush towns. An hour from Jasper you can see the highest point in the Canadian Rockies, Mount Robson (12,972ft/3,954m). Look also for the abundant wildlife, including moose, deer, bald eagles and an occasional bear.

Before the Grand Trunk Railway arrived in 1914, Prince Rupert was an isolated settlement on Kaien Island. Ferry services now operate north from Prince Rupert to Alaska, or south along the British Columbia and Washington coasts to Seattle. Connections can be made in Prince George with the British Columbia Railway service to Vancouver.

The *Skeena* leaves Jasper soon after midday on Sunday, Wednesday and Friday, reaching Prince George by mid-evening. Following an overnight stop in Prince George, trains leave early on Monday, Thursday or Saturday morning to reach Prince Rupert by mid-evening.

Travelling east, the Skeena departs Prince Rupert early on Sunday, Wednesday and Friday morning to reach Prince George by mid-evening. After an overnight stop in Prince George, trains leave early on Monday, Thursday or Saturday morning to reach Jasper by late afternoon.

Complete meals service and bedrooms. No check-in baggage. Economy and Totem class.

VIA uses Prince George's First Avenue and Quebec station, close to downtown. Lockers, vending machines, handcarts, taxi stand. For Prince Rupert and Prince George station information or for reservations call 1 800 561 8630.

## The Corridor Services

VIA's busiest routes are between Quebec City and Windsor as well as to Montreal, Ottawa and Toronto, carrying three million passengers at up to 95mph (150km/h). Montreal and Quebec City are linked by four trains on weekdays, three on Saturday and two on Sunday.

The journey takes just under three hours, and Montreal to Toronto takes less than five hours. Additional services go to Windsor, Sherbrooke, Ottawa (three times daily in each direction) and Niagara Falls (one train daily in addition to Amtrak's *Maple Leaf*). Many trains offer VIA 1 as well as economy class service and have telephones on board.

The *Enterprise* service between Montreal and Toronto leaves both cities just before midnight for an overnight journey. First class sleeping accommodation is available, with access to the Park Car.

### Major stations

**Quebec City** The refurbished Gare du Palais is at 450 rue de la Gare du Palais; tel: 524 3590. Open 06.00–20.30. Quebec's 600-room Hotel Château de Frontenac is another which was built in French style by the Canadian Pacific. The hotel's turrets and bastions still provide the city with its most recognisable landmark.

**Montreal Gare Centrale** (Central Station) at 895 rue de la Gauchetière Ouest first opened in 1943. It is also used today by Amtrak and commuter trains. Reservations and information tel: 514 871 1331. Ticket-office open 06.30–20.45. Waiting-room 24 hours. Red Caps, restaurants, shops, taxi stand.

The **Canadian Railway Museum** is at 126 rue St-Pierre, Saint-Constant, Quebec J5A 2G9, located 30 minutes south of Montreal; tel: 450 632 2410 or 450 638 1522; web: www.exporail.org. Over 130 historic locomotives and vehicles are housed in enormous train sheds. The collection includes Canada's oldest surviving steam engine and a steam-operated snow plough (a Canadian invention). A replica steam locomotive operates on summer weekends and the museum opens daily from late June until early September, otherwise at weekends. Admission charge.

For Montreal city information, see also *The Adirondack* (pages 267–9).

**Toronto** Clean, efficient and softly-lit Union Station is at 65 Front W and

York; tel: 416 366 8411. Reservations and information tel: 416 366 8411 (or 1 800 872 7245 for Amtrak). Ticket-office open 07.00–21.00. Waiting-room 07.00–23.30. GO commuter trains operate to Hamilton, Oshawa, Richmond Hill and Georgetown (tel: 869 3200). Lockers, newspapers, Red Caps, restaurants, shops, taxi stand, subway.

For Toronto city information, see also *The Maple Leaf* (pages 303–5).

**Ottawa** A modern station at 200 Tremblay, two miles (3km) from downtown. Reservations and information tel: 613 244 8289. Ticket-office and waiting-room open 05.00–21.00. Lockers, newspapers, Red Caps, restaurants, shops, taxi stand. The **National Museum of Science and Technology** at 1867 St Laurent Blvd displays historic steam engines and 1890s rolling stock (tel: 613 991 3044). Open daily, admission charge.

### The Ocean

The *Ocean* train first ran on July 3 1904, making it Canada's longest running train to have operated over the same line. It takes 18 hours to travel 840 miles (1,352km) along the old Intercolonial Railway (ICR) route between Halifax, Nova Scotia, and Montreal in Quebec. Trains go via New Brunswick and some of the many rural communities of Quebec's south shore, starting out daily (except Tuesday) in both directions.

You leave Halifax early in the afternoon to reach Moncton by early evening, Campbellton in New Brunswick by late evening and Montreal early the following morning. A ferry service connects Levis with Quebec City.

Travelling east, the *Ocean* departs Montreal early in the evening to reach Campbellton early next morning, Moncton by mid-morning and Halifax, Nova Scotia, by mid-afternoon.

Check-in baggage at main stations. Complete meals service, bedrooms, Park Car and Skyline observation car. Economy and Easterly class.

**Halifax** station is at 1161 Hollis; tel: 1 800 561 3952. Ticket-office and waiting-room open 09.00–17.30. Reservations and information tel: 902 429 8421. Lockers, vending machines, newspapers, Red Caps, restaurant, taxi stand.

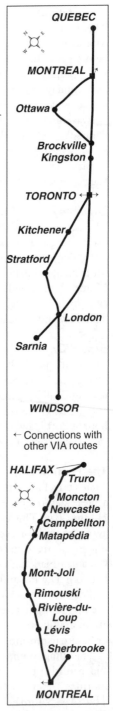

## The Chaleur

This train operates three days a week, following the *Ocean's* route between Montreal and Matapédia, then crossing a tributary of the St Lawrence River before continuing along the beautiful Gaspé peninsula.

Splendidly restored silver trains leave Montreal early on Wednesday, Friday and Sunday evening to reach Matapédia very early the next morning and Gaspé by late morning.

Travelling south, the *Chaleur* leaves Gaspé mid-afternoon on Monday, Thursday and Saturday to reach Matapédia late in the evening and Montreal by early next morning.

Park Car, Skyline Car with observation dome, lounge and café. Check-in baggage. Complete meals service and bedrooms. Economy and Sleeper class.

## Saguenay and Abtibi

The *Saguenay* travels from downtown Montreal to Lac-St-Jean and Jonquière via the forests and lakes of Northern Quebec. The *Abtibi* goes from Montreal to La Tuque then heads northwest through Parent to Senneterre. Stations en route include Jolette, Shawinigan, Saint-Tite and Chambord. Both trains leave Montreal on Monday, Wednesday and Friday mornings, arriving four hours later in Senneterre or Jonquière. Trains depart for Montreal on Tuesday, Thursday and Sunday. Economy class only.

## Bras d'Or

VIA Rail's new, all first class *Bras d'Or* train travels between Sydney and Halifax in Nova Scotia. Departures are from mid-May to mid-September, leaving Halifax every Tuesday morning and arriving in Sydney by late afternoon. Trains depart from Sydney on Wednesday mornings. A stop of one hour at Port Hawkesbury is made in both directions. The train has a Skydome car as well as costumed tour guides, storytellers and musicians.

## The Hudson Bay

Trains travel more than 1,000 miles (1,600km) north from Winnipeg, crossing a bleak desert of ice and snow to Churchill and the polar bear country of Hudson Bay. This is beaver territory, where dams have been known to wash away the track or even wreck a train. The Hudson Bay Railroad opened the line in the 1920s to transport grain for export from Canada's prairies, and the Canadian National's last scheduled steam train (*No. 6043*) made its final run between The Pas and Winnipeg in November 1960.

The *Hudson Bay* leaves Winnipeg late on Sunday, Tuesday and Thursday evening to reach The Pas early next day and Thompson by early evening. You arrive in Gillam around midnight and Churchill early on Tuesday, Thursday or Saturday morning.

Travelling south, trains leave Churchill mid-evening on Tuesday, Thursday and Saturday to reach Gillam early next morning and Thompson by mid-morning. You arrive in The Pas mid-evening and Winnipeg early on Thursday, Saturday or Monday morning.

Book well in advance, especially during summer. Check-in baggage. Complete meals service, bedrooms and roomettes. Economy and Sleeper class.

**Churchill** station is at 74092 Churchill, on the western edge of town. Reservations and information tel: 1 800 561 8630. Left luggage room.

## Other VIA rail trains

On Vancouver Island, the *Malahat* runs daily between Victoria and Courtenay through Malahat Pass and the Cowichan Valley. You leave Victoria early in the morning or Courtenay early in the afternoon for a 140-mile/224km journey lasting four and a half hours. Sunday trains in both directions operate four hours later. Snacks, sandwiches and drinks can be bought during station stops at Nanaimo and Courtenay. Economy class only.

The *Hudson Bay* route connects at The Pas in Manitoba with trains to Lynn Lake. Watch out for polar bear warning signs as you near the edge of the Arctic circle. Trains leave The Pas mid-morning and arrive in Lynn Lake mid-evening on Monday, Wednesday or Friday. You can return from Lynn Lake early on Tuesday, Thursday or Saturday morning to reach The Pas by early evening. Check-in baggage service available. Economy and Sleeper class.

VIA Rail's *Lake Superior* trains depart Sudbury on Tuesday, Thursday and Saturday mornings for a 301-mile (480km) journey to White River in Ontario, arriving by early evening. Travelling east, trains leave White River on Wednesday, Friday and Sunday morning to reach Sudbury by mid-evening. Economy class.

Several VIA trains out of Toronto go to Kingston, Windsor, Stratford and London, Ontario.

## The Rocky Mountaineer

A leisurely two-day, 918-mile (1,469km) journey among the mountains and forests of the Canadian Rockies and on to Calgary makes this one of the most spectacular train trips in the world. The line was part of the now defunct transcontinental *Canadian* train route between Montreal and Vancouver. The *Rocky Mountaineer* was operated as a tourist train by VIA Rail (at a loss) until it was privatised in 1990. Under the ownership of the Great Canadian Railtour Company it has become more popular every year since.

The company is the largest privately-owned passenger rail operator in North America, with more than 300 employees. On September 12 1996 it made the record books by operating the longest passenger train in Canadian history. A total of 37 cars travelled from Vancouver to Kamloops to beat the previous best of 28, set in Regina, Saskatchewan, by the Canadian Pacific's *Dominion* in 1965.

### The routes

The *Rocky Mountaineer* uses Canadian Pacific and Canadian National tracks, as well as (briefly) tracks owned by Burlington Northern and VIA Rail. The

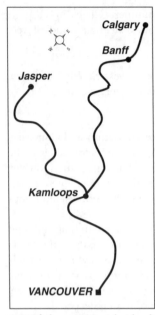

entire journey takes place in daylight so that you can absorb the maximum amount of scenery and see animals such as grazing elk, black and grizzly bears, white-tail deer, moose, mountain goats, coyotes, wolves and big-horn sheep. The thick forests of pine and fir are also home to marmots, porcupines and chipmunks. Much of this wildlife has become accustomed to railroad traffic so this is a great opportunity to see more creatures than would otherwise be possible. Bears, for example, have developed a taste for the grain which leaks out of freight cars and ferments beside the track.

William Cornelius Van Horne, first manager of the Canadian Pacific, famously remarked that 'since we cannot export the scenery, we shall have to import the tourists' and this part of Canada has been doing so ever since. The *Rocky Mountaineer* leaves Vancouver's historic Pacific Central station and crosses the Pitt River on a 1,749ft-long (530m) bridge before following the Fraser River, where seals can sometimes be seen. The passage through the Fraser Canyon was part of the gold rush routes of the late 1880s, when the CN railroad line had to be carved out of the side of the gorge by construction workers using 'dynamite and whisky'.

At Hell's Gate Canyon, so-named because construction work here was so dangerous, a massive rock slide accidentally narrowed the river to 110ft (37m). Look for fish ladders built in the 1940s to allow 40 million sockeye salmon to pass upstream to spawn every year. You continue through a fertile valley of farms and orchards before beginning to climb among snow-capped mountains and glaciers, passing places with names such as Skuzzy Creek, Suicide Rapids and Jaws of Death Gorge. Look for the occasional fields of ginseng, grown under plastic sheets.

After an overnight stop in Kamloops you continue next morning to Jasper by way of the North Thompson River, the Monashee Mountains, Pyramid Falls and Little Hell's Gate. You get an overwhelming view of the highest mountain in the Canadian Rockies, Mount Robson (12,972ft/3,931m) and have the option of continuing on VIA Rail from Jasper, travelling across all of Canada to the Atlantic coast. VIA's *Canadian* train uses the same tracks as the *Rocky Mountaineer* from Vancouver to Jasper but travels partly by night.

An alternative, and usually preferred, *Rocky Mountaineer* train goes from Kamloops across Glacier National Park to Banff and Calgary. You travel among the ranch lands of the South Thompson River then along the fiord-like shores of the Shuswap Lakes. At Silverdale you pass the spot where in 1904 the American Billy Miner and 'Shorty' Dunn carried out Canada's first train hold-up, getting away with $6,000 of gold dust and $50,000 in US bonds. You also pass the spot where their last train robbery (yielding $15 and a handful of liver pills) took place a year and a half later. The gang were captured shortly afterwards by the RCMP, although Miner later escaped from jail.

At Craigellachie you see a stone cairn indicating where the last spike was driven to complete the Canadian Pacific Railroad on November 7 1885. The *Rocky Mountaineer* travels on through Mount Macdonald by way of the Connaught Tunnel, the second-longest (five miles/8km) in North America. Adjacent Macdonald Tunnel is the longest (nine miles/14.5km). Both tunnels were built in the early twentieth century to protect the tracks from heavy snowfalls and avalanches which had caused over 200 deaths. At Stoney Creek a steel arch bridge was constructed in 1929 directly above an 1893 bridge which replaced the original wooden structure.

Beyond the Kicking Horse River you go through two unique spiral tunnels located under Cathedral Mountain and Mount Ogden, excavated between 1907 and 1909. These provide a safer and easier route than the original 'Big Hill', an eight-mile stretch which included a 4.5% grade. The upper Spiral Tunnel is 3,255ft/992m long and turns approximately 250 degrees, emerging 56ft/17m lower than its entrance. The lower tunnel is 2,922ft/890m long, turns 230 degrees and comes out 50ft/15m below. An extra-long freight train may be seen emerging and entering the tunnel simultaneously.

The *Rocky Mountaineer* leaves Vancouver early in the morning to reach Kamloops by late afternoon. After an overnight hotel stop you leave Kamloops early next morning for either Jasper (early evening) or Banff and Calgary (early to mid-evening).

Travelling west, trains leave Calgary early in the morning (or Jasper mid-morning) to reach Kamloops by early evening. After an overnight stop you leave Kamloops early next morning and arrive in Vancouver by late afternoon.

### Facilities

Each air-conditioned train can carry up to 950 passengers in 22 coaches. A boxy, bi-level dome coach at the end of the train has wrap-around windows with flat, vertical areas of glass that make it easy to take distortion-free photographs. Better still, you can take pictures and enjoy the passing scene as the wind rearranges your hair on an open observation platform at the end of the car. Each dome car cost Cdn$1 million, accommodates 72 passengers and was specially built by the Rader company in Colorado. These were the first completely new coaches to be put into service on a Canadian train for 40 years. Similar ones operate on the Alaska Railroad.

RedLeaf service give you a comfortable reclining seat, large picture windows and open-air vestibules. You get complimentary snacks and non-alcoholic drinks as well as an at-your-seat cold meal service. Attendants supply an enthusiastic commentary on the route's history, geography and wildlife. Choose a seat on the left of the train when travelling east, or on the right if going west.

GoldLeaf service is well worth the extra cost, offering access to the dome coach, pre-boarding privileges, an elegant dining lounge, rear observation platform and a superior hotel (dinner included) for the overnight stop in Kamloops. If you ask nicely you may be allowed to travel part of the way on the locomotive platform.

## Timings and booking

The main 20-week season lasts from June to September. Special value seasons with fewer departures operate during April, May and October, making a total of 148 departures. There are 20 Christmas and winter tours, which often include accommodation in grand historic railway hotels. You can book one-way or round-trip and fares start at about US$400. This includes breakfast, lunch and non-alcoholic drinks on board, as well as hotel accommodation in Kamloops. Reduced fares are available for children aged 2–11.

You should book at least 35 days in advance and check in an hour before departure time. Checked baggage (maximum 66lb/30kg) cannot be reclaimed before your final destination (except for Goldleaf passengers) so take a small bag with you for the overnight stop. Special needs can be catered for if notice is given at the time of booking. Smoking is only allowed in certain designated areas.

*Rocky Mountaineer* trains are run by the Great Canadian Railtour Company Ltd, 1150 Station Street, 1st Floor, Vancouver, British Columbia, Canada V6A 2X7; tel: 604 606 7200. Reservations tel: 604 606 7245 (Canada/USA) or 1 800 665 7245; email: reservations@rockymountaineer.com; web: www.rockymountaineer.com.

UK ticket agents include Leisurail (see *Appendix 3*, page 379).

**Calgary** station is at 9th Avenue and Centre. Lockers, newspapers, Red Caps, restaurant, taxi stand. Reservations and information tel: 1 800 561 8630. For information on **The Alberta 2005 Railway Museum** contact PO Box 2442, Station M, Calgary, AB T2P 3C1; tel: 281 5989; web: www.calcna.ab.ca/2005acrm/member.html.

## British Columbia Rail Limited

*Please note that BC Rail ceased operating the following passenger trains in 2002, but it is hoped that another company will take over these services.*
British Columbia Rail was formerly known as the Pacific Great Eastern Railway and before that the Howe Sound Pemberton Valley & Northern Railway, founded in 1908. Unfortunately, BC Rail ceased to operate passenger train services in 2002, although it is hoped that another company, possibly VIA Rail, will take over at least some of the following routes.

BC Rail formerly operated *Cariboo Prospector* self-propelled passenger trains (featuring Budd cars with no visible engines) over a spectacularly scenic 463-mile (740km) route between Vancouver and Prince George, crossing the famous Lion's Gate Bridge built in 1938 to join North Vancouver to Vancouver's Stanley Park. The trains travelled through Horseshoe Bay Tunnel (4,200ft/1,280m long) and passed the snow-covered peak of Mt Garibaldi (8,787ft/2,680m) before snaking through Cheakamus Canyon, where during early summer eagles can be seen nesting along the river. After passing the pinnacle of Brandywine Falls the route climbs 3,000ft/900m among meadows and canyons to Alta Lake, the summit of this line as it passes through the Coast Range.

The *Cariboo Prospector* would then continue among more lakes, mountains and waterfalls before making a a stop at Lillooet, originally called Cayoosh Flats. This was another goldrush town (Mile Zero of the old Cariboo Wagon Road) which began in 1858 to link the gold fields of Bakerville and Wells. At that time there was no city west of Chicago, except for San Francisco, that was bigger than Bakerville. The town has lately been restored as a mining museum.

The line crosses the Fraser River before making a dramatic, winding 3,000ft/900m incline through the Fraser River canyon to the Cariboo Plateau and Kelly Lake, passing Horse Lake (highest elevation on this line), Lone Butte (where an old water tower stands as a symbol of previous railroad days), Williams Lake and Quesnel, travelling into the heart of the Cariboo Region. Until 1952, Quesnel was the most northerly point of the railway.

Trains would cross the 1,023ft/311m long Cottonwood River Bridge then the 920ft/280m long Ahbau Creek Bridge, where in 1952 a silver spike ceremony opened the Quesnel to Prince George line. Prince George, located at the junction of the Fraser and Nechako Rivers, is the railway's main divisional point and a major transportation hub. Freight services continue north to the Peace River country and Fort Nelson, 980 miles (1,577km) from North Vancouver, transporting mainly coal and lumber from Fort St James and McKenzie.

BC Rail's *Cariboo* service included spacious reclining seats, complimentary meals and a licensed bar. Parlour Class on the *Royal Hudson* included either brunch or lunch, depending on the time of travel. The *Pacific Starlight* dinner train used to make a round trip each evening (except Monday and Tuesday) between Vancouver and the calm waters of Porteau Cove by way of Howe Sound. The *Pacific Starlight* used splendid restored period coaches, some dating from the 1930s.

Trains to and from Prince George operated daily from mid-June to mid-September, leaving BC Rail's North Vancouver station at 1311 West First Street early each morning to reach Lillooet by early afternoon. On Sunday, Wednesday and Friday you could continue to Prince George, arriving by mid-evening. Travelling south, trains left Prince George early on Monday, Thursday and Saturday to reach Lillooet by mid-afternoon. From Lillooet, trains departed daily to reach Vancouver by mid-evening.

*Whistler Explorer* trains operated on weekdays between Whistler and Kelly Lake from late May to early October. The round trip started from Whistler early in the morning, arrived in Kelly Lake around midday for lunch then returned by motor coach via Downing Provincial Park to Whistler by early evening. Lunch, afternoon tea and a souvenir memento were included.

The Pacific Starlight dinner train left North Vancouver station early in the evening (except Monday) from early May until the end of September. Trains operated only on Friday and Saturday evenings in October. The Pacific Starlight travelled to Howe Sound and Porteau Cove before making the return journey to North Vancouver, arriving back late in the evening. The rolling stock was purchased by BC Rail in 1997 from the Spirit of Washington dinner train and consisted of nine cars, each with a jazz theme, including two dome cars and six coaches, all refurbished in art deco style. The dome and observation cars previously operated on the Chesapeake & Ohio Railroad, the Western Pacific Railroad and the Great Northern Railroad.

From early May until late September, BC Rail operated the Royal Hudson steam train (Wednesday to Sunday) between Vancouver and Squamish. King George VI and Queen Elizabeth made a royal tour of Canada in 1939, travelling from Quebec City to Vancouver by a train that was 12 cars long (including two vice-regal cars), painted royal blue and aluminium and pulled by Hudson locomotive No. 2850. Hudson No. 2851 was used for the pilot train, carrying officials and press, which preceded the royal train by one hour on its 3,224 (5,188km) mile journey. Royal crowns were attached to the running boards of both locomotives. King George was so impressed that he gave permission for all future Hudson engines to carry his coat of arms and be designated 'Royal Hudsons'.

A sister engine, the *Royal Hudson* 2860, would travel among mountains and forests along the rugged coast of Howe Sound, making it and *3716* the last steam engines still in scheduled mainline service on a North American railway. The coaches dated from the 1940s and included the Mount Garibaldi open observation car once used on Canadian Pacific's Mountaineer between Vancouver and Chicago. Parlour class was available and the single level dome cars had wrap-around windows and at your seat service.

The *Royal Hudson* chugged its way through six tunnels and crossed several high trestles as it travelled through some of Canada's finest scenery. Trains left Vancouver mid-morning and returned mid-afternoon following a two-hour stop in the old logging town of Squamish, where 50 vintage railway cars can be seen at the West Coast Railway Museum. You could either travel both ways by rail or sail one way on the cruise ship Britannia.

BC Rail also ran the historic *No. 3716*, the Port Coquitlam, a steam locomotive built by Montreal Locomotive Works in 1912 and one of the oldest steam engines operating in North America. It transported vintage coaches from North Vancouver to Howe Sound, the Coast Mountains and Whistler then went north to 100 Mile House, once a way station en route to the gold fields. After an overnight stay the train returned south, with another overnight stop in Lillooet. Trips took place in April and October.

BC Rail is based at 1311 West 1st Street, North Vancouver, BC, V7P 1A6. Or write to PO Box 8770, Vancouver, BC, V6B 4X6; tel: 1 800 339 8752 or 604 984 5246; fax 604 984 5505; web: www.bcrail.com/bcrpass.

## The Algoma Central

Trains run for 296 miles (475km) between Sault Ste Marie (pronounced soo-saint-marie) and Hearst in Ontario. You travel a twisting route opened in 1914 among forests, lakes, waterfalls and ravines, where the mountains resemble the Rockies. There are terrific views of the deep Agawa River Canyon and the train makes a two-hour stop for you to admire more closely the 1,500ft/457m high cliffs, pine trees and waterfalls.

Trains operate daily from June to October, leaving Sault Ste Marie early in the morning and returning late in the afternoon. During the foliage season (September to October) you should plan a weekday trip if possible and be sure to book early. Dome Car service includes breakfast, lunch and a separate bar area with private steward.

The Algoma Central's *Snow Train* operates on weekends from January until March, travelling through a snow and ice-encrusted Agawa Canyon. The *Snow Train* makes an overnight stop in the French-Canadian town of Hearst. On certain days throughout the year you can tour the whole length of the railway, including the flat lands of the Clay Belt region with its countless lakes and conifers.

For information or tickets contact the Algoma Central Railway, PO Box 130, 129 Bay Street, Sault Ste Marie, Ontario P6A 6Y2; tel: 705 946 7300; fax 705 541 2989; web: www.agawacanyontourtrain.com.

## The Ontario Northland

In 1932 the Temiskaming & Northern Ontario Railway was built 186 miles (299km) from Cochrane to the Arctic circle across a demanding physical landscape, opening up the north's mining and forest resources. The railway changed its name to the Ontario Northland Railway (ONR) in 1946 and remains principally a freight line, operating to and from northeastern Ontario and northwestern Quebec.

The *Northlander* is a passenger train running between Toronto's Union Station and the town of Cochrane via North Bay, Cobalt and Matheson. It provides large, comfortable seats, wide aisles and picture windows. The **Cochrane Railway and Pioneer Museum** (tel: 705 272 4361) is housed in several old train coaches opposite Cochrane Station. Open daily from June to September, admission charge.

The *Northlander* leaves Toronto for its 440-mile (705km) journey early in the evening every day except Saturday, reaching North Bay by late evening and the gold mining town of Cochrane early the following morning. Travelling south, trains leave Cochrane early in the morning (except Saturday) to reach North Bay by late morning and Toronto by late afternoon. Bus shuttles link Matheson and Timmins with Hearst and Cochrane. Business and Northlander Plus class services include complimentary meals, cellular phones and portable computer terminals.

The ONR's *Polar Bear Express* is a four-hour, 186-mile (300km) ride down the Arctic Watershed, accessible only by rail or plane. You go through a sparsely populated wetland of black spruce forests, lakes, muskeg and scrub, known as 'the bush'. The *Express* proceeds from Cochrane over Ontario's fertile clay belt farmland and Cree Indian territory, crossing the Abitibi and Moose Rivers to Moosoonee on the edge of the Arctic Ocean near James Bay. Only 1,400 people live in Moosoonee, which has no paved roads and is one of Canada's oldest settlements. It was founded by the Hudson's Bay Company in 1673 during French-English rivalry for the fur trade.

Before the T & NO Railway arrived in Moosoonee in 1932 the journey from Cochrane by canoe or snowshoes took ten days. A green railway car on the right of the station houses a museum of the region's natural and cultural history. Nearby Moose Factory Island, with its Hudson Bay post and Cree Cultural Centre, can be visited by tour boat or freighter canoe.

The *Polar Bear Express* operates daily (except Friday) from late June to September, leaving early in the morning and returning late afternoon after a four-hour stopover in Moosoonee. Dress sensibly in case of cool or wet weather and the threat of mosquitoes. Tour guides will answer questions and point out places of interest and the train has a lively piano bar.

The *Little Bear* is a year-round train between Cochrane and Moosoonee. Essentially a freight operation with added passenger cars, this mixed train is less luxurious than the *Polar Bear Express* but provides more contact with local life. One of the last flag stop trains in Canada, it may halt virtually anywhere, perhaps to pick up a fur trapper or canoeist along with his cargo of furs or canoe. The train travels the same route as the *Polar Bear Express*, crossing farmland, bogs, forests and fields of wildflowers. Winters can be very cold, freezing the Moose River solid enough to make a road to Moose Factory Island.

The northbound *Little Bear* leaves Cochrane mid-morning on Monday, Wednesday and Friday to reach Moosoonee by late afternoon. Southbound trains leave Moosoonee early on Tuesday, Thursday and Saturday morning to arrive in Cochrane by early afternoon. Trains run twice weekly during July and August.

Reservations are required for most Ontario Northland trains and should be made well in advance for the *Polar Bear Express*. All trains have air conditioning and are wheelchair accessible. Dining-car or snack bar meals are available. There is no checked baggage service but two carry-on bags are permitted per passenger.

The ONR operates an extensive bus network in northeastern Ontario, as well as ferry services and an airline. The Nor-Pass, available from the beginning of May to the end of September, allows unlimited rail and bus travel throughout the Northland system for 14 days ($179) with an optional seven day extension ($21). For information on this and other ONR services contact the Ontario Northland Railway at Union Station, 65 Front Street W, Toronto, Ontario M5J 1E6; tel: 416 314 3750 or 1 800 268 9281; fax 416 314 3729 or at 555 Oak Street E, North Bay, Ontario P1B 8L3; tel: 705 472 4500; web: www.ontc.on.ca. For information on schedules and fares call 1 800 461 8558.

## Other railways and rail museums in Canada

**Canadian Pacific** The CP is a freight-only railroad but several companies operate over its track, including VIA Rail, the *Rocky Mountaineer* and Vintage Tours of Calgary (CPR-owned). CPR's new Victorian-style pavilion is being constructed in Calgary from the platform behind CP Hotel's Palliser Hotel, and there are further plans to market the glamour and romance of the Canadian Pacific Railway's past. The pavilion will be home to the CP's fleet of vintage business cars, some of the most valuable railway cars in North America. Canadian Pacific will market the storied cars, which can be chartered for scenic cruises in the Rocky Mountains.

Vintage Tours currently operates the *Royal Canadian Pacific*, comprising eight historic cars with carpeted floors, mahogany panelling, inlaid marquetry and cut glass, fine china and white linens to conjure up the service of old. The coaches, built in the early 20th century and named after people or events from the history of Canada, are 80ft/24m long and formerly carried railway executives and other important individuals. Previous travellers on the *Royal Canadian* have included Sir Winston Churchill, Princess Elizabeth and the Duke of Edinburgh.

The *Royal Canadian Pacific*'s Crowsnest excursion makes a three day, 650 mile (1,046km) trip from Calgary to Crowsnest Pass and back to Calgary. The fare includes two nights accommodation at the Palliser Hotel, three nights on board the train, guided tours, meals, baggage handling and admission to off-train tours.

The train heads west from Calgary along the Canadian Pacific Railway main line through the Bow River valley towards the Rocky Mountains. After a short stop in Banff you continue to Lake Louise and the Continental Divide, travelling through the famous Spiral Tunnels into Field, BC, where the train stops for passengers to board a motor coach for a tour of Emerald Lake.

You then depart for Golden, BC, where the train leaves the Canadian Pacific line and goes south along the 'coal route' through beautiful valleys carved by the Columbia River. You also travel through the continent's largest natural wetland, called 'The Rocky Mountain Trench', before making an overnight stop at Invermere. Next morning you travel south to the early 20th century town of Fort Steele, known as Galbraith Ferry during the 1864 Kootenay Gold Rush, then to Cranbrook for a visit to the **Canadian Museum of Rail Travel** (see page 362–3). After re-boarding the train at Fort Steele you travel east to Crowsnest Lake at the top of Crowsnest Pass for a second overnight stop.

The following morning, you leave for Fort McLeod and a guided tour of Head-Smashed-In Buffalo Jump before continuing via the Lethbridge viaduct – the longest and highest bridge of its kind in the world – then on through rolling ranch country to Okotoks. A motor coach takes you to tour a show-jumping establishment at Spruce Meadows before the train returns to Calgary.

Moonlight dining excursions from Calgary to High River provide a luxurious dinner train service for groups (minimum of 20 people, maximum 22), departing mid-evening and returning late evening on most nights of the week as well as at weekends. The company also has plans for Ski Trains to the Bugaboo Mountains and other excursions into the Rocky Mountains. Contact Royal Canadian Pacific, 133 9th Avenue SW, Calgary, AB T2P 2M3; tel: 403 508 1400; web: www.cprtours.com.

Trips can also be booked through West Coast Tours (web: www.wcra.org/tours). For extended stays at one of CP's landmark hotels contact 1 800 441 1414; web: www.cpr.ca.

**The Quebec North Shore and Labrador Railroad** 100 Retty, CP1000, Sept Iles, Quebec G4R 4L5; tel: 418 968 7805; fax 418 968 7183 and Airport Road, Box 1000, Labrador City, NF A2V 2K4; tel: 709 944 8205; fax 709 944 8431. This line was originally built in the early 1950s to move iron ore from Labrador City to a port at Sept Iles on the Gulf of the St Lawrence and the line is still mainly used for freight traffic.

QNS & L trains with Dome cars leave early on Tuesday and Thursday morning from Sept Iles, and on Wednesday and Friday from Labrador City. Some trains go north from Labrador City to Schefferville. For recorded information call 418 968 7539.

**White Pass & Yukon Railway** PO Box 435, Skagway, Alaska 99840, USA; tel: 907 983 2217 or 800 343 7373; web: www.whitepassrailroad.com. A daily coach/train service operates mainly between Whitehorse and Skagway, including a steep narrow-gauge route between Skagway and Fraser. The train hugs precipitous cliffs and crosses flimsy-looking trestle bridges as it follows a route used by many thousands during the 1898 Klondike Goldrush, passing waterfalls, glaciers and tunnels carved out of solid granite. You travel in an 1890s-style coach on the train but the part of the journey between White Pass and Whitehorse is operated by motor coach. The whole journey takes four and a half hours and services run from mid-May until mid-September.

*Summit Excursions* take you from tidewater Skagway to the summit of White Pass, a climb of almost 3,000ft (900m) in only 20 miles (32km). The daily round trip takes three hours.

The *Lake Bennett Adventure* takes you a further 20 miles beyond the summit to Bennett in British Columbia, at the end of the Chilkoot Trail. A two hour layover allows you time to exploring this wonderfully scenic area and to look around the historic displays at the 1903 station. The eight and a half hour, 80 mile (124km) round trips take place each Sunday, Monday and Friday from June to August and the ticket price includes lunch.

On Saturdays from June to August there are steam train excursions on the route to Bennett, and the *Chilkoot Trail* hikers service links Bennett, Fraser and Skagway.

**Canadian Museum of Rail Travel** PO Box 400, 1 Van Horne Street, Cranbrook, BC V1C 4H9; tel: 250 489 3918; web: www.crowsnest.bc.ca/cmrt. The museum includes a beautifully restored *Trans-Canada Limited* first class sleeping car train built in 1929 for the Canadian Pacific Railway. This has 90,000 square feet (8,361m²) of inlaid mahogany and walnut panelling as well as large collections of railway china and silverware. Other trains include the 1907 Soo-Spokane *Train Deluxe*. Expansion plans will enable the museum to display five different train sets showing passenger travel between 1887 and 1955, along with heritage railway buildings such as the 1901 Elko Station. Open daily, admission.

**Elgin County Railway Museum** RR #6, St Thomas, ON, N5P 3T1; tel: 519 631 0936. Located in the 1913 Michigan Central Railway shops on

Wellington Street, the collection includes a Hudson locomotive formerly used by the Canadian National Railway on its Toronto to Montreal corridor. Other locos are displayed along with an NYC Pullman sleeper, *Cascade Lane*.

St Thomas has been an important railway town since 1856 and was known in its heyday as the 'Railway Capital of Canada'. Around 26 railway lines then passed through, including the Wabash, Père Marquette, New York Central and London & Port Stanley. Open daily, admission.

**Winnipeg Railway Museum** Box 48, 123 Main Street, Winnipeg, Manitoba R3C 1A3; tel: 204 942 4632; web: www.icenter.net/~prs. Exhibits include a Midland Railway of Manitoba snow dozer and a combine car (colonist's car) which is now the gift shop. Open Friday, Saturday and Sunday. Admission charge.

**Waterloo–St Jacobs Railway** PO Box 40103 Waterloo Square Postal Station, Waterloo, ON, N2J 4V1; tel: 519 746 1950 or 1 800 754 1054. Four round trips a day (three on Sunday) operate between Waterloo and St Jacobs, west of Toronto. Occasional excursions also go to Elmira. Trains operate daily (weekends in October and November).

**Port Stanley Terminal Rail** 309 Bridge Street, Port Stanley, ON, N5L 1C5; tel: 519 782 3730; web: www.pstr.on.ca. Operates over a seven mile (11km) section of the former London & Port Stanley Railway line between Port Stanley and St Thomas, which opened in 1856. Over 25 million passengers have travelled on the L & PS, many heading for the beach at Port Stanley – 'the Coney Island of the Great Lakes'. Steam trains operated on this route for 59 years, transporting over one million passengers in 1943 alone.

Passenger services were discontinued in 1957 and freight traffic ceased in 1982, but the line was acquired by its present owners the following year and restored by volunteers. Trains again now cross two bridges and travel the banks of Kettle Creek, where you can see apple orchards and deer as well as plants and trees unique to the north shore of Lake Erie.

**Northern Ontario Railroad Museum** Box 26, Bloor Street, Capreol, ON, P0M 1H0; tel: 705 858 5050; web: www.sympatico.ca/normhc. This unique tourist attraction shows the historical impact of railroads in the development of northern Ontario. Open daily.

**Prince George Railway & Forestry Museum** 850 River Road, Prince George, British Columbia V2L 5S8 (adjacent to Cottonwood Island Park); tel: 250 563 7351; web: www.pgrfm.bc.ca. Located on Cottonwood Island, the museum preserves rolling stock and displays the lifestyle of people involved in the railways and industrial development of central British Columbia. Open daily, admission charge.

**Alberta Railway Museum** 34 Street, Edmonton, Alberta; tel: 780 472 6229; web: www.railwaymuseum.ab.ca. The museum has more than 50 pieces of equipment, including cars and locomotives formerly owned by Canadian National and Northern Alberta Railways. The former CN St Albert depot, built in 1902, was moved to the museum grounds in 1973, complete with its station manager's office and functioning telegraph. Open from Victoria Day (the Monday preceding May 25) to Labour Day in September.

Extensive museum archives are located at the City of Edmonton Archives in the Prince of Wales Armouries Heritage Centre, 10440-108 Avenue NW, Edmonton.

On holiday long weekends in August and September, steam engine *No. 1392* pulls a passenger train. The locomotive is powered by diesel on Sundays in July and August.

**American Orient Express** 5100 Main Street, Suite 300, Downers Grove, IL 60515, USA; tel: 630 663 4550 or 1 800 320 4206 (for reservations); web: www.AmericanOrientExpress.com. Luxury blue and gold streamliner-era trains make two journeys each way in July and August between Montreal and Vancouver, following VIA Rail's *Canadian* route for most of the 3,200 mile (5,150km) trip.

The trains are a quarter mile long and consist of restored Pullman-Standard and American Car & Foundry private coaches. The observation car, a veteran of the famed *Twentieth Century Limited*, has a horseshoe bar, a bay window and splendid mahogany woodwork. Expert lecturers and local guides are on board and prices range from $3,990 to $7,290. For more details of *American Orient Express* services and routes see Chapter 2 (page 15).

**Okanagan Valley Wine Train** 11830 Kingsway Avenue, Edmonton, AB, T5G 0X5 (tel: 888 674 8725 in Edmonton, 250 712 9888 in Kelowna); web: www.okanaganwinetrain.com. Trains are operated by Funtrain Canada Inc on tracks belonging to the Canadian National Railway and make six hour excursions through the lush wine and orchard country of British Columbia's Okanagan Valley. The restored vintage coaches are the last surviving rolling stock of the *Super Continental* that operated across Canada in the 1950s and 1960s.

Trains start out from 600 Recreation Avenue in Kelowna and travel north along the shores of Duck, Wood and Kalamalka Lakes, stopping at the historic 1911 station in Vernon before reaching the final destination of Armstrong. Services operate from Wednesday to Sunday between late June and the beginning of September.

**Salem & Hillsborough** 2487 Main Street, Hillsborough, NB, E4H 2X7; tel: 506 734 3195; web: www.shrr.ca. Excursion trains operate over an 11 miles (18km) round trip mostly on Sunday afternoons from mid-June to Labour Day. Foliage specials operate in the fall and dinner trains several times a year. The superb ex-Canadian National steam engine displayed outside the museum was steamed up for the 1998 movie *Paradise Siding*.

**Pacific Wilderness Railway** 1208 Wharf Street, Unit 206, Victoria, BC, V8W 3B9; tel: 250 381 8600 or 1 800 267 0610. Vintage 1950s diesel-electric locomotives pull 1930s open-air coaches with rich, wood-lined interiors and air-conditioned cars from the 1950s. The luxurious first class parlour car dates from 1928.

Trains operate on a two and a half hour round trip from downtown Victoria to the summit of Malahat mountain or a two hour trip that crosses the Arbutus Trestle (247ft/75m high) and the Niagara Canyon Trestle (298ft/91m high). Both trestles are over 400ft/120m long. The railway plans soon to operate using a steam engine and will run between Victoria and Nanaimo over tracks of the former Esquimault & Nanaimo Railway, opened to paying passengers in 1886.

The E & N was the culmination of the railway line promised to join Canadian provinces from east to west. The current narrated tours take place from mid-June to mid-September and on weekends in October.

No passenger trains operate in the Northwest Territories.

### Further reading
The *Trans-Canada Rail Guide* by Melissa Graham (Trailblazer Publications 1996) gives further detailed information about the trans-Canadian services.

## STEAM TRAINS IN CANADA
### The Royal Hudson
British Columbia Rail runs regular *Royal Hudson* steam excursions from its station in North Vancouver (see page 358).

### Alberni Pacific
Operates at weekends and holidays in July and August along the waterfront from downtown Port Alberni to the McLean Hill National Historic Site, which has a 1926 steam sawmill among its 30 preserved buildings. The trip takes about 35 minutes to wind through a forested valley after starting out from a restored 1912 Canadian Pacific station.

The engine is a 1929 Baldwin ex-logging locomotive and the passenger cars are three converted Canadian National transfer cabooses, one of which is open-air. The railway is located on Kingsway at Argyle Street near the Harbour Quay in Port Alberni.

Mail address: Alberni Valley Heritage Network, The Station, Site 125 C14 5633, A Smith Road, Port Alberni, BC, V9Y 7L5; tel: 250 723 1376; web: www.alberniheritage.com.

### Alberta Prairie Railway
Between May and mid-October the Alberta Prairie Railway operates steam train rides lasting up to eight hours through central Alberta, complete with staged robberies by the 'Bolton gang'. Different theme trains run throughout the season and an Alberta roast beef dinner is usually included in the fare. A 1920 Baldwin Consolidation locomotive hauls vintage Canadian Northern

and Canadian National coaches, including an open-air car and the Lone Star Saloon.

Trains travel through Big Valley, the divisional point for the Canadian Northern Railway in the early 1900s when this was a thriving mining centre. Only a few hundred people now live in a community that once numbered 5,000. The restored 1912 station has photographs, blueprints of the gold mine and a complete station master's office.

Contact Alberta Prairie Railway Excursions, PO Box 1600, Stettler, AB T0C 2L0; tel: 403 742 2811 in Stettler, 403 290 0980 in Calgary; web: www.absteamtrain.com.

### East Kootenay

Trains travel through the grounds of Fort Steele Heritage Park in British Columbia, climbing a double loop track to give wonderful views from the Kootenay River lookout point. Locomotive *No. 077* featured in the Jackie Chan movie *Shanghai Noon*.

East Kootenay trains run daily from mid-May to mid-October. Mail address: Fort Steele Heritage Town, 9851 Highway 93/95, Fort Steele, BC, V0B 1N0; tel: 250 417 6000; web: http://fortsteele.bc.ca.

### Hull–Chelsea–Wakefield

A five-hour journey of 36 miles (57km) from Hull, Quebec, taking you through the forests of the Gatineau Hills, Chelsea and Farm Point. Tour guides describe the line's history and trains make a two-hour stop at the pretty village of Wakefield. The 1907 Swedish locomotive, weighing 93 tons, is revolved on Wakefield's hand-cranked turntable and filled at the water-tower.

Daily in July and August; otherwise mostly Tue, Wed and weekends from May to October. Mail address: 165 Deveault Street, Hull, PQ J8Z 1S7; tel: 819 778 7246 or 800 871 7246; fax 819 778 5007; web: www.steamtrain.ca.

### Kamloops Heritage Railway

Currently in the final stages of restoration of the former Canadian National steam locomotive *No. 2141*. Mail address: PO Box 3002, Kamloops, BC, V2C 6B7; tel: 250 374 2141; web: www.kamloopsheritagerailway.com.

### Kettle Valley

Contact the Kettle Valley Heritage Society, 18404 Bathville Road, PO Box 1288, Summerland, BC V0H 1Z0 (tel: 877 494 8424 or 250 494 8422) for details of steam excursions on the Kettle Valley Railway between Summerland in British Columbia and the Trout Creek Bridge. Journeys are two and a half miles (4km) each way, and there are plans to extend operations west to Faulder and east to Penticon, using a Lima locomotive on loan from the British Columbia Forest Museum in Duncan. Operates from May to October. Web: www.kettlevalleyrail.org.

## Prairie Dog Central

The splendid Canadian Pacific engine is the oldest (1882) regularly scheduled operating steam locomotive in North America. This or a vintage diesel takes early 20th century wooden coaches from Inkster Junction in Winnipeg for a two and a half hour, 35-mile (54km) trip over a Canadian National Railways route to Warren, Manitoba, with a stop at Grosse Isle. Other historic Canadian National locomotives are on display in Winnipeg.

Operates on Sunday from May to September. Mail address: The Vintage Locomotive Society Inc, PO Box 33021, RPO Polo Park, Winnipeg, Manitoba R3G 3N4; tel: 204 832 5259; web: www.vintagelocomotivesociety.mb.ca/ index.htm.

## South Simcoe

Based in Tottenham, Ontario, the railway uses a former Canadian Pacific steam engine dating from the 1890s to haul 1920s vintage cars over part of the former Canadian National line between Tottenham and Beeton. Departures are from South Simcoe station at Mill Street West in Tottenham, where there is a museum and freight shed gift shop. This old branch line once connected Hamilton with the shipping ports of Borrie and Collingwood.

Mostly Sun to Wed from May until October. Mail address: PO Box 186, Tottenham, ON, L0G 1W0; tel: 905 936 5815; web: www.steamtrain.com.

Steam trains also operate at:

**Heritage Park Historical Village** 1900 Heritage Drive SW, Calgary, AB T2V 2X3; tel: 403 259 1900.
**Fort Edmonton Park** PO Box 2359, Edmonton, AB T5J 2R7; tel: 780 496 8787. A Lima locomotive (*#2024*) has been saved from the scrap heap and restored to take a passenger train from Midnapore station. Open between May and September.
**British Columbia Forest Museum** 2892 Drinkwater Road, RR #4, Trans Canada Highway, Duncan, BC V9L 3W8.
**Canadian Railway Museum** 120 St Pierre Street, Saint-Constant, PQ J5A 2G9; tel: 450 632 2410; web: www.exporail.org.

## MEASUREMENTS AND CONVERSIONS

| To convert | Multiply by |
|---|---|
| Inches to centimetres | 2.54 |
| Centimetres to inches | 0.3937 |
| Feet to metres | 0.3048 |
| Metres to feet | 3.281 |
| Yards to metres | 0.9144 |
| Metres to yards | 1.094 |
| Miles to kilometres | 1.609 |
| Kilometres to miles | 0.6214 |
| Acres to hectares | 0.4047 |
| Hectares to acres | 2.471 |
| Imperial gallons to litres | 4.546 |
| Litres to imperial gallons | 0.22 |
| US gallons to litres | 3.785 |
| Litres to US gallons | 0.264 |
| Ounces to grams | 28.35 |
| Grams to ounces | 0.03527 |
| Pounds to grams | 453.6 |
| Grams to pounds | 0.002205 |
| Pounds to kilograms | 0.4536 |
| Kilograms to pounds | 2.205 |
| British tons to kilograms | 1016.0 |
| Kilograms to British tons | 0.0009812 |
| US tons to kilograms | 907.0 |
| Kilograms to US tons | 0.000907 |

5 imperial gallons are equal to 6 US gallons
A British ton is 2,240 lbs. A US ton is 2,000 lbs.

### Temperature conversion table
The bold figures in the central columns can be read as either centigrade or fahrenheit.

| °C | | °F | °C | | °F |
|---|---|---|---|---|---|
| −18 | 0 | 32 | 10 | 50 | 122 |
| −15 | 5 | 41 | 13 | 55 | 131 |
| −12 | 10 | 50 | 16 | 60 | 140 |
| −9 | 15 | 59 | 18 | 65 | 149 |
| −7 | 20 | 68 | 21 | 70 | 158 |
| −4 | 25 | 77 | 24 | 75 | 167 |
| −1 | 30 | 86 | 27 | 80 | 176 |
| 2 | 35 | 95 | 32 | 90 | 194 |
| 4 | 40 | 104 | 38 | 100 | 212 |
| 7 | 45 | 113 | 40 | 104 | 219 |

# Appendix

## THE INTERNET

The Internet is an increasingly popular and useful source of up-to-date travel information which you can use to make reservations, check timetables, purchase tickets and keep in touch with people at home (see On-line communications, page 41). Some of the most useful websites for those intending to travel by train are as follows:

## For the USA

**Amtrak** A comprehensive, award-winning site. Web: www.amtrak.com

**USA by Rail** Up-to-date information and tips from other travellers. Web: www.usa-by-rail.com

**Amtrak California** Fare promotions, maps and a quarterly ezine. Web: www.amtrakcalifornia.com

**Amtrak Cascades** For travel between Eugene, Oregon, and Vancouver in Canada. Web: www.wsdot.wa.gov/amtrak

**Coast Starlight** Free gifts and historic Parlor cars. Web: www.coaststarlight.com

**Amtrak Capitol Corridor** For southern California. Web: www.amtrakcapitols.com

**Texas Eagle** Full information for *Texas Eagle* country. Web: www.texaseagle.com

**Friends of Amtrak** An internet advocacy supporting funding for Amtrak. Web: http://trainweb.com/crocon/amtrak

**Amtrak Unlimited** One of the best Amtrak information sources. Web: www.amtraktrains.com

**Amtrak/Passenger Railroad** For travellers, railfans and railroaders. Web: www.trainweb.com/amtrak

**Trainweb** Masses of information about North American trains. Web: www.trainweb.com

**National Rail Page** Lists all national and international rail web sites. Web: www.rrhistorical.com

**Railwaystation** An online community with free stuff for railfans. Web: www.railwaystation.com

**CPRR Photographic History Museum** Stereoviews, engravings, maps, and documents illustrating the history of the Central Pacific Railroad. Web: http://cprr.org

**Railfan** Pictures of trains and other railroad subjects. Web: http://bfcase.railfan.net

**The Railfan Network** By railfans for railfans. Web: www.railfan.net

**RailServe** Over 3,500 rail-related links, forums, railfan chat rooms and more. Web: www.railserve.com

**Riding the Rails** The true story of the boxcar boys and girls of the Great Depression. Web: www.erroluys.com

**RailCenter** News, photos and links for railfans. Web: www.railcenter.com

**Alaska Railroad** Operates out of Anchorage. Web: www.akrr.com
**American Orient Express** Travel in luxury over legendary railway routes. Web: www.travelpower.com/aoe
**Grand Canyon** A steam railway built by the Atchison Topeka & Santa Fe company. Web: www.thetrain.com
**Web Union Station** Tourist railroads and train museums. Web: www.webunionstation.com
**Market Station** An information depot. Web: www.marketstation.com
**Great American Station Foundation** Dedicated to preserving and improving stations. Web: www.stationfoundation.org
**National Association of Railroad Passengers** (NARP) Join and help save the trains. Web: www.narprail.org
**Green Frog Productions** Video, audio and CDs about trains. Web: www.greenfrog.com
**The Railroad Press** Railroad magazine and books with exceptional photography. Web: www.alco628.com
**Railserve Music Page** Links to all kinds of railroad songs. Web: www.railserve.com/music
**Visit USA** General tips and information. Web: www.visitusa.org/index.html
**USA Tourist** The latest tourist developments. Web: www.usatourist.com
**City Net** Advice and information across the USA. Web: www.city.net
**USA Citylink** More about US cities. Web: www.USAcitylink.com

## For Canada
**VIA Rail** Download the latest timetables and request brochures. Web: www.viarail.ca
**British Columbia Rail** Web: www.bcrail.com
**The Rocky Mountaineer** Perhaps the most spectacular train route in North America. Web: www.rkymtnrail.com
**Ontario Northland** From Toronto to the Arctic Circle. Web: www.ontc.on.ca
**Algoma Central** An unofficial web site. Web: www.trainweb.org/algoma
**White Pass & Yukon Railway** Web: www.whitepassrailroad.com
**Discover Canada** General information. Web: www.DiscoverCanada.com
**Canada on City.Net** Web: www.city.net/countries/canada
The official **Canadian government** site is at www.infocan.gc.ca
**Parks Canada** For national parks and heritage sites. Web: www.parkscanada.pch.gc.ca
**Canadian Heritage** Museums and galleries throughout the country. Web: www.chin.gc.ca

## General
**The Cybercafé Search Engine** Lists 2,000 cybercafés in 125 countries. Web: http://cybercaptive.com
**Roadnews** Everything you need to stay connected while travelling. Web: www.roadnews.com
**iAgora** Includes a good selection of links. Web: www.iagora.com
**1travel.com** For airfares and accommodation worldwide. Web: www.1travel.com
**Budget Travel** For travellers of modest means. Web: www.budgettravel.com
**CNN Travel Guide** Travel news and booking information. Web: www.cnn.com/TRAVEL
**Currency Converter** Conversions for 200 different currencies. Web: www.oanda.com/converter/travel

**Electronic Embassy Page** Includes all foreign embassies in the USA. Web: www.embassy.org/embassies

**Epicurious Traveler** Budget travel and discussion forums. Web: http://travel.epicurious.com

**Expedia** For transatlantic flights and much else. Web: www.expedia.co.uk

**EXES Travel Search Engine** Search travel related pages. Web: www.exes.com

**Globetrotters Club** For independent travellers. Web: www.bigfoot.com/~globetrotters

**GoAbroad Home Page** Alternative travel with information on studying and living abroad. Web: www.goabroad.com

**Hostelling International** The 'Worldwide Hostels' section lists hostels in 75 countries. Web: www.iyhf.org

**Internet Guide to Hostelling** One of the largest directories of hostels in the world. Web: www.hostels.com

**Journeywoman Online** Mainly for women travellers. Web: www.journeywoman.com

**Kasbah Travel Information** A search engine with 100,000 sites listed. Web: www.kasbah.com

**Le Travel Store** For travel gear and publications. Web: www.letravelstore.com

**Net News for the Thrifty Traveler** Websites helpful to budget travellers. Web: www.thriftytraveling.org

**Shoestring Travel** Information for budget travellers. Web: www.stratpub.com

**Unet Traveller** Excellent information and resources. Web: www.traveller.eu.net

**Maps** are available at www.pathfinder.com and www.mapquest.com

# Appendix

## USEFUL ADDRESSES
### USA, general
**American Bed & Breakfast Association** PO Box 1387, Midlothian, VA 23113.

**American Hotel Association** Suite 600, 1201 New York Ave, Washington, DC 20005-391; tel: 202 289 3100

**American Youth Hostels** 733 15th Street NW, Suite 840, Washington, DC 20005; tel: 202 783 6161; fax: 202 783 6171; web: www.hiayh.org

**Amtrak Customer Relations Office** 400 N Capitol Street, NW, Washington, DC 20001

**BA Travel Shops** 156 Regent Street, London W1R 6LB; tel: 0845 606 0747 or call telephone sales, 24 hours a day, on 0345 222111; fax 020 7434 4636; web: www.british-airways.com

**Bed & Breakfast in the USA & Canada** Home Base Holidays, 7 Park Avenue, London N13 5PG; tel: 020 8886 8752; fax: 020 8482 4258; web: www.homebase-hols.com

**Bed & Breakfast National Network** PO Box 4616, Springfield, MA 01101; tel: 1 800 884 4288; fax: 401 847 7309; web: www.tnn4bnb.com

**Bed & Breakfast Registry** PO Box 80174, St Paul, MN 55108

**BUNAC** 16 Bowling Green Lane, London EC1R 0QH; tel: 020 7251 3472; email: enquiries@bunac.org.uk; web: www.bunac.org

**Camp America** 37 Queens Gate, London SW7 5HR; tel: 020 7581 7373; fax: 020 7581 7377

**Council Travel** 28A Poland Street, London W1V 3DB; tel: 020 7287 3337 and 205 East 42nd Street, New York, NY 10017; tel: 212 822 2700; web: www.ciee.org/travel/index.htm

**Globespan** Colinton House, 10 West Mill Road, Colinton, Edinburgh EH13 0NX; tel: 0990 561 525; web: www.globespan.com

**Great Rail Journeys** Saviour House, 9 St Saviourgate, York YO1 8NL; tel: 01904 521900; fax: 01904 521905; email: grj@greatrail.com; web: greatrail.com
Offers escorted tours across the USA by rail but cannot arrange tailor-made or ticket-only requests.

**The Great Train Store Company** 14180 Dallas Parkway, Suite 618, Dallas, TX 75240; tel: 214 392 1599

**Greyhound International** PO Box 660362, Dallas, TX 75266-0362; tel: 1 800 229 9424; web: www.greyhound.com

**Hostel Handbook for the USA & Canada** 722 Saint Nicholas Avenue, New York, NY 10031; tel: 212 926 7030; fax 212 9283 0108; web: www.hostelhandbook.com

**Hostelling International (AYH)** 733 15th Street, NW, Suite 840, Washington, DC 20005; tel: 202 783 6161; web: www.hiayh.org

**National Association of Railroad Passengers** 900 2nd Street, NE, #308, Washington, DC 20002; tel: 202 408 8362; web: www.narprail.org

**National Park Service** 1849 C Street NW, Washington, DC 20240; tel: 202 208 6843; web: www.nps.gov

**Pentrex** PO Box 94911, Pasadena, California 91109-4911; tel: 1 800 950 9333; web: www.pentrex.com

**Rail Travel Center** 2 Federal Street, St Albans, Vermont 05478-2035; tel: 1 802 527 1788 or 1 800 458 5394

**Tourist House Association of America** PO Box 355-AA, Greentown, PA 18426; tel: 570 676 3222

**Travel Industry Association of America** 1100 New York Avenue, NW, Suite 450, Washington, DC 20005-3934; tel: 202 408 8422

**United Airlines** PO Box 66100, Chicago, IL 60666; tel: 1 800 589 5582; web: www.ual.com

**US Embassy** 24 Grosvenor Square, London W1A 1AE. Visa information tel: 01891 200 290

**US Immigration and Naturalisation** 425 I Street NW, Washington, DC 20536; tel: 202 307 1501; web: www.ins.usdoj.gov

**US Customs Service** 1300 Pennsylvania Ave NW, Washington, DC 20229; tel: 202 927 5580; web: www.customs.ustreas.gov

**Youth Hostels Association** Trevelyan House, 8 St Stephen's Hill, St Albans, Hertfordshire AL1 2DY; tel: 01727 845 047

**YMCA International** 224 E 47th Street, New York, NY 10017; tel: 212 308 2899; fax: 212 308 3161; web: www.ymca.int

**YWCA National Council** 726 Broadway, New York, NY 10003; tel: 212 614 2700

## Canada, general

**Canada Customs and Excise** 2265 St Laurent Blvd, Ottawa, ON K1G 4K3; tel: 1 800 461 9999; fax: 613 991 9062; web: www.rc.gc.ca

**Canada Customs** c/o Revenue Canada, Mission of Canada to the European Union, Avenue de Tervuren 2, Brussels 1040, Belgium; tel: 00 322 741 0670; fax: 00 322 741 0694

**Canadian High Commission** Canada House, Trafalgar Square, London SW1Y 5BJ; tel: 020 7258 6600

**Canadian High Commission Immigration Division** 38 Grosvenor Street, London W1K 4AA; tel: 020 7258 6600 or 09068 616 644

**Canadian Tourist Office** Macdonald House, 1 Grosvenor Square, London W1X 0AB; tel: 020 7258 6600

**Canadian Airlines International** 23-59 Staines Road, Hounslow, Middlesex TW3 3HE; tel: 020 8577 7722 in London and 0345 7616767 in other areas; fax: 020 7814 1828; web: www.cdnair.ca

**Canadian Pacific Hotels** 62-65 Trafalgar Square, London WC2N 5DY; tel: 020 7389 1126; web: www.cphotels.ca

**CN North America** 935 de la Gauchetière Street West, Montreal, QC H3B 2M9; tel: 514 399 5430

**Hostelling International-Canada** 400–205 Catherine Street, Ottawa, Ontario ON K2P 1C3; tel: 613 237 7884; email: info@hostellingintl.ca; web: www.hihostels.ca

**Hotel Association of Canada** Suite 1016, 130 Albert Street, Ottawa, Ontario ON K1P 5G4; tel: 613 237 7149; web: www.hotels.ca

**Globespan** Colinton House, 10 West Mill Road, Colinton, Edinburgh EH13 0NX; tel: 0131 441 1388 or 0990 561 522 (for reservations); web: www.globespan.com
**Stay'n Save Inns** PO Box 760, Victoria, BC, Canada V8W 2R5; tel: 1 800 663 0298 or 604 273 3311 (outside North America); fax: 604 273 9522; web: www.staynsave.com. Hotels in Vancouver and elsewhere in British Columbia, with rates from Cdn$69.
**VIA Rail Canada Inc** PO Box 8116, Station A, Montreal, QC H3C 3N3; tel: 1 800 561 3949; web: www.viarail.ca
**Visit Canada Centre** PO Box 5396, Northampton NN1 2FA; tel: 0906 871 5000; fax: 0870 165 5665; web: www.travelcanada.ca

## USA state tourism offices

**Alabama** 401 Adams Avenue, Suite 126, PO Box 4927, Montgomery, AL, 36103-4927; tel: 1 800 ALABAMA; web: www.touralabama.org
**Alaska** PO Box 110801, Juneau, AK, 99811-0801; tel: 1 800 862 5275; web: www.dced.state.ak.us/tourism
**Arizona** Suite 4015, 2702 N 3rd Street, Phoenix, AZ, 85009; tel: 1 888 520 3433; web: www.arizonaguide.com
**Arkansas** One Capitol Mall, Little Rock, AR, 72201; tel: 1 800 NATURAL; web: www.arkansas.com
**California** PO Box 1499, Sacramento, CA, 95812; tel: 1 800 GO CALIF; web: http://gocalif.ca.gov
**Colorado** 1625 Broadway, Ste 1700, Denver, CO, 80202; tel: 1 303 892 3885; web: www.colorado.com
**Connecticut** 505 Hudson Street, Hartford, CT, 06106; tel: 1 860 270 8080 or 1 800 CT BOUND; web: www.tourism.state.ct
**Delaware** 99 Kings Highway, Dover, DE, 19901; tel: 1 302 739 4271; web: www.visitdelaware.com
**Florida** Suite 300, 661 East Jefferson Street, Tallahassee, FL, 32301; tel: 850 488 5607; web: www.flausa.com
**Georgia** Tower 2, Suite 1100, 285 Peachtree Center Avenue, NE, Atlanta, GA, 30303; tel: 1 800 VISIT GA; web: www.georgia.org/tourism
**Idaho** 700 West State Street, PO Box 83720, Boise, ID, 83720-0093; tel: 1 800 635 5240; web: www.visitid.org
**Illinois** Bureau of Tourism, State of Illinois Ctr, 100 West Randolph, Ste 3-400, Chicago, IL, 60602; tel: 1 800 2 CONNECT; web: www.enjoyillinois.com
**Indiana** Suite 700, One North Capitol, Indianapolis, IN, 46204-2288; tel: 1 317 232 8860; web: www.enjoyindiana.com
**Iowa** 200 East Grand Avenue, Des Moines, IA, 50309; tel: 1 515 242 4705; web: www.state.ia.us/tourism
**Kansas** Suite 1100, 1000 SW Jackson St, Topeka, KS, 66612-1354; tel: 1 785 296 2009; web: www.travelks.com
**Kentucky** PO Box 211, Dept WWW, Frankfort, KY, 40602; tel: 1 800 225 TRIP; web: www.kentuckytourism.com
**Louisiana** 1051 North Third Street, Rm 313, PO Box 94291, Baton Rouge, LA, 70804-9291; tel: 1 800 334 8626; web: www.louisianatravel.com
**Maine** PO Box 2300, 325-B Water Street, Hallowell, ME, 04347-2300; tel: 1 800 533 9595; web: www.mainetourism.com
**Maryland** 9th Floor, 217 East Redwood Street, Baltimore, MD, 21202; tel: 1 410 767 3400; web: www.mdisfun.org

**Massachusetts** State Transportation Building, 10 Park Plaza, Suite 4510, Boston, MA, 02116; tel: 1 800 227 MASS; web: www.massvacation.com

**Michigan** PO Box 30226, Lansing, MI, 48909; tel: 1 888 78 GREAT; web: www.michigan.org

**Minnesota** 100 Metro Square, 121 Seventh Place East, St. Paul, MN, 55101; tel: 1 800 657 3700; web: www.exploreminnesota.com

**Mississippi** PO Box 849, 550 High Street, 1100 Walter Sillers Building, Jackson, MS, 39205; tel: 1 800 WARMEST; web: www.visitmississippi.org

**Missouri** PO Box 1055, Jefferson City, Truman State Office Bldg, MO, 65102; tel: 573 751 4133 or 1 800 810 5500; web: www.missouritourism.com

**Montana** PO Box 200533, 1424 Ninth Avenue, Helena, MT, 59620-0533; tel: 1 800 VISIT MT; web: http://visitmt.com

**Nebraska** PO Box 98907, Lincoln, NE, 68509-8907; tel: 1 800 228 4307; web: www.visitnebraska.org

**Nevada** 401 North Carson Street, Carson City, NV, 89701-0000; tel: 1 800 NEVADA 8; web: www.travelnevada.com

**New Hampshire** PO Box 1856, Concord, NH, 03302-1856; tel: 1 800 FUN IN NH; web: www.visitnh.gov

**New Jersey** PO Box 820, 20 West State Street, Trenton, NJ, 08625; tel: 1 800 VISIT NJ; web: www.state.nj.us/travel

**New Mexico** PO Box 2002, Lamy Building, 491 Old Santa Fe Trail, Santa Fe, NM, 87501; tel: 1 800 733 6396; web: www.newmexico.org

**New York** PO Box 2603, Albany, NY, 12220-0603; tel: 1 800 CALL NYS; web: www.iloveny.com

**North Carolina** PO Box 29571, Raleigh, NC, 27826-0571; tel: 1 800 VISIT NC; web: www.visitnc.com

**North Dakota** 604 East Boulevard Avenue, Bismarck, ND, 58505-0825; tel: 1 800 435 5663; web: www.ndtourism.com

**Ohio** PO Box 1001, Columbus, OH, 43216-1001; tel: 1 800 BUCKEYE; web: www.ohiotourism.com

**Oklahoma** Room 801, PO Box 52002, Oklahoma City, OK, 73152-2002; tel: 1 800 652 6552; web: www.travelok.com

**Oregon** 775 Summer Street, NE, Salem, OR, 97301-1282; tel: 1 800 547 7842; web: www.traveloregon.com

**Pennsylvania** Commonwealth Keystone Building, 400 North Street, Harrisburg, PA, 17120-0225; tel: 1 800 VISIT PA; web: www.experiencepa.com

**Rhode Island** One West Exchange Street, Providence, RI, 02903; tel: 1 800 556 2484; web: www.visitrhodeisland.com

**South Carolina** Suite 248, 1205 Pendleton Street, Columbia, SC, 29201-0071; tel: 803 734 1700; web: www.discoversouthcarolina.com

**South Dakota** 711 East Wells Avenue, Pierre, SD, 57501-5070; tel: 1 800 SDAKOTA; web: www.travelsd.com

**Tennessee** 320 Sixth Avenue North, Fifth Floor, Nashville, TN, 37243; tel: 1 615 741 2159; web: www.state.tn.us

**Texas** Tourism Division, PO Box 12728, Austin, TX, 78711; tel: 1 800 88 88 TEX; web: www.traveltex.com

**Utah** PO Box 147420, Salt Lake City, UT, 84114-7420; tel: 1 801 538 1030; web: www.utah.com

**Vermont** 6 Baldwin Street, Drawer 33, Montpelier, VT, 05633-1301; tel: 1 800 VERMONT; web: www.1-800-vermont.com

**Virginia** 901 East Byrd Street, Richmond, VA, 23219; tel: 1 800 VISIT VA; web: www.virginia.org

**Washington State** PO Box 42500, Olympia, WA, 98504-2500; tel: 1 800 544 1800; web: www.tourism.wa.gov

**Washington, DC** Suite 200, 1212 New York Avenue, NW, Washington, DC, 20005; tel: 1 800 422 8644; web: www.washington.org

**West Virginia** 90 MacCorkle Ave, South Charleston, WV, 25303; tel: 1 304 558 2200; web: callwva.com

**Wisconsin** 201 W Washington Avenue, PO Box 7976, Madison, WI, 53707-7976; tel: 1 800 432 8747; web: www.travelwisconsin.com

**Wyoming** 214 W 15th Street, Cheyenne, WY, 82002; tel: 1 800 225 5996; web: www.state.wyomingtourism.org

## Tourism offices in Canada

**Alberta** PO Box 2500, Edmonton, Alberta, T5J 2Z4; tel: 1 800 661 8888 or 403 427 4321

**British Columbia** Parliament Buildings, Victoria, British Columbia, V8V 1X4; tel: 1 250 387 1642; web: www.hellobc.com

**Manitoba** Department 20, 155 Carlton St, 7th Floor, Winnipeg, Manitoba, R3C 3H8; tel: 1 800 665 0040 or 204 945 3777; web: www.gov.mb.ca/itt/travel

**New Brunswick** PO Box 12345, Campbellton, New Brunswick, E3N 3T6; tel: 1 800 561 0123; web: www.tourismnewbrunswick.ca

**Newfoundland and Labrador** PO Box 8700, St John's, Newfoundland, A1B 4J6; tel: 1 800 563 6353 or 709 729 2830; web: www.gov.nf.ca/tourism

**Nova Scotia** PO Box 130, Halifax, Nova Scotia, B3J 2M7; tel: 1 800 565 0000; web: http://explorens.com

**Northwest Territories** PO Box 610, 5016 52nd St, Yellowknife, Northwest Territories, X1A 2N5; tel: 1 800 661 0788; web: www.nwtravel.nt.ca

**Ontario** Queen's Park, Toronto, Ontario, M7A 2E5; tel: 1 800 668 2746 or 416 314 0944

**Prince Edward Island** PO Box 2000, Charlottetown, Prince Edward Island, C1A 7M8; tel: 1 888 PEI PLAY or 902 368 4444; web: www.gov.pe.ca

**Quebec** CP 979, Quebec, H3C 2W3; tel: 1 514 873 2015; web: www.bonjourquebec.com

**Saskatchewan** 1922 Park St, Regina, Saskatchewan, S4P 3V7; tel: 1 877 237 2273 or 306 787 2300; web: www.sasktourism.com

**Yukon** PO Box 2703, Whitehorse, Yukon, Y1A 2C6; tel: 1 867 667 5340; web: www.touryukon.com

# Appendix

## TICKETING AGENTS
### Amtrak international sales agents

**Argentina** ASATEJ Group SRL, 835 Florida St, 3rd Floor, 829 Office, Buenos Aires, CP 1005; tel: 11 45118700

Vanguard Marketing, Buenos Aires; tel: 54 11 4328 9415

**Australia**

Asia Pacific Travel Marketing, St David's Hall, 17 Arthur St, Surry Hills, Sydney 2010; tel: 02 9319 6624; fax: 612 93194151; web: www.aptms.com.au

Destination Holidays, #3/36 Main St, Croydon; tel: 03 9725 4655

Spectrum Holidays, 127a Canterbury Rd, Blackburn South, Melbourne, Victoria; tel: 03 9877 3322

Rail Plus, Level 3, 459 Little Collins St, Melbourne, Victoria; tel: 03 9642 8644

Rail Tickets/Concorde International, 310 King St, Melbourne, Victoria; tel: 03 9920 3423

**Austria** Austria Reiseservice, Hessgasse 7, A-1010 Vienna; tel: 01 310 7441

**Bahamas** New Providence Travel, Peek Building, George St, Nassau; tel: 242 322 2548

**Barbados** Paul Foster/Travel Planners, Independence Square, Bridgetown; tel: 246 431 8900

**Belgium** Incento BV, Stationsweg 40, 1404 AP Bussum, The Netherlands; tel: 31 35 695 5111; fax: 31 35 695 5155; web: www.incento.nl

**Bermuda** Meyer Agencies Ltd, 35 Church St, Hamilton; tel: 441 292 4823

**Bolivia** Emete Ltda/Magri Turismo, Av Cap Ravelo Esq, Montevideo VR 1201, La Paz; tel: 2 317 740

**Brazil** GSA Representacoes E Turismo Ltda, Rua Nestor Pestana 125–7, Ste 71/72, São Paulo; tel: 11 257 1177

**Chile** Masterhouse, Estado 10, Piso 11, Santiago; tel: 02 633 4418; fax 56 2 639 7959

**Columbia** Travel Club, Av 19 No 109–21, Bogotá; tel: 01 623 6999

**Costa Rica** Corporación TAM, Calle 1, Av Ctl/1 Ra, San José; tel: 506 256 0276

Suvia Reps, Oficentro Ejecutivo, La Sabana, San José; tel: 506 232 8813.

**Croatia** Mediteran International doo, Kosovelova 2, SI 6320 Portoroz; tel: 3865 67 10 777

**Denmark** Scandinavian Cruise Center, Strandvejen 6, 2100 Copenhagen; tel: 45 39 27 78 00

**Dominican Republic** Turinter, Leopoldo Navarro 4, Santo Domingo; tel: 809 682 4700

**Ecuador** Klein Rep, Ave. Shyris 1000 y Holanda, Quito; tel: 2 265 527

**Finland** Finland Travel Bureau, Kaivokatu 10A, Helsinki; tel: 09 182 6264

**France** Voyageurs du Monde, 55 rue Sainte-Anne, Paris; tel: 01 4286 1730

**Germany** MESO Amerika-Kanada Reisen, Wilmersdorfer Str 94, Berlin; tel: 0180 525 4350

CRD International, North America Travel House, Fleethof, Stadthausbrucke 1–3, 20355 Hamburg; tel: 49 40 300 6160

**Guatemala** GTM, 20 Calle 5-35 Z 10, Plaza Los Arcos, 3er Nivel, Guatemala City; tel: 2 333 6915

**Hong Kong** Travel Advisers Ltd, Rm 906, South Seas Centre, Tower 2, 75 Mody Rd, Kowloon; tel: 2 312 7138

**Hungary** Tradesco Privilege Tours, Papnovelde utc 3, Budapest 1053; tel: 361 485 0400

**India** TCI, 10 Veer Nariman Rd, Fort, Mumbai; tel: 22 202 1881

**Ireland** USIT NOW, 19/21 Aston Quay, O'Connell Bridge, Dublin 2; tel: 01 602 1600

Trailfinders, 415 Dawson St, Dublin 2; tel: 01 677 8444

Trailfinders, 42–44 Fountain St, Belfast; tel: 028 902 7188

**Israel** Tal Aviation Ltd, Migdalor Bldg, 1 Ben Yehuda St, Tel Aviv; tel: 03 795 2144

**Italy** Tabb SRL, Piazza della Republica 28, Milano; tel: 02 657 1141

also at Corso Lione 32, Torino; tel: 011 387 700, Via dei Borromeo 16, Padova; tel: 049 876 2760, and Via Boldrini 22, Bologni; tel: 051 253 538

**Japan** Travel Plaza International; tel: 03 3820 8040

HIS Co Ltd, Hotel & Rail Division, 1st Floor South Gate Building, 5-33-8 Sendagaya Shibuya-ku, Tokyo, Japan 151-0043; tel: 03 5360 4762; fax: 03 5360 4764

United Tours/Fly & Stay Center; tel: 03 5442 0622

Flex International Tours; tel: 03 5470 6164

**Korea** Hana Tour Service Inc, 11f, Hanmi Building, #1 Knogpyung-Dong Chongro-Gu, Seoul; tel: 02 725 1607

**Lithuania** West Express-Turizmo Agentura, A Stulginskio 5, 2001 Vilnius; tel: 3702 222 500

**Malaysia** Diners World Travel, 15th Floor, Meanara, Tan and Tan, 207 Jalan Tun Razak, Kuala Lumpur; tel: 03 261 3522

**Mexico** Sales Internacional SA, Río Nilo 80–501, Mexico City; tel: 5 208 0301

Asesora Publicitaria Turística, Humberto Lobo #520 G-6, Col Del Valle, Monterrey; tel: 52 8335 0384

**Netherlands** Incento BV, Stationsweg 40, 1404 AP Bussum; tel: 35 69 55 111; web: www.incento.nl

**New Zealand** World Rail/Gullivers Pacific, 5th Floor, 66 Wyndham St, Auckland; tel: 09 307 1801

Rail Plus, Level 2, 60 Parnell Rd, Parnell, Auckland; tel: 09 377 4515

**Norway** Nordmanns-Reiser A/S, Radhusgaten 23b, 0158 Oslo; tel: 22 334 530

Geotours/Nordic America Travel, PO Box 8, Sent rum, 0101 Oslo; tel: 22 825 500

NSB Reisebyra, Storingsgt 28, Oslo; tel: 23 151 600

**Pakistan** Columbus Travel, Altaf Hussain Rd, New Chali; tel: 21 236 2308

**Panama** Margo Tours, Calle 51, Bella Vista 24, Panama City; tel: 507 264 4001

**Paraguay** The Ritz Travel, Herrerra 195, Asunción; tel: 21 448 290

**Peru** Lima Reps SA, Av Benavides, 1180 Miraflores, Lima; tel: 14 444 3934

**Singapore** Diners World Travel, 7500 E Beach Rd, The Plaza; tel: 65 292 5522

**Slovenia** Mediteran International doo, Kosovelova 2, SI 6320, Portoroz; tel: 05 67 10 777

**South Africa** World Travel Agency, 8th Floor, Evrite House, 20 De Korte St, Braamfontein, Johannesburg; tel: 011 403 2638

**Spain** Expomundo, Enrique Gardael, Poncela 6, Madrid; tel: 91 780 1253. Also at Diputación, 238, Barcelona; tel: 93 412 5956

**Sweden** Scandinavian Cruise Center, Strandvejen 6, 2100 Copenhagen; tel: 45 3927 7800

**Switzerland** Kuoni Travel Ltd, Neue Hard 7, Neugasse 231, Zurich; tel: 01 277 4580
Hotelplan, Habsburgstrasse 9, Zurich; tel: 01 277 8111
SSR-Reisen, Ankerstrasse 112, Zurich; tel: 01 297 1111
ITV Imholz/Travac, Birmensdorferstrasse 108, Zurich; tel: 01 455 4423. Also at 25 rue
de Monthoux, Geneva; tel: 022 909 7810
Sky Tours Ltd, Freischutzgassel, 3021 Zurich; tel: 01 295 5885
**Taiwan** Golden Formosa Travel Services, No 142 Chung Hsiao East Rd, Sec 4, Taipei
106; tel: 02 775 1138
**Thailand** TV Air Bookings, 795 Silom Rd, Bangkok; tel: 02 233 5160
**United Arab Emirates** Al Tayer Travel, B-65 Sheikh Rashid Building, Al Maktoum
St, Dubai; tel: 4 236 000
**United Kingdom**
Additional tickets locations are available throughout the UK. Check with your local
travel agent.
Leisurail, PO Box 5, 12 Coningsby Rd, Peterborough PE3 8XP; tel: 0870 750 0222; fax:
0870 750 0333
Destination Group, 14 Greville St, London; tel: 020 7400 7099
Trailfinders Ltd, 215 Kensington High St, London W8 6BD; tel: 0207 937 5400
Trailfinders Ltd, 58 Deansgate, Manchester M3 2FF; tel: 0161 839 6969
Trailfinders Ltd, 48 Corn St, Bristol BS1 1HQ; tel: 0117 929 9000
Trailfinders Ltd, 22–24 The Priory, Queensway, Birmingham B4 6BS; tel: 0121 236
1234
Trailfinders Ltd, 254–284 Sauchiehall St, Glasgow G2 3EH; tel: 0141 353 2224
Trailfinders Ltd, 7–9 Ridley Place, Newcastle upon Tyne NE1 8JQ; tel: 0191 261 2345
**Venezuela** Tur V Special Tours, Avenida Francisco de Miranda, Caracas; tel: 2 264
6466

# VIA Rail international sales agents
**Argentina** Vanguard Marketing, Marcelo T De Alvear, 976-3ro K, C1058 AA, Buenos
Aires; tel: 54 11 4328 2563; web: www.vanguardmarketing.com
**Australia** Asia Pacific Travel Marketing, St David's Hall, 17 Arthur St, Surry Hills,
Sydney, NSW 2010; tel: 612 9319 6624; fax: 612 9319 4151; web: www.aptms.com.au
**Austria** Gateway Touristic, Stadplatz 37, A-3400 Klosternneuburg; tel: 011 43 2243 25570
**Brazil** South Marketing International, Av Franklin Roosevelt, 194/505, 20021-120 Rio
de Janeiro; tel: 55021 532 7119
**Denmark** My planet, Noerregade 51, 7500 Holstebro; tel: 97 42 5000; web:
www.benns.com
**France** Express Conseil, 5 bis, rue du Louvre, 75001 Paris; tel: 1 4477 8794; fax: 1 4260
0545
**Germany** Canada Reise Dienst, Rathausplatz 2, 22926 Ahrensburg/Hamburg; tel: 49 40
300 6160; web: www.crd.de
**Hong Kong** Japan Travel Bureau, Room UG305, UG 3rd Floor, Chinachem Golden
Plaza, 77 Mody Rd, Tsimshatsui East, Kowloon; tel: 852 2734 9288
**Israel** TAL Aviation Ltd, 26a Ben Yehuda St, Tel Aviv 63801; tel: 972 3795 2144
**Italy** Kuoni Gastaldi Tours, Mura di S Chiara 1, 16128 Genova; tel: 39 10 59 991, web:
www.kuonigastaldi.it
**Japan** Japan Travel Bureau, 1-6-4 Marunouchi, Chiyoda-ku, Tokyo 100 005; tel: 03
3820 8011
**Korea** Seoul Travel Service Ltd, 5th Floor, Jaeneung Building, 192-11, 1-Ka Ulchiro,
Chung-Ku, Seoul 100-191; tel: 02 755 1144; fax: 02 753 9076; web: www.railpass.co.kr

**Netherlands** Incento BV, PO Box 1067, 1400 BB Bussum; tel: 035 695 5111; fax: 035 695 5155; web: www.incento.nl

**New Zealand** Discover Holidays – Greyhound International, Suite 5A, 1 Montrose Terrace, Private Bag, Mairangi Bay, Auckland 1310; tel: 64 9 479 6555; fax 64 9 479 7525

**Singapore** Travel Pte Ltd, Diners World, 7500 E Beach Rd, #02–201, The Plaza, Singapore 199595; tel: 292 5522; fax: 294 1863; web:dinertravel.com.sg

**Spain** Expomundo, Diputación 238, 3e, 08007 Barcelona; tel: 34 934 12 5956

**Sweden** Tour Canada of Sweden, Box 268, 651 07 Karlstad; tel: 46 5455 6026; fax: 46 5453 2300; web: www.tourcanada.se

**Switzerland** Tui Suisse Ltd (Imholz), Birmensdorferstrasse 108, CH-8036 Zurich; tel: 41 1455 4470; fax: 41 1455 4470; web: www.imholz.ch

**United Kingdom** Leisurail, PO Box 5, 2 Coningsby Rd, Peterborough PE3 8XP; tel: 0870 750 0222; fax: 0870 750 0333; web: www.leisurail.co.uk

**USA** Amtrak, Union Station, 60 Massachusetts Av NE, Washington, DC 20002; tel: 202 906 3000; web: www.amtrak.com

Bradt Travel Guides is a partner to the new 'know before you go' campaign, recently launched by the UK Foreign and Commonwealth Office. By combining the up-to-date advice of the FCO with the in-depth knowledge of Bradt authors, you'll ensure that your trip will be as trouble-free as possible.

**www.fco.gov.uk/knowbeforeyougo**

# Appendix 4

## FURTHER READING
It is obviously impossible to produce any sort of comprehensive reading list on countries so vast as the USA and Canada, and all the more so when they also have such a rich and extensive cultural and literary history of their own. The following suggestions, however, may be of help in providing further information on topics likely to interest rail travellers and those new to North America.

## USA
### Railways
*The Story of American Railroads*, by Stewart H Holbrook (Crown Publishers)
*North America's Great Railroads*, by Thomas York (Brompton Books)
*Encyclopaedia of North American Railroads*, by Aaron E Klein (Bison)
*From Sea to Shining Sea*, by Gavin Young (Hutchinson)
*Making Tracks: An American Odyssey*, by Terry Pindell (Henry Holt)
*Landmarks on the Iron Road*, by William D Middleton (Indiana University Press)
*Historical Atlas of American Railroads*, by John H Stover (Routledge)
*The American Railroad*, by Joe Welsh (Motorbooks International)
*Full Steam Ahead: The Race to Build a Transcontinental Railroad*, by Rhoda Blumberg (National Geographic)
*The Historical Guide to North American Railroads*, by George H Drury (Kalmbach)
*Iron Horses to Promontory*, by Gerald M Best (Golden West Books)
*Donner Pass: Southern Pacific's Sierra Crossing*, by John R Signor (Golden West Books)
*Makin' Tracks*, by Lyn Rhodes Mayer (Praeger)
*Stevens Pass: The Story of Railroading and Recreation in the North Cascades*, by JoAnn Roe (The Mountaineers)
*Empire Express*, by David Howard Bain (Viking)
*Death of the Iron Horse*, by Paul Goble (Aladdin)
*Walt Disney's Railroad Story*, by Michael Broggie (Pentrex)
*Great American Railroad Stations*, by Janet Greenstein Potter (Preservation Press)
*The American Railroad Passenger Car*, by John H White Jr (Johns Hopkins University Press)
*Dining by Rail: A History*, by Ralph W Hidy (Harvard Business School)
*American Steam Locomotive*, by Brian Solomon (Motorbooks International)
*The Story of the Grand Canyon Railway*, by Al Richmond (Grand Canyon Railway)
*Rails to the Rim: Milepost Guide to the Grand Canyon Railway*, by Al Richmond (Grand Canyon Railway)

### General travel
*Live and Work in the USA and Canada*, by Adam Lechmere and Susan Catto (Vacation Work)

*America's Favourite Inns, B & Bs, and Small Hotels: USA and Canada*, by Sandra W Soule (St Martin's Press)
*100 Best Family Resorts in North America*, by Janet Tice (Globe Pequot Press)
*The Bed & Breakfast Encyclopaedia*, by Deborah E Sakach (American Historic Inns)

## General – history, the country, the people
*The American Century*, by Harold Evans (Jonathan Cape)
*A-Z of Modern America*, by Alicia Duchak (Routledge)
*America*, by George B Tindall (W W Norton)
*The American Nation*, by John A Garraty (Longman)
*The American Civil War*, by Brian Holden Reid (Longman)
*American Culture*, edited by Anders Breidlid (Routledge)
*Poplore - Folk and Pop in American Culture*, by G Bluestein (University of Massachusetts Press)
*American Visions*, by Robert Hughes (Harvill Press)
*American Civilisation*, by David Mauk and John Oakland (Routledge)
*Born in the USA*, by T E Scheurer (University of Mississippi)
*An Illustrated History of the US*, by B O'Callaghan (Longman)
*The World Rushed In - the California Gold Rush Experience*, by J S Holliday (Simon and Schuster)
*History of the Donner Party*, by C F McGlashan (Stanford University Press)
*Woody Guthrie*, by Joe Klein (Faber & Faber)
*Movie - Made in America: A Cultural History of American Movies*, by R Skar (Random House)
*Frontiersmen in Blue*, by Robert M Utley (Bison Books)

## Canada
### Railways
*The Trans-Canada Rail Guide*, by Melissa Graham (Trailblazer Publications)
*Steel Across the Shield: Canada Moves West*, by Pierre Berton (McClelland & Stewart)
*The Canadian Pacific Railway*, by John A Eagle (McGill-Queen's University Press)
*Close Ties*, by Ken Cruikshank (McGill-Queen's University Press)
*The Railway King of Canada*, by Rae Fleming (University of British Columbia)
*On the Trail of John Muir*, by Cherry Good (Luath Press)
*On Track*, by Susan McLeod O'Reilly (Canadian Museum of Civilisation)

## General – travel, history, the country, the people
*Living and Working in Canada*, by Benjamin A Kranc (How To Books)
*Canada Traveler's Companion*, by Donald Carroll (Globe Pequot Press)
*The Penguin History of Canada*, by Kenneth McNaught (Penguin)
*Culture Shock: Canada*, by Cheng & Barlas (Kuperard)
*O Canada*, by Jan Morris (Robert Hale)
*Canada from A to Z*, by Bobbie Kalman (Crabtree)
*The Canadians*, by Andrew H Malcolm (St Martin's Press)
*Canada Gazetteer Atlas* (University of Chicago Press)
*Canada's National Parks* (Whitecap Books)
*Carving the Western Path*, by R G Harvey (Heritage House)
*The Cariboo*, by Russell Mussio (Gordon Soules)
*Romantic Days and Nights in Vancouver*, by Richard Cropp (Globe Pequot Press)

# Index

Page references in **bold** indicate major entries

Aberdeen, MD 204
accommodation 38
*Adirondack, The* 260
air and rail travel combined 18
Alaska Railroad 15
Albany, OR 57
Albany-Rensselaer, NY 264, 278
Albuquerque, NM **136**
alcohol 28 (USA), 347 (Canada)
Aldershot, ON 303
Alderson, WV 252
Alexandria, VA 212, 222
Algoma Central Railway 358
Alliance, OH 293
Alpine, TX 159
Alton, IL 171
Altoona, PA 297
*American Orient Express, The* 15, 364
Amherst, MA 271
Amtrak 13, 377
Anaheim, CA 104
Ann Arbor, MI 308
Anniston, AL 218
Antioch-Pittsburg, CA 99
Arkadelphia, AR 175
Ashland, KY 254
Atlanta, GA **216**
Atmore, AL 147
Austin, TX 180
*Auto Train, The* 312

Back Bay Station, MA 192, 275
Bakersfield, CA 101
baggage 27 (USA), 346 (Canada)
Baltimore, MD 205
Baltimore/Washington International, MD 205
Barstow, CA 141
Battle Creek, MI 308
Bay St Louis, MS 148
Beaumont, TX 153

Bellows Falls, VT 271
Benson, AZ 161
Berlin, CT 209
Biloxi, MS 147
Bingen-White Salmon, WA 125
Birmingham, AL 219
Birmingham, MI 311
Bloomington-Normal, IL 170
boarding 20 (USA), 346 (Canada)
Boston, MA **190**, 246, 275
*Bras d'Or, The* 352
Brattleboro, VT 271
Bridgeport, CT 195
British Columbia Rail 356
Brookhaven, MS 186
Browning, MT 120
Bryan, OH 284
Buffalo-Depew, NY 280, 301
Buffalo-Exchange Street, NY 301
Burlington, IA 80
Burlington-Essex Jct, VT 273

Calgary, AB 356
*California Zephyr, The* 75
Canada tourism offices 376
Canadian Pacific Railway 360
*Canadian, The* 348
Cantic, QC 267
Camden, SC 226
*Capitol Limited, The* 286
Carbondale, IL 184
*Cardinal, The* 250
car travel 42
Centralia, IL 184
Centralia, WA 53
*Chaleur, The* 352
Champaign-Urbana, IL 183
Charleston, SC **239**
Charleston, WV 253
Charlotte, NC 214
Charlottesville, VA 213, 250
charter services 31
Chemult, OR 58

Chicago, IL **75**, 108, 127, 168, 182, 259, 285, 293, 299, 306
Chico, CA 59
children on trains 29 (USA), 344 (Canada)
Chipley, FL 146
Churchill, MB 353
Cincinnati, OH **254**
*City of New Orleans, The* 182
Claremont, NH 272
Cleburne, TX 179
Clemson, SC 215
Cleveland, OH **281**, 293
Clifton Forge, VA 251
*Coast Starlight, The* 49
Colfax, CA 97
Columbia, SC 226
Columbus, WI 112
Commerce, CA 103
complaints and suggestions 32 (USA), 347 (Canada)
Connellsville, PA 291
Connersville, IN 256
Corcoran, CA 101
Crawfordsville, IN 258
*Crescent, The* 211
Creston, IA 81
Crestview, FL 146
crime 44
crossing borders 31
Croton-Harmon, NY 262
Culpeper, VA 213
Cumberland, MD 289
customs 31
Cut Bank, MT 119

Dade City, FL 243
Dallas, TX **176**
Danville, VA 214
Davis, CA 61
Dearborn, MI 309
Deerfield Beach, FL 233
DeLand, FL 228
Delray Beach, FL 233
Del Rio, TX 158
Deming, NM 160

Denmark, SC 226
Denver, CO **85**
Detroit, MI **309**
Detroit Lakes, MN 116
Devils Lake, ND 117
dining 26
disabilities, facilities for
    passengers with 29 (USA),
    347 (Canada)
Disneyland 103
Disney World 230
documents 33
Dodge City, KS 131
Dowagiac, MI 307
drink 38
drugs 44
Dunsmuir, CA 59
Dyer, IN 258

East Glacier Park, MT 120
Edmonds, WA 123
Edmonton, AB 349
Effingham, IL 183
Elkhart, IN 284
Elko, NV 93
El Paso, TX 160
Elyria, OH 282
Emeryville, CA 62
*Empire Builder, The* 108
*Empire Builder, The*
    (Spokane–Portland) 124
entertainment 30
Ephrata, WA 121
Erie, PA 280
Essex, MT 120
Eugene, OR 57
Everett, WA 123
Explore America 17

Fargo, ND 116
Fayetteville, NC 238
Flagstaff, AZ 140
Florence, SC 238
food 37
Fort Edward, NY 265
Fort Lauderdale, FL 233
Fort Madison, IA 128
Fort Morgan, CO 84
Fort Worth, TX 178
Fostoria, OH 298
Framingham, MA 276
Fresno, CA 100
Fullerton, CA 103, 142
Fulton, KY 184
further reading 365, 380-1

Gainesville, GA 215
Galesburg, IL 80, 128
Gallup, NM 139

Garden City, KS 132
Gastonia, NC 214
getting there 35
Glasgow, MT 118
Glendale, CA 71
Glenview, IL 109
Glenwood Springs, CO 89
Granby, CO 88
Grand Canyon National
    Park, AZ 140
Grand Forks, ND 117
Grand Junction, CO 89
Great American Vacations 18
Green River, UT 90
Greensboro, NC 214
Greensburg, PA 298
Greenville, SC 215
Greenwood, MS 185
Grimsby, ON 303
group and convention travel
    29
Gulfport, MS 148

Halifax, NS 351
Hamilton, OH 256
Hamlet, NC 225
Hammond, LA 187
Hammond-Whiting, IN 258,
    285, 299, 307
Hanford, CA 100
Harpers Ferry, WV 288
Harrisburg, PA 296
Hartford, CT 209
Hastings, NE 84
Hattiesburg, MS 220
Havre, MT 119
Hazlehurst, MS 186
health regulations 34
Helper, UT 90
High Point, NC 214
Hinton, WV 252
Holdrege, NE 84
Hollywood, FL 234
Homewood, IL 183
Houston, TX **153**
Hudson, NY 263
*Hudson Bay, The* 352
Huntingdon, PA 297
Huntington, WV 253
Hutchinson, KS 131

immigration 34
Indianapolis, IN **256**
insurance 43, 44
Internet, The 369
Irvine, CA 104

Jackson, MI 308
Jackson, MS 186

Jacksonville, FL 144, 227,
    242
Jasper, AB 349
Johnstown, PA 297
Joliet, IL 169

Kalamazoo, MI 307
Kankakee, IL 183
Kansas City, MO **129**
Kelso-Longview, WA 54
Kingman, AZ 141
Kingston, RI 193
Kingstree, SC 238
Kissimmee, FL 231
Klamath Falls, OR 59

La Crosse, WI 113
Lafayette, IN 258
Lafayette, LA 152
La Junta, CO 132
Lake Charles, LA 152
*Lake Cities, The* 307
Lake City, FL 145
Lakeland, FL 245
*Lake Shore Limited, The* 275
Lamar, CO 132
Lamy, NM 135
Lancaster, PA 295
La Plata, MO 128
laptop computers 28
Las Vegas, NM 134
Latrobe, PA 298
Laurel, MS 220
Lawrence, KS 131
Lewistown, PA 296
Libby, MT 121
Lincoln, IL 170
Lincoln, NE 84
Little Rock, AR 174
Longview, TX 176
Lordsburg, NM 161
Los Angeles, CA **71**, 102,
    143, 167
lost property 346
lounge and dome cars 26
Lynchburg, VA 213

Madera, CA 100
Madison, FL 145
Malta, MT 118
Malvern, AR 174
Manassas, VA 212
*Maple Leaf, The* 300
Marshall, TX 176
Martinez, CA 61, 98
Martinsburg, WV 288
Marysville, CA 60
Mattoon, IL 183
Maysville, KY 254

McComb, MS 187
McCook, NE 84
McGregor, TX 179
Memphis, TN 184
Merced, CA 100
Meriden, CT 209
Meridian, MS 220
Metropark, NJ 200
Metropolitan lounge 20
Miami, FL **234**
Michigan City, IN 307
Milwaukee, WI **110**
Mineola, TX 176
Minneapolis, MN **114**
Minot, ND 117
Mobile, AL 147
Modesto, CA 99
money 36
Montgomery, WV 253
Montpelier, VT 272
Montreal, QC **267**, 274, 350
Mount Pleasant, IA 80
Mystic, CT 193

Naperville, IL 79
Nappanee, IN 299
Needles, CA 141
Newark, NJ 200
Newbern-Dyersburg, TN 184
New Carrollton, MD 205
New Haven, CT 194, 209
New Iberia, CA 152
New London, CT 194
New Orleans, LA **148**, 188, 221
Newport News, VA 249
New Rochelle, NY 195
newspapers 42
Newton, KS 131
New York, NY **196**, 211, 222, 237, 242, 261, 275, 294, 301
Niagara Falls, NY 302
Niagara Falls, ON 302
Niles, MI 307
non-Amtrak services 15
*Northeast Corridor, The* 189
*Northeast Corridor, The* (New Haven–Springfield) 209

Oakland, CA 65
Oakville, ON 303
Ocala, FL 243
Oceanside, CA 104
*Ocean, The* 351
Okanagan Valley Wine Train 364
Old Saybrook, CT 194

Olympia/Lacey, WA 53
Omaha, NE **82**
on-board service 31
on-line communications 41
Ontario, CA 167
Ontario Northland Railway 359
Orlando, FL 144, **229**
Osceola, IA 81
other Amtrak trains 312
other VIA Rail trains 353
Ottawa, ON 351
Ottumwa, IA 81
Oxnard, CA 70

*Pacific Surfliner, The* 102
Pacific Wilderness Railway 365
Palatka, FL 228
*Palmetto, The* 242
Palm Springs, CA 167
Paoli, PA 295
Pascagoula, MS 147
Pasco, WA 124
Paso Robles, CA 67
payment 19 (USA), 345 (Canada)
Pensacola, FL 146
Petersburg, VA 224
pets 28 (USA), 346 (Canada)
Philadelphia, PA **201**, 294
Phoenix, AZ **164**
photography 30
Picayune, MS 221
Pittsburgh, PA **291**, 298
Pittsfield, MA 277
Plattsburgh, NY 267
Pomona, CA 167
Pontiac, IL 170, 311
Poplar Bluff, MO 174
Portage, WI 112
Port Henry, NY 266
Portland, OR **55**
postal service 41
Poughkeepsie, NY 263
prices 37
Prince, WV 253
Princeton, IL 79
Prince George Railway 364
Princeton Junction, NJ 200
Providence, RI 192
Provo, UT 91
public holidays 45 (USA), 46 (Canada)

Quebec City, QC 350
Quebec North Shore and Labrador Railroad 362

radios 28 (USA), 346 (Canada)
railfone 30
rail passes 18 (USA), 342 (Canada), 19, 342 (North America)
railroad history 3 (USA), 339 (Canada)
railroad museums (see also 'steam trains') 52, 60, 69, 74, 78, 79, 81, 82, 84, 87, 106, 107, 112, 115, 116, 131, 150, 154, 157, 165, 173, 176, 179, 187, 197, 205, 214, 217, 218, 226, 232, 233, 236, 240, 248, 252, 253, 255, 256, 269, 273, 281, 283, 289, 293, 295, 296, 297, 309 (USA), 350, 351, 358, 359, 361, 362, 363, 364 (Canada)
Raleigh, NC 225
Randolph, VT 272
Raton, NM 133
Red Caps 27
Redding, CA 59
Red Wing, MN 114
refunds 19 (USA), 345 (Canada)
Reno, NV 94
Rensselaer, IN 258
reservations 17 (USA), 344 (Canada)
Rhinecliff, NY 263
Richmond, VA 223, 246
Rochester, NY 280
Rockville, MD 287
Rocky Mount, NC 225, 237
*Rocky Mountaineer, The* 353
Roseville, CA 97
Rouses Point, NY 267
Route 128, MA 192
Royal Oak, MI 311
Rugby, ND 117

Sacramento, CA 60, 97
St Albans, VT 274
St Catharines, ON 302
St Cloud, MN 116
St Lambert, QC 267
St Louis, MO **172**
St Paul, MN **114**
safety 28
*Saguenay and Abtibi, The* 352
Salem, OR 57
Salem & Hillsborough Railway 365
Salinas, CA 66
Salisbury, NC 214

Salt Lake City, UT **91**
San Antonio, TX **155**, 181
San Bernardino, CA 142
Sanderson, TX 158

San Diego, CA **105**
Sandpoint, ID 121
Sandusky, OH 283
Sanford, FL 229
San Francisco, CA **62**, 98
*San Joaquins, The* 98
San Jose, CA 65
San Juan Capistrano, CA 104
San Luis Obispo, CA 67
San Marcos, TX 180
Santa Ana, CA 104
Santa Barbara, CA 69
Santa Fe, NM 135
Sarasota Springs, NY 265
Saskatoon, SK 349
Savannah, GA 226, 241
scenic railroads (see also
  'steam trains') 60, 131, 165,
  257, 271, 277, 308, 309
  (USA), 361, 363 (Canada)
Schenectady, NY 264, 278
Schriever, LA 151
Seattle, WA **50**, 123
Sebring, FL 232
senior citizens 29 (USA), 344
  (Canada)
Sequoia and Kings Canyon
  National Parks, CA 100
sex 45
Shelby, MT 119
Sightseeing 40
*Silver Meteor, The* 237
*Silver Star, The* 222
Simi Valley, CA 70
*Skeena, The* 349
sleeping 23 (USA), 347
  (Canada)
Slidell, LA 221
smoking 28 (USA), 347
  (Canada)
Solana Beach, CA 105
South Bend, IN 284
South Portsmouth, KY 254
Southern Pines, NC 225
*Southwest Chief, The* 127
Sparks, NV 94
Spartanburg, SC 215
Spokane, WA 121, 124
Springfield, IL 170
Springfield, MA 210, 277
Stamford, CT 195
Stanley, ND 117
Staples, MN 116
Staunton, VA 251

steam trains 60, 80, 107, 116,
  135, 140, 165, 178, 217,
  296 308, 317–36 (USA),
  365–7 (Canada)
Stockton, CA 99
students 29, 34, 345
*Sunset Limited, The* 144
Syracuse, NY 279

Tacoma, WA 53
Tallahassee, FL 145
Tampa, FL **243**
Taos, NM 135
Taylor, TX 180
telephones 40 (USA), 347
  (Canada)
Temple, TX 179
Texarkana, AR/TX 175
*Texas Eagle, The* 168
things to take 30
*Three Rivers, The* 294
Thruway buses 20
Thurmond, WV 253
Ticonderoga, NY 266
tickets 16 (USA), 341
  (Canada)
Tijuana (Mexico) 107
timetables 20
time zones 45
tipping 28, 42
Toccoa, GA 215
Toledo, OH 283
Tomah, WI 112
Topeka, KS 131
Toronto, ON **303**, 350
Trenton, NJ 201
Trinidad, CO 133
Truckee, CA 95
Tucson, AZ **162**
Turlock-Denair, CA 99
Tuscaloosa, AL 219
*Twilight Shoreliner, The* 246

useful addresses 372 (USA),
  373 (Canada)
USA state tourism offices
  374
Utica, NY 279

Vancouver, BC 349
Vancouver, WA 54,126
*Vermonter, The* 270
VIA Rail 340, 345, 379
Victorville, CA 142

Waldo, FL 242
Wallingford, CT 209
Walnut Ridge, AR 174
Wasco, CA 101

Washington, DC **205**, 212,
  250, 286
Waterbury, VT 273
Waterloo, IN 284
Waterloo-St Jacobs Railway
  363
weather 35
Wenatchee, WA 121
Westerly, RI 193
West Glacier, MT 120
West Palm Beach, FL 232
Westport, NY 266
when to visit 35
Whitefish, MT 120
Whitehall, NY 265
Whitepass & Yukon Railway
  362
White River Jct, VT 272
White Sulphur Springs, WV
  252
Wildwood, FL 243
Williams, AZ 141
Williamsburg, VA **247**
Williston, ND 117
Wilmington, DE 203
Windsor, CT 210
Windsor Locks, CT 210
Windsor-Mt Ascutney, VT
  272
Winnemucca, NV 94
Winnipeg, MB 349
Winona, MN 113
Winslow, AZ 140
Winter Haven, FL 232, 245
Winter Park, CO 88
Winter Park, FL 229
Wisconsin Dells, WI 112
Wishram, WA 125
Wolf Point, MT 118
Worcester, MA 276
working in the USA 46

Yazoo City, MS 186
Yemassee, SC 241
Yonkers, NY 261
Youngstown, OH 298
Yosemite National Park, CA
  100
Yuma, AZ 166